Looking to the Future

Looking to the Future

Building a Curriculum for Social Activism

Derek Hodson
Ontario Institute for Studies in Education
University of Toronto
Canada
and
University of Auckland
New Zealand

SENSE PUBLISHERS
ROTTERDAM/BOSTON/TAIPEI

A C.I.P. record for this book is available from the Library of Congress.

ISBN: 978-94-6091-470-6 (paperback)
ISBN: 978-94-6091-471-3 (hardback)
ISBN: 978-94-6091-472-0 (e-book)

Published by: Sense Publishers,
P.O. Box 21858,
3001 AW Rotterdam,
The Netherlands
www.sensepublishers.com

Printed on acid-free paper

To Susie – You're at the heart of everything that matters

CONTENTS

PREFACE

In a number of publications (Hodson, 1992a, 1994, 1998a), I have argued that science education is best regarded as comprising three major elements: *learning science* – acquiring and developing conceptual and theoretical knowledge; *learning about science* – developing an understanding of the nature and methods of science, appreciation of its history and development, awareness of the complex interactions among science, technology, society and environment, and sensitivity to the personal, social and ethical implications of particular technologies; and *doing science* – engaging in and developing expertise in scientific inquiry and problem-solving, and developing confidence in tackling a wide range of "real world" tasks and problems. More recently, I have added a fourth component, *engaging in sociopolitical action* – acquiring (through guided participation) the capacity and commitment to take appropriate, responsible and effective action on science/ technology-related matters of social, economic, environmental and moral-ethical concern (Hodson, 2003). This book is largely located in this fourth category of science education.

This book is the third in a series. In the first book, *Towards Scientific Literacy: A Teachers' Guide to the History, Philosophy and Sociology of Science* (Hodson, 2008), I presented a critical reading of the vast and complex literature encompassing the history of science, philosophy of science and sociology of science (HPS). The prime purpose of that book was to identify some key ideas in HPS for inclusion in the school science curriculum, in line with the prominence given to HPS in recent international debate in science education and the numerous influential reports on science education that identify the centrality of HPS to scientific literacy. Discussion focused on those elements of the history, philosophy and sociology of science that would enable all students to leave school with robust knowledge about the nature of scientific inquiry and theory building, an understanding of the role and status of scientific knowledge, an ability to understand and use the language of science appropriately and effectively, the capacity to analyze, synthesize and evaluate knowledge claims, some insight into the sociocultural, economic and political factors that impact the priorities and conduct of science, and a developing capacity to deal with the moral-ethical issues that attend some scientific and technological developments. The second book in the series, *Teaching and Learning about Science: Language, Theories, Methods, History, Traditions and Values* (Hodson, 2009a), discussed ways in which that particular selection of HPS ideas can be assembled into a robust and coherent curriculum, and presented to students in ways that are meaningful, motivating and successful. The overarching goal is taken to be the attainment of *critical scientific literacy*, that is, an understanding of some of the major concepts, ideas and theories of science, an awareness of their history and development, and ability to use them appropriately and effectively, together with the capacity to think critically about the nature of any new scientific knowledge presented by teachers or encountered in textbooks, scientific journals, popular magazines, news-papers, television programmes and Internet websites – in particular, how that knowledge was generated and validated, the evidence that supports it (and opposes it) and the arguments used to sustain it. Such understanding includes layers of refinement relating to the role and status of scientific knowledge, the degree to which scientific knowledge is socially constructed, and its function as both a complex of explanatory systems and a constellation of instrumental devices for prediction and control. Critical scientific literacy also includes an awareness of the institutional characteristics of the community of scientists, including its forms of patronage and control, and some appreciation of the complex interactions of science, technology, society and environment. It includes a comprehensive understanding of scientific language and its deployment, an understanding of the nature of scientific argumentation, and the capacity to read, interpret and evaluate scientific text in whatever form it is encountered. It entails being able to deploy some robust criteria of demarcation in order to distinguish between good science and bad science, detect error, bias and fraud, and recognize pseudoscience and non-science masquerading as science.

One of the major rationales for promoting critical scientific literacy, and for learning *about* science, scientists, scientific inquiry and scientific argumentation, is the need to furnish students with the knowledge, skills and attitudes to address socioscientific and environmental issues in a critical way and to reach informed decisions on a range of science-related and technology-related issues that impact them, their immediate family and friends, the surrounding local, national and global community, and the planet as a whole. In other words, scientific literacy plays a key role in building informed and responsible citizenship and contributing to environmentally responsible behaviour. Just as the most effective way of learning to do science is by doing science, so one of the best ways of learning to address socioscientific issues is by addressing socioscientific issues (SSI). Put simply, addressing SSI is an essential component of any curriculum aiming to teach students *about* science and promote critical scientific literacy. It would be difficult to contemplate (and perhaps more difficult to justify) a course on "The Bicycle" that describes the basic structure of the bicycle and the function of each of its components, provides a history of the bicycle and the sociocultural circumstances of its invention (asking questions such as "Why didn't the Romans invent the bicycle?), examines the aesthetics of bicycle design and the economics of bicycle manufacture (including the move to Third World manufacture), compares and contrasts bicycle use in various countries for leisure, racing and basic transportation, engages students in case studies such as the Tour de France, the brief life of autocycles and drug use in Olympic cycling, shows movies about cycling, and so on, but doesn't actually involve students in riding a bicycle. By analogy, we cannot expect students to acquire the necessary knowledge, skills, attitudes and other attributes to examine SSI in later life simply as a by-product of studying HPS issues. We have to provide abundant opportunities in the curriculum to use that knowledge for real problem solving activities in the context of SSI, and we have to provide students with explicit advice and appropriate support in doing so. Traditional science teaching emphasizes the logical progression of particular scientific advances and the overall coherence of scientific knowledge; the controversial nature of science is omitted, except for reference to one or two famous historical examples. In contrast, the use of SSI emphasizes the problematic, conjectural, interpretive and controversial aspects of science and scientific investigation, and puts pedagogical emphasis firmly on debate, critique and argumentation. As Bell and Lin (2000) and Mason and Boscolo (2002) argue, addressing controversies not only engages students' NOS understanding and capacity for argumentation but also contributes to their development. Also by teaching through debate and argumentation, students improve their language skills, refine their understanding of the nature and role of debate in science, and are introduced to the disciplines that comprise public discourse about SSI – principally, politics, law, economics and ethics. Regrettably, constraints on space precluded a discussion in the second book of how critical consideration of SSI can be built into the science curriculum. Issues pertinent to building such a curriculum, and its associated politicization of students and teachers, is the focus of this book.

Widely known as the Crick report, *Education for Citizenship and the Teaching of Democracy in Schools* (QCA, 1998) stated that "We aim at no less than a change in the political culture of this country both nationally and locally: for people to think of themselves as active citizens, willing, able and equipped to have an influence in public life and with the critical capacities to weigh evidence before speaking and acting; to build on and to extend radically to young people the best in existing traditions of community involvement and public service, and to make them individually confident in finding new forms of involvement" (p. 7). The curriculum advocated in this book reflects a desire to contribute to this goal through science education by: (i) identifying and investigating a series of SSI (many of them to be chosen by the students); (ii) taking account of the beliefs, attitudes, interests and values of the various stakeholders; (iii) evaluating alternative viewpoints with respect to scientific, social, political, cultural, economic, aesthetic, moral-ethical, emotional and historical considerations; (iv) reaching a justifiable position on the issue and formulating a persuasive argument for it; (v) searching for solutions to any problems that arise; (vi) choosing an appropriate and justifiable course of action; (vii) taking action; and (viii) evaluating its consequences. In my view, STS or STSE education has afforded too low a priority to the promotion of critical thinking, and has largely ignored sociopolitical activism. The curriculum advocated in this book seeks to extend the somewhat limited goals of contemporary STS and STSE practice. It is an attempt to foster the understanding, knowledge, skills, attitudes, values and commitments that lead to socially and environmentally responsible civic engagement. It is an attempt to educate and motivate a generation of citizens to build a better world.

Derek Hodson
Auckland
September, 2010

ACKNOWLEDGEMENTS

Because my teaching career extends over forty years, and includes spells in UK, Canada, New Zealand and Hong Kong, it is difficult, if not impossible, to identify by name all those who have influenced me and shaped my thoughts and practice as a teacher, researcher and writer. Nevertheless, I do want to acknowledge one or two pivotal influences.

As an undergraduate at the University of Manchester Institute of Science and Technology I had the great good fortune to attend a series of lectures by David Theobald, author of *An Introduction to the Philosophy of Science* (Methuen, 1968). I thank David for triggering my longstanding interest in philosophy of science. My postgraduate years at UMIST and my developing understanding of chemistry were ably and sensitively fostered by Geoff Holt, who later became my PhD supervisor. Above all, Geoff gave me the confidence to admit my ignorance and to take intellectual risks. My early years as a teacher were immeasurably enriched by interactions with the students at Sevenoaks School (Kent). They taught me far more than I taught them. I also learned a great deal about teaching science from two teachers of English at the school: Alan Hurd and Richard Hanson. Teaching at Rannoch School (an independent school in North Perthshire based on the educational philosophy of Kurt Hahn), Welshpool High School (an 11–18 comprehensive school in mid-Wales) and Yale College (a sixth form college in Wrexham) enabled me to test and refine these ideas in three very different educational contexts. Throughout the succeeding years spent in teacher education and educational research my thinking has been sharpened and my views extended and further refined through discussions with colleagues and graduate students, particularly at the Ontario Institute for Studies in Education, the University of Hong Kong and the University of Auckland. I hereby acknowledge my indebtedness to all those people, too numerous to mention by name.

At a personal level, I owe a huge debt to my paternal grandfather (Herbert Hodson), who gave me my early interest in science and politics, and to my grandmother (Emma Hodson) for constant inspiration and love during my early childhood years. I owe an even greater debt to my mother (May) for teaching me what it means to be a man, to my father (Albert) for teaching me the virtues of humility and perseverance (though I regret they are often imperfectly practiced), to my sister (Maureen) for crucial support during the difficult years following the premature deaths of our parents, to my daughter (Julie) and son (Gareth) for giving me the great joys of fatherhood, and to my beloved grandchildren (Sam, Emma and Ben) for bringing the wonders of grandparenthood. Above all, I acknowledge my indebtedness to my wife, Sue Hodson, my friend and companion for fifty years. To you, Susie, I extend my heartfelt thanks, unending love and admiration. This book could not have been written without your unwavering love, inspiration, encouragement and support. You may not have all the answers… just the ones that matter.

If we teach today as we taught yesterday, we rob our children of tomorrow

John Dewey

SCIENTIFIC LITERACY REVISITED

In recent decades, the notion of *scientific literacy* has become increasingly prominent in international debate about science education, a trend mirrored by a similarly expanding interest in technological literacy and environmental literacy[1]. Although a number of writers have traced the history and evolving definition of scientific literacy (Gräber & Bolte, 1997; Laugksch, 2000; De Boer, 2001; Ryder, 2001; McEneaney, 2003; Roberts, 2007; Dillon, 2009), there is some value in revisiting that history and development here, albeit very briefly.

The term seems to have first appeared in the US educational literature about 50 years ago, in papers by Paul Hurd (1958) and Richard McCurdy (1958). DeBoer (2001) also cites the Rockefeller Brothers Fund (1958) report *The Pursuit of Excellence* (p. 369) as a pioneer user of the term: "Just as we must insist that every scientist be broadly educated, so we must see to it that every educated person be literate in science" (p. 586). At about the same time, Fitzpatrick (1960) remarked: "If the Zeitgeist is to be favorable to the scientific enterprise, including both academic and industrial programs, the public must possess some degree of scientific literacy, at least enough to appreciate the general nature of scientific endeavor and its potential contributions to a better way of life... No citizen, whether or not he is engaged in scientific endeavors, can be literate in the modern sense until he has understanding and appreciation of science and its work" (p. 6). He concludes: "The ultimate fate of the scientific enterprise is in no small degree dependent upon establishing a species of scientific literacy in the general population" (p. 169). Similarly, Alan Waterman (at that time, Director of the National Science Foundation) noted that it was a matter of urgency that "the level of scientific literacy on the part of the general public be markedly raised... progress in science depends to a considerable extent on public understanding and support" (Waterman, 1960, p. 1349).

Although the term scientific literacy was enthusiastically taken up by many science educators as a useful slogan or rallying call (see Roberts, 1983, 2007), there was little in the way of precise or agreed meaning until Pella et al. (1966) suggested that it comprises an understanding of the basic concepts of science, the nature of science, the ethics that control scientists in their work, the interrelationships of science and society, the interrelationships of science and the humanities, and the differences between science and technology. Almost a quarter century later, the authors of *Science for All Americans* (AAAS 1989) drew upon very similar categories to define a scientifically literate person as "one who is aware that science, mathematics, and technology are interdependent human enterprises with strengths and limitations; understands key concepts and principles of science; is familiar with the natural world and recognizes both its diversity and unity; and uses scientific knowledge and scientific ways of thinking for individual and social purposes" (p. 4).

On the other side of the Atlantic Ocean, the long-standing tradition of concern for "the public understanding of science" dates back to the early years of the 19th Century (Jenkins, 1990). As Jenkins notes, science was vigorously promoted through the activities of the numerous Mechanics' Institutes and Literary and Philosophical Societies, and further supported by public lectures, scientific demonstrations and "a remarkable variety of books, journals, tracts, pamphlets and magazines, many of which would be categorized today as 'teach yourself publications'" (p. 43). In the middle years of the 20th Century, inspired in large part by the work of J.D. Bernal, the Movement for Social Responsibility in Science shifted the emphasis for the public understanding of science very sharply in the direction of sociopolitical concerns. In more recent times, the Royal Society (1985) shifted the emphasis yet again, noting that improving public understanding of science is "an investment in the future; not a luxury to be indulged in if and when resources allow" (p. 9). The argument that scientific literacy "can be a major element in promoting national prosperity, in raising the quality of public and private decision making and in enriching the life of the individual" (Royal Society, 1985, p. 9) highlights the key distinction between those who see scientific literacy as the possession of knowledge, skills and attitudes essential to a career as a professional scientist, engineer or technician and those who see it as the capacity to access, read and understand material with a scientific and/or technological dimension, make a careful appraisal of it, and use that evaluation to inform everyday decisions, including those made at the ballot box. Roberts (2007) refers to these contrasting views as "Vision 1" or "literacy *within* science" (focusing on the products of science and the processes by which they are generated and validated) and "Vision 2" or "literacy *about* science" (focusing on the ability to address socioscientific issues). Interestingly, and importantly in the context of this book, Roberts (2007) notes that "Vision 2 subsumes Vision 1, but the converse is not necessarily so" (p. 768).

Debate about what scientific literacy might comprise is necessarily influenced by arguments about *why* we need it and *why* we should promote its attainment in school. Thomas and Durant (1987) have categorized such arguments into three groups: (i) perceived benefits to science, (ii) benefits to individuals, and (iii) benefits to society as a whole. Benefits to science are seen largely in terms of increased numbers of recruits to science-based professions (including medicine and engineering), greater support for scientific, technological and medical research, and more realistic public expectations of science. Little by way of elaboration needs to be said about the first argument, save to note that increased recruitment might also result in increased diversity within the community of scientists. As Helen Longino (1990) and Sandra Harding (1991) argue, increased numbers of women, members of ethnic minority groups and other groups traditionally under-served by science education and under-represented in science-related and technology-related professions would do much to enrich these professions and might serve to re-direct and reorient priorities for research and development - a matter that will be addressed, albeit briefly, later in the book. With regard to the other perceived benefits for science, Jenkins (1994a) makes the related point that enhanced public understanding of science would enable scientists to be more effective in countering opposition from religious fundamentalist groups, animal rights activists and others who might seek to constrain or curtail scientific inquiry. In similar vein, Shamos (1993) states that enhanced scientific literacy is a defence against what he sees as the anti-science and neo-Luddite movements that are, in his words, "threatening to undermine science". The school science curriculum, he argues, "should be the forum for debunking the attempts of such fringe elements to distort the public mind, first by exposing their tactics, and then by stressing over and over again the central role in science of objective, reproducible evidence" (p. 71).

It is probably true to say that there has been a significant decline in public confidence in science and scientists in recent years as a consequence of the BSE episode (the so-called "mad cow disease") in the United Kingdom and concerns about bird flu, swine flu, SARS, West Nile Virus and other transmissible diseases. Skepticism is now rife regarding the bland assurances provided by supposed experts about health risks associated with nuclear power stations, overhead power lines and mobile phones. There is unease about the emergence of so-called 'superbugs' in hospitals, anxiety about the environmental impact of genetically engineered crops, concern about pesticide residues, growth hormones, antibiotics and other contaminants in our food, and so on. There is considerable anxiety about the possibility of a link between the MMR vaccine and autism, and a strong suspicion (rightly or wrongly) that government health authorities do not reveal all that they know. Jasanoff (1997) uses the term "civic dislocation" to describe situations in which a mismatch develops between what the scientific establishment and governmental institutions are supposed to do and are expected to do for the public, in terms of providing guarantees of safety and advice on dealing with increased risks, and what they actually do in times of crisis. At times of civic dislocation, citizens develop a deep distrust of governments and scientists and they look elsewhere for information, advice and reassurance, as evident in the BSE episode in the mid-1990s and the swine flu episode in 2009.

> It is a telling irony that, at the height of the scare over BSE, the British public seemed to get more direct information and advice from their supermarkets than their government… Vulnerable to even the slightest fluctuations in consumer confidence, the food industry was prepared to give more information, promise more controls, and offer more choices to consumers than the government agencies charged with protecting public health. (Jasanoff, 1997, p. 230)

Among some sections of the public there is mounting concern about the increasing domination of scientific and technological research by commercial, governmental and military interests, the increasing vulnerability of science and scientists to the pressures of capitalism and politics, and the increased secrecy and distortion by vested interest that result. The close link between science and commerce in the field of genetic engineering has been a particular trigger for deepening mistrust of scientists. Indeed, Ho (1997) claims, rightly or wrongly, that "practically all established molecular geneticists have some direct or indirect connection with industry, which will set limits on what the scientists can and will do research on… compromising their integrity as independent scientists" (p. 155), while Bencze et al. (2009) state that a close review of 70 research articles concerning the effectiveness of "calcium channel blockers" revealed that 96% of the authors citing positive results had financial ties to companies producing the drugs. As a consequence of revelations such as these, as Barad (2000) notes, "the public senses that scientists are not owning up to their biases, commitments, assumptions, and presuppositions, or to base human weaknesses such as the drive for wealth, fame, tenure, or other forms of power" (p. 229). In its third report, the (UK) House of Lords Select Committee on Science and Technology commented on what it perceives as a "crisis of trust":

> Society's relationship with science is in a critical phase... On the one hand, there has never been a time when the issues involving science were more exciting, the public more interested, or the opportunities more apparent. On the other hand, public confidence in scientific advice to Government has been rocked by a series of events, culminating in the BSE fiasco, and many people are deeply uneasy about the huge opportunities presented by areas of science including biotechnology and information technology, which seem to be advancing far ahead of their awareness and assent. In turn, public unease, mistrust and occasional outright hostility are breeding a climate of deep anxiety among scientists themselves. (Select Committee, 2000, p. 11)

There is some evidence that public trust in science and scientists is linked to the context and institution in which the work is conducted: university scientists enjoy higher levels of trust than scientists employed in industry because they are perceived as more benevolent and more likely to generate outcomes of benefit to the community (Yearley, 2000; Hargreaves et al., 2002; Chalmers & Nicol, 2004; Critchley, 2008).

Confidence and trust in scientists, continuing public support for science, trust in scientists, and the high levels of public funding science currently enjoys, all depend on citizens having some general understanding of what scientists do and how they do it. Since a great deal of financial support for scientific research derives from public funds, the self-interests of scientists would seem to demand that they keep the tax-payer well-informed about scientific research – in particular, about what they choose to investigate, the methods they employ, how they validate their research findings and theoretical conclusions, and where, how and to whom they disseminate their work. In developing this line of argument, Schwab (1962) advocated a shift of emphasis in school science away from the learning of scientific knowledge (the products of science) towards an understanding of the processes of scientific inquiry (how science is done) because that would ensure "a public which is aware of the conditions and character of scientific enquiry, which understands the anxieties and disappointments that attend it, and which is, therefore, prepared to give science the continuing support which it requires" (p. 38). Similarly, Shortland (1988) states that confidence in scientists and public support for science depend on "at least a minimum level of general knowledge about what scientists do" (p. 307). More significantly, support depends on whether the public *values* what scientists do. It would be naïve to assume that enhanced scientific literacy will inevitably translate into simple trust of scientists and unqualified support for the work they choose to do. A scientifically literate population, with a rational view of the world, a predis-position to think critically, and the capacity to appraise scientific evidence for themselves, may prove to be skeptical, suspicious or even distrustful of scientists, and therefore much more likely to *challenge* the nature of scientific research and the direction of technological innovation than to extend unconditional approval. However, between the extremes of simple acquiescence with everything that scientists choose to do and deep suspicion or even open hostility towards what they do, is the goal we should be seeking through school science education: a citizenry able to engage critically with the issues pertaining to scientific and technological practice and the arguments that scientists and engineers deploy. There is also an urgent need for scientists to develop better mechanisms for communication and consultation with the public – see, for example, the recommendations of the Office of Science and Technology and the Wellcome Trust (2001)[2].

Arguments that scientific and technological literacy brings benefits to *individuals* come in a variety of forms. It is commonly argued, for example, that scientifically and technologically literate individuals have access to a wide range of employment opportunities and are well-positioned to respond positively and competently to the introduction of new technologies in the workplace: "More and more jobs demand advanced skills, requiring that people be able to learn, reason, think creatively, make decisions, and solve problems. An understanding of science and the process of science contributes in an essential way to these skills" (National Research Council, 1996, p. 2). In recent years, this has been especially true in industries that make extensive use of information and communications technology (ICT). Of course, we should ask whether young people do still aspire to build careers in science. Data compiled by Jenkins and Nelson (2005) suggests that this is no longer the case in the United Kingdom, though other data accumulated by the Relevance of Science Education project (ROSE), of which the Jenkins and Nelson study forms a part, indicates that aspirations for scientific careers are still strongly held in the Developing world. In addition, it is argued that those who are scientifically literate are better able to cope with the demands of everyday life in an increasingly technology-dominated society, although even casual observation of technological innovation shows that advances are generally in the direction of increased user-friendliness, so that in many cases *less* expertise is needed to cope with a new technology than was needed for the old. Moreover, individuals can function perfectly well in their daily lives without knowing very much science because they often have access to expertise whenever they need it, although that raises a key question about trust of experts (see discussion later in this chapter and in chapter 2).

A stronger case is that scientifically literate individuals are better positioned to evaluate and respond appropriately to the supposed scientific evidence used by advertizing agencies and the science-related arguments deployed by politicians, and better equipped to make important decisions that affect their health, security and economic well-being, resulting in better informed consumers and more critical citizens who can use their knowledge and understanding in ways that 'make a difference' to their own and their family's lives. As will be argued in later chapters, the curriculum I advocate in this book seeks to prepare students to deal critically and effectively with social, economic, ethical and environmental issues that are science-related and technology-related, foster a determination to work tirelessly in the interests of social and environmental health, and make positive contributions to the life of the local, regional, national and global community and to the well-being of other species As the authors of *Benchmarks for Scientific Literacy* (AAAS, 1993) suggest, "People who are literate in science... are able to use the habits of mind and knowledge of science, mathematics, and technology they have acquired to think about and make sense of many of the ideas, claims, and events that they encounter in everyday life" (p. 322). The point at issue here is that some scientific knowledge, skills and attitudes are essential for everyday life in a complex, rapidly changing and science/technology-dominated society. As individuals, each of us is faced with making decisions about whether or not to use a mobile phone, eat genetically modified food or give our children the MMR vaccine. As a society, we need to form an opinion and possibly make decisions about cloning and stem cell research, appropriate use of energy, mineral and water resources, toxic waste disposal, and so on. It is alarming to note that research by Kempton et al. (1995) and Hogan (2002a) shows that many adults, as well as school age students, reach important decisions on socioscientific issues on the basis of incomplete or incorrect knowledge, or even no knowledge at all.

To say that we are living in an era of rapid and far-reaching change, the outcomes of which are sometimes well beyond prediction, is not to say anything new or particularly startling. But it is something to which educators, and especially science educators, need to respond. Major social, economic and political changes, many occurring on a global scale, are coincident with equally profound changes in the generation, organization and transmission of knowledge and information. Previous barriers of time and space have been largely overcome. This instant interconnectivity has intensified all aspects of human life, requiring that we respond to changes and proposals for change within a very short period of time. For many, life in this complex and changing world can be cognitively challenging, emotionally unsettling and increasingly stressful. Writing nearly 20 years ago, Anthony Giddens (1991) noted that "the crisis-prone nature of late modernity... has unsettling consequences in two respects: it fuels a general climate of uncertainty which an individual finds disturbing no matter how far he seeks to put it to the back of his mind; and it inevitably exposes everyone to a diversity of crisis situations... which may sometimes threaten the very core of self-identity" (p. 184). We also live in an era that generates increasing numbers of moral-ethical dilemmas but offers fewer moral certainties – an issue to be addressed in chapter 7. Scientific literacy is essential in helping students to cope with life in this constantly changing and uncertain world and is the principal means of averting the nightmare world that Carl Sagan (1995) so gloomily speculated on in his book, *The Demon-Haunted World*.

I have a foreboding of... when awesome technological powers are in the hands of the very few, and no one representing the public interest can even grasp the issues; when the people have lost the ability to set their own agendas or knowledgeably question those in authority; when, clutching our crystals and nervously consulting our horoscopes, our critical faculties in decline, unable to distinguish between what feels good and what's true, we slide, almost without noticing, back into superstition and darkness. (p. 25)

Some years ago, Neil Postman (1992) described American society as a "technopoly" in which citizens are socialized into accepting without question any statement by a supposed scientific 'expert' if it is presented in a way that readers or listeners perceive to be 'scientific' and is claimed to derive from a research study conducted at a reputable university (no matter whether that claim is true or false).

The world we live in is very nearly incomprehensible to most of us. There is almost no fact, whether actual or imagined, that will surprise us for very long, since we have no comprehensive and consistent picture of the world that would make the fact appear as an unacceptable contradiction. We believe because there is no reason not to believe. (p. 58)

Those with little knowledge of science, especially with little knowledge of the nature of science, can be led to accept as dogma almost any knowledge that they don't fully understand, led to accept way too much on faith and on trust, led to believe that science has all the answers to all of our problems. Central to this disturbing situation, of course, is uncritical acceptance of the myth of an all-powerful route to certain knowledge via the scientific method. It is also the case that those who believe in the certainty of knowledge and in the inevitability of successful outcomes to scientific research, both of which are among the myths perpetrated by traditional science education and are prominent features of the popular public image of science, are likely to have unrealistic expectations of science and to become impatient when scientists do not immediately 'deliver' on society's wants and needs. The following extracts from official documents published over a 25-year period give something of the flavour of this particular argument for scientific literacy.

Personal decisions, for example about diet, smoking, vaccination, screening programmes or safety in the home and at work, should all be helped by some understanding of the underlying science. Greater familiarity with the nature and findings of science will also help the individual to resist pseudo-scientific information. An uninformed public is very vulnerable to misleading ideas on, for example, diet or alternative medicine. (Royal Society, 1985, p. 10)

When people know how scientists go about their work and reach scientific conclusions and what the limitations of such conclusions are, they are more likely to react thoughtfully to scientific claims and less likely to reject them out of hand or accept them uncritically. (AAAS, 1993, p. 3)

An important life skill for young people is the capacity to draw appropriate and guarded conclusions from evidence and information given to them, to criticize claims made by others on the basis of the evidence put forward, and to distinguish opinion from evidence-based statements. (OECD, 2003, p. 132)

There is obviously a need to prepare young people for a future that will require good scientific knowledge and an understanding of technology. Science literacy is important for understanding environmental, medical,

> economic and other issues that confront modern societies, which rely heavily
> on technological and scientific advances of increasing complexity. (High
> Level Group on Science Education, 2007, p. 6)

Some have argued for the cultural, aesthetic and moral-ethical benefits conferred on individuals by scientific literacy. It is nearly fifty years since C.P. Snow (1962) asserted that science is "the most beautiful and wonderful collective work of the mind of man" and that it is as crucial to contemporary culture as literature, music and fine art. In similar vein, Warren Weaver (1966) stated that "the capacity of science progressively to reveal the order and beauty of the universe, from the most evanescent elementary particle up through the atom, the molecule, the cell, man, our earth with all its teeming life, the solar system, the metagalaxy, and the vastness of the universe itself, all this constitutes the real reason, the incontrovertible reason, why science is important, and why its interpretation to all men is a task of such difficulty, urgency, significance and dignity" (p. 50). More recently, Richard Dawkins (1998) has remarked: "the feeling of awed wonder that science can give us is one of the highest experiences of which the human psyche is capable. It is a deep aesthetic passion to rank with the finest that music and poetry can deliver" (p. x). Others have claimed, somewhat extravagantly, that appreciation of the ethical standards and code of responsible behaviour within the scientific community will lead to more ethical behaviour in the wider community – that is, the pursuit of scientific truth regardless of personal interests, ambitions and prejudice (part of the traditional image of the objective and dispassionate scientist) makes science a powerful carrier of moral values and ethical principles. Shortland (1988) summarizes this rationale as follows: "the internal norms or values of science are so far above those of everyday life that their transfer into a wider culture would signal a major advance in human civilization" (p. 310). Harré (1986) presents a similar argument: "the scientific community exhibits a model or ideal of rational cooperation set within a strict moral order, the whole having no parallel in any other human activity" (p. 1). The authors of *Science for All Americans* (AAAS, 1989) spell out some of these moral values as follows: "Science is in many respects the systematic application of some highly regarded human values – integrity, diligence, fairness, curiosity, openness to new ideas, skepticism, and imagination" (p. 201). Studying science, scientists and scientific practice will, they argue, help to instill these values in students. In other words, scientific literacy doesn't just result in more skilled and more knowledgeable people, it results in *wiser* people, that is, people well-equipped to make morally and ethically superior decisions.

Arguments that increased scientific literacy brings benefits to society as a whole include the familiar and increasingly pervasive economic argument and the claim that it can enhance democracy and promote more responsible citizenship. The first argument sees science education as having a key role in stimulating growth, enhancing economic competitiveness and reducing unemployment levels to a socially and politically acceptable level. In this scenario, science education is closely linked to the development of the problem-solving capabilities of students, where the problems to be solved are seen in terms of market competition, innovation and entrepreneurship. Thus, the National Science Education Standards (NRC, 1996) state that one of the key purposes of science education is to "increase economic productivity through the use of knowledge, understanding, and skills of the scientifically literate" (p. 13). It is a view long promoted by the Government of Canada:

> Our future prosperity will depend on our ability to respond creatively to the opportunities and challenges posed by rapid change in fields such as information technologies, new materials, biotechnologies and telecommunications... To meet the challenges of a technologically driven economy, we must not only upgrade the skills of our work force, we must also foster a lifelong learning culture to encourage the continuous learning needed in an environment of constant change. (Government of Canada, 1991, pp. 12 & 14)

Similarly, the authors of an Ontario Ministry of Education and Training (2000) document on curriculum planning and assessment state that the curriculum has been designed to ensure that its graduates are well prepared "to compete successfully in a global economy and a rapidly changing world" (p. 3). Thus, scientific literacy is regarded as a form of human capital that builds, sustains and develops the economic well-being of a nation. Put simply, continued economic development brought about by enhanced competitiveness in international markets (regarded as incontrovertibly a 'good thing') depends on science-based research and development, technological innovation and a steady supply of scientists, engineers and technicians, all of which ultimately depend on public support for state-funded science and technology education in school[3]. Moreover, the argument goes, increased scientific literacy is likely to sustain high levels of consumer demand for the technologies that are perceived by such scientifically literate individuals as highly desirable. At some stage in their school science education, students should be asked to consider whether globalization *ought* be regarded as an unqualified 'good thing' and whether the economic benefits of scientific and technological development are equitably distributed (see discussion in chapter 5).

The case for scientific literacy as a means of enhancing democracy and responsible citizenship is just as strongly made as the economic argument, though by different stakeholders and interest groups. Thomas and Durant (1987) note that increased scientific literacy "may be thought to promote more democratic decision-making (by encouraging people to exercise their democratic rights), which may be regarded as good in and of itself; but in addition, it may be thought to promote more effective decision-making (by encouraging people to exercise their democratic right wisely)" (p. 5). In the words of Chen and Novick (1984), enhanced scientific literacy is a means "to avert the situation where social values, individual involvement, responsibility, community participation and the very heart of democratic decision making will be dominated and practiced by a small elite" (p. 425). Democracy is strengthened when *all* citizens are equipped to confront and evaluate socioscientific issues (SSI) knowledgeably and rationally, rather than (or as well as) emotionally, and to make informed decisions on matters of personal and public concern. Those who are scientifically illiterate are in many ways disempowered and excluded from active civic participation. It is little wonder, then, that Tate (2001) declares access to high quality science education to be a civil rights issue. The following remarks can be taken as illustrative of the scientific literacy for democratic citizenship argument.

> Science education must serve as a foundation for the education of an informed citizenry who participate in the freedoms and powers of a modern, democratic, technological society. With the rapid development of scientific knowledge and the advent of new technologies, all members of society must have an understanding of the implications of that knowledge upon individuals, communities, and the 'global village' in which we now live. (Berkowitz & Simmons, 2003, p. 117)

> Few individuals have an elementary understanding of how the scientific enterprise operates. This lack of understanding is potentially harmful, particularly in societies where citizens have a voice in science funding decisions, evaluating policy matters and weighing scientific evidence provided in legal proceedings. At the foundation of many illogical decisions and unreasonable positions are misunderstandings of the character of science. (McComas, 1998, p. 511)

Of course, as both Tytler (2007) and Levinson (2010) remind us, the notion of science education for citizenship raises a whole raft of questions about the kind of citizen and the kind of society we have in mind, and about what constitutes *informed* and *responsible* citizenship. As Davies (2004) points out, not all science educators who are keen to implement science education for citizenship have a clearly articulated notion of what responsible citizenship entails and how science education can play a part in helping students achieve it. He quotes at length from Gamarnikow and Green's (2000) argument that it so often "reproduces a version of citizenship education unlikely to challenge the social mechanisms of inequality reproduction" (p. 1757). There is an all-too-common and depressing tendency to equate science education for citizenship simply with the inclusion of common everyday examples of 'science in the real world' as a way of motivating students and enhancing conceptual (and possibly procedural) understanding. In other words, the citizenship element is a mere enabling tactic; the real goal is enhanced understanding of science content, and the broader underlying goal is education for social reproduction. When education is geared towards preservation of the existing social order, as most education is, students are prepared to be obedient, deferential, compliant and willing to take their place within existing hierarchical social structures. In general, citizens are expected to leave daily decision-making and policy setting to their elected representatives, in collaboration with the industrial, financial and military sectors (see Levinson (2010) for a fuller discussion of this "deficit model" of citizenship and science education for citizenship). However, if education is geared towards social critique and social transformation, as argued throughout this book, students are prepared to be informed, critical and active citizens who expect (and demand) to be full participants in the decision-making processes within local, regional, national and international communities.

Westheimer and Kahne (2004) draw some useful distinctions among three alternative conceptions of citizenship: the *personally responsible citizen*, the *participatory citizen* and the *justice-oriented citizen*. In addition to paying taxes, obeying laws and voting in elections, the personally responsible citizen is strongly motivated to recycle, use public transport, pick up litter, donate blood and contribute to food and clothing banks, and may do volunteer work in soup kitchens and homes for the elderly. The participatory citizen is involved in organizing and participating in community-based efforts to care for those in need, promote social development and clean up the environment. Justice-oriented citizens respond critically to social, political and economic structures, seek out and address areas of injustice, and endeavour to effect systemic and significant change. The stance adopted in this book is that while each of these orientations is important, none is sufficient in itself. Putting emphasis on individual character and behaviour can divert attention from analysis of the social, economic and political forces that underpin SSI and the search for systemic solutions. In its neglect of the forces that shape society, it can create a politically conservative vision of the role of government, foster blind loyalty or unthinking obedience, and stoke up jingoistic sentiments. At a practical level, it fails to appreciate that individual actions are sometimes insufficient to effect significant change, and that only collective actions can succeed. Encouraging participation in collective actions doesn't necessarily develop students' ability to analyze and critique social and cultural practices or to identify the root causes of problems. It doesn't always help them to recognize underlying ideologies and values, detect vested interests or ascertain the ways in which wealth, power, gender and race impact on fairness, equity and social justice. Thus, it can reinforce rather than challenge existing norms and practices. However, emphasis on critique may only succeed in producing 'armchair activists': people who can hold articulate and politically astute conversations with like-minded individuals, or argue persuasively with political opponents, but don't ever do anything about the causes they seem to care so much about. In short, the unthinking participation that can sometimes occur under the participatory citizenship model can become no more than thoughtful inaction under the social justice model. The kind of citizenship envisaged in this book entails all three perspectives. Chapter 7 has a great deal to say about what it means to be personally responsible; chapters 3 and 9 discuss ways in students can be taught about action and learn through action; every chapter promotes, to some extent, the principles of social critique and pursuit of justice, though chapters 3, 4, 5, 8 and 9 have most to say on these matters. Also relevant to this multi-citizenship notion is Battistoni's (2002) discussion of what he calls "civic participation skills", including basic scientific, technological, economic, social and political knowledge, ability to evaluate knowledge and information quickly and critically, and bring it to bear on particular issues and problems, capacity to communicate confidently, effectively and persuasively in public settings, willingness to listen to others, and ability to collaborate in seeking and implementing solutions. Every chapter contributes something of relevance to the development of these attributes.

The authors of *Science For All Americans* (AAAS, 1989), arguing for the role of scientific literacy in fostering a more socially compassionate and environmentally responsible democracy, state that science education can (and should) "help students to develop the understandings and habits of mind they need to become compassionate human beings able to think for themselves and to face life head on. It should equip them also to participate thoughtfully with fellow citizens in building and protecting a society that is open, decent, and vital" (p. xiii). Moreover, they say, science education can provide the knowledge needed "to develop effective solutions to... global and local problems" and can foster "the kind of intelligent respect for nature that should inform decisions on the uses of technology", without which "we are in danger of recklessly destroying our life-support system" (p. 12). In further elaborating this kind of argument, the OECD's Programme for International Student Achievement (PISA) proposes that a scientifically literate person is "able to combine science knowledge with the ability to draw evidence-based conclusions in order to understand and help make decisions about the natural world and the changes made to it through human activity" (OECD, 1998, p. 5) and has "a willingness to engage in science-related issues, and with the ideas of science, as a reflective citizen... having opinions and participating in... current and future science-based issues" (OECD, 2006, p. 24). In other words, scientific literacy is the driving force for sociopolitical action – an argument that will be explored at length in later chapters. Roth and Calabrese Barton (2004) make essentially the same point: "critical scientific literacy is inextricably linked with social and political literacy in the service of social responsibility" (p. 10). It should not be thought of as a property of individuals, they argue, but as a characteristic of everyday situations in which citizen science occurs. In common with Roth and Lee (2002, 2004) and Roth (2003, 2009a), they recognize that significant impact on decision-making regarding SSI is more likely through collective action than individual efforts, thus shifting the ultimate focus of education for scientific literacy towards effective public practice, summed up by the increasingly popular notion of *enhanced public engagement with science*.

> First, we propose that scientific literacy is a property of collective situations and characterizes interactions irreducible to characteristics of individuals. Second, we propose to think of science not as a single normative framework for rationality but merely as one of many resources that people can draw on in everyday collective decision-making processes. Third, we propose that people learn by participating in activities that are meaningful because they serve general (common) interests and, in this, contribute to the community at large rather than making learning a goal of its own. (Roth & Calabrese Barton, 2004, p. 22).

> Scientific literacy, to be of any use in the everyday life of individuals and collectives, has to be thought of not as lodged in the heads of people and not as to be found *in* the properties of collectives. Rather, we should think of scientific literacy as *an emergent feature* of *collective praxis* so that it can only be observed while people engage one another and as an effect of these interactions. (Roth, 2009, p. 23)

In other words, scientific literacy is something that emerges and develops as a group of people, some of whom may be scientists, confront a socioscientific issue and collectively work towards a solution. Appropriate expertise develops as the situation requires. While I acknowledge that collective action with regard to SSI is often necessary and is frequently more productive than individual actions (see chapter 3), and while I accept that one can legitimately regard a community as having collective scientific literacy, and while I acknowledge that an individual's level of scientific literacy is likely to be substantially enhanced by participating in collective actions focused on SSI, I do not accept the proposition that individual levels of scientific literacy cannot be discerned and should not be cultivated. Nor do I accept the proposition implied in much of Wolff-Michael Roth's recent work, that science education should be de-institutionalized.

One further argument for seeking enhanced scientific literacy is that it might also be the most effective way to address the naïve trust that many students have in the Internet. It seems that many students accept anything and everything they locate on the Internet as valid and reliable; they form their views on all manner of topics after a few minutes Google searching or consulting Wikipedia. Enhanced scientific literacy is also a powerful means to combat the increasingly pervasive influence of 'alternative sciences' such as iridology, aromatherapy and reflexology, and the increasing susceptibility of people to the blandishments of purveyors of miracle cures, revolutionary diets, body enhancement techniques and procedures, and the healing properties of crystals.

In a succinct summary of the foregoing arguments, Symington and Tytler (2004), writing from an Australian perspective, consider school science education to have five key purposes.

- The *cultural* purpose is to ensure that all members of society develop an understanding of the scope of science and its applications within contemporary culture.
- The *democratic* purpose is to ensure that students develop sufficient scientific knowledge and sufficient confidence in science to be involved in debate and decision-making about scientific and technological issues.
- The *economic* purpose is to ensure a regular supply of people with strong backgrounds in science and technology in business and public life, and in science-related and technology-related careers, to secure the country's future prosperity.
- The *personal development* purpose is to ensure that all members of society benefit from the contribution that the values and skills of science can make to their ability to learn and operate successfully throughout life.
- The *utilitarian* purpose is to ensure that all members of society have sufficient knowledge of science to operate effectively and critically in activities where science can make a contribution to their personal well-being and quality of life.

A few years earlier, Driver et al. (1996) had generated a broadly similar list, save that the personal development purpose was replaced by a moral argument: "that the practice of science embodies norms and commitments, which are of wider value" (p. 11).

SCIENTIFIC LITERACIES

Michaels and O'Connor (1990) make the point that literacy is inherently a *plural* notion.

> We each have, and indeed fail to have, many different literacies. Each of these literacies is an integration of ways of thinking, talking, interacting and valuing, in addition to reading and writing... ways of being in the world and ways of making meaning. (p. 11)

In response to the diversity of arguments for promoting it, Shen (1975) identified three categories of scientific literacy: *practical, civic* and *cultural*. Practical scientific literacy is knowledge that can be used by individuals to cope with life's everyday problems (diet, health, consumer preferences, technological competence, and so on); civic scientific literacy comprises the knowledge, skills, attitudes and values necessary to play a full and active part in decision-making in key areas such as energy policy, use of natural resources, environmental protection and moral-ethical considerations relating to medical and technological innovations; cultural scientific literacy includes knowledge of the major ideas and theories of science, and the sociocultural and intellectual environment in which they were produced. The term cultural scientific literacy is used to signal belief that the fundamental theories of science collectively constitute a cultural heritage and resource to which everyone should have access. Layton et al. (1993) have described this aspect of scientific literacy as "recognition and appreciation of 'the cathedrals of science', science as a majestic achievement of the human intellect and spirit" (p. 15). Wellington (2001) reaches a conclusion similar to Shen's when he argues that there are three basic justifications for curriculum content: (i) intrinsic value (cultural scientific literacy), (ii) citizenship needs (civic scientific literacy), and (iii) utilitarian arguments (practical scientific literacy). Shamos (1995) also deploys a three-fold categorization of scientific literacy, but unlike Shen and Wellington he sees his categories as hierarchical. For Shamos, *cultural* scientific literacy is the simplest, most basic level of literacy. It comprises the scientific understanding needed to make sense of articles in newspapers and magazines, and programmes on television, communicate with elected representatives, and follow debates on public issues with a science and technology dimension. *Functional* scientific literacy builds on cultural scientific literacy by "requiring that the individual not only have command of a science lexicon, but also be able to converse, read, and write coherently, using such science terms in a perhaps non-technical but nevertheless meaningful context" (Shamos, 1995, p. 8). *True* scientific literacy, as Shamos calls it, involves knowledge and understanding of major scientific theories, including "how they were arrived at, and why they are widely accepted, how science achieves order out of a random universe... the role of experiment... the importance of proper questioning, of analytical and deductive reasoning, of logical thought processes, and of reliance on objective evidence" (p. 89). Bybee (1997) also arranges conceptions of scientific literacy into a hierarchy: *nominal* scientific literacy (knowing scientific words but not always understanding their meaning); *functional* scientific literacy (being able to read and write science using simple and appropriate vocabulary, but with little understanding of larger conceptual frameworks); *conceptual and procedural* scientific literacy (a thorough understanding of both the conceptual and procedural bases of science); and *multidisciplinary* or *multidimensional* scientific literacy (a thorough and robust understanding of the conceptual and procedural structures of science, together with knowledge of the history of science, an understanding of the nature of science and appreciation of the complex interactions among science, technology and society)[4].

Bybee's notion of multidisciplinary scientific literacy raises some important questions about technology, the relationship between science and technology, and the meaning of technological literacy. While science can be regarded as a search for explanations of phenomena and events in the natural world, technology is the means by which people modify nature to meet their needs and wants, and better serve their interests (see Price and Cross (1995) for an extended discussion of science as *explanation* and technology as *knowhow*). While it is easy to think of technology in terms of artifacts (televisions, computers and microwave ovens; pesticides, fertilizers and antibiotics; automobiles, high speed trains and space stations; high-rise office blocks, water treatment plants and power stations; and so on), it is important to remember that it also includes the knowledge, skills and infrastructure necessary for the design, manufacture, operation and maintenance of those artifacts. Thus, Wajcman (2004) describes technology as "a seamless web or network combining artifacts, people, organizations, cultural meanings and knowledge" (p. 106). In his classic work, *The Culture of Technology*, Arnold Pacey (1983) defines technological products and practices in terms of a *technical* aspect (knowledge, skills, techniques, tools, machines, resources, materials and people), an *organizational* aspect (including economic and industrial activity, professional activity, users, consumers and trade unions) and a *cultural* aspect (goals, values, beliefs, aspirations, ethical codes, creative endeavour, etc.). Similarly, Carl Mitcham (1994) conceptualizes technology in terms of four aspects: (i) as objects, artifacts and products; (ii) as a distinctive form of knowledge, separate from science; (iii) as a cluster of processes (designing, constructing or manufacturing, evaluating, systematizing, etc.); and (iv) as volition (the notion that technology is part of our human will and, therefore, an intrinsic part of our culture). Importantly, in the context of this book, both writers note that technology reflects our needs, interests, values and aspirations. The key point is that technological artifacts are conceived, developed, manufactured and marketed as part of economic and social activity, and often have profound implications and consequences well beyond the immediate sphere of their deployment. For example, the invention of the motor car created the need for driving conventions and road rules, a legal framework for dealing with those who violate the rules, an insurance and vehicle licensing system, a means of training, testing and licensing drivers, the establishment of a car repair industry and an advertizing, marketing and retail industry, all in addition to the research and development activity within the motor vehicle design and manufacturing industry itself.

Although there are some important differences between them in terms of purposes, concepts, procedures and criteria for judging acceptability of solutions, science and technology are closely related. For example, scientific understanding of the natural world is the basis for much of contemporary technological development and, in turn, technology is essential to much contemporary scientific research, and in fields such as high energy physics and nanotechnology it is very difficult, if not impossible, to disentangle science and technology. For these reasons, some commentators choose to speak of *technoscience*. Johnson (1989) sums up the relationship between science and technology as follows:

> Technology is the application of knowledge, tools, and skills to solve practical problems and extend human capabilities. Technology is best described as process, but it is commonly known by its products and their effects on society.

It is enhanced by the discoveries of science and shaped by the designs of engineering. It is conceived by inventors and planners, raised to fruition by the work of entrepreneurs, and implemented and used by society... Technology's role is doing, making and implementing things. The principles of science, whether discovered or not, underlie technology. The results and actions of technology are subject to the laws of nature, even though technology has often preceded or even spawned the discovery of the science on which it is based. (p. 1 – cited by Lewis & Gagel, 1992, p. 127)

As noted in Hodson (2009a), there is sometimes considerable value in teachers emphasizing the differences between science and technology, and sometimes it is more important and more interesting to direct attention to the similarities. On occasions, it is important for students to think in a purely scientific way; on other occasions, it is crucial that they learn to think in a technological way (e.g., like an architect, doctor or engineer). And sometimes, especially when addressing complex real world issues and problems, it is necessary to draw on knowledge from a range of disciplines other than science and technology.

Discussion of what constitutes technological literacy (and, therefore, priorities for technology education) can be found in Dyrenfurth and Kozak (1991), Lewis and Gagel (1992), Layton (1993), Waetjen (1993), Barnett (1995), Gagel (1997), Jenkins (1997a,b), Bugliarello (2000), Petrina (2000), Cajas (2001, 2002), Gräber et al. (2002), DeVries (2005), Dakers (2006), Jones (2006), France (2007), Rose (2007)), Jones and de Vries (2009) and Williams (2009). While issues of definition will not be revisited here, I do wish to draw attention to David Layton's (1993) classification in terms of six "functional competencies".

- Technological awareness or *receiver competence*: the ability to recognize technology in use and acknowledge its possibilities.
- Technological application or *user competence*: the ability to use technology for specific purposes.
- Technological capability or *maker competence*: the ability to design and make artifacts.
- Technological impact assessment or *monitoring competence*: the ability to assess the personal and social implications of a technological development.
- Technological consciousness or *paradigmatic competence*: an acceptance of, and an ability to work within, a 'mental set' that defines what constitutes a problem, circumscribes what counts as a solution and prescribes the criteria in terms of which all technological activity is to be evaluated.
- Technological evaluation or *critic competence*: the ability to judge the worth of a technological development in the light of personal values and to step outside the 'mental set' to evaluate its wider impact.

A similar approach has been adopted by Gräber et al. (2002), culminating in a 7-component competency-based model of technological literacy comprising subject competence, epistemological competence, learning competence (using different learning strategies to build personal scientific knowledge), social competence (ability to work in a team on matters relating to science and technology), procedural competence, communicative competence and ethical competence. Although these other, more complex characterizations of technological literacy have been advanced, it is sufficient for my purposes to regard it as having the same three dimensions as scientific literacy, as envisaged by Shen (1975) – namely, *practical, civic* and *cultural.*

Any discussion of technological literacy inevitably raises important issues relating to computer technology. The World Wide Web, computer-aided design, word processing, data processing and electronic transfer of information have become the engines of economic growth and have fundamentally changed the ways we learn, communicate and do business. The notion of *computer literacy* extends well beyond the acquisition of basic computer skills and the capacity to use computer technology to gather and communicate information. It now encompasses: (i) the capacity to evaluate information for accuracy, relevance and appropriateness; (ii) the ability to detect implied meaning, bias and vested interest; (ii) awareness of the legal issues and moral-ethical dilemmas associated with open access to information, censorship and data protection; and (iv) sensitive and critical understanding of the socio-economic, political and cultural impact of computer technology and the globalization it has accelerated - issues to be addressed in subsequent chapters.

Scientific literacy also presupposes a reasonable level of literacy in its fundamental sense (Wellington & Osborne, 2001; Norris & Phillips, 2003; Fang, 2005; Yore & Treagust, 2006). Scientific knowledge cannot be articulated and communicated except through text and its associated symbols, diagrams, graphs and equations. Thus, engagement in science, contribution to debate about science and access to science education are not possible without a reasonable level of literacy. Moreover, the specialized language of science makes it possible for scientists to construct an alternative interpretation and explanation of events and phenomena to that provided by ordinary, everyday language. It is scientific language that shapes our ideas, provides the means for constructing scientific understanding and explanations, enables us to communicate the purposes, procedures, findings, conclusions and implications of our inquiries, and allows us to relate our work to existing knowledge and understanding. Indeed, it could be said that learning the language of science is synonymous with (or certainly coincident with) learning science.

> Without text, the social practices that make science possible could not be engaged: (a) the recording and presentation and re-presentation of data; (b) the encoding and preservation of accepted science for other scientists; (c) the peer reviewing of ideas by scientists anywhere in the world; (d) the critical re-examination of ideas once published; (e) the future connecting of ideas that were developed previously; (f) the communication of scientific ideas between those who have never met, even between those who did not live contemporaneously; (g) the encoding of variant positions; and (h) the focusing of concerted attention on a fixed set of ideas for the purpose of interpretation, prediction, explanation, or test. The practices centrally involve texts, through their creation in writing and their interpretation, analysis, and critique through reading. (Norris & Phillips, 2008, p. 256)

If it is correct that most people, including many still in school, obtain most of their knowledge of contemporary science and technology from television, newspapers, magazines and the Internet (National Science Board, 1998; Select Committee,

2000; Falk, 2009), then the capacity for active critical engagement with text is a crucial element of scientific literacy. Indeed, it could be claimed that it is the *most important* element.

> To be fully scientifically literate, students need to be able to distinguish among good science, bad science and non-science, make critical judgements about what to believe, and use scientific information and knowledge to inform decision making at the personal, employment and community level. In other words, they need to be *critical consumers* of science. This entails recognizing that scientific text is a cultural artifact, and so may carry implicit messages relating to interests, values, power, class, gender, ethnicity and sexual orientation. (Hodson, 2008, p. 3)

Because meaning in science is also conveyed through symbols, graphs, diagrams, tables, charts, chemical formulae, reaction equations, 3-D models, mathematical expressions, photographs, computer-generated images, body scans and so on, Lemke (1998) refers to the language of science as "multi-modal communication". Any one scientific text might contain an array of such modes of communication, such that it may be more appropriate to refer to the *languages* of science.

> Science does not speak of the world in the language of words alone, and in many cases it simply cannot do so. The natural language of science is a synergistic integration of words, diagrams, pictures, graphs, maps, equations, tables, charts, and other forms of visual mathematical expression. (Lemke, 1998, p. 3)

Thus, the overall meaning of a scientific text or a science lesson is built by combining a partial meaning from the words with a partial meaning from the diagrams, equations and other "inscriptional devices" (as Latour, 1990, calls them) and a partial meaning from the mathematics. The key to effective communication in science, and to understanding the communications of others, resides in appreciation of how these different forms of representation interact and support each other (Sherin, 2001; Ainsworth, 2006; Moje, 2008; Tang & Moje, 2010). Indeed, Tang and Moje (2010) define scientific literacy as "the cultural practices that encompass specific ways of talking, writing, viewing, drawing, graphing, and acting, within a specialized discourse community" (p. 83). Most significant of all is critical media literacy, an issue to be discussed in chapter 2. For the purposes of this book, I am defining media literacy as the ability to access, analyze, evaluate and produce communications in a variety of forms. A media literate person can think critically about what they see, hear and read (and what they wish to say) in books, newspapers, magazines, television, radio, movies, music, advertizing, video games and the Internet, and can respond critically and appropriately to emerging communications technology. As Hornig Priest (2006) reminds us, media literacy is important "not because media directly determine (or ever fully reflect) public opinion, but because media accounts express relevant values and beliefs, help confer legitimacy to or discredit particular groups by treating them as part of the mainstream or as marginal, and therefore indirectly affect which perspectives do or do not ultimately come to dominate collective discourse and decision-making" (p. 58).

Scientific literacy also presupposes some basic understanding of mathematics, such as familiarity with simple algebraic equations and their manipulation, the capacity to interpret graphical and numerical data, and sufficient knowledge of statistics and the mathematics of probability to understand issues of risk, uncertainty and cost-benefit analysis. It also presupposes some historical understanding of the role of mathematics in both theory building and design of investigative procedures in science, medicine and engineering, and the capacity to recognize situations in which mathematics and/or statistics are being misused. A discussion of what constitutes mathematical literacy is well outside the scope of this book. Noss (1998), English (2002), Jablonka (2003) and Yore et al. (2007) provide some valuable perspectives on the question. As an aside, I would argue that overcoming so-called "maths phobia" and addressing the distrust with which many people regard any argument that deploys statistics (because, they say, "statistics can prove anything!") are much more important elements of building scientific and technological literacy than many science teachers recognize.

The notion of *environmental literacy* is also enormously helpful in building a comprehensive picture of scientific and technological literacy, especially in relation to critical consideration of environmental issues and other SSI. Indeed, given the accelerating pace of environmental degradation, it is now abundantly clear that the planet can no longer accommodate a scientifically illiterate, technologically illiterate, environmentally illiterate, uncritical and uncaring yet technologically powerful species. In the words of Carl Sagan (1995):

> The consequences of scientific illiteracy are far more dangerous in our time than in any that has come before. It's perilous and foolhardy for the average citizen to remain ignorant about global warming, say, or ozone depletion, air pollution, toxic and radioactive wastes, acid rain, topsoil erosion, tropical deforestation, exponential population growth. (p. 6)

The consequences of *not* giving prominence to environmental literacy in the curriculum are vividly illustrated by David Orr (1992).

> A generation of ecological yahoos without a clue why the color of the water in their rivers is related to their food supply, or why storms are becoming more severe as the planet warms. The same persons as adults will create businesses, vote, have families, and above all, consume. If they come to reflect on the discrepancy between the splendor of their private lives in a hotter, more toxic and violent world, as ecological illiterates they will have roughly the same success as one trying to balance a checkbook without knowing arithmetic. (p. 86)

Although the term environmental literacy is not universally accepted, with some writers opting for "environmental awareness", "ecological literacy", "environmental responsibility" or even "ecological/environmental citizenship" (Hart, 2007), there is some general agreement on its major components. For example, environmental literacy necessarily includes a clear and robust understanding of a range of biological concepts, ideas and theories, including: cycles, flows and fluctuations (energy, weather, etc.); population concepts (including limiting factors and carrying capacity); interactions, interdependence and coevolution; communities and ecosystems; diversity, change, succession and homeostasis; food webs; mechanisms of climate change and ozone depletion; and so on. It includes the ability to adopt systems thinking to address the complex interactions between human society and the natural world. It includes attitudes and values that reflect feelings of concern for the environment and foster both a sensitive environmental ethic and a sense of responsibility to address issues and resolve environmental problems through participation and action, both as individuals and as members of groups. Like scientific literacy, it includes the adoption of a critical attitude towards received information, skepticism about extravagant claims, and a determination to subject all expressed opinions to close scrutiny.

It is interesting to trace the development of the concept of environmental literacy and shifts in views about the aim/purpose of environmental education. As long ago as 1976, the Belgrade Charter stated that the goal of environmental education is "to develop a world population that is aware of, and concerned about, the environment and its associated problems, and which has the knowledge, skills, attitudes, motivations and commitment to work individually and collectively toward solutions of current problems and the prevention of new ones (UNESCO-UNEP, 1976, p. 2). It is both noteworthy and surprising that words like *society*, *economics*, *politics* and *development* were entirely absent. Nearly 15 years later, Marcinkowski et al. (1990) stated that the aim of environmental education is "to aid citizens in becoming environmentally knowledgeable and, above all, skilled and dedicated for working, individually and collectively, toward achieving and/or maintaining a dynamic equilibrium between quality of life and quality of environment" (p. 1). At about the same time, Brennan (1994) defined an environmentally literate citizen as one who "will have a blend of ecological sensitivity, moral maturity, and informed awareness of natural processes that would make her or him unlikely to contribute to further degradation of natural process at either individual or corporate levels" (p. 5). In an attempt to impose a more rigorous theoretical structure, Marcinkowski (1991) generated a set of nine statements to characterize the nature of environmental literacy.

1. An awareness and sensitivity towards the environment.
2. An attitude of respect for the natural environment, and concern for the nature and magnitude of human impact on it.
3. Knowledge and understanding of how natural systems work, and how social systems interact with natural systems.
4. An understanding of environmental problems and issues (local, regional, national, international and global).
5. The skills required to analyze, synthesize and evaluate information about environmental problems/issues, using both primary and secondary sources.
6. A sense of personal investment, responsibility and motivation to work individually and collectively towards the resolution of environmental problems and issues.
7. Knowledge of strategies available for addressing environmental problems and issues.

8. The skills required to develop, implement and evaluate both single strategies and composite plans for remediation of environmental problems and issues.
9. Active involvement at all levels in working towards the resolution of environmental problems and issues.

Of course, literacy (whether it is literacy in its fundamental sense, scientific literacy, technological literacy or environmental literacy) is not a state that an individual can be deemed to have attained when a particular level of understanding is reached. It is not simply a matter of being literate or illiterate. Rather, there are levels of literacy distributed along a continuum. Accordingly, Roth (1992) developed a framework of knowledge, skills, affective attributes and behaviours arranged into what he calls *nominal, functional* and *operational* forms of environmental competence. Those at the nominal level have "a very rudimentary knowledge of how natural systems work and how human social systems interact with them"; at the fundamental level, they are "aware and concerned about the negative interactions between these systems in terms of at least one or more issues and have developed the skills to analyze, synthesize, and evaluate information about them using primary and secondary sources"; and at the operational level, they "routinely evaluate the impacts and consequences of actions, gathering and synthesizing pertinent information, choosing among alternatives, and advocating action positions and taking actions that work to sustain or enhance a healthy environment" (p. 26). This idea of environmental competencies was also used by Lemons (1991): the ability to apply ecological principles to the analysis of environmental issues, including the analysis of alternative solutions to problems; the ability to understand how political, economic, social, literary, religious and philosophical traditions and activities influence the environment; the ability to understand the role of citizen participation in solving environmental problems; and the ability to apply action-oriented problem-solving skills to achieve conduct appropriate to environmental protection. These same elements are included in John Smyth's (1995) hierarchical ordering of environmental *awareness*, environmental *literacy*, environmental *responsibility*, environmental *competence* and environmental *citizenship*. They are reflected, too, in the distinction drawn by Berkowitz et al. (2005) between *ecological literacy* ("the ability to use ecological understanding, thinking and habits of mind for living in, enjoying, and/or studying the environment") and *ecological citizenship* ("having the motivation, self-confidence and awareness of one's values, and the practical wisdom and ability to put one's civics and ecological literacy into action" (p. 228)[5]. Drawing on a perceived parallel with notions of functional, cultural and critical literacy (Williams & Snipper, 1990), Stables (1998) postulates three dimensions of environmental literacy: *functional* environmental literacy – understanding of the language, concepts and principles used to describe and theorize the natural and built environments, together with the skills needed to gather further knowledge and information; *cultural* environmental literacy – an understanding of how the natural environment has been shaped by human beings as well as by weather, glaciation and volcanic activity, together with appreciation of the significance of natural images and landscapes in human culture; *critical* environmental literacy – understanding of the economic, social and political factors that contribute to environmental change, how decisions that impact the environment are made and how decision-making might be influenced and re-directed.

It would be a relatively straightforward matter to incorporate this 3-fold classifica-tion, together with elements of the notion of environmental competencies advanced by Lemons (1991) and Roth (1992), into an extended definition of practical scientific literacy, civic scientific literacy and cultural scientific literacy.

Before leaving this discussion, it is important to note that Stables and Bishop (2001) draw a distinction between what they call "weak environmental literacy", as defined by Marcinkowski (1991) and Roth (1992), and their own notion of "strong environmental literacy" based on a broad view of literacy in its fundamental sense. The gist of their argument is that we can consider the environment as *text*[6]. Like text, the sense that we make of 'environment', both individually and collectively, is infused with a raft of historical, cultural and aesthetic dimensions, as well as scientific aspects. It follows that there is no one 'correct way' of understanding the environment; different cultural and social groups will hold different views and will identify different aspects as significant and different issues as problematic. Some key differences in how environmental literacy is perceived are evident in the wide range of approaches to environmental education. Lucie Sauvé (2005) identifies as many as fifteen overlapping approaches or "currents of intervention", as she calls them, each of which embodies a particular conception of the environment, a distinctive aim (although it may be implicit rather than explicit) and a preferred pedagogy[7]. As will become evident in subsequent chapters, the approach to science and technology education advocated in this book includes elements of almost all of these approaches, most notably the scientific, problem-solving, socially critical and values-centred "currents" will be utilized in chapter 3, the naturalist, feminist, ethnographic, values-centred, holistic, sustainability and eco-education "currents" will be discussed in chapter 8, and the humanist/mesological, bioregionalist and praxic "currents" will be prominent in chapter 9.

Also before leaving this discussion, and as a way of preparing the ground a little for discussion in chapters 3, 5, 8 and 9, it is important to comment on the problematic nature of concepts such as "sustainable development" and "education for sustainable development". Perhaps the most widely quoted definition of sustainable development is that proposed by Brundtland (1987):

> Sustainable development is development that meets the needs of the present without compromising the ability of future generations to meet their own needs... Sustainable development requires meeting the basic needs of all and extending to all the opportunity to fulfil their aspirations for a better life. (p. 8)

In a broadly similar definition, the UK Government (1996) stated that sustainable development means reconciling two aspirations: (i) achieving economic development to secure rising standards of living both now and in the future, and (ii) protecting and enhancing the environment now and for the future. A decade later, the Forum for the Future (2007) defined sustainable development as "a dynamic process, which enables all people to realize their potential and improve their quality of life in ways which simultaneously protect and enhance the Earth's life support systems" (www.forumforthefuture.org/what-is-sd). As Dissinger (1990), Shiva (1992), Smyth (1995), Dobson (1996), Stables (1996), Palmer (1998), Bonnett (1999, 2002, 2007), Sauvé (1999), Stables and Scott (1999), Rauch (2002), Robinson (2004), Elshof

(2005), Jickling (2005), Ashe et al. (2007), Jickling and Wals (2008), Kahn (2008), Stevenson (2008), Räthzel and Uzzell (2009) and Selby (2010) point out, such definitions are not just problematic, they are internally contradictory. Indeed, Bonnett (2002) remarks that the wide appeal of the term "sustainable development" is rooted in its ambiguous and paradoxical nature.

> By seeming to combine the highly desired goal of development with the equally highly desired goal of conservation of valuable things endangered, it is... set up as a goal which is so obviously attractive as to divert attention from its problematic nature. Sustainable development is something *everyone* can subscribe to, from enlightened captains of modern industry to subsistence farmers – the former concerned to create the conditions for sustained economic growth, the latter concerned to survive into the future and perhaps better their material lot there. Any problems are perceived not with the goal itself, but only with the means of achieving it. (p. 11, emphasis in original)

Exploiting such ambiguities enables politicians, industrialists and policy makers to give the impression that they wish to sustain natural ecosystems while pursuing development policies that are almost guaranteed to exacerbate the problems of environmental degradation. The problems, inconsistencies and irreconcilabilities of "sustainable development" begin to show up when questions are asked about precisely what is to be sustained, for whom, and for how long, by what means, and under what conditions. Gilbert Rist (1997) comments as follows: "For ecologists... sustainable development implies a production level that can be borne by the eco-system, and can therefore be kept up in the long-term... The dominant interpretation is quite different. It sees 'sustainable development' as an invitation to keep up 'development', that is, economic growth... The thing that is meant to be sustained really is 'development' not the tolerance capacity of the eco-system or of human societies" (pp. 192–194). This commitment to continued or even extended economic growth raises all kinds of questions about what "protecting and enhancing the environment" might mean. Yet the term *sustainable development* continues to be widely used and widely applauded as a desirable goal. As Jickling and Wals (2008) observe, "the interests of groups with radically different ideas about what should be sustained, are masked by illusions of shared understandings, values, and visions of the future" (p. 14). They liken this situation to Orwellian "double-think" in which people hold contradictory meanings for the same term and accept them both. Chapter 5 will address curriculum issues relevant to inculcating a more critical and politicized approach to questions of economic growth and sustainability, while chapter 8 will explore notions of sustainability and education for sustainability in greater depth. The link between environmental education and sustainable develop-ment is clearly spelled out in *Agenda 21*, the report of the 1992 Earth Summit.

> Education is critical for promoting sustainable development and improving the capacity of the people to address environment and development issues... It is critical for achieving environmental and ethical awareness, values and attitudes, skills and behaviour consistent with sustainable development and for effective public participation in decision-making. (UNCED, 1992, chapter 36: 2)

A follow-up document to chapter 36, *Reshaping Education for Sustainable Development*, stated: "The function of education in sustainable development is mainly to develop human capital and encourage technical progress, as well as fostering the cultural conditions favoring social and economic change... ensuring rapid and more equitable economic growth while diminishing environmental impacts" (Albala-Bertrand, 1992, p. 3). However, the precise nature of the relationship envisaged between environmental education and sustainable development is somewhat unclear. As McKeown and Hopkins (2003) point out, some writers, commentators and educators see education for sustainable development as an overarching umbrella, to which environmental education, science, mathematics, economics, social studies and many other disciplines can contribute. Others see consideration of sustainability issues as a part of environmental education. John Elliott (1999) draws an important distinction between an approach to environmental education in which students are expected to acquire a pre-specified body of knowledge, adopt a particular set of attitudes, subscribe to a prescribed set of values, and engage in a raft of designated behaviours, and an approach in which the goal is to foster a rational and critical approach to consideration of environmental issues and to their solution at the local, regional, national and global levels. My advocacy of this second approach, which Elliott calls the democratic approach, carries with it an acknowledgement that the idea of sustainable *development* as envisaged by Brundtland et al. (1987) is a nonsense and should be replaced by the notion of *sustainability*, not least because it raises important questions about our conception of the natural environment and our role/place within it. It is both interesting and encouraging that Canada's national environmental education plan is titled "*A Framework for Environmental Learning and Sustainability*" (Government of Canada, 2002).

Finally, Hart and Nolan (1999) note that although the field of environmental education appears to be fragmented, and beset with some radical differences in approach, researchers are interweaving their work in ways that advance environmental education discourse. Sammel (2003) goes further, suggesting that "the existence of conflicting paradigms in environmental education may drive the process of change in much the same way as debates about the appropriateness of competing paradigms in science drives the process of scientific advancement" (p. 31).

EXPERTS AND AUTHORITIES

In the contemporary world we are increasingly dependent on experts. As Jasanoff (1997) comments, "Without authoritative, expert institutions, we could not be reasonably sure that the air is safe to breathe, that aeroplanes will take off and land safely, that new medical treatments will not unexpectedly kill patients... that the food we buy is safe to eat. Lives lacking such assurance would be impossibly difficult to cope with, both pragmatically and psychologically" (p. 223). When dealing with socioscientific issues and appraising new technologies, individuals will only rarely have access to all the relevant data. In consequence, we depend on others to inform us and advise us. For example, we are increasingly dependent on scientists, the inquiries they conduct, and the agencies that report their studies, to tell us about the safety hazards associated with various products and procedures, the toxic effects of pesticides, pharmaceuticals and other materials we encounter in everyday life, the risks associated with post-menopausal HRT, the optimal frequency of mammograms, the threats to our health posed by the proximity of toxic waste dumps, nuclear power plants and overhead power lines, and the large-scale compromising of environmental health through loss of biodiversity, increasing desertification, pollution and global warming. However, it is highly undesirable to cede all deliberation and *all* policy decisions to a particular small group of experts. We need to know when to accept and when to question, when to trust and when to distrust. It is crucial, therefore, that each of us understands how reliable and valid data are collected and interpreted, and that each of us recognizes the tentative character of scientific knowledge. Hence the emphasis given to NOS understanding in earlier discussion. It is crucial, too, that we understand the ways in which all manner of human interests can and do shape scientific inquiry and its interpretation and reporting. Without this insight, we have no alternative but to take reports that blame or exonerate at face value, and to accept all claims to scientific knowledge as 'proven'.

Fourez (1997) argues that knowing when scientists and other 'experts' can be trusted and when their motives and/or methods should be called into question is a key element of scientific literacy. His point is that while there is often a need to access and utilize expert opinion, we do not need to do so uncritically. We can evaluate the quality of data and argument for ourselves, we can look at the extent of agreement among experts and the focus of any disagreements, and we can look at the 'track record' of all those who profess expertise. Walton (1997) provides a list of questions we should ask when addressing an expert's claim(s). Is the utterance within the scientist's field of expertise? Is the cited expert really an expert (as distinct from someone with a well-publicized but unsubstantiated opinion that is quoted because of popularity or celebrity status)? How authoritative is the expert? Is the expert recognized by colleagues as a leader in the field? Is the expert recognized as honest and reliable? If there is disagreement among scientists, are alternative views acknowledged and addressed Is supporting evidence available and the utterance in accordance with this evidence? Is the expert's utterance clear and intelligible, and correctly interpreted? In similar vein, Norris (1995) makes the point that "nonscientists' belief or disbelief in scientific propositions is not based on direct evidence for or against those propositions but, rather, on reasons for believing or disbelieving the scientists who assert them" (p. 206). Ungar (2000) wryly observes that with increasing research specialization, the domain covered by any claimed expertise is continuously shrinking, creating a "knowledge-ignorance paradox" in which the growth of specialized knowledge results in a simultaneous increase in ignorance of related fields, requiring us to consult an ever-expanding range of experts.

Clearly, the independent justification of most of our beliefs is just not possible. Even those at the cutting edge of research must take on trust much of the knowledge they deploy, including the knowledge underpinning the design and utilization of the complex modern instrumental techniques on which so much contemporary research depends. To deal with this situation, Hardwig (1991) proposes the *principle of testimony*: "If A has good reasons to believe that B has good reasons to believe p, then A has good reasons to believe p" (p. 697). In essence, he argues that A's good reasons depend on whether B can be regarded as truthful, competent and conscientious. In short, it isn't possible to draw a sharp distinction between evaluation of the research and evaluation of the trustworthiness of the researcher. This principle of testimony also applies to the relationship between laypersons and 'experts'. Generally, neither members of the public nor journalists and documentary makers have access to original empirical data, or to details of research methods, and so must decide the extent to which they can trust particular researchers and research groups to be honest in their reporting. Code (1987) notes that "one of the most important and difficult steps in learning who can be trusted is realizing that authority cannot create truth" (p. 248). Balance is the key: not blind acceptance of the views espoused by those who are seen, or see themselves, as experts; not cynicism and distrust of all experts. Guy Claxton (1997) captures the essence of this position particularly well: "[students] need to be able to see through the claims of Science to truth, universality, and trustworthiness, while at the same time not jumping out of the frying-pan of awe and gullibility, in the face of Science's smugness and superiority, into the fire of an equally dangerous and simplistic cynicism, or into the arms of the pseudo-certainties of the New Age" (p. 84, capitals in original). Balance is encapsulated in the notion of intellectual independence. As Munby (1980) notes: "One can be said to be intellectually independent when one has all the resources necessary for judging the truth of a knowledge claim independently of other people" (p. 15). Ratcliffe and Grace (2003) cite a study published by the Office of Science and Technology and the Wellcome Trust, in 2000, indicating that people tend to trust sources seen as neutral and independent, such as university scientists, scientists working for research charities or health campaigning groups, and presenters of television news broadcasts and documentaries. The least trusted sources are politicians and newspapers. Sources seen as having a vested interest, such as environmental activist groups, well-known scientists and the popular scientific press, rank somewhere in between in terms of trustworthiness. In Elliott's (2006) study, students were particularly skeptical about the relationship between science, the media and government. Often, there is an 'asymmetry of trust': episodes that weaken or threaten trust in science tend to receive greater exposure in the media and live longer in the public memory than episodes that seek to build or consolidate confidence in science and scientists. Chapter 6 includes details of some research findings relating to the trust that students and teachers place in published material relating to SSI, and their reasons for doing so. Chapter 6 also engages in discussion of how students' levels of critique and discernment can be enhanced.

Given the increasing calls for public consultation on matters such as funding priorities for scientific research and the acceptability of developments in genetic engineering (including calls such as those made in this book), it is pertinent to ask about the confidence and trust that scientists, politicians and business leaders have in the lay public to undertake these monitoring tasks responsibly and effectively. The scientists interviewed by Michael and Brown (2005) about issues relating to xeno-transplantation tended to regard the public as insufficiently prepared, especially on technical matters, unsystematic and likely to conflate issues that they believe should be kept separate, fickle, unpredictable, and likely to be swayed by strong rhetoric. Moreover, they said that the tendency to generalize from one or two unfortunate examples has resulted in the increasingly distrustful public noted in earlier in this chapter. Bucchi and Neresini (2008) argue that experts themselves may reinforce the perception of the public as "ignorant". They report on a Canadian study of communications between doctors and their patients that used questionnaires to assess patients' medical knowledge and doctors' estimates of patients' knowledge. While 75.8% of patients were seen to be "well-informed", in the sense of providing correct answers to questionnaire items, less than 50% of doctors were able to estimate their patients' knowledge accurately. Moreover and alarmingly, the authors report, even when doctors realized that patients didn't understand they failed to adjust their style of communication. By making no attempt to communicate effectively, they compounded their patients' ignorance.

Of particular relevance here is Michel Callon's (1999) 3-fold characterization of laypersons' involvement with scientists in the management of SSI. In the *deficit model*, it is assumed that only scientists are able to grasp the full complexity of the science and citizens have to be properly informed or "brought up to speed"[8]; in the *public debate model*, citizens' knowledge is recognized as different from scientists' knowledge but valuable for enriching and contextualizing the issues and problems; in *the co-production of knowledge model*, citizens are regarded as having a key role in defining the issues/problems, identifying both the kind of knowledge to be accessed and the particular scientists and engineers consulted, and producing and disseminating the report, conclusions and policy decisions. These three models of citizen involvement will be revisited in chapters 4 and 9.

CRITICAL SCIENTIFIC LITERACY

As noted in earlier discussion and will become more apparent in chapters 3 and 5, I share the views of Tate (2001) and Calabrese Barton (2002) that the science curriculum should be concerned with civil rights and civil responsibilities, and should be framed around ideas of equity and social justice. I also share the views expressed by Lee and Roth (2002) that science education should not be seen as a preparation for a future life but as an active participation in the community here and now. To fulfill this role, students need to be able to judge the validity of a knowledge claim independently of other people, tell the difference between good science and bad science, and between science and non-science, and recognize misuse of science, biased or fraudulent science and unwarranted claims whenever and wherever they encounter them. It is for these reasons that I choose to adopt the term *critical scientific, technological and environmental literacy*, though for convenience and economy of space I will shorten it to critical scientific literacy. Its repeated use throughout this book carries the message that the most important function of scientific literacy is to confer a measure of intellectual independence and personal autonomy: first, an independence from authority; second, a disposition to test the plausibility and applicability of principles and ideas for oneself, whether by experience or by a critical evaluation of the testimony of others; third, an inclination to look beyond the superficial and to address the ideological underpinnings of science and technology, the economic and political structures that sustain them, and the norms and practices that accommodate some views and some participants but marginalize or exclude others; fourth, sensitivity to the complex interactions of class, race, gender, language, knowledge and power; fifth, an ability to form intentions and choose a course of action in accordance with a scale of values that is self-formulated; sixth, a commitment to criticism and constant re-evaluation of one's own knowledge, beliefs, attitudes and values. In other words, the fundamental purpose of critical scientific literacy is to help people think for themselves and reach their own conclusions about a range of issues that have a scientific, technological and/or environmental dimension. Use of "critical" as a qualifier for the term scientific literacy also carries with it a commitment to a much more rigorous, analytical, logical, thorough, open-minded, skeptical and reflective approach to school science education than is usual. It signals my advocacy of a much more politicized and issues-based science education, a central goal of which is to equip students with the capacity and commitment to take appropriate, responsible and effective action on matters of social, economic, environmental and moral-ethical concern (Hodson, 1999, 2003). This position aligns very closely with that advocated by McLaren and Lankshear (1993): "Critical literacy, as we are using the term, becomes the interpretation of the social present for the purpose of transforming the cultural life of certain groups, for questioning tacit assumptions and unarticulated presuppositions of current cultural and social formations and the subjectivities and capacities for agenthood that they foster. It aims at understanding the ongoing social struggles over the signs of culture and over the definition of social reality – over what is considered legitimate and preferred meaning at any given historical moment" (p. 413).

Hurd (1998) sums up part of this *critical* dimension of scientific literacy, and its roots in learning *about* science, when he defines a scientifically literate person as someone who "distinguishes experts from the uninformed, theory from dogma, data from myth and folklore, science from pseudo-science, evidence from propaganda, facts from fiction, sense from nonsense, and knowledge from opinion... Recognizes the cumulative, tentative, and skeptical nature of science, the limitations of scientific inquiry and causal explanations, the need for sufficient evidence and established knowledge to support or reject claims, the environmental, social, political and economic impact of science and technology, and the influence society has on science and technology" (p. 24). What Hurd doesn't emphasize to any significant extent is that this kind of understanding needs to be developed in such a way that students can see the sociopolitical embeddedness of science and technology. If science continues to be presented as an exercise in abstract puzzle solving, devoid of social, political, economic and cultural influences and consequences, citizens will continue to see contemporary SSI as predominantly technical problems, for which experts can be relied upon to provide the solutions. What we should be seeking instead is political engagement of citizens in monitoring and, to an extent, directing the course of scientific and technological development. It is both timely and encouraging, then, that the so-called Crick Report, *Education for Citizenship and the Teaching of Democracy in Schools*, has prompted the establishment of citizenship education comprising three strands – social and moral responsibility, community involvement, political literacy - as a mandatory part of the curriculum of all subjects in England and Wales. The declared aim of this initiative is:

... a change in the political culture of this country both nationally and locally: for people to think of themselves as active citizens, willing, able and equipped to have an influence in public life and with the critical capacities to weigh evidence before speaking and acting; to build on and to extend radically to young people the best in existing traditions of community involvement and public service, and to make them individually confident in finding new forms of involvement and action. (Qualifications & Curriculum Authority, 1998, p. 8)

The focus of this book is the kind of science education that is necessary for active and responsible citizenship, a form of science education that can equip students with the capacity and commitment to take appropriate, responsible and effective action on matters of social, economic, environmental and moral-ethical concern. In other words, the principal concern of this book is civic scientific literacy, as defined by Shen (1975) and Wellington (2001), and now re-defined as *critical* scientific literacy. While I recognize that civic, cultural and practical scientific literacy overlap, and that all three are important focuses for the school science curriculum, I believe that civic scientific literacy does warrant some measure of priority. In similar vein, the authors of *Beyond 2000: Science Education for the Future* (Millar & Osborne, 1998) state that science education between the ages of 5 and 16 (the years of compulsory schooling in the UK) should comprise a course to enhance general scientific literacy, with more specialized science education delayed to later years: "the structure of the science curriculum needs to differentiate more explicitly between those elements designed to enhance 'scientific literacy', and those designed as the early stages of a specialist training in science, so that the requirement for the latter does not come to distort the former" (p. 10)[9]. Similar sentiments are expressed by Smith and Gunstone (2009).

The drive to equip students with an understanding of science in its social, cultural, economic and political contexts is, of course, the underpinning rationale of the so-called science-technology-society (STS) approach, more recently expanded to STSE (where E stands for environment). James Gallagher (1971), one of the pioneers of STS education, captures its overall flavour particularly well.

For future citizens in a democracy, understanding the interrelations of science, technology, and society may be as important as understanding the concepts and processes of science. An awareness of the interrelations between science, technology, and society may be a prerequisite to intelligent action on the part of a future electorate and their chosen leaders. (p. 337)

STS has always been a purposefully ill-defined field that leaves ample scope for different interpretations, curriculum emphases and pedagogical approaches, and much has changed over the years in terms of its priorities and relative emphases (Fensham, 1988; Cheek, 1992; Bybee, 1993; Layton, 1993; Solomon, 1993; Yager & Tamir, 1993; Zoller, 1993; Bybee & DeBoer, 1994; Solomon & Aikenhead, 1994; Yager & Lutz, 1995; Yager, 1996; Kumar & Berlin, 1998; Kumar, 2000; Kumar & Chubin, 2000; Gaskell, 2001; Aikenhead, 2003; Pedretti, 2003; Solomon, 2003; Barrett & Pedretti, 2006; Tal & Kedmi, 2006; Nashon et al., 2008; Turner, 2008; Lee, 2010). Aikenhead (2005, 2006) describes how the early emphasis on values and social responsibility was systematized by utilizing a theoretical framework deriving from the sociology of science: (i) the interactions of science and scientists with social dimensions, issues and institutions *external* to the community of scientists, and (ii) the social interactions of scientists *within* the scientific community. Driver et al. (1996) refer to these two elements as "science *in* society" and "science *as* society" (p. 12). Both emphases have remained strong, though much has changed with respect to the sociopolitical and economic contexts in which educators and scientists work and in our understanding of key issues in the history, philosophy and sociology of science. Much has changed, too, in our theoretical knowledge concerning the ways in which students learn science and learn *about* science. Interestingly, as consideration of the nature of science has become a much more prominent part of regular science curricula, even a central part in many educational jurisdictions, so emphasis in STSE education has shifted much more towards confrontation of socioscientific issues (SSI).

Ratcliffe and Grace (2003) have identified a number of key features of socio-scientific issues. They have a basis in science, frequently at the frontiers of scientific knowledge, where data and evidence may be incomplete, conflicting or confusing; they involve the formation of opinions and making of choices at a personal and societal level; they address local, national and/or global issues, with attendant political and societal implications; they involve some cost-benefit analysis in which probability and risk interact with values; and they often feature prominently in the media. Zeidler et al. (2005) contrast SSI-oriented teaching with STS or STSE education in terms of its emphasis on developing habits of mind (specifically, developing skepticism, maintaining open-mindedness, acquiring the capacity for critical thinking, recognizing that there are multiple forms of inquiry, accepting ambiguity, and searching for data-driven knowledge) and "empowering students to consider how science-based issues reflect, in part, moral principles and elements of virtue that encompass their own lives, as well as the physical and social world around them" (p. 357)[10]. They argue that while STS education emphasizes the impact of scientific and technological development on society, it does not focus explicitly on the moral-ethical issues embedded in decision-making: "STS(E) education as currently practiced... only 'points out' ethical dilemmas or contro-versies, but does not necessarily exploit the inherent pedagogical power of discourse, reasoned argumentation, explicit NOS considerations, emotive, developmental, cultural or epistemological connections within the issues themselves... nor does it consider the moral or character development of students" (p. 359). In consequence, they say, STS education has become marginalized. Similar arguments can be found in Zeidler and Sadler (2008a,b) and Zeidler et al. (2009). Authors of pioneering initiatives such as *Science and Society* and *Science in a Social Context* (SISCON) in the UK, *PLON* in the Netherlands, and *Science: A Way of Knowing* in Saskatchewan (Canada), might be very surprised to read that their courses (even back then) did not include such matters, and many others currently teaching and researching in STSE education may be surprised to hear that they have been "marginalized". In an interesting reversal of these propositions, Hughes (2000) argues that STS has marginalized SSI, and simultaneously reinforced gender inequity by promoting a masculinist 'hard science' view to the exclusion of the 'softer' socioscience orientations (her words, not mine) that allow for contextualized examination of issues and values implicit in scientific development.

When socioscience is the icing on the cake, not an essential basic ingredient, part of a good-quality product but not fundamental to teaching science, dominant discourses of science as an abstract body of knowledge are not destabilized and implicit gender hierarchical binaries are readily reinforced. (p. 347).

As Bingle and Gaskell (1994) note, STS education tends to emphasize what Latour (1987) calls "ready made science" (with all its attendant implicit messages about certainty) rather than "science-in-the-making" (with its emphasis on social construction). Interestingly, Simmons and Zeidler (2003) argue that it is the priority given to science-in-the-making through consideration of *controversial* SSI that gives the SSI approach its special character: "Using controversial socioscientific issues as a foundation for individual consideration and group interaction provides an environment where students can and *will* develop their critical thinking and moral reasoning" (p. 83, emphasis added). In a further attempt at delineation, Zeidler et al. (2002) claim that the SSI approach has much broader scope, in that it "subsumes all that STS has to offer, while also considering the ethical dimensions of science, the moral reasoning of the child, and the emotional development of the student" (p. 344). It is also important to consider the myriad ways in which the concerns and priorities of the SSI-oriented approach overlap with those of many other movements and initiatives – principally, science education for citizenship, science education for public understanding, public awareness or public participation, education for sustainability, multicultural and antiracist science education, global education and peace studies.

It is not my intention to become embroiled in a 'turf war' or to engage in evaluation of claims by rival camps that ought to be 'fighting the same battle'. My view is that neither STSE nor SSI-oriented teaching go far enough. For my taste, both are too conservative. My inclination is towards a much more radical, politicized form of SSI-oriented teaching and learning in which students not only address complex and often controversial SSI, and formulate their own position concerning them, but also prepare for, and engage in, sociopolitical actions that they believe will 'make a difference'. Of course, adoption of this curriculum stance raises some important pedagogical issues, which will be addressed in chapters 2 and 6.

CONFRONTING SOCIOSCIENTIFIC ISSUES

It seems almost self-evident that the most effective way of learning to confront SSI is by confronting SSI, provided there are appropriate levels of guidance and support. What I have in mind is a 3-phase approach involving *modelling* (the teacher demonstrates and explains the desired or appropriate approach), *guided practice* (students perform specified tasks with help and support from the teacher) and *application* (students perform independently of the teacher). Teacher modelling (phase 1) is predicated on the assumption that careful observation of someone skilled in the approach will facilitate the learning of successful strategies for addressing SSI. In the second phase (guided practice), students work through a carefully sequenced programme of investigative exercises, during which the teacher's role is to act as learning resource, facilitator, consultant and critic. The assumption is that students will become more expert in addressing SSI as a consequence of practice and experience, through evaluative feedback provided by the teacher and generated in inter-group criticism and discussion, and through intra-group reflection on the activity, both as it progresses and on completion. This is the stage during which teacher and students are *co-investigators*, with both parties asking questions, contributing ideas, making criticisms and lending support. This means that teachers are learning, too! To be intellectually independent, however, students must eventually be able to manage without teacher assistance and take responsibility for planning, conducting and reporting their own inquiries (the application stage). In other words, learning as assisted performance must enable students, in time, to use their knowledge to address new issues, build new understanding and make decisions on where they stand in relation to an issue.

It also seems self-evident that if students are to get to grips with SSI at any level beyond the merely superficial they need relevant scientific knowledge. Common sense would seem to indicate that content knowledge is crucial, and that those who know more about the topic/issue under consideration will be better positioned to understand the underlying issues, evaluate different positions, reach their own conclusions, make an informed decision on where they stand in relation to the issue, and argue their point of view. It is unsurprising, therefore, that consumers' ability to make sense of advertizing claims for cosmetics and so-called "functional foods" (e.g., those touted as useful for lowering cholesterol or "balancing your stomach's good and bad bacteria"), and to reject those making spurious claims, is closely linked to their level of education in science (Dodds, et al., 2008). Similarly, Keselman et al. (2004) found that the capacity of Grade 7 and Grade 9 students to reason about information concerning HIV-AIDS, accessed via a simulated Website, and to deal with myths about HIV-AIDS[11], bore a direct relation to the nature and extent of their knowledge of biology, particularly the characteristics of viruses, mechanisms of infection, and the nature of the immune system. In a subsequent study, Keselman et al. (2007) found that structured writing activities involving a measure of role play had substantial positive impact on students' acquisition of scientific knowledge relevant to consideration of the myths, and on their capacity to use it appropriately. Earlier, Wynne et al. (2001) had shown how a group of high school students were able to use their knowledge of meiosis, often in "very sophisticated ways", to address some complex issues in genetics, and Lewis and Leach (2006) had found that the quality of discussion of issues relating to genetic engineering is substantially enhanced by basic understanding of genetics. The latter authors note that the necessary level of understanding is "relatively modest" and fairly easily achieved. Similarly, Sadler and Zeidler (2005) note that students with deeper understanding of genetics made fewer errors of reasoning and made more frequent and explicit reference to content knowledge in their reasoning about gene therapy and cloning than students with more naïve understanding. A study by Sadler and Donnelly (2006), also in the context of gene therapy and cloning, concludes that a minimum level of basic biological knowledge is essential if students are to understand the nature of the problem and what might constitute appropriate evidence on which to base their decision-making. Beyond that, the authors say, there is little evidence that background knowledge in genetics impacts significantly on ability to build arguments and establish points of view. What may be much more important is *context* knowledge – in this case, specific knowledge of gene therapy and cloning. In a closely related study, Sadler and Fowler (2006) show that College-level science majors with advanced biological knowledge (that may have included knowledge of genetic technologies) significantly outperformed both non-science majors and high school students in the sense of making repeated, explicit and appropriate reference to scientific knowledge in construction and criticism of arguments. In other words, when students' science content knowledge is extensive in depth, breadth and organization it does make a difference to their ability to deploy it effectively in unfamiliar contexts (Ryder, 2001). Yang's (2004) study of Taiwanese Grade 10 students indicates that male students are more likely than female students to have background knowledge relevant to SSI contexts, and to have more confidence in their ability to deploy it in social contexts. Interestingly, they are also more likely to be naively trusting of experts. Studies by Patronis et al. (1999), Hogan (2002a), Dawson and Schibeci (2003), Sadler (2004), Sadler and Zeidler (2004), Zeidler et al. (2002, 2005) and Dawson (2007) provide further confirmation of the importance of science content knowledge.

Sometimes specialized knowledge well beyond science is needed. For example, in order to address the "septic tank crisis" in their school (see discussion in chapter 9), students in Pedretti's (1997) study needed to know about the water cycle, of course, but also about septic tank systems, waste management practices, filtration methods, environmental hazards and local government regulations. In Hogan's (2002) study of Grade 8 students addressing water management issues concerning the impact of invasive zebra mussels on the Hudson River ecology, students had difficulty in adapting their scientific knowledge and understanding to a real world and changing context. They were intent on looking for simple, rather than multiple cause and effect relationships and seemed unable to take the long-term perspective demanded by systems thinking. As will be discussed in chapter 8, the shift to systems thinking is key to the critical scientific literacy necessary for addressing environmental issues. Also of relevance here is the study of problem-solving strategies employed by 14–17 year-old students conducted by Reid and Yang (2002). The authors concluded that knowledge seems to exist in long term memory as relatively independent "islands". Students have great difficulty in linking these islands of knowledge; they have problems in accessing usable knowledge when the problem situation is novel to them (i.e., they have problems in *applying* knowledge); they frequently make inappropriate or unhelpful links. Common sense suggests that students will become more expert in accessing and deploying their knowledge through teacher guidance, support and criticism, further experience, and critical reflection.

A key question concerns the manner in which relevant scientific knowledge should be acquired. Should it be through prior instruction or on a 'need to know' basis when dealing with a particular issue? As is so often the case in education, there is no universal answer; different situations demand different approaches and different SSI create widely different knowledge needs. Clearly, the notions of cultural scientific literacy and practical scientific literacy require that a substantial amount of scientific content is taught, but this book is not concerned with the selection of that science content, nor with discussion of how to bring about an appropriate level of understanding of the important ideas, principles, models and theories of science. My only comment on the matter at this stage is that I wish to endorse my previous promotion of a *personalized* approach to learning (Hodson, 1998a), that is, attending to the particular needs, interests, experiences, aspirations and values of every learner, and to the affective and social dimensions of learning environments. The key to successful learning of science content (or anything else, for that matter) lies in the creation of a supportive and emotionally safe learning environment for all students. The notion of *scaffolding* is particularly helpful (Wood et al., 1976; Collins et al., 1989; Stone, 1993, 1998; Hogan & Pressley, 1997). Scaffolding involves the teacher (or a knowledgeable 'other') adjusting the complexity of the learning task so that the learner is able to solve a problem, perform a task or achieve a goal that would be beyond their unassisted efforts. Scaffolding should not alter the overall structure of the learning task. Rather, it should adjust the precise nature of the learner's participation as the teacher assumes responsibility for those aspects of the task that require knowledge or skills that the learner doesn't yet possess. In a scaffolded task, teacher assistance is only considered productive if the learner has fully comprehended the purpose and structure of the task, understands why the particular strategies were employed, and appreciates how the conclusions have been reached. Only in these circumstances will assistance be educative, criticism productive and feedback effective. These mattters are discussed at greater length in Hodson and Hodson (1998a,b). One further point is worth making: as the literature on problem-based learning makes abundantly clear, content learning is often more secure, more robust and 'longer lasting' when it is embedded in open-ended problem situations. By grounding content in socially and personally relevant contexts, an SSI-oriented approach provides the motivation that is absent from current abstract, de-contextualized approaches and forms a base from which students can construct understanding that is personally relevant, meaningful and important. It also provides increased opportunities for active learning, inquiry-based learning, collaborative learning and direct experience of the situatedness and multidimensionality of scientific and technological practice.

As an aside, it is both interesting and important to note that Aikenhead (2005, 2006) identifies seven categories of scientific knowledge: *wish-they-knew* science is the high status academic knowledge needed for successful university study and a future career as a scientist; *functional* science is the science needed by those who use science-related and technology-related knowledge in their day-to-day work (such knowledge is often learned on-the-job); *need-to-know* science is that used by the lay public in confronting real life SSI (described by Layton et al. (1993) as "practical knowledge for action" – see later in this chapter); *have-cause-to-know* science is knowledge designated by experts as necessary for dealing with real life matters (it often contrasts sharply with knowledge in the previous category, as discussion later in the chapter makes clear); *enticed-to-know* science is knowledge that attracts attention through its prominence in the media, including the Internet (it often focuses on issues of risk and moral-ethical dilemmas); *personal-curiosity* science is knowledge identified by individuals as important for all manner of personal or idiosyncratic reasons; *science-as-culture* is the knowledge needed for active and effective participation in particular sub-cultural or community groups and/ or effective communication with those employed in those groups (including, for example, the public health system, local council planning services and environmental activist groups). The notion of critical scientific literacy developed in the previous chapter encompasses knowledge embedded in several of Aikenhead's seven categories.

NATURE OF SCIENCE

It is clear that no science curriculum can equip citizens with thorough first-hand knowledge of all the science underlying every important issue. Indeed, much of the scientific knowledge students need to know in order to make important decisions on the many important SSI they will encounter during their lifetimes has yet to be discovered. However, we *do* know what knowledge, skills and attitudes are essential for appraising scientific reports, evaluating scientific arguments and moving towards a personal opinion about the science and technology dimensions of real world issues. It includes understanding of the status of scientific knowledge, the ways in which it is generated, communicated and scrutinized by the community of scientists, and the extent to which it can be relied upon to inform critical decisions about SSI. As the authors of the American *National Science Education Standards* document comment: "A literate citizen should be able to evaluate the quality of scientific information on the basis of its source and the methods used to generate it" (National Research Council, 1996, p. 22). In other words, students need to have a clear understanding of what counts as *good* science, that is, a well-designed inquiry and a well-argued conclusion. They need to be able to interpret reports, make sense of disagreements, evaluate knowledge claims, scrutinize arguments, distinguish among facts, arguments and opinions, make judgements about good science, bad science and non-science, detect error, bias and vested interest, and so on. Clearly, students' NOS knowledge and views will impact on the way they address SSI, but not always in a simple, straightforward and predictable way (Ryder, 2001; Zeidler et al., 2002). There is a complex, reflexive interaction: more sophisticated NOS views open up new possibilities for scrutinizing SSI; engagement with important and personally significant SSI enhances and refines NOS understanding.

The traditional school curriculum emphasis on *what* we know rather than *how* we know too often leaves students only able to justify their beliefs by reference to the authority of the teacher or textbook. As Östman (1998) points out, the constant focus on a "correct explanations" approach encourages and reinforces the "companion meaning" that the products of the scientific enterprise are "something that everyone will agree upon, if they just use their senses to smell, taste, listen to, and look at nature" (p. 57). In other words, science is seen as a simple and straightforward route to the truth about the universe; scientific knowledge is seen as authoritative; students are steered towards conformity with received 'official' views rather than towards intellectual independence. As a consequence, they do not attempt to justify their beliefs in terms of careful consideration of the evidence and arguments. Instead, they simply assert their beliefs, and possibly cite the teacher, textbook or Internet site as an authority. They do not recognize that differences of opinion result from adoption of different theoretical perspectives and different interpretations of data. Rather, as Smith et al. (2000) note, "they assume that these differences stem from inadequate knowledge, deception, or deceit, and will ultimately be re-solved when all the facts are known or when one looks at the facts in an unbiased manner" (p. 352). Driver et al. (1996) and Larochelle and Désautels (2001) also remark on the widespread tendency for students to believe that disagreement between scientists is a consequence of insufficient data, and that disputes will be resolved satisfactorily when additional data are accumulated. Although the openness of science to criticism is seen by scientists and philosophers of science as one of its major strengths, it is seen by some members of the public, and by many students, as a sign that all is not well. As Ziman (2000) comments: "Nobody expects a group of lawyers, politicians, theologians or doctors to have identical expert views. But any outward sign of disagreement amongst scientists is taken as a grave weakness" (p. 254). In Bader's (2003) study, students urged scientists who disagreed (in this case, on climate change) to "work together" and conduct their research "at the same place", while Frewer et al. (2003) observe that many scientists have become reluctant to make any public statements on uncertainty in science on the grounds that it might further undermine the credibility of science and scientists.

The key point is that every citizen needs sufficient understanding *about* the relevant science (if not understanding *of* the science) in order to play a part in public debate about SSI. Every citizen needs to develop what Lorraine Code (1987) calls "a policy of circumspection" and what McPeck (1981) calls "reflective skepticism" – that is, the disposition to question and to seek the opinions of others on the science that underpins the issues they confront in everyday life. Duschl et al. (2007) express very similar views: "Students need to develop a shared understanding of the norms of participation in science. This includes social norms for constructing and presenting argument and engaging in scientific debates. It also includes habits of mind, such as adopting a critical stance, willingness to ask questions and seek help, and developing a sense of appropriate trust and skepticism" (p. 40). Citizens who do not understand how scientific research is done, and how scientific research is scrutinized for validity and reliability, have little option but to accept the pronouncements and recommendations of those they perceive to be 'experts' or are persuaded to accept as such (an issue raised in chapter 1 and discussed further in chapter 4). Abd-El-Khalick (2003) makes the point that students who believe that decisions about scientific knowledge are always rational, value-free and unproblematic (i.e., they hold a highly stereotyped view of scientific rationality) may come to regard scientific thinking as inapplicable or irrelevant to the messy and uncertain business of everyday decision-making. In other words, they will regard decision-making with respect to SSI as qualitatively different from decision-making in science. Moreover, there is a danger that those who have understood that science is sometimes tentative, provisional and impregnated with human values may come to believe that science cannot provide any answers at all, and that any view is as good as any other. This kind of naïve relativism is just as harmful as scientistic views that science is all-powerful and all-knowing. Zeidler et al. (2005) express the view that students with naïve, distorted and confused NOS views are just as likely to dismiss scientific knowledge as irrelevant to decision-making about SSI because "they tend to distort whatever data, evidence, or knowledge claims are available to them for the purpose of supporting a predetermined viewpoint with respect to the issue under consideration" (p. 363). Fundamental to the ability to deal critically with SSI is the kind of understanding of scientific argumentation and scientific justification discussed at length in Hodson (2009a).

Kolstø (2001) sums up the NOS knowledge and understanding needed for addressing SSI in terms of eight major elements: (i) the ability to distinguish between science-in-the-making, where dispute, disagreement and uncertainty are to be expected, and ready-made science, on which we can rely; (ii) recognizing that sociocultural, political, economic and religious factors can impact on "the science that gets done", to use Robert Young's (1987) memorable phrase, and on the knowledge claims that are accepted; (iii) ability to evaluate the quality of scientific and statistical evidence, and to judge the appropriateness of anecdotal and experiential knowledge; (iv) ability to appraise the degree of support for a knowledge claim and the quality of the argument that establishes the warrant for belief; (v) a skeptical approach that includes both a critical, questioning stance and a commitment not to jump to conclusions until compelling evidence and arguments have been assembled; (vi) awareness of the importance of contextual factors when evaluating knowledge claims, including the social status of the actors and their institutional allegiance; (vii) sensitivity to the underlying values, ideologies and potential for bias in the design and reporting of scientific investigations; and (viii) awareness of the constraints that might limit the application of generalized theoretical knowledge to particular real world situations. With regard to reports of specific research studies, a simple checklist of questions can be enormously helpful. For example, who conducted the research and where was it conducted? How was the research funded? Was the research sponsored and, if so, by whom? What is being claimed?

What evidence supports the claim? How was the evidence collected? How was the evidence interpreted? What assumptions are made and what theories are used in arguing from evidence to conclusion? Do the authors use well-established theory or do they challenge such theories? Are alternative interpretations and conclusions possible? What additional evidence would help to clarify or resolve issues? Have there been other studies conducted by these scientists or by others?

Students' ability to interpret and make appropriate use of scientific reports hinges, in part, on their understanding of "concepts of evidence", which Gott and Duggan (1996) and Gott et al. (2003) see as comprising three broad categories: (i) concepts associated with design, including variable identification, fair test, sample size and variable type; (ii) concepts associated with measurement, including relative scale, range of interval, choice of instrument, repeatability and accuracy; and (iii) concepts associated with handling data, such as use of tables and graphs. Similar thinking underpins the notion of *evidentiary competence* (Jeong et al., 2007). The thirteen components of evidentiary competence postulated by the authors relate principally to experimental investigations. At the planning stage, they include identification of data relevant to the investigation, understanding of dependent and independent variables, choice of appropriate sample size and design of fair tests. At the data collection stage, they include the need for objectivity and accuracy in data collection and establishment of reliability through successive replication. At the interpretation stage, they include the ability to interpret graphs and tables of data, how to code their own data in these ways, and how to deal with anomalous data. This kind of NOS understanding is, of course, enormously enhanced by opportunities for students to do science for themselves and by themselves, that is, choosing the focus for the investigation, designing and conducting the inquiry, interpreting and reporting the findings, and arguing for the significance of the conclusions.

Over the past two decades, understanding the nature of science (NOS) has become accepted as a major component of scientific literacy and an important learning objective in the science curriculum of many countries. However, while there have been numerous efforts to develop more effective NOS-oriented curricula, robust understanding of NOS for all is still far from being achieved. Indeed, it has been consistently reported that both students and teachers have inadequate, incomplete or confused NOS understanding (Lederman, 1992; Rampal, 1992; Driver et al., 1996; Moseley & Norris, 1999; Ryder et al., 1999; Abd-El-Khalick & Lederman, 2000a,b; Hogan & Maglienti, 2001; Moss et al., 2001; Finson, 2002; Lunn, 2002; Kang et al., 2005; Irez, 2006; Akerson & Hanuscin, 2007; Apostolou & Koulaidis, 2010). Although there are occasionally some striking differences, students from a wide variety of cultural contexts tend to share common misunderstandings about science, scientists and scientific practice (Chambers, 1983; Griffiths & Barman, 1995; She, 1995, 1998; Sumrall, 1995; Parsons, 1997; Song & Kim, 1999; Mbajiorgu & Iloputaife, 2001; Finson, 2002, 2003; Fung, 2002; Liu & Lederman, 2002, 2007; Rubin et al., 2003; Dogan & Abd-El-Khalick, 2008; Koren & Bar, 2009). Two points are worth making. First, it is evident that the goal of improving NOS understanding is often prejudiced by stereotyped images of science and scientists consciously or unconsciously built into school science curricula (Hodson, 1998b; Milne, 1998; Bell et al., 2003) and perpetuated by science textbooks (McComas,

1998; Abd-El-Khalick, 2001; Knain, 2001; Abd-El-Khalick et al., 2008; van Eijck & Roth, 2008; Kosso, 2009)[12]. This should be a relatively easy problem to fix. Second, research has shown that, in general, an *explicit* approach is much more effective than an *implicit* approach in fostering more sophisticated conceptions of NOS among students, preservice teachers and practising teachers (Abd-El-Khalick & Lederman, 2000a; Abd-El-Khalick, 2001, 2005; Khishfe & Abd-El-Khalick, 2002; Bell, 2004; Khishfe, 2008). This distinction resides not so much in differences in the kind of activities used (hands-on inquiries, historical case studies, lectures and readings, for example) as in the "extent to which learners are provided (or helped to come to grips) with the conceptual tools, such as some key aspects of NOS, that would enable them to think about and reflect on the activities in which they are engaged" (Abd-El-Khalick & Lederman, 2000a, p. 690). In an explicit approach, NOS understanding is regarded as 'content', to be approached carefully and systematically, as with any other lesson content. It should be noted that regarding NOS knowledge as content does not entail a didactic or teacher-centred approach or the imposition of a particular view through exercise of teacher authority, but it does entail rejection of the belief that NOS understanding will just develop in students as a consequence of engaging in other learning activities. Most effective of all are approaches that have a substantial reflective component. For example, Lucas and Roth (1996) report substantial gains in NOS understanding during a course incorporating readings on NOS, reflective essays and class discussions, and opportunities for self-directed laboratory experiences; Akerson et al. (2000) report substantial improvements in elementary student teachers' NOS views when the science methods course required reflection on NOS, both orally and in writing, following a series of readings, case studies, debates and other activities. Akerson and Volrich (2006) note substantial improvement in the NOS understanding of Grade 1 students when the teacher made repeated and explicit reference to NOS issues (focused largely on scientific observation, the tentativeness of scientific knowledge and creativity in science), encouraged students to keep a journal related to any NOS issues arising, and finished each lesson with class discussion triggered by the question, "How is what we did like what scientists do?" Heap (2006) also points out the centrality of reflection (in her case, the use of reflective journals) in changing, developing and consolidating NOS understanding. When coupled with opportunities to conduct both teacher-guided and student-designed investigations, explicit and reflective instructional approaches can even bring about favourable shifts in NOS understanding in children at the Grades 1 and 2 level (Akerson & Donnnelly, 2010).

Howe and Rudge (2005), Adúriz-Bravo and Izquierdo-Aymerich (2009) and Rudge and Howe (2009) argue that an explicit reflective approach is particularly effective when guided historical case studies are used to engage students in the kinds of reasoning used by scientists originally struggling to make sense of phenomena and events and construct satisfactory explanations. Three other research studies are noteworthy: Schwartz et al. (2004) found that preservice teachers' NOS understanding was favourably enhanced when their course included a research component and journals-based assignments; Morrison et al. (2009) report that substantial gains in NOS understanding are achieved when explicit, reflective instruction in NOS is augmented by opportunities to interview practising scientists about their work and/or undertake some job sharing; while Abd-El-Khalick and Akerson (2009) report similar major gains in the NOS understanding of preservice elementary teachers when explicit, reflective instruction is supported by use of metacognitive strategies (especially concept mapping), opportunities to research the development of their peers' NOS understanding, and use of case studies of elementary science classes oriented towards NOS teaching. Again, there are clear messages from the research about how best to proceed. My own views on how we can build and implement a curriculum to achieve enhanced levels of NOS understanding are discussed at length in Hodson (2009a).

It is both notable and disappointing that the gains in NOS understanding consequent on exposure to explicit, reflective instruction are considerably less substantial in relation to the sociocultural dimensions of science than with other NOS elements. Moss et al. (2001) state that, in general, Grade 11 and 12 students' understanding of the nature of scientific knowledge (for example, that it requires evidence, and is tentative and developmental) is more complete than their understanding of the scientific enterprise. If the term "scientific enterprise" is taken to include internal and external social factors that impact on the conduct of science, and is not restricted to the specific methods employed in particular scientific inquiries (or to what some teachers continue to refer to as "*the* scientific method"), then I would readily concur. Many students continue to believe that science occurs in something of a sociocultural vacuum – a view held by both preservice and inservice science teachers in Tairab's (2001) study and reinforced by the almost exclusive content orientation of many school science textbooks. Even when curriculum materials put emphasis on NOS understanding, the focus is almost exclusively on epistemological issues, with a consequent neglect of the social dimensions of scientific practice (Zemplén, 2009). Akerson et al. (2000) speculate that poor understanding in this aspect of NOS is a consequence of the subtleties of the subjective and sociocultural influences on scientific practice being impossible to capture in a short course (in their case, for preservice teachers). One or two brief examples will not achieve it; detailed and richly textured case studies (both contemporary and historical) may do so. Dass (2005) reaches essentially the same conclusion when accounting for why a semester-long undergraduate history of science course focused on the sociocultural and political context of major scientific advances achieved only "modest gains". I would argue that disappointing outcomes are also a consequence of uncertainty about intended learning outcomes in this particular NOS domain, the inadequacy of assessment procedures for capturing student understanding, low levels of confidence in teaching these aspects of the curriculum, and the pervasiveness and power of images of science and scientists acquired through informal learning channels. If teachers are unclear about precise learning goals relating to the sociocultural dimensions of science, as many are likely to be, there is likely to be a lack of clarity in lesson design. Hodson (2009a) addresses these matters at greater length.

It is also the case that students' understanding of the nature of technology (NOT) and of the relationships between science and technology are just as poorly developed as their NOS views. Students often see technology solely in terms of computers, televisions and mobile phones, emphasize the products of technology to the virtual exclusion of technology as a creative and socially embedded practice, and see technology primarily as applied science (De Klerk Wolters et al., 1990; Burns, 1992; Rennie & Jarvis, 1995a,b,c; Jarvis & Rennie, 1996; Jones, 1997; McCormick, 1997; Cajas, 2001; deVries, 2005; Scherz & Oren, 2006; Constantinou et al., 2010). Not surprisingly, students are often unclear about the distinctions between and the relationship between science and technology, using *ad hoc* criteria to address particular cases. Only when prompted do they realize that many technologies pre-date the science that now explains them. Two points are worth making. First, students' conceptions of technology will influence the ways in which they address technological aspects of SSI, just as teachers' conceptions of technology will influence their design of learning experiences and selection of curriculum materials. Second, students' views of technology can be changed quite substantially by curriculum interventions focused on NOT, just as their NOS views can be changed.

PRACTICAL KNOWLEDGE FOR ACTION

Of course, knowledge requirements are not restricted to science and nature of science or nature of technology. Those wishing to assess likely risks from the proximity of overhead power lines or nuclear power stations, the dumping of toxic waste and the frequent use of mobile phones, for example, will need considerable relevant technological knowledge. Trying to ascertain ahead of time exactly what technological knowledge will be required to address a range of SSI is virtually impossible, especially since many of the SSI being studied will have been chosen by the students. The practice of enabling students to access knowledge as the need arises would seem to be the only practical solution. Although it is possible to build a curriculum that includes some basic technological knowledge, it makes eminently greater sense to focus this part of the curriculum on learning *about* technology, as encapsulated in notions of technological competence (see chapter 1).

An intriguing study by Layton et al. (1993) investigated the kind of knowledge accumulated and deployed by non-scientists to address specific needs, interests and issues, and to solve problems in everyday life. The study focused on four groups: parents of children with Down Syndrome (or Down's syndrome, as it is more commonly known in the United Kingdom); elderly people trying to cope with domestic energy problems (and seeking to reduce their power bills); local government officials responsible for waste disposal; and people working at, or living close to, the Sellafield nuclear processing facility in West Cumbria (UK), who might be considered at risk from potential radiation leaks. What is striking about the research findings is the way in which concerned citizens built "practical knowledge for action". Applicable only in the particular situation under consideration, this cluster of knowledge and skills often constituted understanding that was very different from the scientific knowledge normally presented in school[13]. Although it frequently included fragments of scientific knowledge, that knowledge was adapted, modified and augmented to address specific purposes and problems more directly. It was used alongside *alternative* scientific knowledge (what some have called "folk science") and highly idiosyncratic judgements deriving from personal experience.

For example, the knowledge commonly deployed in addressing domestic energy problems had more in common with caloric theory than kinetic theory, and many of the elderly people who were interviewed perceived *cold* as an entity with distinct properties of its own, rather than recognizing it as the absence of heat. In other words, they developed an explanatory system rooted very firmly in personal experience of living in a draughty home. As Jenkins (2000) observes, the scientific knowledge learned in school is often irrelevant or no more than marginal to decisions about practical action: "Addressing satisfactorily the coldness of a room by closing a door, double glazing one or more windows, or insulating the walls and ceiling does not require an understanding of cold as the absence of heat conceptualized in terms of molecular motion" (p. 210). In evaluating the usefulness of scientific knowledge, non-standard criteria were often employed. For example, open fires were often preferred to more efficient forms of heating because they are "cosy", and draught excluders were rejected on grounds of social acceptability ("they are naff!"). Brian Wynne (1989, 1991, 1995, 1996) provides a number of striking examples of the gap between scientific knowledge and lay knowledge. For example, his study of the "radioactive sheep" crisis following the Chernobyl nuclear power station accident (in 1986) reveals that British Government scientists had seriously under-estimated the likelihood that sheep in Cumbria and Wales had been contaminated. Their initial assessments had to be substantially revised, resulting in a two-year ban on sale and slaughter of sheep for human consumption. In contrast, the local sheep farmers initially had more reliable knowledge deriving from first-hand experience of the terrain, local waterways, plant behaviour (especially uptake of nutrients) and sheep grazing habits. This gap between the abstract and formalized knowledge of experts and the context-based knowledge of the farmers led to the conviction among local residents that the Government was concerned to "hush up" the affair. Also relevant here is Irwin's (1995) analysis of the treatment of British farmworkers by an expert committee examining the safety of organophosphate pesticides. The committee concluded that the materials were safe so long as they were used properly; the farmworkers, who believed that their health was at risk, rejected this assertion on the grounds that the so-called 'proper procedures' were impractical in a real farming situation. It is disturbing to note that the farmworkers' views were dismissed as "anecdotal and unreliable". A further example is Bloor's (2000) study of a group of coal miners fighting conventional scientific understanding of pneumoconiosis ("black lung"). Faced with a similar situation to the farmworkers in Irwin's story, the miners succeeded in publicizing their views about the connection between coal dust and pulmonary disease by recruiting and coaching their own 'expert witnesses'. As Irwin (2008) comments, they were successful in gaining compensation for industrial injury because they combined highly personal knowledge, scientific knowledge and knowledge of how to "work the system".

In everyday situations, scientific knowledge delivered by supposed 'experts' can sometimes be rejected or regarded with deep suspicion because it is not tailored to specific needs, interests and social circumstances, or because it fails to take account of other agendas. It may also be rejected because the 'experts' who deliver scientific knowledge are sometimes regarded as not entirely trustworthy, that is, they are seen to be biased or to have a vested interest. In the case of the Down

Syndrome parents, knowledge delivered by means of information leaflets was seen as singularly unhelpful. As Layton et al. (1993) comment, it was too often "a message of despair when they were desperate for one of hope" (p. 57). Knowledge was offered "in the wrong form, reflecting priorities different from those of practical action; in the wrong way, discounting understandings which parents had wrought from experience; and, often, at the wrong time, serving the convenience of donors, ignoring emotional traumas which parents might be undergoing, and undiscerning of the moment of need" (p. 58). Thomas (1997) cites a study reported by Irwin et al. (1996) in which residents in housing complexes located close to potentially hazardous industrial sites also responded negatively to expert scientific knowledge. Because it was couched in inaccessible language and seemed unable to answer their most pressing questions, it simply promoted dissatisfaction, elevated anxiety levels and exacerbated feelings of powerlessness. From the perspectives being addressed in this book, it is noteworthy that reports of potential health hazards associated with use of mobile phones is summarily dismissed by most people because of the perceived social value of the technology (Burgess, 2004; Drake, 2006), just as publicizing the known health risks associated with smoking fails to deter many young people from taking up the habit because of the social cachet smoking brings in some youth cultures. Wynne (1995) refers to episodes like this as the *social construction of ignorance*: the deliberate avoidance of scientific knowledge because it is perceived as contrary to one's interests or too much in the other party's interests (as in, "they are just trying to sell us something"). For example, workers at the Sellafield nuclear processing plant told researchers that they avoided scientific knowledge that could have helped them to assess health risks more effectively because trying to resolve the various controversies would be too time-consuming, and being too conscious of risks would raise anxiety levels. In addition, they didn't want to signal mistrust of the staff whose job it is to assess risks and institute safety procedures. In a study conducted by Lambert and Rose (1996), most of the patients diagnosed with *familial hypercholesterolaemia* (a genetically transmitted inability to metabolize lipids that greatly increases an individual's susceptibility to cardiac arrest) constructed personal knowledge for action that sought to balance scientific knowledge concerning above-average risk of premature death with consideration of the implications of a more restricted lifestyle, opting for a compromise between risk-reducing action (particularly, strict dietary control) and maintaining an enjoyable social life.

What these studies show is that people faced with making important decisions in everyday life may not always use 'pure' scientific knowledge. They may use restricted or adapted scientific meanings; they may incorporate knowledge from areas outside science; they may rely heavily on hunch, intuition, personal experience and testimony from other non-scientists. This complex of knowledge is assembled into a highly personal and context-specific repertoire for thinking about issues, solving problems and reaching decisions. To be useful in practical contexts, abstract, idealized science has to be adapted and modified to take account of the complexity and non-uniformity of the real world. In David Layton's (1991) words, "the scientific knowledge offered or accessible to people is rarely usable without being reworked and contextualized. This involves, at least, its integration with other, situation-specific knowledge, often personal to individuals, as well as with judgments of other kinds" (p. 58). To address SSI in class in any meaningful way students may need to engage in a similar kind of re-working of scientific knowledge to that of engineers addressing complex practical problems and lay people confronting science-related dilemmas in daily life: "Adjusting the level of abstraction, 'repackaging' knowledge to bring together components of scientific knowledge that pedagogical and disciplinary considerations have uncoupled, and 'recontextualizing' scientific knowledge to reassimilate the messy realities that have been idealized in order to shape and address a problem with the rigour deemed necessary to move towards a scientific solution" (Jenkins, 1994b, p. 601).

In an attempt to theorize these matters, and explain the ways in which a group of residents in an area with a high level of background radiation learned about radiation hazards and evaluated the potential threat to their health, Alsop (1999) developed what he calls the Informal Conceptual Change Model (ICCM). The model, which has ready application to all SSI, comprises three theoretical dimensions: the *cognitive* (the way learners make sense of the relevant science and their views of its consistency, reliability and truthfulness), the *affective* (the way they feel about the issue and how their emotions influence their learning) and the *conative* (the usefulness of scientific information in meeting their specific needs and concerns)[14]. The cognitive dimension includes the relevant science and NOS understanding related to consistency and reliability of the data and rationalizations. Drawing on earlier work by Watts and Alsop (1997), Alsop explains the affective dimension in terms of how *salient* (noticeable, prominent or important in some way), *palatable* (appealing or agreeable) and *germane* (personally relevant) a particular idea is perceived to be. The conative perspective focuses on questions such as: How can I use this knowledge? Does it empower me to act? Does it help me to solve problems? Alsop (1999) describes the conative perspective in terms of three major components: trust (the extent to which knowledge provided by 'experts' can be relied upon), control (the extent to which an individual feels that knowledge can be used to influence or change a particular situation) and actionable (an idea that is very closely related to the notion of practical knowledge for action discussed earlier).

LANGUAGE ISSUES

If students are to address SSI thoroughly and critically, they also need the language skills to access knowledge from various sources and the ability to express their knowledge, views, opinions and values in a form appropriate to the audience being addressed.

> Beyond vocabulary and background facts, there are discourse-specific ways in which arguments are made, in which certain kinds of information must be foregrounded and used as evidence. There are discourse-specific ways in which you must infer connections or 'get the point'. Different discourses require very different ways of 'reading between the lines'... Becoming literate in any particular domain involves learning a specific discourse – particular ways of thinking, acting, valuing. (Michaels & O'Connor, 1990, p. 12)

CHAPTER 2

We need to focus students' attention very firmly on the language of science, scientific communication and scientific argumentation. As Goldman and Bisanz (2002) note, there are three major categories of communication of scientific information in our society: communication among scientists through research journals and conference papers; popularization and dissemination of information generated by the scientific community via newspapers, magazines and television; and formal education via textbooks and other curriculum materials. We need to ensure that students develop the necessary critical reading skills for all three types of text. Proficient and critical reading, whether first order or second order literature, involves more than just recognizing all the words and being able to locate specific information; it also involves the ability to: (i) determine when something is an observation, an inference, a hypothesis, a conclusion or an assumption; (ii) distinguish between an explanation and the evidence for it; and (iii) recognize when the author is asserting a claim to 'scientific truth', expressing doubt or engaging in speculation. Without this level of interpretation the reader will fail to grasp the essential scientific meaning. In practice, many students are unaware of inconsistencies in what they read, unable to assess the reliability of data and detect bias, and only moderately capable of relating what they read to what they already know. In general, they are poor at distinguishing claims from evidence, evidence from conclusions, and beliefs from inferences (Goldman & Bisanz, 2002). Like everything else in science education, critical reading skills need to be modelled and taught, carefully and systematically. Specifically, students need advice, criticism and support in their efforts to connect items of information within and across texts, evaluate the validity and reliability of all information used, weigh the rival merits of alternatives, assess consistency and inconsistency, and seek to resolve inconsistencies by gathering further information. These matters are discussed at greater length in Hodson (2009a), alongside a critical review of the now extensive research literature on reading and writing for learning in science.

What is too often unrecognized by science teachers, science textbooks and curricula, and by the wider public, is that dispute is one of the key driving forces of science. Real science is impregnated with claims, counter claims, argument and dispute. Arguments concerning the appropriateness of experimental design, the interpretation of evidence and the validity of knowledge claims are located at the core of scientific practice. Arguments are used to answer questions, resolve issues and settle disputes. In everyday life, decision-making on SSI is based largely on evaluation of information, views and reports made available via newspapers, magazines, television, radio and the Internet. Citizens need to understand the standards, norms and conventions of scientific argumentation in order to judge the rival merits of competing arguments and engage meaningfully in debate on socioscientific issues. The ability to judge the nature of the evidence presented and its validity, reliability and appropriateness, the interpretation and utilization of that data, and the chain of argument substantiating the claims, are crucial to good decision-making. Students need to know the kinds of knowledge claims that scientists make and how they advance them. In particular, the form, structure and language of scientific arguments, the kind of evidence invoked and how it is organized and deployed, and the ways in which theory is used and the work of other scientists cited to strengthen the case. Neglect of scientific argumentation in the school science curriculum gives the impression that science is the unproblematic accumulation of data and theory. In consequence, students are puzzled and may even be alarmed by reports of disagreements among scientists on matters of contemporary importance. They are also unable to address in a critical and confident way the claims and counter claims impregnating the socioscientific issues with which they are confronted in daily life. Being able to assemble coherent arguments and evaluate the arguments of others, especially those appearing in the media, is crucial if students are to understand the basis of knowledge claims they encounter and make decisions about where they stand on important issues.

A number of science educators have recently turned their attention to these matters and to what had previously been a shamefully neglected area of research and curriculum development. The research agenda set out by Newton et al. (1999), Driver et al. (2000), Osborne (2001), Duschl and Osborne (2002), Erduran et al. (2004), Osborne et al. (2004), Simon et al. (2006), Bricker and Bell (2008), Duschl (2008), Jiménez-Aleixandre and Erduran (2008), Berland and Reiser (2009), and others, focuses on the following questions: Why is argumentation important? What are the distinctive features of scientific argumentation? How can it be taught? What strategies are available? To what extent and in what ways are the strategies successful? What problems arise and how can the difficulties be overcome? This research is discussed at length in Hodson (2009a) and will not be reviewed here, save to note its key features and to emphasize its obvious relevance to SSI-oriented teaching and learning.

Many science educators have used Stephen Toulmin's (1958) description of the structure of an argument in terms of six components:

– *Claim* - makes an assertion or states a conclusion.
– *Data* - states the evidence used to provide support for the claim.
– *Warrant* - explains or justifies the relationship between the evidence and the claim.
– *Qualifier* - indicates the degree of reliance to be placed on the conclusions and/or the conditions under which the claim is to be taken as 'true'.
– *Backing* - states the additional evidential, theoretical and methodological assumptions underlying the warrant and establishing the validity of the argument.
– *Rebuttal* - identifies circumstances in which the claim can no longer be sustained or introduces reservations that question the data, warrant, backing or qualifier of an argument.

The six components comprise two *levels* of argumentation: first, the construction of a basic argument establishes the relation between a claim and the evidence in support of it, and states the justification for this relationship; second, backing, rebutting and qualifying the justification complements and extends the basic argument. Each component in the model is, in effect, an answer to a question: what is being asserted? (*claim*); what evidence supports the claim? (*data*); what reasons, principles, rules or values justify the conclusion? (*warrant*); how likely is it that the conclusion is true? (*qualifier*); what theoretical assumptions justify the line of reasoning and establish the trustworthiness of the claim? (*backing*); under what circumstance(s) would the argument break down? (*rebuttal*). In constructing a 5-level analytical framework for assessing the quality of an argument, Zeidler et al. (2003), Erduran et al. (2004) and Osborne et al. (2004) place considerable emphasis on the systematic consideration of rebuttals. Thus, level 1 arguments comprise a simple claim versus a counter-claim, or a claim versus a claim; level 2 arguments consist of claims with data, warrants or backings, but no rebuttals; level 3 arguments involve a series of claims or counter-claims with data, warrants or backings and the occasional weak rebuttal; level 4 arguments have a clearly identifiable rebuttal, and may have several claims and counter-claims as well, though this is not necessary; level 5 or extended arguments have more than one rebuttal.

Research findings from studies using the Toulmin framework are somewhat mixed. For example, Bell and Linn (2000) conclude that students tend to rely on data to support their claims, but rarely use warrants or backings, while Jiménez-Aleixandre et al. (2000) found that many students don't even use data to support their claims. One major problem is that the Toulmin model is deceptively simple and straightforward, and its deployment in science education research to monitor the development of students' argumentation skills is beset with difficulties – most notably, the difficulty of determining exactly what counts as *claim, data, warrant* and *backing* in a particular set of circumstances (Erduran et al., 2004). Thus, ascertaining the extent to which students have made use of data, warrants, backings and qualifiers to support arguments, and the extent to which they use rebuttals to elaborate and extend or oppose an argument, can be problematic. Even with written arguments, the deployment of Toulmin's model as a research tool can sometimes be difficult; with verbal arguments, it is even more problematic. The natural flow of conversation can serve to disrupt the logical structure of the argument. Moreover, students often use language that is vague or ambiguous, and they frequently contradict themselves as they struggle to sort out their ideas. Boundaries between the categories of argument become blurred and fluid, with key elements in the argument being implied rather than explicitly stated. They may even be conveyed by gesture. In addition, elements of an argument may be omitted because the arguer simply assumes that it is already well-known and doesn't need to be re-stated. In short, real face-to-face argument is dynamic and interactive. Moreover, in trying to ascertain students' capabilities it is essential to take account of the context in which the argument is located, and its familiarity and interest for the student. Even with written arguments, the venue can impact substantially on the way the argument is presented, with important variations among research articles, conference presentations, email communications, grant proposals, textbooks and magazine articles.

In an attempt to sidestep these problems, Zohar and Nemet (2002) collapsed *data, warrants* and *backings* into a single category of *justifications*. McNeill et al. (2006) also reduced Toulmin's model to just three components: *claim, evidence* (or data) and *reasoning* (a combination of warrant and backing, deployed as considered appropriate). In the Zohar and Nemet scheme, the criteria for the classification of justifications is: (a) no consideration of scientific knowledge; (b) inaccurate scientific knowledge; (c) non-specific scientific knowledge; and (d) correct scientific knowledge. Schwarz et al. (2003) advance a case for evaluating arguments in terms of argument type, soundness of argument, overall number of reasons, number of reasons supporting counter-arguments, and types of reasons (including logical, concept-rich and theory-based reasons, appeals to authority, everyday common sense and personal experiences, and attempts to tease out the consequences of holding a particular view or engaging in a particular kind of action). Their notion of a hierarchy of arguments ranges from *simple assertions* (a conclusion unsupported by any kind of justification) through *one-sided arguments* (for which one or two reasons may be advanced) and *two-sided arguments* (including reasons that both support and challenge the conclusion, but do not weigh their rival merits) to *compound arguments* (replete with multiple reasons and critically evaluated counter-arguments)[15]. Sandoval and Millwood's (2005) approach focuses attention on two components of the argument: (i) the epistemological quality of the argument, that is, the extent to which the student has cited sufficient data in warranting a claim, written a coherent explanation and made appropriate use of inscriptions (graphs, tables, equations, etc.); and (ii) its conceptual quality and appropriateness, that is, how well the student has articulated the claims within an appropriate theoretical framework and warranted those claims using appropriate data. Sampson and Clark's (2006) detailed review of the field expresses dissatisfaction with all schemes so far used by science educators to evaluate the quality of scientific arguments. They suggest that instead of focusing on technical issues relating to the precise structure of an argument, teachers should pay attention to such matters as: the kinds of claims advanced and whether they are well supported by the evidence; whether all the evidence has been utilized and discrepancies accounted for; whether the sources of data and the methods by which data were accumulated have been critically examined; how (or if) alternative claims are acknowledged, their weaknesses pinpointed and conclusions rejected. Before leaving this discussion it is worth mentioning Jiménez-Aleixandre and Federico-Agraso's (2009) advocacy of a framework broadly similar to "epistemic quality" comprising three criteria: *pertinence* - the extent to which evidence relates directly and umambiguously to the claims; *sufficiency* – whether the evidence is sufficient to support the claims; and *coordination* – whether the items of evidence are coordinated across different epistemic levels. This latter criterion relates to the ways in which details of procedures, data readings, data trends, graphs, and so on, are related to theoretical propositions. Falk and Yarden (2009) identify two kinds of coordination practices: *research-oriented coordination*, which links research questions, hypotheses, methods, data, theoretical issues and application of findings; and *text-oriented coordination*, which focuses on the function, organization and genre of the text. Not surprisingly, the authors found that when evaluating specially adapted primary literature (in biotechnology), students used the former coordination practices for appraising the Research Design and Results sections and the latter practices for judging the quality of the Discussion section.

Research shows that students do improve their capacity for constructing and presenting effective arguments through practice, though not always as rapidly and predictably as we might wish (Jiménez-Aleixandre et al., 2000; Zoller et al., 2000; Osborne et al., 2004; Garcia-Mila & Andersen, 2008). What is clear is that development of those skills is a long-term undertaking, and one or two brief experiences will not suffice. As with NOS, teaching of argumentation needs to be explicit and systematically planned. A number of researchers have shown how the quality of students' arguments can be considerably enhanced by judicious scaffolding, use of writing frames, encouraging student reflection, fostering metacognition and providing timely and constructive feedback (Kuhn et al., 2000, 2008; Bell, 2002; Cho & Jonassen, 2002; Engle & Conant, 2002; Zembal-Saul et al., 2002; Nussbaum & Sinatra, 2003; Felton, 2004; Nussbaum & Kardash, 2005; Sandoval & Millwood, 2005; Erduran, 2006; Chinn, 2006; Kenyon et al., 2006; McNeill et al., 2006; Andriessen, 2007; McNeill & Krajcik, 2007, 2008; Reigosa & Jiménez-Aleixandre, 2007; Chinn & Samarapungavan, 2008; Jiménez-Aleixandre, 2008; Varelas et al., 2008; Berland & Reiser, 2009; McNeill, 2009; Dawson & Venville, 2010; Kuhn, 2010). Of particular value in this context is the learning progression devised by Berland and McNeill (2010) as a description of how students' argumentation skills develop and as a set of guidelines for how teachers can support and enhance that development. It comprises three dimensions: *instructional context, argumentative product* and *argumentative process*. In terms of the first dimension, the instructional context must be rich enough to enable multiple perspectives and must require the use of evidence to resolve any significant differences in perspective. The authors identify four "leverage points" impacting the complexity and, therefore, the fruitfulness of the problem: the complexity of the problem, the size of the data set, the appropriateness of the data, and the sophistication and availability of scaffolds. Key factors relating to the product include the ways in which arguments are supported and whether they include rebuttals, and the appropriateness and sufficiency of the supporting data. The argumentative process is described in terms of argumentative functions and the spontaneity of student contributions. The authors identify four utterance functions, arranged as a hierachy: (i) individuals stating and defending claims; (ii) individuals questioning one another's claims and defence; (iii) individuals evaluating one another's claims and defence; and (iv) individuals revising their own and others' claims. With regard to spontaneity, there is a progression from activities that are initiated or prompted by the teacher, through those that are negotiated between teacher and students, to those initiated, conducted and evaluated by students.

MEDIA LITERACY

Because much of the information needed to address SSI is of the science-in-the-making kind, rather than well-established science, and may even be located at or near the cutting edge of research, it is unlikely that students will be able to locate it in traditional sources of information like textbooks and reference books. It will need to be accessed from magazines, newspapers, TV and radio broadcasts, publications of special interest groups and the Internet, thus raising important issues of *media literacy*. Being media literate means being able to access, comprehend, analyze, evaluate, compare and contrast information from a variety of sources and utilize that information judiciously and appropriately to synthesize one's own detailed summary of the topic or issue under consideration. It means recognizing that the deployment of particular language, symbols, images and sound in a multimedia presentation can each play a role in determining a message's impact, and will have a profound influence on its perceived value and credibility. It means being able to ascertain the writer's purpose and intent, determine any sub-text and implicit meaning, detect bias and vested interest. It means being able to distinguish between good, reliable information and poor, unreliable information. It involves the ability to recognize what Burbules and Callister (2000) call *misinformation, malinformation, messed-up information* and *useless information*. Students who are media literate understand that those skilled in producing printed, graphic and spoken media use particular vocabulary, grammar, syntax, metaphor and referencing to capture our attention, trigger our emotions, persuade us of a point of view and, on occasions, by-pass our critical faculties altogether.

Overall, research paints a pretty depressing picture of the ability of students, at both school and university level, to read media reports with the kind of under-standing encapsulated in the notion of critical scientific literacy (Norris & Phillips, 1994, 2008; Korpan et al., 1997; Phillips & Norris, 1999; Norris, et al., 2003; Penney et al., 2003). Phillips and Norris (1999) identify three major student 'stances' towards reports of science in newspapers and magazines. In the *critical* stance, readers attempt to reach an interpretation that takes account of the text information and how it is presented in relation to their own prior beliefs, sometimes producing a new mental model or representation of the phenomenon or events under consideration. Those readers adopting the *domination* stance allow prior beliefs to overwhelm text information, reinterpreting it (sometimes implausibly) to make it consistent with their existing frameworks and beliefs. In stark contrast, the *deferential* stance allows the text to overwhelm prior beliefs, resulting in blind (though perhaps only temporary) acceptance of views expressed in the text and implicit trust in the author. Disturbingly, this latter position seems to be the most common stance among high school students.

Many students accept media-based information at face value; they focus on superficial features of the material and are easily seduced by the razzamatazz of presentation. Students need to be made aware, if they are not already aware, that the popular press invariably over-simplifies complex issues and that information from such sources is often incomplete, sometimes purposefully so, and often highly selective. It may be confused, confusing or deliberately misleading, as in the case of government-sponsored reporting in the UK at the time of the Chernobyl nuclear power station disaster in the mid 1980s and the BSE episode in the 1990s. Unbalanced reporting can arise because of journalists' honest attempts to be even-handed and to present "both sides of the story". Science is built on skepticism, and presentation of conflicting data, counter arguments and alternative conclusions is a key element in the public scrutiny that eventually leads to consensus. But consensus is not unanimity; dissenting voices can always be found, even for well-established scientific knowledge, and laudable efforts by journalists to be 'objective' in their reporting can sometimes result in outlandish views, poorly substantiated views and even discredited views being reported as legitimate alternatives to mainstream scientific opinion (Friedman et al., 1999; Weigold, 2001). This commitment to even-handed reporting is sometimes exploited by those with a vested interest in manufacturing doubt about scientific findings perceived to be counter to their interests, as in the case of the tobacco industry's attempts to cast doubt on the link between smoking and lung cancer (see chapter 7). Coverage of global warming and climate change is another case of the press reporting major differences of opinion on matters where there is clear scientific consensus, as discussed in chapter 8. This is certainly not to argue for a popular press that is slavishly subservient to the scientific establishment; rather, it is to argue for readers to be constantly vigilant.

An analysis by Zimmerman et al. (2001) of articles and news reports published in a range of newspapers and magazines in Canada and the United States over a one-month period showed that they routinely failed to provide information about where the research was originally published, and who funded it, and only very rarely presented full details of research design or included critical comments by other experts in the research field[16]. Reporters frequently omit discussion of the limitations, subtleties and nuances of the research because such details might detract from a story's clarity, impact, conciseness and ability to hold the reader's attention. While numerical data is often used to create an impression of care, precision and authority, carefully selected and sometimes highly dubious statistics are commonly used to mislead or concentrate attention on particular aspects of the report, to the exclusion of others. Hence Benjamin Disraeli's famous remark, later popularized by Mark Twain, that (in politics) there are three kinds of lies: *lies, damn lies* and *statistics*. Also relevant is the old joke that 72.5% of statistics are made up on the spur of the moment. To compound the problems, readers may do little more than 'skim read' the report or watch 'with one eye only' while attending to other matters or engaging in other activities. Material may be biased and may use a range of journalistic techniques such as emotive language, hyperbole and innuendo, provocative pictures and images, and emotionally manipulative background music, to persuade readers, viewers and listeners of a particular point of view. As Nelkin (1987) observes, "selective use of adjectives can trivialize an event or render it important; marginalize some groups, empower others; define an issue as a problem or reduce it to a routine" (p. 11). In a study of the metaphors used by British newspapers in their reporting of developments in biotechnology, Liakopoulos (2002) found many metaphors intended to convey a positive image of bio-technology (including: *revolution, breakthrough, major step, golden opportunity, potential goldmine, miracle,* and *opening the door*) and many intended to create a negative response (including: *Pandora's box, threat, rogue virus, killer plants, Frankenfoods, Nazi-like eugenics, playing God,* and *unnatural selection*). Describing biotechnologists as mad scientists, evil geniuses or Frankenstein figures leaves little doubt about the position the reader is expected to adopt. Jensen (2008) provides similar examples of highly selective language use to support or oppose stem cell research. Somewhat earlier analyses of press coverage of genetic engineering revealed what Mulkay (1993) called an oscillating "rhetoric of hope and fear" and van Dijck (1998) called a hybrid discourse of "promise and concern". An analysis of more recent British newspaper reports concerning GM foods conducted by Augoustinos et al. (2010) reveals a consistent pro-GM position in *The Times* and *The Sun*, where opposition to GM foods and concerns expressed by critics about possible environmental and health risks were commonly described as "irrational", "unscientific", "scaremongering", "ignorant" and "anti-science", and a consistent anti-GM position in *The Guardian* and *The Daily Mail*, where reporters tend to emphasize public anxieties (portrayed as "reasonable"), the vested economic interests of biotechnology companies and the political interests of the British government. Essentially the same conclusions concerning the same four newspapers were reached by Cook et al. (2006)[17]. In his survey of newspaper reporting of biotechnology issues in the United States, Germany and UK, Listerman (2010) identifies five distinct ways of framing the discussion: *utility* – Nature is a resource to be used by people as long as it is beneficial and profitable to do so; *risk* – complex technology is risky because it has impacts on Nature that cannot always be predicted and managed; *control* – since each alteration has an impact, the changes on Nature and society inflicted by humanity must be under strict control and carefully regulated through political authority; *fate* – we cannot control the changes in Nature but only try to cope with the consequences; *morality* – all technological activities raise moral-ethical issues. American reports tended to emphasize the utilitarian aspect (i.e., benefits to people and the economy), German and British reports put much greater emphasis on risk and moral-ethical issues.

Although newspaper and television news editors necessarily consider very carefully the quality and significance of the science they include, they are likely to be even more strongly influenced by other considerations: (i) what they deem to be interesting to readers/viewers and whether the primary motive is to inform, entertain, provoke, advocate, defend or oppose a particular view/development; (ii) the extent to which sensationalist reporting and emphasis on novelty and rarity might gain additional readers/viewers, or lose some; (iii) the vested interest that newspaper proprietors or broadcast station owners might have; (iv) the need to meet advertisers' expectations and attract new advertizing clients; (v) the strong desire to claim an 'exclusive'; (vi) how conveniently the item matches the 'house style' and the time and space available; (vii) the availability of appropriate experts for consultation; and (viii) the urgency of meeting a deadline. At a general level, students need to consider the following questions. Who determines what we see and hear in the media? How is this information monitored, filtered and edited? Who provides information to the media, and why? Why is a particular story covered? How is a particular story framed and how is a particular position evaluated? Why are some views emphasized or even magnified, while others are downplayed or ignored altogether? While the media can quite rightly be accused, on occasions, of distorting research results, sowing seeds of distrust and acting as an *agent provocateur*, they also provide much needed recognition for scientific research, raise public awareness of important developments and sometimes 'blow the whistle' on overt vested interest, bias and fraud. A democratic and open society is premissed on the free flow of information among its citizens. It is here that the media plays a crucial role, but can only do so when there is a wide variety of newspapers, magazines, Internet websites, writers and editors to ensure diversity of views. When control and ownership are vested in the hands of a few individuals and corporations, opponents can be easily discredited, alternative views suppressed and dissident voices marginalized or silenced. In their haste to meet a deadline, or in their desire to present a particular position on an issue, journalists may neglect to include the voices of people who could invest their coverage with alternative perspectives and different experiences. As Conrad (1999) notes, on medical matters, the voices of patients and their carers/advocates are often absent, although a survey conducted by Hivon et al. (2010) of the coverage in Canadian news media of two controversial therapeutic interventions (electroconvulsive therapy (ECT) and the use of cyclo-oxygenase-2 (COX-2) drugs in treatment of arthritis) and two contentious screening tests (first-trimester prenatal screening for Down syndrome and prostate-specific antigen (PSA) screening for asymptomatic men) showed that the voices of patient associations, patients and their families were well represented, and in the case of ECT they came close to those of scientists and medics in terms of overall representation.

In an extended discussion of the politics of news media, Graber et al. (1998) make a plea for diversity that parallels the argument used throughout this book for diversity within the community of scientists and engineers, and the various funding agencies, and within the bodies that make decisions on curriculum, assessment programmes and other educational issues. As with many aspects of SSI, it may well be that the extent and prominence of media coverage of the views of any particular group of people reflects the political literacy and political power of the group and its ability to contact and influence journalists. Media coverage can be impacted by whether those affected by the condition are numerous and urbanized or isolated and widely scattered, robust and able-bodied or infirm, young or old, men or women, socially privileged or disadvantaged and marginalized. These kinds of issues are discussed in chapter 9 in relation to community-based action. Would-be activists can draw great encouragement from Epstein's (1995, 1996, 1997) compelling account of how AIDS activists, with virtually no formal education in science, acquired sufficient scientific knowledge and political expertise to be become effective and respected participants in the design, conduct, interpretation and reporting of clinical trials of a range of AIDS-therapy drugs and in the design and implementation of treatment protocols. In a later work, Epstein (2008) discusses how other patient and patient advocacy groups have had a profound impact of public perceptions of a wide range of medical conditions, changed the ways in which the condition is characterized and diagnosed, stimulated technological innovation, and brought about significant modifications to the attitudes of health practitioners, management of patients, research priorities and protocols, health policy and the cost and availability of drugs. Also of interest is Jensen's (2008) account of how patient groups have been instrumental in constructing the generally favourable view of "therapeutic cloning" (the use of embryonic stem cells in medical research) in the British press.

Clearly, a reasonable level of media literacy is essential if students are to confront SSI in a rational and critical way. Bryant and Zillmann (1986), Nelkin (1987, 1995), Dunwoody (1993, 1999), Stocking and Holstein (1993), Stocking (1999), Miller and Kimmel (2001), Spinks (2001), Nisbet and Lewenstein (2002), Reah (2002) and Ten Eyck (2005) provide wide-ranging discussions of journalistic techniques, McClune and Jarman (2010) provide details from interviews with 26 recognized authorities on science in the media focusing on the knowledge, skills and attitudes they consider essential to critical reading of science-based news reports, while Dimopoulos and Koulaidis (2003) show how habits of careful, critical reading of newspaper reports can be successfully taught and can prove invaluable in helping students to identify the key social actors and forces that impact decision-making in both the private and public sectors. Experience in combining informational text with language specifically chosen to engage readers' attention, surprise or shock them, incite anger, generate sympathy or sway their thinking, is invaluable in understanding the ways in which the media seek to manipulate public opinion. Students can learn much about media techniques by playing the devil's advocate - for example, by writing short articles to endorse opinions they do not hold or views they actively oppose. They might learn to detect bias and distortion by engaging in it, that is, by writing text using only data, statistics, examples and 'expert testimony' that are favourable to a particular viewpoint, and ignoring all other. Marks and Eilks (2009) describe an interesting project in which Grade 10 students investigated the use of synthetic musk in the detergents and soap industry, particularly in the manufacture of perfumes and shower gels. Although the early carcinogenic nitromusks have now been mostly replaced, the materials currently in use continue to pose health risks, largely through their hormone-activating and allergenic properties, and create a raft of environmental problems, most of which have gone unreported in the news media. They enter wastewater systems in huge volumes, pass through the sewage system largely unaltered and are discharged into streams, rivers and lakes. Increasingly high levels of synthetic musks are now being encountered in the fatty tissues of oily fish and may be responsible for falling fertility levels in male fish. They have also been detected in human tissue – most alarmingly, in breast milk. After studying the relevant chemistry, the students prepared some shower gels and subjected them to tests for consumer preference. Then they worked in groups to compile a video report to reflect the viewpoints of four constituencies: consumer protection agencies, the cosmetics industry, environmental protection groups and the authorities responsible for wastewater disposal.

There is considerable value in encouraging students to collect, display, criticize, compare and contrast samples of writing on SSI from newspapers and popular magazines, textbooks of various styles, science-oriented magazines, academic journals, museum exhibits, works of fiction, Websites and interactive media, together with clips from works of fiction, movies, cartoons, advertisements and product labels. Of course, reading or watching media reports of science may be a new experience for many students, and so provision of guidelines may be essential in ensuring that they direct their attention to key aspects of the report, such as use of provocative headlines and illustrations, editorializing, identification (or not) of information sources, omission of alternative views, portrayal of scientists in favourable or unfavourable light, balance, bias, thoroughness of content coverage, and so on. Some kind of media checklist might be extremely helpful in helping to build up students' critical reading skills. Who is the author (or speaker) and what is the author's purpose? Who is the audience? How is the message tailored to that audience? Is the information complete? Are there proper citations of the sources of information? What techniques and what language are used to attract and maintain audience attention? What is assumed or left implicit? Are there any discernible underlying values and attitudes? What information and points of view are omitted? And so on.

In recent years, the Internet has become the dominant medium through which the public (including students) access knowledge and information, in all areas and disciplines. For example, Falk (2009) reports that 87% of a representative sample of US citizens state that they gather scientific information from the Internet, compared with 10% in a similar survey conducted in 2000[18]. When students seek to extract, evaluate and utilize information from the Internet and from multimedia materials, rather than from solely print-based media, movies and television, they are increasingly vulnerable to biased, distorted, confused, inaccurate and untruthful material, and so even more in need of supportive, critical guidance. Like all forms of communication, the Internet is vulnerable to messages that reflect the vested interests of governments, business, media corporations and advertisers; it is subject to the kind of cultural control and censorship that seeks to privilege particular beliefs, values and practice, and to marginalize, exclude or misrepresent others. Those with power and influence may attempt to restrict the messages and voices of those who might wish to express counter views. As discussed in chapter 3, there is enormous potential for both good and bad. In Dahlberg's (2005) view, the bad seems to be winning: "the Internet's potential for extending strong democratic culture through critical communication is being undermined by a coporate colonization of cyberspace" (p. 160). Brem et al. (2001) have studied the ability of students in Grades 9, 11 and 12 to evaluate information located on Websites of varying quality, including some hoax sites. Despite lots of preparatory work and continuing support from teachers, students frequently failed to differentiate between the quality of the science and the nature of the reporting and presentation, often equating amount of detail with quality. Students were often unable to assess the accuracy, judge the credibility and evaluate the site's use of evidence to substantiate knowledge claims. Because students tended to rely on common sense as their principal guide, rather than careful analysis and critical reflection, they were too easily seduced by whatever attractive surface features the authors deployed. In a similar study at the Grade 6 level, Wallace et al. (2000) found that students usually concentrated on the search aspects of the task and their ability to navigate a range of sites, and neglected to evaluate the quality of the science they located. Often they searched for key words and then slavishly copied the chunk of text in which they had located them into their notebooks.

Tsai (2004a, b) and Wu and Tsai (2005) have developed a conceptual framework, named *Information Commitments* (ICs), to describe and evaluate the strategies and standards used by students in their Internet-based searches. ICs address issues such as use of a simple keywords search versus more sophisticated concept-based searches, the value placed on ease of searching and retrieving information versus relevance and quality of information, whether students considered the reputation of the Website, and whether they cross-checked information against other Websites, printed texts and the findings of their peers. Among students aged 16 to 18 in a number of schools in northern Taiwan, Lin and Tsai (2008) found that those with more sophisticated NOS views tended to adopt more sophisticated ICs, used a greater range of sites, sought to ascertain the trustworthiness and reputation of the sites accessed, and were much more likely to engage in cross-checking of information. This research may provide some useful guidelines for how teachers can provide advice, guidelines and critical support to assist students in enhancing their web literacy.

Although it is well outside the scope of this book, it is important to acknowledge the urgency of broadening our conception of literacy and media literacy. Presentation of information is increasingly multimodal, combining text with complex and overlapping visual and audio messages and creating the need for a new kind of multimodal literacy. In the words of Carmen Luke (2000), "the cyberspace navigator must draw on a range of knowledges about traditional and newly blended genres or representational conventions, cultural and symbolic codes, as well as linguistically coded and software-driven meanings. Moreover, the lateral connectedness of hypertext information, which users access by clicking on buttons or hotlinks, immerses navigators in an inter-textual and multimodal universe of visual, audio, symbolic, and linguistic meaning systems. In hypertext navigation, reading, writing, and communicating are not linear or unimodal (that is, exclusively language and print-based), but demand a multimodal reading of laterally connected, multi-embedded, and further hotlinked information resources variously coded in animation, symbols, print text, photos, movie clips or three-dimensional and manoeuvrable graphics" (p. 73). When we consider the additional need to understand the specialist registers of various technical and professional communities, the variations in language use introduced by text speak and rap music, the genres favoured by politicians, the military and the world of advertizing, and so on, it may well be that it is more appropriate to refer to the need for students to be "multiliterate".

Kress (2003) notes that while "language-as-speech" is likely to remain the primary mode of human communication, "language-as-writing" is rapidly being displaced by "language-as-images" and combinations of images. Ulmer (2003) likens this shift towards what he calls "electracy" to the shift from orality to literacy at the dawn of the print age. Among the many new demands is the problem of distinguishing among data and images that are uninterpreted, neutral, authentic, manipulated, artificial and sometimes provocatively slanted to express a particular viewpoint and exclude others. There was a time when we could say: "the camera never lies". Photoshop has changed all that, and as Donna Haraway (1997) comments, "there are no unmediated photographs... only highly specific visual possibilities, each with a wonderfully detailed, active, partial way of organizing worlds" (p. 177). It has always been the case that scientific data obtained by means of sophisticated technology is both theory-impregnated and mediated by the decisions of scientists and technicians about how to collect, organize and display data. This is particularly evident in relation to contemporary medical technology. Computerized tomography, ultrasound, PET scanners and magnetic resonance imaging do not produce photo-graphs, but mathematically constructed representations, as Burri and Dumit (2008) comment in their discussion of MRI.

> Scientists and technicians make decisions about parameters such as the number and thickness of the cross-sectional slices, the angle they are to be taken from, and the scale or resolution of the image data. Decisions also have to be made when it comes to post-processing the images on the screen: perspectives can be rotated, contrast modified, and colors chosen for scientific publications. These specific decisions do not depend on technical and professional standards alone but also on cultural and aesthetic conventions or individual preferences. (p. 301)

In elaboration of the ways in which images are manipulated to suit a particular sociocultural context, the authors note some intriguing differences in the ways ultrasound images of early-stage foetuses are deployed in different cultural contexts in relation to different levels of anxiety, hope, excitement, privacy and publicity, and are sometimes used by advertisers and anti-abortion groups to project a particular message.

DEALING WITH CONTROVERSIAL ISSUES

Many SSI are highly controversial: GM crops, governmental DNA banks, gene therapy, cloning, stem cell research, health hazards associated with mobile phones and overhead power lines, toxic waste disposal, euthanasia, abortion, nuclear power generation and nuclear weapons, deep space exploration, xenotransplantation, animal experiments, food irradiation, compulsory MMR vaccination, smart ID cards, priorities for deployment of scarce resources for medical services and for medical research, and ways to deal with ozone depletion, desertification, loss of biodiversity and other environmental crises. An issue can be regarded as controversial when: (i) the scientific information required to formulate a judgement about it is incomplete, insufficient, inconclusive or extremely complex and difficult to interpret, and (ii) judgement involves consideration of factors rooted in social, political, economic, cultural, religious, environmental, aesthetic and/or moral-ethical concerns, beliefs, values and feelings, concerning which, people may hold widely varying positions. It is also the case that the dispute should have persisted for some time (brief differences of opinion are not usually regarded as controversial) and should involve more than two people. Implied, too, is public interest in resolving the conflict because of its significance to decision-making about how best to proceed. Dearden (1981) sums up the situation as follows: "A matter is controversial if contrary views can be held on it without those views being contrary to reason. This can be the case, for example, where insufficient evidence is held in order to decide the controversy, or, where the outcomes depend on future events that cannot be predicted with certainty, and where judgement about the issue depends on how to weigh or give value to the various information that is known about the issue" (p. 38). While these characteristics presuppose that the issue is reasonably well articulated and key differences are open to public scrutiny, it is important to recognize, as Levinson (2006) reminds us, that there can be situations where "a significant group of people might keep their interchanges with the rest of society to a minimum, where there may be no forum for exchange of views or where they might feel intimidated by expressing their opinions" (p. 1204). He continues as follows: "Social consensus could be based around a point of view that is generally seen as commonsense, which an outsider perceives as deeply wrong and possibly offensive, but the modes for articulating disagreement are not available to the outsider" (Levinson, 2006, p. 1204). On occasions, SSI are heavily impregnated with business interests, military concerns and political imperatives that are socially or politically difficult to oppose. In many contexts, independent and critical consideration of SSI is vulnerable to pressure from social groups seeking to advance particular views and values.

Teachers wishing to incorporate controversial SSI into their curriculum cannot avoid consideration of the values inherent in the issues. Indeed, for Zeidler et al. (2005) this is the very *raison d'etre* for including SSI in the curriculum. David

Layton (1986) identifies three possible stances on values education: (i) *inculcation* – particular values are instilled through repeated exemplification and reinforcement; (ii) *moral development* – students are helped to develop more complex moral reasoning patterns; and (iii) *clarification* – students are helped to identify their own values and those of others. As Ratcliffe and Grace (2003) observe, "which of these three dominates [is adopted] depends on the age of the students, the curriculum context and teacher disposition" (p. 23). It also depends, in large measure, on directives issued by school Principals and governing bodies, Ministries of Education and other local education authorities, their capacity and willingness to use sanctions against teachers who might adopt a contrary position, and the courage of teachers to resist attempts at control. It is deplorable that all five teachers interviewed by McGinnis and Simmons (1999) felt so intimidated by the prevailing social climate that they expressed support for an STS orientation but avoided controversial topics, especially those that might challenge religious views of a fundamental nature or the practices of local industries. Similarly, Sammel and Zandvliet (2003) note that most approaches to SSI in school are conducted within teachers' perceptions of "politically acceptable limits". The primary thrust of the politicized science education being advocated in his book entails being critical of industrial, business, military and wider social practices, and where considered necessary, seeking change. Causing surprise, discomfort or offence to one or two parents, school officials, local residents or business interests is simply the price we have to pay in the struggle to create and sustain a 'better world' and a more just, equitable and honourable society. It is imperative that teachers find the courage, enlist the support of others and mobilize the resources to be much more challenging, critical and politicized in their approach. From my point of view, it is enormously encouraging that the Qualifications and Curriculum Authority in the United Kingdom regard teachers as having a *duty* to prepare students to deal with controversial issues.

> Education should not attempt to shelter our nation's children from even the harsher controversies of adult life, but should prepare them to deal with such controversies knowledgeably, sensibly, tolerantly and morally. (QCA, 1998, p. 56)

Once teachers decide to include controversial issues in the curriculum, they have to decide the most appropriate way to do so. Should the teacher take a neutral position, adopt the devil's advocate role or try to present a balanced view? In a deliberate move to renounce the position of the teacher as an authority figure on all matters, the *Humanities Curriculum Project* in the late 1960s and early 1970s proposed that teachers act as a neutral chair during class discussion and debate on controversial issues relating to poverty, race relations and gender inequality (Ruddock, 1986; Stenhouse, 1970, 1983). One form of neutrality, *affirmative neutrality*, describes a situation in which teachers present multiple sides of a controversy without revealing which side they support. In *procedural neutrality*, information about the controversy and different points of view are elicited from the students, possibly after opportunity for library-based or Internet-based research. Without neutrality (procedural or affirmative), Stenhouse (1970) argued, "the inescapable authority position of the teacher in the classroom is such that his [sic] view will be given an undue emphasis and regard which will seriously limit the readiness of the students to consider other views" (p. 7). Quite apart from the danger of encouraging relativism, where any idea is accepted as long as it is someone's opinion, this is a position that seriously threatens the teacher's credibility and invites the reasonable question: Do you not have a view, Miss? It is absurd for teachers to pretend that they don't have a view. It is deplorable for teachers to refuse to state their view, while simultaneously requiring students to state their views. The guidelines issued by the Qualifications and Curriculum Authority (QCA, 2000, p. 35) on presenting a 'balanced view' direct the teacher to avoid bias by *resisting the temptation* to:

- highlight a particular selection of facts or items of evidence, thereby giving them a greater importance than other equally relevant information;
- present information as if it is not open to alternative interpretation or qualification or contradiction;
- set themselves up as the sole authority not only on matters of 'fact' but also on matters of opinion;
- present opinions and other value judgements as if they are facts;
- give their own accounts of the views of others instead of using the actual claims and assertions as expressed by various interest groups themselves;
- reveal their own preferences by facial expressions, gestures, tones of voice, etc.;
- imply preferences through choice of respondents to contribute their views to a discussion;
- allow a consensus of opinion that emerges too readily to remain unchallenged.

The notion of presenting a 'balanced view' is extremely problematic. What counts as balance? Whose judgement of balance and selection of perspectives is to count? Who decides what counts as relevant or not relevant, accurate or inaccurate, admissible or inadmissible, important or unimportant? Who decides what should be regarded as facts and what is deemed to be opinion? If all students express similat views, who will provide the alternatives? How should the teacher or the class respond to opinions that seem designed for no other reason than to shock, provoke or 'wind people up'? The key point is that *all* views embody a particular position, and that position needs to be rationalized and justified if indoctrination is to be avoided. Both teachers and students need to recognize that although 'balance' can never be fully achieved, all parties can be forewarned about bias and distortion and forearmed to recognize and deal with it. This is just as important for teachers selecting curriculum materials as it is for students working with them. Oulton et al. (2004) argue that developing a *generic* understanding of the nature of controversy and the ability to deal with it is more important than developing students' ability to address any particular issue. In other words, understanding the nature of controversy is step number one. Teachers need to make it explicit to students that views may differ because they are based on different information, different interpretations of the same information or differences in worldviews, values, attitudes, interests, experiences, feelings or emotions. Students need to know that different value judgements are sometimes a consequence of differences in moral codes or ethical principles deriving from different religious, political or philosophical positions. As Ratcliffe and Grace (2003) comment, following the QCA guidelines to the letter in pursuit of a supposed evenhandedness would prevent students from developing the critical skills necessary for judging the worth and validity of different positions. Following the guidelines would require teachers to give equal time, consideration and weight to views and arguments that are clearly not of equal merit. Moreover, teachers' views are likely to be evident to students anyway from the questions they ask and the ways in which they respond to (or ignore) student comments, and through tone of voice, maintenance of eye contact (or not), and the ever-potent and revealing classroom body language.

When they come to approach a *particular* controversial SSI, students need to ascertain the nature and extent of the disagreement. Is it a consequence of insufficient evidence, evidence of the 'wrong kind', evidence that is conflicting, confusing or inconsistent, or too complex and difficult to interpret? Is the problem of resolution located in the absence of clear criteria for making a judgement? Is it the case that different criteria point to different solutions or actions? And so on. They may also need to know in what ways personal feelings and emotions or personal experiences are likely to impact the way the issue, the data or the interpretation and conclusion are evaluated. This applies just as much to their evaluation of the teacher's views as it does to the evaluation of their own views, the views of other students, and the views expressed in the materials under consideration. Indeed, I am in full agreement with Oulton et al. (2004) when they state that: "acceptance that all materials and judgements about teaching and learning strategies are open to bias leads us to argue that teachers should make their position explicit at the start of the exercise so the pupils are aware of potential bias in the way the teacher has arranged the experience and in what they say and do" (p. 417). These authors proceed to add a rider: "This increased openness would not remove from pupils and teachers alike the right to remain silent on some matters that they do not wish to make public" (p. 417). While I acknowledge the right of an individual student to remain silent, I would not extend that privilege to teachers. Nor would I be supportive of teachers who used their own views as justification for excluding opportunities for students to address issues such as abortion, birth control, genetic engineering and cloning. I believe that it is incumbent on teachers to make provision for students to address a wide range of controversial SSI, particularly those in which they express an interest and those with direct impact on their lives. And I believe that it is incumbent on teachers to share their views on these matters with students and to make explicit the ways in which they have arrived at their particular position. It is also incumbent on teachers to adopt the same stance of critical reflection and open-mindedness that they demand of their students, and to be willing to change or modify their views in the light of new evidence, a new way of interpreting evidence, a reappraisal of underlying values, or whatever. Some years ago, Kelly (1986) proposed the broadly similar approach of "committed impartiality", in which teachers present multiple sides of an issue or argument and, at some stage, share their own views with the class. In my view, it is crucial that teachers identify, clarify and challenge the assumptions of *all* positions (including their own), acknowledge the influence of sociocultural context, religious beliefs, emotions and feelings, address issues of rationality, equity and social justice, and encourage critical reflection. Kelly (1986) argued that when students are encouraged to debate and challenge their teacher's ideas without fear of sanctions, they not only develop argumentation skills, but also build the courage for social commitment. According to Kelly, the balance between personal commitment and impartiality catalyses students' ability to think and argue critically and to express themselves courageously: "When students are treated as colleagues, they feel more grown up" (p. 194).

In discussing the nature of scientific rationality, Helen Longino (1990, 1994, 2002) identifies four conditions that a community of practitioners must be able to meet if consensus is to count as valid and reliable knowledge rather than mere opinion, illustrating her argument in relation to the social organization of the community of scientists. First, she says, there are public forums for the presentation and criticism of evidence, methods, assumptions and reasoning – in particular, conferences, academic journals and the system of peer review. Second, there are shared and publicly available standards that critics invoke in appraising work, including but not restricted to empirical adequacy. Third, the scientific community makes changes and adjustments in response to critical debate, and is clearly seen by practitioners and members of the public to do so. Fourth, the right to submit work for peer appraisal and criticism is open to all practitioners; so, too, the right to publicly criticize the work of others. Further, the critical scrutiny exerted on scientific ideas by peer review and public critique via conferences and journals is the centrepiece of scientific rationality and a guarantee of the objectivity and robustness of the knowledge developed (see chapter 4 for further discussion).

> The formal requirement of demonstrable evidential relevance constitutes a standard of rationality and acceptability independent of and external to any particular research program or scientific theory. The satisfaction of this standard by any program or theory, secured, as has been argued, by intersubjective criticism, is what constitutes its objectivity. (Longino, 1990, p. 75)

In addressing SSI in class, teachers should work to establish similar procedures and standards, with "every member of the community… regarded as capable of contributing to its constructive and critical dialogue" (Longino, 1990, p. 132). Of course, students' views and the actions that may follow from them are likely to be strongly influenced by emotions and feelings, by personal experiences and the experiences of friends and family, and by socioculturally determined predispositions and worldviews. A student's sense of identity, comprising ethnicity, gender, social class, family and community relationships, economic status and personal experiences extending over many years, will impact on their values, priorities and preferences. It should go without saying that teachers introducing SSI into the curriculum need to be sensitive to these influences, as discussed in the next section of this chapter.

Because values and moral-ethical concerns and personal experiences will play a crucial role in the way students address controversial SSI, we should take steps to assist them in dealing with these matters in a more careful and effective way. Ralph Levinson (2008) makes a powerful case for the role of personal narratives in teaching and learning about controversial SSI, on the grounds that they act as a bridge between formal science and personal experience, provide graphic illustration of social, cultural, political and religious viewpoints, and help to reinforce or problematize warrants and generate rebuttals. Most importantly, personal narratives help students to see issues and events from the standpoint of those who do not share their own views or experiences. We also need to assist students in recognizing the ways in which values impregnate and underpin all SSI and help them to recognize the value-laden nature of scientific practice itself, including the ways in which science often reflects the interests, values and biases of those who produce it. We need to assist students in clarifying their own value positions and in considering what counts as 'right action' in particular circumstances. Values in science and science education are discussed at greater length in chapters 4 and 5. The teaching of ethics is discussed in chapter 7.

AFFECTIVE AND SOCIAL DIMENSIONS OF LEARNING

Although some specific pedagogical issues related to an SSI-oriented approach will be discussed in chapter 6, it is important also to address some more general teaching and learning concerns, particularly with regard to the affective and social dimensions of learning. More than 40 years ago, David Ausubel (1968) famously remarked: "If I had to reduce all of educational psychology to just a single principle, I would say this: Find out what the learner already knows and teach him accordingly" (p. 337). Following these comments and the accumulation of a vast body of research into students' alternative conceptions in science extending over some two decades[19], a number of so-called "constructivist approaches" to teaching and learning science were developed and became widely accepted as the new orthodoxy of science teaching in many countries around the world. While these schemes differ a little in detail, they have certain features in common, and can be usefully summarized as follows.
- Identify students' ideas and views.
- Create opportunities for students to explore their ideas and test their robustness in explaining phenomena, accounting for events and making predictions.
- Provide stimuli for students to develop, modify and, where necessary, change their ideas and views.
- Support their attempts to re-think and reconstruct their ideas and views.
In what is probably the most widely cited science education article of the 1980s and 1990s, Posner et al. (1982) argued that new learning can be brought about only when learners are dissatisfied with their current beliefs/understanding and have ready access to a new or better idea. Also, to be acceptable the new idea must meet certain conditions: (i) it must be *intelligible* (understandable) – that is, the learner must understand what it means and how it can and should be used; (ii) it must be *plausible* (reasonable) – that is, it should be consistent with and be able to be reconciled with other aspects of the student's understanding; and (iii) it must be *fruitful* (productive) – that is, it should have the capacity to provide something of value to the learner by solving important problems, facilitating new learning, addressing concerns, making valid and reliable predictions, suggesting new explanatory possibilities or providing new insight. In summary, conceptual change is made possible when students understand the limitations of their current views and recognize the need to replace them. Dissatisfaction with an existing idea may reside in its failure to predict correctly or to control events beyond its previous restricted context, that is, it is no longer fruitful in the new situations the learner has to confront. It may also be located in recognition that the new view meets the conditions of intelligibility and plausibility

more satisfactorily than the existing idea. Taking this view at face value, Hewson and Thorley (1989) describe the conceptual change approach to teaching and learning science as a matter of changing the status of rival conceptions with respect to the three conditions of intelligibility, plausibility and fruitfulness. Put simply, the teacher's task is to lower the status of the students' existing ideas and raise the status of the new one. It is assumed that feelings of surprise, puzzlement, unease or curiosity occasioned by the demonstrated inadequacy of existing ideas to explain the new event or phenomenon will act as both a motivating factor and a stimulus for conceptual change. It is further assumed that the collision of existing ideas with new experiences precipitates what Piaget calls "cognitive disequilibrium", the resolution of which is achieved by cognitive restructuring.

> A necessary condition for cognitive restructuring is an opportunity for repeated, exploratory, inquiry-oriented behaviors about an event or phenomena in order to realize that the intact schema option is no longer tenable, and that the only reasonable option is to revise one's cognitive structure so as to be more consistent with one's experience (data, measurements, or observations). (Saunders, 1992, p. 138)

However, a host of writers (including West & Pines, 1983; Salmon, 1988; Claxton, 1991; Bloom, 1992a,b; Pintrich et al., 1993; Demastes et al., 1995; Watts & Alsop, 1997; Dole & Sinatra, 1998; Pintrich, 1999; Alsop and Watts, 2000, 2003; Zembylas, 2002a; Hennessey, 2003; Sinatra & Pintrich, 2003; Kelly, 2004; Alsop, 2005; Sinatra, 2005; Johnston et al., 2006; Nieswandt, 2007; Littledyke, 2008) have pointed out the ways in which this rationalist view of learning fails to acknowledge the complexity, uncertainty and fragility of learning and its susceptibility to a whole array of personal and social influences. Any or all of the following could impact on learning: previous experiences; emotions, feelings, values and aesthetics; personal goals and motivation levels; views of learning; social norms and aspirations; general feelings of well-being and satisfaction. It is easy to see how feelings of wonder, awe, delight, amusement, curiosity, indifference, anxiety, uncertainty, boredom, happiness, sadness, indignation, anger, fear, disgust and horror could impact in different ways on a learning task – sometimes favourably with respect to learning and sometimes unfavourably. So, too, could a student's level of interest, perception of relevance and self-interest, feelings of satisfaction/dissatisfaction, confidence and pride, and their self-image and sense of identity. Aesthetic, political, economic and moral-ethical concerns also play a role. Put simply, how students *feel* about the ideas being presented to them, for whatever reasons, will influence their learning. Bloom (1992a) shows how emotions, values and aesthetics can influence not only students' willingness or reluctance to engage in a learning task, bur also the kinds of meanings that they construct – in the case of the data he presents, about earthworms. Students are likely to have strong emotional commitment to ideas that they have used successfully in the past, especially in contexts they regard as personally and/or socially important. Indeed, some ideas are so much a part of the student's everyday life that they are used automatically and unconsciously. Changing them is not easy, especially when they continue to be used by peers, within family groups and in the wider society. Abelson (1986) describes some views as being like "possessions";

they have become so much a part of the student's views of self and sense of identity, sometimes held in the face of otherwise substantial changes, that if ever they were abandoned or replaced it would only be with the greatest reluctance and an acute sense of loss and discomfort. When teachers make the assumption that learning science and learning *about* science are entirely rational activities, and that a clear understanding of the evidential justification of an idea or the logical case for a particular viewpoint will result in ready acceptance by the student, they fail to account satisfactorily for why some students who seem to have the requisite prior knowledge, and the intellectual capability to appraise the evidence and argument, fail to engage in cognitive restructuring. They also tacitly accept the obverse: that when students decline to accept a particular idea it is because they don't understand the scientific argument that supports it. As a consequence, they may misdirect their teaching efforts and, in doing so, may reinforce the student's reluctance to accept it. The substance of the foregoing argument is eloquently summarized by Caine and Caine (1991).

> We do not simply learn. What we learn is influenced and organized by emotions and mind-sets based on expectancy, personal biases and prejudices, degrees of self-esteem, and the need for social interaction. Emotions operate on many levels, somewhat like the weather. They are ongoing, and the emotional impact of any lesson may continue to reverberate long after the specific event. (p. 82)

Not only has the rhetoric of constructivism frequently neglected the affective dimension of learning, it has also consistently neglected the social dimension. Many constructivist writers have failed to acknowledge that in addition to being driven by the need to make personal sense of the world around them, learners also have to integrate their understanding into the various social contexts in which they are located in ways that are socially acceptable. While constructivists talk at length about finding effective ways of replacing students' commonsense, everyday knowledge with scientific knowledge, they fail to afford sufficient importance to the fact that it is consensus within social groups that gives status and stability to knowledge and understanding. After all, it is called *common sense* because it is the sense that is common to the group. It seems that each of us, whether adult or child, needs the approval and support of someone else in order to feel comfortable with our ideas. Thus, we often talk as much to get reassurance from others about our ideas as we do to convince others of our views. As Solomon (1987) says, "We take it for granted that those who are close to us see the world as we do, but, through social exchanges, we seek always to have this reconfirmed" (p. 67). These social exchanges also serve to establish what others think and, thereby, to assist the learning of knowledge that has been validated and approved by the social groups to which we belong. It follows that if we are to change students' commonsense knowledge, or expand and develop it in order to incorporate scientific ways of understanding, we need to take account of the social forces that will resist change and those that will assist or promote it, and we need to pay much greater attention to the various social contexts in which students move.

One of those social contexts is, of course, the classroom itself. Classrooms are very public places and much learning occurs in group settings. It would be surprising, therefore, if school-based learning were not greatly influenced by interactions with peers, just as they are influenced by interactions with teachers. In small-group work, for example, it could be argued that the quality of learning is just as much a function of interpersonal relations as it is a function of the cognitive capabilities of the group members. In other words, the social, affective and cognitive are inextricably intertwined. In whole-class activities, learners struggling to make sense of the lesson do so in an environment in which social interaction plays a profound and complex role. Students have many social goals, including making friends, impressing others and establishing social status, perhaps attracting a boyfriend or girlfriend, and so on, any or all of which can interfere with the supposedly rational processes of learning. These 'goals for classroom life' will have significant impact on learning as individuals negotiate for themselves a role that maximizes personal benefits, minimizes risks and threats to feelings of personal well-being, and helps them build a sense of personal identity. They will have a profound influence on the likelihood of students replacing their existing ideas with the idea proffered by the teacher, another student or a textbook.

> Changing your mind is not simply a matter of rational decision-making. It is a social process with social consequences. It is not simply about what is right or what is true in the narrow rationalist sense; it is always also about who we are, about who we like, about who treats us with respect, about how we feel about ourselves and others. In a community, individuals are not simply free to change their minds. The practical reality is that we are dependent on one another for our survival, and all cultures reflect this fact by making the viability of beliefs contingent on their consequences for the community. (Lemke, 2001, p. 301)

If students are to understand how scientific knowledge is negotiated and deployed within the community of practitioners, and subsequently used to promote particular positions regarding SSI, they need some direct experience of critique and negotiation. They need the opportunity to construct, discuss and debate the merits of their ideas with others. If they are to achieve the intellectual independence we seek, students have to be afforded a substantial measure of responsibility for their own learning. Student-led discussion in small groups is ideal for supporting students as they generate theoretical explanations, build on each other's ideas and subject ideas to rigorous criticism. Subsequent large group discussion or formal presentation encourages clarity of expression and careful consideration of possible counter arguments. Van Zee and Minstrell (1997) contrast traditional teacher-dominated class-room talk with what they call "reflective discourse", during which three conditions are met: "(i) students express their own thoughts, comments and questions, (ii) the teacher and individual students engage in an extended series of questioning exchanges that help students better articulate their beliefs and conceptions, (iii) student/student exchanges involve one student trying to understand the thinking of another" (p. 209). But the kind of productive talk envisaged by van Zee and Minstrell doesn't just happen; it has to be carefully planned and sustained by judicious teacher inter-ventions. Ultimately, the success of talk-based classroom activities depends on establishing a classroom environment in which student-student interaction is encouraged and supported. A half century ago, Rokeach (1960) observed that some students are more open to new ideas than others, and that these differences are present from an early age. For some, reluctance to change ideas seems to stem from a deep-seated fear of uncertainty. Such students are distrustful of new ideas unless they are presented authoritatively and they seek certainty in knowledge, rather than the ambiguity, uncertainty, fluidity and context-dependence characteristic of SSI and environmental concerns. A very supportive classroom environment is essential if these students are to accommodate to a learning style in which they are encouraged to express their own views, argue for their developing ideas, consider a wide range of alternatives and engage in the cut and thrust of debate. Students need to feel comfortable to listen to the ideas of others, question them, introduce their own ideas, accept criticism, work with others to articulate, modify and develop ideas, and build towards shared understanding.

My own research with Canadian students in Grades 6 to 12 shows that without considerable groundwork by the teacher, free exchange of ideas and criticism is quite rare and meaning is established only tentatively and hesitantly. On occasions, meaning is imposed by bold assertions from the more confident group members, rather than negotiated within the group. Often, genuine understanding doesn't develop because the group feels the need to reach early and easy consensus. In other words, their task orientation (commitment to 'getting the job done') curtails the time needed for matters to be thoroughly discussed. Depending on students' previous experience of group learning methods, it may be necessary to lay down robust procedural guidelines. Too often, teachers neglect to do so, and fail to provide students with sufficient explicit guidance. In consequence, students commonly lack clear, shared understanding of the purpose of many of the activities in which they are engaged; they are often confused, unfocused, unproductive and apathetic. When explicit guidance *is* provided, students can be enthusiastic and effective in sharing, criticizing and re-constructing their views and ideas (Barnes & Todd, 1995; Mercer, 1995, 1996). They need to know, for example, the appropriate way to *present* an argument, *listen* to an argument and *respond* to an argument; they need to know how to criticize, accept criticism, argue and reach consensus. This form of learning can be catastrophically undermined if students don't have the necessary language and social skills to participate appropriately. It can also be catastrophically undermined if learners are unable to deal with the complex and powerful emotions raised by consideration of SSI (a matter to be discussed in chapter 6).

The social context in which the student is located outside school is also a major factor impacting learning. Rejecting knowledge and beliefs that are strongly held within social groups to which the student belongs, or wishes to belong, may be so emotionally stressful that it becomes virtually impossible. Similarly, accepting views that are in opposition to the dominant views within those groups is likely to be a formidable undertaking. At the most extreme, it can be a matter of acquiring and using an alternative worldview, that is, the scientific worldview rather than the worldview that is dominant within those out-of-school contexts (see discussion in chapter 4). Every individual is a member of several social groupings: family group, ethnic group, friendship group, employment group, possibly a religious group, sports group, leisure pursuits group, local community group or Internet chatroom and listserv group. Effective participation in these groups requires appropriate subcultural knowledge and skills, shared understanding, beliefs, language, code of behaviour, aspirations, values and expectations. As people move from one social context to another, they are invariably required to change their way of speaking, acting and interacting with others in order to be accepted within the group. School is also a distinctive subculture with *its* own language, code of behaviour, values, goals and expectations. So, too, of course, is science and the school version of it. The greater the differences between a student's home and peer group subculture and the subcultures of school and school science, the more difficulties the student will encounter in "crossing the border", that is, in gaining access to school science and being successful there. Costa (1995) describes the ways in which students from different subcultural backgrounds effect (or not) the transition into the subculture of school science. She describes various patterns in relationships between students' social worlds and their success in school science in terms of five broad categories of student:

- *Potential scientists* – for whom the worlds of family and friends are congruent with the worlds of school and science, and the transition into the culture of school science is smooth and unproblematic. These students have educational aspirations and career plans in which science has a prominent role.
- *Other smart kids* – for whom the worlds of family and friends are congruent with school, but not with science. These students can manage the transition into the culture of school science without too much difficulty. While science is not personally interesting to them, they recognize its 'gatekeeper role' and can make instrumental use of it in pursuit of other educational goals.
- *"I don't know" students* – for whom the worlds of family and friends are inconsistent with both school and science. Transition into the culture of school science is hazardous, though possible at some personal cost. Often, these students find a way of meeting the demands of the system and obtaining reasonable grades without ever really understanding the material[20].
- *Outsiders* – for whom the worlds of family and friends are discordant with both school and science. These students tend to be disillusioned with or alienated from school in general, so that transition into the culture of school science is virtually impossible. They neither know nor care about science.
- *Inside outsiders* – for whom the worlds of family and friends are irreconcilable with the world of school but potentially compatible with the world of science. Although these students have a natural interest in the physical world and the intellectual ability to cope with science, transition into the culture of school science is prevented by a lack of support both inside and outside school and by their distrust of schools and teachers.

These five student 'types' experience the same science curriculum in very different ways, their experiences being positive or negative to the extent that the values, beliefs and expectations of their family and peer groups are consistent with those of science and the classroom[21]. In Costa's California-based study, all students in the inside outsider category (the group that is potentially well-disposed towards science but is so hostile to school that border crossings are not even attempted) were African Americans. Just as significant is the observation that most of those for whom transition into the world of school science was smooth and unproblematic were from White middle-class family groups. It is also the case that transitions were generally smoother for boys than for girls. Most importantly, the categories are not fixed and may shift quite substantially when the educational situation or scientific context changes.

If successful learning depends on learners exploring and developing their personal store of knowledge, and if a significant part of that personal knowledge is experientially and socioculturally determined, and includes powerful affective components, then a student's social and cultural identity becomes a significant factor affecting learning. In other words, a student's gender, ethnicity, religion, moral-ethical values and politics, as well as their emotional well-being, impact very substantially on learning. It is fair to say that many teachers have seriously under-estimated the difficulties faced by some students. As Lemke (2001) comments, a student "spends most of every day, before and after science class, in other subject-area classes, in social interactions in school but outside the curriculum, and in life outside school. We have imagined that the few minutes of the science lesson somehow create an isolated and nearly autonomous learning universe, ignoring the sociocultural reality that students' beliefs, attitudes, values, and personal identities – all of which are critical to their achievement in science learning – are formed along trajectories that pass briefly through our classes" (p. 305). In effect, then, the science teacher's job can be seen as helping students to gain an understanding of what, for many, are alien cultures (the subcultures of science, school and school science) and to assist them in moving freely and painlessly within and between these subcultures and the subcultures of home and community (Aikenhead, 1996, 1997, 2006; Cobern & Aikenhead, 1998; Aikenhead & Jegede, 1999; Hodson, 2001). Others see the science teacher's role more as a matter of assisting students in deploying more effectively the cultural resources that they bring with them (Seilor, 2001) or as a matter of seeking to merge the "first space" of school science with the "second space" of the home to create a "third space" that brings together the different knowledges, discourses, relationships, aspirations and values in ways that enable new knowledge and discourse to emerge and new identities to be forged (Gutiérrez et al., 1999; Moje et al., 2001, 2004; Gutiérrez, 2008; Zembylas & Avraamidou, 2008). Calabrese Barton et al. (2008) see the science classroom as creating multiple hybrid spaces, depending on the nature of the activity (whole class settings, small group work, individual study, and so on). Within these different spaces there are opportunities for students to craft new forms of participation and construct new identities or, of course, to consolidate or modify existing identities. Issues of identity are discussed further in chapters 3 and 9.

The foregoing discussion suggests that the list of conditions for conceptual change set out by Posner et al. (1982) needs to incorporate an additional element: that students *feel comfortable* with the new idea, in the sense that it meets their emotional needs and is "culturally safe" and socially acceptable or, at least, non-threatening. Watts and Alsop (1997) and Alsop (1999) argue that for new knowledge to be acceptable, it needs to be *salient, palatable* and *germane*. In other words, material has to be noticeable, engaging, stimulating or startling, it has to be appealing and agreeable (certainly not disagreeable or disturbing), and it has to be recognized as relevant to the learner's personal needs, interests and aspirations. If this complex of affective and social factors is as important as I am arguing with respect to learning science content and NOS knowledge, how much more significant is it likely to be with regard to controversial and often emotionally charged SSI and environmental concerns? This fusion of the cognitive, affective, aesthetic and social, too often absent from the science classroom, is essential to the kind of radical shift in attitudes and values on which sociopolitical action depends. Some teachers will see this in a positive light, and will seek to use these affective and social dimensions as a stimulus to engaging students' interest in SSI, getting them to consider moral-ethical issues, and building their commitment to social action (Macy, 1983; Alsop, 2001; Alsop & Watts, 2002; Matthews et al., 2002). Others will see it as constituting a set of problems: how to deal with controversy, how to create the right learning conditions, how to help students cope with powerful emotions, and so on – matters to which I will return in chapter 6.

BUILDING A CURRICULUM

As argued earlier, science and technology education has the responsibility of educating students about the complex but intimate relationships among the technological products we consume, the processes that produce them, the values that underpin our needs and wishes to acquire them, and the biosphere that sustains us. It has the responsibility of presenting students with the moral-ethical dilemmas arising from developments in medicine and biotechnology. It has the responsibility of assisting students to confront all socioscientific issues rationally, critically, vigorously, fearlessly and confidently, and to argue strongly, appropriately and persuasively for their own views. It has the responsibility of motivating and enabling students to address and challenge taken-for-granted assumptions, commonly expressed views and ideas, 'received wisdom' and dominant perspectives. It has the responsibility of encouraging students to question their own beliefs, attitudes and values, address any inconsistencies, and consider the appropriateness of their daily behaviour. It has the responsibility of preparing students for sociopolitical action, and giving them some experience of such action. Failing to do these things, on spurious grounds of disciplinary purity or rigour, or the desire to present science as 'value free', is simply reinforcing the *status quo* and contributing to the problems our society currently faces. As Martin Luther King said, in a somewhat different context, "If you are not part of the solution, you are part of the problem". At about the same time, Noam Chomsky (1969) wrote: "Intellectuals are in a position to expose the lies of governments, to analyze actions according to their causes and motives and often hidden intentions. In the Western world at least, they have the power that comes from political liberty, from access to information and freedom of expression. For a privileged minority, Western democracy provides the leisure, the facilities and the training to see the truth lying hidden behind the veil of distortion and misrepresentation, ideology and class interest through which the events of current history are presented to us" (p. 256). If we don't exercise that capacity for intellectual independence, scepticism and critique, and encourage our students to do so, we become passive agents for corporate, government and military interests rather than active agents for the common good. We are, therefore, implicated in what Chomsky calls the "manufacture of consent".

Steven Lukes (1974) notes three ways in which control of thought, values and aspirations is maintained: first, legal coercion; second, the power of setting the agenda for public debate and decision-making; third, socialization through formal and informal education, including the popular media. With regard to setting the agenda, Bakhtin (1981) reminds us that language is not neutral; it does not pass freely and easily between individuals; its acquisition changes the learner in several important respects and may impact on her/his sense of self, sometimes positively and sometimes negatively. It carries a substantial sub-textual cargo of meaning (culturally determined assumptions, beliefs, values and attitudes) that is intended to create a particular view of the world and to foster particular attitudes, behaviours and habits. Its power is located in the ways in which it determines how we think about society and our relations with others, and in its impact on how we act in the world. When deployed effectively and continuously, it creates a particular social reality, a reality that is firmly in the interests of those who are able to impose their own language on others. Indeed, rhetoric becomes reality and those who think differently, and have different values, are regarded as deviant or aberrant. People learn to speak and to think in particular ways through socialization into the linguistic conventions and practices of particular communities. In that sense, control is exerted through language even on the thoughts that cross our minds. Common strategies include presenting one's own position as natural or as plain common sense, thus implying that there is a conspiracy among one's opponents to deny the truth or to promote what is fashionable or 'politically correct' (itself a term that has acquired substantial pejorative connotations).

> This is a powerful technique. First, it assumes that there are no *genuine* arguments against the chosen position; any opposing views are thereby positioned as false, insincere or self-serving. Second, the technique presents the speaker as someone brave or honest enough to speak the (previously) unspeakable. Hence the moral high ground is assumed and opponents are further denigrated. (Gillborn, 1997, p. 353)

Lukes (1974) comments: "Is it not the supreme and most insidious exercise of power to prevent people, to whatever degree, from having grievances by shaping their perceptions, cognitions and preferences in such a way that they accept their role in the existing order of things, either because they can see or imagine no alternative to it, or because they see it as natural and unchangeable?" (p. 24). As Cohen (2001) notes, "without being told what to think about (or what not to think about), and without being punished for 'knowing' the wrong things, societies arrive at unwritten agreements about what can be publicly remembered and acknowledged" (p. 10). It is this catalogue of "unwritten agreements" that my issues-based and action-oriented science and technology curriculum seeks to challenge and, when deemed necessary, overturn in favour of an alternative rooted in principles of freedom, equity, social justice and environmental responsibility.

Chomsky (1991) speaks about two other ways in which governments, corporations and the media "manufacture consent": (i) using "diversions" such as sport and pop culture to distract people away from paying attention to important issues and problems, or seeking to take action; and (ii) fostering "irrational jingoism", that is, a narrow-minded chauvinism that overlooks problematic issues in the cause of national cohesion and unity. Gramsci (1971) also describes how the manufacture and reproduction of consent is made possible through the construction of a "common sense" view in which the particular interests of the dominant elite are presented as in the interests of everyone. In the contemporary world, the mass media play a key role through the careful monitoring, sorting, editing and encoding of information, presenting some items as important and truthful, while opposing, marginalizing devaluing or ignoring alternative views. It is the power of the media to manipulate public opinion that forms the bedrock of political compliance, mass loyalty and consumer demand. As Jurgen Habermas (1996) notes, the media "collect information, make decisions about the selection and presentation of 'programs' and to a certain extent control the entry of topics, contributions, and authors into the mass-media dominated public sphere" (p. 376). As argued in chapter 2, high levels of media literacy are essential if students are to confront SSI critically and independently, and recognize the underlying value positions of different viewpoints. Newman (2006) expresses this position particularly well.

If we are to engage in learning in order to act on and change our social and political world, then we need to examine who is trying to lay out our futures for us, who is telling us what we should and should not do, who is holding us back, and who is preventing us from acting effectively in our own and other's interests. We need to do our learning by identifying and naming the wielders of power, analyzing the kinds of power they hold and, where we deem that power to be malign, examining the ways in which they use it. (p. 10)

Gerard Fourez's (1982) "liberation ethics" are enormously helpful in this context: "the task of ethics must begin with analysing the established power relationships, laying bare a given society's inner institutional relationships and decoding its legitimating myths" (p. viii). Fourez suggests that people's actions are determined far more by reflection on personal experience and the actions of others than they are by some normative absolutes of behaviour. In his words, people are "called" to respond to others and make meaning of their lives based on these calls. It is vitally important, therefore, that teachers encourage students to deconstruct social norms and practices and to recognize, for example, how the social pressure for increased consumption (acquiring material goods) promulgated by media advertizing serves the interests of business and those in positions of power, and has led to the current crop of environmental and social crises. Through critical examination of the social production of values and ideologies, students can be freed from the constraints of current environmentally destructive rhetoric. In deconstructing their own conditioning, they become liberated from current dominating relationships and are led to consider alternatives. Freed from these constraints, students can make calls on others and stand in solidarity with them in promoting an alternative ethic. The significance of collaboration with others will become apparent in chapter 9.

Our language use also impacts on how others perceive *us*, because it signals our sociocultural affiliations. In the words of Nancy Brickhouse (2001), "learning is not merely a matter of acquiring knowledge, it is a matter of deciding what kind of person you are and want to be and engaging in those activities that make one a part of the relevant communities" (p. 286). A significant part of the curriculum approach advocated in this book involves students confronting key questions about the sociopolitical and economic rationale, attitudes and values underpinning scientific and technological practice and the science and technology curriculum in school and university, and asking themselves what kind of person they want to be. It involves a critical appraisal of a wide range of alternative perspectives. An early step in challenging and then seeking to change perceptions involves drawing attention to the ways in which everyday language predisposes us to think in particular ways and helping students to recognize how their own attitudes, beliefs, actions and values are shaped by the prevailing sociocultural context in which they live and the language they speak every day.

Inevitably, there are those who seek to maintain science education's current preoccupation with abstract, theoretical knowledge and with pre-professional preparation courses, and some who regard the reformulation of science education in terms of more overtly political goals as undesirable. Restriction of an issues-based curriculum to the level of theoretical and technical considerations only is seen by many as 'politically safe' because of its supposed neutral stance. It is my contention that it is *not* neutral. Rather, it implicitly supports current social practices, institutions and values. Insofar as it fails to address underlying sociopolitical and economic issues, excludes consideration of social alternatives, sustains a 'technocratic' approach to the confrontation of problems, and fails to equip students with the capacity to intervene, the so-called 'neutral' approach reinforces the societal values that have created the problems, and so has to be regarded as education for social reproduction and even as education *against* the environment. Of course, schools have a key role to play in social reproduction, and it does no-one any good to pretend otherwise. Schools seek to reproduce in students the language, knowledge, skills, codes of behaviour, attitudes and values that underpin existing social beliefs, patterns and practices. They seek to provide students with socially approved frameworks for understanding and interpreting the world in which they live, and try to assist them in finding meaning, purpose and direction in their lives in ways that reflect 'mainstream' values, attitudes and aspirations. And much of that is both essential and laudable. What I am advocating, *in addition*, is that students are enculturated into a critical frame of mind that enables them to turn a critical spotlight on society, and its values and practices, make judgments about what is desirable and undesirable, and seek to reinforce the former and 'do something' to change the latter. As curriculum builders and teachers, we have a choice: we can encourage or we can discourage the development and utilization of students' critical capabilities for examining the prevailing political, social and cultural dimensions of society and the part they play, or could play, in sustaining or changing current structures, attitudes and conventions (see Berlak and Berlak (1981) for an extended discussion of education for social change).

If it is true that schools foster social stability, it follows that in a society characterized by political and economic inequality, school will play a key role in maintaining and legitimizing that inequality.

> This system of structured inequality is integral to capitalism, and its strength and stability rest upon the fact that most people see it as natural and inevitable. The victims of the system tend to blame not the system for its inequalities, but themselves for their failure to 'make it'. In this way, the dominant groups in society maintain their hegemony. They do not have to use coercion or physical force. They persuade those they dominate that this is simply the way the world works. Indeed, they probably believe it quite sincerely. As a result, awkward questions are not asked. The *status quo* is maintained. (Osborne, 1991, p. 46)

The curriculum I am advocating seeks to challenge the view that these things are natural and inevitable. It aims to encourage and support students to ask awkward questions, formulate an alternative view of what is desirable, and work towards changing the *status quo*, both within and between societies. The kind of social reconstruction I envisage includes the confrontation and eventual elimination of racism, sexism, classism, homophobia and other forms of discrimination, scapegoating and injustice; it includes the confrontation and elimination of all forms of social and economic injustice; it includes a substantial shift away from unthinking and unlimited consumerism towards a more environmentally sustainable lifestyle that promotes the adoption of appropriate technology. It is based on respect for others (including non-humans), concern for and active involvement in the local community, and a commitment to open-mindedness, consideration of alternatives, critical reflection, dialogue with diverse others, and involvement in responsible action. In short, the curriculum proposals outlined in this book are unashamedly political. They are intended to produce social activists: people with the courage to fight for what is right, good and just; people who will work to re-fashion society along more socially-just lines; people who will work vigorously in the best interests of the biosphere. It is here that the curriculum deviates sharply from most of the STS or STSE courses currently in use.

In building this alternative curriculum, or any curriculum for that matter, we need to pay very careful attention to the values we wish to promote, and to the values that might be implicit in the materials and methods we employ. This is not to say that we should seek to indoctrinate students, on the one hand, or try to present a 'value-free' education, on the other. While the former is ethically unacceptable (though clearly discernible in many science and technology curricula, as a number of critical theorists have pointed out), the latter is impossible. Addressing SSI necessarily entails consideration of values. Indeed, for Zeidler et al. (2006), as noted in chapter 2, this is the very *raison d'etre* for including SSI in the curriculum. But whose knowledge, beliefs, values and attitudes are to be included? And whose are to be marginalized or excluded? My own view is that we should present students with diverse views and controversial views, and the arguments used to sustain them. If we are to prepare students to deal with controversial issues rationally, diligently, tolerantly and morally, we need to ensure that they have the knowledge, skills, attitudes and confidence to scrutinize diverse views, analyse and evaluate them, recognize inconsistencies, contradictions and inadequacies, reach their own conclusions, argue coherently and persuasively for their views, use them in making decisions about what is right, good and just in a particular context or situation, and formulate appropriate and effective courses of action. As argued throughout this book, the curriculum I advocate is anchored in notions of critical scientific literacy (as defined in chapter 1), media literacy and political literacy. It is also rooted very firmly in a commitment to reject actions that are merely convenient, expedient or in our own interests in favour of careful and critical consideration of what is good, just and honourable. In other words, as discussed in chapter 7, it is inextricably linked with teaching ethics and promoting moral development.

To reiterate the position stated in chapter 1, the focus of this book is the kind of science education that is necessary for active and responsible citizenship, the kind of science education that can equip students with the capacity and commitment to take appropriate, responsible and effective action on matters of social, economic, environmental and moral-ethical concern. The prime purpose is to enable young citizens to look critically at the society we have, and the values that sustain it, and to ask what can and should be changed in order to achieve a more socially just democracy and to bring about more environmentally sustainable lifestyles, especially in the industrialized countries of the world. This view of science education is overtly and unashamedly political. It takes the Advisory Group on Education for Citizenship and the Teaching of Democracy in Schools (QCA, 1998) at its word – not just education *about* citizenship, but education *for* citizenship.

> Citizenship education is education *for* citizenship, *behaving and acting as a citizen*, therefore it is not just knowledge of citizenship and civic society; it also implies developing values, skills and understanding. (p. 13, emphasis added)

The shift in curriculum perspective I am advocating is away from the traditional form of science education, with its emphasis almost solely on the acquisition of content knowledge and procedural skills, and towards an SSI-oriented and highly politicized science and technology curriculum that goes well beyond the usual focus of STS or STSE curricula. This shift can be regarded as a shift from a predominantly *transmission* view of education (or what Freire called a "banking education" view[22], in which there is (essentially) a one-way movement of knowledge, skills and values *from* the teacher *to* the student, through a *transactional* view in which due consideration is taken of students' existing knowledge and experience and attempts are made to engage students in problem-solving, to a *transformative/ emancipatory* approach in which students (alongside their teachers) adopt and further develop a critical stance towards the knowledge, skills and values included in the curriculum and represented in society. It is tempting to see these three views as alternatives. I am more inclined to the view that they represent increasing inclusivity, that is, the transaction position includes the transmission position focus on knowledge acquisition and retention and applies it to problem-solving, while the transformative position incorporates the cognitive thrust of the transaction position within a broader, more inclusive and more politicized approach. Of course, all three positions reflect a sociopolitical stance, ranging from a concern to reproduce mainstream knowledge, beliefs and values, and thereby maintain the existing social order, to a commitment to work towards social change. As Richard Shaull (1970) notes in his Foreword to Paolo Freire's *Pedagogy of the Oppressed*, "there is no such thing as a neutral educational process. Education either functions as an instrument which is used to facilitate the integration of the younger generation into the logic and practice of the present system and bring about conformity to it, or it becomes the 'practice of freedom', the means by which men and women deal critically and creatively with reality and discover how to participate in the transformation of their world" (p. 15). He also notes that "the development of an educational methodology that facilitates this process will inevitably lead to tension and conflict" (p. 15) – an issue that will be addressed later in this chapter and in chapters 8 and 9.

The proposed shift of emphasis can also be interpreted in terms of Habermas's (1971, 1972) theory of knowledge and human interests. *Technical rationality* and the goal of self-interest is apparent in the economic rationalist goals of efficiency and production, and in the desire to control and exploit the environment in pursuit of short term economic gains (a goal implicit, and sometimes explicit, in many recent official curriculum documents); *interpretive or hermeneutic rationality* is apparent in the desire to gain a clearer understanding of the multitude of competing human interests from the perspectives of the various actors and, thereby, a better understanding of the underlying causes of social disadvantage and environmental degradation (the goal of some STSE curricula); *critical rationality* is apparent in the emancipatory goal of self-critical reflective knowledge, free from the ideologically oriented interests of particular individuals and groups, that can form the basis for the kind of social action that reforms society and its practices (the goal of the curriculum I am proposing). In the words of Henry Giroux (1988), the goal of this latter kind of curriculum is "not only (to) empower students by giving them the knowledge and social skills they will need to be able to function in the larger society as critical agents, but also educate them for transformative action. That means educating them to take risks, to struggle for institutional change, and to fight both *against* oppression and *for* democracy... in the interest of creating a truly democratic society" (p. xxxiii).

BUILDING A COHERENT CURRICULUM

The first step in the politicization of science education is to establish the focus on SSI, that is, provide students with the opportunity to confront real world issues that have a scientific, technological or environmental dimension. The second step in building such a curriculum is to identify the most appropriate SSI and organize them into a coherent and theoretically justifiable curriculum. Of course, this is no easy matter. What might be the criteria for inclusion? Student interest? Perceived importance in contemporary society? Cutting edge science? Controversy? Ready availability of curriculum resources? In the Western contemporary world, technology is all pervasive; its social and environmental impact is clear; its disconcerting social implications and disturbing moral-ethical dilemmas are made apparent almost every day in popular newspapers, TV news bulletins and Internet postings. In many ways, it is much easier to recognize how technology is determined by the socio-cultural context in which it is located than to see how science is driven by such factors. It is much easier to see the social and environmental impact of technology than to see the ways in which science impacts on society and environment. For these kinds of reasons, it makes good sense to use problems and issues in technology and engineering as the major vehicles for contextualizing the science curriculum. This is categorically not an argument against teaching science; rather, it is an argument for teaching the science that informs an understanding of everyday technological problems and may assist students in reaching tentative solutions about where they stand on key SSI. In constructing a new science and technology curriculum for the 21st century, my inclination is to provide a mix of local, regional/national and global issues, and a range of idiosyncratic personal interests, focusing on seven areas of concern: human health; land, water and mineral resources; food and agriculture; energy resources, consumption levels and sustainabaility; industry (including manufacturing industry, the leisure and service industries, biotechnology, and so on); information transfer and transportation; ethics and social responsibility (i.e., freedom and control in science and technology). Although my focus in this book is science and technology education in the Western world, it is apparent that very similar concerns impact curriculum debate in the Developing world (Vlaardingerbroek, 1998; Dillon & Tearney, 2002; Lee & Roth, 2002). Indeed, science teachers in Vlaardingerbroek's (1998) Botswana-based study regard "reducing the spread of HIV/AIDS" as the principal goal of science education, while "promoting environmental awareness and an active interest in preserving and maintaining the natural environment", "promoting healthy diet and avoidance of drugs" and "promoting human population control" are ranked third, fourth and fifth.

As argued in Hodson (1994, 2003, 2009b, 2010), the kind of issues-based approach I am advocating can be organized in terms of four levels of sophistication.

- *Level 1*: Appreciating the societal impact of scientific and technological change, and recognizing that science and technology are, to a significant extent, culturally determined.
- *Level 2*: Recognizing that decisions about scientific and technological development are taken in pursuit of particular interests, and that benefits accruing to some may be at the expense of others. Recognizing that scientific and technological development are inextricably linked with the distribution of wealth and power.
- *Level 3*: Developing one's own views and establishing one's own underlying value positions.
- *Level 4*: Preparing for and taking action on socioscientific and environmental issues.

Contrary to the impression created by some school science textbooks, science is not propelled exclusively by its own internal logic or by a simple search for the truth. Rather, it is motivated and shaped by the personal beliefs, values, aspirations and political attitudes of its practitioners and the individuals, groups and organizations willing and able to provide the necessary funding. Necessarily, it reflects the history, power structure and political climate of the community in which it is embedded. Necessarily, it reflects the prevailing social, economic, political and moral-ethical attitudes and values of that community. In the memorable words of Robert Young (1987), "Science is not something in the sky, not a set of eternal truths waiting for discovery. Science is practice. There is no other science than the science that gets done. The science that exists is the record of the questions that it has occurred to scientists to ask, the proposals that get funded, the paths that get pursued... Nature 'answers' only the questions that get asked and pursued long enough to lead to results that enter the public domain. Whether or not they get answered, how far they get pursued, are matters for a given society, its educational system, its patronage system and its funding bodies" (pp. 18 & 19). However, although it would be grossly misleading to believe that there is only one conceivable representation of the world, or that we can know what the world is like independently of our conceptual structures, it does not follow that the world is merely a construct of the human mind, that our knowledge is purely arbitrary, or that individuals are free to fabricate any view of the world that happens to suit them. Social construction does not mean social determination. The admission that descriptions and explanations could be different does not reduce knowledge to mere fashion, prejudice, social convention or the outcome of a power struggle. The world does limit us in some ways, and it 'bites back' when we seriously misjudge its nature, as discussed in chapter 8 with respect to environmental issues. Scientific knowledge is a product of the interaction between the external real world and our intellectual needs and capabilities. Of course, what we contribute to that interaction changes over time in response to social, cultural and political change, technological innovation and new theorizing. And it varies with our knowledge, needs, interests, aspirations and values as economists, politicians, religious leaders, philosophers, scientists, engineers, and so on. While social, cultural, economic and political forces do not determine how the natural world is constituted or how it behaves, they do 'open our eyes' in particular ways, direct our attention to particular phenomena and events, and impact on the ways in which we make sense of them. Lorraine Code (2000) refers to this complex of interactions as "mitigated epistemological relativism". In turn, revolutionary scientific thinking such as Darwin's theory of evolution and Einstein's relativity theory can change quite radically the ways in which people talk, think and act. In other words, science is both culturally dependent and culturally transforming. It arises directly from the social mileu, from the problems we encounter, the needs and interests we develop, and the questions we ask, and it impacts very directly and profoundly on the social, cultural and economic fabric of society, including the language in which we express our thoughts and the ways in which we conduct our daily lives.

If it is true that science is socially constructed and socially transforming, how much more is it the case that technology is socially constructed and socially transforming? Indeed, technology is sometimes defined as the means by which people modify nature to meet their needs and wants, and better serve their interests. Technologies emerge in particular social, cultural and economic contexts and become established as part of the social fabric of everyday life, thereby shaping the lives of people and other species, and impacting significantly on the environment as a whole. Put simply, technologies shape and are shaped by social practices. As Jasanoff (2004) puts it, technology "both embeds and is embedded in social practices, identities, norms, conventions, discourses, instruments and institutions – in short, in all the building blocks of what we term the social" (p. 3). Robert Pool's (1997) study of the nuclear power industry shows how prevailing differences in sociopolitical climate in different countries determined whether the technology was adopted or rejected, how it developed (if it did), and the extent to which it gained public acceptance. In similar vein, Cheek (2009) states that technologically superior solutions sometimes fail to gain acceptance because of inadequate investment, lack of political support and low levels of public interest or confidence, citing the steam car of the 1930s (compared with petrol-driven cars) as an example. Although it is usually only the affluent members of society who have early access to new technologies, ever-increasing production levels, manufacturing innovation, low costs and extensive advertizing eventually ensure much more widespread ownership and use, with consequent massive changes in daily life – as witness, the uptake of motor cars, household electricity supply, telephones, radio, television, washing machines, personal computers and mobile phones. For these reasons, history of technology may be more appropriate and effective than history of science in bringing about awareness of the sociocultural embeddedness of science and technology, the values that create and sustain particular priorities for research and development, the moral-ethical dilemmas arising, and the social, emotional and environmental issues and problems that may arise from deployment of new science and new technologies.

At curriculum level 1, discussion might focus on the ways in which the science of Galileo, Newton, Darwin and Einstein changed our perception of humanity's place in the universe and precipitated enormous changes in the way people address many of the issues encountered in daily life. It might examine how recent developments in gene therapy and gene manipulation have thrown into question our notions of life and death and our views about what is natural and what is artificial, presented us with profound moral-ethical problems, and posed some major challenges to our concepts of freedom, equality, democracy and personal identity. Case studies of major technological inventions such as the steam engine, the internal combustion engine, the printing press and the computer can be used to show how technology can precipitate far-reaching social and economic changes that impact the lives of almost everyone on the planet. In Layton's (1993) words, "an artifact can reshape people's values and call new ones into play. It makes possible new kinds of action between which people have to choose" (p. 31).

'Level one awareness' also includes recognition that large-scale technological innovation is a complex, far-reaching and not entirely predictable activity. It can result in unexpected benefits, unanticipated costs and unforeseen risks. The benefits of scientific and technological innovations are sometimes accompanied by problems: the urgent need for many people to develop new skills, challenging and sometimes disconcerting social changes, radical changes in lifestyle, hazards to human health, environmental degradation, major moral-ethical dilemmas, and sometimes restriction rather than enhancement of individual freedom and choice. The extent to which technology can have social, political, economic and environmental impact well beyond that imagined by scientists and engineers is well illustrated in D.E. Nye's (1990) book, *Electrifying America*.

In the United States electrification was not a 'thing' that came from outside society and had an 'impact'; rather, it was an internal development shaped by its social context. Put another way, each technology is an extension of human lives: someone makes it, someone owns it, some oppose it, many use it, and all interpret it. The electric streetcar, for example, provided transportation, but there was more to it than that. Street traction companies were led into the related businesses of advertizing, real estate speculation, selling surplus electrical energy, running amusement parks, and hauling light freight. Americans used the trolley to transform the urban landscape, making possible an enlarged city, reaching far out into the countryside and integrating smaller hamlets into the urban market. Riding the trolley became a new kind of tourism, and it became a subject of painting and poetry. The popular acceptance of the trolley car also raised political issues. Who should own and control it? Should its workers unionize? Did the streetcar lead to urban concentration or diffusion, and which was desirable? Like every technology, the electric streetcar implied several businesses, opened new social agendas, and raised political questions. It was not a thing in isolation, but an open-ended set of problems and possibilities. (pp. ix–x)

Too often the seductive power of new and powerful technologies blind us to their unexpected adverse consequences and the values that accompany them. For example, computer technology has vastly enhanced our ability to access, manipulate, store and communicate information on all manner of things, but it has led to a massive increase in paper consumption, created an almost insatiable demand for related technologies (printers, scanners, copiers, and so on), impacted our sense of identity and our style of communication with others, and through in-built obsolescence has created a spiralling consumer demand for new machines and the related problems of how to dispose of the old ones. The spread of computer technology in non-Western societies has vastly increased opportunities for rapid communication but has played a significant role in undermining traditional forms of knowledge, communication and moral authority. While computer technology has created some new employment opportunities, it has also led to widespread redundancies and redeployments, and to extensive "outsourcing" to locations where costs are lower. Not least among these concerns, it has substantially increased the ability of employers and governments to monitor the activities of employees and citizens. While email, and the immediate downloading of attached files, has opened up enormous possibilities for rapid communication and transfer of data, it has created some problems of privacy and ownership. Because email messages are assigned traceable number codes, almost any message can be tracked and made available to others, possibly in modified form. On a similar note, Steve Keirl (2006) asks us to be a little more critical in our views about the value of mobile phones.

We can phone someone in the full knowledge that our location, duration of use, and whom we contacted are readily logged. Our call may be monitored, trawled or tapped. Employers can tell us when to have the phone switched on (the phone as dog lead). Answering machines and caller identification let us screen callers – including friends and relatives – before we speak with them. Phoning call-centers lets us use menus, join queues, and listen to music. Researchers and marketers contact us without invitation. We cannot avoid the unwanted call signals and conversations of others in public places. (p. 84)

David Barlex (2006) notes some of the unanticipated consequences, some beneficial and some harmful, resulting from the development of the internal combustion engine.

To accommodate the needs of the motorist (and to provide for movement of goods by lorries and tankers), a large network of roads and motorways have developed. The use of motor vehicles on this transport network contributes significantly to pollution of the atmosphere and global warming. Learning to drive and acquiring a motorcar have become a rite of passage for most young adults, male and female, in many countries. The opportunity to move from your place of birth to new and different places, to gain employment, to meet new people, to form friendships and relationships is facilitated by the motorcar. This physical and social mobility can have a deleterious effect on small, localized communities... Since the first road-crash fatality in 1896, motor vehicles have claimed an estimated 30 million lives globally. On average, someone dies in a motor-vehicle crash each minute... When the motorcar was invented and the automobile industry was born, no one envisaged that subsequent design iterations would be responsible for environmental damage, social upheaval, and a colossal death-toll. (p. 184)

He goes on to ask whether those who developed the early motor vehicles would have heeded warnings about the likely harm to the planet, the erosion of family values, decline in the quality of urban life, and the deaths of millions of people in traffic accidents. His answer is "of course not", because they would have thought such outcomes highly unlikely and would have assumed that future generations would attend to any problems as they arose. There is an important lesson here about vigilance and prompt action that relates to all scientific and technological developments. Technologies almost always develop faster than our awareness of the problems, understanding of the associated ethical issues, and development of legal constraints. Realization of the full extent of the hazards often comes very late, as in the case of DDT and CFCs. We also have to contend with our tendency to bury our heads in the sand and hope that problems will either go away or will be solved by new scientific discoveries or technological innovations, as graphically illustrated in the recent movie *The Age of Stupid* (playing in Auckland cinemas as I write these words). Even more disturbingly, the hazards may be known but they are ignored because it is more convenient to 'carry on as usual', while 'doing something' may be difficult or expensive. The hazards may go undetected for a long time. The impact may primarily affect those with little or no power to protest, organize concerted counter-actions, demand change, and/or seek recompense. For these reasons, it is important to ensure that there is wider and more critical scrutiny of our policies and priorities for scientific research and technological development by a more diverse group of people, and closer monitoring of all trials and implementations. It would be utter folly to allow these matters to be decided simply by the career interests of scientists and engineers and/or the profit motive of multinational companies.

At a much more overt political level, students should be invited to consider how technology can be used to liberate or to oppress - again in relation to the prevailing sociopolitical climate. For example, new forms of ICT such as cell phones, email and the Internet, create opportunities and possibilities that would have been unimaginable just a few years ago. Cheap, lightweight and "go anywhere" technologies have shifted, broadened, fragmented and redefined the basis of communicative power and shown that governments, NGOs, business corporations and the military can no longer exploit public ignorance or exert absolute control over news and information. The long-standing assumption of a gulf in time between the initial news of an event and the emergence of a detailed account of the events, during which the story can be edited and manipulated to reflect particular interests, is fast being eliminated. Within minutes, the public has access to vivid and authentic impressions of what is happening, even in remote parts of the world. There is no longer time for governments and other interested parties to pre-empt, mediate or suppress information. Because these new portable technologies are available to almost everyone, a new capacity for instant scrutiny, and an attendant call for greater accountability, has emerged. Nik Gowing's superb BBC documentary, *Skyful of Lies* (www.bbc.com/skyfuloflies)[23], provides some striking examples that would be ideal for school use, including the mobilization of opposition demonstrators in the aftermath of the disputed 2009 Iranian election, the exposing of government incompetence and seeming indifference in the wake of hurricane Katrina, and revelations concerning the conduct of the Israeli military in Gaza, police brutality against members of the public in a host of countries, and systematic lying by the US military and NATO regarding civilian deaths in Afghanistan and Iraq and the gross indecencies attending the execution of Saddam Hussain.

Gowing (2009) also reports some fascinating examples of the deliberate blurring of media demarcation lines. For example, in late 2008, the mass circulation German newspaper *Bild* joined with supermarket chain Lidl to sell easy-to-use digital cameras for €70 to develop its "volksjournalismus" (people's journalism) project. The result, says Gowing, will be "a staff increase of 82 million" (p. 16). An earlier example of people's journalism was the establishment of *Oh My News*, a South Korean newspaper founded in 2000 with the slogan: "Every citizen is a reporter" and followed four years later by *Oh My News International* (http://english.ohmy news.com). Other examples include the collaboration of the non-professional photo-sharing site Flickr with the professional agency Getty Images and the establishment by the Big Pictures agency of the *Mr Paparazzi* Website, through which members of the public are encouraged to sell photos of "celebrities" under the catch line "Now EVERYONE'S a paparazzo". Mobile phones, email, blogs and sites like You Tube, Facebook, My Space, Twitter and Second Life facilitate the quick and effective exchange of ideas, values, beliefs and experiences, foster critical response to these communications, and enable virtual communities to be built with diverse others, even across national boundaries. New modes of communicative design, including peer-to-peer sharing and open publishing platforms like blogging and wikis, have created a space for alternative politics, cultures and voices. And have created new opportunities for collective intervention to address common issues and problems. It is much easier to become familiar with a diverse range of viewpoints, interact directly with those who share one's views, and those who oppose them, and establish one's own position within the debate by means of a wiki, Webpage or listserv than it would be to research, compose, produce and disseminate a paper publication of the same scope. As Remtulla (2008) comments, "Burgeoning coalitions of activists, citizens, social movements, select governments, and private enterprises that aim to address environmental devastation and the global ecological crisis serve as powerful exemplars of (a) the coming together of civic engagement, civil society, and the Internet; and (b) how people around the world may be brought together in the public sphere... in a massive demonstration of global solidarity" (p. 268). Hess et al. (2008) report on the sometimes spectacular successes of patient groups and patient advocate groups in using these technologies to disseminate information, challenge research priorities, change policy and establish new treatment regimes. Those opposed to GM foods technology have also made extensive use of ICT to publicize their arguments and organize protest activities (Purdue, 2000; Bauer & Gaskell, 2001). Of course, the other side of the coin is that new ICT enable much more extensive surveillance, interception and corruption of messages.

PRIORITIES, INTERESTS, VALUES AND SOCIAL JUSTICE

Questions need to be asked about what scientific research gets funded and which technologies are pursued, the underlying rationale and justification for those decisions, the perceived social, economic and environmental effects, any moral-ethical issues raised, and what adverse impacts there might be. In their different ways, both historical case studies and science fiction stories can assist students in recognizing the uncertainty, potential risks and contested and politicized nature of science and technology. Students need to know that risk is an inherent characteristic of life in a modern technology-rich society (Beck, 1992, 2000) and that media (or curriculum) presentation of technology as exclusively beneficial is either hopelessly naïve or, more likely, deliberately misleading in an attempt to manipulate opinion, fuel production and consumption, and garner increased sales. They also need to know that while a few people in the affluent parts of the world enjoy the benefits of new sophisticated technologies, up to two-thirds of the world's population have no access to even the most basic technologies. Worse still, much of the world's population do not enjoy what those in the West (North) quite rightly regard as basic human needs: clean water, adequate food, good health and access to education. The Nuffield *Design and Technology Project* (see Kent, 1998), targeted at 11 to 14 year-olds, includes an activity in which students identify all those likely to be affected by a particular innovative technology, coding their views in terms of "winners" and "losers", and then seeking to reach a balanced viewpoint on the desirability of the innovation. Students are then divided into two groups: those who believe the innovation to be worthwhile, on balance, and those who are opposed to it. Each group writes a brief report on the reasoning underpinning their decision and identifies the factors that might lead them to change their view[24]. Contemporary developments in biotechnology might make a suitable focus for this kind of activity. Steven Best and Douglas Kellner (2002) identify the issues so clearly and elegantly that I feel it appropriate to quote their words at length.

> Defenders of biotechnology extol its potential to increase food production and quality; to cure diseases and prolong human life; and to better understand human beings and nature in order to advance the goals of science. Its critics claim that genetic engineering of food will produce Frankenfoods that pollute the food supply with potentially harmful products; that biotechnology-out-of-control could devastate the environment, biodiversity and human life itself; that animal and human cloning will breed monstrosities; that a dangerous new eugenics is on the horizon; and that the manipulation of embryonic stem cells violates the principle of respect for life and destroys a bona fide 'human being'. (p. 440)

In addition to the moral-ethical issues raised by cloning and stem cell research, students might be asked to consider why the deployment of genetically modified (GM) plants is being extensively promoted by multinational companies like

Monsanto. Is it because agricultural production cannot be maintained at levels necessary for meeting the nutritional needs of the burgeoning world population? Is it because so much of the annual harvest is lost to the pests and diseases that GM plants can be designed to resist? Or is it because increasing dependence of farmers on GM plants is in the financial interests of the companies holding the patents? Students might be asked to consider the environmental risks that would inevitably follow from the loss of genetic richness and variance, and whether such risks should be taken without more widespread consultation. They might look into the possibility of unanticipated risks, particularly mutations and extinctions, arising from interactions of GM plants with insects and other plants. With regard to risk assessment, students might consider the likely effectiveness of protocols for ensuring that environmental risks associated with the introduction of transgenic organisms are minimized. They might consider who sets the procedures and standards, and whether it is likely that the protocols will be faithfully performed and monitored by all farmers. Of course, standard risk assessment methods do not address what we might call the "social risks" surrounding the monopolization of the world's food supply in the hands of one or two giant companies and the impoverishment and dislocation of small-scale farming communities, but these are important considerations for presenting to students. On an ethically-related issue, students might be asked to consider why drug companies consistently decline to engage in research and development directed towards combating and treating diseases such as malaria, trypanosomiasis (sleeping sickness) and schistosomiasis (bilharzia), while directing massive resources towards research into heart disease and cancer. Some attention might also be given to consideration of the practicality and possible adverse outcomes of some of the more extreme measures that have been suggested for dealing with climate change, such as spraying micron-sized particles of seawater into the air to make clouds whiter so that they reflect more light, deploying wave-powered pumps in the Pacific Ocean to revive the phytoplankton that converts carbon dioxide into living matter, diffracting the power of the sun by placing trillions of lenses in space (in effect, creating a 250,000 square kilometre sunshade), deploying thousands of satellites to gather the energy of the sun and beam it back to Earth as microwave energy for conversion into electricity, creating artificial trees to suck carbon dioxide out of the atmosphere, and scrubbing carbon dioxide from the air using a giant 120-metre high contraption that sucks in air at one end, sprays it with sodium hydroxide solution, and expels 'clean air' at the other end.

Much of STS, STSE and environmental education, while recognizing some of the adverse features of development, is currently pitched at the level where decision-making about scientific and technological development is seen simply as a matter of reaching consensus or effecting a compromise regarding pros and cons (what Levinson (2010) calls the "dialogic/deliberative" approach to citizenship education). It presupposes that debate is open to everyone, a wide range of viewpoints will be heard, and decisions will be reached by rational argument and careful consideration of alternatives. In contrast, the intention at curriculum level 2 is to enable students to recognize that scientific and technological decisions are usually taken in pursuit of particular interests, justified by particular values and sometimes implemented by those with sufficient economic or political power to override the needs and interests of others. Moreover, what benefits some may harm others, that is, the advantages and disadvantages of scientific and technological developments often impact differentially. Thus, the consumption-oriented lifestyle in the industrialized nations creates contaminated environments that impact disproportionately on those groups of people least able to protect themselves. In Western countries, the garbage from urban consumption is sent to incinerator plants, waste dumps and landfill facilities located overwhelmingly in urban and rural communities of colour, poverty and social disadvantage. The wealthy can significantly reduce their level of risk and exposure to toxic effluent by moving home; the politically powerful can do so by ensuring that the installation is cited elsewhere. The poor and the powerless are left to deal with the hazards and problems as best they can. A case study of the Bhopal disaster would provide a particularly graphic illustration, although similar (if not such extreme) injustices occur in most countries. For example, although the US Environmental Protection Agency (1998) states that no group of people, including racial, ethnic or socioeconomic groups, should bear a disproportionate share of the negative environmental consequences resulting from industrial, municipal and commercial operations or the execution of federal, state, local and tribal programmes and policies, Bullard and Johnson (2000) allege that governments at both federal and local levels fail to prevent unequal enforcement of environmental and health laws, differential exposure of some populations to harmful chemicals, pesticides and other toxins, discriminatory zoning and land use practices, and exclusionary methods that prevent some individuals and groups from participating in decision-making and policy making, or seriously limit their participation.

> The dominant environmental protection paradigm institutionalizes unequal enforcement; trades human health for profit; places the burden of proof on the 'victims' and not the polluting industry; legitimates human exposure to harmful chemicals, pesticides and hazardous substances; promotes 'risky' technologies; exploits the vulnerability of economically and politically disenfranchised communities; subsidizes ecological destruction; creates an industry around risk assessment and risk management; delays cleanup actions; and fails to develop pollution prevention as the overarching and dominant strategy. (p. 558)

These authors also draw attention to the environmental problems created by the vast number of industrial installations, known locally as maquiladoras, located along the US-Mexico border. Toxic waste is routinely dumped into sewers and rivers, including those from which local communities obtain their drinking water, and in the desert. Bullard and Johnson (2000) report that in the border cities of Brownsville (Texas) and Matamoras (Mexico), the incidence of children born with *anencephaly*, that is, born without a forebrain, is four times the national average, and that affected families have filed lawsuits against 88 of the area's 100 maquiladoras for exposing the community to xylene[25] – thought to be the cause of these birth defects and known to cause brain haemorrhages and lung and kidney damage. Minaya and Downing (nd) have since reported that many of the lawsuits have been settled out of court and much stricter controls on dumping of toxic waste have been established, although they note that local community activists, health professionals and the more outspoken employees of the maquiladoras allege continuing disregard of regulations.

It is here that the radical political character of the curriculum begins to emerge. It is here that teachers can begin to provide illustrations of Sandra Harding's (1998) assertion that "scientific and technological changes are inherently political, since they redistribute the costs and benefits of nature's resources in new ways. They tend to widen any pre-existing gaps between the haves and the have-nots unless issues of just distribution are directly addressed" (p. 50). It is the intention of the curriculum being discussed here that students *will* address issues of equity and justice. It is my contention that a healthy democracy requires a citizenry sensitive to the ways in which economic and political power are used to privilege some members of society at the expense of others, and requires a citizenry that is willing and able to do something to address these inequities and injustices. Kyle (1997) makes a similar case for a reorientation of educational priorities.

> One fifth of our global citizenry reside in urban areas where air pollution (both indoor air pollution and urban air pollution) exceeds healthful levels. Throughout the world, human health and aquatic life is compromised as effluents are released to waterways with minimal or no treatment. While the green agenda remains an important focus of global environmental concern, perhaps it is time for science educators to engage students and community members in issues associated with the 'brown' agenda – the problems of poverty, pollution, and environmental hazards in urban communities around the world. In doing so, citizens may see the ways in which urban and global concerns are intrinsically linked. (p. 2)[26]

As Dos Santos (2009) notes, urban populations are growing at roughly three times the rate of rural populations and marginalized communities living in a state of severe poverty have mushroomed around many cities. These communities are generally characterized by high crime rates, environmental pollution, ecological degradation and chronic overcrowding. In the cities of Developing countries these communities often do not have a reliable supply of clean water and electricity or an efficient sewage system. The politicized issues-based curriculum I am advocating is concerned, in part, to equip people living in socially under-served urban localities with the knowledge, attitudes and skills to mobilize their communities for action. It is here that Wolff-Michael Roth's (2003, 2009a) notion of scientific literacy as "an emergent feature of collective practice" (see chapter 1) becomes important, as will be elaborated in chapter 9. The proposed curriculum is also about equipping those students who may eventually be in powerful positions in government, business and industry with a sense of compassion for those less fortunate than themselves and a sense of outrage at continuing social injustice at both local and global levels. And it is about enabling everyone to be more socially and environmentally aware, and more concerned to reconstruct society at the local, regional, national and international level along more socially just and environmentally responsible lines.

Those curricula that take the trouble to address the symptoms of Third World poverty (malnutrition and famine, inadequate sanitation, and the high incidence of diseases such as rickets, tuberculosis and cholera, for example) usually neglect to include a sociopolitical and historical analysis of the major causes. Often= they treat poverty, poor health and malnutrition as a simple consequence of climatic harshness, overpopulation and ignorance. By contrast, the approach being advocated here would recognize the widespread indifference of Western governments to Third World health issues and the role played by Western governments and business interests in controlling the production and distribution of resources, including examples of the systematic appropriation of Third World land and water resources for producing cash crops for export to the West, often resulting in lower prices for farmers, increased vulnerability of crops to pests (and the consequent increased reliance on chemical controls), soil impoverishment and top soil depletion, increased poverty, insecurity and eventual dispossession. Third World countries are often forced to accept Western technology and Western agricultural practices, including widespread use of fertilizers to increase crop yield, herbicides and insecticides for weed and pest control, mechanized farming and irrigation practices, and even adoption of genetically engineered crops, in exchange for other forms of economic aid and military support. Such high cost inputs may not be affordable or ecologically sustainable. Chopra (2009) describes how the introduction of Western-style agribusiness methods, including widespread use of chemical fertilizers, pesticides, growth hormones and antibiotics, extensive forest clearance, introduction of genetically modified plants and animals, and the recycling of slaughterhouse refuse as animal feed, has had disastrous ecological impact in many parts of India. The water table has dropped to alarmingly low levels; the earthworm population has been devastated, with major adverse impact on the quality of topsoil; many species of bees, butterflies and birds, essential to the pollination process, are in serious decline; nitrogen-fixing bacteria are almost extinct; and the numbers of insect eaters such as frogs and lizards are much reduced, with consequent decline in the numbers of predators that feed on them (eagles, hawks, etc.) and the vultures that dispose of the 'leftovers'. Equally disastrous has been the negative impact on the lives of subsistence farmers. In most science and technology curricula, exploitation of Third World countries is not mentioned or is implicitly accepted as an acceptable and 'natural' consequence of international trade. Students presented with suitable case studies would quickly recognize that critical consideration of scientific and technological development is inextricably linked with questions about the distribution of wealth and power, that science and technology serve the rich and the powerful in ways that are often prejudicial to the interests and well-being of the poor and powerless, sometimes giving rise to further inequalities and injustices, and that material benefits in the West (North) are often achieved at the expense of those living in the Developing world. Moreover, they would begin to see the ways in which problems of environmental degradation are rooted in societal practices and in the values and interests that sustain and legitimate them.

Questions need to be asked about who funds science and technology, and why, whether the public has a voice, how consent is manufactured and opinion manipulated, and so on. We need to ask: Who benefits? Who loses? What are the personal, social, cultural and environmental consequences of following a particular course of action? What alternatives are available? It is here that the concerns of science, technology and environmental education should (but often don't) intersect with those of multicultural and antiracist education (see Bryant, 1995; Warren, 1996; Hodson, 1999). The frequency with which environmental degradation impacts the poor, the disadvantaged, the marginalized and the powerless much more than the rich and powerful warrants use of the term *environmental racism*. For example, substances deemed dangerous to the environment, and hence banned in countries of the rich North, are still exported to the Developing countries of the economically challenged South, and pharmaceuticals banned in the West are routinely sold, distributed and used in Developing countries (Petryna et al., 2006). French nuclear weapons testing in the 1990s was conducted not in the French countryside but in the islands of the South Pacific still under French colonial administration. Highly toxic waste is routinely shipped from the United States, where it was created, to impoverished countries like Guinea-Bissau and Sierra Leone in exchange for economic aid. Polybrominated diphenyl ethers (PBDEs), widely used as a fire retardant in the manufacture of furniture, are increasingly being found in the tissues of people and animals living in Arctic regions, and now constitute a major health hazard for those Indigenous peoples who hunt and eat 'wild food'. Environmental degradation is accompanied by extensive social degradation and impoverishment. The Third World factories and sweatshops making cheap goods for Western/ Northern markets often make extensive use of child labour, frequently operate under highly unpleasant, unsanitary and unsafe working conditions, and routinely deny workers basic rights (including fair wages) and trade union representation. Rainforest destruction in pursuit of profits for logging companies and cattle ranchers often precipitates loss of traditional lifestyle and social disruption among powerless Indigenous groups. Indeed, most environmental problems can be interpreted as social justice issues: race/ethnicity, gender and class are major factors determining who controls and benefits from the businesses and institutions that cause environmental degradation, and who experiences the adverse impact. As Bullard (1993) comments, "social inequality and imbalances of power are at the heart of environmental degradation, resource depletion, pollution and even overpopulation. The environmental crisis can simply not be solved effectively without social justice" (p. 23).

Climate change is an issue of global environmental justice/injustice in several senses. First, the wealthy industrialized countries of the Northern hemisphere contribute disproportionately high levels of carbon dioxide emissions per capita. It is estimated that the richest 20% of the world's population is responsible for over 60% of current greenhouse gas emissions[27]. Second, inadequate infrastructure, material resources and technological capability make it likely that the impact of climate change will be more severe in poor countries. For example, rising sea levels will displace many more people in Bangladesh, Tuvalu and the Maldives than in the Netherlands, a similarly low-lying country[28]; and the food insecurity, water shortages, spread of infectious diseases and population displacement that will result from climate change are likely to be considerably more severe in Africa than elsewhere. Third, climate change treaty negotiations have always favoured the economically and politically powerful countries of the industrialized world. There is also a significant inter-generational equity issue: those living today and enjoying the benefits of modern technology and industrial production are impacting on the planet's resources, atmosphere, oceans, ecosystems and climate in ways that severely reduce its capacity to sustain a reasonable quality of life for future generations. Sadly, as van Gorder (2007) observes, "most educational systems have no mechanism to foster within the privileged the self-defeating notion that they enjoy the benefit of their lives by impoverishing and oppressing others. Injustice is either obscured in the immediate or highlighted in the remote and distant" (p. 13). The curriculum being advocated in this book is an attempt to change that situation.

ADDRESSING SOME KEY ISSUES

It is fairly easy to see the potential for politicization in the seven areas of concern listed earlier.

-   Human Health - health goals in North America versus those in the Developing world, priorities in health spending, gender issues relating to 'body image', plastic surgery for merely "cosmetic" purposes, stress-related disorders, abortion, xenotransplantation, compulsory MMR vaccination, availability of *Gardasil*, antibiotics resistance and "superbugs", impact of advertizing on diet, alcohol consumption and smoking.
-   Land, Water and Mineral Resources - land usage issues, including Aboriginal land rights and efforts to formulate an Antarctic Treaty, deforestation and desertification, toxic waste disposal, water pollution issues, wetlands destruction, fluoridation, sustainable consumption, rainforest clearance, loss of biodiversity, population control measures.
-   Food and Agriculture - the politics of starvation, factory farming, genetically modified food crops, food irradiation, social and environmental impact of growing cash crops for Western consumption in the Developing world, soil erosion, increasing urban development, issues relating to processing, packaging and transportation of food.
-   Energy Resources - renewable energy sources, the politics of the petroleum industry (including ecological disasters such as the oil spills from the Exxon Valdez tanker, in 1989, and the Deepwater Horizon drilling rig, in 2010), consumption and lifestyle issues, nuclear power generation, ecological, economic and social issues relating to large scale biofuel production.
-   Industry – power usage and waste disposal issues, employment considerations versus environmental impact, sustainability issues, automation and job loss, child labour and unhealthy work conditions in Third World manufacturing.
-   IT and Transportation - data protection issues, widespread use of surveillance techniques, cultural imperialism, vehicle emission controls, environmental and social impact of air travel.
-   Ethics - cloning, stem cell research, 'designer babies', Third World organ donors, ethics of professional practice and the idea of a Hippocratic oath for scientists and engineers[29], DNA fingerprinting and governmental DNA banks, euthanasia and countless other issues.

It is also relatively easy to see how these areas of concern lend themselves to treatment at the four levels of sophistication. At level 1, students are made aware of the societal and environmental impact of science and technology and alerted to the existence of alternative technologies, with different impact. At level 2, they are sensitized to the sociopolitical nature of scientific and technological practice, asking questions such as: Who are the stakeholders? What are their interests? Whose voices are heard and whose are marginalized or ignored? What intentions or motives guide the decision-making? Who benefits? Who is harmed? Is this just and equitable? Does this decision promote the common good or serve the needs of environmental protection? Should we support or oppose this development? Curriculum level 3 is concerned primarily with supporting students in their attempts to formulate their own opinions on important issues and establish their own value positions, rather than with promoting the 'official' or textbook view (the prime motive of what Levinson (2010) calls the "deficit view" of citizenship education). It focuses much more overtly than traditional STS or STSE education on values clarification, developing strong feelings about issues, addressing moral-ethical concerns, and actively thinking about what it means to act wisely, justly and 'rightly' in particular social, political and environmental contexts, for which the frameworks for ethical reasoning outlined in chapter 7 are crucial. This phase is also about becoming committed to the fight to establish more socially just and environmentally sustainable practices and building the confidence, mindset, insights and skills necessary for effective and responsible change advocacy and change agency. It has much in common with the goals of Peace Education (Brock-Utne, 1987; Hicks, 1988; Reardon, 1988; Smith & Carson, 1998; Selby, 2000; Haavelsrud, 2010), Multicultural and Antiracist Education (Hodson, 1993, 1999; Sleeter, 1996; Dei, 2010; Hines, 2003), Global Education (Pike & Selby, 1987; Fien, 1989; Hicks & Steiner, 1989; Pike, 2000; Gaudelli, 2003; White & Openshaw, 2005; Hicks & Holden, 2007b) and Humane Education (Selby, 1994a,b, 1995). It begins with the fostering of self-esteem and personal well-being in each individual, and extends to acceptance of diversity in ideas, opinions, perspectives, practices and values, concern for the welfare of others, respect for the rights of others, building empathy and mutual trust, the pursuit of fairness, equity, justice and freedom, cooperative decision-making, creative resolution of disagreements and conflict between individuals, within and between communities, and throughout the world. It is driven by a deep commitment to *anti-discriminatory* education, that is, exposing the common roots of sexism, racism, homophobia, Eurocentrism and Westism (or Northism) in the tendency to dichotomize and generate a sense of *other*, and working actively to confront the "us and them" mentality that invariably sees "us" as the norm, the desirable and the superior. It culminates in a commitment to the belief that alternative voices can and should be heard in order that decisions in science and technology reflect wisdom and justice, rather than powerful sectional interests. Maxwell (1984, 1992) defines wisdom as the capacity to realize what is of value in life for oneself and others. He continues as follows: "In a world in which international affairs are conducted at the intellectual and moral level of gang warfare (as they all too often are), the mere provision of new knowledge and technology, dissociated from a more fundamental concern to help humanity resolve its conflicts and problems of living in more cooperative ways, is an obvious recipe for disaster. It merely increases our power to *act*, without at the same time increasing our power to act humanely, cooperatively and rationally... We urgently need a new, more rational kind of academic inquiry, which gives intellectual priority to the tasks of articulating our problems of living, proposing and critically assessing possible cooperative solutions" (Maxwell, 1992, p. 207).

At level 4, students acquire the knowledge and skills to intervene effectively in decision-making processes in order to ensure that alternative voices, and their underlying interests and values, are brought to bear on policy decisions. To reiterate, it is important for students to learn that scientific/technological activity is influenced by a complex of social, political and economic forces, and it is important for them to formulate their own views on a range of contemporary issues and problems, and to care passionately about them. But the curriculum needs to take them further. Students need to learn how to participate, and they need to experience participation. Moreover, they need to encourage others to participate, too: parents, grandparents, friends, relatives, neighbours, local businesses, etc. It is not enough for students to be armchair critics! As Kyle (1996) puts it: "Education must be transformed from the passive, technical, and apolitical orientation that is reflective of most students' school-based experiences to an active, critical, and politicized life-long endeavour that transcends the boundaries of classrooms and schools" (p. 1). In words that would have substantial currency in my native North of England working class community, students need to "put their money where their mouth is!", that is, they need to engage in action rather than just talk about it (Hodson, 2009b). Indeed, all of us (students, teachers and other citizens) need to do so. With that in mind, I have much in sympathy with Elam and Bertilsson's (2003) notion of the *radical scientific citizen*.

> The radical scientific citizen is fully prepared to participate in demonstrations… street marches, boycotts and sit-ins and other means of publicly confronting those ruling over science and technology… While the scientific citizen as activist may be taking a partisan position in defence of a particular individual or group in society, they are also understood as assuming a moral stance in defence of general ethico-political principles… which are accepted as existing through many different and conflicting interpretations… and subjecting them to continuous contestation. (p. 245).

Thus, the final (fourth) level of sophistication in this issues-based approach is concerned with students findings ways of putting their values and convictions into action, helping them to prepare for and engage in responsible action, and assisting them in developing the skills, attitudes and values that will enable them to take control of their lives, cooperate with others to bring about change, and work towards a more just and sustainable world in which power, wealth and resources are more equitably shared.

PREPARING FOR AND TAKING ACTION

Among the keys to action on socioscientific and environmental issues are *knowledge, ownership, attitudes, values, commitment, sense of responsibility, empowerment* and *high self-esteem*. In other words, those who act are those who have: a deep understanding of the issues (and their economic, political, social, moral-ethical and environmental implications); a personal investment in addressing issues and a commitment to solving problems; values supportive of individual autonomy, civic and environmental responsibility, freedom, equality and social justice; knowledge of how to ensure that their own voice is heard and acknowledged; awareness of the range of interventions that are possible; and confidence that their actions can make a difference. Hines et al. (1986) also identify economic constraints and social pressures as key factors. *Prosocial behaviour*, defined by Eisenberg and Miller (1987) as "voluntary intentional behaviour that results in benefits for another", seems more likely when individuals are free from economic pressures, have met their own immediate needs satisfactorily, and are supported by their peers and immediate family. Put simply, when money is tight, decisions about courses of action will be strongly influenced by cost. For example, energy-efficient technology is often expensive to install, so the "payback time" needs to be short. Moreover, few people will take actions to protect the environment if they entail personal inconvenience, and even fewer will take actions that require radical changes to their lifestyle or incur substantial costs. Batson (1994) argues that prosocial behaviour can be motivated by any of four factors: *egoism, collectivism, altruism* and *principalism*. Egosim is a self-interest motivation, that is, the goal is to enhance one's own welfare – for example, choosing to take public transport (rather than drive a car) because it saves money[30]. The goal of collectivism is to increase the well-being or welfare of one or more individuals other than oneself. Principalism is behaviour motivated by some moral-ethical principal. In similar vein, but writing with specific reference to environmental concerns, Stern et al. (1993) and Stern and Dietz (1994) identify three different value orientations: *egoistic* values, *social-altruistic* values and *biospheric* values (though I would prefer the term bio-centric values – see chapter 8). Egoistic values predispose people to protect aspects of the environment that affect them personally or to oppose protection of the environment if the personal costs are too high. Social-altruistic values lead individuals to act on issues in relation to costs and benefits to others - individuals, groups, neighbourhoods, social networks, countries, or all humanity. Biospheric/biocentric values result in actions taken in the interests of all living things. It seems self-evident that concern about the environment and consistent environmentally responsible behaviour will be motivated by the extent to which people define themselves as independent from others, interdependent with other people or interdependent with all living creatures – matters that will be discussed at length in chapter 8.

Social norms, family customs and strong role models might also be expected to be influential. If a particular attitude or a set of values is constantly reinforced by those we respect, the associated action is more likely to follow than it is in a situation where we seem to be alone in our views. Pruneau et al. (2007) report that only a handful of Canadian teachers changed their level of electricity consumption or their driving patterns following a 6-day professional development course on climate change. However, the few who did change their behaviour said that it was participation in a community of like-minded people that had prompted the change. Also writing from a Canadian perspective, McKenzie-Mohr and Smith (1999) advocate the use of *social marketing techniques*: target audiences are defined (those deemed most likely to change behaviour and/or those whose behaviour most needs to be changed); specific barriers (both internal and external) are identified; and programmes are designed to reach the target audience by using "behaviour change tools" that utilize the lifestyle characteristics of the target group to provide personally meaningful and lifestyle-relevant information on the issue and the problematic behaviour, the consequences of that behaviour, and the benefits of changing behaviour. The advantage of such approaches, which have been widely used in anti-smoking and HIV-AIDS awareness campaigns, is that it starts with people's usual behaviour and "works backwards" to find tactics suited to changing that behaviour. Sometimes, a range of behaviours may assist the resolution of a problem. For example, the levels of landfill dumping can be reduced by recycling, reducing consumption or re-use of materials. Similarly, greenhouse gas emissions can be reduced by carpooling, using public transport, bicycling, working from home, improved home insulation, installation of energy-saving light bulbs, lowering thermostat temperatures in winter and not using air conditioning in summer. While it may be desirable to promote all these behaviours, the resources needed to do so may be prohibitive. With community-based social marketing, writes McKenzie-Mohr (2000), priorities are established in response to three questions: What is the potential impact of each of the proposed behaviours? What barriers might work against the adoption of these behaviours? What resources are available to help overcome these barriers?

Bator and Cialdini (2000) discuss the range of factors that need to be taken into account in the design of the public service announcements that might constitute part of a social marketing campaign. For example, it is important to consider how the message should be delivered – for example, by television, radio, newspaper, magazine, flyer or the Internet. And to consider who should be employed to deliver it - scientist, environmentalist, well-known 'personality' or 'typical citizen'. A crucial question concerns the appropriateness and likely effectiveness of different styles of message, that is, considerations relating to language use, hyperbole, shock, repetition, and whether the message is alarmist or hopeful. In terms of effectiveness, much might depend on whether the message uses a direct or indirect approach, whether the target behaviour is an immediate or long-term goal, and whether the message is aimed at encouraging a new behaviour or stopping/curtailing an existing one. While these considerations are important, and will be raised in later discussions, it is important to emphasize that the critical scientific literacy envisaged in this book entails ceding responsibility for students/citizens to work out for themselves what would constitute appropriate and socially and environmentally responsible behaviour in any particular set of circumstances. Critical scientific literacy, allied to a measure of political literacy, readily translates into thoughtful, responsible behaviour.

Writing from the perspective of environmental education, Jensen (2002) categorizes the knowledge that is likely to inform and promote sociopolitical action and pro-environmental behaviour into four dimensions: (i) scientific and technological knowledge that informs the issue or problem; (ii) knowledge about the underlying social, political and economic issues, conditions and structures, and how they contribute to creating social and environmental problems; (iii) knowledge about how to bring about changes in society through direct or indirect action; and (iv) knowledge about the likely outcome or direction of possible actions, and the desirability of those outcomes. Although formulated as a model for environmental education, it is reasonable to suppose that Jensen's arguments are applicable to all forms of SSI-oriented action. Little needs to be said about dimensions 1 and 2 in Jensen's framework beyond the discussion earlier in this and preceding chapters.

With regard to dimension 3, students need knowledge of actions that are likely to have positive impact, and knowledge of how to engage in them. It is essential that they gain robust knowledge of the social, legal and political system(s) that prevail in the communities in which they live, and develop a clear understanding of how decisions are made within local, regional and national government, and within industry, commerce and the military. Without knowledge of where and with whom power of decision-making is located, and awareness of the mechanisms by which decisions are reached, intervention is not possible. Thus, the curriculum I propose requires a concurrent programme designed to achieve a measure of *political literacy*, including knowledge of how to engage in collective action with individuals who have different competencies, backgrounds and attitudes, but share a common interest in a particular SSI (see chapter 8 for further discussion). Dimension 3 also includes knowledge of likely sympathisers and potential allies, and strategies for encouraging cooperative action and group interventions. What Jensen does not mention, but would seem to be a part of dimension 3 knowledge, is the NOS-oriented knowledge that would enable students to appraise the statements, reports and arguments of scientists, politicians and journalists, and to present their own supporting or opposing arguments in a coherent, robust and convincing way (see Hodson, 2009a, for a lengthy discussion of this aspect of science education). Jensen's fourth category includes awareness of how (and why) others have sought to bring about change and entails formulation of a vision of the kind of world in which we (and our families and communities) wish to live. It is important for students to explore and develop their ideas, visions, dreams and aspirations for themselves, for their neighbours and families, and for the wider communities at the local, regional, national and global levels – a clear overlap with Futures Studies (Cornish, 1977, Slaughter, 1988, 2005; Hicks & Holden, 1995; Bell, 1997; Gidley, 1998; Hicks & Slaughter, 1998; Jones, 1998; Sardar, 1999; Dator, 2002; Hicks, 2002; Gidley et al., 2004; Lloyd & Wallace, 2004) and values education (see discussion in chapters 7 and 8). An essential step in cultivating the critical scientific and technological literacy on which socio-political action depends is the application of a social and political critique capable of challenging the notion of technological determinism (see chapter 5). As Hutchinson (1996) comments: "Whether in relation to our schools, our societies or our species, when taken-for-granted ways of thinking about the future are left unexamined, a closure of horizons occurs – futures are foreclosed and 'inevitabilities' are confirmed as 'realism'" (p. 48). Dimension 4 is also evident in the cultivation of a sense of place (and strong affection for it), commitment to community activism, and building feelings of responsibility, ownership and empowerment. These matters will be discussed more fully in chapter 9.

There is, of course, a substantial body of research evidence attesting to the positive correlation between self-esteem and academic attainment (Lawrence, 1988; Helmke & van Aken, 1995; Marsh & Yeung, 1997; Bong & Skaalvik, 2003; Nieswandt, 2007). In essence, this research tells us that students with high self-esteem are likely to be socially and academically confident, they will be eager for new learning and new challenges, they will persist longer on difficult tasks and feel less anxious about learning tasks, and they will more readily take risks in learning. In contrast, students with low self-esteem will lack confidence and will tend to shy away from both social interaction and collaborative learning opportunities. These students tend to avoid risky learning because they anticipate failure or even humiliation. Lawrence (1988) also argues that students with high self-esteem will probably be more altruistic and hold positive attitudes towards others, while low self-image can lead to negative attitudes and behaviours towards others, both in school and in the wider community. Some thirty years ago, Prutzman et al. (1978) argued that "poor self-image is at the root of many conflicts that exist in school today" (p. 35) on the grounds that it is difficult to feel positive about others if we don't feel positive about ourselves. Strong links have also been identified between level of self-esteem and commitment to democratic values and procedures: "Perhaps the dominant factor in sapping our courage to stand against prejudice is the erosion of our sense of worth. The more we question our worth the more easily we are controlled" (Cell, 1984, p. 24). It follows that a positive self-image and feelings of self-worth foster a desire for self-determination. Of particular significance in the context of the curriculum proposal discussed here is the likelihood that individuals with high self-esteem will be more prepared to take action when faced with challenge or crisis, while those with lower self-esteem may adopt an attitude of resignation, despair and powerlessness, and may expect that someone else will attend to the problem. Classroom strategies for enhancing self-esteem are beyond the scope of this book, but see Selby (1995).

Personal investment in an issue and commitment to problem solving and action derive, in part, from emotional involvement. The stronger one's emotional involvement, the more likely one is to take positive action – a situation that is well illustrated in students' responses to SSI when they impact directly on their own lives, or those of family members and those in the local community (see discussion in chapter 9). Reliance on secondary experience, information and knowledge, which is likely to be the case for many students for many SSI, removes them emotionally from the issue and is likely to result in non-involvement and non-action. It easy to react to sudden and catastrophic change brought about by earthquakes and tsunamis, but environmental degradation and climate change are both slow and cumulative. There is a tendency, therefore, to over-estimate the long-term significance of hurricanes and earthquakes and seriously under-estimate the long-term significance of small increases in the mean temperature of the oceans. Large-scale, global environmental problems (such as ozone depletion, loss of habitat and greenhouse gas build-up) are not immediately tangible. We don't see it happen and so it 'slips off the radar'. The time lag between the emission of greenhouse gases and their effects on the climate impedes a proper understanding of the relationship. So, too, the anticipated time lag between any actions taken to reduce emissions and the positive effects they might produce. For many people in the affluent West/North, tangible impact is elsewhere: melting ice caps in Antarctica, rising sea levels in the islands of the South Pacific, pollution of waterways in China. For many people, the fact that the effects are not uniform across different parts of the world seems to be at variance with predictions that associate climate change with mean increase in temperature across the globe. Moreover, predictions by the IPCC and other bodies lose precision at finer geographical scales and so may seem to contradict local experience (González-Gaudiano & Meira-Cartea, 2010)[31]. Thus, environmental degradation and climate change are seen as distant or future problems, not immediate and local ones.

Despite repeated warnings from climate change scientists that the longer we delay measures to reduce greenhouse gas emissions the deeper and more irreversible the consequences will be, significant action at the political level is not forthcoming. Many aspects of SSI relating to health, resource use, industrial practice and information technology may also seem distant to students. Making these issues real means finding ways to stimulate, provoke, irritate, offend, outrage, amuse or delight students as a way of gaining their attention and building involvement and commitment. We need to find ways to make the impact more real, to precipitate feelings of fear, anger, sadness, pain, empathy, compassion and guilt, and link them to positive feelings of agency, control and empowerment. As discussed in chapter 2, emotional involvement can be fostered through case studies, drama and role play, literature, art, photographs, movies and music, site visits, interviews, and so on. Interestingly, Lester et al. (2006) have shown that carefully designed writing activities can also play an important role in developing personal investment in an issue and in increasing students' awareness of the need for sociopolitical action, especially when students assume the role of investigative journalist. It seems also that informal learning experiences may be more effective than formal schooling in bringing about awareness of issues, attitudinal shifts, values reorientation and willingness to engage in sociopolitical action. Chapter 8 discusses these matters at greater length.

The final link in the chain connecting knowledge, values and attitudes to action involves the notions of *identity* and *agency*. Clearly, an individual student can be a member of several different sociocultural groups: family, friends, school (including particular classes), sports teams and other social groups, and groups based on broader defining characteristics such as gender, class, ethnicity, sexual orientation, language preferences, nationality/citizenship, political or religious affiliations, and so on. Functioning comfortably within these groups requires an individual to adopt a particular identity (or a series of identities), characterized by a distinctive language, code of behaviour, expressed beliefs, values and attitudes. Moving comfortably between the groups entails a reasonable facility in *changing* identities, that is, being able to 'wear different hats' as the social situation shifts. Perspectives from the literature of situated cognition suggest that learning can be thought of as a process of identity formation and identity modification (Lave & Wenger, 1991). As students decide what kind of people they are and what kind of people they aspire to be[32], they seek to acquire the knowledge, skills, attitudes, beliefs and values needed for effective participation in particular "communities of practice". While the processes of identity construction and development are, in one sense, an individual matter, they are also socially situated (see discussion in chapter 2). An identity has both an 'inner life' (in the individual's mind) and an outer manifestation; it comprises our conception of ourselves, the ways in which that conception is presented to the world via our utterances and actions, and the ways in which others interpret those manifestations and respond to them. Our cluster of identities is the principal factor shaping our interactions with others and, in turn, these identities are shaped by our interactions. At any one time, some aspects of an individual's identity are clear, constant and stable, while other aspects may be confused, ambiguous and unstable (Britzman, 1992; Gee, 2002). As individuals experience the world and interact with other people, their conceptions of the world and other people change, the ways in which they see themselves change, and the ways in which others see them may change. And, of course, the communities to which an individual belongs, or aspires to belong, will also change.

> An identity, then, is a layering of events of participation and reification by which our experience and its social interpretation inform each other. As we encounter our effects on the world and develop our relations with others, these layers build upon each other to produce our identity as a very complex interweaving of participative experience and reification projections. Bringing the two together through the negotiation of meaning, we construct who we are. (Wenger, 1998, p. 151)

Agency is defined by Holland et al. (1998) as establishing conscious control of one's behaviour, that is, gaining the capacity, power and confidence to act purposefully and reflectively. Inden (2000) provides a much more elaborate definition of human agency as "the realized capacity of people to act upon their world and not only to know about or give personal or intersubjective significance to it. That capacity is the power of people to act purposively and reflectively, in more or less complex interrelationships with one another, to reiterate and remake the world in which they live, in circumstances where they may consider different courses of action possible and desirable, though not necessarily from the same point of view" (p. 23). In other words, agency is the conscious role we choose to play in order to express our sense of identity. Thus, the goal in stages 3 and 4 of the model of an issues-based curriculum proposed earlier in the chapter can be seen as the drive to establish, clarify and stabilize a sense of identity as a sociopolitical activist and as an agent of change. The goal is that students identify themselves as willing and able to engage in critical discussion of SSI, willing and able to formulate, organize and engage in sociopolitical action aimed at addressing problems, raising public awareness, and finding solutions. The goal, also, is that students develop high levels of self-efficacy[33]. When individuals feel that their actions will make a difference there is much more incentive to engage in them (Bandura, 1977, 1986, 1993; Devine-Wright, et al., 2004; Schreiner et al., 2005). Similarly, when individuals feel that their actions are likely to be ineffective, they are likely to retreat into apathy and a sense of resignation. Despite the seemingly self-evident nature of this first proposition, studies by Fortner et al. (2000) in the United States and Boyes et al. (2009) in Australia show that individuals are sometimes unwilling to undertake actions even when they have a strong belief in their effectiveness, especially if the action involves additional expense or inconvenience. Additionally, individuals are often willing to take actions that are inexpensive, don't inconvenience them too much and are socially reinforced, even when they regard them as somewhat ineffective.

Identity and agency have a marked moral-ethical component and may ultimately be dependent on students developing all four dimensions of moral development outlined by Rest et al. (1974, 1986), Rest (1986) and Thoma and Rest (1999): *moral sensitivity* – interpreting the situation, considering how various actions would affect the parties concerned, imagining cause-effect chains of events, and being aware that there is a moral problem when it exists; *moral judgement* – judging which action would be most justifiable in a moral sense; *moral motivation* – being committed to a moral course of action, valuing moral values over other values, and taking personal responsibility for moral outcomes; *moral character* – persisting in a moral task, having courage, overcoming fatigue and temptations, and implementing subroutines that serve a moral goal. If these dimensions of moral development are seen as a hierarchy, it is students' *moral character* that will ultimately determine whether students become sociopolitical and environmental activists and agents of social reconstruction.

It is my firm belief that the likelihood of students becoming active citizens is increased substantially by encouraging them to take action *now* (in school), and by providing opportunities for them to do so. And by giving examples of successful actions and interventions engaged in by others. With respect to an environmental focus (by way of illustration), suitable action might include any (or all) of the following: conducting surveys of dump sites, public footpaths and environmentally sensitive areas, monitoring pollution levels in local waterways, disseminating advice to householders, farmers and local industries on safe disposal of toxic waste, generating data for community groups such as birdwatchers and ramblers, establishing neighbourhood 'nature watch' initiatives, instituting recycling programmes for glass, paper and aluminium cans, organizing consumer boycotts of environmentally unsafe products and practices, publishing newsletters, lobbying local government officials on policy matters and regulations (for example, traffic conditions and recreational facilities), working on environmental clean-up projects, establishing an 'adopt a stream' scheme, creating nature trails, conservation ponds and butterfly gardens, planting trees, building a community garden, designing, building and installing nesting boxes for endangered birds or bats, organizing a school 'environmental awareness day', setting up a garbage-free lunch programme, assuming responsibility for environmental enhancement of the school grounds (including planting of indigenous species and encouragement of biodiversity), monitoring the school's consumption of energy and material resources in order to formulate more appropriate practices (including use of solar panels, for example), reducing water consumption through recycling schemes, monitoring use and disposal of potentially hazardous materials within the school, setting up a "green purchasing" network, and so on. Suitable actions on other matters might include: making public statements and writing letters, building informative Websites, writing to newspapers, organizing petitions and community meetings, working for local action groups and citizen working groups, making posters, distributing leaflets, demonstrating, making informative multimedia materials for public education, and exerting political pressure through regular involvement in local government affairs.

It is sometimes useful to distinguish between *direct* and *indirect* action. The former includes such things as recycling, cleaning up a stream or a beach, building a compost heap, using a bicycle rather than a car or bus, switching off lights, and using 'green bags' at the supermarket; the latter includes compiling petitions, distributing leaflets, writing to newspapers and making submissions to the local council. Jensen and Schnack (1997) characterize these two kinds of action in terms of orientation towards people-environment relations or people-people relations. Oddly, some environmental educators tend to de-value indirect actions as "mere classroom exercises", while extolling the virtues of direct action. Before reaching such a judgement we should look carefully at the likely *effectiveness* and *social significance* of particular actions, both in the short-term and long-term. While direct action can be enormously important and can have some significant impact, it can also divert attention from the root causes of the problem in our social, political and economic activities. It fails to confront the real causes and agents of environmental degradation, avoids critique and questioning, and "deceptively universalizes the different positions individuals have in relation to the distribution of environmental resources, risks, responsibilities, and decision-making power" (Lousley, 1999, p. 299). It depoliticizes environmental problems and shifts the burden of responsibility onto individuals and families and away from governments, corporations, the policies that might have long-term and significant impact, and the political negotiations that might lead to change. Cleaning up a beach will have immediate beneficial impact, but without an investigation of the causes and appropriate intervention aimed at those causes, there will be no long-lasting solution. Although reducing our personal use of cars is a small step in reducing air pollution and conserving energy, it fails to tackle the ways in which sociopolitical decisions about modern urban developments have made the car a virtually indispensable means of transport. While recycling and buying so-called 'environmentally friendly' products enable us to feel that we are 'doing something', they may have no impact whatsoever on the underlying social and economic structures that have created the problems. Indeed, engaging in recycling might even be an emotional justification for (even more) consumption. On occasions, the increased consumption of 'green products' negates the very benefits the product was intended to confer – for example, the gains achieved through more fuel-efficient car engines are lost when motorists simply drive more because they can now afford to do so. Setting up a recycling programme may prolong the active life of one or two landfill sites but it doesn't address (and it certainly doesn't change) the unsustainable economy of resource use, production and consumption. In Cheryl Lousley's (1999) words, "Recycling and green consumerism are responses to middle-class environmental problems, relevant in areas where there are no hazardous waste sites and industries, where transportation is accessible and affordable, where water, foodcrops, and fish are available and safe to consume, and where families have sufficient income to over-consume" (p. 300). Also writing about "green consumersism", Sandilands (1993) comments: "People are increasingly less willing to purchase goods that have been developed at the expense of small animals' lives, that have been wrapped at the expense of old-growth forests, or that have been chlorine bleached at the expense of entire ecosystems; people are increasingly more willing to purchase organic, or energy-conserving, or recycled goods, to change what they buy in order to demonstrate and foster environmental responsibility. And certainly the consumer has the power to change what gets produced... But, as a whole, green consumerism masks more problems than it solves" (p. 43).

Jensen and Schnack (1997) draw a distinction between *activities* and *actions*. For them, actions must be consciously chosen and focused on solutions to the problem or issue being addressed, or directed towards changing the conditions or circumstances that led to the problem(s). Thus, investigating nitrate and phosphate levels in waterways is classified as an activity; boycotting chemically-based agricultural products and promoting the use of organic fertilisers is classified as an action[34]. Conducting the analysis, publicizing the data arising from it, identifying the likely cause of the pollution as 'run off' from local farms and parks, alerting farmers, ground maintenance staff in sports facilities, park keepers and domestic gardeners to both the causes and the adverse environmental impact of chemically-based products, making them aware of organic alternatives, and encouraging farm suppliers and garden centres to promote those organic alternatives, would be classified as a complex of activity, direct action and indirect action. The optimum approach would seem to be a blend of direct and indirect action. Of course, indirect action needs to be *authentic* action: not just a classroom exercise in which a letter to an imaginary newspaper editor is composed, but a real letter to a real newspaper editor, to express real concerns or to make a series of real debating points or policy recommendations, or the preparation of a report for submission to a local government body, or provision of material assistance for an individual or group involved in a local dispute. In these circumstances, a great deal of knowledge is required, including a substantial measure of argumentation and media literacy skills. From a curriculum or pedagogical perspective, some very obvious distinctions can be drawn between simple and quickly achieved actions (building nesting boxes or cleaning up a stream), those that require a sustained commitment over time (establishing and maintaining a fish hatchery or taking responsibility for managing a conservation area) and those that require a substantial level of political literacy (lobbying for policy changes, drafting legislation and filing law suits against those who violate existing codes and regulations). For these reasons, Roth (2010) is at some pains to distinguish among actions, activities and activism. In a more elaborate categorization, Stern (2000) distinguishes among *environmental activism* (participation in activities organized by Greenpeace, Friends of the Earth, Sea Shepherd, etc.), *non-activist political behaviours* (voting, joining a community group), *consumer behaviours* (buying 'green' products, recycling), *ecosystem behaviours* (installing nesting boxes, cleaning up a stream) and *behaviours specific to our expertise or workplace* (reducing both resource consumption and waste generation). Another useful distinctions, drawn by Stern (2000), is that between "private sphere" actions and "public sphere" actions, and the further elaboration by Menzel and Bögeholz (2010) into activism (e.g., participating in public demonstrations), non-activist public sphere actions (e.g., signing petitions), private sphere actions (e.g., green purchasing) and public sphere actions (e.g., fostering recycling in the workforce)[35]. From a school perspective, there is also much value in distinguishing actions that are student initiated from those that are teacher initiated. Adapting the work of Arnstein (1979), Roger Hart (1992, 2008) outlines a "ladder of student participation", ranging from actions that are assigned by the teacher, through those that are decided by teachers after consultation with students, initiated by teachers but negotiated with students, initiated and directed by students, to those initiated by students and carried out in collaboration with adults. This ladder metaphor is especially useful in theorizing about community-based actions (see chapter 9).

In discussing energy usage, Gardner and Stern (2002) state that, in the industrialized world, individual consumption accounts for approximately one third of a country's total energy consumption, with business, industry, government institutions and the military consuming the remaining two thirds. Analysis of waste production and its attendant pollution reveals similar disproportionality. In consequence, private actions are likely to be fairly limited in their impact. Much more effective are collective actions that can exert pressure on governments and industry to take responsibility for environmental protection, establish more rigorous standards for energy consumption and greenhouse gas emissions, dismantle barriers to change and constraints on environmental protection, provide incentives and create alternatives for private actions and proenvironmental behaviour. The power of individual consumers to change their buying patterns is readily countered by the power, will and organization of producers, advertisers and retailers, and by the compliance or intransigence of governments. As Chawla and Flanders Cushing (2005) put it, "People cannot purchase energy efficient cars, use public transportation or travel on bikeways, for example, unless business and Governments make these choices available" (p. 441). Similarly, one's freedom to buy local products and eat locally-grown, organic produce is sometimes thwarted by the forces of globalization, industrialization of agriculture and marketing policies, especially for those who cannot afford the extra costs that would be involved. Mitchell et al. (1997) remind us that changes at fundamental levels will only result when three key elements of persuasion are in place: *legitimacy* – perception that the action is desirable or morally right; *urgency* – the need for the issue to be addressed quickly; and *power* – the capacity to force another to do something counter to their current practice, using financial means, voting power, etc. It is group action that provides this final element. Collective action is probably the only way that fundamental change in our society can be brought about – a matter to be addressed in chapter 9.

The foregoing discussion of direct and indirect action, activities and action, and individual versus collective action suggests that a key part of preparing for action involves identifying action possibilities, assessing their feasibility and appropriateness, ascertaining constraints and barriers, resolving any disagreements among those who will be involved, looking closely at the actions taken by others (and the extent to which they have been successful) and establishing priorities in terms of what actions are most urgently needed (and can be undertaken fairly quickly) and what actions are needed in the longer term. It is essential, too, that all actions taken by students are critically evaluated and committed to an action database for use by others. From a teaching perspective, it is important that care is taken to ensure both the appropriateness of a set of actions for the particular students involved and the communities in which the actions will be situated, and the overall practicality of the project in terms of time and resources. As noted several times in this book and discussed at length in chapter 10, an action-oriented curriculum can generate considerable controversy and may provoke opposition from other teachers, school administrators, parents and members of the local community. While recycling, cleaning up the beach, building nesting boxes or working in the local food bank or shelter for the homeless are safe, benign and non-controversial, challenging local councils, staging demonstrations, conducting vigils and organizing boycotts may raise parental anxiety levels, offend the local community and lead to sustained opposition. Teachers need to be prepared for backlash and they need courage to fly in the face of this opposition. Implementing this kind of curriculum is not 'an easy ride'.

LEARNING *ABOUT, THROUGH* AND *FROM* ACTION

McClaren and Hammond (2005) draw distinctions between learning *about* action, learning *through* action and learning *from* action. Learning *about* action focuses on learning the skills and strategies of sociopolitical action using movies, biographies and autobiographies, case studies and simulations, role-play and dramatic recon-structions. Providing students with examples of successful action taking, preferably involving other students, fosters the belief that they can changes things, too. It is here that an action database can be especially useful. Learning *through* action comprises direct involvement in action-oriented projects outside the classroom that have tangible outcomes and consequences. While some projects may be chosen and organized by the teacher, especially in the early years, it is important to involve students as quickly as possible in selecting and planning for themselves the actions to be taken. Learning *from* action occurs when students evaluate the plans, strategies, processes and outcomes of their own action projects and those of others. "Debriefing", as some would call it, entails compilation of a record of what happened or what the students perceive to have happened, an attempt to say why (or why not), and reflection by all parties on the significance of the action for themselves and for the community. It almost goes without saying that the process is facilitated by keeping careful logs and journals, consulting with others, sharing experiences and feelings, and communicating with those who were not involved. There is value, too, in recruiting members of the community to act as critical reviewers.

Students can gain experience of action via the familiar 3-phase apprenticeship approach.
- *Modelling* - the teacher demonstrates and explains the desired behaviour, and provides illustrative examples.
- *Guided practice* - students perform specified tasks within an overall action strategy with the help and support of the teacher.
- *Application* - students function independently of the teacher.

In short, it is assumed that students will become more expert in planning, executing and evaluating sociopolitical action by observing teachers or other 'experts' as they engage in action, practising the various sub-skills under controlled conditions, taking increasing levels of responsibility for planning and organizing the action, and engaging with critical evaluative feedback provided by the teacher and generated in inter-group criticism and discussion, and by means of intra-group reflection on the activity, both as it progresses and on completion. Initially, the teacher is responsible for planning the actions and directing the actions of students. However, if students are to achieve intellectual independence, they must eventually take responsibility for their own learning and for planning, executing and reporting their own projects. In other words, learning as assisted performance must enable students, in time, to go beyond what they have learned and to use their knowledge and skills in creative ways, for addressing different issues, solving novel problems and building new understanding. Consequently, alongside the modelled investigations, students should work through a carefully sequenced programme of exercises, during which the teacher's role is to act as learning resource, facilitator, consultant and critic. Complex problems and interventions can sometimes be broken down into a series of smaller problems and suitable interventions, including relatively simple activities in which careful planning by the teacher can almost guarantee that students will succeed, while also creating opportunities for students to act independently of the teacher, thus building confidence and enhancing motivation for assuming greater autonomy. These exercises provide opportunities for students to learn through a cycle of practice and reflection, and to achieve, with the careful assistance and support of the teacher, and of each other, a level of sophistication and performance they could not achieve unaided. In this guided practice phase, teacher and students are *co-activists*, with both parties asking questions, contributing ideas, making criticisms and lending support. Thus, the teacher's role shifts from instructor/demonstrator to director/ facilitator. Clearly, such activities will only be productive if teachers and students are able to establish a learning community characterized by respect for diversity, trust, willingness to engage in collaborative learning and eagerness to contribute to the learning of all members of the community. Eventually, as students gain experience and take on increasing control of decision-making, they can proceed independently: choosing their own topics, problems and situations, and approaching them in their own way. From this point on, students are responsible for the whole process, from initial problem identification to final evaluation. Students identify the issue or problem, collect, organize and analyse information, define the problem from a variety of perspectives, identify, consider and select alternative actions to take, develop and carry out a plan of action, and evaluate the outcome and the entire undertaking As a consequence, they experience both "the excitement of successes and the agony that arises from inadequate planning and bad decisions" (Brusic, 1992, p. 49). Throughout these activities the teacher's role is crucial: model activist, advisor, learning resource, facilitator, consultant, emotional support and critic. Also, because students are given the opportunity to experience failure as well as success, it is imperative that the class atmosphere is both forgiving and supportive.

Crucial to the notion of apprenticeship is a continuing dialogue about the way the activity is progressing, including frank discussion of problems encountered, avenues that prove fruitless, and barriers to progress that prove insurmountable. Crucial also, if the goal is for students to gain understanding of authentic socio-political action, is constant comparison between what students are doing in their project and what others have done (using the aforementioned database). By engaging in interventions and action-oriented projects alongside a trusted and skilled critic, students increase both their understanding of what constitutes sociopolitical action and their capacity to engage in it successfully. In other words, social activism is a reflexive activity: current knowledge and expertise informs and determines the conduct of the activity and, simultaneously, involvement in actions (and critical reflection on them) refines knowledge and sharpens expertise. In Patemen's (1970) words, "participation develops and fosters the very qualities necessary for it; the more individuals participate the better they become able to do so" (p. 42). As noted in the Preface to this book, I have long argued for a key distinction to be drawn between learning *about* science (concern with HPS issues and STSE dimensions) and *doing* science (gaining first hand experience of scientific investigation). Part of that argument is based on my contention that doing science entails experiential and affective components that can only be acquired by engaging in the activity for oneself and by oneself. This complex of experience-based understanding builds up over time into expertise and connoisseurship. In contrast to the stereotyped description of "the scientific method" still found in some science textbooks and curriculum documents, I would argue that scientists refine their approach to an investigation, develop greater understanding of it and devise more appropriate and productive ways of proceeding *all at the same time*. As soon as an idea is developed and an investigation is begun, ideas, plans and procedures are all subjected to evaluation. Sometimes that evaluation leads to new ideas, to further and different investigative methods, or even to a complete re-casting of the original idea and re-formulation of the underlying problem. Thus, almost every move that a scientist makes during an inquiry changes the situation in some way, so that the next decision is made and the next action is taken in an altered context. Consequently, *doing* science is an holistic and fluid activity, not a matter of following a strictly defined set of actions formulated well in advance. Science is an organic, dynamic, interactive activity, a constant interplay of thought and action. As it proceeds, the whole is continuously evaluated, re-planned and re-directed. The path from initial idea to final conclusions may involve many backtracks, re-starts, short cuts and dead ends. In other words, *doing* science is an untidy, unpredictable activity that requires each scientist to devise her or his own course of action. In that sense, science has no one method, no set of rules or sequence of steps that can, and should, be applied in all situations. Rather, it requires scientists to 'think on their feet' and adapt their strategy to the changing situation. In doing so, they draw on previous experience, adapt it to the new context, and make extensive use of their intuitive sense of what needs to be done. I would make the same case, in part, for learning *through* action: certain knowledge, skills, attitudes and feelings gained through action are simply not available from classroom presentations or exercises, or even from simulations, no matter how well-designed and realistic they may be. One cannot understand all the nuances and complexities of an issue or a problem without becoming immersed in attempts to solve it. Moreover, just as students *doing* science quickly learn that plans cannot always be straightforwardly put into practice, so those engaging in action-oriented projects learn that real world situations are often ill-defined, confused, confusing, fluid and unpredictable. In consequence, they may have to modify and adapt their plans, re-think their strategies and try again. Sperling (2009) urges teachers to introduce students to the idea of SMART plans, that is, plans that are specific, measurable, attainable, realistic and timely. Good advice, certainly, but the reality is that the smartest plans in prospect may prove otherwise in practice. And coming to that realization, and seeking to ascertain why the plan proved less than ideal, is a crucial part of the learning experience. So, too, of course, is simply engaging in action. Even though an action may not solve a problem, reach a satisfactory conclusion or have significant environmental impact, it may still have great significance in terms of personal growth, fostering positive attitudes and building commitment – as Short (2010) reminds us.

As well as teaching students the need to be sufficiently resilient and determined to try again, experiences of failure may also impress upon them the need to mobilize others and to engage in collective action. As discussed in chapter 8 (with respect to environmental issues), collective actions are often more effective than individual actions and, in some circumstances, may be the only means of bringing about change. Interestingly, Roth (2009a) reformulates the Vygotskian notion of zone of proximal development to refer to what can be achieved through community-based collaborative efforts compared with what can be achieved by individuals. A key part of preparation for activism, then, is helping students to recognize, mobilize and coordinate the knowledge and skills that are distributed across communities. As Roth and Calabrese Barton (2004) state: "Education needs to focus on the individual as an integral and constitutive part of the collective, and on the distributed nature of knowledge and skill... (and) we have to begin thinking about the modes by which individuals with different expertise coparticipate in resolving the complex problems that their communities, countries, and humanity as a whole face today" (p. 13). Roth (2009a) argues that it matters very little who, within the group, has particular knowledge and skills, provided that there is collective scientific literacy (and, presumably, collective political literacy, too). While I recognize this as an entirely reasonable proposition from the perspective of the group and the likelihood of successful action, I regard it as a wholly unacceptable stance to take with respect to individuals. As discussed in chapter 1, my principal concern is to achieve an acceptable and empowering level of critical scientific literacy for *every* citizen. However, I do regard the establishment of a sense of identity as a member of the local community as a vital element in preparation for activism.

In advocating this 4-level curriculum model (which Levinson (2010) might characterize as a combination of the "conflict and dissent" mode of citizenship education and "science education through praxis"), my intention is not to suggest that all action and preparation for action is delayed until the final years of schooling. Rather, students should proceed to whatever level is appropriate to the topic in hand, the learning opportunities it presents, and the stage of intellectual and emotional development of the students. In some areas of concern it is relatively easy for students to be organized or to organize themselves for action; in other areas it is more difficult. It is also the case that for some topics level 3 is more demanding than level 4. For example, it is easier to take action on recycling than to reach a considered and critical judgement of recycling versus reduced consumption versus use of alternative materials. Further, it is highly unlikely that all students will be motivated by the same issues, problems, experiences or situations. Nor will all students be in a position to make substantial changes to their daily behaviour and routines, and more particularly in the context of education at the school level, effect changes in their family's behaviour and routines. Individuals can also vary quite substantially in their disposition to act (that is, in terms of differences in knowledge, self-esteem, values, commitment, emotional involvement, and so on). Clearly, these variations make it difficult to plan an action-oriented curriculum for all. But there is no reason why we should expect different students and groups of students to participate in the same project. Different views and different priorities could (or should) lead to involvement in different projects. One final point: it is important that a particular action is not viewed as an end in itself. Students need opportunities to evaluate the action taken, reflect on its nature and impact, and possibly re-formulate the action. The simple point is that an *action orientation* and an *action competence* (as Jensen, 2004, calls it) are established over time and are rooted in reflective practice.

Several years ago, in an effort to construct a curriculum able to educate for global citizenship, or "world citizenship" as they call it, Parker et al. (1999) consulted a panel of 182 scholars, practitioners and policy leaders in science, technology, the arts, health, education, politics and government, business, industry and labour concerning: (i) the complex global crises that humanity will face over the next 25 years, (ii) the human characteristics needed for dealing with these crises, and (iii) the educational strategies capable of developing these characteristics. The panel, drawn from nine countries in four geopolitical regions (East Asia, Southeast Asia, Europe and North America) reached a high level of consensus on the issues and challenges: the widening gap between rich and poor, scarcity of resources, loss of privacy, environmental deterioration, loss of biodiversity, burgeoning population leading to increased poverty and conflict, increased levels of regulation and control, increase in drugs-related urban crime, continued growth in consumerism, decline in social responsibility and sense of community. There was consensus, too, on eight characteristics considered essential to addressing these problems: (i) ability to address problems as a member of a global society; (ii) capacity to work with others in a cooperative way and to take responsibility for one's roles/duties within society; (iii) understanding, accepting, appreciating and tolerating cultural differences; (iv) ability to think in a critical and systematic way; (v) willingness to resolve conflicts peacefully; (vi) willingness and ability to participate in politics at local, national and international levels; (vii) willingness to change one's lifestyle and consumption habits to protect the environment; and (viii) ability to be sensitive towards and to defend human rights. The educational strategies considered necessary can be summed up as follows: development of critical thinking; ensuring diversity of perspectives among teachers and curriculum materials; cooperative learning; inculcating cross-cultural sensitivity; and providing opportunities for community action and involvement. The panel proposed the construction of a curriculum around six ethics-related issues and questions relating to equity and fairness, privacy and access to information, environmental stewardship and human prosperity, population growth, genetic engineering and child welfare, universalism and particularism in respect of prevailing values, and power relationships within and between societies. In several senses, the issues-based curriculum outlined in this book can be regarded as a version of this curriculum implemented in the field of STSE education.

CHAPTER 4

TURNING THE SPOTLIGHT ON SCIENCE

In addition to addressing a number of topical and controversial SSI (health hazards associated with mobile phones, xenotransplantation, stem cell research, GM foods, and the like), the curriculum needs to turn the critical spotlight on science itself. In particular, encouraging students to direct careful and critical attention to the role and status of scientific knowledge, the procedures by which scientific knowledge is generated, validated and disseminated, the language in which it is communicated to other scientists, students and the wider public, the values that underpin the conduct of scientists, the moral-ethical issues raised by contemporary scientific developments, and the wider social, political and economic climate in which science is practised. If teachers are to present science and scientific practice in a critical light, they need reliable information about the kind of understanding their students are likely to have already. Methods for ascertaining those views, including questionnaires and surveys, interviews, small group discussions, writing tasks and classroom observations (particularly in the context of hands-on activities), have been extensively reviewed by Hodson (2008, 2009a) and will not be revisited here. While it is always dangerous to generalize from research findings, it is fair to say, as noted in chapter 2, that many students (and their teachers) hold confused, confusing, misleading or downright false views about science, scientists and scientific practice[36], views that are compounded by similarly inadequate/unsatisfactory views located in science textbooks and curriculum materials, projected via the so-called "hidden curriculum", encountered through informal learning experiences in museums, zoos and science centres, and promulgated by the popular media.

A quarter century ago, as part of a major survey of Canadian science education conducted by the Science Council of Canada, Nadeau and Désautels (1984) identified what they called five "mythical values stances" suffusing science education: (i) *naïve realism* – science gives access to truth about the universe; (ii) *blissful empiricism* – science is the meticulous, orderly and exhaustive gathering of data; (iii) *credulous experimentation* – experiments can conclusively verify hypotheses; (iv) *excessive rationalism* – science proceeds solely by logic and rational appraisal; and (v) *blind idealism* – scientists are completely disinterested, objective beings. The cumulative message is that science has an all-purpose, straightforward and reliable method of ascertaining the truth about the universe, with the certainty of scientific knowledge being located in objective observation, extensive data collection and experimental verification. Moreover, scientists are rational, logical, open-minded and intellectually honest people who are required, by their commitment to the scientific enterprise, to adopt a disinterested, value-free and analytical stance. A decade and a half later, Hodson (1998b) argued that a number of myths and falsehoods about science continue to be transmitted by teachers, consciously or unconsciously, and by curriculum materials: observation provides direct and reliable access to secure knowledge; science starts with observation; science proceeds via induction; experiments are decisive; science comprises discrete, generic processes; scientific inquiry is a simple, algorithmic procedure; science is a value-free activity; science is an exclusively Western, post-Renaissance activity; the so-called "scientific attitudes" are essential to the effective practice of science; all scientists possess these attitudes. I have addressed the epistemological and methodological issues elsewhere (Hodson, 2008, 2009a); here, I intend to concentrate on the values issues encapsulated in these myths and falsehoods.

For convenience, values associated with science can be divided into two broad groups: those *internal* to science (that is, the values that govern the conduct of individual scientists and the mechanisms through which the community monitors that conduct and appraises the knowledge generated) and those *external* to science (that is, the values of the wider community that are likely to impact on science, scientific policy and the establishment of research and development priorities). In the terms used by Helen Longino (1990), this is a distinction between the *constitutive* values of science (the drive to meet criteria of truth, accuracy, precision, simplicity, predictive capability, breadth of scope and problem-solving capability) and the *contextual* values that impregnate the personal, social and cultural context in which science is organized, supported, financed and conducted. Allchin (1999) draws a similar distinction between the *epistemic* values of science and the *cultural* values that infuse scientific practice. Throughout this chapter, the term 'values' is taken to mean "the principles, fundamental convictions, ideals, standards, or life stances which act as general guides or as points of reference in decision-making or the evaluation of beliefs or actions and which are closely connected to personal integrity and personal identity" (Halstead, 1996, p. 5).

THE CONSTITUTIVE VALUES OF SCIENCE

Science is a creative, collaborative and culturally embedded activity in which valid and reliable knowledge is generated through diverse, rigorously monitored methods and validated by critical evaluation within the community of practitioners. All scientific knowledge, while stable and able to be used in further inquiry and theory-building, is subject to change, modification or rejection in the light of new evidence or a new way of making sense of existing evidence. As a set of rigorous methods, science embodies a number of values: orderliness, care and precision, meticulous and critical attentiveness, accuracy, reliability and replicability. The knowledge generated by scientists also has to conform to certain values: clarity, coherence, universalism, stability, tentativeness and fecundity/fruitfulness (in the sense of solving problems and having predictive capability). Elegance, simplicity and parsimony can also be significant factors in gaining support for a theory. As Richard Feynman (1965) remarked: "You can recognize truth by its beauty and simplicity... When you get it right, it is obvious that it is right. The truth always turns out to be simpler than you thought" (p. 171)[37]. It seems also that many scientists are driven to look for common explanations or common *kinds* of explanations. Consequently, a new theory is more likely to be accepted when it is consistent with other well-established theories; it is less likely to be accepted when it is in conflict with them (Laudan, 1977). Thus, Copernican theory had some initial problems because it was inconsistent with Aristotelian physics, a problem that was solved by Galileo. Holton (1975, 1978, 1981) argues that scientific thought is also governed by what he calls "themata": thematic presuppositions or predispositions to think and theorize in particular ways. He identifies fifty or so antithetical dyads, and occasional triads, that constitute the core underlying values of science and form the essential framework for building scientific theories. Examples include complexity-simplicity, reductionism-holism, hierarchy-unity, synthesis-analysis and constancy/equilibrium-evolution-catastrophic change. Holton (1988) also notes the conscious or unconscious preoccupation with symmetry shown by many scientists.

Practitioners are expected to display and practice certain personal values: objectivity, rationality, intellectual integrity, accuracy, diligence, open-mindedness, self-criticism, skepticism and circumspection (in the sense of suspending judgement until all the evidence is in hand). In addition, they are expected to be dispassionate and disinterested. All knowledge claims must be treated skeptically until their validity can be judged according to the weight of evidence; all evidence is carefully considered before decisions about validity are made; the idiosyncratic prejudices of individual scientists do not intrude into the decision-making. In choosing to become a scientist, one makes a commitment to "a set of preferences for such things as a non-dogmatic, anti-fideistic, critical attitude in which strength of belief is attuned to evidence, and for 'open horizons' over closures" (Suchting, 1995, p. 16). Nearly 70 sixty years ago, Robert Merton identified four "functional norms" or "institutional imperatives" that govern the practice of science and the behaviour of individual scientists, whether or not they are aware of it (Merton, 1973)[38]. These norms are not explicitly taught; rather, newcomers are socialized into the conventions of scientific practice through the example set by more senior scientists. Merton argued that these norms constitute the most effective and efficient way of generating new scientific knowledge and provide a set of "moral imperatives" that serves to ensure good and proper conduct.

- *Universalism* – science is universal (i.e., its validity is independent of the context in which it is generated or the context in which it is used) because evaluation of knowledge claims in science uses objective, rational and impersonal criteria rather than criteria based on personal, national or political interests, and is independent of the reputation of the particular scientist or scientists involved. Science is also universal in the sense that access to the community is open to all, regardless of gender, race, ethnicity, sexual orientation and social status.
- *Communality* – science is a cooperative endeavour and the knowledge it generates is publicly owned. Scientists are required to act 'in the common good', avoid secrecy and publish details of their investigations, methods, findings and conclusions so that all scientists may use and build upon the work of others.
- *Disinterestedness* – science is a search for truth simply for its own sake, free from political or economic motivation or strictures, and with no vested interest in the outcome. Attempts to exploit the ignorance or credulity of non-scientists or to fabricate results in pursuit of commercial or personal gain are strictly outside the code of approved scientific conduct.

- *Organized scepticism* – all scientific knowledge, together with the methods by which it is produced, is subject to rigorous scrutiny by the community of scientists in conformity with clearly established procedures. Criteria include methodological appropriateness, a clearly expressed chain of argument from data to conclusions, and testability. The "emotional neutrality" of these procedures ensures that all knowledge claims are treated similarly, regardless of their origin.

Two additional norms have been proposed by Barber (1962): (i) *rationality* – science uses rational methods to generate and validate its claims to knowledge; and (ii) *emotional neutrality* – scientists are not so committed to an existing theory or procedure that they will decline to reject it or adopt an alternative when empirical evidence points to it[39]. Because science is a communal practice, scientists have to trust that everyone will conform to these community-approved norms and standards, unless or until they learn otherwise. Moreover, since no scientist can be expert in all aspects of science it is essential to have trust in the work of scientists working in related fields, and in the work of those who design the complex laboratory instruments on which so much modern science depends. Without mutual trust, the scientific enterprise cannot function effectively or productively.

Many contemporary sociologists of science argue that Merton's norms of scientific conduct do not really *guide* practice; rather, they are used retrospectively by scientists to dignify what they have done, and to impress non-scientists. Mitroff (1974), for example, suggests that the "emotional neutrality" of organized scepticism is frequently over-ruled by the "emotional commitment" of scientists struggling to overcome difficulties and setbacks. Indeed, he postulates a counter-norm for each of the norms listed above.

- *Particularism* – the personal or professional attributes of the researcher, and the status of the institution in which it is conducted, are frequently taken into account in the evaluation of scientific contributions.
- *Solitariness* – ownership and control of distribution of scientific knowledge reside with the individual scientist or group of scientists who produced it. On occasions, results are withheld until a patent has been secured or delayed until their announcement will have greater impact.
- *Interestedness* – many scientists have personal agendas for engaging in particular research and may have a vested interest in the outcomes, even more so when research is funded by commercial organizations.
- *Exercise of judgement* – the expert opinion of experienced scientists plays a prominent role in the evaluation of knowledge claims. Moreover, the research of newcomers is subject to much more rigorous checks than the work of established scientists.
- *Non-rationality* – scientists do not always act in a fully functional manner and scientific advances can result from non-rational as well as rational actions.
- *Emotional commitment* – commitment to a theory is essential for its advancement; disinterest leads to stagnation. On occasions, however, commitment in spite of substantial contrary evidence becomes unreasonable.

Mitroff argues that scientists simply act as they see fit and attempt to rationalize, justify and dignify it afterwards. Hence, he argues, rather than regarding science as a distinctive way of proceeding, to which all scientists have to conform, it makes more sense to regard science as (no more than) what scientists actually do. Conventions such as Mertonian norms do not direct the actions of scientists, they are simply what the collective actions of scientists amount to – at least, in their retrospective rationalizations. In Mulkay's (1979) words, "it seems more appropriate to portray the 'norms of science', not as defining clear social obligations to which scientists conform, but as flexible vocabularies employed by participants in their attempts to negotiate suitable meanings for their own and others' acts in various social contexts" (p. 72).

A significant mismatch centres on the cluster of personal characteristics and attributes that have long been regarded by science educators as essential for the successful pursuit of science and, so the commonly used science curriculum rhetoric goes, are clearly exhibited in the day-to-day practice of successful scientists: superior intelligence, objectivity, rationality, emotional neutrality, open-mindedness, willing-ness to suspend judgement, intellectual integrity and communality (see Gauld, 1982). Like Mertonian norms, these so-called *scientific attitudes* are said to guarantee proper scientific practice by ensuring that: (i) all knowledge claims are treated sceptically until their validity can be judged according to the weight of evidence; (ii) all evidence is carefully considered before decisions about validity are made; and (iii) the idiosyncratic prejudices of individual scientists do not intrude into the decision making. In traditional science curricula, 'evidence' is always taken to mean empirical evidence, that is, agreement with the 'observed facts'. Thus, proper scientific practice is seen to comprise a dispassionate appraisal of that empirical evidence (the 'facts') before any decision about acceptability is taken.

It is now 50 years since Roe (1961) suggested that scientists rarely possess these scientific attitudes, although (she says) they think that they do. They, too, subscribe to the myth of the emotionally-detached, disinterested and impartial scientist. Or they continue to promote this false image because they perceive it to be in their interests to imply a connection between the disinterested approach and the truth of the findings as a means of ensuring high levels of public funding for scientific research[40]. Roe concludes: "The creative scientist, whatever his field, is very deeply involved emotionally and personally in his work" (p. 456). Mahoney's (1979) conclusions about the attitudes and characteristics of scientists make particularly interesting reading: (i) superior intelligence is neither a prerequisite nor a correlate of high scientific achievement; (ii) scientists are often illogical in their work, particularly when defending a preferred view or attacking a rival one; (iii) scientists' per-ceptions of reality are dramatically influenced by their theoretical expectations; (iv) scientists are often selective, expedient and not immune to "perceptual bias" and distortion of the data; (v) scientists are among the most passionate of professionals, and their theoretical and personal biases often colour their alleged openness to the data; (vi) scientists are often dogmatically tenacious and inflexible in their opinions, even when contradictory evidence is overwhelming; (vii) scientists are skilled in "expedient reasoning", that is, bending their arguments to fit their purposes; (viii) scientists are not paragons of humility and disinterest - rather, they are often selfish, ambitious and petulant defenders of personal recognition and territoriality, with vitriolic episodes and bitter disputes over personal credit and priority being common; (ix) scientists often behave in ways that conflict with the supposed communal sharing of knowledge, that is, they are frequently secretive, suspicious of others, and prone to suppressing data until they have established priority of discovery; (x) far from being a "suspender of judgement", the scientist is often an "impetuous truth-spinner" who rushes to hypotheses and theories long before the data warrants. Following their study of scientists and engineers involved in NASA's Apollo Project, Mitroff and Mason (1974) concluded that scientists are arranged along a continuum from *extreme speculative scientists*, who "wouldn't hesitate to build a whole theory of the solar system based on no data at all", to *data bound scientists*, who "wouldn't be able to save their own hide if a fire was burning next to them because they'd never have enough data to prove the fire was really there" (p. 1508). These conclusions echo Mahoney's (1979) description of a continuum of scientists ranging from *speculophobics*, "scientists who devoutly avoid any ventures beyond the data", to *hypothophiliacs*, "scientists who need less than a hint of evidence to draw sweeping generalizations and construct ambitious models" (p. 357). Contrary to the school textbook stereotype, the scientists who produce the most significant work are those who disregard the so-called scientific attitudes. Careful attention to detail and painstaking accumulation of data are both crucial to good science and to the effective conduct of laboratory testing, the maintenance of safety, and the sound operation of science-based industries, but theoretical breakthroughs are made principally by those who 'break the rules' and act in accordance with Paul Feyerabend's (1975) dictum that "anything goes". This can be taken as a reminder that science teachers need to provide students with experiences capable of developing both sets of attributes.

So what should we take as an authentic view of scientific practice? Although many scientists would be reluctant to accept the findings of the plethora of recent sociological and ethnographic studies as an authentic or true version of what happens in science laboratories, most practising scientists would readily acknowledge the significant role that can be played by intuition, hunch, luck, greed, personal needs, publishing pressures, and the like. They might admit to Knorr-Cetina's (1995) assertion that scientists can, on occasions, be guilty of practices that are not entirely "open and above board", such as hoarding of information, implementing personal and group biases, engaging in plagiarism, showing blind trust in their own data or theory while dismissing those of rivals without sufficient consideration. Many would also acknowledge that *competition* plays a key role and, for some, may even be the major driving force. As David Hull (1988) observes, as long as there are rewards for publishing papers, formulating new theoretical propositions and developing new techniques and instruments, there will be scientists ready and willing to produce them, and many who will strive to be the 'first' or the 'best'. Of course, competition can also lead to wasteful duplication of research and, in the rush to publish, to the generation of substandard work and the publication of incomplete studies. Even worse, it can lead to attempts to mislead competitors, steal other scientists' results, discredit other researchers by spreading false information about them, and the regrettably all-too-common tactic of releasing part of the research findings in support of an alternative explanation/theory in a deliberate attempt to mislead or distract competitors (Monhardt et al., 1999; Wong & Hodson, 2009, 2010). Following their study of "sharp practice" by scientists involved in government-funded research, Broad and Wade (1982) concluded: "Scientists are not different from other people. In donning the white coat at the laboratory door, they do not step aside from the passion, ambitions, and failings that animate those in other walks of life" (p. 19).

In a piece originally published in 1945, Karl Popper noted that scientific objectivity is a community-based characteristic (scientific community, that is), not a characteristic of the individual scientist.

> What we call 'scientific objectivity' is not the product of the individual scientist's impartiality, but a product of the social or public character of scientific method; and the individual scientist's impartiality is, so far as it exists, not the source but rather the result of this socially or institutionally organized objectivity of science. (Popper, 1966, p. 217)

The key point is that we *improve* our science because of constant critical scrutiny by people with wide and varied experience, a range of interests and a diversity of value positions. Over time, we identify wrong science, incompetent science, poorly designed science and bad science (such as science with clear evidence of bias), we detect and expose fraud, and we differentiate science from non-science. The point at issue for the science curriculum is that all accepted scientific knowledge has a well-argued and well-supported warrant for belief – a warrant that holds until there are compelling reasons to revise our conclusions. While acknowledging that conclusive verification of theories is not possible, this position recognizes that science makes progress. Progress arises from continual criticism and efforts to meet criticisms through modification and/or replacement of theoretical structures. As Rorty (1991) argues, what makes science 'special' is that scientists have done a better job than most other groups in implementing certain values – in particular, reliance on persuasion rather than coercion, and willingness to consider alternative ideas. In summary, science is characterized by the same messy and conflicting human values, diverse attitudes, influence of reputation, power differentials, social negotiation and social construction as all other spheres of human activity, though it has socially organized methods of appraisal (both of procedures and products) that ensure the identification of less than exemplary conduct and less than exemplary science.

CONTEXTUAL VALUES

What an individual scientist regards as important, puzzling or worthy of attention is a consequence of her/his *personal framework of understanding*, an idea developed at length in Hodson (1998a). This unique and complex array of conceptual and procedural knowledge, ideas, beliefs, experiences, feelings, values, expectations and aspirations, what Giere (1988) refers to as "cognitive resources", will determine the questions that are asked and the problems that are pursued, guide the way investigations are designed and conducted, and influence the way data are interpreted and conclusions are drawn. Further, because scientific practice is located in a social context (at the level of research teams, the wider scientific community, and society as a whole), the ideas, beliefs and values prevailing in those social milieux will impact on scientists and influence their judgements on all manner of things. Thus, the focus of scientific attention and, therefore, the subject matter generated are to some extent a reflection of the needs, interests, motives and aspirations of the scientists themselves, the key decision-makers within the scientific community, and the wider society. In other words, science is to some degree a product of its time and place, and subject to the values that pertain in the society that supports and sustains it. A key question for us, as curriculum builders and teachers, is whether these social, cultural and economic factors constitute the main driving force for science or whether they are influences that simply make science a human and, therefore, imperfect but intriguing endeavour. Some sociologists of science extend acknowledgement of social *influences* on scientific practice to a position that embraces social *determination* of scientific knowledge. In other words, science is a social construct and possibly *no more than* a social construct. Put more baldly, scientific knowledge is 'what scientists say it is', for the reasons they construct and choose. It could be otherwise. It has no special status. Science is 'no better' than any other knowledge about natural phenomena and events; it is just 'different'. For reasons discussed at length in Hodson (2008) and noted in chapter 3, I believe that we should reject the proposition that science is entirely determined by a combination of self-interest and political expediency, just as we should reject the proposition that it comprises a proven and certain body of fixed knowledge. The compromise or balanced position is that science has developed some very robust, reliable and trustworthy methods, particularly its system for rigorously scrutinizing all claims to knowledge through peer review, but the knowledge produced and the methods by which it is generated and evaluated are profoundly influenced by social, economic and moral-ethical considerations. Values impregnate science at many levels, though the nature of those values and the extent of their influence will change over time. Sociocultural pressures can function to oppose or even exclude particular lines of research and explanation, while encouraging others. For example, the most strenuous objections to Charles Darwin's *The Origin of Species* did not concern its empirical inadequacy but the value-laden nature of its theoretical constructs. Similar problems confronted both Newton and Copernicus.

> What chiefly troubled Copernicus' critics were doubts about how heliocentric astronomy could be integrated within a broader framework of assumptions about the natural world – a framework which had been systematically and progressively articulated since antiquity. (Laudan, 1977, p. 46)

To be admitted to the corpus of approved scientific knowledge, theories have to be socially, culturally, politically and emotionally acceptable, as well as cognitively and epistemologically acceptable. Bloor (1974) comments as follows: "The ideas that are in people's minds are in the currency of their time and place... The terms in which they think do not emanate from their subjective psyches. They come from the public domain *into* their heads during socialization" (p. 71). Such is the power of day-to-day socialization processes that many value-laden assumptions remain unrecognized and unchallenged. As Rose (1997) points out, because modern science is hegemonic its underlying assumptions appear to be natural and universal. The great and "ultimately damaging achievement" of science, she says, "is to appear as a culture with no culture" (p. 61). Thus, unless there are substantial moral-ethical issues involved, as in recent research in the biological sciences, the priorities and practices of science usually go unchallenged. The words of Robert Young (1987), quoted more fully in chapter 3, provide a succinct summary of the situation: "There is no other science than the science that gets done. The science that exists is the record of the questions that it has occurred to scientists to ask, the proposals that get funded, the paths that get pursued... matters for a given society, its educational system, its patronage system and its funding bodies" (pp. 18 & 19).

Recognizing that science is a social activity, that the focus for scientific investigation is chosen by people for all manner of sociocultural reasons, and that the methods and procedures of science were established by people and are sustained by authority and custom, is not to say that the scientific knowledge produced is empirically inadequate, socially expedient, irrationally believed or likely to be false. In Hilary Putnam's (2004) words, "Recognizing that our judgements claim objectivity and recognizing that they are shaped by a particular culture and by a particular problematic situation are not incompatible" (p. 45). Rationality can be retained in our account of science while simultaneously acknowledging its socio-cultural embeddedness. We can be confident that the methods of appraisal we choose to employ produce knowledge that is robust enough to solve empirical and conceptual problems, and has some direct relationship to the actual world. Indeed, we choose particular methods because they have some objective value in helping us to reach our principal goal of 'getting a handle on the nature of reality'. The rationality of science is located in careful and critical experimentation, observation and argument, and in critical scrutiny of the procedures and products of the enterprise by other practitioners. It is a community-regulated and community-monitored rationality. As noted in chapter 2, Helen Longino (1990, 2002) has postulated four social norms to guide the practice of science: (i) equality of intellectual authority (or what she now calls "tempered equality" in acknowledgement of differences in expertise and experience); (ii) some shared values, especially the valuing of empirical success; (iii) public forums for criticism (conferences, responses to journal articles, etc.); and (iv) responsiveness to criticism. In other words, science is socially constructed through critical debate. And those involved in it have a commitment to maintain certain rigorous debating standards. Longino (1990) makes the crucial point that "it is the social character of scientific knowledge that both protects it from and renders it vulnerable to social and political interests and values" (p. 12). This organized skepticism, as she calls it, which is primarily the collective responsibility of the editors and referees of reputable science journals, ensures that the accumulated store of scientific knowledge reflects rigorously scrutinized claims and supporting arguments rather than the idiosyncratic opinions and interpretations of individual scientists (see discussion later in the chapter). The scientific knowledge that goes into school textbooks has survived this critical scrutiny and in doing so has taken on the appearance of objectivity and certainty.

Because science is often presented in the school science curriculum in a-historical ways, it gives the appearance of being value-free. Sometimes it is only through historical case studies and biographical material that the idiosyncratic features of a theory's origin and the underlying values of the cultural context that produced it become apparent. So, as a first step in opening students eyes' to sociocultural influences on science, teachers might consider using a number of case studies of important scientific developments. It is often much easier to identify the ways in which values relating to social class, religion, gender and politics impacted on science at other times and in other places than to detect such influences in the contemporary world (that is, *here* and *now*). Of course, we can only fully understand the past from the perspectives then current; the intellectual standards of the present sometimes have little relevance to a genuine understanding of events in the distant past. Accounts that are more faithful to historical circumstances and sociocultural influences require consideration of the various by-ways, diversions, false paths and dead ends of science, recognition that science is frequently complex and uncertain, and acknowledgement that not all inquiries are fruitful. A 'proper' history of science attends to both the theoretical and practical problems that motivated new ideas and new procedures, and takes cognizance of the metaphysics and worldview prevailing at the time. In these respects, 'time slices' rather than 'vertical history' may be more appropriate for the curriculum, that is, consideration of the range of ideas current at any one time, how these ideas were generated, and how they were received, interpreted, modified and utilized in further work. Once students have gained the habit of scrutinizing science and scientific activity from these perspectives, they have acquired a powerful means of addressing contemporary practice in science and technology.

WORLDVIEW THEORY

At a fundamental level, acceptance or rejection of new ideas, formulation of new courses of action, and implementation of those actions, are governed by the expectations we have about what the world is like, how we reason about it and make sense of it. Science has to fit with those expectations. Stephen Pepper (1942) refers to these fundamental beliefs as *world hypotheses*[41], though *worldview* has become a more widely used term in recent years. It is our worldview that determines how we interpret reality, how we make sense of our experiences, how we see ourselves as human beings in relation to others and the world as a whole. It determines our values, aspirations and sense of responsibility. Although a simple and precise definition of worldview isn't readily available, it can conveniently be regarded as a set of presuppositions (assumptions that may be true, partially true or entirely false) that we consciously and/or unconsciously hold about the world, sometimes consistently and coherently, sometimes inconsistently and erratically. Individuals are socialized into the dominant worldview of the society in which they live, and that worldview becomes so much a part of their lives that it is largely 'invisible' to them. It is everywhere reflected in what people say and do, in movies, radio and television programmes, newspapers, magazines, music, drama, and in government debate and policy making, formal education, and our science and technology. Kearney (1984) refers to worldview as "culturally organized macrothought: those dynamically inter-related basic assumptions of a people that determine much of their behavior and decision making, as well as organizing much of their body of symbolic creations... and ethnophilosophy in general" (p. 1). He identifies seven major components of a worldview: *the Self, the Non-Self or Other, classification, relationship, causality, space* and *time*. Kearney refers to these items as "universals" because they are, he argues, universal in their significance across cultures, though they vary in nature and detail. While each component is distinctive in some way, it is the interactions among the universals that most effectively sum up the way a particular cultural group sees the world. Capra (1983) describes what he calls the Cartesian/Newtonian worldview underpinning modern science, and most of school science, in terms of five main ideas: (i) there is a fundamental division between mind and matter; (ii) nature is a mechanism that works according to exact and universal laws; (iii) reality comprises a multiplicity of building blocks, which collectively constitute the whole; (iv) the scientific method is assumed to be the only valid way to ascertain the true nature of phenomena; (v) the goal of science is to understand nature so that it can serve human wants, needs and interests[42]. In similar vein, Gauch (2009) refers to a number of "pillars of scientific thinking", including an assumption that the physical world that science seeks to understand is real, the presupposition that the world is orderly and comprehensible, a demand for evidence to support conclusions and explanations, and reliance on logical argument. Smolicz and Nunan (1975) had earlier identified four "ideological pivots" inherent in scientific practice and in the image of science presented through the science curriculum. First, *anthropocentrism*: the view of mankind[43] as the technologically powerful manipulator and controller of nature, with science as the means by which we control the environment and shape it to meet our interests and needs. Of particular interest in this "nature in the service of man" view is the underlying assumption that we have the *right* to control and manipulate the natural environment – a value position that will be revisited in chapter 8. Second, *quantification*: scientists are regarded not just as observers, but also as measurers and quantifiers. Whatever exists in nature can (and should) be explained in mathematical terms, best of all by means of equations. Third, *positivistic faith*: faith in the inevitable linear progress of science towards "truth about the world", with the certainty of this knowledge being underpinned by an all-powerful and all-purpose scientific method. Fourth, the *analytical ideal*: the assumption that phenomena and events are best studied and explained via analysis; an entirely mechanistic view of the world which assumes that the whole is simply, and no more than, the sum of its parts. According to Smolicz and Nunan (1975), these values and principles become incorporated into scientists' background assumptions and are used unquestioningly to inform scientific practice.

In his seminal work, *The Geography of Thought*, Richard Nisbett (2003) draws attention to what he considers to be key differences in worldview between Europeans and East Asians. European thought, he says, "rests on the assumption that the behavior of objects – physical, animal, and human – can be understood in terms of straightforward rules" (p. xvi). He notes that Westerners see the world in analytic, atomistic terms; they see objects as discrete and separate from their environments; they see events as progressing in linear fashion; they have a strong interest in categorization, which helps them to know what rules to apply to the objects under consideration. Moreover, because of the high priority afforded to the resolution of inconsistencies and contradictions, formal logic plays a key role in problem-solving. In contrast, he says, East Asians "attend to objects in their broad context…

Understanding events always requires consideration of a host of factors that operate in relation to one another in no simple, deterministic way" (p. xvi). They regard the world as complex and highly changeable and its components as interrelated; they see events as moving in cycles between extremes. Their lack of concern about contradiction and their emphasis on "the middle way" results in formal logic playing little role in problem-solving. When confronted with two apparently contradictory propositions, Westerners tend to polarize their beliefs, while Easterners move towards equal acceptance of both propositions. In consequence, Easterners are not as surprised by unanticipated outcomes as Westerners. Nisbett's conclusion is that "Easterners are almost surely closer to the truth than Westerners in their belief that the world is a highly complicated place and Westerners are undoubtedly often far too simple-minded in their explicit models of the world. Easterners' failure to be surprised as often as they should may be a small price to pay for their greater attunement to a range of possible causal factors. On the other hand, is seems fairly clear that simple models are the most useful ones – at least in science – because they're easier to disprove and consequently to improve upon" (Nisbett, 2003, p. 134). He further argues that Westerners have a much greater tendency to categorize objects than do East Asians, find it easier to learn new categories by applying rules about properties to particular cases, and make more inductive use of categories, that is, they have a greater tendency to generalize from particular instances of a category to other instances or to the category as a whole. For Easterners, explicit modelling or rule making is less characteristic of causal explanations; they are less likely to use rules to understand the world, less likely to make use of categories, and find it hard to learn categories by applying explicit rules. The significance of these distinctions for consideration of environmental issues will be addressed in chapter 8.

Clearly, those with a pre-existing worldview that is in harmony with the scientific perspective described by Capra (1983) and Smolicz and Nunan (1975) will find it easier to learn science because it 'makes sense' to them in terms of fundamental assumptions and underlying values. Science teaching will support and enhance their pre-existing worldview. Those whose worldview differs substantially may experience difficulties in learning science. As Cobern (1995) says, "One scientist trying to convince a colleague, or even a scientist from another field, is not the same as trying to convince those outside the scientific community" (p. 289). When there is a clash of worldviews the situation is, he says, like Charles Darwin presenting his book, *The Origin of Species*, to a public with very different, religion-based views about origins. Speaker and audience don't share the same fundamental ideas about the world and so may 'talk past each other'. Mutual incomprehension is, indeed, a poor basis for effective teacher-student relationships! Numerous problems of this kind have been identified, in a number of widely different sociocultural contexts (North America, West Africa, Southern Africa, New Zealand and Japan, for example), by writers such as Locust (1988), Aikenhead (1996, 1997, 2001a, 2005), Kawasaki (1996), Jegede (1998), Batisste (2000), McKinley (2005), Brandt (2008), Keane (2008) and Hansson and Lindahl (2010). The problems run considerably deeper than cognitive or epistemological concerns. Science teaching may threaten, disrupt, overpower, marginalize and eventually displace long-standing beliefs and values that underpin some students' sense of personal and cultural identity. In other words, students become assimilated into the dominant scientific cultural traditions at the expense of their other beliefs and values. Alternatively, students may resist what they perceive as an attempt at displacing their worldview and decide that science is not for them. For some students, religion may be one of those sociocuturally located factors that impact quite substantially on their response to science in school, especially in the context of evolutionary theory or the moral-ethical issues surrounding genetic engineering and stem cell research (Dagher & BouJaoude, 1997, 2005; Roth & Alexander, 1997; Rudolph & Stewart, 1998; Ayala, 2000; Sinatra et al., 2003; Abd-El-Khalick & Akerson, 2004; Reiss, 2007a,b, 2010a; Donnelly et al., 2009; Stolberg, 2010). Indeed, in some circumstances and with some individuals, it may well act as a boundary condition for entertaining scientific explanations at all or even participating in discussion; in effect, acting as a kind of roadblock that prevents students from recognizing and attending critically to data and ideas that are seen as constituting a challenge to religious convictions (Samarapungavan, 1997). Bybee (2001), Griffith and Brem (2004), Anderson (2007), Jones and Reiss (2007), Hermann (2008), Hildebrand et al. (2008), Martin-Hanson (2008) and Goldstein and Kyzer (2009) discuss pedagogical approaches suitable for teaching evolution as a controversial topic to students with strong religious beliefs, largely from a US perspective. Edis (2007) and Mansour (2008) address this same issue from an Islamic perspective. Interestingly, strongly held beliefs (religious or otherwise) do not always or necessarily prevent students from understanding and being able to use scientific knowledge that contradicts them. Demastes et al. (1995), for example, show that some students can construct a perfectly adequate scientific understanding of evolution despite rejecting its truthfulness on grounds of strong religious beliefs concerning creationism (see also, Sinatra et al., 2003). It seems that both knowledge structures (evolution and creationism) can co-exist within an individual's personal framework of understanding because they are used for different purposes.

Similar considerations hold at the community of scientists level with respect to theory acceptance/rejection. As Laudan (1977) argues, when the basic premisses of a theory are in conflict with the prevalent worldview, the theory is considered problematic and will stand a good chance of being rejected. When the premisses and the dominant worldview are consonant, the problematic nature of the theory is resolved and acceptance is much more likely, provided that certain other criteria are also met. Following Laudan's logic, because our society is sexist and gender biased, a sexist theory would be unproblematic if it is androcentric (male-oriented) but problematic if it is gynocentred (female-oriented). A female-oriented science would be counter normative; it would conflict with the prevailing social climate; it would struggle to gain acceptance.

BIAS AND DISTORTION

This might be an appropriate point at which to raise the issue of sensitizing students to the inherent gender bias and ethnic bias in science. There is substantial evidence of gender bias in science: first, in the history of science and technology and the ignorance, neglect and suppression of women's contributions, and sometimes their false attribution to men; second, in the institutions of science, from which women were historically excluded and within which, even today, women are still under-represented (especially at senior levels), disadvantaged and made to feel unwelcome and uncomfortable – sometimes overtly, more often covertly; third, in the priorities for scientific research and development (which often fail to reflect women's interests, concerns and needs), and in the language of science, its concepts, theories, methods, criteria of judgement, forms of argument and underlying values. Gender studies in science comprise a vast literature, which cannot be addressed within the confines of this book. Useful starting points for teachers wishing to acquire some awareness of this literature are Harding and Hintikka (1983), Bleier (1984), Code (1991), Shepherd (1993), Keller and Longino (1996), Harding (1998), Kleinman (1998), Etkowitz et al. (2000, 2008), Fox (2001), Lederman and Bartsch (2001), Rosser (2004), Miller et al. (2006) and Rolin (2008).

A 'common sense' explanation for this gender bias runs along the following lines: since most scientists, for whatever social reasons, have been male, there is good reason to expect that the science produced will be androcentric (male-centred and male-biased) simply because it reflects the outlook, interests, priorities and experiences of those who produced it. In addition to being profoundly influenced by their own individual preferences, experiences and feelings, these male scientists are subject to all the social, political, economic, religious, technological and moral-ethical forces that impact society and work towards the formation of particular attitudes, values and ways of thinking. Thus, they are 'children of their time and place', just like everyone else, and if it is legitimate to refer to masculine ways of thinking, then science could be expected to reflect them. For example, three of the "ideological pivots" identified by Smolicz and Nunan (1975) as impregnating science – anthropocentrism, quantitative methodology and analysis – could be regarded as masculine. The feminine equivalents would be biocentrism, qualitative methodology and holism. Some would regard science's fondness for dichotomies, hierarchies, linear reasoning, and the search for clear and direct cause and effect relationships, as masculine concerns. At the risk of trading in stereotypes, women could be said to be more concerned with webs of relationships, interconnections, interdependence and intuition. The underlying values of science relating to control and manipulation of the natural environment could also be considered masculine. Even the language of science and the style of reporting in the third person, past tense and passive voice have been labelled masculine. Furthermore, the argument goes, because science plays such a powerful ideological role in our society it has functioned to legitimate social inequality between the sexes – in other words, to discriminate against women. For many years, women were denied access to science, presumably in order to retain power and influence in the hands of men. In more recent years, with the removal of formal barriers to access, the masculine face of science has functioned to dissuade, limit or restrict access by making women feel uncomfortable or 'out of place'. In a society where one gender (or one race) is dominant there is likely to be a disproportionate distribution of resources, with the greater share going to the dominant group and the inequity being justified on the basis of presumed inherent differences between dominant and subordinate groups. It is likely, then, that science will have been used, consciously or unconsciously, to benefit those in power and to exclude or disadvantage those already on the margins.

Because all members of society are subject to the powerful socialization processes that result in bias, it is not always easy to identify it in contemporary science and technology. It can be invisible and, of course, all the more insidious for that. The gender bias in events that occurred elsewhere and at other times is usually much easier for students to recognize. A suitable historical case study would be Elizabeth Fee's (1979) account of craniology. She states that 19th Century anthropologists 'knew' that women are less intelligent than men but, as scientists, they needed the evidence provided by measurement of skulls. Measurement based on cranial volume indicates that elephants are more intelligent than humans, so volume had to be rejected as the principal indicator of intelligence. The ratio of brain size to body weight indicates that birds are more intelligent than humans, so other increasingly complex measurements were made to ensure that conclusions didn't violate prior understanding of the intellectual status of humans. Allchin (2004a) notes that the leading American craniologist, Samuel Morton, was highly selective in deciding which particular skulls to measure, thus ensuring confirmation of the prior belief that men are more intelligent than women. This basic deviation from good scientific practice went undetected until Alice Lee and Marie Lewenz pointed it out, and used more sophisticated statistics than Morton's to reinterpret the data. Interestingly, they reached the opposite conclusion to Morton: women are more intelligent than men. The field of primatology provides further compelling evidence that a change of perspective, from male to female, brings about a change in conceptualization. For example, Fedigan (1986) discusses what she calls the "baboonization" of primatology in the 1950s: savannah baboons, one of the most aggressive and male-dominated of all primates, was established as the preferred model for ancestral human populations, despite knowledge of other, less aggressive primate populations, because its behaviour conformed to male scientists' presuppositions of primate behavior based on human characteristics. Haraway (1989) has shown how these initial androcentric assumptions, and the language in which they were expressed, were challenged by a group of women scientists and re-shaped into alternative accounts and explanations of primate behaviour and social organization. In Helen Longino's (1990) words, "The existence of dominance structures in primate troops is 'obvious' until a different way of describing the interactions shows us that dominance is an interpretation of behaviour arising from the researchers' assumptions and expectations of social behaviour" (p. 221).

Discussion might turn to turn to the ways in which bias can be so extreme that it results in the systematic and organized misuse of science for social and political ends. A prime example is the suppression of Darwinian ideas underpinning evolutionary biology in the Stalinist Soviet Union in favour of Trofim Lysenko's theorizing about Lamarkism, on the grounds that transmission of acquired characteristics (acquired through hard work or by living a virtuous life, that is) was much more compatible with Marxist-Leninist ideology. Lysenko's argument was that all differences between individuals are due to environmental effects and, therefore, organisms can be radically modified by exposing them to environmental challenges. He claimed that the production of new crops and the adaptation of existing crops to new habitats need not involve the long processes of selective breeding, as claimed by scientists in the Capitalist world, but can be simply and quickly achieved by exposing seeds and young plants to suitable modifying conditions. The disastrous agricultural consequences of adopting this ideologically inspired stance are described by Joravsy (1970), Lewontin and Levins (1976) and Lecourt (1977).

Scientific racism is a term that has been widely used to describe the ways in which science, scientific research and scientific argument are used to justify discrimination, disadvantage and oppression of others. Suitable examples for school use include the 19th Century misuse of the Darwinian principle of natural selection to argue that white Europeans are superior to Africans in evolutionary terms, and so provide a spurious justification for colonization, and even slavery (Fryer, 1984; Gould, 1981a,b, 1995), and the eugenics programme in the United States, United Kingdom and Nazi Germany (Wegner, 1991). Seldon (2000) provides a richly detailed account of the ways in which knowledge of heredity was used in the United States in the 1920s and 1930s to promote the notion of "societal improvement" through selective breeding and sterilization, discourage inter-racial marriage and restrict immigration from Southern Europe. Black (2003) also documents this history, together with the work of Francis Galton, Karl Pearson and Robert Rintoul in the UK and the full horrors of the pursuit of "genetic purity" in Nazi Germany. More recent examples of scientific racism include the low priority afforded to research on sickle cell anaemia (a disease that primarily affects those of African descent) and systematic misinformation about the condition to exclude African Americans from active flying duties in the US Air Force and prevent them achieving flight status with some commercial airlines (Michaelson, 1987; SSCR, 1987; Dyson, 2005; Howe, 2007; Rudge & Howe, 2009), and the continuing misrepresentation of research by psychologists such as Eysenck and Jensen to claim the intellectual superiority of Caucasians (see Rushton, 1997, 2000; Rushton & Jensen, 2005). On this latter topic, Brush (1989) provides powerful food for thought in his description of the background to the Stanford-Binet IQ test, still widely used as a supposedly objective measure of intellectual capacity, and the basis of the Scholastic Aptitude Tests (SATs) for college entrance in the United States.

> When Lewis Terman tried out the first version of his intelligence test on white California schoolchildren, he found that the average score for girls was a little higher than for boys of the same age. This result was inconsistent with his preconception that males are at least as smart as females. So he balanced the test items on which boys tended to do better against those on which girls do better, in such a way that the average score would be 100 for each sex... But when Terman and other psychologists administered the test to Blacks and found that they scored several points below Whites on the average, they did not make a similar revision to equalize the average scores; they were content with the 'discovery' that Whites are smarter than Blacks. (p. 65)

CONTEMPORARY SCIENTIFIC PRACTICE

In the traditional forms of 'basic' or 'fundamental' research envisaged by Merton (1973), usually located in universities and/or government research institutes, so-called 'pure scientists' constitute their own audience: they determine the research goals, recognize competence, reward originality and achievement, legitimate their own conduct and discourage attempts at outside interference. In the contemporary world, universities are under increasing public pressure to deliver more obvious value for money, and to undertake research that is likely to have practical utility or direct commercial value. There are increasingly loud calls for closer links between academia and industry. In this changed sociopolitical environment, scientists are now required to practice what Ziman (2000) calls *post-academic* science[44]. Because contemporary scientific research is often dependent on expensive technology, it must meet the needs and serve the interests of those sponsors whose funds provide the resources. Research is often multidisciplinary and involves large groups of scientists, sometimes extending across a number of different institutions, working on problems that they have not posed, either individually or as a group. Within these teams, individual scientists may have little or no understanding of the overall thrust of the research, no knowledge of their collaborators at a personal level, and no ownership of the scientific knowledge that results. Indeed, there is a marked trend towards patenting, privatization and commodification of knowledge.

> Post-academic research is usually undertaken as a succession of 'projects', each justified in advance to a funding body whose members are usually not scientists. As the competition for funds intensifies, project proposals are forced to become more and more specific about the expected outcomes of the research, including its wider economic and social impact. This is no longer a matter for individual researchers to determine for themselves. Universities and research institutes are no longer deemed to be devoted entirely to the pursuit of knowledge for its own sake. They are encouraged to seek industrial funding for commissioned research, and to exploit to the full any patentable discoveries made by their academic staffs, especially when there is a smell of commercial profit in the air (Ziman, 1998, p. 1813).

A number of governments and universities have moved to privatize their research establishments, that is, sell institutes or laboratories engaged in potentially commercially lucrative research areas to industry and business interests, or turn them into independent companies, which are often located in science parks (Stankiewicz, 1994)[45]. In consequence, scientists have lost a substantial measure of autonomy. In many universities, the research agenda no longer includes so-called "blue skies" research (i.e., fundamental research), as emphasis shifts to "market-oriented research", "outcomes-driven research" and ever-shortening "delivery times". As Carter (2008a) comments, the increasing amounts of time that scientists now have to devote to filing applications for external research funding, publicizing their investigative capability (in an effort to secure a contract), and completing "accountability indicators", has radically changed the nature of their work (see Hargreaves Heap, 2002, for an account of the impact of the Research Assessment Exercise on universities in the United Kingdom). Fuller (2000) takes this observation a step further: "Scientists today spend an increasing amount of time on entrepreneurial, managerial and accounting tasks at the expense of 'research' in the traditional sense of doing experiments, consulting the literature, and the like... The seat of 'real' creativity would seem to lie in the tactics one uses to sustain funding and earn credibility, especially given the growing number of competitors who are trying to do exactly the same thing... The scientist's primary function is now a sophisticated form of publicity-seeking and record-keeping that enables others, both scientists and non-scientists, to legitimate or delegitimate certain courses of action" (p. 43). Many researchers are now so dependent on government contracts, commercial sponsorship and/or closely defined employment contracts that they become, in all but name, agents of government policy and particular business interests. In some situations they are advocates for a particular point of view rather than disinterested arbiters of the 'truth'. Many scientists are employed on contracts that prevent them from disclosing all their results. As Ziman (2000) comments, they are forced to trade the academic kudos of publication in refereed journals for the material benefit of a job or a share in whatever profit there might be from a patented invention. Varma's (2000) study of the work of scientists in industry paints a similar picture of disturbing changes in the way research is conducted: customization of research to achieve marketable outcomes, contract funding and strict budget constraints, flexible but strictly temporary teams of researchers assembled for specific projects, and a shift in the criteria for research appraisal from the quality and significance of the science to cost effectiveness. Slaughter and Leslie (1997) and Slaughter and Rhoades (2004) use the term academic capitalism to describe this radical shift in the norms of scientific practice. In a further parallel with contemporary trends in business life precipitated by deregulation and globalization, Fuller (2000) notes that research and development work, like manufacturing, computer-based business and communications organization, is increasingly being "outsourced" to the Developing world, where scientific and engineering expertise is high but labour and capitalization costs are low.

The vested interests of the military and commercial sponsors of research, particularly tobacco companies, the petroleum industry, the food processing industry, pharmaceutical companies and the nuclear power industry, can often be detected not just in research priorities but also in research design, especially in terms of what and how data are collected, manipulated and presented. More subtly, in what data are *not* collected, what findings are omitted from reports and whose voices are silenced. Commercial interests may influence the way research findings are made public (press conferences rather than publication in academic journals, for example) and the way in which the impact of adverse data is minimized, marginalized, hidden or ignored. For example, in publicizing the value of oral contraceptives and hormone replacement therapy, the increased risks of cervical cancer, breast cancer and thromboembolism are often given little attention. Following critical scrutiny of 70 research articles focused on calcium channel blockers (CCBs), used to treat hypertension, Stelfox et al. (1998) concluded that there was a "strong association" between authors' opinions about the safety of CCBs and "their financial relationships with pharmaceutical manufacturers". There are many examples of industry actively using the news media to manipulate public opinion by seeking to discredit science that threatens its interests – most prominently, in recent years, the petroleum industry's efforts to manufacture doubt about global warming (see chapter 8). Brown and Lyons (1992) describe the efforts of the chemical industry to suppress and/or misrepresent evidence that CFCs damage the ozone layer, while Stocking and Holstein (2009) give details of the concerted efforts of the pig farming industry to discredit research that catalogued the health hazards related to industrialized pig farming (particularly, groundwater contamination) and to suppress data showing that such installations were differentially sited in areas populated by poor African-Americans. Not only were attacks directed at the research but also at the researcher himself and his professional integrity. As Martin (1999) reports, attacks on researchers who accumulate unwelcome data (unwelcome to the company, that is) or express counter views are not uncommon: "Some of the methods used to attack dissenting scholars include ostracism, petty harassment, withdrawal of research grants, blocking of appointments or promotions, punitive transfers, reprimands, demotions, spreading of rumors, dismissal and blacklisting" (p. 346). Underhand tactics are not restricted to manipulation of public opinion through the press. For example, in 2001, TAP Pharmaceuticals was fined US$875 million for health care fraud in relation to its anti-cancer drug Lupron. Angell (2004) reports that charges to which TAP pleaded guilty included bribing doctors with televisions, VCRs, trips to resorts, cash in the form of "educational grants" (to be used for any purpose whatsoever) and free or heavily discounted drugs, for which the physicians were encouraged to bill Medicare at the full commercial price. In September 2009, Pfizer was fined US$2.3 billion for providing financial rewards and other inducements to encourage general practitioners to prescribe drugs for uses not approved by the FDA, principally the use of Bextra, a drug developed to treat arthritis, as a general analgesic. Interestingly, the drug has now been withdrawn from use altogether. Other charges related to misuse of the antipsychotic drug Geodon, the antibiotic Zyvox, and the epilepsy treatment drug Lyrica.

In summary, science is no longer the disinterested search for truth and the free and open exchange of information portrayed in the school textbook versions of science. Rather, it is a highly competitive enterprise in which scientists may be driven by self-interest and career building, desire for public recognition, financial inducements provided by business and commerce, or the 'political imperatives' of military interests. Interestingly, and in contrast to Ziman's pessimism about the impact of competition on contemporary science, Paul Kitcher (1993) and Miriam Solomon (2001) argue that intense competition and distribution of research efforts across large teams is enormously beneficial to science because it guarantees a much higher level of critical scrutiny as competitors seek to promote their views and defend them against the claims of others. Debate is both quickened and deepened, they argue, when individual researchers or research teams pursue different theories and/or different research strategies. A more cynical interpretation of this state of affairs is that the science that "gets done" (Young, 1987) is the science that is in the interests of the rich and powerful, the self-interest of particular influential scientists, or the interests of the companies or government agencies providing the research funding. Among the most disturbing features of contemporary science is the effective privatization of knowledge. Science is increasingly conducted behind closed doors, in the sense that many procedures and findings remain secret or they are protected by patenting, thus removing them from critical scrutiny by the community of scientists[46]. The scope of what can be patented has been progressively and systematically broadened, such that the very notion of public accessibility to the store of contemporary scientific knowledge is under threat (Mirowski & Sent, 2008).

It seems that the realities of contemporary science are in direct contradiction of three, if not all four, of the functional norms identified by Merton. Communality, disinterestedness and organized skepticism have been replaced by "the entrepreneurial spirit and economic growth, such that scientific intellectual creativity seems to have become synonymous with commodity" (Carter, 2008a, p. 626). Within this new reality and the blurring of distinctions between university and corporate sponsor, the entrepreneurial enthusiasm and expertise of a new crop of scientists seems to have set aside all scruples about who owns the knowledge produced by their research efforts. Perhaps the most striking example of the entrepreneurial scientist is Craig Venter, at one time a scientist on the human genome project and now leading the race to create artificial life (see chapter 7).

> The new academic-industry and non-profit-for-profit liaisons have led to changes in the ethical norms of scientific and medical researchers. The consequences are that secrecy has replaced openness; privatization of knowledge has replaced communitarian values; and commodification of discovery has replaced the idea that university-generated knowledge is a free good, a part of the social commons. The rapid growth of entrepreneurship in universities has resulted in an unprecedented rise in conflicts of interest, specifically in areas sensitive to public concerns. Conflicts of interest among scientists has been linked to research bias as well as the loss of a socially valuable ethical norm – disinterestedness – among academic researchers. As universities turn their scientific laboratories into commercial enterprise zones and as they select their faculty to realize these goals, fewer opportunities will exist in academia for public-interest science – an inestimable loss to society. (Krimsky, 2003, p. 7)

Teachers and students should ask whether Merton was right or wrong about the norms of scientific conduct. Is there, for example, a key distinction between 'science as it ought to be conducted' (Mertonian norms) and 'science as it is currently practiced' (the underlying values of post-academic science)? If there is any substance to a claim of collision between ideal and actual practice, what is an appropriate view of science to present to students in school science classes? And if we feel it necessary, what can we do to ensure that future scientific practice more closely aligns with the ideal?

Once we choose to present science in the school curriculum as a human practice, embedded in the sociocultural milieu of contemporary society, we necessarily acknowledge that it is vulnerable, on occasions, to bias, the influence of vested interest, distortion and misuse. There are many situations in which scientists, sometimes unconsciously and sometimes deliberately, deviate from the community-approved code of scientific conduct. In urging science teachers to lift the lid of this particular Pandora's box and reveal the real nature of the relationship between science and business, Bencze (2008) itemizes in spectacularly incriminating style the ways in which Mertonian norms are routinely, systematically and cynically violated in pursuit of company profit. By making students aware, we forearm them, make them more vigilant, enhance their critical scientific literacy, and increase the likelihood that they will become politically active citizens. Later chapters look at the kinds of actions that students might take. One further question remains: if we choose to include these matters in the school science and technology curriculum, how soon would it be appropriate to do so, and to what extent? It would be a gross disservice to students (and to scientists) to suggest that all contemporary scientists working in industry are routinely engaged in shady and ethically dubious activities, just as it would be a gross disservice to suggest that all scientists are 'squeaky clean' in this respect. It is important for students to know that, now and again, there are highly regrettable incidences of bias, distortion, manipulation and mis-representation of data, suppression of 'inconvenient findings', discrediting of legitimate opponents, and outright fraud. As discussed at length in Hodson (2009a), it would be valuable to include in the curriculum some examples of overt fraud[47]. Suitable candidates include the Piltdown Man forgery and the more recent *archaeo-raptor liaoningensis* hoax, the discredited work of the psychologist Cyril Burt and cardiologist John Darsee, the Bell Laboratories affair involving Jan Hendrick Schon, and the more recent scandal over Hwang Woo-Suk's faked stem cell research. I am not trying to be deliberately evasive when I state that only the classroom teacher can judge when students are mature enough, intellectually and emotionally, to address these issues in a suitably critical and reflective fashion. With regard to the Hwang case, there are some valuable opportunities for enhancing students' media literacy by looking at the nature of press coverage of the events, particularly the change in reporting style from the initial announcement of the publication of Hwang's research findings in a prestigious international journal (*Science*), through the several press conferences and the subsequent valorization of Hwang as a hero (except, of course, in newspapers consistently opposed to stem cell research), the later reporting of allegations of unethical conduct (by investigative journalists working for *PD-Notebook*, a news magazine programme on Korean television's MBC channel), to subsequent revelations about the nature and extent of the fraud, Hwang's public apology and resignation from his position at Seoul National University (Augoustinos et al., 2009; Haran & Kitzinger, 2009; Park et al., 2009)[48]. Predictably, several mainstream scientific and medical journals later heralded the exposure of Hwang's fraud as a triumph for peer review and critical scrutiny within the research community.

Since the pioneering work of Latour and Woolgar (1979), there have been numerous sociological and ethnographic studies of the day-to-day lives of scientists - for example, Latour, 1986; Knorr-Cetina, 1981, 1995; Knorr-Cetina & Mulkay, 1983; Lynch, 1985, 1997; Pickering, 1992. However, this kind of academic analysis is likely to be singularly unappealing to school-age students. As Bryce (2010) argues, there is likely to be much more appeal and much more insight into the difficulties, pressures, intrigues, personal conflicts and moral dilemmas of scientific life in fictionalized accounts, such as the science fiction novels of Gregory Benfield and the work of Carl Djerassi (described by the author himself as "science in fiction").

CHANGING SCIENCE

It is now widely accepted that empirical data are rarely sufficient in themselves to establish the validity of a scientific theory. Other criteria have to be invoked, including simplicity, scope, internal and external consistency, fruitfulness and technological success. It is also the case that many citizens no longer consider that the priorities for scientific research should be set simply by the 'desire to find out' or priorities for technological development set solely by corporate and military interests. By encouraging individuals of varying backgrounds, experience and value positions to participate in the critical appraisal of research and development proposals and claims to new scientific knowledge, we can ensure that science and technology are subjected to more vigorous and rigorous critical scrutiny. This assertion is based on the assumption that a change of background assumptions can sometimes lead to a revision of the value placed on particular science and particular technology, a change in perception of the status of evidence and the plausibility of explanations, a change in views about priorities for research and development, and even a change in the way a scientific investigation is conceptualized, designed, conducted and reported. In Helen Longino's (1997) words, "the ideal state is not the having of a single best account, but the existence of a plurality of theoretical orientations that make both possible the elaboration of particular models of the phenomenal world and serve as resources for criticism of each other" (p. 29).

In elaborating these views, Longino (1997) advocates an approach in which traditional epistemic values such as consistency with established knowledge, simplicity and generalized explanatory power are replaced with values such as *novelty, ontological heterogeneity* and *complexity of relationship*. Valuing novelty leads to a preference for theories that differ in significant ways from currently accepted theories with respect to the entities they postulate or the nature of the explanation. The goal of ontological heterogeneity leads to a preference for theories that invoke a range of causal entities rather than theories that postulate only one kind of causally efficacious entity or seek to use hierarchically-based reasoning to reduce explanations to just one causal entity. Seeking complexity of relationship results in a preference for theories that regard relationships between entities as interactive rather than unidirectional, and multi-factored rather than single-factored on grounds that they offer "protection against the unconscious perpetuation of the sexism and androcentrism of traditional theorizing" (Longino, 1997, p. 21). She also advocates the decentralization of power within the scientific community – in her words, "empowerment of the many rather than the concentration of power among the few" (p. 25). As Sandra Harding (1991) comments, exposing science to the scrutiny of those with alternative viewpoints, particularly those of oppressed and marginalized groups, increases the objectivity of research by "bringing scientific observation and the perception of the need for explanation to bear on assumptions and practices that appear natural or unremarkable from the perspective of the lives of [those] in the dominant group" (p. 150). What Harding is emphasizing is that it is easier to identify problematic assumptions underpinning science when one does not hold the same values as the scientist(s) in question. In other words, a plurality of values within the community establishes a system of epistemic checks and balances, with the ultimate justification for any knowledge claim lying in the inter-subjective judgement of the community of practitioners. A process of "transformative interrogation", as Longino (1990) calls it, determines which social values are retained and which are eliminated at any one time; it seeks to minimize the domination of science by any particular set of values deemed prejudicial to the objectivity of science.

That theory which is the product of the most inclusive scientific community is better, other things being equal, than that which is the product of the most exclusive. It is better not as measured against some independently accessible reality but better as measured against the cognitive needs of a genuinely democratic community. This suggests that the problem of developing a new science is the problem of creating a new social and political reality. (Longino, 1990, p. 214)

Of course, the way in which the community of scientists exercises public scrutiny at any one time is subject to a whole range of social, cultural, political and economic factors, and the inclination of individual scientists to be persuaded by a particular argument or to be swayed by particular evidence depends, in part, on their background knowledge, assumptions and values. It is also the case that critical standards can vary substantially from community to community, and even from journal to journal. In these respects, as Longino states, the procedures of scientific appraisal are vulnerable to charges of social relativism. The resilience of science in the face of such charges is a consequence of its openness to criticism by individuals of diverse backgrounds, experiences, interests and underlying values. Questions will be asked about the appropriateness, extent and accuracy of the data, how it was collected and interpreted, and whether the conclusions follow directly from the data, and so on. The explanation will be scrutinized for internal consistency and for consistency with other accepted theories. Particular attention will be directed to the background theory and assumptions underpinning the research design, and to the deployment of auxiliary theories and choice of instrumentation and measurement methods. The possibility that these questions may be answered differently by different appraisers, and that different perspectives will be brought to bear in the appraisal process, is the reason for upholding the principle of academic equality and is one of the guarantees of scientific objectivity, because only conclusions that are robust across varying interpretations and differing criteria will survive to become part of the corpus of accepted knowledge. Sandra Harding (1991) refers to this as a shift from *weak objectivity*, based on traditional scientific values of disinterestedness, impartiality and impersonality as guarantors of the validity and reliability of particular evidential support, to *strong objectivity*, based on diverse interpretations of what constitutes evidence, and why. Only conclusions that are robust across varying interpretations and differing criteria will survive to become part of the corpus of accepted knowledge. By seeking to exclude contextual beliefs and values from the appraisal of scientific knowledge, and by failing to acknowledge influences on the ways in which particular scientists see and shape the world, traditional methods fail to recognize the beneficial as well as the injurious effects they can exert on the conduct of science. In contrast, strong objectivity explicitly identifies the role that the researcher, her/his perspectives and interests, and the specific socio-cultural context of the research, play in the production of scientific knowledge[49].

Strong objectivity requires that the subject of knowledge be placed on the same critical, causal plane as the objects of knowledge. Thus strong objectivity requires what we can think of as 'strong reflexivity'. Culturewide (or nearly culturewide) beliefs function as evidence at every stage in scientific inquiry:

in the selection of problems, the formation of hypotheses, the design of research (including the organization of research communities), the collection of data, the interpretation of data, decisions about when to stop research, the way results of research are reported, and so on. (Harding, 2004, p. 136).

Better scientific knowledge does not result from trying to eliminate subjectivity, and conforming to some spurious notion of objectivity, but from critical consideration of the contextual values that influence or *should* influence the scientific enterprise. Kourany (2003) has argued that in choosing between empirically under-determined theories we should adopt criteria that promote egalitarian goals relating to gender, race and ethnicity, sexual orientation, age and other struggles for social justice, freedom and elimination of poverty. For example, theories or models that posit "complexity of relationship" or that treat relationships between entities and processes as mutually interactive rather than unidirectional and hierarchical promote egalatariansm better than simpler models that only posit unidirectional causal relation-ships. As Intemann (2008) comments, "theories and models that treat relationships as complex are more likely to treat causal actors as having equally important and valuable roles" (p. 1071). In Kourany's view, research priorities and research policy should be determined by these same egalatarian goals. Sharon Crasnow (2008) develops a similar argument in her notion of "model-based objectivity". Modelling always involves values-based decisions and the preferences resulting from those chosen values will be reflected in the model that is built. It is crucial that we direct careful and critical attention to the values we hold, both implicitly and explicitly.

> Since models are tools, like all tools, each is designed for specific purposes. Modeling requires making choices about the world; we focus on the features that we believe are salient to what we want. As a result, what we value is an integral part of the construction of the model. In this way, values are intrinsic to science and to our negotiating our way through the world in general. Model-based objectivity directs us to examine our social values as one of a group of factors directing our choice of characteristics. (Crasnow, 2008, p. 1101)

While model-based objectivity appears to make science relative to interests and goals, charges of relativism can be avoided if we are able to make objective decisions about the values we incorporate. In other words, we can have value commitments and still have objective scientific knowledge if we are rational and objective in making our decision about the values we incorporate. For Crasnow, that decision needs to be in favour of the things we value for their contribution to human well-being and, I would add, environmental health (a discussion that will be revisited in chapter 8).

> Model-based objectivity turns the problem of science and values on its head. Instead of asking how science can manage to be objective even though values play an intrinsic role in knowledge production, I am claiming that since values do play a role, we should be asking questions about the objectivity of value claims. We should be holding and operating with values that are objectively based in projects which will be better for human beings, allowing

humans to achieve goals that are more closely tied to their flourishing. (Crasnow, 2008, p. 1105)

Longino (1997) expresses broadly similar views: "Research that alleviates human needs, especially those traditionally attended by women, such as care of the young, weak, and infirm or feeding the hungry, should be preferred over research for military purposes or for knowledge's sake" (p. 23). However, as noted earlier, Ziman's (2000) description and evaluation of "post-academic science" suggests that research priorities are largely determined by the interests of the military, by the priorities of the pharmaceutical industry, chemical industry, petroleum industry, agribusiness and biotechnology firms, or by the government on behalf of these industries. In consequence, we have "agricultural research that revolves around pesticides, herbicides and growth hormones, and other petrochemicals, of little help to smaller, poorer farmers around the world; and medical research that revolves around expensive high-tech treatments and cures rather than the less lucrative preventive knowledge that would help so many more people, especially poorer people" (Kourany, 2003, p. 9). Using Sandra Harding's notion of strong objectivity and Sharon Crasnow's idea of model-based objectivity to justify replacing one set of social goals by another set that is more favourable to human well-being and environmental health would not pose insurmountable problems for the validity and reliability of scientific knowledge, though it would have enormous implications for the lives of millions of people.

Both these perspectives on scientific objectivity also raise the question of increased public participation in the determination of priorities for scientific and technological development and the monitoring of scientific practice. Numerous research studies have shown that scientists and policy makers frequently conceptualize the public as having insufficient scientific knowledge to reach rational decisions about scientific and technological matters, even those that directly concern them. Public opposition to new science or new technological developments is often attributed to lack of knowledge, fear of the unknown, irrational reasoning, lack of vision or emotionally-driven Luddite tendencies (Gregory & Miller, 1998; Collins & Evans, 2002; Bäckstrand, 2003). Scientists and journalists have been encouraged to make up for this perceived shortfall in public understanding by reducing the complexity of the science presented to the public to a level that is more readily understood and, therefore, more likely to be approved and accepted by the public. Michel Callon (1999) labels this the *deficit view* or *public education model* of public participation: not only must scientists teach the public everything they need to know (or that scientists, politicians and corporations want them to know), he says, they also have nothing to learn from the public.

> Science is a separate institution governed by its own norms. To succeed in its knowledge enterprise and guard against all forms of contamination, it has to protect itself from lay knowledge... The public does not participate directly in knowledge production; it consists of individuals who, either as citizens or as consumers, delegate the satisfaction of their expectations and demands to intermediaries who are in direct contact with scientists... The crucial point in the model is the existence of trusting relationships between lay people and

scientists. As soon as mistrust sets in, all relationships, as well as the balance between them, are threatened. This mistrust may have multiple origins, for example: scientists are unable to cope with the unintended results which affect the public in unexpected ways, or scientists are divided and reflect an image of an uncertain and controversial science... Whatever the case may be, the true cause is the illiteracy and ignorance of the public which transform it into easy prey for beliefs and passions. The only antidote to the poison of mistrust is to intensify educational and informative actions. (pp. 82 & 83)

In recent years, there have been some very welcome signs of a shift away from this deficit model, including the following comments in the Royal Society's (2004) *Science in Society Report*: "The implied relationship that support for science can be achieved through better communication overlooks the fact that different groups may frame scientific issues differently. The [deficit] approach did not adequately conceptualise how publics' views and attitudes towards science were embedded within wider social, political and institutional understamdings, and risks discounting the role of local knowledge and different public values in science debates" (p. 11). What is needed, as a matter of some urgency, is better understanding and communication across the scientist-public divide – in both directions. With his distinctive wit, Ralph Levinson (1999) comments that we need SUP (Scientists Understanding People) just as much as we need PUS (Public Understanding of Science). But "before SUP", he says, "could we not have Scientists Learning to Understand the Responses of People, SLURP?" (p. 52).

As noted in chapter 1, Callon (1999) postulates two alternatives to the deficit model: the *public debate model* and the *co-production of knowledge model*. In the former approach, scientists interact with the public through surveys, referendums, symposia, focus groups, citizen panels, and so on. Of course, citizens are unlikely to be unanimous in their views; rather, they form sub-groups with divergent interests, needs, experiences and viewpoints. Citizens' knowledge, while different from that of scientists (as discussed in chapter 2), is regarded as enriching, complexifying, contextualizing and problematizing scientific knowledge. However, as with the deficit model, the public debate model ascribes roles in the production of scientific knowledge in asymmetric fashion, with the public having some input into the establishment of research and development priorities, and sometimes into the ways in which findings are applied, but little or no involvement in the intervening steps. In the co-production model, there is a wholesale redistribution of roles: scientific knowledge is regarded as the product of processes in which citizens and scientists collaborate closely at all stages. Citizens are seen to possess knowledge and experience that is vital to defining what counts as a problem, relevant to the design, conduct and evaluation of scientific research, and important in determining the composition of research teams and dissemination of findings. Moreover, the complexity, uncertainty and contextual dependence of problem solutions make it imperative that the views and experiences of those most affected are at the core of decision-making.

In this model the role of non-specialists in the production of knowledge and know-how is essential. In Model 1 the constant concern is to do away with local knowledge and beliefs; in Model 2, it is to take account of it only for the purpose of enriching official expertise. In the third model the dynamics of knowledge is the result of a constantly renewed tension between the production of standardised and universal knowledge on one hand, and the production of knowledge that takes into account the complexity of singular local situations, on the other hand. These two forms of knowledge are not totally compatible, as in Model 1, nor are they produced independently from each other as in Model 2; they are the common by-product of a single process in which the different actors, both specialists and non-specialists, work in close collaboration. (Callon, 1999, p. 89)

In similar vein, Nowotny et al. (2001, 2003) argue for the establishment of a "mode-2 society" in which scientific practice is increasingly "socially embedded" and "socially robust", while Jasanoff (2005) postulates the notion of "civic epistemologies" to describe the public forms of reasoning that would drive such a society. These more radical forms of civic engagement, or the variants that can be achieved for involvement of school-age students, form a major part of discussion in chapter 9.

The gist of the foregoing discussion is succinctly summarized by Helen Longino (1990): "If we recognize... that knowledge is shaped by the assumptions, values, and interests of a culture and that, within limits, one can choose one's culture, then it's clear that as scientists/theorists we have a choice. We can continue to do establishment science, comfortably wrapped in the myths of scientific rhetoric or we can alter our intellectual allegiances" (p. 191). One of the key purposes of this book is to lay the foundations for future scientists and citizens to engage in close critical scrutiny of the enterprise of science and, where necessary, change their "intellectual allegiances". Increased levels of public involvement in the regulation of science and the establishment of research priorities will ensure that future research is more likely to be directed towards matters of public good and less likely to be conducted in pursuit of commercial interests. The curriculum advocated in this book is intended to raise awareness of these issues and to foster commitment to those higher levels of public involvement. Some examples of collaborations between scientists and the lay public, or between various expert communities and non-expert communities (the terminology preferred by Evans and Plows, 2007) are discussed in chapter 9.

CHAPTER 5

TURNING THE SPOTLIGHT ON SCIENCE EDUCATION

In addition to looking critically at the values that underpin science and scientific practice, students and their teachers should turn the critical spotlight on the values, both explicit and implicit, that impregnate science education. Values are projected through the school science curriculum in all manner of ways, despite the claims of many teachers that they adopt a 'neutral' approach. Regardless of whether individual teachers recognize it, or not, values are embedded in our choice of curriculum content, teaching and learning methods, assessment/evaluation strategies and resource materials, and in the examples of science and scientists we use, the classroom language we deploy, and the ways in which we interact with students, other teachers and parents. Even the laboratories and the school buildings carry messages about environmental values, attitudes towards technology, policy on energy consumption, waste disposal, water usage, and so on. Decisions about how the school day is organized, the balance between competition or collaboration, the ways in which students are encouraged to behave towards each other, both in class and out of class, expectations about unquestioning obedience to authority versus independent thinking, and the relative emphasis placed on academic achievement, sporting prowess, creative endeavour and community-oriented work, are all heavily impregnated with values. In a curriculum oriented towards critique and action, all of these are important focuses for student and teacher attention.

As Hildebrand (2007) points out, the values embedded in a curriculum plan (the *intended* curriculum) derive from three major sources: science values, education values and the values of the surrounding society – each of which is a highly contested domain. A particular intended curriculum embodies a particular selection (from all that is available) made by particular people at a particular time in pursuit of particular goals, purposes and interests, with different stakeholders (teachers, parents, politicians, scientists, business and industry, for example) seeking to promote their own values, attitudes and interests. Sometimes particular values items are consciously selected; sometimes the selection process is unconscious or intuitive, thus reflecting the prevailing sociocultural climate in which some value positions are so pervasive that they are virtually 'invisible'. There are occasions and situations in which the values embedded in a curriculum are made explicit to the teachers who are charged with the responsibility of implementing that curriculum, and to the students who will study it; more often, values remain implicit. Because values are often highly contested, and because curriculum decision-making is usually in the hands of a small cadre of powerful individuals, the value-laden nature of curriculum is problematic. *What* values are included? *Whose* values are included?

More importantly, perhaps, whose values are *excluded*? What is made *explicit* and what remains *implicit*? It is vital that all curricula are held up to rigorous critical scrutiny, with opportunities for alternative voices to be heard and alternative values to be acknowledged and, where appropriate, incorporated into a modified curriculum. For these reasons, greater diversity within the bodies that make decisions about science education is essential, just as greater diversity is essential within the bodies that determine policy in relation to scientific research and technological development, and within bodies that make decisions at the local, regional and global levels about SSI (see discussion in the previous chapter).

When they come to read, interpret and implement an intended curriculum, classroom teachers interact with these embedded values, sometimes consciously and sometimes unconsciously, adding, deleting and modifying certain value positions as they feel interested, willing and able to do so. Choice of teaching and learning methods, curriculum materials and assessment and evaluation strategies also embody all kinds of value judgements relating to scientific knowledge, education, teaching, learning, students, teachers, language use, interactions among teachers and students, and codes of classroom behaviour – matters well beyond the scope of this book, except for my advocacy of an "ethically attentive practice" and the promotion of the "communicative virtues" (see chapter 6 for a discussion of these two notions), and a plea for teachers to become much more aware of how their own values influence what they consider it important to teach and learn, and how those embedded values impact on students. A further phase of filtering and modifying occurs when students respond to their perceptions of the values embedded in the curriculum and choose what they will attend to and what they will oppose or ignore. Of course, *students'* assumptions, beliefs, values, preferences, feelings and attitudes, themselves a consequence of sociocultural environment, impact very profoundly on the ways in which they perceive and respond to curriculum experiences, play a large part in determining the kind of questions they ask and the topics they pursue, and are largely responsible for their decisions about whether (or not) to continue studying science and seeking a career in science and science-related professions. In urging teachers and curriculum developers to pay much closer attention to students' perspectives, Howes (2002) develops what she calls "kid marks" (in contrast to the now all-too-familiar "benchmarks" that litter many official curriculum documents). Empathy and commitment to democratic goals figure prominently in students' espoused values – for example, although objectivity in science is seen as a desirable but difficult goal to achieve, students believe that scientists should also engage their emotions, feelings and care for others, science should be a moral enterprise in which scientists accept that they carry a huge social and environmental responsibility, and the priorities and practices of science should be subject to criticism by the wider community.

It follows that when we talk about values in the curriculum, it is important to be clear whether we refer to the intended, enacted, null, hidden or attained curriculum. It is equally important for teachers to strive to make all curriculum values explicit both to themselves and to their students, subject them to critical scrutiny, and seek to modify and enrich them in pursuit of the diversity essential to an inclusive and welcoming science curriculum.

The value position of one particular intended science curriculum was impressed upon me, and even more brutally impressed on my students, in my very first year as a teacher in a school making use of the early Nuffield Biology (1966) curriculum. In a chapter entitled "How Living Things Begin", intended for 11-year olds, students are instructed to break open hens' eggs that have been incubated to various stages of development.

> After chipping away the surface of the egg as you did before, break it into a warm Petri dish and, with blunt seekers, push the embryo to the edge of the yolk. The embryo will still be attached to the yolk by blood vessels, so you will have to cut these with scissors in order to free the chick completely. The chick dies almost immediately... so it will not feel anything now... With the help of your partner straighten the embryo out... and measure its length from point A (the mid-brain) to point B (the tail). (Nuffield Biology, Text 1, 1966, p. 95)

A subsequent exercise involves flooding the embryo with warm saline solution to prolong its life so that the heartbeat can be observed. When this has been done, the "unused embryos" are discarded by flushing them down the sink. In the *Teachers' Guide* for the revised edition of the course (Revised Nuffield Biology, 1974), published some eight years later, the activity was substantially modified, though it seems that the authors were reacting rather more to the horrified reaction of students than to the underlying ethical position when they said that "while some children find looking at the stages in the development of chick embryos fascinating, others find it distasteful and are distressed by it" (p. 45). Strong feelings of revulsion towards dissection in science class, and a consequent lowering of self efficacy levels among students, are also noted by Holstermann et al. (2009). Elsewhere in the Nuffield Biology course, students are invited to conduct experiments on the larval or maggot stage of houseflies, subjecting them to variations in temperature, humidity, light intensity levels, and the like, simply to "observe how they behave". Of course, such emotionally insensitive and ethically questionable activities were not, and are not, confined to Nuffield science programmes. I located each of the following activities in science textbooks intended for use in US high schools: the diet of mice is controlled to show the effects of malnutrition; frogs are placed into iced water to slow down metabolism and simulate hibernation; a jar containing fruit flies is sealed to demonstrate that they die when the oxygen is used up; a drop of dilute sulphuric acid is put into a tank of fish to show the effects of external stimuli. Each example serves to illustrate a very clear value position: it is acceptable to starve, ill-treat, harass, terrorize, cripple or kill other animals in order to pursue our own interests in knowledge accumulation.

Each year, thousands of animals are subjected to inhumane conditions in laboratories. They may be injected with foreign substances in order for scientists to study their effects, after which they are usually killed in order to dissect them for post-mortem examination. This is a value position to which teachers should respond, and invite their students to respond. Most governments have regulations governing the use of animals in research, testing and education, but we might ask students to consider whether they consider these regulations adequate for ensuring basic animal welfare. It is important for both teachers and students to ask whether dissection of animals is an acceptable activity for the school science curriculum, especially when there are many alternatives in the form of readily available computer simulations and multimedia materials (Balcombe, 2000; Predavec, 2001; Jukes & Chiuia, 2003; Smith & Smith, 2004; Lalley et al., 2010). As Orlans (1988), Balcombe (1997), Madrazo (2002), PETA (2004), Hart et al. (2008), Hug (2008) and Oakley (2009) point out, strong objections can and should be levelled against the practice in respect of moral-ethical considerations, values projected, emotional impact on students, health hazards related to the toxicity of formaldehyde, environ- mental consequences (especially when animals such as frogs are obtained from the wild), minimal pedagogical value and, of course, violation of some cultural and religious beliefs, customs and traditions. We might also ask students whether they trust scientists in universities, industry and government agencies to tell the truth about their use of animals, and what actions they would take to express their concerns[50]. It is important, too, that students are asked to consider the ethical issues raised by factory farming, including the conditions under which animals are raised, the ways in which they are transported and killed, and the use of selective breeding, genetic manipulation and growth hormones to increase meat production regardless of the impact on the animals' quality of life. David Selby (1995) engages in a lengthy and insightful discussion of these matters and the wider issues of animal welfare (pets, farm animals, conservation, hunting, the fur industry, use of animal parts in traditional medicines, and so on). Stanisstreet and Williams (1993), Stanisstreet et al. (1994), Foster et al. (1995), Doster et al. (1997) and Barr and Herzog (2000) report on research studies investigating the views of high school students on these matters. Chapters 7 and 8 include some further discussion of these and related issues.

It is important to note that attempting to present science in a supposedly value- free way is, in itself, a value position (Layton, 1986). If, in a chemistry course, for example, teaching about water is restricted to consideration of its solvent capability, its molecular shape and the phenomenon of hydrogen bonding (all important aspects of the chemistry of water, of course), and there is no reference to problems of ensuring an adequate supply of clean water for many people in the Developing world, the unspoken value judgement is that abstract theory is more important than social awareness. A discussion of the electrolysis of brine that concentrates on the electrode processes but excludes questions about the safe disposal of the toxic mercury residue makes the same kind of value judgement with respect to environ- mental responsibility. These messages, both explicit and implicit, are everywhere in science education. They constitute a very powerful statement about science and raise important questions about the underlying values of both science and science education, and whether they can (and should) be changed. If teachers are bold enough to address the real nature of contemporary scientific practice, as argued in the previous chapter, and if they are courageous enough to address the moral-ethical issues discussed in chapter 7, the cat will be well and truly out of the bag: science and technology are categorically *not* value-free. Bowers (2001) uses a particularly powerful exemplar to make the same point: "That scientists willingly worked on a

Monsanto project to create a toxin-producing gene that would have forced poor farmers to depend on purchased seeds for the next year's planting should lead any thinking person to question the wisdom of treating education in the sciences as entirely separate from moral issues" (p. 172).

It is also important to remind students (and teachers) that informal science education experiences via the press, television and movies, visits to museums and science centres, and activities in outdoor pursuits establishments, are also heavily impregnated with values. Rennie (2007) describes the ways in which particular science facts (assuming that there are such things) are selected, modified and packaged by museum curators into a "science story" for presentation to the public. As she comments, "the choices made in this restructuring process depend on the purpose and imbue the story with the values of the interpreter" (p. 202). As in a classroom, when an individual engages with this "science story", whether in the form of a newspaper report, broadcasted television programme or museum exhibit, what is understood and what is learned may be unpredictable and unique to the individual because the particular person-story interaction depends on the individual's knowledge, beliefs, interests, experiences, values, attitudes and, as Rennie reminds us, on their prime motivation for engaging with the story.

THE CONSUMERIST AGENDA

A substantial number of recent curriculum documents (in many different countries) put considerable emphasis on what they consider to be the key role of science and technology (and science and technology education) in promoting economic growth and technological development. In many educational jurisdictions students are confronted on a daily basis with a curriculum language that promotes economic globalization, increasing production and unlimited expansion, sees unfettered technological production and spiralling consumption as progress, and regards job satisfaction as the accumulation of wealth and material goods. This doesn't mean that every lesson is ideologically-driven; rather, the effect is cumulative, extending over weeks, months and years. The net effect is to persuade most students that these 'realities' are normal, natural, inevitable and in everyone's best interests.

> The rule of market forces now in force further heightens the false understanding that the principal social objectives of all countries are consumption and accumulation, twin objectives to be enforced through the two complementary strategies of the carrot of consumerism, through which a system of total demand is created, and the competitive stick of enforced economic participation. (Odora Hoppers, 2000, p. 102)

> The idea of the 'consumer' is crucial... For neoliberals, the world in essence is a vast supermarket. 'Consumer choice' is the guarantor of democracy... Thus, democracy is turned into consumption practices... the ideal of the citizen is that of purchaser. (Apple, 2001a, p. 39)

Bencze (2001) has argued that contemporary science education for the majority of students is, in effect, an *apprenticeship for consumership*, that is, it seeks to create "a large mass of relatively scientifically and technologically illiterate citizens who simultaneously serve as loyal workers and voracious, unquestioning consumers"

(p. 350). According to Bencze, key elements contributing to this goal include: (i) *compartmentalization* – teaching science as discrete units prevents students gaining an understanding of complex inter-relationships among science, technology, society and environment; (ii) *standardization* – homogenization of students renders them more susceptible to mass marketing; (iii) *intensification* – an overloaded curriculum leads teachers to fall back on didactic methods and neglect opportunities for discussion and critique; (iv) *idealization* – part of the myth-making of school science education is that science has an all-purpose and powerful method of ascertaining the truth, scientists always act in an altruistic and ethically exemplary way, and the knowledge produced is value-free and trustworthy; (v) *regulation* – because decisions about what to study, how to investigate and how to present findings are all under strict teacher control, students do not develop the skills and attitudes needed for independent problem-solving; (vi) *saturation* – students are given the impression that science has solved most problems, so there is little need to question, speculate or investigate; and (vi) *isolation* – the traditional emphasis on working individually severely reduces the opportunity to engage in the group discussion, collective critique and collaborative decision-making that is essential for addressing SSI. There are strong echoes here and in Bencze et al. (2009), which adds the further elements of *confusion* (consequent upon a seriously overloaded curriculum) and *de-skilling* (as a consequence of insufficient opportunities for students to direct and control their own learning), of Michael Apple's (1993) assertion that in the new economy-driven educational climate, students are no longer seen as people who will participate in the struggle to build and rebuild the social, educational, political and economic future, but as consumers: freedom is "no longer defined as participating in building the common good, but as living in an unfettered commercial market, with the education system… integrated into the mechanisms of such a market" (p. 116).

Arguing along similar lines, Lee and Roth (2002) assert that in contemporary science education "both the subject matter and the method of instruction are not geared toward generating a scientifically literate populace, but rather function like a Fordian production line in a Foucauldian (disciplining) institution that forms employees of a certain class for a limited number of powerful institutions" (p. 42) and sees education itself as one more product or commodity like cars, televisions, coffee and bread. What is being created here is an education "fit for business", that is, an approach at primary, secondary and tertiary levels that is designed to provide what business considers the appropriately skilled workforce and to generate the attitudes and instill the values that will be supportive of the competitive marketplace. Marshall (1995) uses the term "busnocratic rationality" to describe the curriculum emphasis on acquisition of skills rather than knowledge building, and on information and information retrieval rather than knowledge, understanding and wisdom. He notes also the accompanying notion that it should be *consumers* of education (i.e., business interests and employers) rather than the *clients* (students) or *providers* (educators) who determine curriculum, define and measure quality in education, and set standards of attainment. Moreover, he argues, these standards are set in such a way that they ensure a largely uneducated, uncritical and undemanding workforce to fill society's low-paid jobs, with any shortfall being filled by immigration (see also Stromquist & Monkman, 2000). Lankshear et al. (1996) argue that the pressures exerted by business and industry on schools to provide more "job ready" people can be seen as part of an overt sociotechnical engineering practice in which new capitalism is creating "new kinds of people by changing not just their overt viewpoints but their actual practices" (p. 22). In short, the business community is re-engineering people in its own image! As Saul (1997) and Crossley and Watson (2003) observe, at an international level, the World Bank is a major agency of promotion for this neoliberalist corporate agenda. Jickling and Wals (2008) spell out the situation very clearly: "For institutions such as the World Bank, education appears simply and solely about preparing individuals to join the local labour market to nourish the global marketplace and satisfy corporate needs. As a result, education is less and less seen as a public good, and the state's role in providing citizens with the best possible education is diminished" (p. 2). Other noticeable trends in the commodification of education and knowledge include the growth of private training and educational establishments (and the associated erosion of traditional provision) and the franchising and satellite broadcasting of educational prorammes.

In many countries in the industrialized world, governments have reduced individual and company taxation and reduced regulation of business activities such as transnational trade, while decreasing spending on social programmes, including health and education, and privatizing what had previously been state-owned and state-operated services such as public transport, power and water supply, and telecommunications (McMurty, 1999). Carter (2008a) observes that "public sector reform typically involves the adoption of business practices such as privatization, strategic planning, regulation and quality assurance, with performance judged against indicators or standards. We see here a new kind of nation state: smaller, more centralized and geared to work as a regulator and auditor, rather than an agent for redistribution and social justice" (p. 620). Apple (2001a) sees a powerful alliance among enthusiasts for the neo-liberal marketization of education, neo-conservatives who want "a return to higher standards and a 'common culture', authoritarian populist religious fundamentalists deeply worried about secularity and the preservation of their own traditions, and particular factions of the professionally oriented new middle class who are committed to the ideology and techniques of accountability, measurement and 'management'" (p. 103). Carter (2005) argues along similar lines:

Neoliberalism 'marketizes' everything, even notions of subjectivity, desire, success, democracy, and citizenship, in economic terms. At the same time neo-conservatism works to preserve traditional forms of privilege and marginalize authentic democratic and social justice agendas. More sinister still is the success with which both ideologies have colonized the rhetoric so at the very time reforms appear to be more just and equitable, they actually work in opaque ways against those they purport to help... Neoliberal and neoconservative forces work in tandem to marketize and reform and, as reform proceeds, to (re)distribute power back to traditional elites, effectively rejecting recent progressive liberal moves to increase equality and social redress... Democracy [has been redefined] as largely synonymous with capitalism, so that consumption becomes the new form of democratic participation, and equity becomes isomorphic with increased choice. (pp. 571 & 565)

In the so-called 'knowledge economy', businesses need only a relatively small number of people who are knowledge creators and managers, whom Apple (2001b) calls "symbolic analyzers" (those who can analyze and manipulate words, numbers, visual representations and other symbols) and a much larger number of less skilled and less knowledgeable workers who can and will follow instructions (Bencze & Alsop, 2007; Gee et al., 1996; Lankshear, 2000; Carter, 2009; Bencze, 2010). Thus, school science education functions to select and educate the "relatively small group of students who may work as engineers and scientists to help companies develop and manage mechanisms of production (and consumption) of goods and services... (and) large groups of citizens who may function best as compliant workers and as enthusiastic purchasers of products and services of business and industry" (Bencze, 2004, p. 193). For the majority, emphasis is not on the development of critical thinking but on the mastery of a given body of knowledge. Assessment and evaluation are seen as a means of monitoring the system to determine its efficiency. The result is an education that focuses on that which is easily and reliably assessed. As Noble (1998) comments, business benefits from "a school system that will utilize sophisticated performance measures and standards to sort students and to provide a relatively reliable supply of... adaptable, flexible, loyal, mindful, expendable, 'trainable' workers" (p. 281). Hence the rush in many countries around the world to establish so-called "standards of performance" monitored by an imposed regime of systematic and regular assessment via standardized tests.

> When applying a neoconservative framework to education, one imagines a system where components respond according to the principles of excellence and competition, such as when businesses survive or fail based upon their ability to respond to their clients. Likewise, neoconservative policy subjects individual teachers... and school systems to similar criteria. Instead of monetary gains as the measuring tool, test performance is the educational standard by which people and institutions are sorted into winners and losers. (Settlage & Meadows, 2002, p. 5)

Education authorities insist that students, classes, schools and whole education systems show quantifiable results, with testing regimes monitoring outcomes and positioning everyone so that improvements can be claimed by the authorities and any shortfalls or deficiencies blamed on teachers (Carter, 2005). There is no research evidence whatsoever indicating that the imposition of these so-called "educational standards" is linked to continued or enhanced enhanced economic growth, yet many governments, business leaders, industrialists and citizens act as though there is. As Apple (1999, 2000, 2001a) argues, these educational standards embody both neoliberal concerns for increased accountability, surveillance and regulation and neoconservative desires for a return to "real learning" and "real knowledge". In this kind of technocratic approach to education, efficiency, marketability and accountability are regarded as the ultimate virtues. Alsop (2009) notes that the impact of this kind of thinking on Ontario schools has been considerable. It is now rare, he says, to find teachers who are prepared to question Ministry of Education directives, much less to design and implement curriculum experiences that challenge these new societal assumptions or address controversial issues. Instead, most teachers comply with all policy guidelines, ensure coverage of the prescribed curriculum content as efficiently as possible, avoid anything controversial, implement standardized assessment schemes to measure designated learning outcomes, and fill in the myriad boxes in the ever-expanding catalogue of official report cards. Tan (2009) observes an increased emphasis on teaching for the test (including increased teacher preparation time, class time and financial resources) and increasing marginalization of any material that is not part of the designated examinable syllabus. My own view, as expressed at length in Hodson (1992b, 1993b), is that these testing regimes are philosophically unsound (because they are not based on a valid model of science or scientific literacy), educationally worthless (because they trivialize learning), pedagogically dangerous (because they encourage bad teaching), professionally debasing (because they de-skill teachers) and socially undesirable (because of some powerful hidden and not-so-hidden messages about control and compliance). They are also morally repugnant, because they are based on market values, seek to objectify people, regard knowledge as a commodity to be traded for marks and grades, disallow freedom of expression, and stifle creativity.

Before leaving this discussion it is important to note that schools are under increasing pressure to seek sponsorship for all manner of things, from school sports teams and drama productions to computer laboratories. There is pressure, at least in New Zealand and Australia, to recruit increasing numbers of overseas fee-paying students, especially from East Asia. There is increasing use of curriculum materials generated by multinationals, in which there is often a great deal of quite overt propaganda designed to increase marketability and generate a more favourable PR image. Ross (2000) is one of several writers to draw attention to this disturbing trend.

> While your local high school hasn't yet been bought out by McDonald's, many educators already use teaching aids and packets of materials, 'donated' by companies, that are crammed with industry propaganda designed to instill product awareness among young consumers: lessons about the history of the potato chip, sponsored by the Snack Food Association, or literacy programs that reward students who reach monthly reading goals with Pizza Hut slices. (p. 24)

Sometimes the alliance of business and education (and the underlying motivation for the alliance) is quite overt. Goodman and Saltman (2002), for example, comment on BPAmoco's iMPACT curriculum materials, designed for middle school science programmes: "Amoco's curriculum produces ideologies of consumerism that bolster its global corporate agenda and it does so under the guise of disinterested scientific knowledge, benevolent technology, and innocent entertainment" (p. 68). Sometimes the corporate agenda is less immediately apparent, though it is nonetheless pervasive and powerful.

BECOMING MORE CRITICAL

There are many important questions to be asked of students and their teachers with respect to continued economic growth, ever-increasing production, and spiralling levels of material consumption. While enhanced production levels provide the material benefits we crave, they also create many of the social and environmental problems that currently plague us. For many people, feelings of satisfaction and contentment, self-identity, self-expression and personal ambition are intimately bound up with consumption and acquisition of material goods. The old and familiar are constantly being replaced with something new – in reality, with something more profitable for the manufacturer and retailer. There is a constant barrage of advertizing on television and computer screens, at sporting events and the movies, and in buses, subway cars, railway stations, museums and art galleries (indeed, anywhere where people gather), all of which is designed to make people want things they had never previously considered and to create a culture of instant gratification in a world of seemingly endless abundance. Feelings of dissatisfaction, deprivation and lack of fulfillment become associated with not having the latest product. In Bauman's (2007) words, "the search for individual pleasures articulated by the currently offered commodities, a search guided and constantly redirected and refocused by the successive advertizing campaigns, provides the sole acceptable – indeed badly needed and welcome – substitute for both the uplifting solidarity of work-mates and the glowing warmth of caring-for-and-being-cared-by the near and dear inside the family home and its immediate neighbourhood" (p. 29).

The great triumph of the business and industrial sector, and the disaster from an environmental perspective, is to have created and imposed on a large mass of people the idea that acquisition of material goods is central to their lives and their sense of personal fulfillment. Some years ago, Daly (1991) coined the term "growthmania" to describe the orientation of contemporary Western society towards continued economic growth: "Economic growth is held to be the cure of poverty, unemployment, debt repayment, inflation, balance of payment deficits, pollution, depletion, the population explosion, crime, divorce, and drug addiction. In short, economic growth is both the panacea and the *summum bonum*" (p. 183). So successful has this campaign been that many people endlessly search for new goods and the latest designs, regardless of the fact that there appear to be no tangible or meaningful benefits. Particular norms of beauty, fashion and style are created and applied in advertizing campaigns to persuade targeted social groups that they must acquire the goods that will help them meet these standards. Technological products, especially clothes, cosmetics and mobile phones, are used to signal the wearer's or the user's sense of style, social group membership and socioeconomic status. Intensive advertizing seeks to generate a distinctive brand identity, consciousness, desire and loyalty, with the company logo being worn to signal membership of a particular sub-cultural group. Particular products are equated with particular ideas, attributes, attitudes and values, and become associated with particular people, especially sports stars and the so-called "celebrities" of popular culture. The seductive lure of supposedly ever more desirable goods is used by advertisers to make and shape people's sense of identity, with choice of car, clothes and mobile phone, together with preferences of particular music and movies, being used to signal who we are and who we would like to be. In teen culture, brands and products have come to determine who is "in" and who is "out", who is cool and who is not, who is likely to have friends and high social status, and who is ostracized, isolated or ridiculed (Seiter, 1993; Schor, 2004). As Quart (2003) notes: "Teens suffer more than any other sector of society for this wall-to-wall selling. They are at least as anxious as their parents about having enough money and maintaining their social class, a fear that they have been taught is best allayed by more *branded* gear. And they have taken to branding themselves, believing that the only way to participate in the world is to turn oneself into a corporate product or a corporate spy to help promote the products to other kids" (p. xiii). In short, people have become what they consume. In the words of Alastair McIntosh (2008), "[Consumerism] keeps us narcissistically at a child-like level of immaturity, seeking only the next fix" (p. 176). That fix also includes the fix that comes from the advertizing-induced craving for junk foods. There seems to be no limit to what advertisers will do to get young children to crave products with high levels of sugar and fat, making them increasingly vulnerable to obesity and type II diabetes. For these kinds of reasons, McGregor (2003) sees consumers as victims, but largely victims of their own making.

> People behave as they do in a consumer society because they are so in-doctrinated into the logic of the market that they cannot 'see' anything wrong with what they are doing. Because they do not critically challenge the market ideology, and what it means to live in a consumer society, they actually contribute to their own oppression. (p. 3)

Advertizers recognize only too well that children are the key focus in gaining access to the family budget: "They are the first adopters and users of many of the new technologies. They are the household members with the most passionate consumer desires, and are most closely tethered to products, brands, and the latest trends" (Schor, 2004, p. 11). The advertizing bombardment begins very early in life. As Cope and Kalantzis (2000) note, and I know only too well from my inter-actions with my beloved grandchildren, even a substantial component of the culture of childhood seems now to be made up of "interwoven narratives and commodities that cross television, toys, fast-food packaging, video games, T-shirts, bed linen, pencil cases, and lunch boxes" (p. 16). Bakan (2004) makes the same point: "Children's worlds (are) increasingly defined by profit-driven synergies among megacorporations, a kind of corporate 'enclosure of childhood' is taking place, with children living more and more of their lives inside 'brand enclosures" (p. 127).

However, as Steve Keirl (2006) notes, when we put on a pair of the latest jeans, having previously ensured that they have the desired designer label, we pay little heed to the social, economic and ecological footprint[51]: "Brass rivets from Namibian copper and Australian zinc; zip teeth from Japan; zip tape from France; thread made from petroleum in Japan and subsequently spun in Ireland; synthetic indigo dye which when discarded cuts out light in water and so kills fish and plants; labor carried out in Tunisia, paying about $A1.50 per hour; and cotton probably grown in a Majority World country using large amounts of water and probably a genetically modified seed" (p. 86). Petrina (2000b) carries out a similar ecological and social justice accounting exercise for a pair of branded trainers.

> The leather upper of the shoes, consisting of about twenty parts, is typically from cows raised and slaughtered in Texas. The hides are shipped to Asia and

treated through a chemical-intensive chrome tanning process, with a by-product of toxins dumped into an Asian river. The synthetic parts of the shoes are made from petroleum-based chemicals from Saudi Arabia, and distilled and cracked in a Korean refinery, with wastes again making their way into rivers. The midsole is ethylene vinyl acetate foam which requires a number of processes to synthesise. The sole is made from styrene-butadiene rubber, synthesized from Saudi petroleum in a Taiwanese factory. In the factory, the sole is moulded and cut, generating the largest amount of solid waste in the shoe production process. The shoes are assembled in a Tangerang factory or similar Asian factories. Most of the assembly is done through the labour of children and women cutting, gluing, and sewing under sweatshop conditions of high temperatures... and toxic fumes from solvent-based toluene glues and paint. Their average wage is about 15 cents per hour over their 65 hour work week... The finished shoes are hand packed with light-weight tissue from Sumatran rain forest trees and placed in a box. The unbleached, corrugated cardboard for the shoe box was made in a closed-loop paper mill in New Mexico. The shoe box itself is folded in a mill in Los Angeles and shipped to Asia. The boxed shoes are shipped as cargo back to the west coast of the US, transported to local outlets, purchased for about $60.00 to $150.00 (ESD) per pair, and worn for occasions that have nothing to do with sports or training. The average pair of cross-trainers lasts less than a year and usually ends up in a landfill. (p 216)

Many products are created almost solely for profit, no matter what the real need, social and environmental cost, or moral-ethical desirability. Bakan (2004) charac-terizes this pursuit of profit regardless of cost to people and environment as pathological: "The corporation's legally defined mandate is to pursue, relentlessly and without exception, its own self-interest, regardless of the often harmful cones-quences it might cause to others. As a result, I argue, the corporation is a pathological institution, a dangerous possessor of the great power it wields over people and societies" (p. 1) and, of course, over the natural environment. It is estimated that up to 80% of energy used and carbon dioxide emitted in the industrialized world is a direct consequence of consumer demand (Curran & de Sherbinin, 2004). For example, the 'must have' status of sport utility vehicles (SUVs), which consume one third more fuel and create 75% more pollution than regular saloon cars, has led to Americans wasting 70 billion gallons of petrol (gasoline) over the past ten years. For what, one wonders?

Both the formal school curriculum and the very powerful hidden curriculum, together with the informal curriculum mediated by the mass media, play a role in reproducing the socially and environmentally unsustainable values of the affluent, acquisitive, consumer society, including the unquestioned assumption of the importance of continued economic growth, the priority of self, and the correctness of allowing market forces to determine economic and social policy, priorities for scientific and technological development, and the agenda for environmental protection (or lack of it). Sadly, research suggests that technology teachers are often the most enthusiastic supporters of the culture of consumption (Holdsworth & Conway, 1999; Elshof, 2001). By fostering this culture of consumption, we prepare students for a life that works against the environmental conditions necessary to sustain that lifestyle. Indeed, any lifestyle! In Petrina's (2000b) words, "we teach in full knowledge of an insane contradiction" (p. 215). In illustration of how the consumer mentality invades the classroom, Elshof (2009b) describes an activity developed for the school technology curriculum in which groups of students design, build, test and race a model Indy or F1 car, quoting the promotional material sent to teachers: "Just like the real world they must incorporate marketing and seek sponsors to compete regionally, nationally, and internationally" (p. 49). As Elshof comments: "Just like the real world is exactly the problem" (p. 50). Carter and Dediwalage (2010) report that even a project specifically designed to provide a science curriculum oriented towards sustainable living, named *Sustainable Living by the Bay*, and focused ostensibly on responsible water and energy use and waste management in the Port Phillip Bay area of Victoria (Australia), can become permeated with globalization rhetoric and emphasis on innovation, competitiveness and ensuring a ready supply of scientists and technologists to underpin economic growth.

There are some important questions we should be asking students about the pros and cons of our consumer culture. Do we need all these goods? Are they really worth the social and environmental cost? Do we want a society that gives priority to economic values or one that gives priority to quality of life – for all people. It is the relentless drive to create new products and new markets, the in-built obsolescence that constantly creates new demands, and the ever-escalating cycle of material and energy consumption, manufacturing production and contamination through waste disposal, exacerbated by a burgeoning world population, that is primarily responsible for the rapid changes we are now witnessing in natural systems. The current and rapidly deepening ecological crises are directly tied to mass production and hyper-consumption, aided and abetted by advertizing and political propaganda. We have entered what Daly (1991) calls "terminal hyper-growthmania: "When we deplete geological capital and ecological life-support systems and count that depletion as net current income, then we arrive at our present state of terminal hyper-growthmania" (p. 183). It is a terminal condition because we are exploiting renewable resources at a rate that now exceeds the self-renewing capability of natural systems. We need a radical re-think of the underlying idea that everything that can be made, should be made, marketed, purchased and (relatively soon) discarded in favour of a newer, brighter, glossier or more powerful alternative. But, as Shiva (2008) comments, such is the current political milieu and the determination to defend and enlarge markets, that even when it is clear that climate change demands radical changes in our patterns of production and consumption, and the values that underpin them, many are still preoccupied with protecting market structures and mechanisms.

Quite apart from the damaging environmental impact, high levels of material consumption can have an adverse impact on our emotional well-being. Hamilton and Denniss (2006) refer to the debilitating condition of *affluenza*. Its characteristics include: "the bloated, sluggish and unfulfilled feeling that results from efforts to keep up with the Joneses... An epidemic of stress, overwork, waste and indebtedness caused by the dogged pursuit of the (consumerist) dream... (and) an unsustainable addiction to economic growth" (p. 3). In like vein, Schumaker (2001) comments: "A strong materialist orientation has been associated with diminished life satisfaction, impaired self-esteem, dissatisfaction with friendships and leisure activities, and a pre-disposition to depression... [and] features in the worrying rash of 'consumption disorders' such as compulsive shopping, consumer vertigo and kleptomania. Hyper-materialism also features predominantly in the emerging plagues of 'existential disorders' such as chronic boredom, ennui, jadedness, purposelessness, meaning-lessness and alienation" (p. 35). The incessant brand consciousness among young people (see above) has generated massively increased levels of teasing and bullying – often with tragic results. The constant craving for increased flexibility, power, connectivity and speed through ever more sophisticated ICT devices has spawned a deluge of information and a rash of virtually meaningless communications that have created a form of ignorance through overload. This excess of what we might call "information noise" builds up stress levels in many people to an intolerable level. Kasser (2002) presents similar arguments in his book *The High Price of Materialism*.

These high levels of stress and feelings of anxiety, dissatisfaction, boredom and alienation have themselves become a commercial target, with pharmaceutical companies rushing to sell us the cure to our problems in the form of sleeping pills, anti-depressants, vitamin supplements, and the like. As Hamilton and Denniss (2005) observe, drug companies engage in *disease-mongering*: "describing, medicalising and exaggerating normal problems and turning them into clinical conditions" (p. 120). Once there is a diagnosable condition, there is a potential market for a new medication, fuelled by the now all-too-prevalent direct-to-consumer advertizing (Mintzes, 2002). Moynihan et al. (2002) provide a number of striking examples of such cynical disease-mongering, including the characterization of common adolescent shyness as "social adjustment disorder", to be treated with antidepressant drug Aurorix, and the elevation of what had previously been a mild functional disorder requiring little more than reassurance about its benign natural cause into a serious medical condition warranting the specialist term "irritable bowel disorder" and needing "a clinically proven treatment" – the drug Lotronez[52]. Most outrageous of all has been the attempts by pharmaceutical companies responding to the massive profits accruing to Pfizer from sales of Viagra to define "female sexual dysfunction" and turn it into a medical condition treatable with drugs (Moynihan, 2003). Equally disturbing is the increasing trend to towards treating dissatisfactions through breast implants, nose reconstructions, liposuction, "tummy tucks", facelifts, botox injections, toe shortening, navel repositioning, vaginal reconstruction (or "vaginal rejuvenation" as some Websites describe it), and all the other heavily marketed and publicized procedures of the cosmetic surgery industry – procedures that are increasingly and alarmingly being promoted to teenagers (Quart, 2003). Hamilton and Denniss (2005) comment: "The traditional role of doctors is to consider the patient's symptoms, make a diagnosis and recommend a treatment, but in the case of most cosmetic surgery the media manufacture the symptoms and make the diagnosis and the 'patient' then tells the doctor what the treatment should be" (p. 129).

QUESTIONING GLOBALIZATION

There are also many questions that teachers and students should ask about globaliz-ation. What began as a means for some companies to conduct business more efficiently and more profitably by outsourcing some manufacturing, generating some new markets for existing products and creating markets for new products, has now extended to a major global trend through which "the world is rapidly being integrated into one economic space via increased international trade, the inter-nationalization of production and financial markets, the internationalization of a commodity culture promoted by an increasingly networked global telecommunic-ations system" (Gibson-Graham, 1996, p. 121).

> For the first time in the development of markets, global modes of production can commodify almost everything on a planned, rational, mass scale. Not only can the raw resources of the Earth, the manufactured things of factory production and the social services of human interaction be submitted to a business logic of exchange, but also words, codes, memories, sounds, images and symbols can be designed as value adding, fungible products for rapid transit through mass markets as instruments of production, accumulation, reproduction and circulation. Even life itself, whether in the form of designer genes, engineered tomatoes, bionic joints, synthetic skin, or patented mice, is being turned into a commodity. (Luke, 2001, p. 196)

Because globalization refers to capital, labour, markets, communications, scientific and technological innovation, production and resources, and much more besides, writers such as Waters (1995), Little (1996), Jameson (1998), Delanty (1999), Beck (2000), Harvey (2000) and Stromquist and Monkman (2000) find it useful to organize patterns of globalization into three major and mutually reinforcing agenda: *economic* globalization (including the opening of economies to free market control, competitive penetration of each other's markets, intensified competition, relocation of manufacturing to low-cost parts of the world, new sources of wealth (and poverty), new alliances, and new forms of exchange); *political* globalization (deregulation and abandonment of exchange controls, tariffs and subsidies, changed relationships between nation state, capital and individuals, shift of power from citizens to corporations, commodification of education, and so on); and *cultural* globalization (such as increased mobility of people, goods, information, knowledge and services, development of new information, communications and transport technologies, and cultural imperialism, including the spread of Western lifestyle options and the establishment of English as a global language). The dominant discourse on globalization, including that in the school curriculum, is optimistic, with considerable emphasis on the advantages created by the open, highly connected and competitive markets and by economic and cultural exchange. But, for some, the reality may be rather different. As with any change, there are winners and losers. Globalization has impacted the lives of citizens and nations to differing degrees and with a differing mix of positive and negative effects.

> On the surface, [globalization] is instant financial trading, mobile phones, McDonald's, Starbuck's, holidays booked on the net. Beneath this gloss, it is

the globalization of poverty, a world where most human beings never make a phone call and live on less than two dollars a day, where 6,000 children die every day from diarrhoea because most have no access to clean water. (Pilger, 2002, p. 2)

While globalization has made a few people very rich indeed, it has worsened the quality of life for many people in the Developing and Under-developed world. The relocation of manufacturing industry to the Developing world has led to widespread exploitation of labour, social disruption and environmental degradation. Developing countries are often put into the situation of introducing the technological products and practices of alien cultures without relevant experience or education, without the necessary resources, and at the expense of their own cultural heritage. Un-scrupulous multinationals can make easy profits in these conditions and can operate with freedom from any effective control of labour conditions and environmental standards. The increasing urbanization disrupts traditional mechanisms of social stability, precipitating massive increases in alcohol abuse, drug taking, crime and prostitution. Meanwhile, the financial benefits drain away to more affluent societies. Western propaganda and advertizing have concocted a spurious but seemingly glamorous culture of over-consumption and over-indulgence, which threatens to undermine social stability, weaken traditional values, dilute local culture and impose English as the language of modernity and popular culture. Organizations like CNN and Disney promote "America" as a kind of brand name for all that is considered desirable in life. In the cities of Developing countries, McDonald's, KFC and Dunkin' Donuts spring up on every street corner. American fashions in clothes and popular music are slavishly mimicked, and the lives of Hollywood "personalities" are followed in all their excruciatingly banal detail. In pursuit of this transplanted cultural dream, there is a major drift of people from rural areas to work in the sweatshops and factories that provide the consumer goods for the West. Students should know that there are many citizens in the economically under-developed parts of the world who see globalization as a renewed form of colonization, a form of cultural and economic imperialism that threatens to destroy rather than foster their economic and social well-being, that commodifies both natural resources and people, locates them on the periphery of key decision-making (or excludes them entirely) and compounds their powerlessness, poverty and dispossession (Muchie & Li, 2006). As Roseneau (1992), Saul (1997, 2005), Larner (2000), Lawton et al. (2000), Bakan (2004) and others observe, the self-serving policies that international organizations such as the IMF, World Bank, World Trade Organization, OECD and G-7 (now G-20) impose on many Under-developed and Developing nations constitute "governance without government". Nation states are in danger of being reduced to the level of simple mechanisms for implementing the policies of transnational corporations at the local level.

Multinational corporations now electronically 'network' the remotest parts of the country into a vast and increasingly international consumer market. Decisions made in corporate headquarters increasingly disrupt the interdependencies of entire communities by downsizing the workforce. And their advertizing budgets lead to shaping the most basic sense of an individual's taken-for-granted 'reality' to fit the technologically based vision of progress and, in the process, delegitimate traditional beliefs and practices that represented an alternative basis of community life. A similar commoditizing mentality and concentration of power permeates governmental institutions, the medical establishment, and public schools and universities. (Bowers, 1977, p. 37)

It is the executive directors of these powerful banks and transnational corporations that can direct, or at least influence, the policies of individual countries and national economies by integrating them into regional or global economies, and by making it increasingly impossible for them to regulate and control their own affairs. (Crossley & Watson, 2003, p. 103)

While neo-liberalism may mean less government, it does not follow that there is less governance. While on the one hand neo-liberalism problematises the state and is concerned to specify its limits through the invocation of individual choice, on the other hand it involves forms of governance that encourage both institutions and individuals to conform to the norms of the market. (Larner, 2000, p. 12)

Behind the imperative of globalization stands the military, technological, and economic power of the West. These powers have rights without qualifications, including the right to *prop up dictatorships* and undermine popular democracy if those democracies are not in step with the wishes of the Western powers; the right to *create a strong transnational state* that dictates economic policy including manufacturing, media and communications, and institutions in which a participant takes place in a fairly rigid hierarchy of domination, implementing orders from above, transmitting them downwards; the right to *construct the parameters of meaning*; and the right to *intellectual property* – the misnomer for the rising tide of doctrines designed to ensure that the US-based corporations control the technology of the future, including biotechnology, which in turn will allow those state-subsidized private enterprises of the West to control health and agriculture as well as the means to life of all humanity. (Odora Hoppers, 2000, p. 103).

REDIRECTING TECHNOLOGY

Making points closely related to the issues raised earlier in this chapter, Beyer (1998) paints a particularly bleak picture of contemporary society when he says that we live "in a democratic-capitalist social order in which commodity fetishism, the rule of the market, patriarchy, and White Supremacy constrain, distort, and oppress the expression of many individuals' humanity and their ability to act democratically" (p. 260). Dobbin (1998) is equally dark in his vision: "Thousands of years of human development and progress are reduced to the pursuit of 'efficiency', our collective will is declared meaningless compared to the values of the marketplace, and communitarian values are rejected in favour of the survival of the fittest. A thinly disguised barbarism now passes for, is in fact promoted as, a global human objective" (p. 1). Muchie and Li (2006) express very similar sentiments.

Money has acquired a value and purpose of its own. Far from being a servant of human transaction, it has become a tyrant that requires human submission. It has turned into an overall measure, index, standard and yardstick by which human worth has been ultimately expressed. If wealthy, one is right, if poor one is wrong... The human soul has been battered with the artillery of the ideology of commodification. Morality and ethics have fallen to the same commodity transaction. (p. 38)

These authors certainly paint a bleak picture of contemporary society. But it is a picture we can change. And, I believe, the place to begin that process of change is in school. Hence my advocacy throughout this book of a school science and technology curriculum that fosters an enhanced, critical scientific literacy and promotes the politicization of students, that is, a curriculum that will enable students to resist the culture of consumerism and compliance, encourage them to fight for social justice, and lead them to conduct their lives in an environmentally responsible way. For the past sixty years or more, we have been socialized by politicians, economists, industrialists, business leaders, primary producers of various kinds (especially the mining and petroleum industries), retailers, advertisers, and even waste disposal managers and taxation department personnel, into believing that we never have enough in terms of consumer goods and can never have too much. It is this belief that now threatens our social, economic and environmental security. We have to change. And we have to change *now*. In the words of Muchie and Li (2006), "A vision of human and social well-being for technological development is a *moral minimum* if the planet is to save itself from blindly following an amoral technological self-momentum mainly guided by the military and the instrumental greed of the burgeoning corporate-military power" (p. 35, emphasis added). It is a matter of some urgency that citizens begin to reflect on and voice their opinions on "deeper issues related to how well-being and happiness can be fostered not merely through the dominant logic of economic accumulation and competition, but also... through intelligent use of new technologies to enrich life and living for ordinary people everywhere" (Muchie & Li, 2006, p. 36).

As teachers, we have to choose whether to continue preparing students intellectually, attitudinally and morally to be part of the existing corporate-dominated, market-oriented, competitive and exploitative society or whether we will use the science curriculum to challenge this ideology, seek an alternative, and work towards far-reaching social change driven by principles of social justice and environmental responsibility. In David Orr's (1994) words, "The disordering of ecological systems and of the greater bio-geochemical cycles of the earth reflects a prior disorder in the thought, perception, imagination, intellectual priorities and loyalties inherent in the industrial mind. Ultimately, the ecological crisis concerns how we think and the institutions that purport to shape and refine the capacity to think" (p. 2). My agenda for science and technology education can be clearly stated: a shift from what Freire (2004) calls "the narrow and mean ethic of profit and the market" to a society that has concern for the well-being of all the people, and for ensuring and sustaining the health of both the natural and the built environments. Kyle (2006) talks about developing a new concept of globalization: "We must transcend the present-day notions and tensions associated with globalization and move beyond the narrow focus of trade and financer that has distorted international discourse... (but) forging a harmonious global community will only be possible if it is based on universal principles of respecting human rights, meeting basic human needs, and preserving the natural environment for future generations" (p. 5).

Of course, the values underpinning this approach cannot and should not be imposed on students from outside. Rather, they must be fostered from within (as discussed in chapters 6 and 7). Nevertheless, the overall message is clear: we need to go beyond the idea that efficiency, productivity and consumption are a good thing regardless of side effects in terms of human suffering and environmental damage. The ideology of consumption needs to be challenged by concepts of sustainability, social justice and more appropriate lifestyle. In making this case, Beck (1997) calls for a "technology of doubt" that would help us to adopt guiding principles other than economic efficiency, utility, marketability and productivity – for example, uncertainty, ambivalence, fantasy, pluralism and contextuality.

Sadly, many science and technology curricula continue to reflect (if not actively promote) the values, attitudes, ways of thinking and social structures that have fostered the economic, social and political systems responsible for current social and environmental crises. Many curricula continue to promote the notion of unlimited economic growth, increased levels of production and consumption, and accelerating globalization, and disregard the social and environmental consequences. What should be at issue is not the pursuit of short-term economic gain but concern for long-term environmental and social health. Many science and technology curricula continue to promote the view that energy production based on oil or coal consumption, conventional hydro power and/or nuclear power are the only viable alternatives, dismissing the use of wind, solar, tidal and biomass energy production as 'cranky', economically disadvantageous or hopelessly futuristic. We should ask whose interests are served by failing to make students aware of alternatives and, therefore, much more likely to demand alternatives. Certainly not the interests of the wider global community or of the planet as a whole! Addressing alternative values rooted in ecofeminism and/or in the perspectives of Indigenous peoples (see discussion in chapter 8) can lay the groundwork for a serious consideration of alternative, more environmentally sustainable and appropriate technologies, which Budgett-Meakin (1992) characterizes as technologies that are sensitive to the immediate social, cultural and economic circumstances, capitalize on local skills, ingenuity and materials, make sparing and responsible use of non-renewable resources, and are controlled by the community, thereby resulting in increased self-respect and self-reliance. Adoption of appropriate technology entails rejection of any technology that violates our moral-ethical principles, exploits or disadvantages minority groups, or has adverse environmental impact[53]. The goal is the widespread adoption of a *humanized* technology: a technology more in harmony with people and with nature, a technology that is energy-conserving and materials-conserving[54]. In other words, a technology based on renewable resources and recycling, and on durability rather than in-built obsolescence and deterioration. If teachers are not introducing students to the principles of ecologically sound technologies they are implicated in an agenda that continues to exploit and impoverish the natural environment[55]. As Elshof

(2009a) puts it, "the future course of human technological development must be *'biosphere friendly'* or the world they help us create will not be *'homo sapiens friendly'*" (p. 133). Biosphere friendly technologies, which are often promoted initially by environmental movements and social activists, can sometimes grow into mainstream and very lucrative industries. Examples include energy generation through wind power, the now ready availability of pesticide-free and chemical fertiliser-free "organic foods" and the elevation of simple recycling practices into very elaborate waste management businesses.

A number of technology educators have outlined innovative approaches to technology education for sustainability – most notably, Petrina (1998, 2000a,b), Pavlova (2005, 2006, 2009) Elshof (2006, 2009a,b) and Williams (2009). Pavlova (2005) spells out her particular vision as follows:

> The involvement of students in democratic debates on the future outlines of technological development; development of their social and ecological sensitivities; avoiding orienting their solutions to the standard of business efficiency and profitability criteria only; helping them to distinguish real needs from desires; discussing the role of designed objects in the life of contemporary society; putting more emphasis on... the aesthetic aspects of life that can provide existential meaning for people; challenging the way people are manipulated through advertizing and cultivation of their desires; developing an active/creative attitude towards problems... teaching students to formulate problems (not only being involved in problem solving); challenging consumer oriented design; looking at design as one source of inspiration, not as a source of economic utility; and developing social responsibility. (p. 212)

Although discussion of such notions as industrial ecology, dematerialization, eco-efficiency and biomimicry[56] is outside the scope of this book, it should be noted that for Elshof (2009b) they are essential components of a new thrust in technology education. His priorities include: (i) fostering a sense of stewardship for the natural systems from which we draw resources; (ii) fostering an appreciation of inter-dependence among communities and their ecosystems; (iii) appreciating that the perspectives of "ecological economics" should be used to inform decision-making about technological developments; and (iv) developing an understanding of inter-generational responsibilities when designing technologies. The concept of "ecological footprint" (Rees, 1992) is a simple and helpful idea for students to use in examining why current lifestyles in the West/North are no longer ecologically sustainable (see endnote 51). So, too, the notion of a "social footprint", in the sense of impact on the social fabric of communities engaged in primary agricultural production (including disruption by the imposition of Western agribusiness practices), mining, oil production and various forms of manufacturing industry. The notion of social footprint includes wider issues relating to social justice and human rights, and specific issues relating to working conditions, trade union representation and worker safety. With respect to these matters, Petrina (2000b) urges us to present students with the following raft of questions: How much energy does the product or process require over its lifetime? Are renewable or sustainable resources used? And if not, why not? Are there less energy-intensive and longer-lived alternatives? Are local resources and labour used in extraction and manufacturing? If not, why not? What hazardous gaseous, aqueous and solid wastes are created and which ecologies and communities are exposed to this waste? Can waste be reduced through alternative materials and techniques? Are there any other health and safety hazards associated with the product or manufacturing process? How much energy is needed for transporting the materials and product? How easy is it to maintain and recycle the product? Who is responsible for maintenance? How much maintenance is required over its lifetime? How resource-intensive is this maintenance? What wastes are produced during maintenance? Can the product be recycled or reused at the end of its useful life? Do different materials offer better chances of resource recovery at the end of the product's like? Do we really need this product?

Drawing on the work of Layton (1993) and Petrina (1998), Leo Elshof (2006) refers to this approach as developing "product critique". The emphasis is on developing a form of technological connoisseurship that assists students in valuing, acquiring and using only those products that are ethically defensible, functional, durable and ecologically responsible. However, despite efforts we might make to answer these questions in ways that reflect sound eco-friendly design, it is clear that it will never add up to sustainability unless we substantially reduce production and consumption. Technology education needs to focus on reduction in production, consumption and waste. And reduction is essentially about a reordering of values. In McKibben's (2007) words, "We will have to make the biggest changes to our daily habits in generations – and the biggest change, as well, to our worldview, our sense of what constitutes progress" (p. 2). The kind of shift in values and worldview that will be needed is discussed in chapter 8.

One crucial element of the politicized science and technology education being advocated in this book is rejection of the notion of *technological determinism* that pervades so many science fiction stories and movies, and much popular writing on technology, that is, the idea that the pace and direction of technological change are inevitable and irresistible, that current technology determines future technology and human beings must adapt to its dictates (see Winner (1977), Smith & Marx (1994) and Wyatt (2008) for an extended discussion). Remarks such as "You can't stop progress", "It's inevitable" and "That's what we will have to get used to" are commonplace. They reveal a strong sense of individual and collective disempowerment and a feeling that technological change and development are in the hands of others, if not of technology itself. They also seem top absolve us from responsibility for the technologies we design, produce and use, and simultaneously provide an easy justification for employers who wish to downsize, redeploy workers or reorganize working practices. We should ask how this state of affairs has come about. In part, it is because we are often unaware of the alternatives that failed to make it to the marketplace. Given the huge teams of designers, engineers, manufacturers, marketing executives, advertisers and retailers involved in the technological-manufacturing enterprise, and the ways in which decision-making in large organizations is sub-divided and compartmentalized, this awareness may not even be available to those involved in it. As in post-academic or post-normal science (see chapter 4), very few participants will have a comprehensive overview of the design-manufacturing-marketing processes. In addition, powerful corporations and governments may have a vested interest in suppressing alternatives or even awareness of alternatives. Most importantly, according to Sclove (1995), "we lack a societal custom of subjecting technologies to critical democratic scrutiny. In the absence of a democratic technological politics, it has become customary to let combinations of distant bureaucracies or depersonalized market forces introduce technological systems that no single individual, group, or organization consciously chose or governs. This supports the false inference that because no particular person or group chose, the result is natural rather than a partly explicit, partly tacit social product" (p. 104). In part, it is this deficiency that the curriculum advocated in this book is designed to ameliorate. If our curriculum goal is the pursuit of critical scientific and technological literacy, we need to present students with a social and political critique capable of challenging the notion of technological determinism. We *can* control technology and its environmental and social impact, if we have the will and political literacy to do so. More significantly, we can *control the controllers* and redirect technology in such a way that adverse environmental impact is substantially reduced (if not entirely eliminated) and issues of freedom, equality and justice are kept in the forefront of discussion during the establishment of policy. We can, and should, promote the notion of *technological choice*, whereby citizens decide for themselves the kind of technology they will and will not use.

As discussed earlier in this book, and noted at some length by Bowers (2002), developments in science and technology are currently guided by the interests of elite groups whose members have little understanding *of*, little interest *in*, and take no responsibility *for* the culturally and environmentally transforming effects of unbridled development, especially on the already marginalized groups in society and the already compromised and fragile ecosystems. They have even less concern with how the changes precipitated by their drive to maximize production and consumption, create new technologies, and engage in ethically dubious science and biotechnology, will impact on the quality of life of future generations. Given past history, it is easy to imagine a situation in which the benefits of any chosen new technologies are appropriated disproportionately by the rich and powerful, further widening the gap between rich and poor, between the haves and have nots. It is here, in attending to these matters and opening students' eyes to alternatives, that *Futures Studies*, as envisaged by Cornish (1977), Slaughter (1988, 2005), Hicks and Holden (1995), Bell (1997), Gidley (1998), Hicks and Slaughter (1998), Jones (1998), Sardar (1999), Dator (2002), Hicks (2002), Gidley et al. (2004) and Lloyd and Wallace (2004), can be particularly effective. The guiding principles of Futures Studies or Futures Education set out by Cornish (1977, p. 223) are especially helpful: (i) the future is not fixed, but consists of a variety of alternatives among which we can choose; (ii) choice is necessary - refusing to choose is itself a choice; (iii) small changes through time can become major changes; (iv) the future world is likely to be different in many respects from the present world; (v) people are responsible for their future; the future doesn't just happen to them; and (vi) methods successful in the past may not necessarily work in the future, due to changed circumstances. In Newman's (2006) words, "If we are to engage in learning in order to act on and change our social or political world, then we need to examine who is trying to lay out our futures for us, who is telling us what we should and should not do, who is holding us back, and who is preventing us from acting effectively in our own and other's interests. We need to do our learning by identifying and naming the wielders of power, analysing the kinds of power they hold and, where we deem that power to be malign, examining the ways they use it" (p. 10). We need to find an acceptable balance between unbridled technological optimism that believes things will inevitably get better as new technological innovations come on stream and the debilitating technological pessimism that predicts an inevitable social collapse and environmental catastrophe. We need to break free from our past, plan for the future we want, and resist the future we don't want. Futures education helps students to clarify their hopes and fears about the future in order to move beyond passive forecasting about "how it is likely to be" to the generation of ideas about the sort of future they want as the basis for planning and action (see discussion in chapter 8)[57]. Futures Education also provides valuable opportunities for introducing students to the principles of participatory democracy (Holden, 1998) and provides a springboard for preparing students for individual and collective action (see chapter 9).

It is now a well-worn cliché to say that we live in a global village, and that what we do in our own backyard can impact quite significantly on people living elsewhere in the world. What is also true is that our actions now impact on the lives of future citizens. The ethics of previous generations have dealt almost exclusively with relations among people alive at the same time. In startling contrast, the pace of contemporary technological development makes an urgent issue of relations with those as yet unborn. In recognizing this new reality we would do well to heed the wisdom (both ancient and contemporary) of the First Nations people of North America.

> Treat the Earth well. It was not given to you by your parents; it was loaned to you by your children. We do not inherit the Earth from our ancestors, we borrow it from our children. (Native American Proverb)

> If you see things in terms of circles and cycles, and if you care about the survival of your children, then you begin to engage in commonsense practices. By trial and error, over thousands of years, perhaps, you can learn how to do things right. You learn to live in a way that keeps in mind, as native elders put it, seven generations. You ask yourself – as an individual and as a nation – how will the actions I take affect the seven generations to come? You do not think in terms of a four-year presidency or a yearly national budget, artificial creations that mean nothing positive in terms of the health of the Earth and the people. You say to yourself, what will happen if I cut these trees and the birds can no longer rest there? What will happen if I kill the female deer who has a fawn so that no animals survive to bring a new generation into the world? What will happen if I divert the course of this river or build a dam so that the fish and animals and plants downstream are deprived of water? What will happen if I put all the animals in my game bag? (Bruchac, 1993, pp. 12 & 13)

Generally, in the contemporary Western world our focus of attention, our thinking and planning, and our actions are geared to the present or the immediate future.

In Kyle's (1999) words, "We live in a world that has an obsession with the present. Society-at-large is behaving as though we have no children" (p. 13). It is a matter of some urgency that we change our focus. It is not too much of an exaggeration to say that the degree to which young citizens incorporate sustainable practices into their professional and personal lives will determine the quality of life for future generations. The curriculum has a crucial role to play in teaching them how to exercise the enormous power of technology responsibly, carefully and compassionately, and in the interests of *all* living creatures. Decisions about how life will be lived by our grandchildren are being made now. The time is long past when the notion of 'alternative technology' (less resource-greedy technology) can be equated with the somewhat pejorative term of 'alternative lifestyle'. The time is long past when one can assume that technological developments are universally beneficial (if, indeed, there ever was such a time). The time is long past when we can regard the planet's resources as inexhaustible and its capacity to absorb our waste products as unlimited. The time is long past when we can ignore the social and moral-ethical implications of our science and technology. If we are to ensure the quality of life of future citizens, those now in school need to get used to subjecting scientific and technological practice to close and intense critical scrutiny, they need to find ways to make their voices heard in the various decision-making forums, and they need to find ways to create the kind of future they want.

Nearly 20 years ago (July 30, 1993), the Supreme Court of the Philippines ruled that a group of children had the right to sue on behalf of future generations in relation to environmental protection, specifically the right to preserve "the rhythm and harmony of nature", including "the judicious disposition, utilization, management, renewal and conservation of the country's forests, minerals, land, waters, fisheries, wildlife, off-shore areas and other natural resources"[58]. The children, represented by the Philippines Ecological Network, a Manila-based environmental group, sought to stop the logging of the nation's dwindling old-growth rainforests, arguing that continued deforestation would cause irreparable injury to their generation and succeeding ones, and would violate their constitutional right to a balanced and healthy ecology. The Court ruled that the children did have the necessary legal standing to defend their generation's right to a sound environment and to seek to preserve that right for future generations. In underwriting the concept of intergenerational responsibility, the Court declared that every generation has a responsibility to the next generation "to preserve that rhythm and harmony for the full enjoyment of a balanced and healthful ecology". Sadly, the legislation doesn't seem to have stopped the voracious logging companies plundering the country's forests. Indeed, between 1990 and 2005, the country lost one third of its forest cover. The current deforestation rate is about 2%, much of it illegal (see http://rainforests. mongabay.com). Nevertheless, the principle is clear: citizens have an ethical responsibility towards the well-being of future generations and have the moral right to use that principle to oppose developments that might threaten it. Amongst the many other goals relating to social justice, the curriculum I am promoting seeks to encourage students to claim this right and exercise this responsibility.

TAKING A STANCE AND TAKING ACTION

The extent to which science and technology teachers are able and willing to challenge the pervasive rhetoric of consumerism and globalization, and encourage students to think and act differently, is a matter of personality, political outlook and values. At the very least, they need to give serious consideration to the message about globalization that is embedded in the science and technology curriculum they implement. At the very least, they should assist students in recognizing the links among consumerism, environmental degradation and social injustice. Thus far, the choice of most teachers seems to have been to reflect (if not actively promote) the values, attitudes, ways of thinking and social structures that have fostered the economic, social and political systems responsible for current social and environmental crises. It is a matter of considerable urgency that we change the way we think, and change the science and technology education that has for too long maintained a particular way of thinking.

Further to discussion in chapter 3 on the factors that encourage or discourage sociopolitical action, and so might influence teachers in taking action (or not) on the kind of curriculum they promote, Gardner and Stern (2002) state that whether or not people take action in accordance with their knowledge, beliefs, attitudes and values (or espoused values) depends to a large extent on their perception of the nature and extent of the barriers to action and the cost in terms of time, resources and inconvenience. Many people know about the health risks of smoking, excessive alcohol consumption, drug use and unprotected sex in ignorance of their partner's health status, but their behaviour doesn't always reflect that knowledge. Similarly, many people express concern about environmental degradation but they live their lives as if they don't know about it or don't care about it.

> The very danger signals that should rivet our attention, summon up the blood, and bond us in collective action, tend to have the opposite effect. They make us want to pull down the blinds and busy ourselves with other things. Our desire for distraction supports billion-dollar industries which tell us everything will be all right so long as we buy this car or that deodorant. We eat meat from factory-farmed animals and produce grown by agribusiness, knowing of the pesticides and hormones they contain, but preferring not to think they'll cause us harm. We buy clothes without noticing where they are made, preferring not to think of the sweatshops they may have come from. We don't bother voting, or if we do, we vote for candidates we may not believe will address the real problems, hoping against all previous experience that they will suddenly awaken and act boldly to save us. (Macy & Brown, 1998, p. 26)

Stanley Cohen draws a distinction between *literal denial* (simply asserting that something is untrue or didn't happen) and *interpretive denial* (accepting the facts but advancing an alternative interpretation or explanation). Even when they know, and even when they claim to care, some people may still turn a blind eye, look the other way or claim that "it's not my responsibility". Cohen (2001) refers to this kind of response as *implicatory denial*, illustrating it as follows: "The facts of children starving to death in Somalia, mass rape of women in Bosnia, a massacre in East Timor, homeless people in ours streets are recognized, but are not seen as psychologically disturbing or as carrying a moral imperative to act" (p. 9). Two closely related defence mechanisms are *rational distancing* and *delegation*. In the former, an individual is well aware of the issues and problems but no longer feels any emotions about them; in the latter, individuals seek to absolve themselves of responsibility by blaming others for the problems. It is also the case that people tend to compartmentalize their concerns and their behaviours, such that responsible and ethically sound behaviour in one context is not always indicative of responsible and ethically sound behaviour in another context, even when closely related. Thus, supposedly 'environmentally aware' and 'environmentally conscious' individuals who conserve water and power in the home, use recycled paper products, and only buy organic vegetables, may drive a gas-guzzling SUV and make frequent use of long-haul air travel solely for vacations, while those who buy a hybrid car and install energy saving heating and lighting in their homes may still dispose of highly toxic cleaning materials down the kitchen sink and may be unconcerned about factory farming and child labour in Third World sweatshops. Sandra Postel (1992) argues that the ubiquity and strength of these self-duping behaviours, denials and defensive mechanisms are such that *psychology*, just as much as science and technology, will determine the fate of the Earth.

> Action depends on overcoming denial, among the most paralysing of human responses. While it affects most of us in varying degrees, denial runs particularly deep among those with heavy stakes in the status quo... This denial can be as dangerous to a society and the natural environment as an alcoholic's denial is to his or her family. Because they fail to see the addiction as the principal threat to their own well-being, alcoholics often end up destroying their own lives. Rather than facing the truth, denial's victims choose slow suicide. In a similar way, by pursuing lifestyles and economic goals that ravage the environment, we sacrifice long-term health and well-being for immediate gratification – a trade-off that cannot yield a happy ending. (p. 4)

While I acknowledge the power and logic of Postel's argument, I feel that we need to go much further, and look at the reasons why self-deception is so common. We need to look closely at the emotions, values and aspirations that underpin our tendency to self-deceive. The simple point is that it is almost always much easier to proclaim that one cares about an issue than to do something about it, and to do it consistently, coherently and effectively. As Curtin (1991, 2007) reminds us, it is important to distinguish between caring *about* and caring *for*. Put simply, our values are worth nothing until we live them. Rhetoric and espoused values won't bring about social justice and won't save the planet. We must change our behaviour and we must take action to change the behaviour of others. A politicized ethic of care (caring *for*) entails active involvement in a local manifestation of a particular problem or issue, exploration of the complex sociopolitical context in which the problem/issue is located, attempts to resolve conflicts of interest, and a commitment to taking appropriate sociopolitical action, both individually and collectively (as discussed further in chapter 9). In the context of discussions in this chapter, are we prepared to publicize unethical and environmentally unsafe practices in local industries or lobby against international trade agreements like GATT and NAFTA that endanger ecosystems through their lax environmental protection legislation and undermine social and economic justice for many of the world's marginalized peoples? Are we prepared to boycott companies that pollute, exploit cheap labour and infringe worker rights? Are we prepared to agitate for more critical scrutiny of advertizing and marketing techniques (especially those directed at the very young) and to protest at local ports about the global arms trade and the exportation of toxic waste to Third World countries? Are we prepared to set up blockades or conduct vigils to protest or disrupt logging of old growth forest, mining operations in environmentally sensitive areas, and construction of yet more motorways and shopping malls in our dwindling countryside? Are we prepared to encourage our students to take such actions, now or in the future?

The point I am trying to make here, somewhat indirectly, is that it is future citizens' moral character and moral courage that will ultimately determine our success in securing the well-being of the planet and the establishment of a more socially-just society. Science and technology education has a key role in building that moral character and fostering the courage and commitment to fight for change. It is significant, then, that Zeidler et al. (2002) emphasize that the SSI-oriented approach prioritizes "the ethical dimensions of science, the moral reasoning of the child, and the emotional development of the student" (p. 344). Chapter 7 focuses on ways to foster moral reasoning.

STRATEGIES, RESPONSIBILITIES AND OUTCOMES

Interest in a particular SSI can be stimulated by means of newspaper and magazine clippings, items from Websites, photographs, movies, radio and television clips, stories, poems, personal oral accounts, anecdotes and testimony (including those provided by classroom visitors), biographies, paintings, cartoons, museum and science centre visits, field trips, site visits, and so on. The chosen issue can be pursued by means of library or Web-based research, whole or small group discussions, debates and 'Town Hall meetings', use of critical incidents and case studies (including consultation of the primary research literature), project work, problem-based learning, games, role play, drama, simulations and interactive media. Two points can be made. First, we need to pay heed to the old phrase "Horses for Courses". An approach that is well-suited to one issue may be ill-suited to another. Teachers need to look carefully at the strengths and weaknesses of particular approaches in relation to particular SSI and particular groups of students. Second, we need to ensure variety of approach. Almost any approach can become tedious and unproductive if over-used.

Conventional debates, which require students to speak in their own voices and express their own views, can be enormously beneficial in helping students to clarify and articulate their views, criticize the views of others, accept criticism, and collaborate with others to reach consensus. However, they can also be intimidating and stressful for some students. Speaking in someone else's voice and expressing someone else's views, as in role-plays, can reduce stress and ensure greater involvement. And, of course, can be very effective in helping to build empathy with those most impacted by a particular SSI or by environmental degradation Paradoxically, the distancing afforded by the fictional aspects of drama and role-play can enable students to reflect more thoroughly and more securely on the basic underlying issues, and can highlight perspectives that would otherwise remain hidden (Simonneaux, 2001; 2008). For example, to investigate concerns about potential threats to health from mobile phone use, Albe (2008a,b) cast her students in the role of expert witnesses in the trial of an employer being sued by an employee for health problems allegedly caused by excessive mobile phone use in the work place. In like manner, Jiménez-Aleixandre and Pereiro-Muñoz (2002, 2005) created a simulated consultancy activity focused on a wetlands environmental management problem. The activity, in which 38 Grade 11 students participated, involved a research-based fieldtrip and the preparation of reports dealing with technical issues relating to laying a network of pipelines within the wetlands area to drain effluent from local housing, an industrial site and a granite quarry. Reports also addressed the economic benefits of new employment opportunities and some relevant conservation issues. The activity culminated in interviews with two outside "experts": the engineer who had developed the teaching materials and the President of an environmental activist group. The authors report that the students' reasoning and the arguments they generated were very similar to those produced by the experts, with good use of conceptual understanding, awareness of economic considerations and sound environmental values. Watts et al. (1997) describe a role-play activity in which students (in Brazil and the United Kingdom) undertook a "Commission of Inquiry" to establish the needs, costs, benefits and risks associated with the construction and operation of nuclear power stations. The students also role-played the making of a television documentary focused on a nuclear accident that had occurred in the city of Goiania, in Brazil, in the late 1980s. For a project focused on environmental considerations in industrial planning, Dori and Herscovitz (1999) employed an open-ended PBL approach in which students were assigned the role of experts in a jigsaw-based approach. Flores and Tobin (2003) describe an approach in which they made use of the primary research literature relating to the environmental impact of GM plants, augmented by study guides to assist students in interpreting the often complex and inconclusive science. The study guides included essays written by the researchers as exemplars of how to make effective use of published material to formulate a personal viewpoint. In a role-play based on US Senate hearings on global climate change, Harwood et al. (2002) randomly assigned preservice elementary school teachers the role of a Senator or a representative of one of six special interest groups: the Sierra Club, Greenpeace, the US Environmental Protection Agency, the California State Governor's Office, the Center for Disease Control and the Greening Earth Society (a group, funded by the mining industry, that regards increasing carbon dioxide levels in the atmosphere as beneficial – see www.greeningtheearthsociety.com) The authors report that the research in which students engaged to fulfil the assigned roles had substantial impact on their understanding of climate change. Moreover, the experience of role-play (for many, it was a first time experience) made them enthusiastic to use this approach in their own classrooms. Ballantyne et al. (2001a) describe an approach using De Bono's (1992) "six thinking hats" approach[59] to study a local environmental problem. Following a teacher-led investigation of air pollution attributed to heavy traffic flow in the area adjacent to the school, students formed into small groups to address an environmental problem of their choice: air pollution, noise pollution, water pollution, graffiti, urban development, declining koala numbers, litter, animal abuse or the problems caused by stray dogs. Students considered how they felt about the issue/problem (red hat), gathered pertinent information from a wide variety of primary and secondary sources (white hat), considered the pros and cons of the various solutions proposed by scientists, politicians, community groups and environmental action groups (yellow and black hats) and formulated alternative solutions (green hat). Throughout the activity, the students kept log books, and at the end they compiled an evaluation report and a set of recommendations (blue hat).

Kolstø (2000) describes an approach to SSI based on the Consensus Conferences established by the Danish Technology Council in the 1990s to involve lay people more closely in policy making[60]. In the school version, which he calls *consensus projects*, students are divided into a number of 'expert groups' and one 'lay group'. The task of the former is to access a wide range of sources from which to gather information, interpretive knowledge and opinion on a designated aspect of a particular SSI, preferably of a controversial nature (GM foods, stem cell research, cloning, recycling, location of waste dumps and nuclear power generation have all been addressed). Each expert group presents its findings and recommendations to the lay group and defends its data and conclusions against criticisms from fellow students and the class teacher. Once the lay group has listened to the reports of the various expert groups, its members seek to reach consensus in an open debate, with the other students acting as participant audience. During both these phases the teacher's role is to ask questions, seek clarification and stimulate debate and critical thinking. Next, the lay group writes a report outlining its conclusions and rationale. Kolstø argues that reaching consensus is desirable for pedagogical purposes, principally for stimulating the debate and argument that a straight vote on pros and cons would preempt. If the lay group cannot reach consensus, its members make a clear statement concerning aspects of the issue on which they agree and disagree, and give their reasons for doing so. Each group produces a final report that takes account of issues raised in the debate.

Multimedia materials and Internet-based activities are particularly well suited to a curriculum focus on SSI. Among the best known examples is the Web-based Inquiry Science Environment (WISE), developed by Bell and Linn (2000), which enables students to access and investigate a wide range of SSI, many of a controversial nature. For example, Seethaler and Linn (2004) report the favourable impact of this approach on students' ability to argue the pros and cons of genetically modified foods. Furberg and Lundvigsen (2008) have done similar work addressing some social and moral-ethical aspects of genetics. Barab et al. (2007) report on a fascinating study in which elementary school students (in Grade 4) collect and interpret data in a search for possible causes of a decline in fish stocks in "Taiga Park", a river and lake system created within a multi-user virtual environment known as Quest Atlantis. Using this data, students are required to produce a solution to the problem that balances the scientific evidence they have collected with sociopolitical and economic considerations related to the logging industry (which generates income for the park and provides employment for local people) and the rights and traditions of the Indigenous people living within the park (who are currently not required to follow park protocols on their own land). In *Mine Games*, a 3-D simulation game located at Science World in Vancouver, visitors are introduced to a number of people with views on the proposal to begin mining operations in the neighbourhood of the West Coast township of "Grizzly", including the Mayor, a cross section of the local community, a representative of the local First Nations community, executives from the mining company, local business people and various others with an interest in the issue. After familiarizing themselves with key issues, visitors sit in a tiered debating chamber to discuss their views and reach a decision about whether a mine should be built, and if so, what would be the safest, most economically viable, most beneficial to the local community, and most environmentally sound development. Participation in this phase of the simulation experience, which is known as *Hot Seat*, is facilitated by a mediator with access to a range of interactive multimedia resources. As Pedretti (2004) reports, emotions can run very high as visitors come to identify with particular stakeholders.

On occasions, there are opportunities for students to participate directly in an ongoing SSI, as in Pedretti's (1997) example of the "septic tank problem" (see chapter 9) and Wolf-Michael Roth's work over several years with the residents of the Central Saanich community as they struggled to improve water quality and resolve environmental problems in their area (Roth & Lee, 2002, 2004; Roth et al., 2004; Roth, 2009a,b). Issues arising from this kind of direct action constitute a major part of the discussion in chapter 9.

DISCUSSION, DEBATE AND GROUP WORK

In traditional classrooms, all classroom talk tends to be orchestrated by the teacher. Students speak only when they have been granted permission to do so (usually in response to a raised hand) or when previously nominated by the teacher. There is little or no talk between and among students, and only rarely is talk initiated by students. In general, the teacher decides the focus for discussion and is the final arbiter of what views should be accepted. Such a situation is not conducive to the exploration of ideas and the engagement in criticism and argument that constitutes the SSI-focused and action-oriented approach advocated in this book. Rather, students need direct experience of critique and negotiation, the opportunity to construct, discuss and debate the merits of their ideas with others, and a substantial measure of responsibility for their own learning.

Barnes (1988) distinguishes two kinds of talk, located at opposite ends of a continuum: (i) *exploratory* talk, through which students articulate, consider and reorganize their ideas (in effect, "listening to themselves thinking", as Thier and Daviss (2002) put it); and (ii) *presentational* talk, through which they report to others in a more formal way on what they currently understand or have recently learned. Mercer (1995, 2000) identifies three distinctive categories of student talk in collaborative groups. First, *disputational* talk: an exchange of opposing views in which disagreements are emphasized. Second, *cumulative* talk: students build positively but uncritically on what others say. Third, his particular definition of *exploratory* talk: students engage critically with each other and support each other in collaborative reconstruction of ideas. Mercer et al. (1999) further define exploratory talk as "that in which partners engage critically but constructively with each other's ideas. Statements and suggestions are sought and offered for joint consideration. These may be challenged and counter-challenged, but challenges are justified and alternative hypotheses are offered. In exploratory talk, *knowledge is made publicly accountable* and *reasoning is visible in the talk*" (p. 97, emphasis in original)[61]. There is still a crucial role for the teacher as scientific expert, guide, critical friend and facilitator. First, laying down guidelines and rules concerning how to participate successfully in group discussions: how to argue and negotiate, how to listen, how to give and receive criticism, and so on. Second, pushing students to ascend the hierarchy of talk categories (disputational, cumulative and exploratory). Third, modelling what constitutes a good argument and providing clear advice on how to present a carefully reasoned and well-articulated position. At times, teachers may need to solicit ideas, guide students in appraising, comparing and contrasting them, and assist them in resolving differences and incompatibilities. From time to time they may need to supply additional data, ideas and perspectives. It is important that teachers point out any deficiencies in student reasoning. Ford (2008a) expresses this position particularly well: "The teacher has a voice, and a privileged one, but it is through the role of critiquer that the students themselves are expected to play and are learning to play. Thus, the teacher's critiques should function not only to identify errors, but also to model the kind of thing that students are expected to do with their peers' and with their own knowledge claims" (p. 420). Hogan (1999) has developed an intervention strategy for Grade 8 students called *Thinking Aloud Together*, which aims to help *individuals* understand the nature of collaborative reasoning, the difficulties it sometimes presents, and the tentative nature of its conclusions, and to help *groups of students* plan, monitor, regulate, reflect on, and evaluate their activities. In Hogan's study, the experimental group using this approach did achieve a better understanding of the nature of collaborative reasoning and were able to articulate the processes and procedures in which they had engaged, though they were no more successful than the control group in applying their conceptual knowledge to a novel situation or using scientific reasoning to address an ill-defined problem.

According to Kim and Song (2006), group discussion often proceeds through four stages, regardless of the topic: focusing, exchanging, debating and closing. The first priority is to establish the focus for the discussion and decide on procedures to be adopted. Next, students exchange information, identify gaps in their knowledge and seek to establish appropriate frames of reference. The all-important third phase, in which students criticize the views of others and respond to criticisms of their own ideas can sometimes be curtailed by the desire to effect closure and signal to the teacher that the task has been completed. Clearly, the specific purpose of any class activity should be made explicit, groups should be encouraged to remain 'on task' (while recognizing the importance of 'social talk' in preparing the ground for effective discussion) and time limits should be made clear well in advance. It is important that groups reach an effective and explicit closure to the discussion, though not a premature one. Too often, discussion tails off, becomes fragmented and unclear, or is abruptly stopped by the bell or by teacher intervention. Above all, there must be *authentic* discussion in which the content of the discussion is problematized in some way, students express their views in their own way, diversity of views is encouraged, and the strength of feelings is acknowledged by the teacher. It is crucial that teachers also provide guidance, point students in the direction of additional data or alternative ideas, introduce new ways of thinking and give guidance on appropriate use of specialized language. Tal and Kedmi (2006) sum up these and similar moves on the part of the teacher as "creating a thinking culture". In a "thinking classroom", they say, the teacher stimulates the students to do thoughtful work by constantly switching between individual, small group and whole group activities, asking questions, demanding reasons and evidence for assertions, ensuring that students articulate their position, and so on. In reiterating the importance of creating opportunities for both individual and group work, Peter Taylor (in Taylor et al., 2006) notes that creative thought is often the outcome of personal solitary thought and reflection on it, but the ideas generated can be clarified, enriched and developed, sometimes in ways entirely unanticipated by the originator of the idea, by critique and argument within a group. These group activities can also lead to rejection of the idea, of course. Taylor's (2002) guidelines for teachers wishing to teach critical thinking include items such as the following: help students to generate new questions about issues and raise alternative perspectives; acknowledge and mobilize the diversity within the group, including diversity with respect to intellectual, emotional, situational and relational factors; help students to "clear mental space" so that thoughts below the surface can emerge; teach students to listen well; support them as they journey into the unfamiliar and confront the disconcerting; address feelings of fear, apprehension and uncertainty; be confident, patient and persistent. The impact of students' personal experiences, feelings, attitudes, values and moral-ethical views on their reasoning and decision-making about SSI are addressed later in the chapter.

It has been argued that conversation tools such as online discussion forums and email can be used to help students build effective and supportive learning communities as they seek to clarify and establish shared understanding. Clearly there is much scope for research here. However, discussion of technology-supported discussion and communication tools is well outside the scope of this book. For discussion of such matters, see Mercer and Wegerif (1999), Jonassen & Land (2000), Hill and Hannafin (2001), Reiser (2002, Andriessen et al. (2003), Veerman (2003), Bell (2004), Nussbaum et al. (2004), Seethaler and Linn (2004), de Jong (2006), Andriessen (2007), Clark and Sampson (2007, 2008), Clark et al. (2007, 2008) and Furberg and Ludvigsen (2008).

Whatever approach is taken, it needs to be remembered that discussion, debate and argument can sometimes push students into making up their minds on an issue prematurely and can be impacted very substantially (and not always productively) by social dynamics within the group or the class as a whole. It is crucial, therefore, as noted in chapter 2, that teachers establish an appropriate classroom climate for open and respectful discussion and establish firm and fair rules of conduct - for example, everyone is given time and opportunity to express their views, and participants are not subject to constraints that may prevent them from stating their views. Although Naylor et al. (2007) note some situations in which teachers are better advised to maintain an arms-length approach with regard to organization of discussion procedures, it seems beyond dispute that students need to know that there is an appropriate way to *present* an argument, *listen* to a point of view and *respond* to another student's opinions. They need to know that there is an appropriate way to criticize, accept criticism, argue and reach consensus. In short, students must be sufficiently interested to participate, and there needs to be a safe, trusting, non-threatening and supportive environment in which all students feel confident to contribute and allow each other sufficient 'space' in which to talk, especially when their ideas are tentative and hesitantly expressed. It is important that any feelings of injustice or hurt are dealt with promptly and effectively. Both Solomon (1998) and Boulter and Gilbert (1995) warn teachers against using a confrontational or oppositional approach, urging the adoption of "inclusive language" that (i) encourages sharing of personal thoughts and experiences, rather than demonstrating one's knowledge and skill, and (ii) emphasizes listening, 'creating space' for others and acknowledging all contributions.

As Kutnick and Rogers (1994) note, there can be all manner of social tensions that inhibit effective group work. Groups can become polarized, cliques can develop, individuals can be marginalized or even harassed by others, and some students can become "freeloaders" who rarely contribute but continue to claim the benefits of group efforts. Interactions are profoundly influenced by the status and power of the participants and their conceptions of themselves, the teacher and other students. Those of high academic or social status tend to speak more frequently, and more confidently and assertively. They command more attention and their ideas are more frequently utilized, both by the students and by the teacher (Bianchini, 1997; Moje & Shepardson, 1998). Cornelius and Herrnkohl (2004) note that even in the most open and democratic classroom environments, students can "develop alliances against more 'powerless' groups, namely, students of lower social and economic status" (p. 470). Bianchini (1997, 1999) presents some disturbing evidence of students who are perceived as low status by their peers being denied access to materials and excluded from group discussions. Alarmingly, these are predominantly students from groups that have historically under-achieved in science and are generally under-served by science education, that is, in the American context in which Bianchini works, female students, Latinos/Latinas and African Americans. Whomever students perceive as having ownership of a particular idea or point of view (teacher, textbook author, some adult or peer, or themselves) influences their response to it. It might also affect their future attitude towards the person expressing it. Hatano and Inagaki (1991) note that effective discussion can sometimes be derailed because some students tend to show solidarity with their friends, supporting their ideas regardless of merit. Varelas et al. (2008) comment as follows: "While some children are seen as 'smart', others are seen as 'popular', and their voice is heard in different ways. At times, children are not willing to contradict each other, their ideas are weakly held or the bonds of their friendship are stronger than the power of their ideas" (p. 92). However, these researchers also note that some students act as mediators, making spaces for those with less power.

Clearly, the social and interpersonal skills that students bring to the group can be just as influential as their scientific knowledge and cognitive abilities. Individuals will vary enormously in terms of what they can and are willing to contribute: conceptual knowledge, NOS knowledge, other beliefs, values, attitudes, commitments and dispositions, cognitive skills, metacognitive knowledge and skills, motivational attributes, organizational and regulatory abilities. Groups will be effective to the extent that group members are able and willing to contribute and to utilize the contributions of others. In any discussion group, there will be students who look to dominate and exercise control, those who rarely if ever contribute, those who slavishly accept the views of socially prominent or intellectually capable individuals, and those who seem unable to listen to others or consider their views. Hogan (1998) identified a number of roles consistently adopted by particular students during discussion activities – in her example, discussions focused on model building.

Four roles promoted the group's reasoning processes and led to successful outcomes: promoter of reflection; contributor of content knowledge; creative model builder; and mediator of group interactions and ideas (Hogan's terminology). Four roles had little or no impact, or had an inhibiting effect: promoter of acrimony; promoter of distraction; promoter of simple task completion or unreflective acceptance of ideas; and reticent participant. In the context of SSI decision-making, Ratcliffe (1997, 1999a,b) identifies the key role of students whom she refers to as *information-vigilant*. These students are particularly adept at using information to clarify the advantages and/or disadvantages of particular options.

DEALING WITH THE AFFECTIVE AND SOCIAL DIMENSIONS OF LEARNING

Before leaving this discussion it is important to be reminded that changing one's mind is not always a simple, straightforward business. There can be very significant emotional, attitudinal and social barriers to be overcome, and there can be quite severe emotional and social consequences attending a change of position (see discussion in chapter 2). Both teachers and students need to recognize that each of us, whether student, teacher, scientist or whatever, is a member of a number of sub-cultures, and that we necessarily align with particular views and adopt particular positions with respect to social and cultural conflicts that extend far beyond the classroom, but may have classroom manifestations. Building on previous work by Burbules and Rice (1992), Levinson (2006) identifies what he calls the "communicative virtues" essential to the thorough and effective consideration of controversial issues: patience, tolerance, respect for differences, attentive and thoughtful listening, openness, honest self-expression, adherence to agreed procedures, freedom of expression and equality of opportunity. Successful enactment of these communicative virtues requires that all parties consider them desirable, and requires that teachers make good decisions about intervention. It is important for teachers to consider very carefully when and to what extent they will intervene to raise perspectives that may be absent from class discussion and may not be reflected in the materials currently being utilized - for example, the views of particular ethnic, political and religious minority groups, perspectives of gays and lesbians, concerns of disabled and socio-economically disadvantaged groups.

As noted above, and in chapter 2, the much more open form of learning being advocated in this book can be catastrophically undermined if students don't have the necessary language and social skills to participate appropriately. It can also be catastrophically undermined if learners are unable to deal with the complex and powerful emotions raised by consideration of SSI. Students who have been used to traditional curriculum orientations will be familiar with science being presented as entirely rational, systematic, analytical, depersonalized and unemotional, with few opportunities for exploring feelings, emotions and sentiments[62]. When confronted with an SSI-oriented approach, such students may be surprised and disconcerted by their emotional responses to controversial SSI and environmental issues. They may need considerable support in dealing with their feelings. If learners lack the capacity to handle emotional upsets or to deal with their impulses, it becomes difficult for them to engage in learning activities, evaluate different options, apply mature and reasoned judgement, and take responsibility for synthesizing their views. It is here that notions of *emotional intelligence, emotional literacy* and *emotional competence* can be helpful (Goleman, 1985, 1996, 1998; Saarni, 1990; Salovey & Meyer, 1990; Salovey & Shayter, 1997; Steiner, 1997; Sharp, 2001; Matthews et al., 2004a,b; Zeidner et al., 2009). Although these three terms are closely related, Matthews (2005) chooses to draw a distinction between the individualistic nature of emotional intelligence and the strongly social nature of emotional literacy. Thus, he argues, emotional intelligence refers to an individual's ability to perceive, describe, appraise and express emotions, understand emotions and emotional knowledge, access and/or generate appropriate feelings when they facilitate thought, or manage them productively when they might inhibit, while emotional literacy is the capacity to be receptive to a wide range of feelings, empathize with others, and continuously monitor the emotional climate in which one is located. Emotional competence may be seen as an amalgam of the two. In general, the goal of emotional literacy is awareness and management of one's emotions in both joyful and stressful situations, the confidence and self-assurance to understand one's own emotions, and the capacity to deal with them in a positive and intentional way. It is closely related to notions of self-awareness, self-image, self-esteem and sense of identity, and less directly with self-efficacy and agency (ideas to which I will return in chapters 8 and 10). It is also worth noting the close relationship between emotional literacy and moral-ethical reasoning. As Val Plumwood (1999) observes, "moral reasoning requires some version of empathy, putting ourselves in the other's place, seeing the world to some degree from the perspective of the other with needs and experiences both similar to and different from our own" (p. 75).

Hochschild (1983, 1990, 1993) and Zembylas (2004a,b) use the term *emotional labour* to describe the efforts that teachers make to monitor, regulate and manage both their own emotions and those of their students, while Wood et al. (1976) talk about "frustration control", "stress reduction" and "face saving when students make mistakes" as *scaffolding* activities. Following their lead, the definition of scaffolding adopted in chapter 2 could be extended to include all strategies to foster constructive emotions and/or reduce unconstructive ones, effect a shift from a concern with performance goals to a learning or mastery orientation, generate good learning strategies, foster self-sufficiency beliefs and improved self-esteem. These moves may widen the *zone of proximal development* (Vygotsky, 1978) by providing students with the confidence they need to sustain their learning efforts during difficult tasks, as well as stimulating a willingness to engage with these tasks in the first place (Hodson, 1998a). Roseik (2003) identifies two approaches to emotional scaffolding: *implicit* and *explicit*. Implicit approaches involve teachers in fostering a constructive emotional response to the topic by associating it with something students are likely to find familiar, interesting or enjoyable, or trying to avoid triggering an unconstructive emotional response to the topic that could be a consequence of approaching it in an unfamiliar, unpleasant or disconcerting context. Explicit approaches seek to foster a constructive emotional response to a topic by predicting its occurrence, rationalizing it, and giving students reasons for why the effort to learn is going to be worthwhile for them even when emotionally demanding. In addition, they seek to undermine an unconstructive emotional response by drawing attention to these emotions, setting them in a wider context, and perhaps reassuring students that matters are "not so bad as they seem at present". While it is too elaborate, systematic, algorithmic and prescriptive for my taste, Astleitner's (2000) so-called FEASP approach includes one or two useful ideas among its twenty strategies for managing emotions of fear, envy, anger, sympathy and pleasure, including development of anger management skills, encouraging openness and honesty about one's feelings, strengths and weaknesses, establishment of peer support groups, fostering a learning orientation in preference to a performance orientation[63], using criterion referencing rather than norm referencing for assessment and evaluation purposes, allowing a substantial measure of learner self-determination and self-direction, and frequent use of drama, role-play, and the like. Notwithstanding the problems that teachers will sometimes have to deal with, I would argue that it is the emotional component of SSI that make this kind of teaching and learning so satisfying and so valuable a part of education for citizenship. In the words of Rachel Carson (1965), "It is not half so important to *know* as to *feel*. If facts are the seeds that later produce knowledge and wisdom, then the emotions and the impressions of the senses are the fertile soil in which the seeds must grow" (p. 45).

A wide variety of pedagogical strategies can be used to engage students' interest, personalize and contextualize learning, provoke emotion, generate controversy, stimulate dialogue and debate, promote reflection and, generally, facilitate the affective and social components of learning. For example, a teaching unit on food and nutrition can be extended well beyond the usual scientific matters to include wider health issues such as body image, obesity and anorexia, the fast food industry, advertizing, packaging, transportation issues, waste and pollution, genetically modified crops, industrialized farming, globalization, sustainability, the politics of surplus production, and the attitudes of Western governments to starvation in the Third World. Case studies could be developed to address such value-laden and emotionally charged issues as euthanasia, stem cell research, xenotransplantation, animal experiments, conservation measures for endangered species, factory farming and feral animal management. For example, Buntting and Jones (2009) describe the use of Web-based multimedia resources addressing various strategies for dealing with brushtail possums, which constitute a serious conservation issue in New Zealand. Possums were introduced (from Australia) some 70 years ago in an unsuccessful effort to establish a fur trade; they have adapted well to many New Zealand habitats, have no natural predators, compete with native fauna for food, prey directly on many native birds and insects (many of which are endangered) and spread bovine tuberculosis (at great cost to cattle and deer farmers). Possible solutions, including shooting, trapping, poisoning and all manner of biological controls such as introduced predators, spreading of possum-specific parasites and viruses, and attempts to reduce possum fertility, raise a raft of important ethical and consequential environmental issues for student discussion. Some related ethical issues are discussed in chapter 7, while discussion in chapter 8 raises the question of what counts as *pro-environmental behaviour* and/or *pro-environmental action*. In New Zealand, measures taken to reduce the population of possums could be interpreted as pro-environmental action because they seek to protect and conserve native species. In contrast, possums are protected as a native species in Australia, and in Tasmania are considered an endangered native species. In this context, pro-environmental actions include the careful and systematic monitoring of the number and location of possums, efforts to reduce the population of foxes (an introduced species and a significant predator on possums), and the building and installing of nesting boxes (Birdsall, 2011).

There is abundant evidence of the power of television, movies, drama, role-play, multi-media materials and language-based activities of various kinds to stimulate interest in an issue, provoke an emotional response, present alternative positions, challenge values and precipitate debate. In the words of Alasdair MacIntyre (1981), "I can only answer the question, 'What am I to do?' if I can answer the prior question 'Of what story or stories do I find myself a part?'... Deprive children of stories and you leave them unscripted, anxious stutterers in their actions as in their words. Hence there is no way to give us an understanding of any society, including our own, except through the stock of stories which constitute its initial dramatic resources" (p. 216). Stories juxtapose different opinions, voices and perspectives, encouraging the reader (or listener) to deliberate, evaluate and decide on where they stand, or to adopt a different stance. Through stories, and especially through drama, students are stimulated to address issues and events from the perspectives of others, explore and develop understanding, establish new relationships and consolidate existing ones. In other words, engaging with narrative is as much a way of knowing ourselves as it is a way of understanding the views of others. Improvised drama enables students to enrich these explorations with personal experiences, thoughts and linguistic preferences (O'Neil & Lambert, 1983; Henry, 2000; Schneider et al., 2006). Poetry is an especially powerful means of generating emotional response and provoking the shift of perspective that Girod et al. (2003) call "re-seeing" (see chapter 9). In the words of Percy Bysshe Shelley (1927): "It reproduces the common universe of which we are portions and it purges from our inward sight the film of familiarity which obscures from us the wonder of our being. It compels us to feel that which we perceive and to imagine that which we know. It creates anew the universe after it had been annihilated in our minds by the recurrence of impressions blunted by reiteration" (p. 137). In writing about the power of stories to deal with complex ideas and emotions, Martha Nussbaum (1990) comments: "With respect to certain elements of human life, the terms of the novelist's art are alert winged creatures, perceiving where the blunt terms of ordinary speech, or of abstract theoretical discourse, are blind, acute where they are obtuse, winged where they are dull and heavy" (p. 5). Encouraging students to write poetry and stories creates opportunities for them to explore their ideas, express them in less formal language, manipulate and critique them by placing them in the mouths of others, explore ambiguity and uncertainty, wrestle with dilemmas and, crucially, express the way they feel about their ideas and the ideas of others. Watts (1989, 2001, 2005) and Watts and Barber (1997) have written at length about the educational potential of poetry, and Watts (2000) has complied a collection of poems written by students and teachers[64]. Hipkins (2004) describes an innovative way of engaging affect, empathy and an ethic of care and concern through a combination of games and reflective narrative writing.

However, the greatest power is located in authentic experiences. What an individual experiences first hand, warts and all, can be extraordinarily effective in engaging levels of student attention that can often be maintained sufficiently strongly over time to lead to activist behaviour in later life. A site visit to an intensive poultry farm, a veal-rearing unit or an abattoir, for example, can have a profound and emotionally disturbing, but intellectually powerful impact on students' views of our relationship with animals. As Bowd (1989) observes, "Few members of a junior high school class presented with literature and a lecture on the cruelty of battery hen farming will act to change battery hen farming, although they may express a negative attitude toward the practice. Consider, however, a group that visits such a facility, examines alternative egg producing arrangements, and in this context is required to stop eating battery eggs for a week as part of a project... Their knowledge is less likely to remain inert, and will be accessed and applied to relevant situations outside the classroom context" (p. 56).

SOME RESEARCH FINDINGS

The first point that should be made relates to the extensive evidence that SSI-oriented teaching promotes conceptual understanding (Pedretti, 1999; Zohar & Nemet, 2002; Dawson & Schibeci, 2003; Walker & Zeidler, 2003; Sadler & Zeidler, 2005; Applebaum et al., 2006; Sadler & Fowler, 2006; Yager et al., 2006; Barab et al., 2007; Keselman et al., 2007; Albe, 2008b; Furberg & Ludvigsen, 2008; Norris et al., 2009; Klosterman & Sadler, 2010), the development of NOS understanding (Zeidler et al., 2002, 2009; Tal & Hochberg, 2003; Sadler et al., 2004; Celik & Bayrakçeken, 2006; Khishfe & Lederman, 2006; Lewis et al., 2006; Walker & Zeidler, 2007; Castano, 2008) and the refinement of argumentation skills (Yerrick, 2000; Dori et al., 2003; Kolstø, 2006; McNeil et al., 2006; Tal & Kedmi, 2006; Zeidler & Sadler, 2008a; Fowler et al., 2009; Dawson & Venville, 2010)[65]. It provides opportunities for students to attach personal meaning to science and to connect classroom science to everyday life, thus providing strong motivation and interest for students (Dori et al., 2003; Bennett et al., 2005; Harris & Ratcliffe, 2005; Bulte et al., 2006; Parchmann et al., 2006; Sadler et al., 2007; Albe, 2008a; Zeidler et al., 2009; Dawson, 2010). The critique, argument and debate involved in confronting SSI can stimulate reconceptualization and a re-ordering of ideas, although there are situations in which the conceptual complexities of SSI can cause students to become confused and uncertain of their understanding (Levinson, 2003; Parchmann et al., 2006). And there are situations in which students seek to deploy inappropriate and poorly understood science (Schweizer & Kelly, 2001). In Walker and Zeidler's (2007) study, students developed NOS understanding through the SSI-oriented curriculum activities but were unable to deploy it effectively in subsequent debate. However, despite these one or two unfortunate occurrences, there are some good, strong arguments for using SSI, quite apart from the education for citizenship motivation discussed in chapter 1. SSI-oriented teaching also requires students to confront values and helps them to develop social awareness, empathy, compassion and moral sensitivity (Zeidler & Sadler, 2008a,b; Fowler et al., 2009). Moral sensitivity and associated concepts such as moral reasoning, moral commitment and moral courage will be discussed in chapter 7.

Ratcliffe (1997, 1999a,b) reports that students' ability to form opinions and make decisions about SSI is substantially enhanced by using the following 6-step framework, especially when sufficient time and opportunities are provided for peer group discussion and teachers provide appropriate and timely support and encouragement.

- Identify possible positions on the issue.
- Identify or develop criteria for comparing alternatives.
- Clarify the available information in relation to the criteria.
- Consider the advantages and disadvantages of each option in light of the designated criteria.
- Make a carefully considered and informed decision between/among the options.
- Reflect on the decision-making process, identifying any possible improvements or additional considerations.

The success of this approach, or any other approach, depends on certain conditions being met. For example, as argued in chapter 2, common sense would seem to indicate that content knowledge is crucial, and that those who know more about the topic/issue under consideration will be better positioned to construct arguments, criticize arguments, engage in argumentation, and reach decisions, despite Deanna Kuhn's (1991) assertion that "a large sophisticated knowledge base in a content domain does not determine the quality of thinking skills used in the domain" (p. 39). Three points should be made in response to Kuhn's seemingly ludicrous proposition. First, there is abundant evidence to the contrary, as discussed in chapter 2. Second, students may experience difficulty in deciding what scientific knowledge is relevant to the situation under consideration or may have difficulty in transferring knowledge from an academic context focusing on abstract ideas to a context involving practical, real world issues. Indeed, as Layton et al. (1993) have shown, the knowledge needed to deal with real problems in everyday life (what they call "practical knowledge for action") is often very different in form from school science knowledge (see chapter 2). Also as noted in chapter 2, affording a higher profile to SSI-oriented teaching necessarily entails explicit teaching of critical thinking, argumentation and decision-making, and the development of students' critical reading skills. Phillips and Norris (2009) note that because of poorly developed reading skills, university students often perform no better than high school students at interpreting scientific texts, despite their more extensive content knowledge. My observations suggest that this is especially likely in the case of reports of scientific research relevant to SSI appearing in the popular press. Herein lies my third response to Kuhn's (1991) assertion of the irrelevance of content knowledge. If they are to utilize scientific knowledge effectively in addressing SSI, students need to be taught how to assemble their knowledge into coherent arguments that enable them to reach a decision. Because SSI are typically contentious, ill-structured, open-ended, subject to multiple perspectives, and likely to generate a range of interpretations and solutions, students need explicit guidance on how to evaluate evidence, assess alternatives, establish the validity of claims and address counter positions.

As noted in chapter 2, Sadler et al. (2007) identify four essential components of "good socioscientific reasoning": recognizing the inherent complexity of SSI; being willing to examine the issue(s) from multiple perspectives, acknowledging that further inquiry relating to scientific understanding, social aspects or moral-ethical issues may be necessary before a final decision can be reached; exhibiting skepticism and being alert to the potential for bias and vested interest. Simonneaux and Simonneaux (2009) suggest that there are two additional (or more focused) components that have particular relevance to the decision-making phase: (i) identifying risks and uncertainties, and (ii) taking account of the values and moral-ethical issues – although it could be argued that they already form part of the "complexity" and "multiple perspectives" aspects of socioscientific reasoning identified by Sadler et al. (2007). Students' abilities to reason appropriately and to develop "reflective judgement" (King & Kitchener, 1994, 2002, 2004 – see later discussion) are enhanced by opportunities to discuss important issues with others, share ideas, give and receive criticism, and especially by struggling to reach consensus (see Zeidler et al., (2009) for a discussion of the reflective judgement model in relation to SSI). Without explicit instruction, experience, criticism and support, students' consideration of issues may be shallow, inconsistent, unreflective, incomplete and hasty. Common weaknesses include a reluctance or inability to justify claims properly, deal appropriately with contradictory evidence and address the possibility of counter arguments. For example, in Kortland's (1996) study, middle school students discussing issues related to waste management and recycling tended to limit their arguments to factors that provide direct support for their stated position. No possible counter claims or rebuttals were considered. Studies by Zeidler et al. (2002) and Sadler et al. (2004) indicate that many students are not as critical in their evaluations or as skeptical of presented information as they ought to be. Students usually attribute contradictory conclusions to discrepancies in data or to error, rather than differences in interpretive frameworks. They are extremely unlikely to recognize the influence of vested interest, deliberate distortion or bias. Perhaps this is a consequence of lengthy exposure to traditional styles of science education in which knowledge is presented as authoritative and truthful.

Shafir et al. (2004) note a widespread tendency to weigh positive factors ("pro arguments") more heavily when *choosing* in favour of particular alternatives and to weigh negative reasons ("con arguments") more heavily when *rejecting* alternatives. A study at the Grade 5 level by Schwarz et al. (2003) showed that teacher guidance and frequent opportunities for students to practice their argumentation skills raised the level of students' performance on all measures employed: the *type* of argument (unsupported, one-sided, two-sided or multiple perspectives considered), the *soundness* of the argument (acceptability of argument, relevance of reasons invoked), and the *quality* of the argument (coherence, clarity and the number and significance of abstract ideas deployed). Zohar and Nemet's (2002) study of a group of Grade 9 students showed that explicit instruction in content knowledge and argumentation (structure of arguments, status of evidence, fallacious reasoning, coherence of claims and the criteria distinguishing between good and bad arguments) greatly enhanced the students' ability to construct and evaluate arguments in genetics. A control group that was taught *only* genetics content knowledge did not show any improvement in argumentation skills. Interestingly, the experimental group out-performed the control group in terms of biological knowledge, providing some reinforcement of the frequently made assertion that problem-based learning is a particularly effective context for concept development.

As argued in chapter 2, NOS knowledge concerning the role and status of scientific knowledge, the ways in which scientific knowledge is generated and validated, the tentative and contested nature of scientific knowledge (and, of course, its robustness and dependability once validated), the sociocultural location of scientific practice, and the ever-present danger of bias, distortion and error, can all impact positively and productively on the ways in which a particular knowledge item is regarded and utilized in confronting SSI. Indeed, Kolstø et al. (2006) found that NOS understanding (largely focused on perceptions of "empirical adequacy", investigative methods employed and theoretical justification) played a very prominent part in preservice teachers' evaluation of the significance of the science content of a series of SSI-related articles that had been self-selected by the teachers through Internet search. Zeidler et al. (2002) state that students' NOS views impacted their discussion of animal rights issues in three ways: (i) recognition of the importance of empirical data in reaching any conclusion; (ii) acknowledgement that sociocultural and economic factors might affect how data are collected, interpreted and reported; and (iii) a tendency to separate personal knowledge from scientific knowledge, and to resist the influence of scientific knowledge on personal views. In a debate on global warming based on two purpose-written articles, Sadler et al. (2004) noted that sociocultural influences were strongly invoked by some students and vehemently rejected by others. When asked to compare the two articles in terms of scientific merit and persuasiveness, 40% of the students reported that the article deemed to have "more scientific merit" was also "less persuasive"[66] – a finding that reiterates the need for explicit instruction in argumentation and raises important questions about students' media literacy and their ability to negotiate multiple sources of information and resolve the conflicts that may result. Research by Kolstø (2001b) in the context of controversial issues suggests that sixteen-year olds (at least, in the Norwegian schools he studied) tend to devote more attention to *who* conducted the research than to *how* it was conducted. Their views seem to be easily swayed by the status of the university, research institute or company in which the work was conducted and by the level of confidence in the validity of the data exhibited by the author(s). In a Canadian study, Korpan et al. (1997) gave College level students four (fictitious) news briefs on an issue and asked them to identify what additional information would be needed to confirm the report's findings and conclusions. In contrast to Kolstø's study, the most common request was for details of the research methods employed. Little interest was shown in the identity and personal history of the researcher(s). Even though the formats of the four reports were identical, students made substantially different requests, suggesting that the context in which an SSI is located is a crucial determinant of the knowledge students choose or wish to deploy. After expressing frustration that students often failed to utilize their

NOS knowledge when discussing the topic of genetically modified foods, even when it is well-established and secure NOS understanding, Walker and Zeidler (2007) urge teachers to guide students much more directly in applying NOS considerations as they construct and evaluate arguments.

MULTIPLE PERSPECTIVES REVISITED

Of course, understanding the relevant science and technology, the key items of NOS knowledge (for example, that scientific knowledge is tentative, empirically based, impacted by the scientists' experiences and values, socioculturally embedded and, in part, the product of human imagination and creativity), and knowing what constitutes a sound argument (and how to construct one), are no guarantee that students will be able to use that understanding to address the complexities of SSI and the diversity of views they encapsulate. In the context of SSI, claims often need to extend well beyond scientific considerations, and students need to take account of the wide range of perspectives that can impact people's views, including social, cultural, religious, philosophical, political, legal, economic, moral-ethical, aesthetic and even historical standpoints. Other crucial issues include recognizing the complexity of SSI, acknowledging that further and sometimes extensive research may be needed before a firm conclusion can be reached, adopting the kind of skeptical approach that ensures proper scrutiny of all knowledge claims, and being aware that vested interest can play a major role. As Geddis (1991) notes, we need to teach in ways that encourage students to "uncover how particular knowledge claims may serve the interests of different claimants. If they are able to take other points of view into account in developing their own positions on issues, they need to attempt to unravel the interplay of interests that underlie these points of view" (p. 171). In response to this reality, Sadler et al. (2007) identify *multiple perspective-taking* as a major criterion for evaluating students' arguments in the context of SSI.

In an effort to study the development of students' ability to handle multiple perspectives, Zeidler et al. (2009) have utilized the *Reflective Judgement Model* (RJM), developed by King and Kitchener (1994, 2002, 2004) specifically to describe the reasoning patterns that individuals use in addressing ill-structured problems. The model identifies three major stages: *pre-reflective, quasi-reflective* and *reflective*. The pre-reflective stage is characterized by reliance on an authority figure (teacher, scientist, politician, religious leader, etc.) to determine an absolute truth about matters, a truth that will be accepted regardless of contrary evidence. The quasi-reflective stage is marked by uncertainty and cynicism. There is recognition that authorities are not necessarily or always correct, and that evidence may be manipulated to reflect a particular point of view. At the reflective stage, individuals can appraise evidence and arguments from diverse sources in order to construct their own rationally-argued views. Zeidler et al. (2009) provide some striking evidence that Grade 11 and Grade 12 students who followed a programme requiring them to confront a range of SSI (including organ transplantation, issues relating to passive smoking, marijuana and alcohol use, stem cell research, euthanasia, steroid abuse, cosmetic surgery, excessive fast food consumption and fluoridation of the water supply) developed more sophisticated reflective judgement than students who followed conventional content-oriented courses in anatomy and physiology. Given the complexity and uncertainty associated with many SSI, the values issues raised, the likelihood of involvement at a personal level and the powerful emotions that may be generated, it is inevitable that students' construction, evaluation and response to arguments will vary substantially from context to context, and may even be highly context-specific. There may also need to be substantial differences in relation to the teaching and learning strategies employed. Case studies, debates and role-plays may generate different responses. For example, many students find it easier to address different perspectives when role-playing, that is, when it is not their own ideas that are under scrutiny. When students have a close personal involvement in an issue or problem, they may be reluctant to consider alternatives that threaten their current position.

From a study of publicly available documents, including reports of public meetings, newspaper editorials and government reports, and following interviews with members of the public who had been involved in reaching decisions on rival ways of disposing of recycled liquid fuel, Tytler et al. (2001) identified three types of evidence used by citizens in constructing arguments and reaching decisions about whether they would prefer landfill disposal, high temperature incineration or utilization as fuel in cement kilns: (i) scientific evidence, (ii) informal evidence (common sense, circumstantial evidence and personal experience), and (iii) wider issues related to the framing of the issues. This latter category included questions such as: What should be measured and compared? and What safety limits are appropriate? It also included economic, environmental and moral-ethical considerations. The authors note that informal knowledge was the most significant contribution to decision-making. In a school context, Simonneaux (2001) identified economics, ecology, genetics, wider science considerations, medicine, politics and ethics as areas consulted by students in support of their opinions on issues involving animal transgenesis. Of course, views about what knowledge is considered relevant to a particular discussion will not just vary from topic to topic, it may also vary from individual to individual. Yang and Anderson (2003) identified three different groups of students in respect of their preference for particular information: scientifically oriented students, socially oriented students, and those who are equally disposed to both. When Kolstø (2006) interviewed twenty-two high school students about construction of overhead power lines in residential areas, and the possible increased risk of childhood leukaemia, he found five main kinds of argument, reflecting different use of science and non-science knowledge.

1. The relative risk argument – the risk is low, the costs of alternatives (such as underground lines) are high, so the decision is unproblematic.
2. The precautionary argument – if there is any risk at all overhead lines should not be allowed[67].
3. The uncertainty argument or "decision impossible" – both the precautionary principle and the avoidance of extra costs are valued, but since they cannot both be upheld, students avoid making a decision. The author notes that although the students cited a need for further evidence, they didn't attempt to collect it.

4. The small risk argument – we live with risks all the time and since this risk is small it doesn't constitute a problem (if the risk was bigger, an alternative would need to be sought).

5. The pros and cons argument – the advantages and disadvantages of all approaches are carefully considered.

With respect to the pros and cons argument, research provides some conflicting and ambiguous conclusions. Ratcliffe (1997) suggests that students can compare a given set of options, but only in an unsystematic way; Hogan (1999), Hong and Chang (2004) and Siegel (2006) found that students focused on a limited number of aspects, frequently ruling out some options prematurely and without proper justification in order to reduce the complexity of the task and speed up the decision-making. In the study conducted by Seethaler and Linn (2004), students were able to choose from among a range or options, provide evidence and arguments for their preferred option, and argue against rejected options. Arvai et al. (2004) and Eggert and Bögeholz (2010) urge teachers to model the decision-making process and to teach students some generalized decision-making strategies. I am inclined to the view that decision-making is facilitated by greater scientific understanding, more robust and applicable NOS knowledge, more information about the context and the varied interests of the chief protagonists, interest in the issues and a commitment to solving problems, rather than by knowledge of some supposedly all-purpose algorithm for decision-making.

It is apparent that students differ quite substantially in terms of what they believe will help them to resolve a dilemma and reach a decision on the most desirable course of action. Some students in Kolstø's (2006) study requested more scientific evidence related to the health risks associated with overhead power lines, and whether there was consensus within the scientific community; some requested further information on relative costs; others requested information concerning the views of those likely to be most affected by any decision. This study raises important questions about how we help students to ascertain shortfalls in information, proceed with incomplete information, and establish priorities among competing claims and interests. It is particularly interesting to note that students subscribing to the "relative risk argument" believed that they were pursuing a purely knowledge-based decision. They took the notion of cost-effectiveness as unproblematic, oblivious to the values issues embedded in it. In many situations, it is values conflicts that represent the greatest obstacle to reaching decisions on options. Ways of prioritizing among conflicting values are discussed in chapter 7.

Human beings have always faced environmental risks (earthquakes, storms, floods, forest fires, and the like) and risks to their safety through famine, disease, social unrest and war. In the contemporary world there are all manner of risks at the personal, local, regional, national, international and global levels created by human actions. Indeed, risk is an inherent characteristic of a science-based and technology-based society. Beck (1992, 2000) describes risks as super-national and class-unspecific in terms of causing threats that cannot be delimited in time and place. They cross national borders and they impact people irrespective of age, sex and social status, although as I argued in chapter 3 the impact on the poor and powerless is often proportionally much greater. People's perception of risk is often not rooted in rational appraisal of data; rather, it tends to be intuitive and rooted in emotions. For example, publicity surrounding dramatic and sensational causes of injury and death leads to an over-estimation of risk, while the risk of everyday and ordinary causes is seriously under-estimated. Nor does an individual's perception of risk always lead to appropriate action. Not everyone avoids smoking, unsafe sexual practices or eating food known to be harmful to their health, for example. Interestingly, it seems that we tend to be more accepting of risks undertaken voluntarily (driving a car on a busy highway in bad weather or using a mobile phone, for example) than we are of involuntary risks such as the threat of bird flu or swine flu, the dangers of overhead power lines or the environmental hazards resulting from industrial development. Sometimes our distorted perception of relative risks leads us to nonsensical decisions. For example, some of those who drink so-called "organic wine" do so in order to avoid the approximately 20 parts per million of pesticide residue that "mainstream wine" might contain, yet they seem to have no qualms about continuing to drink up to 14.5% by volume of highly toxic ethanol. As noted above, consideration of risks, hazards and benefits also has a significant political dimension. For example, to whom do the risks and benefits of scientific and technological development accrue? Issues relating to power, wealth and social justice that determine such matters, together with an argument for confronting students with such questions, form the basis of the curriculum proposed in this book.

TRUSR, VALUES, ETHICS, EMOTIONS AND INTUITION

As noted several times in earlier discussion, a major issue in reaching a decision on a particular SSI is knowing *who* and *what* to trust. Can all sources be relied upon to provide high quality, thorough and reliable scientific data? Clearly not! Kolstø (2004) identified four "resolution strategies" used by the 16-year old students he interviewed on the overhead power lines controversy: (i) acceptance of all knowledge claims – that is, taking it for granted that all information and data contained in news briefs, leaflets and reports can be trusted; (ii) evaluation of statements in terms of the level of agreement between different experts and the extent to which the data conformed with their own views and/or "seemed plausible"; (iii) ready acceptance of particular sources of information as trustworthy and authoritative – some students assumed that researchers are trustworthy, others put their faith in newspapers, local residents or the power companies; and (iv) evaluation of sources of information in terms of their perceptions of competence, neutrality, vested interests and underlying value positions. Analysis of written responses to articles on a chosen SSI located by Internet search revealed four major criteria used by preservice secondary school science teachers for judging trustworthiness: (i) empirical and theoretical adequacy, including the amount and consistency of data, coherence of argument, quality of referencing and compatibility with the reviewer's conceptual understanding; (ii) completeness – whether there is sufficient information to reach a conclusion, and whether the argument is complete in the sense that other perspectives are considered, with all theoretical and methodological issues adequately referenced; (iii) social aspects – asking questions such as whether the researcher/ institution is well-respected, whether the underlying values are acceptable, and whether there any evidence of vested interest in the outcome; and (iv) rhetorical devices – use of emotionally manipulative language, personal denigration of those who express opposing views, sensationalist reporting, etc. Kolstø (2004) has used these findings to formulate a set of questions to guide students as they read articles on SSI.

– What are your sources and what is the evidence and documentation for this factual claim?
– Why do you trust these sources?
– Might the sources have interests that could have influenced the views expressed?
– Does there seem to be consensus regarding this knowledge claim within the scientific community?
– Is the source (e.g., an expert) talking within her/his area of expertise?

Pouliot (2008) describes a study in which a group of students investigating concerns about the health risks associated with mobile phone use had very explicit views about the roles, responsibilities and expertise of the different stakeholders in the dispute. They saw scientists as responsible for conducting research and making expert judgments about the harmful effects of the microwaves emitted by cell phones, the phone industry as primarily concerned with commercial aspects of phone use and the establishment of networks, and the government as responsible for overseeing the conduct of the phone industry, establishing safety guidelines and advising the public. They did not see the public as having any direct role, other than as phone users. As the author comments, this is a striking example of what Callon et al. (2009) call a *delegative* approach to the management of SSI: scientists produce knowledge; politicians represent the interests of citizens, regulate any associated manufacturing or distribution of services and provide advice to citizens; citizens have no direct role for knowledge production, representing their own interests or regulating commercial/industrial activity. This is the situation so strongly criticized by Cross and Price (2002):

> The problem of expertise is at the centre of the difficulty of the democratic participation of the public in debate and decision making. It is the role experts are given and the general contempt with which ordinary people are held when attempting to participate that makes it so difficult for the public to have a say. (p. 102)

In stark contrast, Callon et al. (2009) urge us towards a radical reconsideration of procedures for consultation and representation, an alternative conception of expertise and a redistribution of roles and responsibilities with respect to SSI (see also chapter 1 and chapter 4). They argue that through their vested interests, personal involvement and day-to-day experiences, lay persons (whom they call "researchers in the wild") are able to contribute valuable insights that can and should be used to contextualize and refine the lab-based research findings of scientists. This kind of citizen involvement in knowledge production and policy formation, which Callon et al. (2009) refer to as "dialogic democracy", will be discussed at greater length in chapter 9. Pouliot (2009) presents a convincing argument for explicit teaching of Michel Callon's (1999) deficit, public debate and co-production models of scientist-non-scientist interaction (see chapter 4) as a way of sensitizing students to alternative views of the expertise needed for addressing SSI and engaging in sociopolitical activism.

Solomon (1992) reports that self-led discussions of SSI facilitated with seventeen and eighteen-year olds via a series of television programmes focused on organ transplants, nuclear power and genetic engineering were characterized by an initial framing discourse, as students talked about what they had seen and raised matters for discussion, followed by a sequence of negotiation and persuasion in which opinions were exchanged and students tried to persuade others through the use of examples and empathy with the situation(s) rather than through logical argument based on scientific knowledge. Sometimes group discussion resulted in a consensus *moral judgement* and formulation of a strategy for dealing with the issue. Bell and Lederman (2003) found that 85% of the responses of College professors to four SSI (foetal tissue implantation for treatment of Parkinson's disease; relationships among diet, exercise and cancer, and whether certain high risk foodstuffs should be banned; global warming, and whether there should be legally-binding limits on greenhouse gas emissions; the link between smoking and cancer, and whether smoking should be banned in all public buildings) focused primarily on identifying moral-ethical issues, sociopolitical concerns or value judgements, with NOS under- standing playing "an insignificant role for a minority... and no clear role for the majority" (p. 367). Given the particular sample of respondents (university professors with good understanding of NOS issues) and the nature of the SSI addressed and questions asked, these findings are perhaps not surprising (see also, Bell, 2004). A study of students' views of stem cell research, including the use of embryonic stem cells, conducted by Halverson et al. (2009) at the US College level, revealed eight perspectives used by students as lenses through which to reach decisions about acceptability (arranged here from most to least commonly used): benefit to medical practice; ethical considerations; rights of donors, embryos and patients; funding issues; religious concerns; personal experiences and anecdotal stories; political or ideological beliefs; and impact on future scientific research. Only 4% of students were opposed to all forms of stem cell research (100% citing ethical reasons); 36% supported all forms of research; the remaining 60% of students held intermediate views, and most cited more than one of the eight perspectives in support of their views. These results, together with Sadler and Zeidler's (2004) finding that *the majority* of individuals in a sample of College level students construe genetic engineering issues as predominantly moral issues, lends substantial support to early work by Fleming (1986a,b) showing that 70% of the 16 to 18-year olds in his study employed moral reasoning to reach decisions about issues relating to nuclear power generation and genetic engineering, and to Best and Kellner's (2002) argument that all contemporary SSI necessarily integrate scientific, ethical and political perspectives. In discussing the science, ethics and politics of cloning and stem cell research, Best and Kellner (2002) comment: "It is imperative we do not leave the decisions to the scientists, anymore than we would to the theologians (or corporate-hired bioethicists for that matter), for their judgement and objectivity is less than perfect, especially for the majority who are employed by biotechnology corporations and have a vested interest in the hastening and patenting of the brave new world of biotechnology"

(p. 465). Not only *do* students include moral dimensions in their discussions, they *ought* to do so and should be encouraged to do so. Part of the argument I am developing throughout this book is that critical scientific literacy for citizenship entails the ability make moral judgements. The bases on which students might reach these judgements will be discussed in Chapter 7.

In their study of College students' decision-making about environmental issues, Zeidler and Schafer (1984) found that *affect* was a major influence, with decisions reflecting a complex of affect, personal experiences and moral reasoning. In a related study, Simmons and Zeidler (2003) report on a detailed study of the responses of 101 preservice primary school teachers and 137 students in Grades 9 to 12 to questions relating to animal experimentation. They comment that the principal finding of the study (conducted by Zeidler et al., 2002) was "the tendency for students to bestow empirical validity on socio-cultural beliefs and personal opinion" (p. 88). "Time and again", they say, "students conflated the roles of scientific knowledge, opinion and empirical data, sometimes even asserting that knowledge and opinion were virtually equivalent" (p. 88). It was not uncommon for students to disregard or distort empirical evidence that ran counter to their current viewpoint. Not surprisingly, in this context, emotional issues, personal experiences, moral-ethical considerations and religious views impacted very substantially on students' reasoning. In a study involving interviews with College level science and non-science majors concerning a number of genetic engineering dilemmas[68], Sadler and Zeidler (2005b) identified three patterns of student reasoning and decision-making: (i) *rationalistic* – reason-based considerations, including patients' rights, parental responsibilities, side effects, financial costs, availability of other treatment options and discrepancies in access to them; (ii) *emotive* – empathy and concern for the care and well-being of others, often drawing on personal experiences; (iii) *intuitive* – based on immediate affective reactions to the scenario presented, which often couldn't be rationalized. Most intuitive responses were negative: a typical reaction being "It just doesn't feel right". Many participants used multiple reasoning patterns, within which individual elements may or may not support each other, and all used more than one form of reasoning for at least one scenario. When an individual displayed intuitive reasoning alongside emotive and/or rationalistic reasoning, intuitive reasoning always preceded the other(s). Although intuitive reasoning was infrequently employed, it was usually more influential than other forms of reasoning in terms of decision-making, and was rarely changed by subsequent engagement in other forms of reasoning, a finding confirmed by Wu and Tsai (2007) in discussions of nuclear energy by Grade 10 students in a Taiwanese high school. Predictably, in the Sadler and Zeidler study, emotive reasoning and intuitive reasoning were the most context-dependent, with 80% of respondents using it in the context of Huntington's disease but only 10% in the context of gene therapy for enhanced intelligence. Rationalistic reasoning was seen to be the "most transferable" across contexts. While most participants explicitly acknowledged moral-ethical issues, those concerns were not isolated or distinct from other concerns and did not necessarily determine the final decision. In other words, morality, social considerations, emotive factors and personal experiences were subsumed into complex patterns of reasoning.

Not surprisingly, Howes (2002) noted the prevalence of empathy, concern for the well-being of others and personal experiences of family members and friends, as key elements determining the responses of a group of Grade 10 biology students (all were female students) to issues relating to prenatal testing for certain genetic disorders. In a study based in Western Australia, Dawson and Venville (2009) found that intuitve reasoning and emotive reasoning were much more widely used than rational reasoning by Grade 8, Grade 10 and Grade 12 students addressing a range of issues in biotechnology. The researchers also coded the students' argumentation skills as level 1 (claim only), level 2 (claim, data and/or warrant), level 3 (claim, data, warrant, backing or qualifier) or level 4 (claim, data, warrant, backing and qualifier) (see chapter 2 for a discussion of scientific argumentation). For all year groups, level 2 argumentation was the most common (exhibited by 56% of students), levels 1 and 3 were the next most frequent (22% and 17%, respectively), and level 4 was the rarest (5%). Only among those students deemed to be at level 4 was rational reasoning more common than emotive reasoning and intuitive reasoning.

Before leaving this discussion it is important to note that students' reasoning about SSI, especially in relation to health issues, can be substantially impacted by traditional beliefs, Indigenous knowledge and what some have termed "folk biology" (see George & Glasgow, 1988; Au & Romo, 1999; George, 1999a,b; Patel et al., 1999; Gitari, 2003, 2006). It is also important to note Ratcliffe's (1997) disturbing counter-finding that the students in her study were much more likely to use criteria about cost effectiveness and reliability than criteria indicating any moral-ethical considerations, and that selfish criteria were more likely to be used than altruistic ones. Of course, a normative conclusion (what we *should* do and what decision we *should* make) cannot be deduced from observation of the ways in which individuals do behave in particular circumstances, nor should we even attempt to do so. Chapter 7 provides some guidance on how decisions about how we *should* behave might be reached.

PROBLEMS, DIFFICULTIES AND ANXIETIES

Several researchers, including Cross and Price (1996), Roth et al. (1996), McGinnis and Simmons (1999), Hughes (2000), Levinson et al. (2000), Gayford (2002a), Pedretti (2003), Ratcliffe and Grace (2003), Summers et al. (2003), Bryce and Gray (2004), Levinson (2004), Reis and Galvão (2004), Cotton (2006), Lee et al. (2006), Sadler et al. (2006b), Tal and Kedmi (2006), Forbes and Davis (2008), Pedretti et al. (2008) and Tan and Pedretti (2010), have addressed the legion of problems, difficulties and anxieties raised by teachers facing the challenge of incorporating SSI or STSE perspectives into the curriculum. For example, many teachers claim that such approaches take too much time and divert attention away from content aspects of the curriculum, thus "diluting the science curriculum", "reducing science to the level of social science", and "alienating those with a passion for science". There is also concern that the social, economic, historical, political and moral-ethical dimensions of SSI will be poorly addressed because science teachers lack expertise in these areas, with some concern being expressed that this may lead to lower levels of job satisfaction for science teachers, loss of experienced teachers from the profession, and a decline in recruitment. Some teachers are concerned that a shift from the supposed "certainties of science" to the uncertainties of SSI-oriented teaching will constitute a threat to their classroom authority and to their role as "gatekeepers of scientific knowledge". In addition, many who express a tentative interest in teaching about SSI cite lack of time to plan lessons and prepare materials capable of integrating coverage of content with social concerns, economic considerations and moral-ethical dilemmas as a major constraint. Others cite difficulties associated with design of assessment and evaluation strategies. Conventional assessment methods do not cope well when there is no clearly defined outcome, no certain and unambiguous solution; when the curriculum is extended to include sociopolitical action, evaluation is as much about what the community learns from the activity, or how it is changed, as it is about what the students learn. Clearly, much work will be needed to develop appropriate assessment and evaluation strategies if an issues-based curriculum is to become a reality.

A substantial number of science teachers, as well as students, parents, scientists, employers, politicians and others, hold the view that social, political, economic and moral-ethical issues have no place in the science curriculum. Many believe that students are not mature enough to cope with SSI or sufficiently interested in addressing them, though my own research extending over many years, and that reported by Ratcliffe (2007), indicates that these are exactly the things that students *do* wish to address through the science curriculum. There will always be teachers who feel that they lack sufficient basic science knowledge to address complex SSI properly, though this is a relatively easy problem to solve through teacher education. A more difficult problem concerns those teachers who hold naïve NOS views, regard all scientific knowledge as proven, secure, unchallenged and unchallengeable, and present science as though it comprises a body of firmly established, value-free facts. Many students hold similarly naïve NOS views, overlaid with performance-oriented goals related to their image of a 'good student'. In consequence, both teachers and students are driven by the need to 'get the right answer', and so teachers 'short cut' or omit entirely any focus on evidence, argument, values clarification and evaluation. There is an urgent need for a reorientation of priorities, with increasing emphasis on teaching and learning *about* science (Hodson, 2006, 2009a). As noted by Bartholomew et al. (2004), the shift in pedagogy from a preoccupation with content to one that engages students with the processes and practices of science and their associated values has five principal dimensions: (i) a shift from anxiety about their own nature of science knowledge (NOS) to confidence about NOS, (ii) from teacher as dispenser of knowledge to teacher as facilitator of learning, (iii) from use of closed and authoritative classroom discourse to open and dialogic discourse, (iv) from a narrow content focus to development of scientific reasoning, and (v) from prescribed, contrived classroom activities to authentic activities owned by students.

Some teachers claim that they lack resources for addressing SSI. This is patently untrue. Newspapers, television reports and Internet websites abound with suitable material. What these teachers are really claiming is that they do not have access to carefully constructed instructional materials that meet the specifications of the official curriculum. Given the track record of such materials in seeking to promote particular political and economic ideologies or inculcate attitudes and codes of 'good behaviour' derived from particular religious beliefs (Marsden, 2001), it is perhaps no bad thing that teachers lack ready-made 'official' resources. As Cross and Price (1996) point out, there is a danger that large corporations and government agencies will respond to teachers' concerns about lack of materials by producing glossy and user-friendly materials that use sophisticated communications techniques to promote a particular position or point of view that is difficult to counter with the relatively unsophisticated curriculum materials generated by teachers, citing the Australian mining industry's advocacy of uranium mining as a case in point. Discussion in chapter 5 noted just how vigilant teachers need to be in identifying and, where necessary, intervening to counter the values that are likely to be promoted by such materials. In the SSI approach, breadth of perspectives is crucial. As Levinson (2001a) has shown, even teachers who express their intention to encourage students to express and develop their own informed, personal viewpoints can sometimes dominate classroom discussion and engage in inappropriate direction of students. Similarly, classroom observations by Cotton (2006) indicate that teachers' own attitudes as implied by questions asked, views challenged and counter opinions sought (in this case, towards environmental issues) were more influential on student opinion than the teachers had intended or realized. The likelihood of such manipulation of opinion would be considerably greater if teachers were to use a prescriptive text. What teachers *do* need, however, is sound advice on ways to manage active, student-centred learning, develop students' argumentation and critical thinking skills, and assist their ability and willingness to accommodate to ambiguity and uncertainty. It is inevitable that some students will find these experiences disconcerting, or even threatening. Many are not used to knowledge, especially scientific knowledge, being contested; they are used to locating 'correct answers' in textbooks. School often puts high value on students being quietly obedient, whereas addressing SSI requires students to engage in open inquiry, challenge and disagreement (both with other students and teachers). It is also likely that students will be frustrated if the teaching and learning experiences are not well-organized, well-focused, consistently stimulating and concise. As with any classroom situation, boredom sets in when an activity persists for too long, and anxiety develops when students are unclear about what is expected of them and how their work will be assessed. Ambiguity and uncertainty are key elements of most SSI, and cannot be avoided, but students can learn how to deal with them. This does not mean, however, that learning experiences associated with SSI should be vague, ambiguous and poorly structured.

It is inevitable that some teachers will lack confidence and expertise in handling unstructured, open-ended discussions and it is unsurprising that teachers unfamiliar with such an approach commonly express a concern, bordering on anxiety, that they will be accused of bias, and may possibly lay themselves open to charges of in-doctrination. I would make two points in response. First, adoption of the critical approach described in chapter 2 (what Ratcliffe and Grace (2003) refer to as the "stated commitment" approach) constitutes a legitimate defence against such charges[69]. Second, the views of students often indicate the exact opposite, with many of the students with whom I have worked expressing the view that SSI-oriented teaching "opened my eyes to other perspectives", "helped me to sort out my own views" and "enabled me to think more clearly and more carefully" about such matters. Similarly, far from feeling that they had been indoctrinated, students who followed the Open University course *Science Matters*, in the UK, reported that new information provided a stabilizing framework within which existing views could be accommodated and used more critically and more effectively (Thomas, 1997).

There is no doubt that the sheer complexity of the teacher's role in SSI-oriented teaching can be very daunting in prospect: organizer, facilitator, consultant, friendly critic, general arbiter on all manner of disputes and disagreements, examiner, and so on. All I can say is that it gets easier with practice, like everything in the life of a teacher, and that all of us learn by critical reflection on the circumstances in which we may have 'got it wrong' and by striving to work out how we might 'do it better' next time. Rogers et al. (2007) provide much valuable advice in their discussion of what constitutes an "ethically attentive practice". As they point out, moral-ethical issues impregnate all aspects of pedagogy: teacher-student and student-student relationships, engagement with ideas and arguments, willingness to take risks (such as admitting confusion and indecision, stating partly-developed ideas, etc.), respectful listening, and so on. An ethically attentive pedagogy requires that all interactions among teachers and students embody the values of *respect, caring* and *trust*. These key concepts of respect, caring and trust refer to the responsiveness of all classroom participants to classroom events, that is, respect for the rights, responsibilities, views, values and beliefs of others, an ethic of care with respect to other persons and groups, other living things, and the environment as a whole, and trust that the teacher and the students will consistently and unwaveringly uphold these values. A particularly prominent feature of SSI-oriented teaching is negotiation of meaning/ understanding deriving from multiple sources of authority: *disciplinary* authority (the content, methods and arguments of science), *expert* authority (as expressed by teachers, textbooks and socially dominant students) and *experiential* authority (including personal experiences, experiences of family, friends and acquaintances, and anecdotal evidence). In an ethically attentive practice rooted in respect, caring and trust, understanding based on teacher authority is not automatically privileged, as it is in much traditional practice. It sits alongside other perspectives as students negotiate what they consider an appropriate balance among these authorities and develop their own personal commitment to them (or not) by asking questions such as: What is the source of this person's authority? and Are there any good reasons why I should accept or believe what they say? Appropriate moment-by-moment decisions by teachers are key elements in building respect for students' understanding (initial, developing and final understanding) and fostering student autonomy and intellectual independence: "Knowing as a teacher when to speak, when to stay silent, what to attend to, what to leave unaddressed, when to employ humour, and when to be serious are but a few examples where negotiation of authority are implicated in the respect for students' understanding and a desire to promote student autonomy in one's teaching practice" (Rogers et al., 2007, p. 172). The point being made here is that beliefs, understandings and meanings, and especially the values that underpin them, are closely tied to the activities that give rise to them. In summary of their argument, Rogers et al. (2007) state that: (i) fostering rich student understandings requires care/respect in the science classroom and the negotiation of sources of authority; (ii) helping students to translate classroom understandings in science to new contexts requires a focus on learning a practice of reflective engagement on the construction of understanding; and (iii) developing students' capacity to engage successfully in any form of inquiry requires that teachers model social inquiry in the classroom.

If so many science teachers believe that they are ill-equipped to deal with SSI of a controversial nature, would the task be better given to humanities teachers? As Levinson (2001) points out, just because these controversies are located in science and technology does not mean that the science curriculum is always the most appropriate place to deal with them. His questionnaire survey of 1000 schools, with follow-up semi-structured interviews in twenty of them, reveals that humanities teachers believe themselves (not unreasonably) to be more experienced and more adept at dealing with controversial matters, while science teachers expressed concern about the humanities teachers' lack of relevant science knowledge and their tendency (as the science teachers put it) to pay more attention to the persuasiveness of the argument than to scientific validity. Donnelly (1999) presents a similar case for regarding history teachers as better placed than science teachers to promote "disciplined personal judgement... and the handling of inherently uncertain evidence" (p. 32)[70]. I recognize that asking science teachers to take on the role of presenting SSI adds to their already considerable burdens, but I am sure that SSI-oriented teaching is essential to achieving universal scientific literacy and that the science curriculum is the only sensible location for such topics. It would be disastrous if we retreated to teaching science devoid of social context and unrelated to everyday life and its concerns. It would be equally disastrous for students to consider the sociocultural, economic, political and moral-ethical dimensions of SSI, and develop their skills to reason and communicate about them, separate from the scientific knowledge and NOS considerations that should inform the debate. The science curriculum is the appropriate place to deal with all aspects of SSI, but this does not mean that science teachers cannot call on teachers of other subjects as consultants, advisors and occasional classroom visitors[71]. We need to adopt much more flexible, inter-disciplinary approaches. This is a topic well outside the scope of this book, except to mention that Ratcliffe et al. (2004, 2005) and Harris and Ratcliffe (2005) report on the benefits to both teachers and students of a "collapsed day", a cross-curriculum initiative suggested by Levinson and Turner (2001) in their influential report *Valuable Lessons*. Teams of teachers devised a whole-day programme focused on genetic testing and genetic engineering for use in eight schools, using one of three organizational arrangements: (i) teachers taught within their own subject area and students moved to specialist teachers as required (in two schools); (ii) classes undertook activities in the same order with individual teachers supporting activities both within and outside their own area of expertise (in five schools); classes undertook activities in a common order and were team-taught by a pair of teachers from different subject areas (in one school). All three arrangements were successful in generating student interest and fostering learning of the social implications of genetics. Although costs and organizational demands on the schools were high, 94% of the teachers said that they valued the opportunity to share ideas and expertise with teachers in other subject areas, though few were able to identify specific pedagogical expertise they had developed as a direct consequence of the experience.

IN CONCLUSION

Discussion in this chapter suggests the following key influences on students' ability to confront SSI.

1. Relevant conceptual and theoretical knowledge.
2. Ability to identify and access whatever additional scientific knowledge is deemed necessary for the specific context under consideration.
3. NOS knowledge, including the theory dependence of observation and experiment, the relationship of evidence to theory, investigative design, the role and status of scientific knowledge, the sociocultural location of scientific practice, etc.
4. Understanding of scientific argumentation, and the ability to evaluate it and deploy it effectively.
5. Ability to identify and access other knowledge resources as needed (e.g., economic, moral-ethical, legal, sociocultural and religious knowledge).
6. Recognition that personal and social values and perspectives, personal experiences, emotions and feelings can play a major role in considering SSI and will impact on decision-making.
7. Ability to evaluate evidence from many different perspectives, establish priorities, resolve conflicts and dilemmas, reach conclusions and decisions, and justify all decisions or proposed actions.

The argument I wish to promote is that these items constitute the knowledge, skills, attributes and attitudes needed to deal effectively with SSI, both in school and in the wider community, and that they are developed and enriched by that engagement. In other words, critical scientific literacy and consideration of SSI are inextricably intertwined. The course in "Biotechnology, Environment and Related Issues" described by Dori et al. (2003), and encompassing traditional biotechnologies such as cheese and wine making, genetic engineering, the human genome project, DNA finger printing, gene therapy and cloning, provides a compelling illustration of this argument. Further, if personal experiences and personal knowledge play a particularly important role in reasoning about SSI, we need to provide ample opportunities for students to explore their *personal framework of understanding* in relation to 'official' scientific knowledge and what Layton et al. (1993) call "practical knowledge for action". As argued at length in Hodson (1998a, 2009a), reading, writing and talking activities, movies and multimedia materials, visits to museums, and so on, are invaluable ways of exploring personal understanding. In the context of SSI-oriented teaching, it is very important to include a range of local issues, with direct impact on the students themselves. Ownership of issues and personal identification are the key to serious consideration of SSI and development of the attitudes that might lead to students being politically active as adult members of the community.

Hence, while consideration of global issues such as climate change and generalized discussion of topics such as genetic engineering are important components of an SSI-oriented curriculum, it is crucial that teachers find a way of helping students to see the *personal* relevance of these issues. Students need an opportunity to express their emotions and feelings regarding SSI. Rather than aiming to suppress them in favour of a detached 'scientific rationality', as so often in the past, we should be encouraging students to express their feelings, personal beliefs and values, and showing them that we recognize and value them as key components of responsible decision-making. This is not to say that emotive and intuitive reasoning should be exempt from challenge, any more than religious views should be exempt from challenge. A crucial element in critical thinking is knowing how to balance these different perspectives and/or prioritize among them. What is appropriate depends on the context and one's familiarity with it and personal involvement in it. Another point relevant to Deanna Kuhn's claim that students' arguments are independent of their scientific knowledge is that students may simply choose *not* to deploy scientific knowledge on any particular occasion, and may do so for all kinds of unexplained (and even possibly unexplainable) reasons.

Because making decisions about sensible priorities is context-specific, it is a skill that cannot be taught in a simple straightforward way. Rather, it develops over time, with experience of addressing SSI in a safe and supportive environment. What students also learn through experience is the sheer complexity and fluidity of reasoning about ill-defined, multi-faceted and contentious problems and issues with no clear-cut answers and solutions. It quickly becomes clear that the whole basis of an argument can shift when new information becomes available or when a new perspective or argument is introduced. Thinking shifts as students begin to evaluate arguments and consider the pros and cons of different positions. Experiencing the fluid, fuzzy and uncertain nature of the discussion is an essential step in the development of critical scientific literacy and the knowledge, skills, values and attitudes needed for responsible citizenship.

CHAPTER 7

TEACHING ETHICS

As noted in chapter 6, almost any discussion of a topical SSI is likely to raise questions about what is the *right* decision and what *ought* we to do? For example, should any individual with a disabling genetic condition be able to have gene therapy using material from embryonic stem cells? Should prenatal genetic testing be readily available and selective abortion of a foetus with a severe genetic disorder be permitted? Parents can already choose the sex of their child; soon scientists may be able to isolate and remove the genes that increase the likelihood of schizophrenia, obesity, alcoholism, ADHD, and a host of fatal or disabling conditions. Should such genetic engineering, when possible, be permissible[72]? As Conway (2000) points out, the effect (if not the intent) of these actions should be considered eugenic because they put value on one kind of person at the expense of another. Indeed, they consciously seek to eliminate the less valued.

> The first (step) is to characterize disease as genetic, the second is to characterize as a disease every abnormality that is genetic. Plainly, if we follow that logic, the outcome will be, via the processes of privatized or 'domestic' eugenics, a population that is normalized according to whatever is perceived as 'normal' at the time the technology becomes available. (Appleyard, 1999, p. 139)

It might soon become possible for prospective parents to choose the colour of a child's hair and eyes or to select any other characteristics they regard as desirable. Here there is a clear eugenic intent. Should this be permissible? As Finkler (2000) and Finkler et al. (2003) point out, this new genetic technology is increasingly being used to transform a healthy person into a patient with symptoms and a designated condition or syndrome, thereby placing increasing emphasis on biological rather than social and environmental determinants of health and ill-health. This trend, which Lippman (1998) earlier referred to as *geneticization*, brings with it a wide range of ethical issues concerning privacy, discrimination, inequality and justice.

> Using diagnostic technologies to name and classify diseases not only provides a means for generalizing across populations, time, and locales but also provides a rationale for justifying giving or withholding treatments and labeling individuals and groups as being ill, aberrant, or 'at risk'... When data are used to create categories based on probability and risk... new forms of subjectivity are created... When applied to other nonmedical institutional settings, such categories have far-reaching implications for governance and for individual lives. Susceptibility to substance abuse or chemical sensitivity, potential psychiatric disorders, probability of manifesting a genetic disorder,

or even being in the state of carrying a gene can have serious consequences in terms of workplace discrimination or the courts. (Hogle, 2008, pp. 849 & 850)

There are many other ethics-related questions that we might put to students. Should public drinking water supplies be fluoridated because it reduces the cost of dental care? Should certain rights relating to freedom and protection from harassment be extended to the great apes[73]? Should parents be required to ensure that their children receive the MMR vaccination regardless of any anxiety they may have about attendant risks, on the grounds that it is in the best interests of the wider community? More topically, should *Gardasil*, which has been shown to be 100% effective against human papillomavirus (HPV), the major cause of cervical cancer, be made available to all girls before they become sexually active, regardless of parental wishes[74]? Is ADHD an over-diagnosed condition and is the use of Ritalin merely a convenient way to render supposedly disruptive children submissive and compliant? What risks to health and privacy are likely to arise from current developments in nanotechnology and what ethical issues are raised by them?

Recent developments in biotechnology raise many important questions and concerns about whether certain lines of research should be permitted. For example, the work of Craig Venter shifts the focus from *reading* a genetic code to *writing* one – that is, not just modifying an existing organism to ensure "more favoured characteristics", but making an entirely new one. Venter's Websites (www.jcvi.org and www.tigr.org) state that his research involves building new organisms from strands of DNA disarmingly called "biobricks". In May 2010, he and his co-workers published an article in *Science Express* (www.sciencemag.org/cgi/content/abstract/science.1190719) describing the stepwise creation of a bacterial chromosome and the successful transfer of it into a bacterium, where it replaced the native DNA. Driven by the synthetic genome, the microbial cell began replicating and making a new set of proteins (over 1 billion replication events, to date).

We report the design, synthesis and assembly of the 1.08-Mbp *Mycoplasma mycoides* JCVI-syn1.0 genome starting from digitized genome sequence information and its transplantation into a *Mycoplasma capricolum* recipient cell to create new *Mycoplasma mycoides* cells that are controlled only by the synthetic chromosome. The only DNA in the cells is the designed synthetic DNA sequence, including 'watermark' sequences and other designed gene deletions and polymorphisms, and mutations acquired during the building process. The new cells have expected phenotypic properties and are capable of continuous self-replication. (Gibson, et al., 2010, p. 1)

The paper goes on to describe how the research team had sequenced the 600,000-base chromosome of a bacterium *Mycoplasma genitalium* as long ago as 1995, and in 2008 had created an artificial chromosome that matched *Mycoplasma genitalium*'s but also contained "watermark DNA sequences" that would enable the researchers to distinguish the synthetic genome from the natural one. Transplanting the genome into a recipient cell in order to establish a cell controlled only by the synthetic genome (to be called, somewhat provocatively, *Mycoplasma laboratorium*) proved difficult because of the extremely slow growth rate of *Mycoplasma genitalium*.

Attention then shifted to the 1 million-base genome of the much faster growing *Mycoplasma mycoides*, with the successful outcome described earlier. Because the genome was transplanted into an existing cell it would be incorrect to refer to this achievement as the creation of a truly synthetic life form. Nevertheless, it is a remarkable achievement and brings us a little closer to Venter's goal of producing synthetic bacteria that will soak up enormous amounts of carbon dioxide, thus solving the global warming crisis, provide alternative food sources, and create new fuels and pharmaceuticals. Although there will be substantial upfront research costs, this kind of synthetic biology promises (threatens?) to become readily available. No expensive resources or highly specialized technical knowledge will be required, and herein lies the problem: how to regulate the research and how to ensure adequate levels of environmental protection. It is all too easy to imagine a nightmare scenario in which synthetic bacteria 'escape' from a laboratory, interact with 'wild bacteria' and mutate into organisms that we never envisaged, about which we have no knowledge, and over which we have little or no control. It is all too easy to imagine the potential in Venter's work for terrorism and warfare.

Stem cell research poses another raft of ethical problems. There is, of course, an important distinction to be drawn between adult stem cells derived from blood, bone marrow, fat and other tissues, and embryonic stem cells from discarded IVF cultures, aborted foetuses or embryos created in the laboratory. Embryonic stem cells are more plentiful and easier to extract; they can be grown and made to multiply in the laboratory more easily; they are more pliable and so have much more regenerative potential. In short, they are of much greater value in research and more likely to result in the development of innovative medical treatments. However, for some people, the distinction between embryonic stem cells and adult stem cells also constitutes a boundary between ethically acceptable and ethically unacceptable practice. For others, the boundary may lie in the distinction between stem cells from "IVF discards" and those from embryos cloned specifically for research purposes. Those who draw the ethical distinction at this point argue that using cells from embryos left over from IVF treatments, which otherwise would be destroyed, is substantially less objectionable than cloning an embryo in order to "harvest" its cells, and then destroying it. Ultimately, the debate hinges on the philosophical issue of what constitutes a human being and the ethical issue of whose rights should have priority. Does human life begin at the point of conception, at the moment of implantation in the uterus, at the onset of the development process, at the point when a backbone and organs begin to develop, or at the point when the foetus is capable of survival outside the mother, with or without sophisticated technological support? The issue of relative rights is much more complex than the issue of the relative rights of mother and foetus that students will (or might) have addressed in discussion of abortion.

We live in an increasingly pluralist society, within which we cannot assume a shared set of moral values. Reaching agreement is difficult. One response is to allow the views of the majority to prevail – a position that necessarily disregards or marginalizes the needs, interests, values and rights of minorities. Even critical discourse between and among all interested parties may fail to bring about consensus.

And even if consensus were reached there would be no guarantee that it had reached the *right* answer. Asking questions about what we *ought* to do raises questions and concerns about morality (what it is right or wrong to do) and ethics (the reasons and justifications for judging these things to be right or wrong). In other words, ethics is the process of rational inquiry by which we decide on issues of right (good) and wrong (bad) as applied to people and their actions. Reiss (1999) characterizes the distinction as follows:

> We all make moral decisions daily on matters about what is the right thing to do, and we may give much thought, little thought or practically no thought at all to these decisions. Ethics, though, is the particular discipline which tries to probe the reasoning behind our moral life, especially by critically examining and analysing the concepts and principles which are or could be used to justify our moral choices and actions. (p. 125)

In order to ascertain what is right/good or wrong/bad we may appeal to some authority (for many, this would be God's authority), to sociocultural tradition and precedent (sometimes enshrined in laws), or to human reasoning. Consideration of religion-based morality is outside the scope of this book. Peter Singer's (1991) edited collection, *A Companion to Ethics*, provides much valuable background on ethics from the perspective of Judaism (Kellner, 1991)), Christianity (Preston, 1991), Islam (Nanji, 1991), Hinduism (Bilimoria, 1991), Buddhism (de Silva, 1991) and classical Chinese philosophy (Hansen, 1991). With regard to the second option (tradition and precedent), there is a marked tendency in these post-modernist times to suggest that a wide range of judgements is possible, depending on the sociocultural context, and that no one view is to be preferred to any other; they are just "different". In Donald Culpitt's (1991) words: "Another story, another truth". I have little patience with this position. I share Mary Warnock's (1996) conviction that this "politically-correct orthodoxy" needs to be re-examined "before it under-mines, as it threatens to do, any possible use of a moral vocabulary within which some things may be designated good or virtuous, others wrong, wicked or vicious, and within which also some people may be told unequivocally that their behaviour is morally intolerable" (p. 48). When adopting the third route of appeal to human reasoning (the preference in this book), one can be confident about the validity of an ethical conclusion, says Reiss (1999), if three criteria are met: "First, if the arguments that lead to the particular conclusion are reasoned with internal consistency. Secondly, if the arguments are conducted within one or more well established ethical frameworks. Thirdly, if there exists among relevantly interested parties a significant degree of consensus, arising from a process of genuine debate, about the validity of the conclusions" (p. 126). I am certainly not advocating that students be required to follow a rigorous course in moral philosophy, but I am advocating that they be equipped with some intellectual tools for addressing and resolving contentious issues that cannot be solved solely by scientific considerations.

The least sophisticated and least satisfying argument is that moral values reflect our personal desires and interests, a position described by moral philosophers as *egoism*. In short, everyone is driven by self-interest and is motivated only to satisfy their own desires. Thus, when we try to convince others that something is good, or ought to be done, we are attempting to get them to think and act as *we* think they should, and in accordance with *our* interests. Of course, this theory fails to explain why individuals frequently act in ways that are patently *not* in their interest - parents' behaviour with respect to their children, for example. This cannot be explained unless we reduce self-interest to the base level of surviving long enough and in good enough physical condition to engage in reproduction and raise offspring to a position from which they can reproduce, thereby ensuring the survival of some of our genes. A further objection to egoism is that it may constitute a theory of how people *do* behave but it is not a theory of how we *ought* to behave. *Ethical egoism* meets this particular objection by asserting that it is rational to act in one's own interests (the principle of rational egoism) and that we ought to act rationally (the principle of ethical rationality). Thus, when we act in ways that conflict with our own interests we are acting irrationally. This depressing and unappealing theory simply invites us to focus attention on ascertaining our own interests and how to pursue them.

Social construct theory (or *social contract theory*, as it is sometimes called) takes the position that it is advantageous to each individual if everyone agrees to refrain from actions that are harmful or hurtful to others. Over time, conventions conducive to social harmony and individual well-being have been developed, and each of us is socialized into valuing what others around us value. Put simply, it is to our advantage if people do not steal from us, lie to us or break promises, so we agree not to do those things to them. The driving force is still egoistic (our own interests) but in order that we benefit we agree to abide by established social conventions. As Singer (1993) notes, when there are discrepancies in power and resources among individuals it is no longer to the advantage of those powerful individuals to abide by the social contract. It would be in their interests to take advantage of those who are weaker than they are and less able to harm them. Of course, that wouldn't make their actions right, it would simply make them rational from an egoistic perspective.

Consequentialist theories aim to settle the question of what is the right thing to do by considering the likely consequences of a particular action. According to Jeremy Bentham's *utilitarian theory*, the goodness of an action is to be measured in terms of the pleasure or pain that results from it. For utilitarians, any question about good/bad conduct (no matter whether it concerns animal welfare, genetic engineering, disposal of toxic waste or responses to environmental crises) can be answered by the extent to which it maximizes pleasure and minimizes pain. Not entirely tongue-in-cheek, Reiss (1999) points out that one advantage of utilitarianism is that it takes pleasure seriously: "The general public may sometimes suspect that ethics is all about telling people what not to do. Utilitarianism simply says that people should do what maximizes the total amount of pleasure in the world" (p. 127). Of course, there is the problem of defining pleasure and ascertaining how it can be measured. Should it be interpreted as general well-being or happiness? How would we compare the rival claims of material gratification, aesthetic delight, intellectual joy and sexual satisfaction? If the principle of maximizing pleasure is replaced with maximizing the satisfaction of preferences, as some have suggested, do these difficulties disappear? One potential solution is to seek to maximize the welfare of society and the individuals who comprise it. If we accept this position, then in our actions towards others we should aim to do what we believe is in their interests and the interests of the community (see Singer, 1993). When faced with a choice, our obligation is to act in response to our perception of (long term) needs rather than (short term) wants, on the grounds that basic human needs (health, food, shelter, knowledge, skills, etc.) are easier to ascertain and of greater importance than individual preferences. This is particularly relevant in a school situation: we should, the argument goes, act in accordance with the students' interests and not necessarily in accordance with what they are interested in. My own views on this question have been expressed at length in Hodson (1998a). Of course, it isn't always possible to foresee the consequences of a particular action sufficiently well to know if it would satisfy the criterion of enhanced welfare. Also, as Fullick and Ratcliffe (1996) point out, "it seems that things we do in secret, and which never have any further consequences, are acceptable under consequentialist theories, even if those are things that are intuitively wrong" (p. 16). A further problem is that consequentialism can lead to otherwise unacceptable acts and behaviours on the grounds that they promise favourable consequences for the majority. Consequentialism forbids nothing on principle. Indeed, utilitarian or consequentialist arguments have been used "to justify suppression of free speech, suppression of free association, suppression of free publication, and a variety of other freedoms which we feel are natural rights which all people should be able to enjoy" (Fuller & Ratcliffe, 1996, p. 17).

Deontological ethics is concerned with actions that can be judged right or wrong in themselves, regardless of the consequences. It seeks to establish a system of rights, duties and obligations of various kinds, such that a duty in one direction (e.g., to tell the truth) entails a reciprocal right (e.g., to be told the truth by others). The most important principles concern *autonomy* and *justice*. People act autonomously when they are free and able to make and implement their own informed decisions. Thus, autonomy is the foundation of individual rights, including the right to respect, free association and free speech. Morality is not based on our role in the social order but on the rights that establish a social order through moral agreements between autonomous agents. In other words, social order depends on universal rights. Immanuel Kant coined the term "categorical imperative" for the demand that any principle should be rejected if it cannot be adopted as a universal principle: "Act only according to the maxim by which you can at the same time will that it should become a universal law" (cited by Johnson, 1989, p. 199). O'Neill (1991) explains how the categorical imperative justifies the principle of keeping promises. If everyone keeps promises there is a social stability on which all can rely; it is wrong to break a promise because if the principle of breaking promises were to be extended universally, the moral principle of promising would break down and this particular social stability would be lost. "False promising is not wrong because of its unpleasant consequences, as the consequentialist would have it, but it is wrong because it cannot be willed as a universal principle. It is self-defeating, it is acting according to a self-contradictory maxim" (Fullick & Ratcliffe, 1996, p. 18).

Justice, a key element in both social contract theories and deontological ethics, is about fair treatment and the fair distribution of resources and opportunities. John Rawls (1957, 1971) notes that in any social organization or practice there are often quite major differences among people's wishes, desires, claims for privileges, benefits, and so on. Not all these claims can be satisfied together and the satisfaction of some will inevitably exclude satisfaction of others. For Rawls, the goal is to seek a proper balance of competing claims; therein, he says, resides justice. Our rights within a just practice are those claims that are allowed; our obligations or duties are those actions required of us by the practice. Rawls argues that ethical principles can be derived from an imaginary choice in which those choosing do not know whether they will be the ones who gain or lose by the principles they select. The principles of a just practice are established, he says, on the basis of what kind of social organization of that practice would be acceptable to the participants in the practice if they did not know what role they would play in the practice. If the freedom of every individual in the practice were so well balanced against the freedom of every other individual in the practice that there would be *no preferred role*, then the practice is just. That is, if no role in the practice is seen to have an advantage over the other roles, the practice is just. Rawls (1957) goes on to assert that:

> A practice will strike the parties as fair if none feels that, by participating in it, he, or any of the others, is taken advantage of, or forced to give in to claims which he does not regard as legitimate. This implies that each has a conception of legitimate claims which he thinks it reasonable that others as well as himself should acknowledge... A practice is just, then, when it satisfies the principles which those who participate in it could propose to one another for mutual acceptance... Persons engaged in a just, or fair, practice can face one another honestly, and support their respective positions, should they appear questionable, by reference to principles which it is reasonable to expect each to accept. (Rawls, 1957, cited by Johnson, 1989, pp. 402 & 403)

In similar vein, Kohlberg (1971, 1973) argues that to be taken as sound, moral judgements have to be *reversible*. In other words, what is right, fair and just in any conflict situation can be judged by applying the principle of reversibility.

> To say that rights and duties are correlative is to say that one can move from rights to duties and back without change or distortion. Universalizability and consistency are fully attained by the reversibility of prescriptions of actions. Reversibility of moral judgment is what is ultimately meant by the criterion of the fairness of the moral decision. (Kohlberg, 1973, p. 641)

Virtue ethics has its origins in the writing of Plato and Aristotle. In essence, it attempts to answer the question: What would a good person do in a particular situation? However, instead of emphasizing rules of conduct and action, it focuses on the development of character traits such as kindness and generosity that will increase the likelihood of good actions and the elimination of personal characteristics such as greed, jealousy and irascibility that would decrease the likelihood. Whereas deontology and consequentialism are concerned with right action, virtue ethics is concerned with the good life and the kind of person we should aim to be. Clearly, a question such as "what is the right action?" is significantly different from "what kind of person should I be and how should I live?" While the former deals with specific dilemmas, the latter is a question about how to conduct one's life, in general. Instead of asking what is the right act here and now, in these particular circumstances, virtue ethics asks what kind of person should I be in order to make good decisions and take proper action on every occasion. The central concept of virtue ethics is *eudaimonia*, variously translated as happiness, flourishing, well-being, contentment and fulfillment[75]. For Aristotle and modern virtue ethicists such as Philippa Foot (1978, 2001), Alasdair MacIntyre (1981) and Rosalind Hursthouse (1999), eudaimonia is the proper or fundamental goal of human life, an outcome that can be reached by practising the virtues. It is not just that the virtues lead to the good life (e.g., if you are good, you are rewarded); rather, a virtuous life *is* the good life because the exercise of our rational capacities in pursuit of the virtues is its own reward.

Aristotle categorized virtues into *moral* virtues and *intellectual* virtues. Among the former are courage, temperance, generosity, benevolence, patience, tolerance, truthfulness, modesty, compassion and righteous indignation; among the latter are knowledge, common sense, intuition, wisdom, resourcefulness, creativity and sound judgement. Aristotle considered each of the moral virtues as a midpoint (the "golden mean") between two corresponding vices. For example, the virtue of courage is the mean between the two vices of cowardice (the disposition to act more fearfully and hesitantly than the situation deserves) and foolhardiness (the disposition to pay too little heed to the possible adverse consequences of an action). In other words, courage is the disposition to show the amount of fear and apprehension appropriate to the situation. Virtue "lies in a mean", says Aristotle, because the right response to each situation is neither too much nor too little. Virtue is the *appropriate* response to particular situations and particular people. The virtues are closely associated with feelings and emotions. For example, courage is associated with fear, modesty with feelings of shame, and kindness with empathy towards others. The virtue "lies in the mean" because it involves displaying the appropriate amount of emotion in a given set of circumstances[76].

While intellectual virtues are developed through formal and informal educational processes, moral virtues are cultivated by habit and reflection. To become a generous person one must get into the habit of being generous; to become patient, one needs to practice patience. In both cases, one needs to reflect on whether one's behaviour in a given set of circumstances was generous and/or patient. In other words, virtue ethics is a theory of action: having virtuous inner dispositions involves being moved to act in accordance with them – for example, realizing that kindness is the appropriate response to a situation leads one to act kindly. Moreover, character traits should be stable, consistent and reliable dispositions, so that if an individual possesses the character trait of kindness, we would expect her or him to act kindly in all sorts of situations, towards all kinds of people, and to do so consistently over a long period of time, even when it is difficult to do so. It is important to recognize that moral character develops over time. People are born with, or acquire very early, all kinds of natural tendencies, some of which are positive (such as a placid and friendly nature) and some negative (such as an irascible or jealous nature). These natural tendencies can be encouraged and developed, or discouraged and thwarted, by the influences to which one is exposed when growing up. A range of people, experiences and events may affect one's character development: parents, siblings, teachers, peers, role models, other community members, the encouragement and attention one receives, one's exposure to different situations, stimuli, challenges and constraints. Together, they shape and develop our character through a long and gradual process of education and habituation.

Virtue ethics presupposes that people have some capacity to shape their own character. Thus, moral education and development is a major part of virtue ethics and is greatly assisted in its early stages by the availability of good role models. The virtuous agent acts as a role model and the student of virtue emulates her or his example. Initially this is a process of habituating oneself in "right action". However, the virtuous agent does not act properly out of an unreflective, habituated response, but has come to recognize the value of virtue and why it is the *appropriate* response. Virtue involves knowledge, understanding and choice, and a virtuous act is chosen knowingly for its own sake. It is not enough to act kindly in an unthinking way, by accident, or because everyone else is doing so; one must act kindly because one recognizes that this is the right way to behave. In the words of Alasdair MacIntyre (1981), virtue "is at variance with central features of the modern economic order and more especially its individualism, its acquisitiveness and its elevation of the values of the market to a central social position" (p. 237). It isn't possible, he says, to be both modern and moral because "the fully autonomous self knows no morality other than the expression of its own desires and principles" (p. 211). The significance of these remarks in terms of the relationships among science, technology, society and environment was a focus of discussion in chapters 3 and 5, and will be revisited in chapters 8 and 9.

Following Aristotle, many virtue ethicists draw a distinction between full or perfect virtue and "continence", or strength of will. The fully virtuous do what they should without an attendant struggle against contrary desires; the "continent" have to control a desire or temptation to do otherwise. Many would argue that there is something particularly admirable about people who manage to act well when it is especially hard for them to do so, but as Foot (1978) points out, the plausibility of this depends on precisely what makes it hard. Another way in which one can fall short of full virtue is through lack of *phronesis*, that is, lack of moral or practical wisdom. Given that good intentions are intentions to act well or "to do the right thing", we can say that practical wisdom is the knowledge or understanding that enables its possessor to do just that, in any given situation. Practical wisdom is the capacity to adapt one's behaviour to the complexity of particular situations, to be sensitive to the various factors that might indicate a particular course of action as good/right or bad/wrong.

The ethics of care (or care-based morality) is a variant of virtue ethics motivated to some degree by an assertion that men think in masculine terms, like *power* and *control*, while women think in feminine terms, like *caring* and *nurturing*. Theorists

such as Gilligan (1982), Noddings (1984, 1995), Baier (1985) and Tronto (1987) call
for a change in how we view morality and the virtues that underpin it, advocating a
shift towards virtues that are traditionally (or stereotypically, for some) exemplified
by women, such as taking care of others, patience, the ability to nurture, self-
sacrifice, and so on. It is argued that these virtues have been marginalized because
Western society has not adequately valued the contributions traditionally made by
women. While those writing in this area do not always make an explicit connection
with virtue ethics, there is much in the discussions that is central to virtue ethics.
Care-based morality rejects the notion that a single and simple formula exists for
solving moral problems. Rather, morality is inextricably linked to the contexts of
individual situations and the people involved. Indeed, the care perspective prescribes
a far more relational approach, with emotions such as sympathy and empathy
contributing very significantly to decisions about proper actions, with a corres-
pondingly smaller emphasis on a system of rules. Gilligan (1982) notes that women
tend to apply a contextual or "relational" problem-solving strategy to moral conflicts
because they are disposed, in general, to perceive such conflicts in accordance with
"the parameters of connection". In contrast, men are more likely to apply a system
of rules and principles to the resolution of moral conflicts because they are
disposed, in general, to perceive such conflicts in terms of justice and fairness only.
In other words, men and women differ in "their approach to conflict resolution –
that is in their use rather than their understanding of the logic of rules and justice"
(p. 2).

Virtue ethics has been criticized on the grounds that it is unable to provide
action-guidance and, therefore, rather than being a normative rival to utilitarian and
deontological ethics it is no more than an invitation to identify a moral exemplar or
role model and do what she/he would do. In response, Hursthouse (1991) notes that
a great deal of specific action guidance can be found in rules employing the virtue
and vice terms (what she calls "v-rules"), such as: "Do what is honest and charitable"
and "Do not do what is dishonest/uncharitable". Much valuable action guidance
comes from avoiding courses of action that would be irresponsible, inconsiderate,
selfish, mercenary, indiscreet, tactless, unsympathetic, incautious, presumptuous,
hypocritical, self-indulgent, vindictive, calculating and/or ungrateful. Critics also
charge virtue ethics with cultural relativism. Clearly, action does not occur in a
sociocultural vacuum, and different societies encourage different virtues and vices.
If different cultures embody different virtues, it follows that the v-rules will identify
actions as right or wrong only in relation to a particular culture. Two responses can
be made. First, while cultural relativism is a major challenge, it is just as much a
problem for social contract, utilitarian and deontological ethics. The cultural
variation in character traits regarded as virtues is no greater than cultural variation
in rules and norms of conduct. A second and bolder strategy, adopted by Martha
Nussbaum (1988), is to claim that Aristotle's virtues are absolutes. Much cultural
disagreement arises, Nussbaum says, from local misunderstandings of the virtues,
but the virtues themselves are not relative to culture. Justice, temperance, generosity,
and the like, are essential elements of human well-being and flourish across all
societies and for all time. Furthermore, Nussbaum argues, in any given society a

virtuous character trait has universal applicability. It is inconsistent, for example, to claim a certain character trait as a female virtue while at the same time not proposing it as a male virtue. In contrast, MacIntyre (1981) argues that virtues are, and necessarily must be, grounded in a particular time and place. What counts as virtue in 4th Century Athens would be a ludicrous guide to proper behaviour in 21st Century Toronto or Auckland. However, MacIntyre argues, this does not necessarily commit one to a belief that particular accounts of the virtues are static. Moral activity and reflection (that is, attempts to ascertain and practice the virtues) constitute intellectual and cultural resources that allow people to change the ethos of their own society – a key element in the politicized science and technology education advocated in this book.

While I am strongly inclined in my own life towards virtue ethics as a way of deciding issues relating to personal actions and behaviour, I recognize that different individuals may still arrive at different conclusions concerning a particular SSI. It is here that Mary Warnock's (1998) distinction between private (or personal) morality and public morality can be helpful. Public morality, the kind embodied in legislation concerning genetic engineering, animal welfare and the location of toxic waste dumps, for example, is based on values considered "*acceptable* to the majority".

> There is a difference between what is a generally agreed moral view… and a morality which, though not agreed, is nevertheless broadly *acceptable*. When I first came across the use of the word 'acceptable' in this kind of context, I thought of it as typical civil servant cop-out. It was, I thought, mealy-mouthed. They, the civil servants, did not want to use strong and definitive words which would commit them, words like 'right' and 'wrong'. But I came to see that I was here confusing private with public morality. In public issues where there is radical difference of moral opinion (as between those who think that the early embryo should have the same moral status as a child and those who do not), and where no compromise is possible, the concept of the acceptable is a useful and indeed indispensable one. (Warnock, 1998, p. 70)

Of course, acceptable does not mean *right* and certainly does not preclude an individual acting otherwise, although *unacceptable* might be more likely to preclude contrary action.

ETHICS AND NON-HUMANS

We should also ask whether it is sufficient only to consider *people* in reaching our decisions on the ethical dimensions of SSI. What status should be afforded to other species in our moral-ethical reasoning? Such questions arise in relation to experiments on animals, of course, and in relation to xenotransplantation, rainforest clearance (with its accompanying destruction of habitat) and industrialized farming methods (including intensive poultry farming and use of hormones to increase milk production). Regan (1983, 1985), Singer (1993, 2002), Scruton (1996), Rowlands (1998) and Donovan and Adams (2007) provide extensive discussion of animals' rights issues that would do much to inform student debate on industrialized farming, animal experiments and other aspects of our relationships with animals[77], while Andrew and Robottom (2001) engage in an insightful discussion of the issues with respect to pest eradication - specifically, rabbits in Australia.

Deontological ethics relating to the right of respectful treatment for autonomous beings would seem to rule out rights for all creatures other than *homo sapiens*, and possibly great apes, on the grounds that other creatures are incapable of acting as moral beings. Not so for utilitarianism. Both Singer and Regan point out that if an animal has the ability to feel pain and experience pleasure then it has interests that utilitarian consequentialism would seem to uphold. At the very least, this position demands that: (i) farm animals are not subjected to de-beaking, de-horning, castration, tail docking, branding, force feeding, indiscriminate use of growth hormones and antibiotics, separation of mother and young, breaking up of herds, and so on; (ii) species-appropriate living conditions are provided for all animals, including pigs, cows, horses and chickens, comprising adequate space and light, proper bedding material and adequate cover from the sun and rain; and (iii) pain-free methods are used to kill both farmed animals and those species deemed to be pests[78].

In addition to the inhumane conditions of factory farming and industrialized slaughterhouses, millions of animals are subjected to the horrors of laboratory experimentation. When animals are used in laboratory experiments there is an assumption that in some way they model a range of human states, conditions, diseases and responses, both physical and psychological. Without that assumption the experiments would have no value. It follows that the animals chosen for the experiments are also likely to feel a measure of physical pain and/or emotional distress that echoes the likely human responses to the circumstances of the experiment. It is important for students to consider the ethical issues raised by such recognition, especially with regard to the testing of cosmetics, food additives and the like[79]. Hampson (1989) comments as follows: "It is an evil to allow people to suffer and die if that suffering and death can be prevented by drugs, by vaccination, by surgery. It is an evil for us not to exploit our full intellectual potential, not to push back the frontiers of knowledge. But the means by which we have to do so, are also evil. They involve the imprisonment, suffering and death of countless millions of sentient creatures" (p. 106). She proceeds to make a powerful case for reducing the number of animal experiments (arguing that up to 60% of them are unnecessary and/or of limited value when results are applied to human beings[80]), finding alternatives (such as *in vitro* experiments), and refining the procedures so that the experiments we do conduct are less inhumane and more informative (see also, Balls and Southee, 1989). Both Sapontzis (1995) and the Physicians Committee for Responsible Medicine (2007) report on the unacceptably high levels of pain, fear, deprivation, frustration and distress experienced by animals through every stage of the progression from capture to death, or for those specially bred for the purpose, from birth to death.

According to Linzey (1989), the first person to use the term "rights" in relation to animals was Thomas Trynon in the 17th Century. In a piece titled "Complaints of the birds and fowls of heaven to their Creator", published in 1688, Trynon gives voice to the animals as they plead for justice:

But tell us, O men! We pray you to tell us what injuries have we committed to forfeit? What laws have we broken, or what cause given you, whereby you can pretend a right to invade and violate our part, and natural rights, and to assault and destroy us, as if we wee aggressors are no better than thieves, robbers and murderers, fit to be extirpated out of creation... From whence did thou (O man) derive thy authority for killing thy inferiors, merely because they are such, or for destroying their natural rights and privileges? (cited by Linzey, 1989, p. 36)

Of course, many students would regard the idea that animals have rights as bizarre. In this event, we should encourage students to shift the focus from arguments for *rights* to consideration of our *responsibilities* towards other living things. The key issue for students to consider is how we can act ethically towards animals within a cultural context (the West) that exploits them on a massive scale: on the farm, in movies, circuses and marine centres, in the laboratory and in the wild through hunting and pest control.

The term "pest", as Andrew and Robottom (2001) point out, is a social construct that seems to legitimate different treatment for different species, rather like the notion of "plants" and "weeds" justifies the gardener's discriminatory actions. In Australia, rabbits and cane toads are not afforded the same consideration as "valued species" such as indigenous animals like wombats, Tasmanian devils and hooded parrots, especially when the indigenous creatures are also endangered. Rabbits and cane toads are both introduced species, and are increasingly so numerous that normal rabbit behaviour conflicts with the interests of farmers and cane toad behaviour conflicts with the interests of native snakes, which have no immunity to cane toad venom and no instinct to avoid them. Students might be asked to consider whether conflict of interest with people or with highly valued species justifies inhumane methods of destruction, an issue that arises in New Zealand in relation to the damage inflicted by the brush tailed possum, an introduced species, and the measures adopted to reduce numbers (see discussion in chapter 6). They might also be asked to consider some of the differences in our relationships with animals that are a source of food and of revenue for farmers (such as pigs and sheep), those we regard as companions (dogs and cats), and those we regard as pests (mice, ants and snails). The language we use reveals some substantial differences in our attitudes towards different species. While cats and dogs are often described in the most affectionate terms, with frequent reference to their companionship, faithfulness, intelligence and endearing qualities, "pests" such as rats and foxes are described in highly anthropomorphic terms, including sly, cunning, devious, ruthless, cowardly, blood-thirsty and filthy. There is no doubt that cuddly and photogenic creatures like pandas and koalas are more favourably regarded and receive more considerate treatment than creepy, slimy and ugly ones (beetles, slugs and worms) – a tendency that Peter Singer refers to as "speciesism". Tucker (1989) comments that in children's literature, "vegetarian animals like rabbits or horses tend always to emerge as lovable, whereas predators such as foxes, or carrion eaters like vultures, all with their own equally important part in general ecology, still come off as natural villains" (p. 168), with the wolf as the arch villain. Interestingly, rabbits are variously regarded as a source of food, as suitable 'objects' for experimentation, as pets, and as pests to be eliminated in whatever way proves economically viable. Of course, it doesn't matter much to the rabbit how it is *regarded*, but it does matter how it is *treated*. Students might be asked to reflect on the notion of speciesism. They might be asked to consider why, in Western society, it is generally considered acceptable to eat sheep but not dogs, and to eat fish but not dolphins. If sentience is the criterion, why would we allow pigs, probably the most sentient, intelligent and socially aware of domesticated animals, to be treated in such inhumane ways. Posing such a question reminds us that scientific knowledge and rationality is sometimes insufficient for decision-making. Nor can ethics always assist us. In many situations, as discussed in chapter 6, decision-making is determined by emotions and deeply held feelings.

Selby (1995) describes an activity in which students are asked "Where do you draw the line?" with respect to various uses of animals: farming for milk, eggs and meat; using horses and oxen for pulling carts, and horses and camels for riding; the fur trade; dog fighting; animal experiments; dissection of animals for educational purposes; keeping animals in zoos and safari parks; using them in circuses and movies; and so on. Some research findings on students' views about such matters, including the use of genetically engineered animals in research, can be found in Stanisstreet and Williams (1993), Stanisstreet et al. (1993), Foster et al. (1994), Hill et al. (1999) and Dawson (2007). Students might be invited to discuss their feelings about the kind of experiments involving living things discussed in chapter 5, including the ways in which the animals – usually frogs, rats or dogfish – are collected, transported, handled, maintained and killed. They might be asked to ponder why some scientists who are opposed to the cloning of human beings do not also regard the cloning of animals as ethically problematic. Since the cloning of Dolly the sheep by Ian Wilmut and his colleagues at the Roslin Institute, in March 1997, scientists have engineered many varieties of transgenic animals and have cloned a whole range of animals, including sheep, cows, goats, pigs, mice, rats, cats and monkeys. As Best and Kellner (2002) observe, it is the combination of genetic engineering and cloning that presents a whole raft of new ethical issues[81]: "In a potent combination, genetic engineering and cloning technologies are used together in order, first, to custom design a transgenic animal to suit the needs of science and industry (the distinction is irrevocably blurred) and, second, to mass produce the hybrid creation endlessly for profitable peddling of medical and agricultural markets" (p. 44). In addition to the ethical issues raised by genetically engineered changes in animal characteristics created to benefit the meat and dairy industries, students might be asked to consider the ethical issues raised by research such as: (i) genetically engineering pigs as sources of organs for future transplantation into humans by eliminating the protein that is usually rejected by the human immune system; (ii) genetically engineering animals to be much more susceptible to the particular diseases scientists wish to study; and (iii) so-called "pharmaceutical farming" (or *pharming*, to its critics), that is, the practice of genetically modifying animals to secrete therapeutic proteins and medicines in their milk. In this "Brave New Barnyard" of genetic engineering, as Best and Kellner (2002) call it, cows are genetically engineered to produce lactoferrin (a human protein useful for treating infections), goats to generate antithrombin III (a human protein that can prevent blood clotting) and serum albumin (which regulates transfer of fluids in the body), and sheep to secrete alpha antitrypsin (a drug used to treat cystic fibrosis). In another highly innovative but ethically dubious development, scientists employed by Nexia Bio-technologies have implanted a spider gene into goats so that their milk produces a super strong material – trademarked as *Biosteel* – that can be used in various aerospace and engineering applications that require light but strong materials, including the manufacture of bulletproof vests (see www.nexiabiotechnologies.com).

One of the purposes of these ethics-focused classroom activities is to impress upon students that the ways in which we treat animals tell us a great deal about ourselves, and possibly a great deal about the ways in which we are likely to treat other people. In other words, discussing issues relating to animal welfare may be a good entry point to consideration of wider social justice issues. More importantly, perhaps, a change in students' views about the proper way to treat animals may effect a shift in the way they treat other people. It is now more than a century since Sarah Eddy (1897) pointed out this connection: "Society first said that needless suffering should be prevented. Society now says that children should not be permitted to cause pain because of the effect on the children themselves" (cited by Finch, 1989, p. 66). In 1933, the National Parent-Teacher Association in the United States noted that "children trained to extend justice, kindness and mercy to animals become more just, kind and considerate in their relations with one another... The cultivation of the spirit of kindness to animals is but the starting point toward that larger humanity that includes one's fellow of every race and clime" (cited by Selby, 1995, p. 3). Of course, not everyone shares this view. As Cindy Milburn (1989) observes: "To many people it is inconceivable that we should measure our civilization by the way we treat animals. To others it is inconceivable that we should not" (p. 73).

Before leaving this discussion, it is important to note that it may be unreasonable to expect humans to value all other life forms equally, and in all circumstances. For example, Mueller (2009) asks why we would value "pesky critters such as the protozoan *Plasmodium falciparum*, that causes malaria; and hookworms, and liver flukes, and organisms that cause river blindness, dengue fever, yellow fever, cholera, typhoid, leprosy, and tuberculosis" (p. 1038). It is not unreasonable, in some situations, to act in the interests of our own species, and against the interests of other species. To this effect, Sterba (2001) formulates two "practical principles" for ecological ethics: (i) *the principle of human defence* – actions that defend oneself and other human beings against harmful aggression are permissible even when they necessitate killing or harming individual animals or plants, or even destroying whole species or ecosystems; and (ii) *the principle of human preservation* – actions that are necessary for meeting one's basic needs or the basic needs of other human beings are permissible even when they entail compromise to or denial of the basic needs of individual animals and plants. However, actions that meet non-basic or luxury needs of humans are prohibited when they impact negatively on the basic needs of individual animals and plants, or on whole species or ecosystems.

On a related matter, students might also be asked whether mining, forestry and other exploitative industries should be permitted in environmentally fragile areas.

Is the destruction of habitat and possible extinction of a species an acceptable price to pay for increased employment opportunities and company profits? In addressing the question of what constitutes an appropriate *environmental ethic*, Elliot (1991) considers a range of arguments underpinning *human-centred* ethics (environmental policies should be evaluated solely on the basis of how they affect humans), *animal-centred* ethics (evaluation should include the interests of all non-human animals) and *life-centred* ethics (we should consider the impact on entire ecosystems, including plants, algae and single-celled organisms). We should also, as Elliott reminds us, ask questions about our ethical relationship to the non-living environment. What ought to be our responsibilities and duties towards not only the oceans, rivers, forests and mountains, but also towards the planet's atmosphere and lithosphere? At the very least, we have an obligation to future generations, just as we have an obligation to people living elsewhere from the immediate site of our actions. Wellington (2004) uses this set of obligations to formulate what he calls "science-based" ideas and principles to guide our moral-ethical decisions and determine our actions, including acknowledgement that the Earth's resources are finite and not always renewable or replenishable, awareness of our ecological footprints (and that resource use is unevenly distributed around the world), and recognition of the interconnectedness of all living things. Chapter 8 will address these matters at greater length.

WHY AND HOW TO TEACH ETHICS

Reiss (1999) asks us to ponder the question, "Why teach ethics?" In other words, what are the aims of teaching ethics in science? Or elsewhere in the curriculum, for that matter. One answer is that scientific practice has its own code of ethics and scientific literacy demands that students be aware of it and act in accordance with it when conducting their own scientific work. In addition to ethical considerations relating to choice of research priorities, ethical conduct entails a requirement to collect data honestly, state conclusions with clarity and without distortion or bias, accept criticism willingly, defend one's views rationally, and so on, although Hall (2004) maintains that these are not so much moral-ethical values as methodological requirements: "scientists do not adhere to these requirements because they are moral but because they are a necessary (but not sufficient) condition for admission to the community of scientists" (p. 25). Proper ethical conduct also extends to considerations relating to plagiarism, fair treatment of technicians, students and colleagues, and proper conduct when reviewing and responding to the work of other scientists. The entire scientific enterprise is based on trust: trust in the moral-ethical values that underpin the identification of research priorities and the daily conduct of scientists, trust in the validity of currently accepted scientific knowledge (until there is strong evidence to support its replacement), and trust that all practitioners accept and adhere to particular standards in the collection and presentation of data and the construction of scientific arguments (Norris, 1995; Harding & Hare, 2000; Gaon & Norris, 2001). In short, scientists need to know that they can trust the work of other scientists (including other members of their own research team) and that their own work will be accepted as trustworthy. Without such trust in each other the scientific enterprise cannot function effectively and productively. The independent justification of most of our beliefs is just not possible and, as discussed in chapter 4, even those at the cutting edge of research must take on trust much of the knowledge they deploy, including the knowledge underpinning the design and utilization of the many complex modern instrumental techniques on which so much contemporary research depends. As Lorraine Code (1987) points out, there is a complex network of interdependence that constitutes an *epistemic contract* among scientists.

> Scientists themselves must rely heavily for their facts upon the authority they acknowledge in their fellow scientists. They use the results of sciences other than their own and of other scientists in different areas of their own field, results they may feel neither called upon *nor* competent to test for themselves... For this interdependence to be workable, there must be a tacit basis of trust and trustworthiness... a sort of *epistemic contract*. (Code, 1987, p. 230, emphasis added)

Just as it would be dishonest of science teachers to pretend that individual scientists do not, from time to time, make mistakes and errors of judgement, it is also dishonest to deny, trivialize or remain silent about sharp practice, misconduct and fraud in science. Errors can arise through (i) hasty, inattentive, negligent or careless data collection, (ii) inadvertent mistakes in preparing materials or taking measurements, (iii) reliance during the design and performance of experiments on theories that later turn out to be false or incomplete, (iv) failure to recognize other significant factors impacting behaviour, or (v) inadequate testing or failure to test at all. As discussed in chapter 4, in the highly competitive world of contemporary scientific research, with the constant need to secure research funding and generate publications, scientists are sometimes tempted to 'cut corners', be less rigorous than perhaps they should, overstate their case, or make premature claims. Stealing data from other research groups, trying to mislead competitors by publishing erroneous or incomplete data, and using delaying tactics when reviewing articles for publication written by rivals, are more common than science teachers might suppose (Wong & Hodson, 2009, 2010). How much of this less-than-savoury tale should we tell students? Should school science education address issues of scientific misconduct and fraud? Borrowing from Allchin's (2004a) argument for teaching about errors in science, one could argue that studying *mis*conduct in science is a powerful way of educating students about *proper* conduct as well as reinforcing their understanding of the sociocultural climate that seduces some scientists to violate the code. Misconduct involves such things as plagiarism (of ideas and data), failing to acknowledge co-workers as authors, simultaneous publication of the same data in different locations, failure to acknowledge involvement of (or funding by) commercial enterprises, use of threats and bribes to influence other scientists, falsification and fabrication of data, including concealment of 'inconvenient data'. It does not include errors in recording, selecting and analyzing data, or errors of judgement and interpretation. Clearly, it is very important to distinguish between what is intended and what is unintended.

The issue of fraud in science was discussed in chapter 4, and some suitable examples for study in the school curriculum were identified (see, also, later discussion in this chapter). Fraud is, of course, potentially devastating to science because it undermines the trust that other scientists need to have in published work, including scientific knowledge on which they may wish to build their own research endeavours.

The commitment to conduct their work in an ethically responsible way does not entail a requirement for scientists to be silent on science policy issues, research priorities and controversial SSI. It is important to remember, as discussed several times in this book, that scientific practice is a values-impregnated activity. Failure to criticize ethically indefensible or questionable values implicitly gives assent to them. Not all positions are equally defensible; if they are not, then proper ethical conduct and scientific objectivity requires one to acknowledge it and act appropriately. As Lemons (1995) comments, "objectivity represented as neutrality in the face of possible significant hazards or threats is to serve the interests of those responsible for the threats... objectivity represented as neutrality ignores the fact that objectivity is negotiated and discovered socially through grappling with alternative points of view... objectivity represented as neutrality can sanction ethical relativism and therefore serve the interests of injustice" (p. 106). Donnelly (2004) provides a discussion of some of these matters, including comments on the particular ethical issues raised by experiments involving living things. A consideration of issues relating to informed consent and non-manipulative and non-exploitative treatment of human subjects extends beyond the scope of this chapter; issues concerning what counts as ethical treatment of animals were briefly raised earlier in the chapter.

Kovac (1999) discusses several approaches to teaching professional ethics, including formal courses, use of case studies and what he calls "the ethics moment" (dealing with issues as they arise in the design and conduct of particular investigations). Research by Clarkeburn (2003) reveals a depressingly low level of ethical awareness among undergraduate science students, though the author does show that awareness increases substantially and rapidly when students are engaged in what she calls "ethics-sensitizing activities". Ethics has a much higher profile in engineering and medical education, where programmes have often been in place for many years. Both these areas can provide interesting issues for school-age students to consider. For example, engineers have a great deal of freedom in terms of what they create and, therefore, carry the responsibility to use that power and influence wisely, fairly and ethically. All stages of engineering practice, from initial problem definition and design brief, through evaluation of alternatives to eventual design implementation, involve engineers in trying to balance and trade-off issues relating to technical feasibility, client wishes, legal constraints, social and environmental impact, costs and aesthetics, requiring them to make decisions that are value-laden and have ethical dimensions. Medicine raises all kinds of ethical problems relating to medical priorities, treatment routines and research protocols, together with issues such as xenotransplantation, organ donation, euthanasia and sophisticated birth technology. In addressing the ethical issues surrounding clinical trials of drugs and experimental medical treatments (including diets), Weinstein (2008) asks whether the notion of "informed consent" needs to be substantially extended beyond consideration of potential risks and benefits to include frank discussion of the purposes of the research (including profit motives), ownership of data collected, and the criteria used to select the "treatment population". The latter issue relates to the all-too-common practice of recruiting the poor and marginalized through use of financial incentives and targeting people who are clearly ill-equipped in terms of scientific literacy to make a genuinely informed and responsible decision about their involvement.

Drawing on the work of Davis (1999), Michael Reiss (1999) identifies four additional justifications for teaching ethics: (i) *raising ethical sensitivity* – helping students to recognize previously 'invisible' moral-ethical issues in everyday situations and events; (ii) *increasing ethical knowledge* – providing students with the intellectual resources to recognize the relationships among interests, rights, duties and obligations; (iii) *improving ethical judgement* – providing experiences that increase the likelihood that students reach ethically defensible decisions on issues; and (iv) *fostering ethical conduct* – equipping students with the knowledge, skills, attitudes and experiences that can lead to behaviour and actions that are ethically sound. Put more simply, since students will meet moral dilemmas in many aspects of their lives, teachers have a moral duty to help them acquire the means to address such dilemmas critically and confidently. Ability to do so in the context of SSI is, of course, a key component of critical scientific literacy. Students need to be morally literate if they are to engage in debate about SSI and contribute to decision-making at a local, regional, national and international level. They need a high level of moral-ethical literacy in order to contribute to debate about how to solve the world's current environmental crises and ensure a reasonable quality of life for future generations. In short, an understanding of ethics and facility in reaching decisions on moral-ethical issues are needed for social reconstruction and for effecting change in the way we conduct our lives.

According to Rest (1986) and Rest et al. (1986), individuals will only act in a morally appropriate and defensible way if they have developed *moral sensitivity, moral reasoning, moral commitment* and *moral courage*. Moral sensitivity is the ability to recognize when a situation has a moral dimension (as in the definition proposed by Reiss, above), and to recognize how it will be perceived differently and will impact differently on different people. It presupposes a measure of emotional literacy, including feelings of sympathy, empathy and compassion (see discussion in chapter 6). Moral reasoning is the capacity to formulate a course of action and provide a well-argued defence for it. Moral commitment is the willingness to choose the most moral course of action, regardless of personal concerns and interests. Moral courage is the determination to follow through with one's moral commitment regardless of obstacles and opposition. Developing these attributes requires that students be presented with a wide range of situations that require a moral judgement to be made (see Rest et al., 1974). As Tirri and Pehkonen (2002) note, such judgements vary enormously with content and context, with the same student using very different moral principles on different occasions. Haidt (2001) postulates the notion of *moral intuition*, that is, a "gut feeling" that something is either right or wrong[82]. Moral judgements, Haidt argues, are arrived at quickly and effortlessly through moral intuition; moral reasoning is a much slower and more controlled process of searching for arguments that will constitute a *post-hoc* justification for that intuitive moral judgement. In other words, moral reasoning is the retrospective rationalization of judgements that have already been reached by intuition, and are rarely changed by subsequent reasoning. Students are more likely to change their views when they are confronted with the well-articulated moral reasoning of teachers, peers, family members or some other highly regarded person, or when they are suddenly confronted with, or immersed in an SSI at a personal level. Role play can also be very effective. Simply by putting oneself into the shoes of another person, one may instantly feel pain, sympathy or other vicarious emotional responses that can trigger moral reflection and a change of view. Indeed, some would argue that mature moral-ethical reasoning presupposes a capacity to empathize with others, and to see the world from a range of human perspectives.

Of course, this is an aspect of education that is deeply controversial, especially in our increasingly pluralist society. It therefore behoves teachers to teach ethics in an ethically responsible way and to exhibit in their teaching the approach they seek to develop in their students. Reference has already been made in chapter 6 to the comments of Rogers et al. (2007) on the nature of an "ethically attentive practice" and to my advocacy of "the communicative virtues" (Levinson, 2006). Both these notions are central to this current discussion. So, too, are the principles of communicative ethics developed by Jurgen Habermas (1990): discourse must be free of violence and the use of force or social and economic power, and be restricted only by universal ethical principles. Everyone with competence to speak (and interest in doing so) is permitted to take part in the discourse, allowed to express her/his attitudes, desires and needs, introduce any assertion into the discourse, and question any assertion introduced by others. No-one may be prevented by internal or external coercion from exercising these rights. Fullick and Ratcliffe (1996) suggest that a basic principle of an ethical education is the right of students to address science-related issues that they feel may affect their lives. In consequence, they argue, teachers have the duty to provide students with the opportunity to exercise this right. Fulfilling this duty requires teachers to foster respect for rational inquiry, encourage open-mindedness, cultivate a willingness to listen to and respect the points of view of others and take steps to avoid hasty judgement, develop students' awareness of similarities and differences in ethical interpretations of issues, and avoid indoctrination. With a diverse student body, the task is not a simple one. However, teachers can learn to proceed cautiously and respectfully, and to develop students' abilities to do likewise. I am in total sympathy with David Selby's (1995) assertion that "the role of the teacher combines a comforting of the agitated and an agitating of the comfortable" (p. 42). The former encompasses: (i) challenging the views of students without undermining their confidence and self-esteem; (ii) ensuring that the source of discomfort is identified and dealt with sensitively; (iii) providing students with the opportunity to 'think on their feet' in order to respond immediately, but also to reflect on their views in order to reach a considered decision; and (iv) being unafraid to say "I don't know" or "I can't decide" (thus reinforcing the view that good answers, let alone right answers, are difficult to reach). "Agitating the comfortable" requires teachers to raise provocative, challenging and controversial matters, and demand that students confront them, too. It requires them to assist students in reconciling conflicts and reaching reasoned conclusions on proper actions in difficult, complex and sometimes uncertain circumstances. As discussed at length in chapter 10, teachers need to be aware of the ways in which discussion of SSI (and ethical dimensions in particular) might disturb, upset or antagonize students, parents, school Principals and governors, religious leaders, local industry chiefs, politicians, and so on. Teachers themselves need the moral commitment and moral courage they aim to develop in their students. Socioscientific issues are too important for teachers to be frightened into avoiding them.

Fullick and Ratcliffe (1996) describe a number of strategies that can help to direct student attention to the ethical concerns embedded in SSI and assist them in dealing with ethical dilemmas in a systematic and rational way. Strategies include: consequence mapping or "future wheels" (through which students are asked to consider a range of personal, social, economic, legal, environmental and ethical implications surrounding an issue and the possible responses to it); use of a goals-rights-duties framework (for each player or constituency involved in a controversy, students consider the intentions, rights/expectations and obligations towards others and the environment); and group discussions around carefully focused questions (oral or written questions direct student attention to the nature of the problem, possible solutions, reasons why one solution may be preferred to another, and stimulate reflection on students' own value positions). Pfeiffer (1992) has developed the RESOLVEDD strategy for dealing with personal ethical conflicts.

R Review of the history, background and details of the situation.
E Estimation of the conflict or problem one confronts.
S Solutions deemed to be possible in the situation are listed, grouped and reduced to a small number of main solutions.
O Outcomes or consequences of each main solution are described.
L Likely impact of main solutions on people's lives are noted.
V Values upheld and compromised by main solutions are examined.
E Evaluation and refining of main solutions and search for other solutions in light of relevant value conflicts.
D Decision one arrives at is clarified, refined and supported.
D Defence of the decision against objections and major weaknesses.

In addition to publishing case studies of a wide range of issues in biotechnology, the New Zealand Biotechnology Learning Hub (www.biotechlearn.org.nz) provides support for students addressing ethical issues in the form of two interactive "thinking tools". The "ethics thinking tool" enables students to structure and evaluate their ideas in relation to four sets of ethical guidelines: benefits and harms; rights and responsibilities; freedom of choice; virtues[83]. The "futures thinking tool" encourages students to consider the existing situation, analyze trends, identify the driving forces and causes of those trends, identify possible and probable futures, and select preferred futures. Use of these tools, together with a wide range of other teaching and learning strategies, is discussed by several authors in the edited collection: *Ethics in the Science and Technology Classroom* (Jones et al., 2010). Other organizations providing valuable ethics-oriented teaching materials via the

Internet include: the Bioethics Education Project (www.beep.ac.uk), the University of Iowa Bioethics Outreach Program (www.bioethics.iastate.edu), the ShiPS Teachers' Network (www.umn.educ/ships/ethics) and the Eubios Ethics Institute (www.eubios.info/index).

Although it was designed for *evaluating* students' moral reasoning, Lind's (2008) Moral Judgment Test could be usefully employed as a teaching and learning strategy. After being presented with a moral dilemma, students are asked to judge whether the protagonist's decision was right or wrong, and to provide their reasoning. Thereafter, they are presented with six arguments in favour of the decision and six arguments opposing it, each of which is written to reflect one of Kohlberg's (1984) six stages of moral development: obedience and punishment orientation; self-interest; interpersonal accord and conformity; maintaining social order; social contract and individual rights; universal ethical principles. Acknowledging that it can sometimes be difficult to apply Kohlberg's model, Jones et al. (2007) and Reiss (2010b) have developed a series of indicators of progression (or trends) in ethical thinking that may have more immediate classroom utility.

- From viewing an ethical issue in purely personal terms to adopting the perspectives of one's peers, followed by those of the wider community and, finally, those of people globally.
- From holding an egocentric position to following social rules, then to adhering to reasoned principles.
- From being able to use one ethical framework to being able to use two or three.
- From considering only humans to considering other sentient animals, and finally to consideration of entire ecosystems.
- From an orientation to the present to an orientation towards the future.
- From using one's current knowledge to searching for and considering new ideas.
- From a single perspective to multiple perspectives.
- From focus on one's own values to acknowledging and considering the values of others.
- From simple acceptance of ethical frameworks to rigorous critique of them.
- From a dependence on consulting frameworks before using them to internalization, personalization and intuitive use of them.

Sherborne (2004) describes some less-structured but highly motivating approaches, including a card game focused on organ transplants and the need to obtain consent from family members of potential donors on life support, or already deceased, a simulated television discussion of the scientific, legal and ethical issues surrounding the pre-implantation screening of embryos created by IVF to detect genetic disorders, and the involvement of students in editing video material on bioterrorism for broadcasting as a television news item. In the latter activity, students are asked to select video items, order them into a story and provide a suitable commentary, thus requiring them to identify and prioritize risks and benefits associated with research into viruses and bacteria, consider the possibility of bioterrorist activity, evaluate strategies for defence, and decide what is in the best interests of viewers in terms of balancing awareness and anxiety. Evaluation of existing print, video and multimedia reports provides valuable opportunities for students to explore some issues in depth while contributing to their media literacy by gaining further insight into the techniques used to generate emotions such as hope, optimism, anxiety, fear and anger in readers/viewers. De Luca (2010) discusses how stories of various kinds can be used to sensitize students to ethical issues and raise awareness of alternative viewpoints located in different cultural traditions (see also, discussion in chapter 6), while Odegaard (2003, 2004) provides helpful guidelines and graphic illustration of the use of role play and drama (both writing dramatic pieces and performing them) in sensitizing students to the likely impact of ethical dilemmas on the lives of those involved. In summary, literature, movies, drama, poetry, debates and Town Hall meetings, case studies and student-led seminars all have an important role to play, as does extended project work, preparation of a detailed report on the ethical issues surrounding a topical SSI, and simple 'off-the-cuff' class discussion in response to a news item raised by a student. Kempton (2004) suggests the use of paintings, cartoons, newspaper advertisements and spoof/satirical 'adverts' such as those produced by Adbusters.

LEARNING THROUGH CASE STUDIES

Although students do not employ the sophisticated reasoning that a medical ethicist, philosopher or medical geneticist might use to reach decisions on ethical issues relating to genetic disorders, as studies by Dawson and Taylor (2004) and Lindahl (2009) reveal, there is ample evidence that with practice they get better at it. It is worth noting that numerous studies, from Rosenthal and Jacobsen (1968) to Rubie-Davies (2006), have shown that teacher expectation is a powerful influence on student performance. Interestingly, it seems that high teacher expectations are particularly important in assisting students to deal appropriately and effectively with the ethical dimensions of SSI (Hanegan et al., 2008). The kind of ethical dilemmas described by Solomon (1992), Bell and Lederman (2003), Sadler and Zeidler (2004, 2005b), Dawson and Venville (2009) and Halverson et al. (2009) (see chapter 6) provide valuable opportunities for students to practice, critique and develop their ethical reasoning, even at the elementary school level (Buntting & Ryan, 2010). A topical and important focus might be the ethical issues raised by GM foods and the processes used to create them, for which Frewer et al. (1997), Pascalev (2003) and Knight (2009) provide some suitable background information. One dividing line between supporters and opponents of genetic modification is whether genetic manipulation is simply an extension of selective breeding practices (used by farmers for millennia) or whether they are fundamentally different processes. For some, genetic manipulation is ethically acceptable for plants, but not for animals. Others might draw the line of acceptability/unacceptability at the "mixing of plant and animal DNA", or of either with human DNA. There is value, too, in students looking at the prime motivation for developing GM crops. Is it a bold attempt to increase food production by creating high-yielding plants, pest-resistant plants, herbicide-resistant plants and plants that can grow well in arid regions? Or is it a means of creating a monopoly for the biotechnology companies like Monsanto that have patented the plants? One possible answer to these questions can be found in Conway's (2000) observation that the reality of the GM revolution in many African countries is that food insecurity has dramatically increased and many peasant farmers have been drawn into debt, sometimes leading to dispossession and suicide. Another answer might be found in Baskaran and Boden's (2006) account of Monsanto's questionable conduct in relation to GM crops and the herbicide *Roundup*. Conway (2000) also discusses what has become known as *bio-piracy*: companies and research institutes scour the forests of India, Southeast Asia, Africa and South America to identify plants with potentially high commercial value, isolate and modify their genes, and then patent them and the new plants they derive from them. Local people then have to pay to have access to plants that they have nurtured and used for millennia. Many countries in the South are attempting to resist this bio-piracy by establishing legal systems to safeguard public access to biological and genetic resources and to all forms of traditional knowledge (Simpson et al., 1997). The most celebrated example of these efforts in recent years has been the lengthy fight to annul the patents held on products derived from the bark, leaves and seeds of the neem tree, which generations of people living in India and Burma have used as insecticides, spermicides, medicines and cosmetics. Case studies can be designed to enable students to consider the ethical dimensions of the risks and uncertainties that surround the release of genetically modified plants and animals into the natural environment – for example, the risk of unanticipated interaction with humans (or other animals) such as allergic reactions to the proteins used to code genetic sequences or antibiotic resistance being transferred from transgenic foods or the risk that a modified plant may interact with other plants and/or with insects to produce robust, invasive and herbicide-resistant 'weeds' or voracious, insecticide-resistant pests. While biotechnology companies are, of course, keen to downplay or even ridicule these concerns, there are important questions to be asked about the rights of people to be protected from unnecessary risks undertaken in pursuit of the commercial interests of others. There is a situation here that exactly mirrors the paradox identified earlier in this chapter in relation to animal experiments. As Yearley (2008) points out, "GM seed companies are keen to stress the distinctiveness of their products. GM material can only be patented because it is demonstrably novel. How then can one be sure that it is novel enough to merit patent protection but not so novel that differences beyond the level of substantial equivalence may not turn out to matter a decade or two into the future?" (p. 932).

Intelligence testing, and the attempts to link intelligence to gender, race and ethnicity, provides another fruitful area for student research. The gender and racial bias underpinning the development of the Stanford-Binet IQ test has already been mentioned (chapter 5). Even more ethically dubious is the work of Phillipe Rushton in pursuit of a link between race and cognitive ability (Rushton, 1997, 2000; Rushton & Jensen, 2005). From such studies, students can learn how easy it is to be seduced by sophisticated statistical techniques into assigning actual physical properties to abstract mathematical entities[84], especially when they serve to reinforce our own prejudices and further an ethically questionable agenda. Case studies of bias in science, scientific malpractice, unethical conduct and fraud, together with the deliberate misuse of science and what has been termed *scientific racism* would be particularly valuable here (see chapter 4). At the most extreme, examples of the horrific experiments on human subjects conducted by Nazi scientists studying hypothermia and the physiological effects of various poisons could be used to set the scene (Proctor, 1991; Caplan, 1992). The kinds of socio-cultural prejudices underpinning the science of phrenology (Shapin, 1979; Hodson & Prophet, 1986; Sadler & Zeidler, 2003) and the eugenics movement (Gould, 1995; Black, 2003) provide further examples of the ways in which science has been used to pursue particularly odious social and political agendas. Students might also be asked to ponder the assertion by Duster (1990/2003) that human molecular biology constitutes a "backdoor to eugenics" (see earlier discussion). Interestingly, Jallinoja and Azo (2000) report that such fears are greater among those with greater know-ledge of genetics. As noted in chapter 4, there is enormous value in considering some specific incidents of malpractice and in examining cases of scientific fraud, such as the Piltdown Man forgery and the now discredited work of Cyril Burt, John Darsee, Jan Hendrick Schon and Hwang Woo-Suk.

Sadler and Zeidler (2003) describe several examples of unethical science conducted by governments and business, including the Tuskegee syphilis experiments, in which African American males with syphilis were left untreated in order to monitor the "natural course of the disease", a programme that was maintained from 1932 to 1972[85]. During the 1970s, a similar experiment involving the withholding of treatment for cervical cancer was conducted in New Zealand. For more than a decade, beginning in 1966, Dr Hubert Green of Auckland's National Women's Hospital adopted a "wait and see" approach to women presenting with abnormal cervical lesions, known as *carcinoma in situ* (CIS), instead of adopting the usual practice of removing them immediately on detection by routine "pap smear" tests. Many of the women (22%) subjected to this experimental "conservative approach", most of whom did not know that they were being studied or that they were being treated in an unorthodox way, went on to develop invasive cancer of the cervix or vagina and had to undergo radical surgery such as hysterectomy. As many as 27 women in the experimental group died, that is, 9% of the experimental group compared with 0.5% of the group treated in the more usual way. These events were brought to public attention by Sandra Coney and Phillida Bunkle in an article titled "An unfortunate experiment at National Women's", published in *Metro* magazine in June 1987. Subsequently, in 1988, an inquiry headed by Judge Silvia Cartwright declared Green's treatment to be unethical and the management of his patients to be inadequate. Among other episodes discussed by Sadler and Zeidler (2003) are the reckless disregard of the safety of both civilians and military personnel during the testing of nuclear weapons by the United States[86] and the cynical distortion, misrepresentation and suppression of data on the harmful effects of cigarette smoke by the tobacco industry[87].

Students might also research the circumstances that led to the Pfizer pharmaceutical company being fined US$2.3 billion for inducing physicians to prescribe drugs for uses not approved by the FDA (see chapter 4) or the circumstances surrounding Borden Chemicals being fined US$3.5 million for storing hazardous waste illegally, failing to install adequate containment systems, burning hazardous waste without a permit, neglecting to report the release of hazardous chemicals into the air, contaminating groundwater beneath the plant site in Geismar (Louisiana) and shipping toxic waste overseas without EPA permission. At a more general level, students might consider the global trade in pharmaceuticals and the ways in which major drug companies sometimes use spurious data concerning research and development costs in support of pricing policies in situations where those factors are not significant – a tactic that artificially inflates the price of particular drugs. Angell (2004) states that most major drug companies spend at least twice as much on marketing as they do on research and development, and may spend even more on actions designed to prevent or delay the introduction by competitors of generic versions of their own established "brand name" drugs. Moreover, Angell (2004) claims, most of the R&D budget is directed towards designing higher-priced minor modifications of existing medicines (what she calls "me-too drugs") – a move that effectively extends the patent rights. Considerable resources are then deployed in persuading physicians to prescribe them. Companies also routinely engage in so-called "market segmentation" policies, that is, fixing the price of drugs differently in different countries irrespective of actual production costs. Further, as Bencze (2008) points out, some ethically very dubious tactics are sometimes employed during clinical trials to enhance the chances of FDA approval, including "use of small sample sizes, younger, healthier subjects (who may be less susceptible to negative side effects), lower doses than those to be prescribed, higher doses of the new drug tested against lower doses of the old drug (for which the patent period had expired), ineffective drug delivery techniques for tests of older drugs that companies want off the market, and short test periods" (p. 306). Zavetoski et al. (2004b) report that some pharmaceutical companies have been known to set up "front groups" masquerading as patient advocacy groups in order to build up demand for a particular drug and/or put pressure on the FDA and Medicare for drug approval. It is also the case that researchers under contract to drug companies are often prevented from publishing any negative data from clinical trials (see Bencze et al. (2009) for examples).

Sadler and Zeidler (2003) advocate that students also look carefully and critically at situations in which scientific/technological interventions based on poorly designed scientific investigations, faulty reasoning, hasty conclusions, and economic pressure to reach a solution, have led to enormously damaging environmental impact. Their principal examples are the deployment of DDT and CFCs. They also discuss examples of the unanticipated consequences of introducing exotic species in an effort to change the ecological balance. For example, melaleuca trees, native to Australia and Papua New Guinea, were introduced into Florida in an attempt to soak up water and convert land deemed to be "unproductive swampland" into land suitable for farming and building. The trees have adapted spectacularly well to their new environment, displacing native species (and the plants and animals that depended on them) and impacting the fragile wetlands ecosystem of the Everglades to such an extent that a wetlands restoration scheme costing hundreds of millions of dollars is now necessary. The introduction of possums into New Zealand and cane toads into the sugar plantations of Queensland would also make excellent case studies, as would the injustices (especially the massive increase in local food prices) resulting from the widespread appropriation of agricultural land in Africa for producing biofuels.

In common with many other curriculum innovations, introduction of moral-ethical dilemmas and problem-solving raises questions about assessment and evaluation. A particular concern is the development of methods capable of addressing the subtle nuances involved in the rational weighing of alternatives that precedes complex judgement calls. Assessment methods need to be sufficiently open-ended to allow students to demonstrate their awareness of ambiguity and context-dependence and their skills of analysis, evaluation and synthesis. Conner (2004) describes some innovative approaches using reflective journals and both peer and self-assessment. As part of the Salters-Nuffield Advanced Level biology programme for 16–18 year-olds in the UK, in which students are introduced to four frameworks for ethical reasoning (utilitarianism, rights and duties, autonomous reasoning, and virtue ethics), there is a requirement for students to submit a report on a biology-related SSI or on a fieldtrip or site visit. Reiss (2008) reports that ethical reasoning was employed in all the scripts he examined dealing with global warming and that students were able to reason validly and systematically about ethical matters. He notes a marked preference for utilitarian reasoning: 16 out of the 17 scripts examined, compared with 4 out of 17 employing arguments about rights and duties, 3 out of 17 making reference to autonomy, and only one using virtue ethics. He also notes the preponderance of anthropocentric reasoning – an issue to be addressed in chapter 8.

CONFRONTING ENVIRONMENTAL ISSUES

To say that there are important questions to be asked about the nature, extent and seriousness of the environmental degradation we face, and about what can and should be done to address it, is not to say anything new or particularly startling. As David Orr (1994) comments, "the truth is that many things on which our future health and prosperity depend are in dire jeopardy: climate stability, the resilience and productivity of natural systems, the beauty of the natural world, and biological diversity" (p. 7). Elsewhere, Orr (1992) concludes that the environmental crisis is "not only a permanent feature of the public agenda, for all practical purposes it is *the* agenda. No other issue of politics, economics, and public policy will remain unaffected by the crisis of resources, population, climate change, species extinction, acid rain, deforestation, ozone depletion and soil loss. Sustainability is about the terms and conditions of human survival, and yet we still educate at all levels as if no such crisis existed" (p. 83). Science and technology education, and in particular the kind of action-oriented approach advocated in this book, needs to grasp this particular nettle before it is too late.

Despite the efforts of environmental scientists and environmental activists, many citizens remain blissfully unaware of the extent of the problems. Or they deny the evidence. Or they blithely assume that science and technology will solve the problems anyway, regardless of their extent. Many people experience difficulty in acknowledging the extent of the world's problems, the levels of suffering and deprivation involved, and the dangers of failing to act. An innate protective instinct can result in what Walsh (1992) calls "psychic numbing" that denies both the reality and our part in creating it. Kahn (1999) coined the expression "environmental generational amnesia" to explain some aspects of our society's persistent blindness to the extent of the crises.

> People may take the natural environment they encounter during childhood as the norm against which to measure environmental degradation later in their life. The crux here is that with each ensuing generation, the amount of environmental degradation increases, but each generation takes that amount as the norm, as the nondegraded condition. The upside is that each generation starts afresh, unencumbered mentally by the environmental mistakes and misdeeds of previous generations. The downside is that each of us can have difficulty understanding in a direct, experiential way that nature as experienced in our childhood is not the norm, but is already environmentally degraded. (p. 7)

Orr (1994) identifies a number of barriers that prevent us from appreciating the scale and extent of the environmental problems we face and acknowledging the need for radical changes in the way we live, including an unwillingness to accept that science and technology cannot solve all our problems, the lack of a *biophilic* imagination[88], and being comfortable with ugliness. This third barrier is not quite as surprising as it initially seems when notice is taken of Orr's (1994) comment that ugliness is not just an aesthetic issue, it is a sign of disease and malaise in society: "Show me the hamburger stands, neon ticky-tacky strips leading toward every city in America, and the shopping malls, and I'll show you devastated rain forests, a decaying countryside, a politically dependent population, and toxic waste dumps" (p. 88). In formulating an approach to environmental problems suitable for school, we need to keep these barriers and these defensive tendencies firmly in mind.

More than thirty years ago, Arthur Lucas (1979) characterized approaches to environmental education as education *about* the environment (development of cognitive understanding of environmental matters and the acquisition of skills used in extending that understanding), education *in* and *through* the environment (direct experience of studying and working outdoors, often seen as having motivational and context-setting value), and education *for* the environment (inculcating values and attitudes consistent with a concern for environmental protection, sustainability and regeneration). Education *about* the environment has the longest tradition and in many parts of the world it is still the dominant form of environmental education - certainly in Canada, as Russell et al. (2001) and Lin (2002) argue. Because of its emphasis on content knowledge it tends to promote a technocentric view of environmental problems, that is, the view that most environmental problems can be addressed and resolved by proper application of scientific knowledge and procedures, and by better resource management.

> The technocentric world view promoted by education *about* the environment ignores the important qualitative dimension of the majority of environmental issues which involve 'quality of life' or 'social need' concerns – emotions, beliefs, aspirations, aesthetics and, perhaps most important of all, vested interests. It could be argued that a view of the resolution of environmental problems that stresses the role of technical rationality (i.e., the processes of an objective, applied science method) creates a false impression of the way these issues are resolved. (Robottom, 1987, p. 104)

It could be argued that the technocratic approach to environmental issues, through its prioritization of human needs and interests, has contributed substantially to the perpetuation of attitudes and values that have led to the environmental crises we now face. It could also be argued that education *about* the environment, education *in* the environment and education *for* the environment can be characterized in terms of the Habermasian notion of knowledge-constitutive interest: *technical, practical* and *emancipatory*. In other words, the three styles of environmental education are shaped in accordance with the particular human interests they serve. The technical interest is governed by people's interest in acquiring knowledge that is instrumental, explanatory, causal and able to facilitate technical control over events and provide solutions to problems and issues in the environment. The practical interest seeks to clarify the issues, engage in meaningful communication and dialogue with diverse stakeholders and generate knowledge in the form of interpretive understanding that can inform and guide both personal and collective judgements. The emancipatory interest seeks freedom and personal autonomy through an understanding of how one's thoughts and actions (and the thoughts and actions of others) are shaped, influenced and ultimately distorted by constraints of authority, ignorance, custom, tradition and vested interest. While this characterization may have some theoretical value, it seems to locate the three forms of environmental education in a hierarchy of value. My own view is that all three are essential; none is sufficient in itself. As noted in chapter 2, those students who know more about the topic/issue under consideration will be better positioned to understand the underlying issues, evaluate different positions, reach their own conclusions, make an informed decision on where they stand in relation to the issue, and argue their point of view. In other words, education *about* the environment is a crucial precursor to education *for* the environment, and as I will argue in chapter 9, education *in* the environment is a particularly effective way of sensitizing students to environmental issues and cultivating the values that lead to a commitment to work *for* the environment.

EDUCATION *ABOUT* THE ENVIRONMENT

Adopting the Ausubelian principle of starting with students' existing knowledge, it is important for teachers to know as much as possible about students' existing conceptions of the environment and the values they hold with respect to it. Studies conducted in Australia (Connell et al., 1998, 1999; Payne, 1998a,b; Walker et al., 1999; Loughland et al., 2002, 2003), the United Kingdom (Bonnett & Williams, 1998; Myers et al., 1999, 2000; Littledyke, 2004), Sweden (Gooch, 1995; Alerby, 2000), China (Yeung, 1998; Ma, 2009), the Netherlands (Kuhlemeier et al., 1999), Greece (Flogaitis & Agelidou, 2003) and the United States (Cobern et al., 1999; Rickinson, 2001; Shepardson, 2005; Shepardson et al., 2007; Desjean-Perrotta et al., 2008) reveal that many students (and often their teachers, too) have a fairly unsophisticated view of the environment as "a place where plants and animals live". There is often only scant understanding that humans are part of the environment and have impact on it, and many students omit entirely any consideration of urban environments and human-managed landscapes. Research using the New Environmental Paradigm-Human Exception Paradigm (NEP-HEP) scale developed by Dunlap and van Liere (1978), which includes items related to "the need for natural balance" and "limits to human impact on nature" (NEP dimension) and items expressed in anthropocentric terms regarding the view that humankind is different from and has control over nature (HEP dimension), reveal similarly confused and uncertain views among students (Bechtel et al., 1999; Kim, 1999; Corral-Verdugo & Armendáriz, 2000; van Petegem & Blieck, 2006). Cajete (1999) comments that some students suffer from *biophobia*: "a fear of nature reflected in the culturally conditioned tendency to affiliate with technology and human artefacts and to concentrate primarily on human interests when relating to the natural world" (p. 190). Biophobic attitudes exist along a continuum ranging from discomfort in natural places to active contempt or disregard for anything that is not human-made or managed by people[89]. Disturbingly, Rickinson (2001) notes that young children sometimes see the environment as threatening and potentially dangerous. Wals (1994) reports, for example, that a number of students from inner-city Detroit felt that "nature itself can be scary because of the dangerous animals that wander around, but the real danger comes from the people who are there and the fact that there is no familiar place to escape to" (p. 189). Similarly, Bonnett and Williams (1998) report that some of the children in their UK-based survey expressed a fear of "being mugged" when they are in the countryside. Parental anxiety about the safety of their children, fuelled by sensationalist media reporting, results in many children choosing to avoid open countryside and woodlands, resulting in what Louv (2005) calls "nature deficit disorder". Bixler and Floyd (1997) also report on fear of snakes, insects and spiders and a generalized fear of woodlands among their Texas-based high school students. Many students also expressed feelings of disgust at the dirtiness and smelliness of the outdoors, and discomfort at the weather, which they perceived as being more extreme in the country than in the city. Addressing these feelings is clearly a matter of some urgency.

Numerous research studies conducted over the past two decades show that both students' and teachers' knowledge of specific environmental issues such as the causes, consequences and appropriate responses to acid rain, atmospheric pollution, ozone depletion, desertification, loss of biodiversity and climate change are often incomplete and/or confused, and so constitute a formidable barrier to politicization of students and preparation for action[90]. Boyes and Stanisstreet (1993) conclude that many students "are unable to disentangle a whole series of environmental problems from their, sometimes overlapping, causes, and therefore assume a generality that all 'environmentally friendly' actions will 'help' all environmental problems" (p. 551). Rickinson (2001) notes that there are substantial variations in environmental know-ledge in relation to gender, age, socioeconomic status and geographical location[91]. In general, it seems that girls tend to know more than boys about environmental issues in the immediate locality and to express more concern about them, especially when they relate to health and human welfare, while boys are more aware of global, longer-term issues of a more abstract nature[92]. Very few students, of either sex, seem to have a clear understanding of *sustainability* or *sustainable development* (Walshe, 2008), which is unsurprising in the light of the confusions surrounding use of the terms in the media and in curriculum documents, as discussed in chapter 1 and later in this chapter. Clearly, a great deal of groundwork is needed before students have sufficient understanding of environmental problems to provide a sound basis for decisions to be made on possible interventions, with Chenhansa and Schleppegrell (1998) emphasizing the key role of precise, unambiguous and concrete language. Too often, they say, use of overly abstract and indirect language impedes a full understanding of complex issues and obscures both the causes and possible solutions of environmental problems[93]. Once again, it is important to note that both students and adults (including teachers) obtain the bulk of their knowledge about environ-mental issues from newspapers, television and the Internet, thus reiterating the call for attention to be directed towards enhancing students' media literacy.

There would be enormous value in different groups of students taking responsibility for collecting reliable up-to-date data on the nature and extent of environmental problems. At the local level, focusing on problems such as air and water pollution, encroaching urbanization and loss of recreational space; at the global level, focusing on matters such as top soil loss, deforestation, wetlands destruction, ozone depletion, species loss and declining fish stocks. They might also look at data on population growth, income levels (especially the gap between rich and poor, both within and between countries), levels of malnutrition and starvation, expenditure on arms and warfare compared with spending on health and education, access to clean drinking water and effective sanitation, per capita energy consumption, and so on. The most serious problem, of course, is global warming and the consequent climate change. In 2007, the Intergovernmental Panel on Climate Change (IPCC) stated: "Warming of the climate system is unequivocal, as is now evident from observations of increases in global average air and ocean temperatures, widespread melting of snow and ice, and rising global average sea level" (p. 1). Predictions are that the mean surface air temperature will rise by 1.8C to 6.4C (with a best estimate of 4.0C) during the 21st Century, and ocean levels will rise by 0.18 to 0.59 metres. Gelbspan (2005) comments as follows: "As we continue to pump gasified carbon and other greenhouse gases into the atmosphere, nature is beginning to respond with furious energy. Storms are becoming more violent, droughts more prolonged, downpours more torrential, and heat waves more intense. As we humans heat the far North and melt the polar ice, nature repays us – at least in the short term – with crueller, more severe winters, as the melting ice chills the south-flowing currents from the Arctic Circle and the northeasters whip the cold air into bitter and seemingly interminable winters" (p. 189). More than 15 years previously, Bill McKibben (1989) had written about "the end of nature", by which he meant that human beings have become so powerful and so dangerous that they have usurped the power of nature, though they have done so in ignorance of the consequences and in the absence, thus far, of the will to relinquish that power.

> We can no longer imagine that we are part of something larger than ourselves – that is what all this boils down to. We used to be. When we were only a few hundred million, or only a billion or two, and the atmosphere had the composition it would have had without us... there was the possibility that something larger than us... reigned over us... But now we make that world, affect its every operation. As a result, there is no-one by our side... And there is nobody above us... Our actions will determine the level of the sea, and change the course and destination of every drop of precipitation. That is, I suppose, the victory we have been pointing to since the eviction from Eden – the domination some have always dreamed of. But... it is a brutish, cloddish power... We sit astride the world like some military dictator – we are able to wreak violence with great efficiency and to destroy all that is good and worthwhile, but not to exercise power to any real end. (McKibben, 1999, pp. 83–84)

Just how much time we have left in which to respond to climate change is hotly debated among scientists (Kolbert, 2007). Whatever the specific prediction we choose to accept, it is clear that the window of opportunity is narrowing fast and, for some, it may already be too late (Lovelock, 2006, 2009; Romm, 2007). Incredibly, some scientists, business executives, politicians and media commentators continue to deny the data or claim that the changes are natural rather than anthropogenic. There are powerful voices in society seeking to suppress information and spread *disinformation* about climate change, and to claim that environmental crises are fictions generated by environmental activists to support their own agendas and generate funding for further research. Terms like "scare mongering", "greenhouse alarmists" and "prophets of doom" are commonplace in the conservative-oriented press. So, too, are appellations that now carry a pejorative tone: "greenie", "tree hugger" and "the Greenpeace crowd". This should serve to remind us, once again, of the need to ensure that students develop high levels of media literacy (see discussion in chapter 2). The charitable view is that journalists give more column space to the anti-environmentalist lobby than is scientifically justified because they are keen to be seen by readers as presenting "both sides of the story". However, this journalistic commitment to the principles of objective reporting is often cynically manipulated by those with a vested interest in manufacturing opposition to the mainstream scientific view. Further, increasing levels of corporate control of the popular media can result in some important scientific data being deliberately withheld, misrepresented or trivialized, and in dissenting voices being over-represented. In the cause of manipulating public opinion, environmentalists are demonized as "ecoterrorists" and protesters are represented as trouble-makers. Consultants are employed and primed by the fossil-fuel industry to cast doubt on the underlying science, while corporate-funded "research centres" and "think tanks" like the National Center for Policy Analysis, Competitive Enterprise Institute, Marshall Institute and Cato Institute are set up to generate conflicting data and present conflicting views about the causes of global warming.

McCright and Dunlap (2000) identify three main strands in the construction of the anti-environmentalist position. First, criticism of the evidentiary basis of global warming, including allegations of inconclusive, confused, flawed or contradictory research data, suggestions that there is no scientific consensus, accusations of wildly exaggerated predictions (such as the IPCC prediction of the total melting of the Himalayan glaciers by 2035 – see chapter 3, especially endnote 31), and even accusations that scientists have falsified data to exaggerate the problems, as in the run-up to the 2009 Copenhagen Conference on Climate Change. Given the discussion in chapter 4 focusing on the ways in which scientists sometimes manipulate data to serve the needs and interests of their employers, it isn't possible merely to shrug off allegations of falsified or distorted data on the grounds that scientists don't do that sort of thing, although substantiating the allegations would seem to imply a vast conspiracy involving most (if not all) scientists who have published material on the topic, whatever their role, status and expertise. At the time I was writing these words, Associated Press had just released details of its review of the 1023 email messages stolen from the Climate Research Unit at the University of East Anglia and posted online, and allegedly revealing how scientists had fabricated or manipulated climate data to support the environmentalist lobby. In the three weeks leading up to the Copenhagen conference, a number of Republican congressmen in the United States, together with former US Vice-Presidential candidate Sarah Palin, called for an independent investigation, a delay in US Environmental Protection Agency regulation of greenhouse gas emissions, and/or outright boycott of the conference on the grounds that the emails revealed a "culture of corruption" among climate scientists. The five reviewing journalists found no evidence that data had been misrepresented, manipulated or faked. Some of the emails expressed disquiet about why data and theoretical models didn't always match - a common occurrence in science; some noted the importance of presenting the data in the most persuasive way possible - precisely what all good research papers are designed and intended to do. The review found some evidence of an increasing reluctance to release data to some of the more vociferous critics of climate change science, largely because of the frequent and often frivolous requests for data that were subsequently made in a clear attempt to divert scientists from their work. A second strategy identified by McCright and Dunlap (2000) is to proclaim the "benefits of global warming" (should it occur), including lower heating bills, reduced transportation delays, fewer accidents in winter, an expanding tourism market in regions such as Alaska and Northern Canada, all-year-round navigable passages through the Arctic, and anticipated benefits to agricultural production. The third and the most vociferous counter-claim strategy focuses on the negative effects of proposed international legislation of greenhouse gas emissions. These include predictions of a "devastating impact" on the economy, economic disadvantage resulting from Developing nations not being held to the same targets and standards as the industrialized world, loss of sovereignty (because decisions are made by bureaucrats in the UN or similar body) and threats to national security resulting from inspection demands.

In commenting on what he calls the "junk science" deployed by lobby groups with names such as Friends of Science, the Natural Resources Stewardship Project and the International Climate Coalition to discredit the work of environmentalists and climate change scientists, and to delay the introduction of stringent carbon emissions legislation, Elshof (2009b) describes tactics that are eerily reminiscent of the tactics used by proponents of creation science and intelligent design to undermine the teaching of evolution in schools. For example, multiple publication of essentially the same meagre data with change of title and re-ordering of the authors' names – a technique that is also widely used by drug companies as a way of implying (but not presenting) a substantial body of research support (Greenberg, 2003). A related tactic uses multiple names and Websites for what is basically the same organization in order to maximize exposure and create the impression that the denial group is substantial in numbers. Elshof (2009b) continues as follows: "These groups often use the bandwagon effect to self-referentially refer to their own non-peer reviewed 'papers' or press releases produced by the 'other' organizations as 'evidence' that their message has wider credibility. This manipulation is often called the 'echo chamber' effect in which inactivists quote and promote each other's junkscience, until the PR 'echo' sounds louder than it would otherwise" (p. 51). Dispensa and Brulle (2003), McCright and Dunlap (2003), Corbett and Durfee (2004) and Mooney (2005) have also written at length about the distortion in the conservative-oriented press of scientific data on global warming, climate change, ozone depletion, environmental pollution and declining fish stocks. This socioculturally constructed culture of denial is both widespread and persuasive, and is reinforced by favourable images of high levels of production and consumption in shopping malls, advertizing posters and the mass media. As Norgaard (2006) comments: "With the protection afforded by material resources, ecological collapse seems a fanciful issue to those in the 'safe' and 'stable' societies of the North as we buy our fruits and vegetables from South America, our furniture from Southeast Asia, and send our wastes into the common atmosphere" (p. 367).

In his extensive survey of research findings on students' environmental concerns, Rickinson (2001) notes substantial variation among students in different parts of the world, although most students tend to regard global and national issues as more serious than local ones (see also: Dunlap et al., 1993; Uzzell, 1999, 2000). A consequence of such views is that many students feel powerless and "unable to make a difference" in respect of the "big issues". Moreover, many feel that others are unable to make a difference either. Indeed, in many parts of the world, young people are pessimistic about the future, with few believing that substantial progress will be made in solving the various environmental crises (Heilbroner, 1995; Hicks & Holden, 1995, 2007; Hicks, 1996; Oscarsson, 1996; Hutchinson, 1997; Barraza, 1999; Connell et al., 1999; Eckersley, 1999, 2002; Gidley & Inayatullah, 2002; Rubin, 2002; Bentley et al., 2004; Holden, 2007). It should be noted that low levels of perceived self-efficacy and personal empowerment regarding global environ-mental problems are also the norm among adults (Levy-Leboyer & Duron, 1991; Uzzell, 2000). It should also be noted that students in the survey conducted by Jenkins and Pell (2006) were not nearly so pessimistic, with 40% of the 1277 respondents believing that solutions to environmental problems will be found, though only 6% said that they would be willing to make personal sacrifices to help achieve solutions[94].

If left unattended, feelings of pessimism and powerlessness can easily lead to apathy regarding pro-environmental action, just as they can lead to lack of personal involvement with respect to other SSI. If we are to build a curriculum that leads to meaningful action, we need to ensure that students are well informed, articulate and confident in their ability to "do something". Therefore, as David Selby (1995) comments, in a somewhat different context, "the role of the teacher combines a comforting of the agitated and an agitating of the comfortable" (p. 42) (see also, chapter 7). Comforting the agitated involves demonstrating to students that the situation is not hopeless; agitating the comfortable is alerting otherwise complacent individuals to some of the harsher realities. But raising awareness needs to be conducted carefully. As Hillcoat et al. (1995), Jensen and Schnack (1997), Kaplan (2000), Hicks and Bord (2001), Corcoran (2004), West (2004), Nicholson-Cole (2005), Kefford (2006) and Mueller (2009) note, constant emphasis on environmental problems and disasters, and overuse of the term crisis, can be counterproductive. Some young people already have to confront problems like drug and alcohol abuse, AIDS, family breakdown and divorce, sub-standard housing, poor sanitation, street crime and violence, gang activity, peer pressure and bullying, high levels of youth unemployment, and discrimination of various kinds. Presenting them with a whole battery of additional and seemingly intractable problems may be more than they can handle. By spending massive amounts of time itemizing environmental problems, some approaches to environmental education can exacerbate feelings of anxiety, despair, powerlessness and hopelessness, leading to what Sobel (1996) calls *ecophobia:* "fear of oil spills, rainforest destruction, whale hunting, acid rain, the ozone hole, and Lyme disease. Fear of just being outside" (p. 5). When compounded by feelings of being unable to change the situation (in psychological language, issues of locus of control and self-efficacy), anxiety can quickly lead to apathy and feelings of resignation. Over-exposure to crises can also result in desensitization or "compassion fatigue". It can lead individuals to adopt one of a number of defence mechanisms aimed at reducing these negative and uncomfortable feelings, principally denial and the kind of displacement behaviour in which individuals attempt to stave off anxiety about environmental degradation through continued, or even increased, material acquisition and consumption – popularly known as "retail therapy". As noted in chapter 5, Stanley Cohen (2001) identifies three categories of denial: *literal denial* is a simple assertion that something is untrue or didn't happen; *interpretive denial* admits the facts, but posits a different interpretation and explanation; *implicatory denial* admits the facts and possibly the explanation, too, but minimizes or denies the sociocultural, political and/or moral-ethical implications. All three categories of denial are evident with respect to climate change. All three categories should be targets for the school science curriculum.

Opotow and Weiss (2000) also identify three kinds of denial: *denial of outcome severity, denial of stakeholder inclusion* and *denial of self-involvement*. Denial of outcome severity includes disregarding, ignoring, distorting or minimizing harmful outcomes, asserting that exposure or injury is an isolated and unlikely event rather than routine, frequent and persistent, masking and sanitizing harmful outcomes with palliative terminology and euphemisms, and invoking different levels of harm as acceptable for different social groups. Denial of stakeholder inclusion includes making unflattering between-group comparisons to bolster one's own ideological position at the expense of others, emphasizing only the negative attributes and arguments of others in order to discredit, exclude or trivialize others' interests, knowledge and/or stake in a dispute, regarding others stakeholders with disdain, denigrating them or denying their entitlement to the same resources, rights and dignity expected for oneself. Denial of self-involvement includes victim blaming, asserting that one's own contribution to environmental problems is minimal, claiming that environmental damage is a consequence of collective rather than individual decisions and actions, shifting all responsibility to governments, industry and the military, and casting oneself as 'environmentally clean' in comparison with the irresponsible and reprehensible behaviour of others. Again, all these forms of denial are evident in the climate change debate, and all should be targets for school science and technology education. Rippetoe and Rogers (1987) identify three other emotion-focused responses to potential and imminent crises and dangers: *wishful thinking* (simplistic and/or unrealistic expectations, such as relying on scientific advances or technological innovation to solve all the problems), *religious faith* (hope based on reliance on an outside power) and *fatalism* (accepting the inevitability of the un-avoidable). Disturbingly, some people resort to *rational distancing*, that is, no longer feeling any emotions about the issues – similar to the "psychic numbing" referred to earlier. And in some instances there is a socially constructed silence that deliberately avoids mentioning the issues that most disturb us – what has become known as "the elephant in the room"[95]. Zerubavel (2006) provides a fascinating insight into the ways in which various "elephants" are constructed and maintained.

Rogers and Tough (1996) sum up the complexity and emotional hazards of dealing with environmental crises and possible future scenarios, and the tendency to use defensive strategies, as follows:

> Coming to grips with the complexity of the world's problems, confronting uncertainty about the future, and critically examining deeply held worldviews may cause emotional and existential turmoil. To try to cope with the onslaught of thoughts and feelings, people may resort to using defence mechanisms such as denial, suppression, intellectualisation or projection. Consequently, rather than being truly able to face the future, the protective defence mechanisms may cause people to retreat or disconnect from reality. Thus paradoxically, the learning process may lead to paralysis rather than mobilising informed choice and action. (p. 492)

To enable students to address environmental issues carefully and critically, teachers need to help students build their self-esteem and foster their feelings of empowerment. Students need to know that they can be forces of constructive change, and that their involvement is both needed and valued. In other words, education should be geared towards replacing feelings of apathy and powerlessness with the feeling that, as individuals or as a group, they can *make a difference*. It is important, as Huckle (1990), Hicks (1998) and Summers and Kruger (2003) emphasize, to foster feelings of optimism for the future: "We should build environmental success stories into our curriculum and develop awareness of sources of hope in a world where new and appropriate technologies now offer liberation to all" (Huckle, 1990, p. 159). It is here that Futures Studies has a key role to play (see discussion and references cited in chapter 5). In Bell's (1997) words, the purpose of Futures Studies is "to discover or invent, examine and evaluate, and propose possible, probable and preferable futures. Futurists seek to know what can or could be (the possible), what is likely to be (the probable), and what ought to be (the preferable)" (p. 73). In an increasingly polluted and climatically unstable world that is rapidly running out of readily accessible sources of energy and raw materials, and having to face continuing population growth towards a predicted 9.2 billion by 2050[96], an alternative view of the future, and the determination to achieve it, is not just idle fantasy, it is an urgent necessity. We need to move beyond crisis management to coherent, systematic and responsible planning for the kind of future that will provide environmental security and social justice for all. Eckersley (1999) notes that among the 15–24 year-old Australians involved in his study, the dominant perception is that the gap between preferred and probable futures is widening. The approach being advocated in this book seeks to equip students with the critical thinking skills to analyse various scenarios for the future, the open-mindedness to consider a wide range of options, the level of moral judgement necessary for deciding what is good, just and honourable, the commitment that comes from emotional involvement in issues, and the political literacy and moral courage to take effective and appropriate action, thereby *narrowing* the gap between desirable and probable futures. Arguing along similar lines, Timberlake (1992) expresses deep reservations about too early and too intense a focus on problems and crises, and urges teachers to focus instead on actions that might lead to a better future.

Let us not labour to stuff environmental problems – pollution, poisons and population – into young heads too early. Let us instead teach the young to use their heads to be environmentally active citizens... Such an approach might actually produce a critical mass of adults who feel a responsibility to change things for the better – environmentally, socially, in health care, education, etc. They might start acting like citizens rather than subjects. (p. 3)

Schreiner et al. (2005) suggest the kind of questions with which we should confront students – in their example, with respect to climate change, though the questions can be raised with respect to almost any SSI.
– What do we think, feel, hope and fear in relation to the issue or problem?
– Who has the power in this situation and how do they use it?
– What would things look like in a more just and sustainable future?
– What values will we use to guide our choices?
– What are the possible courses of action?
– How shall we implement our plan of action in school, at home and in the community?

Drama, especially improvized drama, may be a particularly effective way of exploring alternative futures. As Varelas et al. (2010) argue, drama enables students to move back and forth between the real world (here and now) and various imagined worlds, and to link their own experiences, feelings, values and aspirations to those of others. Reading, writing and discussing science fiction may fulfil a similar role. It is clear that personal experience also plays a key role in sensitizing students to SSI and environmental problems, and in encouraging activism. For example, Kahn and Friedman (1995) and Mohai and Bryant (1998) show that African-Americans who live in poor neighbourhoods are generally more concerned about their environments than those in more affluent areas, while Taskin (2009) reports that Turkish students living in shantytowns (the author's expression) are more aware of environmental problems than those living in up-market suburban areas, and so more likely to engage in action. Moreover, subsequent actions and interventionist behaviour are more likely to persist when rooted in, and driven by, significant and emotionally charged personal experience, that is, if a person's "heart is in it". Conversely, if behaviour change is in response to imposed regulations, external incentives or general feelings of anxiety, it is more likely to be superficial, temporary and prone to reversion (Maiteny, 2002). The curriculum outlined in chapter 3 aims to sensitize students to a number of SSI through direct experience, to provide other experiences that engage students' emotions and challenge their values, and to build a sense of identity, agency and self-efficacy as a social activist.

EDUCATION *FOR* THE ENVIRONMENT

In recent years, there have been some encouraging signs that the tide of curricular opinion may be shifting towards education *for* the environment and the adoption of a more *ecocentric* view of environmental issues. Fien (1993a) defines ecocentricity as having "a high regard for nature; respect for the natural and social limits to growth; empathy with other species, other people and future generations; support for careful planning in order to minimise threats to nature and the quality of life;

and a desire for change in the way most societies conduct their economic and political affairs" (p. 4). More recently, the years 2005–2014 were designated by the United Nations as a Decade of Education for Sustainable Development, the overall goal of which is to "integrate the principles, values, and practices of sustainable development into all aspects of education and learning. This educational effort will encourage changes in behaviour that will create a more sustainable future in terms of environmental integrity, economic viability, and a just society for present and future generations"[97]. Equally encouraging is an Ontario Ministry of Education report on future environmental education initiatives:

> Over the past decade, changes in the earth's environment and its natural systems have emerged as a matter of increasingly urgent concern around the world. While the issues are complex and diverse, there is a shared and universal recognition that solutions will arise only through committed action on a global, national, regional, local, and individual scale. Schools have a vital role to play in preparing our young people to take their place as informed, engaged, and empowered citizens who will be pivotal in shaping the future of our communities, our province, our country, and our global environment. (Ministry of Education, Ontario, 2007, p. 1)

One of the central planks of education *for* the environment is the inculcation of what Kollmus and Argyeman (2002) call *pro-environmental behaviour*: "behaviour that consciously seeks to minimize the negative impact of one's actions on the natural and built world" (p. 240). Stephen Gough (2002a) takes issue with the assumption that the notion of "pro-environmental behaviour" is simple, straightforward and un-problematic. Rather, he argues that it is highly context-specific, citing the example of European Union environmental regulations that mandated a clean-up of parts of the North Sea coastline. In recent years, as a consequence of this legislation, discharges of waste and sewage have been drastically reduced, with disastrous consequences for the large populations of seabirds that had come to depend on this effluent as a food source. In these circumstances, Gough says, we need to ask what actions are "pro-environmental". A similar situation arises with regard to the significantly different attitudes towards, and treatment of brush tailed possums in Australia and New Zealand (see chapters 6 and 7). Gough (2002b) also notes that environmental knowledge, values and attitudes sometimes follow from observation of pro-environmental behaviour exhibited by a well-respected individual or group. In other words, the causative direction is reversed. Perhaps there is a need to distinguish behaviour that is pro-environmental in intent from behaviour that is pro-environmental in terms of impact. Some behaviours intended to be pro-environmental may not have the desired impact – for example, many people continue to believe that avoiding the use of aerosol cans can protect the ozone layer, even though the production of CFCs has been banned for some twenty years[98]. Courtney-Hall and Rogers (2002) also note that the definition adopted by Kollmus and Argeyman (2002) excludes all non-conscious, habituative behaviour, whatever its value and effectiveness, even though we all strive to make 'good actions' second nature, that is, unconsciously engaged in. As a result, they argue, "much behaviour that should be counted as environmentally virtuous is rendered invisible by this exclusion, particularly behaviour that is no longer consciously chosen each time it is performed because it is enacted out of habit (e.g., turning off lights or weeding without herbicides) and behaviour that is enacted out of deeply rooted values and inclinations rather than out of a conscious choice to minimize negative environmental impacts (e.g., sharing equipment with neighbours, teaching neighbourhood children about plants and insects; watching the sunset and giving thanks for life)" (p. 288). Moreover, some behaviours can be judged as pro-environmental in an indirect way, that is, they bring about changes in policy or impact on commodity prices, consumption levels or consumer preferences that, in turn, have direct impact on the environment (see chapter 3 for a discussion of direct and indirect action). Most significant of all, however, is the seeming imposition of a specified list of approved behaviours. As Courtney-Hall and Rogers (2002) comment, "Once we locate 'behaviour change' at the top of the educational agenda, it is all too easy for schooling to slip from education to indoctrination. It is also all too easy for students to catch on quickly, and to develop the attitude of giving their teachers what they seem to want to hear" (p. 285). Similar concerns are expressed by Jickling (2003) and by McClaren and Hammond (2005), who summarize their concerns on this issue as follows: "The challenge... is to find ways to develop a curriculum... in which students can critically consider environmental issues, examine possible courses of action, and take action as integral parts of educational experience without recruiting them to selected causes or policies and indoctrinating them to particular ideologies" (p. 274). In short, rather than telling people what they should and shouldn't do, we should enable them to figure it out for themselves. In a sense, this mirrors the distinction that has been drawn between the *moralistic* and *democratic* approaches to health education and environmental education (Jensen, 2000; Schnack, 2008). The moralistic approach is predominantly instrumental, aiming to change individuals' lifestyle and behaviour in particular ways, while the democratic approach aims to involve students in critical consideration of issues and in making informed choice about personal behaviour.

Another central pillar of education *for* the environment is the notion of sustainable development. However, as noted in chapter 1, we need to look critically at what the notion of "sustainable development" actually means. "Sustainability" implies respect for and maintenance of nature's processes, cycles and rhythms; "development" suggests a concern with maintaining (or even increasing) supplies of raw materials and usable energy, increasing levels of production, consumption and waste, accumulation of capital, and maximizing returns on investment. As Bonnett (2007) remarks, "One cannot help thinking that a certain sleight-of-hand is in play when the ultimately unsustainable assumption of continuous (material) economic growth is apparently brought into harmony with a much vaunted eco-friendliness" (p. 710). How can continued economic growth be compatible with sustainability when present levels of resource consumption and waste production are already unsustainable? The maintenance of the current affluent lifestyle in the industrialized North/West, and its eventual extension to all people in the world, is an absurd ambition. The planet cannot even maintain current levels of consumption and waste, let alone an increased level for an increased population (world population is predicted to rise from its current 6.8 billion to 7.6 billion by 2020, and 9.2 billion by 2050). As Jickling and Wals (2008) note, "comparing the sustaining of ecological processes with the sustaining of consumerism reveals inconsistencies and incompatibilities of values, yet many people, conditioned to think that sustainable development is inherently good, will promote both at the same time" (p. 14). Arguing along similar lines, Lélé (1991) describes the notion of sustainable development as a "metafix" that unites everybody "from the profit-minded industrialist and risk-minimizing subsistence farmer to the equity-seeking social worker, the pollution-concerned or wildlife-loving First Worlder, the growth-maximizing policy maker, the goal-orientated bureaucrat, and therefore, the vote-counting politician" (p. 613). The notion of sustainable development is popular with governments and industrialists because it retains the principle of development. It is comforting to individuals in the North/West because it holds out the prospect of some continuity and stability in a world of rapid and far-reaching change. It is popular in Developing countries because it is seen to offer hope for a better share of the world's wealth and resources. However, as Rist (1997) comments: "The growth policy supposed to reduce poverty and stabilise the ecosystems hardly differs at all from the policy which historically opened the gulf between rich and poor and placed the environment in danger" (p. 186). McKibben (2007) expresses similar views: "Growth is no longer making most people wealthier, but instead generating inequality and insecurity. And growth is bumping against physical limits so profound – like climate change and peak oil – that continuing to expand the economy may be impossible; *the very attempt may be dangerous*" (p. 2, emphasis added).

Leaving aside speculation on whether advocacy of economic growth as a solution to the problems of environmental degradation, poverty and social injustice for which it is largely responsible is simply naïve, provocatively perverse or deliberately deceptive, it is clear that the notion of sustainable development is fraught with unresolved issues and problems.

> Sustainable for how long: a generation, one century, a millennium, ten millennia? Sustainable at what level of human appropriation: individual households, local villages, major cities, entire nations, global economies? Sustainable for whom: all humans alive now, all humans that will ever live, all living beings living at this time, all living beings that will ever live? Sustainable under what conditions: for contemporary transnational capitalism, for low-impact Neolithic hunters and gatherers, for some space-faring global empire? Sustainable development of what: personal income, social complexity, gross national product, material frugality, individual consumption, ecological diversity. (Luke, 1995, p. 21)

The stark reality is that not everything can be sustained, and as soon as debate focuses on what is to be sustained, and at what level and for how long, there is a whole raft of social, political, economic, scientific and technological factors to be taken into account and some key decisions on underlying values to be made. If we are to ensure our survival as a species, and the survival of other species, and if we are to ensure an acceptable standard of living for all citizens, we need to engage in critical scrutiny of our current priorities and values, we need to resolve differences between what people need, what they want and what the planet can sustain and accommodate, and we need to make some drastic changes in the way we live. Issues have to be fully explored, problems diagnosed, plans formulated and evaluated, decisions made and changes implemented. To paraphrase Räthzel and Uzzell (1999), the bottom line is that learning to live sustainably is non-negotiable, simply because the Earth's resources and capacity to absorb and accommodate anthropogenic impact is finite. In contrast, except in relation to basic survival needs, our needs and wants are relative, negotiable and able to be met in a variety of ways because they are the product of social, cultural, economic and political activity.

As Courtney-Hall (1997) points out, education is the key to effecting the kind of societal changes that will be necessary. First, because the changes will encompass changes in lifestyle that will be quite profound and potentially disconcerting for many people in industrialized societies. They run counter to the goals, aspirations and desires instilled in us by the popular media, current consumerist rhetoric and advertizing. Second, because the reforms will require both new and differently applied knowledge and skills, together with considerable political will. In sum, she says, "they involve altered expectations, altered daily life practices, altered work practices, altered regulatory and enforcement practices, altered infrastructures, altered understandings of responsibilities and rights, greater citizen involvement in decision-making and implementation, and even altered taxation systems" (p. 365). Because these changes cannot be imposed on people, at least not in democratic societies, and cannot be achieved entirely by legislative and fiscal measures, education will be crucial – not only school-based education, but education in informal settings such as parks and gardens, nature centres, science centres and environmental clubs, education in the home, the workplace and community centres, education through advertizing and public notices, education through leisure activities, education through the news media and through movies, theatre, literature, music and dance, education through examples set by prominent members of the community, education through peer group pressure. Unprecedented levels of cooperation, support and collaboration will be necessary among national and local governments, government agencies and public services, research establishments, environmental groups, formal and informal educational institutions, the business and industrial sector, trade unions, cultural and community organizations, youth groups, voluntary organizations, and so on. As far as school-based education is concerned, devising a curriculum for sustainability requires that we focus attention on the knowledge, skills, attitudes and values needed by citizens to bring about a society that is ecologically sustainable, socially sustainable, economically sustainable, and politically sustainable (Fien, 1998).

Similar views are encapsulated in the way Hill et al. (2003) relate sustainability to ways of thinking about the world, and to forms of social and personal practice that lead to: ethical, empowered and personally fulfilled individuals; communities built on collaborative engagement, tolerance and equity; social systems and institutions that are participatory, transparent and just; and environmental practices that value and sustain biodiversity and life-supporting ecological processes. In essence, these are the underlying values of UNESCO's (2005, p. 16) statement designating the period 2005 to 2014 as a decade of education for sustainable development.

– Respect for the dignity and human rights of all people throughout the world and a commitment to social and economic justice for all.
– Respect for the human rights of future generations and a commitment to inter-generational responsibility.

- Respect and care for the greater community of life in all its diversity, which involves the protection and restoration of the Earth's ecosystems.
- Respect for cultural diversity and a commitment to build, locally and globally, a culture of tolerance, non-violence and peace.

ENVIRONMENT AS A SOCIAL CONSTRUCT

In an issues-based curriculum oriented towards sociopolitical action, as outlined in chapter 3, it is not acceptable to regard environmental problems and exploitation of vulnerable people as matters of careless industrialization and inexpert management of natural resources, or as an inevitable but unfortunate aspect of progress. Such an approach ignores the underlying causes of the problems: the values underpinning industrialization, ever-increasing levels of production and consumption, the profligate use of natural resources, the exploitation of cheap labour, and lax environmental controls. It is dangerously misleading because it suggests that science itself can solve the problems by simple technical means. In that sense, the approach depoliticizes the issues, thereby removing them from the 'realm of possibility' within which ordinary people see themselves as capable of intervention. As a consequence, dealing with environmental problems is left to experts and officials, and ordinary citizens are disempowered. Education for sociopolitical action entails recognizing that the environment is not a 'given'; rather, it is a *social construct*. It is a social construct in three senses. First, the environment is a human habitat. It is a place where we live. By living, and seeking to live more comfortably, we act upon and change the natural environment, constructing and reconstructing it through our social actions. Indeed, very few parts of the planet are free of humankind's intervention. Continuing rainforest clearance in countries such as Brazil and Indonesia, in pursuit of short-term economic gain, is the most spectacular example of change, of course, but even the large so-called 'unspoiled' areas of European, Canadian, American and New Zealand countryside show the indelible imprint of previous generations of agricultural workers. Of course, modern technology has substantially escalated both the scale and extent of these transformations. Further, because of limitations in our knowledge, the changes brought about by human actions are never wholly predictable (as discussed in chapter 3). Moreover, different groups of people may perceive the changes differently, and with different degrees of approval and disapproval, precipitating further actions and further changes. And so on. Second, as briefly noted in chapter 1, we perceive the environment in a way that is dependent on the prevailing sociocultural framework. In addition to scientific-ecological consider-ations, our notion of environment includes a complex of cultural, aesthetic, emotional and historical dimensions, and a range of economic and political dimensions, too. The historical dimension is important because it tells us how a particular environment came to be as it is; it tells us about the particular ways in which a group of people have perceived their environment, notes any differences among the views of different stakeholders, and suggests ways in which we might perceive the environment differently. To have a chance of creating a better world we need a cultural history of landscape or environment, that is, an understanding of the cultural perspectives that govern our response, and governed the responses of previous generations, to our surroundings. The environment is also a social construct in the sense that we share it with other people and other species, and so we have a *shared* responsibility for its care and protection. Lijmbach et al. (2002) describe an action research project in which a group of researchers from a number of disciplines (including science, sociology, education and philosophy) worked together to produce a series of teaching modules for primary and secondary schools that promote such pluralistic views of the environment. By raising awareness of alternative viewpoints, the materials stimulate debate, foster critical reflection and lead to further research in an effort to clarify uncertainties and resolve disputes.

To acknowledge the internal dimensions of environment, Canadian ecologist Pierre Dansereau (1975) adopts the notion of *inscape* from poet Gerard Manley Hopkins. *Inscape* is to be juxtaposed with *landscape* (the external dimension). As Smyth (1995) comments, "Our perceptions of our external environment (the landscape) are always modified by our internal environment of needs and appetites, memories and visions; both our perceptions and our responses to it are selected and interpreted under their influence (the inscape). Our inscape is thus different from both the landscape around us and the inscapes of others, yet this is the environment to which our own behaviour is responding" (p. 4). In other words, the very notion of "environment" is a social construct, and so could be different. Indeed, as discussed by Caduto and Bruchac (1988), Maybury-Lewis (1991), Knudtson and Suzuki (1992), Cajete (1994, 1999, 2000b), Kawagley et al. (1998), Maurial (1999), Semken (1999), Battiste and Henderson (2000, 2005), Kalland (2000), Grim (2001), Bandeira et al. (2002), Riggs (2003, 2005), Chinn (2006), Aikenhead and Ogawa (2007), Keane (2008) and Beckford et al. (2010), many Indigenous peoples do perceive it in significantly different ways: there is a sense of empathy and kinship with other forms of life and reciprocity between the human and natural worlds, with resources seen as gifts; wisdom and ethics are derived from direct experience with the natural world; it is recognized that nature will always possess unfathomable mysteries; the human role is to participate in the orderly designs of nature; people have responsibility for maintaining a harmonious relationship with the natural world. Contrast these elements with their equivalents in the prevailing Western position: a sense of separateness from and superiority over non-human forms of life; natural resources are available for unilateral human exploitation; human reason transcends the natural world and can produce insights independently; nature is completely decipherable by the rational human mind; the human role is to dissect, analyze and manipulate nature for its own

Accepting the environment as a social construct helps us to realize that environmental problems are not problems 'out there', in our surroundings. Rather, they are problems 'in our heads', that is, in the way we choose to make sense of the world as a guide to our actions. They are pre-eminently social problems, that is, problems of people, their lifestyles and their relations with the natural world. By encouraging students to recognize the ways in which the environment is socially constructed, we can challenge the notion that environmental problems are 'natural' and inevitable. If environment is a social construct, environmental problems are social problems, caused by societal practices and structures, and justified by society's current values. It follows that solving environmental problems means addressing and changing the social conditions that give rise to them and the values that sustain them. Environmental problems will not just 'go away'. Nor will they be solved by a quick 'technical fix' while we blithely maintain our profligate lifestyle. It is abundantly clear that without changes in our political and social priorities, and the values that underpin them, no amount of scientific theorizing or technological innovation will lead to environmentally sustainable lifestyles and to environmental rehabilitation. We know full well that indiscriminate clearance of tropical rainforest for agricultural production brings about local problems of erosion, floods and fuel wood shortage, and global problems related to global warming, climate change and loss of bio-diversity, but while science provides an understanding of these issues and of the value of the forest, it doesn't contribute much to solving the problems of continuing destruction. Solutions will be found, if at all, by dealing with issues relating to poverty (both individual and national), through education (especially of women), by changing patterns of land ownership and the terms of international trade and, especially, by addressing burgeoning population growth. On this latter point, it is important to note that in those countries where birth rates have declined, the influential factors have not been more (scientific) understanding of fertility, but availability of cheap/free contraceptives, less dependence on children as a source of labour and as insurance against old age or accident, decreased child mortality through better health care, and greater educational and employment opportunities for women.

To reiterate, the planet can no longer sustain our present Western/Northern way of life. We have to change it! If people have created social structures, living conditions and ways of thinking and acting that are oppressive of the less powerful and injurious to the environment, they can also create structures, conditions, thought systems, values and practices that foster freedom, equality, justice and environmental well-being. But changing our way of life entails changing our values and changing the way we view the environment. Joseph Bruchac (1993) of the Abenaki nation of Vermont expresses it far more powerfully.

> If we see 'the Earth' as the web of life that sustains us, then there is no question that the web is weakened, that the Earth is sick. But if we look at it from another side, from the view of the living Earth itself, then the sickness is not that of the planet, the sickness is embodied in human beings, and, if carried to its illogical conclusion, it will kill us. Human self-importance is a big part of the problem. It is because we human beings have one power that no other creatures have – the power to upset the natural balance – that we are so dangerous. (p. 8)

It follows that an environmental education, like all aspects of the science and technology curriculum being promoted in this book, should promote critical analysis of the sociopolitical realities underpinning environmental issues and problems, including rigorous and vigorous analysis of the motivations, intentions, positions, justifications, arguments, values (both implicit and explicit) and decisions of the various stakeholders and protagonists in a given situation. In short, science education for sociopolitical action is inescapably an exercise in values clarification and values change. This basic argument is strongly endorsed by the UNESCO (2002)

report *Education for Sustainability*: "Success in the struggle for sustainable development requires an approach to education that strengthens our engagement in support
of other values – especially justice and fairness – and the awareness that we
share a common destiny with others. Ultimately, sustainability will depend on
changes in behaviour and lifestyles, changes which will need to be motivated by a
shift in values and rooted in the cultural and moral precepts upon which behaviour
is based. Without change of this kind, even the most enlightened legislation, the
cleanest technology, the most sophisticated research will not succeed in steering
society towards the long-term goal of sustainability" (p. 11). Acid rain, global
climate change, toxic waste, the threat of nuclear holocaust, ozone depletion, loss
of biodiversity, increasing deforestation and desertification are all located in our
impoverished values. As Ernst Schumacher said in his book *Small is Beautiful*,
nearly forty years ago, we have to reject our current values of bigger, faster and
more powerful, our current preoccupation with higher production and wealth generation, in favour of an orientation towards "the organic, the gentle, the non-violent,
the elegant and beautiful" (Schumacher, 1973, p. 29). In similar vein, Wendell
Berry (1990) states that we must "achieve the character and acquire the skills to
live much poorer than we do. We must waste less, we must do more for ourselves
and each other" (p. 19). Berry (1990) goes on to argue that human welfare should
not be located in the values of the marketplace but in relationships that can emerge
among people and landscapes where care and community rather than commercial
success are the central aims. In similar vein, David Orr (1992) states that "the
difference between a humane and sustainable world and a technological nightmare
will ultimately be decided by people capable of acting with wisdom, foresight, and
love, which is to say, with virtue" (p. 182) – a ringing endorsement of the proposal
in chapter 7 to focus student attention on virtue ethics.

Of course, in seeking to change the way we live in the West/North, we need to
take account of the aspirations of those living in the Developing world and in the
rapidly growing consumer societies of China and India. As long ago as 1983,
O'Riordan argued that it is both immoral and futile to teach about "living within
the confines of natural replenishability if only a few get the advantages and the rest
increasingly suffer" (p. 11). There are no moral grounds whatsoever for the view
that people in the rich industrialized countries can/should continue their profligate
energy and resource use to sustain their present levels of consumption and
associated high pollution levels, while expecting those in the Developing world to
hold back on their own economic development. Why would the Developing
nations currently undertaking large-scale industrialization limit their economic
growth in order to help solve the problems created by the wealthy industrialized
nations unless those wealthy nations are also willing to undertake massive reform
of their practices? We need solidarity with the world's poor and underprivileged,
and we need solutions in which everyone can play a part.

CHANGING OUR WORLDVIEW

Ultimately, it is our worldview that determines how we interpret reality, how we
make sense of our experiences, and how we see ourselves as human beings in

relation to others and the world as a whole. It determines our values, aspirations and overall sense of responsibility. Both teachers and students (and scientists, too) should ask whether the continued promotion of the Cartesian/Newtonian worldview described by Fritjof Capra (1983), and briefly outlined in chapter 4, is a good or bad thing. According to Capra, it is a bad thing because it cannot adequately describe and explain the complexities of the world in which we now live. In his view, we need to shift from traditional mechanistic thinking, with its simple linear chain of cause and effect ascertained through close experimental control, to a more holistic and flexible systems-style of thinking that is able to deal with complex webs of relationships, multiple interdependencies, feedback systems, unpredictability, uncertainty, long-term consequences and side effects. Our current dilemma, he states, is that "we are trying to apply the concepts of an outdated world view – the mechanistic world view of Cartesian-Newtonian science – to a reality that can no longer be understood in terms of these concepts. We live today in a globally interconnected world, in which biological, psychological, social, and environmental phenomena are all interdependent. To describe this world appropriately we need an ecological perspective which the Cartesian world view does not offer" (Capra, 1983, p. 15). Likewise, many SSI and related problems are not susceptible to being decomposed and handled in one dimension at a time; rather, they need to be considered in all their systemic complexity, fluidity and uncertainty.

Wilber (1995) goes further and contends that the environmental crises we currently face are, in fact, a *direct consequence* of acting in accordance with this mechanistic worldview - a view that he describes as *fractured* or *broken*: "A worldview that drastically separates mind and body, subject and object, culture and nature, thoughts and things, values and facts, spirit and matter, human and nonhuman; a worldview that is dualistic, mechanistic, atomistic, anthropocentric, and pathologically hierarchical – a worldview that, in short, erroneously separates humans from, and often unnecessarily elevates humans above, the rest of the fabric of reality, a broken worldview that alienates men and women from the intricate web of patterns and relationships that constitute the very nature of life and Earth and cosmos" (p. 4). Linear, mechanistic and individualistic thinking has created the problems. In short, a fragmented or disintegrated worldview creates a disintegrating world: loss of biodiversity, greater gaps between rich and poor, destruction of local economies, loss of cultural diversity, major distortion of the life support cycles of the planet, and so on. Fifteen years before Wilbur's remarks. physicist David Bohm (1980) had expressed a broadly similar point of view: "It is not an accident that our fragmentary form of thought is leading to such a widespread range of crises, social, political, economic, ecological, psychological, etc. in the individual and in society as a whole. Such a mode of thought implies unending development of chaotic and meaningless conflict" (p. 16). Wilber (1995) argues that the only way to ameliorate the planetary and societal crises we currently face is to replace this "fractured worldview" with a worldview that is "more holistic, more relational, more integrative, more Earth-honoring, and less arrogantly human-centred. A worldview, in short, that honors the entire web of life, a web that has intrinsic value in and of itself, but a web that, not incidentally, is the bone and marrow of our own existence as well" (p. 4). When we acknowledge that our worldview influences how we live, and we decide to change it and interpret the world *differently*, we change our understanding of what is acceptable and what is possible, and new horizons for action become available.

The element of the Western (scientific) worldview that is most in need of urgent reappraisal is *anthropocentrism*, identified by Smolicz and Nunan (1975) some 35 years ago as one of the ideological pivots of Western science and science education (see chapter 4). As many scholars have argued, anthropocentric thinking and the consequent objectification of nature is the root cause of the several global environmental crises that confront contemporary society and contributes substantially to a huge raft of social problems (Corcoran & Sievers, 1994; Russell & Bell, 1996; Bell & Russell, 1999, 2000). By objectifying nature, people absolve themselves of any moral responsibility for the care and preservation of the natural environment and justify their continued exploitation of natural resources and other life forms.

As Neil Evernden (1985) argues, the "real authorities" in any culture are the unquestioned assumptions, values, beliefs and attitudes that are buried so deeply in our belief systems, worldviews and social norms that they are 'invisible'. Anthropocentrism is such an authority. It is so deeply ingrained, and so consistently acted upon, that it is largely 'invisible'; it is taken-for-granted and so passes unnoticed, and when it is noticed, it is regarded as 'natural'. In other words, for many people it is an unremarked and/or unchallenged part of the accepted social fabric and of the science curriculum, at least in the West/North. As Sandra Harding (1986) might put it, examples of anthropocentrism, like sexism, racism, classism and heterosexism, are evident in "those places where speakers reveal the assumptions they think they do not need to defend, beliefs they expect to share with their audiences" (p. 112). The pervasiveness of anthropocentrism is evident in our common everyday language. We subdue Mother Nature, conquer high mountains and virgin territory, tame the jungle, rape the countryside, achieve mastery over the elements, manage, exploit and control natural resources, penetrate previously unknown areas, overcome physical obstacles, push back frontiers, extend boundaries, and so on. It is evident in the way we construct the natural world as a 'resource' to serve humanity's needs and interests. It is evident in the way non-human beings are invariably described by their physical characteristics and 'functions', and in the disturbing reality that many students rarely (if ever) experience non-humans alive, in natural settings, or unmediated by books, computers, videos or laboratory equipment (Bell & Russell, 1999). It is evident, too, in the treatment of animals in school (as discussed in chapters 5 and 7). Oakley (2009) estimates that about 80% of students in American and Canadian schools will carry out at least one dissection during their K-12 science education. As Selby (1995) comments, dissection positions animals as "mere commodities, disposable resources for our curiosity and convenience, possessing no value in their own right" (p. 255)[99]. Oakley (2009) goes on to comment: "As the animal's body is cut open and cut up, there is a reduction of the entire being to a few selected components deemed noteworthy or interesting to the observer, while the rest of the animal is ignored. Students who dissect animals are usually asked to identify particular organs or systems in the animal, which reduces the animal to parts that are considered significant while decontextualizing those parts from the whole" (p. 61). The stereotypical scientific values of impartiality, neutrality and disengagement seem, by definition, to exclude relationships of care, sympathy and engagement with the fate and well-being of what is known and studied. But the ultimate expression of anthropocentrism is the genetic modification of animals and animal cloning to serve human interests. As Jeremy Rifkin (1997) remarks: "Reducing the animal kingdom to customized, mass-produced replications of specific genotypes is the final articulation of the mechanistic, industrial frame of mind. A world where all life is transformed into engineering standards and made to conform to market values is a dystopian nightmare, and needs to be opposed by every caring and compassionate human being who believes in the intrinsic value of life" (p. 35). Both chapter 5 and chapter 7 include some discussion of the moral-ethical issues raised by the technology of genetic manipulation.

Seeking to effect change from this anthropocentric milieu entails identifying, challenging and overturning all these hidden and taken-for-granted assumptions and replacing them with a *biocentric* ethic comprising the following elements: (i) all things in the biosphere have intrinsic value and an equal right to exist alongside humans; (ii) the natural world is not just a resource for human use; and (iii) all life forms are inextricably interconnected (Russell, 1997). For me, adoption of such an ethic also entails cultivation of a sense of compassion and caring towards both human and non-human species, having a concern for maintaining the existence of biological and cultural diversity, and challenging and rejecting all forms of discrimination. It is worth noting that some authors use the term *ecocentric* in preference to *biocentric*, presumably on the grounds that it includes a concern for entire ecosystems, not just the plants and animals that live in them. The argument that we should shift towards biocentric or ecocentric thinking is not new. Indeed, it has been a feature of educational debate for many years, for example in the writing of Lucas (1979) and O'Riordan (1983). Building on and critiquing O'Riordan's earlier conceptualization of environmental education, John Fien (1993a,b) places worldviews on a continuum of "environmental politics" extending from those who are "technocentrics" to those who are "biocentrics". A technocentric worldview regards people as separate from nature and sees nature as a resource to be conserved in the interests of people through efficient management; a biocentric or ecocentric worldview holds that people are part of nature, nature should be conserved for its own sake, and nature provides a metaphor for morality and a guide to the way we should live. A technocentrist view acknowledges that environmental problems exist, but believes that science and technology will solve them (or, at least, manage them) and allow for continued growth. Biocentrists are under no such illusions.

Some teaching and learning activities that might contribute to this shift in beliefs, values and behaviour are discussed in chapter 9, although it is worth commenting here that almost any activity that reduces an individual's sense of unfamiliarity or discomfort with nature (for example, walking in the forest, camping in the mountains, building a nesting box or caring for an animal) will assist the shift towards bio-centrism. As an aside, it is worth noting Liu and Lederman's (2007) finding that student teachers with an "informed" NOS understanding were more inclined to adopt a biocentric outlook than those with "naïve" NOS understanding (the authors' terms). In exploring young children's moral reasoning with respect to environmental issues, Kahn (2001) describes a significant transition from biocentrism based on *isomorphic reasoning* to biocentrism based on *transmorphic reasoning*. The former is evident when children compare animals directly with humans, reasoning that their needs and desires are exactly the same as ours, and therefore they merit the same moral consideration as people. For example, "fishes want to live freely, just like we live freely" and "If we don't like to live surrounded by trash, then the fish won't like it either". Transmorphic reasoning is evident when children establish moral rights based on characteristics, needs and behaviours that may be substantially different from those of humans, but nonetheless warrant acknowledgement and consideration. Interestingly, in a later study, Kahn (2002) found that biocentric reasoning was no more prevalent in a forest-dwelling community in Brazil than in urban areas such as Houston (Texas), and were lower than levels found in Lisboa (Lisbon, Portugal). An additional point I wish to make here is that endeavouring to shift students' thinking from an anthropocentric to a biocentric ethic necessarily carries with it a commitment to humane education (Selby, 1994 a,b; 1995; Weil, 2004). Through consideration of the ways in which human society treats animals, humane education seeks to challenge "the selfish and anthropocentric attitudes that have encouraged exploitation of each other, animals and the world to the point where we are now threatening our very survival on this planet. Humane education aims to provide the basis for responsible planetary citizenship" (Milburn, 1992, p. 2). In the words of Patty Finch (1989): "Without humane education, environmental education reaches the mountains, but not the trapped coyote; the oceans, but not the aquarium-bound whale; the Arctic, but not the clubbed seal; the cities, but not the stray dog; the open ranges, but not the cinched rodeo horse; the farmlands, but not the crated veal calf; the endangered species, but not the abused animals" (p. 69).

In most jurisdictions, education in science, technology and environmental studies has yet to effect a shift from anthropocentrism to biocentrism, and seems unlikely to do so any time soon. It still rests, in Noel Gough's (1990) words, on a "shallow environmentalism – a narrow instrumental response to circumstances that inconvenience us" (p. 14). In a later work, Gough (1991) suggests that the discourse of environmental education in popular textbooks and prominent policy documents is "constructed so as to reinforce the dominant assumptions of modernism... By reinforcing modern industrialized societies' high status forms of knowledge (like science, technology and economics) in environmental curricula, we are exacerbating many of the problems that we are attempting to resolve" (p. 3). Even the notion of education *for* the environment is, in Gough's (1987) view, both patronizing and anthropocentric: "Who are we to say what is 'good for' the environment and which environment is '*the* environment' anyway?" (p. 40). He argues that education *with* the environment is a much better reflection of the ecocentric position because it implies that "learning is not a transfer of something by someone to someone, but it is a relationship... the relationship is considered to be reciprocal" (p. 49). Writing some ten years later, Connie Russell (1997) notes that although there has been some progress, contemporary environmental education curricula still regard the natural environment as a resource for humankind that can be rationally and successfully managed with the appropriate scientific and technological tools. Because the role of humans is still seen as one of stewardship, she says, "[the] position remains anthropocentric; humankind is still considered separate from and superior to nature and must remain in absolute control" (p. 36) – a position exemplified in Sauvé's (2005) description of the "conservationist/resourcist current" in environmental education. Little has occurred in the dozen years since Russell's remarks to suggest that significant curricular change is imminent.

Before leaving this discussion it is important to note Bonnett's (2002) argument that biocentrism runs the risk of divesting us of our essential humanity and distinctiveness as thoughtful creatures. In common with Gough et al. (2000), he notes that all views of reality, that is, all worldviews and all conceptions of the environment, are in some sense anthropocentric because they employ concepts, ideas and theories that are themselves human constructs, and it is highly questionable whether any reality perceived by human beings can be entirely ecocentric. In short, all our thinking, shaped as it is by our experiences, the linguistic resources we possess, and the communities in which we conduct our lives, takes place within traditions and conventions that are heavily anthropocentric

> Things are always revealed to us in a context of human concerns and practices and their reality is therefore always conditioned by such concerns and practices. Notions such as care, sympathy, empathy, identification, responsibility, which… are celebrated by eco-centrism… are only possible… at the human level of conscious functioning… within individual and cultural horizons of significance, and in this sense are indelibly human-related. (Bonnett, 2002, p. 273)

In response to this problem, Bonnett advocates a position that is "neither anthropocentric in the conventional sense of seeing our relationship with the environment as properly orientated around human interests and wants, nor eco-centric, in the sense of subsuming us in, or subordinating us to, some greater whole" (p. 273). Rather, it emphasizes the centrality of human consciousness, and focuses on "human flourishing" (in all its senses) and a concern to "let things be as they are in themselves", that is, to safeguard, preserve and conserve. Lawrence Buell (1995) acknowledges that views, beliefs, attitudes and representations can encompass *varying degrees* of ecocentricity, and has formulated some tentative guidelines for making judgements about its extent in any particular environmental text.

- The non-human environment is present not merely as a framing device, but as a presence that begins to suggest that human history is implicated in natural history.
- The human interest is not understood to be the only legitimate interest.
- Human accountability to the environment is part of the text's ethical orientation.
- Some sense of the environment as a process rather than as a constant or a given is at least implicit in the text.

IN SEARCH OF A CRITIQUE

Feminism is a particularly appropriate critique for STSE education because, firstly, the central concept of "environment" is a gendered social construct, and secondly, the traditional form of environmental education (education *about* the environment) focuses on science, which many scholars regard as a gendered construct. Sandra Harding (1986), for example, argues that generations of male scientists have moved whatever counts as science towards the masculine and what counts as feminine away from science: "[science] is inextricably connected with specifically masculine... needs and desires. Objectivity vs subjectivity, the scientist as knowing object vs the objects of his inquiry, reason vs the emotions, mind vs body – in each case the former has been associated with masculinity and the latter with femininity" (p. 23). In Keller's (1985) words, "women have been the guarantors and protectors of the personal, the emotional, the particular, whereas science – the province par excellence of the impersonal, the rational and the general – has been the preserve of men" (p. 8). Hence some would see the shift from anthropocentrism to biocentrism, and the associated shift in emphasis within environmental education from education *about* the environment to education *for* the environment, as an exercise in feminization. Shifting towards a biocentric ethic entails adoption of feminine conceptions of the self/non-self relationship: "interrelatedness and interconnectedness, wholeness and oneness (of the person and of the planet/universe), inseparability of observer and observed (and knower and known), transcendence of the either-or dichotomies (such as rational/intuitive and subjective/objective), dynamic and organic" (Perreault, 1979, p. 4, p. 8 in parentheses). It entails a shift towards a re-valuing of the intuitive, affective, symbolic, spiritual and artistic. Further, for many feminist scholars, working to re-establish harmony with nature is seen as inseparable from the goal of harmonizing relations among people and, more particularly, among men and women. For Clover et al. (2000), it is also a matter of reclaiming women's traditional role as the prime environmental educators.

> Women are often the first environmental educators. In their homes and communities they pass along a unique understanding of the natural processes which take place around them. For centuries, women have been involved in teaching traditional medicine and health care, seed collection and the maintenance of biodiversity, farming and the processing and preservation of food, forestry and water management, skills which will become increasingly more vital as environmental destruction continues. (p. 18)

In many cultures, sexual symbolism is foundational to the perception of order and relationships in the natural world. As Rosemary Radford Ruether (1975) says, "The psychic organization of consciousness, the dualistic view of the self and the world, the hierarchical concept of society, the relation of humanity and nature, and of God and creation – all these relationships have been modeled on sexual dualism" (p. 3). She argues that in Western societies the fusion of sexual dualism and the hierarchical ordering of nature implicit in the Judaeo-Christian tradition creates a cultural symbolic model of domination-subordination that legitimates the patriarchal ordering of society, the oppression of other racial groups and the appropriation of the right of control over other species. Located at the heart of this complex of symbols is a nature-culture and mind-body dichotomy in which man is identified with culture and the mind (intellectual, autonomous, spiritual, active), and is considered to have a special relationship with God-the-Father, while woman is identified with nature and the body (sensual, passive, dependent, fecund), and is regarded as having a special relationship with Mother Earth. As noted earlier, the pervasive nature of this symbolism is evident in our everyday language and metaphors about man versus nature. In short, we have a language that is rich in images of control, domination and sexual aggression. Since most environmental violence can be seen as a consequence of science and technology – the ideal of masculine control and power – the symbolic equation becomes: *Man/Science & Technology versus Woman/Nature*. It is out of this imagery that ecofeminism emerged (Merchant, 1980, 1992, 1996; Shiva, 1989; Diamond & Orenstein, 1990; Warren, 1990; Rodda, 1991; Birkeland, 1993; Gaard, 1993; Mies & Shiva, 1993; Vance, 1993; Birke, 1986, 1994, Spretnak, 1994; Mellor, 1997, 2003; Sturgeon, 1997; Zell, 1998; Warren, 2000, 2001). Although not by any means a unified field of scholarship, ecofeminist thinking is invaluable in directing attention to the intersection of culture, language, knowledge and power in our conceptions of, and treatment of, the natural environment.

> The primary insight of ecofeminism is that all issues of oppression are interconnected, that to understand how to heal and liberate the world, we must look at the relationships between the various systems by which power is constructed. In an ecofeminist vision, there is no such thing as a struggle for women's rights separate from a struggle to repair the living systems of the earth that sustain life, or a struggle for gender equality that can be divided from a struggle for equality along lines of race, culture, economics, ancestry, religion, sexual orientation, or physical ability. (Diamond, 1994, p. ix)

> A science that does not respect nature's needs and a development that does not respect people's needs inevitably threatens survival. In their fight to survive the onslaughts of both, women have begun a struggle that challenges the most fundamental categories of western patriarchy – its concepts of nature and women, and of science and development. Their ecological struggles are aimed simultaneously at liberating nature from ceaseless exploitation and themselves from marginalization. They are creating a feminist ideology that transcends gender, and a political practice that is humanly inclusive; they are challenging patriarchy's ideological claim to universalism not with another universalising tendency, but with diversity; and they are challenging the dominant concept of power as violence with the alternative of non-violence as power. (Shiva, 1989, p. xvi)

In contradistinction to the coercive, manipulative, exploitative relationship that masculine technology has maintained towards nature, a more sympathetic, intuitive, respectful and loving relationship is advocated. Women, because of their supposed kinship with nature, are especially privileged and equipped to create and sustain this relationship. Thus, matters such as conservation and ecological balance are seen as feminist concerns.

Many scholars see anthropocentrism as a Western, and particularly Judaeo-Christian, view of the environment (see White, 1967; Spring & Spring, 1974; Watanabe, 1974; Schultz et al., 2000).

> And God said unto them, be fruitful, and multiply, and replenish the earth, and subdue it, and have dominion over the fish of the sea, and over the fowl of the air, and over every living thing that moveth upon the earth. (Genesis 1:28, King James version)

What did Christianity tell people about their relations with the environment?... Man named all the animals, thus establishing his dominance over them. God planned all this explicitly for man's benefit and rule; no item in the physical creation had any purpose save to serve man's purposes... Christianity... also insisted that it is God's will that man exploit nature for his proper ends... By destroying pagan animism, Christianity made it possible to exploit nature in a mood of indifference to the feelings of natural objects. (White, 1967, p. 1205)

In the western idea, man was not an ordinary part of nature. He was a specially privileged creature, and nature was subordinate to him... He was master of the natural world, which was at his disposal to analyze, examine, and make use of... since the natural world and the whole universe were manifestations of God's creation, the study of it was not only useful but also a highly esteemed endeavour... Such an outlook provided some of the most important religious motivation which fostered the development of modern science in the Western world. (Watanabe, 1974, p. 280)

Some commentators have cited the anti-environmentalist stance of the George W. Bush administration as a clear reflection of the evangelical and fundamentalist Christian beliefs of many of his supporters. Indeed, some researchers have shown a close correlation between fundamentalist Christian beliefs and attitudes towards the environment (Hand & van Liere, 1984; Eckberg & Blocker, 1989, 1996). Consideration of whether these arguments hold water from a theological perspective, and whether the research does show a connection between Christian beliefs and an anti-environmentalist stance or between some related political beliefs and anti-environmentalism, as Shaiko (1987) argues, are outside the scope of this book, save to note that in responding to Lynn White's assertions, Michael Poole (1998) argues that much hinges on our interpretation of the word "dominion". In Poole's view, it means "lordship" and implies a caretaker or trusteeship role rather than an exploitative one. Nevertheless, as noted in chapter 7, the Catholic Church has opposed the Spanish government's granting of a number of traditional human rights to the great apes on the grounds that the Bible grants human beings dominion over the Earth and all other living things. Further discussion can be found in Woodrum and Hoban (1994), Hitzhusen (2007) and Reiss (2008). For some, shifting to biocentrism would entail a rejection, or at least a modification, of any Christian views they might hold. In contrast, Edwards (2006) argues that all living things reflect the image of God, and so human beings are called upon to love and respect all creatures and to care for all of God's creation.

Toh and Cawagas (2010) state that in Judaism the notion of stewardship is underpinned by the principles of "*bal tashhit* (do not destroy wantonly nor waste resources) and *za'ar baalei hayyim* (pain of living things)", together with observance of *shabbat* (ceasing from work to contemplate the spiritual aspects of life and acknowledge the gifts of God) (p. 178). The same authors point to two key ecologically sound ideas in Islam: the principle of balance or *Mizan* (all living things "have a role and purpose and are related in a state of dynamic balance"); and *Khalifa* or the responsibility principle, "which upholds the role of trusteeship (*amanah*) for the well-being of humanity and all nature" (p. 179). On a related matter, Sardar (1989) states: "Muslim scientists sought to understand, not to dominate the object of their study, their respect for which was almost reverential. Bacon's dictum that 'nature yields her secrets under torture' would have sent shudders down al-Biruni's spine! Humility, recognition of the limitations of the scientific method, respect for the object of study: these primary lessons can be adopted at the very start of the journey to rediscover the heritage and contemporary meaning of Islamic science. And this, in essence, is also the message of Islamic science to the world" (p. 27)[100].

Despite some very obvious distinctions among them, there are some common values, principles and teachings in a number of other religions that promote the principle of living harmoniously with nature. Hinduism is quite explicit in *not* regarding humanity as having a privileged position with respect to other life forms. Nor should people take anything more from the Earth than is necessary for their immediate needs. If this simple convention is accepted, so the argument goes, the Earth will provide for all human needs (Chapple & Tucker, 2000; Prime, 2006). Similarly, Jainism sees all living beings as having a divine soul capable of being released from karma through mental and physical purification, and so calls on believers to be compassionate to all living beings (Chapple, 2002). Buddhism also puts strong emphasis on establishing a "proper relationship" with the natural world (Tucker & Williams, 1997; Brown, 2004). Although Buddhism teaches that humans, unlike other animals, have the capacity to achieve enlightenment, it does not regard humanity as superior to the rest of the natural world. Indeed, recognition of the interdependence of all things and phenomena, together with the values of love, kindness and compassion, require that all living beings are treated in a peaceful and caring way (Tucker & William, 1997; Kaza & Kraft, 2000).

Using a fascinating blend of sociocultural history, philosophy, educational studies and psychology, Richard Nisbett (2003) argues that while Westerners tend towards an analytic view that focuses on perceived salient objects and their particular attributes, East Asians tend towards an holistic view that focuses on continuities in substances and complex interrelationships within the environment (see discussion in chapter 4). For the East Asian, everything in the universe is related to everything else, and one cannot understand the pieces without considering the whole picture. For the Westerner, the whole is best understood through analysis into its component parts, each of which can be studied separately.

> To the Asian, the world is a complex place, composed of continuous substances, understandable in terms of the whole rather than the sum of its parts, and subject more to collective than to personal control. To the Westerner, the world is a relatively simple place, composed of discrete objects that can be understood without undue attention to context, and highly subject to personal control. (p. 100)

According to Fritjof Capra (1977), the Eastern mystical scientific worldview is characterized by "words like 'organic', 'holistic', or 'ecological', since it regards all phenomena in the universe as integral parts of an inseparable, harmonious whole... all things and events... are interrelated and are but different aspects or manifestations of the same ultimate reality... the cosmos is seen as one inseparable reality – forever in motion, alive, organic, spiritual and material at the same time" (pp. 21 & 22). Masakata Ogawa (1998) describes the traditional Japanese concept of *shizen* – a distinctive element of a particular worldview that involves people in an emotional, spiritual and aesthetic engagement in the natural environment. For most Japanese, he argues, the Western emphasis on control and exploitation of nature co-exists with an emphasis on harmony, aesthetics and appreciation of nature: "Everything surrounding human life, the mountains or hills, rivers, earth, plants, trees, insects, fish, or animals, has its own spirit (kami in Japanese), with which people can communicate. Most Japanese feel and are familiar with such spirits... with this kind of feeling and familiarity one cannot regard natural things merely as the objects of Western modern science" (p. 158). Similarly, traditional Chinese teachings rooted in Confucianism and Taoism emphasize the fundamental unity and interdependence of all beings and nature (indeed, the entire universe) and state that we should strive to live in harmony with nature and acquire knowledge of it through experience and reflection, rather than control and manipulation (Girardot et al., 2001). Thus, shifting to a biocentric ethic would seem, for some scholars, to entail a shift away from Western thinking and towards Eastern philosophies (see Callicott, 1994).

Others argue for a rekindling of Aboriginal conceptions of nature[101]. For example, Morrison and Carmody (1997) argue that the worldview of Aboriginal groups in Australia is "that the land and its resources don't exist in isolation from the people. The two are intimately linked, where people are spiritually part of the land, and the land is maintained and cared for by the people. It is not a world view that sees land as a saleable commodity for exploitation, but rather one where the land and the people are one and the same" (p. 2). In making essentially the same point, Aikenhead (1997) notes that the interests of the First Nations people of North America in survival, coexistence and celebration of mystery are not in sympathy with the drive of Western science to achieve mastery over Nature through objective knowledge based on mechanistic explanations. Nor are the holistic perspectives of Aboriginal knowledge, with its "gentle, accommodating, intuitive and spiritual wisdom" in sympathy with reductionist Western science and its "aggressive, manipulative, mechanistic and analytical explanations" (p. 220). Often there are concepts, ideas and principles embedded in a particular way of knowing that cannot be faithfully translated into another language or fully understood from a different cultural standpoint. For example, as Aikenhead and Ogawa (2007) point out, "the noun *knowledge* does not translate easily into most verb-based Indigenous languages" (p. 553). In consequence, these authors prefer to use the expression "Indigenous ways of living in nature" instead of "Indigenous knowledge".

Kawagley and Barnhardt (1999) point out that the Yupiaq people of Alaska believe that all plants, winds, mountains, rivers, lakes and creatures of the Earth possess a spirit, and therefore have consciousness and life, requiring that relationships with them are maintained in a respectful, reciprocal, cooperative and harmonious way, lest the balance be upset. Similarly, the Māori concepts of *whakapapa* (commonly understood as genealogy, but also embracing relationships among all living things and the natural environment), *mauri* (the life essence or life force) and *tikanga* (acting according to what is considered ethically correct or socially appropriate) underpin the principle of *kaitiakitanga*, that is, the obligations and responsibilities to care for the environment and maintain a proper balance (Roberts, 2005; De Luca, 2010). Prior to the adoption of Western technology, Yupiaq people practised what Kawagley et al. (1995) refer to as "soft technology": tool making and use, construction of shelters, making clothes, preparation and preservation of food, and so on, were all carried out with as little harm to the physical and spiritual world as possible. The shamans were the intermediaries between the spiritual and natural world, informing the people of what was appropriate/inappropriate in their interactions with the Earth and ensuring that the overall well-being of the plants and animals on which they depended was maintained. Similarly, the Anglo-Saxon concept of *wyrd* envisages the Earth as a vast and all-encompassing system of links or fibres, rather like a 3-dimensional spider's web extending in both time and space, such that what we do now affects people in the future and what we do here affects people elsewhere. The words of Chief Sealth (or Chief Seattle, as he is now known), spoken to a tribal assembly in the Pacific Northwest in 1854, provide eloquent reinforcement of this view.

> Humankind has not woven the web of life. We are but one thread within it.
> Whatever we do to the web, we do to ourselves. All things are bound together.
> All things connect.

This kind of thinking has its modern equivalent in the work of James Lovelock, at one time an employee of NASA investigating the possibility of life on Mars. Lovelock (1986, 1991, 2000) elaborated on the views of the 18th Century geologist, James Hutton, that the world's self-repairing, self-regulating qualities made it more like an organism than a machine, into his Gaia hypothesis[102], which envisages the Earth as a kind of living, self-regulating organic system (of which we are a part) maintained in homeostasis by the activities of living things through a series of cycles (the rock cycle, the nitrogen cycle, the carbon cycle, etc.): "The temperature, oxidation state, acidity, and certain aspects of the rocks and waters are at any time kept constant... this homeostasis is maintained by active feedback processes operated automatically and unconsciously by the biota" (Lovelock, 1991, p. 19). Pepper (1996) summarizes this notion as follows: "Living things themselves produce the conditions most conducive to their thriving. So they are not passive: they manipulate and radically change environments in ways most favourable to their future development. This makes the whole planet a self-sustaining system: a discrete entity able to maintain its own integrity by responding appropriately to changes via feedback mechanisms. Life and non-life are complementary and collaborating" (p. 21). Discussion of Gaia is outside the scope of this book, save to note that the principal objections focus on its strong teleological aspects (seemingly requiring a measure of foresight and planning) and its over-emphasis on biological regulation. Lovelock responds to these criticisms by noting that the regulation processes should be seen as automatic rather than purposeful or goal-seeking.

For some, the kind of theorizing outlined in this section of the chapter is enormously helpful and sets up an agenda for change; for others, it constitutes unhelpful trading in stereotypes and/or romanticism. We need to be cognizant, for example, of the danger of projecting a romanticized view of traditional/Aboriginal knowledge. Although there may well have been some very significant attitudinal and values differences, from which we can learn a great deal, the principal reason why early cultures impacted much less harmfully on the environment than post-industrial society was a consequence of the much lower population density and the much lower level of technological development (Smithson, 1997). There is also abundant evidence that both hunter-gatherers and early Neolithic agriculturalists did, from time to time, drive other species to extinction (Diamond, 1982; Martin & Klein, 1984), and that this pattern of behaviour continued for thousands of years. However, while past extinctions generally resulted from the over-hunting of vulnerable species (large flightless birds, for example), those of today are due primarily to destruction of habitat. As technological capability increased, the environment increasingly came to be seen as a huge, even limitless resource and a huge dumping ground for waste. However, emerging knowledge of the location and extent of resources, and the capacity to exploit them, was not balanced by utilization of the knowledge of biological systems that earlier people had accumulated. Although some Indigenous communities still retain some of that traditional knowledge, it is fast disappearing as it struggles for status and credibility against the juggernaut of scientific knowledge (Shiva, 1993). Before it is lost for ever, we should look to that knowledge for a measure of guidance and inspiration. The depth of ecological knowledge, its robustness over long periods of time, and its context-specific detail within an overall holistic framework, represent an invaluable framework for addressing current environmental crises. Snively and Corsiglia (2001) note that the spiritual basis of traditional knowledge, which is a major feature distinguishing it from science, incorporates "important ecology, conservation, and sustainable development strategies" (p. 23) – an argument also made by Christie (1991), Chinn (2007) and El-Hani and Bandeira (2008).

Orr (1992, 1994, 1996) points out the prominence given in traditional knowledge to: (i) trans-generational communication (Elders have responsibility for passing on the community's accumulated knowledge and practices); (ii) patterns of civic responsibility and mutual aid to ensure that wealth accumulation is not the paramount goal; and (iii) approaches to home construction, food production and health care that reflect ecological understanding and a deep knowledge and respect of the immediate locality. These three focuses will be revisited in chapter 9 with respect to the action-oriented approach proposed in chapter 3. However, the solution to contemporary environmental problems cannot be found *solely* within the principles and practices of traditional knowledge. Environmental problems are historically, geographically and culturally located (i.e., problems of here and now), and so we must find our own solutions. Demonizing science and technology because of the role they have undoubtedly and often unwittingly played in creating social and environ-mental problems is fruitless and unhelpful, just as uncritical romanticization of Aboriginal beliefs, values and practices or unthinking adoption of feminist rationales or Eastern mysticism are fruitless and unhelpful. Contemporary scientific knowledge and technological innovation can play hugely influential roles in both understanding and ameliorating environmental crises. What best serves the purpose of building the critical scientific literacy essential to responsible citizenship is a *range* of perspectives and a critical evaluation of the values they embody and the practices they promote: scientific *and* traditional, Eastern *and* Western, masculine *and* feminine.

As an aside, it is important to recognize that in a number of countries the introduction of traditional knowledge into the curriculum not only plays a major role in personalizing learning and assisting border crossings into science, it can be a crucial element in cultural stabilization or renewal. Much of this traditional knowledge is under threat. Indeed, much has already been lost. School science education can play a vital role in conserving that knowledge for future generations. The task is to find ways of incorporating traditional knowledge into the curriculum in order to celebrate and maintain important cultural traditions whilst attending to national development priorities that are rooted in contemporary science and technology. It is here, at the intersection of Western science and traditional knowledge, that a recent curriculum initiative in South Africa is important. The goal is to integrate "indigenous knowledge systems" with school science throughout the entire school system (K-12).

> Indigenous or traditional technologies and practices... reflect the wisdom of people who have lived a long time in one place and have a great deal of knowledge about their environment... Much valuable wisdom has been lost in South Africa... and effort is needed now to rediscover it and examine its value for the present day. (Department of Education, RSA, 2002, p. 10)

Ogunniyi (2007a,b) reports that progress to date is encouraging, though many teachers are still uncertain about exactly what is entailed and apprehensive about their ability to engage in the radically different teaching and learning strategies that the new curriculum requires. Closer to my home, it is very encouraging that *Science in the New Zealand Curriculum* (Ministry of Education, 1993) urges teachers to make science more relevant and more accessible to Māori students by acknowledging Tikanga Māori (Māori culture, beliefs and values), using and valuing Te Reo Māori (Māori language) and acknowledging and building on the experiences of Māori students. More significantly, the Ministry of Education (1996) has produced a parallel document, *Pūtaiao: i Roto i Te Marauntanga o Aotearoa*, for schools wishing to teach science through the Māori language. The goal is to teach science from a Māori worldview perspective, including Māori ways of understanding the living world. Elsewhere, Thomson (2003) has worked with Elders in Kenya to identify and categorize knowledge of snakes in the local Keiyo language. Similarly, Gitari (2003, 2006) has sought to integrate traditional knowledge of herbal medicine in rural Kenya into the Kenyan science curriculum [see also, Kithinji, 2000], while Malcolm and Keogh (2004) and Keane (2008) have done similar work with regard to traditional farming methods and views of nature in rural Kwa-Zulu Natal (South Africa). Chinn (2007) has shown how the Hawaiian science curriculum can incorporate traditional cultural practices focused on sustainability issues and development of a sense of place (see chapter 9), while Glasson et al. (2006, 2010) have made similar efforts to incorporate the traditional agricultural practices of Malawi into a science curriculum for sustainability. Sustainability is also the key focus of Prakash's (1999) argument for promoting ecological literacy by giving attention to traditional Punjabi knowledge relating to food production. Further important research along these lines includes June George's (1999a,b) discussion of ways of incorporating the traditional knowledge of fishing communities in

Trinidad and Tobago into the school science curriculum, Tevita Palefau's (2005) study of how traditional knowledge in the Pacific Islands (specifically, the Kingdom of Tonga) can be preserved and incorporated into a science and technology curriculum concerned with economic development and responsible citizenship, and the efforts of educators in the South Western United States to incorporate Indigenous knowledge into the earth sciences curriculum (Bevier et al., 1997; Dubiel et al., 1997; Semken & Morgan, 1997; Riggs, 2005). In addition, Aikenhead (2002) describes how a group of teachers in Northern Saskatchewan worked together to design *Rekindling Traditions*, a Grades 6 to 11 science course incorporating the local community's traditional knowledge, much of which was gathered by the students themselves through interviews with Elders and other knowledgeable people in the community. Lewthwaite and Renaud (2009) describe a similar collaborative initiative to develop and implement a curriculum incorporating traditional Inuit knowledge into the science curriculum for schools in the Qikiqtani (Baffin Island) region of Nunavut.

It almost goes without saying that all developments that seek to integrate science and Indigenous or traditional knowledge need to be wary of the dangers of cultural appropriation, romanticization, distortion and over-simplification (Odora Hoppers, 2002; Reid et al., 2004; van Damme & Neluvhalani, 2004). As Hatcher et al. (2009) point out, by adopting the principles of "two-eyed seeing" some of these dangers can be avoided: "Two-Eyed seeing refers to learning to see from one eye with the strengths of Indigenous ways of knowing and from the other eye with the strengths of Western ways of knowing and to using both of these eyes together... (It) allows the Indigenous Sciences' sense of the whole 'to dance' with the Western Science sense of the parts" (p. 146, capitals in original). Relevant here is Pauline Chinn's (2006) description of an action research approach to designing a culturally appropriate science curriculum for high school students in Hawai'i that involved deep cultural immersion and cooption of persons she calls "cultural translators" into the curriculum development team.

EDUCATION FOR SUSTAINABILITY CITIZENSHIP

Regardless of one's personal position with regard to these ideas and their relevance to the school curriculum, what remains unquestioned is the importance of shifting students' views in the direction of what Arne Naess, Bill Devall and George Sessions refer to as "deep ecology" (Devall & Sessions, 1985; Naess, 1989): (i) the well-being and flourishing of humans and non-human life on Earth have intrinsic value or inherent worth; (ii) the richness and diversity of life forms contribute to the realization of these values, and are values in themselves; (iii) humans have no right to reduce this richness and diversity, except to satisfy vital needs; (iv) the flourishing of human life and cultures is compatible with a substantially smaller human population, and the flourishing of non-human life *requires* a smaller human population; (v) present human interference with the non-human world is excessive, and the situation is rapidly worsening; (vi) policies that affect basic economic, technological and ideological structures must be changed; (vii) those who subscribe to these points are obliged to implement the necessary changes, either directly or indirectly. As Capra (1996) comments: "Deep ecology recognizes the fundamental interdependence of all phenomena and individuals and societies embedded in (and ultimately dependent on) the cyclical processes of nature. Humans are not separate from the natural environment and are just one strand of the web of life" (p. 7).

Appreciating interconnectedness means acquiring an understanding of the relationships that exist between all natural and human made systems, recognizing that all human actions have consequences that will affect a complex global system that includes humans and non-human species, recognizing that the well-being of future generations is deeply dependent on the choices we make *now* and the actions we take *now*, having an awareness of and acting on choices to maintain an ecologically sound and humane lifestyle[103]. It includes awareness of the economic, social and political connections established through the movement of goods, people and information that link all humanity in relationships that are sometimes unjust and inequitable. It includes awareness of the complex interactions among social structures, culture, traditions, philosophy, religion, science, technology, economics, politics, agricultural and industrial practices, and human aspirations, interests and values. It also includes awareness that one's own health, well-being and sense of self will influence, and will be influenced by, the condition of the planet. And, at a personal level, it includes awareness of the interconnectedness of our own cognitive, physical, emotional and spiritual make-up. In other words, to deal adequately with SSI and environmental issues the concepts of interdependence and interconnectedness need to be addressed at multiple levels: intrapersonal, interpersonal, local, regional and global. Reaching this level of understanding entails a rejection of many of the dichotomies arising from the mechanistic/reductionist thinking that is almost all-pervasive in school-based education: local/global; human/ animal; human/environment; nature/culture; masculine/feminine; rational/emotional; mind/body; content/process; and so on. For Capra (1983), the essential shift in values is from independence to interdependence, competition to cooperation, quantity to quality, expansion to conservation, and domination to partnership.

László (2001) describes the inculcation of this clutch of values as the development of a *planetary ethic* - an ethic which "respects the conditions under which all people in the world community can live in dignity and freedom, without destroying each other's chances of livelihood, culture, society, and environment" (p. 78). Laszlo is at some pains to state that abiding by a planetary ethic does not necessarily entail major sacrifices or self-denying behaviour (though not everyone would agree with him on this point). Striving for excellence, beauty, personal growth, enjoyment, even comfort and luxury, is still possible, he argues, provided that we consider the consequences of our actions on the lives and opportunities of others by asking:
– Is the way I live compatible with the rights of others?
– Does it take basic resources from them?
– Does it impact adversely on the environment?

Barry (2006) posits the broadly similar notion of *sustainability citizenship*, which he defines as an "ambitious, multifaceted, and challenging mode of green citizenship, which focuses on the underlying structural causes of environmental degradation and other infringements of sustainable development such as human rights abuses or social injustice" (p. 24). Elizabeth Dowdeswell, former Executive Director of the United Nations Environment Programme (UNEP)[104], expresses the situation with typical clarity and directness: "We have to ask ourselves simple but fundamental questions: How should we live? How much is enough? What way of life ought human beings to pursue? We have to develop the ecological holistic worldview, which connects us with the environment and other people and species, both materially and spiritually. Our task should be... translate [this worldview] into a clear prescription for public policy and behaviour" (Dowdeswell, 1996, p. 8). And, I would add, into curriculum. In similar vein, Princen (2003) coins the notion of "sufficiency" to ask how much we really need to consume in order to live a sustainable but still meaningful and rewarding life, one of the key elements of which is restraint: "using less than what is physically or technically or legally or financially possible" (p. 47). Some of these ideas are encapsulated in the notion of environmental *stewardship* (sometimes included in the wider notion of environmental literacy, as discussed in chapter 1): the moral obligation to care for the environment and to exhibit in one's actions a reverence for the Earth, respect for the integrity of natural systems, and an obligation to future generations. This entails a commitment to using resources wisely, sparingly and efficiently, placing realistic limits on personal consumption and re-aligning expectations, habits and values to reflect an ethic of care. Other elements of an education for sustainability citizenship, or what David Selby (2010) calls *education for sustainable contraction* ("a transformation to less exploitative and environmentally harmonious lfe ways"), include: a robust understanding of interdependence (of society, economy and natural environment); recognizing the importance of diversity (cultural, social, political, economic and biological); acknowledging fundamental rights and responsibilities, and variations in aspirations, needs and interests; having a commitment to promoting freedom, equity and justice, and developing an eagerness to become involved in SSI-related activities within the local community; and a willingness to engage in other forms of sociopolitical action. The ultimate goal of such an education is to prevent problems arising, rather than "tidying up" afterwards.

To paraphrase Robinson and Tinker (1997), the notion of sustainability encompases three "imperatives": the *ecological imperative* is to stay within the biophysical carrying capacity of the planet, the *economic imperative* is to provide an adequate material standard of living for all, the *social imperative* is to provide systems of governance that propagate the values by which people want to live. Meeting these three imperatives necessarily entails resolution of conflicts and contradictions among them, debating and reaching agreement on a wide variety of beliefs, needs, interests, values and aspirations, and addressing issues relating to fairness, equity and social justice. Sustainability, then, is not so much a definable end state as a socio-political process for co-producing a set of possibilities and, eventually, identifying preferred options. Robinson (2004) expresses this view particularly well: "Sustain-ability is... the emergent property of a conversation about what kind of world we collectively want to live in now and in the future. The problem... will not be resolved by new research, better science, and teaching people to understand the true nature of the problems, desirable as these may be. Instead, the way forward involves the development of new forms of partnership, and new tools for creating political dialogue, that frame the problems as questions of political choice, given uncertainty and constraints; that renounce the goal of precise and unambiguous definition and knowledge; and that involve many more people in the conversation" (p. 382). The kinds of partnerships and conversations envisaged by Robinson are the focus for much of chapter 9.

PLACE, COMMUNITY AND COLLECTIVE ACTION

Education *in/through* the environment, or education *with* the environment (to use Gough's (1987) phrase), can play a substantial role in raising environmental awareness, cultivating environmental sensitivity, challenging and re-ordering existing environmental values, and developing new ones. Gough (1989), for example, describes how the kind of experiences advocated by the Earth Education movement (van Matre, 1979, 1990; van Matre & Johnson, 1988; Cohen, 1990; Johnson, 2007) can be utilized in re-orienting students' environmental understanding, taking them beyond the superficial to embrace the complexity, diversity, interconnectedness and dynamic nature of the natural environment. Some years ago, Woolnough and Allsop (1985) talked about the importance of students "getting a feel for phenomena" through hands-on experiences in the laboratory as a prerequisite for good conceptual understanding. The same kind of preparation may be essential to gaining the kind of conceptual understanding of the natural environment that leads to environmental literacy. So many of today's children are strangers to the natural world, spending their time in a world of steel, glass and concrete. For them, nature exists as tiny isolated pockets – a small park, a window box, a tree-lined avenue here and there. Many are so protected and so urbanized that they have never felt the rough bark of a tree, experienced total darkness or silence, seen the full glory of the milky way, heard an owl's call, watched a spider spin a web, or even paddled barefoot in a stream or pond. They haven't walked in the forest, climbed a mountain, sailed down a river or explored a cave. They increasingly live in a virtual environment, with experience mediated by computerized devices that entail sensory deprivation of the natural kind and its substitution by the bleeps and burps of electronic gadgets. In consequence, their understanding of the natural environment is minimal and their attitudes towards it are ill-informed.

> Within the context of cities and suburbs it becomes easier to forget nature and to believe that human beings and our economy are able to exist outside the requirements of the ecosystems we have covered with our highways and shopping malls and skyscrapers. That relationship must be re-established. (Smith & Williams, 1999, p. 7)

What I am advocating as a matter of some urgency is "getting a feel for the environment", that is, building a sense of ecological relationships through powerful emotional experiences outdoors – the kind of experiences so vividly reflected in the poetry of John Keats and Gerard Manley Hopkins. Bonnett (2007) refers to it as "knowledge by acquaintance (knowledge that affects and is capable of engaging all the senses), citing Thoreau's (1949) advice to "Live each season as it passes; breathe the air, drink the drink, taste the fruit, and resign yourself to the influences of each... Open all your pores and bathe in all the tides of Nature, in all her streams and oceans, at all seasons… Grow green with spring, yellow and ripe with autumn" (p. 394). It is experiences like these that enable us to understand and value our place in the natural order of things. Similar proposals have been advanced by Carson (1965), Greenhall Gough (1990), Hungerford and Volk (1990), Nabhan and Trimble (1994), Tilbury (1994), Thomashow (1995), Hutchinson (1998), Eagles and Demare (1999), Bateson, (2000), Palmberg and Kuru (2000), Chawla (2002), Kahn (2002), Kahn and Kellert (2002), Louv (2005), Magntorn and Helldén (2005), Council of Outdoor Educators of Ontario (2007), Littledyke (2008) and Sandell and Öhman (2010). The key emphases are: sharpening the senses (learning to look, listen, smell and feel without the aid and intervention of sophisticated technology); building key ecological concepts – not just as analytical abstractions but as tools for *seeing* and *understanding*; providing opportunities for solitude; making learning a joyful, magical and aesthetically powerful experience; and developing a deep emotional relationship to a particular place (or to several places). We should aim to give all students the opportunity to experience the smells, sights and sounds of the forest, mountains and seashore, the chance to interact with the natural world and take risks, and in the words of Kahn and Kellert (2002), "climb trees, muck about, catch things, and get wet" (p. xvii). Through these experiences, students come to *know* in a different way: "In feeling the resilience of this piece of grass underfoot, this piece of earth to the spade, this piece of wood to the chisel, in feeling the growing chill in the air and apprehending the brooding presence of storm clouds, we engage with the world less through a cognitive ordering and more through a receptive sensing that is less susceptible to abstract generalization and objectification" (Bonnett, 2007b, p. 716). In addition, by learning to be sensitive to the aesthetic and spiritual qualities of caves, volcanoes and forests, rather than seeing them merely as products of erosion, the outcome of geothermal activity and resources for making paper or furniture, our students can recover what many Indigenous peoples around the world have never lost: a sense of unity between humanity and the natural environment. In the words of David Suzuki (1998), "Nothing exists in isolation. Everything – past, present, and future – is part of an uninterrupted continuum. Each rock, stream, and tree, every star, cloud and bird, is part of a single interacting and interdependent whole" (p. 16). Plumwood (1991) sums up the importance of what I have in mind as follows:

Special relationship with, care for, or empathy with particular aspects of nature as experiences rather than with nature as abstraction are essential to provide a depth and type of concern that is not otherwise possible. Care and responsibility for particular animals, trees, and rivers that are known well, loved, and appropriately connected to the self are an important basis for acquiring a wider, more generalized concern. (p. 7)

Similar views are expressed by Paul Shepard (1982) when he says that maturity of thought (*wisdom* rather than mere knowledge) arises from connecting with the Earth in the early years of childhood. Without close contact with the earth, soil, wildlife, trees and animals, he argues, we become *infantile adults*: wanting everything now and new; careless of resources and waste; unable to empathize with others (both human and non-human); prone to violence when frustrated; despising age and denying human natural history. David Orr (1994) talks about the importance of early experiences of nature in building *biophilia*: "If by some fairly young age... nature has not been experienced as a friendly place of adventure and excitement, biophilia will not take hold as it might have. An opportunity will have passed, and thereafter perception and imagination" (p. 143). Clover et al. (2000) advocate outdoor experiences for adults, too, as a means to "heal, re-connect, liberate, empower, create and celebrate" (p. 20). At the risk of 'beating my point to death with a stick', I offer one more quotation, from Stephen Jay Gould (1994), to reinforce my case for outdoor experience: "We cannot win the battle to save species and environment without forging an emotional bond between ourselves and nature as well – for we will not fight in order to save what we do not love... We must have visceral contact in order to love" (p. 44). It is perhaps not surprising, then, that a number of research studies focused on environmental educators, environmental activists and professionals employed in fields ranging from wilderness protection to urban planning reveal that early experiences of natural environments (especially hiking or tramping, camping, canoeing and kayaking, bird watching, fishing and collecting berries), together with the influence of family and friends and involvement in organizations like guides and scouts, were the major factors determining later environmental sensitivity, attitude, values and activist stance (Palmer, 1993; Palmer & Suggate, 1996; Sobel, 1996; Sward, 1996, 1999; Chawla, 1998, 1999, 2008; Palmer et al., 1998; Bogner, 2002; Kellert, 2002; Palmberg & Kuru, 2002; Hsu, 2009; Braun et al., 2010). Similarly, secondary school students who are active in environmental clubs and activist groups report that they also had similar formative experiences as children (Sivek, 2002; Bögeholz, 2006). Negative experiences, such as the destruction of a favourite natural location, increased urbanization, proliferation of waste dumpsites and serious decline in species numbers, can be very significant, too. Bögeholz (2006) makes the interesting and potentially important observation that nature experience is the strongest indicator of future individual, direct pro-environmental behaviour, while experience in environmental organizations is the strongest predictor of indirect and collective action (see chapter 3 for a discussion of these distinctions).

In empirical support of these propositions, Mittelstaedt et al. (1999) report that a one-week experiential programme operated by the Cincinnati Museum Center in an Appalachian wilderness area had immediate impact on the environmental sensitivity and attitudes of the participants, many of whom expressed their intention to engage in more responsible environmental behaviour in the future: not leaving litter, not trampling or picking plants or damaging trees, not harming "bugs, bees, insects or endangered species", trying to be quiet in the forest, not disturbing natural habitats, not wasting water, not generating so much garbage and not causing pollution. Similarly encouraging results are reported by Emmons (1997), Palmer (1998), Dettmann-Easler and Pease (1999), Palmberg and Kuru (2000), Bogner (2002), Brody et al. (2002), Kellert (2002), Knapp and Benton (2006), Ballantyne and Packer (2008), Stern et al. (2008) and Cachelin et al. (2009)[105], though Cook (2008) issues a timely reminder that the nature of the activities in which students engage is a crucial determinant of the learning outcome. It is not just being outside, *per se*; it is 'what you do there' that is key. As Dillon (2003) comments, it would be reckless to assume that "because the body is in the field that the mind is there, too" (p. 219). Park and Chang (1998) report how high school students' ability to identify and explore their feelings about the environment was substantially enhanced by a programme combining outdoor experiences with meditation strategies – an idea with enormous educational potential. Others have advocated raiding Buddhist teachings for further inspiration but, as Scharper (2002) warns, teachers need to be alert to the difficulties of trying to apply ideas and practices outside their original cultural and religious context. It might also be expected that the likelihood of desirable outcomes will be strongly influenced by the attitudes and values exhibited by the educators involved.

Russell and Hodson (2002) suggest that whalewatching and other ecotourist activities (such as safaris, birdwatching, wildlife treks and the wildlife cruises now available in Alaska and the Galapagos Islands) can be particularly effective in preparing the ground for a shift from anthropocentrism to biocentrism and more humane perspectives (see also, Ham & Weiler, 2002; Russon & Russell, 2004; Russell & Russon, 2007). However, as Ballantyne et al. (2007) point out, the presence of humans can sometimes have substantial negative impact on the animals that ecotourists come to see – for example, increased stress, changes in feeding behaviours, disruption of natural behaviours such as nest building and mating rituals, habituation to humans, degradation or destruction of habitat, and even risk of injury. Ensuring minimum impact and providing appropriate visitor preparation are key to the animals' welfare and authenticity of experience, though these goals can be difficult and expensive to achieve. One experience with virtually no impact on the species observed is provided by the Niagara Parks Butterfly Conservatory (in Ontario, Canada). Pedretti and Soren's (2006) discussion of visitors' responses provides eloquent evidence of the potential of such experiences to shift feelings, attitudes and values: a powerful aesthetic and emotional response to being surrounded by such fragile and beautiful creatures; feelings of tranquillity, serenity, peace and relaxation in being away from the stresses of daily life; and a sense of connectedness to nature from immersion (even for just a few hours) in a delicate tropical rain forest environment that contrasts so sharply with the ugly, noisy and polluted urban environment in which visitors say they usually spend so much time. Lindemann-Matthies and Kamer (2006) describe similar kinds of affective responses following visitors' interactive experiences at a Swiss zoo (Tierpark Goldau) focused on a breeding and release programme for the endangered bearded vulture (*Gypaetus barbatus*). As well as observing the birds, visitors can use "touch tables" equipped with skulls, food samples, feathers and soil stained with iron oxide to investigate the bearded vulture's highly unusual habit of deliberately staining its feathers. Indeed, informal learning experiences (or "free choice experiences", as some researchers prefer to call them) in zoos, aquaria, botanical gardens, nature trails, local conservation areas, theme parks, amusement parks, outdoor pursuits centres, science centres, museums and interpretive centres can often be much more effective than formal classroom learning in bringing about awareness of issues, precipitating a shift in values and attitudes, and fostering a willingness to engage in socio-political action (Ramey-Gassert & Walberg, 1994; Meredith et al., 1997; Negra & Manning, 1997; Jeffrey-Clay, 1999; Pedretti, 1999, 2002, 2004; Medved & Oatley, 2000; Falk, 2001; Martin, 2004; Myers et al., 2004; Rennie & Johnston, 2004;

Djerking, 2005; Kola-Olusanya, 2005; Nielsen et al., 2009; Simpson & Parsons, 2009; Stocklmayer et al., 2010). Recent studies by Davidson et al. (2010) and Kisiel (2010) emphasize just how important it is for teachers to work closely with educators in the zoo, aquarium or museum to forge a common agenda, reach consensus on the nature of the proposed experience, and establish a common set of priorities and an agreed approach to teaching and learning.

A sense of wonder and feelings of empathy, respect and compassion towards other living things can also be fostered by such easily organized activities as investigating a rock pool, noting what lives in a wall or hedgerow[106], taking digital photographs to examine the feathers of birds in a suburban garden, watching a spider spin a web, observing insects through a magnifying lens or pond water under a microscope (see Lindemann-Mathies (2005) for further suggestions along these lines). Nor should we under-estimate the value of caring for pets, growing vegetables, observing activity in an ant colony and watching the dramatic events in the life history of frogs and butterflies. An important part of these experiences is the delight that students experience in becoming absorbed in their observations, the feelings of surprise at seeing the world in new ways, the thrill of encountering previously unfamiliar living organisms and habitats, recognizing new possibilities and seeing new relationships (Liston, 2004). Girod et al. (2003) refer to this kind of experience as "re-seeing".

> Re-seeing is an attempt to focus our perception on the nuance and detail of the world. Re-seeing requires that we look carefully when we might be tempted to assume we see everything. Re-seeing is also a disposition that causes us to ask questions of what we perceive, such as 'What's really going on here?' 'Why do things look the way they do?' And 'What kinds of things do I need to know more about to really re-see this?' (p. 579)

Looking at the world with 'different eyes' is important because it leads individuals to understand and value plants and animals that had previously been misunderstood, ignored or unvalued. It is easy to be enthralled by spectacular animals like lions, tigers, giraffes and bears, those that are like ourselves (apes, monkeys and pandas), those that are cute (bushbabies, koalas, squirrels), and those that exhibit intelligent behaviour, make eye contact and communicate by sound (dolphins, sea lions, dogs). It is less easy to care about insects, spiders, snails and worms. Similarly, it is easy to put value on plants with large and colourful flowers or those that bear fruit, while non-flowering plants or those with small and inconspicuous flowers are ignored. They are just part of the habitat of animals! But the current alarming losses of biodiversity makes it imperative that we value all living things. In urging teachers to direct attention towards currently less-favoured creatures, McVay (1993) asks us to ponder the following: "What would happen if every elementary schoolchild chose a creature, whether an ant, a bee, cricket, dragonfly, spider, waterstrider, snake, frog, fly, beetle, or bat, to study and report on repeatedly during his or her first six years of school?" (p. 11). His answer: "The capacity for bioaffiliation in the rising generation would be boundless" (p. 11). There would be enormous value in getting young children to create a story, poem or play about events in the life of a plant or animal, especially from the perspective of a creature that is disliked for some reason – for example, by a child who is frightened of it, by a farmer who sees it as a pest or by a camper who regards it as a nuisance. Many biologists and biology teachers consider anthropomorphism to be bad practice; my view is that it may be essential to successfully combating biophobia. Inspiration for such activities can be found in David Abram's (1996) beautiful description of the problem-solving creativity inherent in the work of spiders as they spin their webs and in Neil Evernden's (1985, 1992) sensitive representation of the daily lives of woodland insects. On a similar theme, Bell et al. (1998) describe how they sought to enrich the study of species extinction and biodiversity for students in three Ontario high schools with an understanding of the issues grounded in an ethic of care and respect, principally by generating a keen understanding of the needs, interests and experiences of *individuals* among the threatened group. By preceding a discussion of the threats to orang-utans from logging, poaching, mining and urban encroachment on habitat with some moving and amusing stories about individual orang-utans (drawn from one of the authors' personal experiences while working in Borneo), they created a situation in which the students could readily appreciate what habitat loss, food stock depletion and population decline would mean at the personal level. Next, students were asked to write a story from the perspective of a Monarch butterfly faced with loss of habitat in Mexico (its winter home) due to careless and unrestricted logging, faced with the concerted efforts of farmers in many parts of Canada (the summer home) to eradicate milkwood (the Monarch's primary food source as a caterpillar) because they see it as a noxious weed, and confronted by a host of hazards on a migration flight of several thousand miles. Follow-up studies looked at the problems faced by bats, condors, beluga whales, elephants and rattlesnakes. By such means, students learn to see plants and animals as members of complex ecological communities characterized by diverse patterns of interaction and constantly changing threats and challenges.

Girod's notion of "re-seeing" also includes the new ways of looking at events and phenomena in the light of newly acquired scientific knowledge. Looking at a landscape through the lens provided by geological knowledge, or at a rainbow with the eyes of a physicist, provides opportunities that were previously absent. The following three quotations should be sufficient to make the point.

The world looks so different after learning science. For example, trees are made of air, primarily. When they are burned, they go back to air, and in the flaming heat is released the flaming heat of the sun which was bound in to convert the air into tree, and in the ash is the small remnant of the part which did not come from air, that came from the solid earth, instead. These are beautiful things, and the content of science is wonderfully full of them. They are very inspiring, and they can be used to inspire others. (Feynman, 1969, p. 320)

It is raining DNA outside. On the bank of the Oxford canal at the bottom of my garden is a large willow tree, and it is pouring downy seeds into the air. There is no consistent air movement, and the seeds are drifting outwards in all directions from the tree. Up and down the canal, as far as my binoculars can reach, the water is white with floating cottony flecks, and we can be sure that they have carpeted the ground to much the same radius in other directions too. The cotton wool is mostly made of cellulose, and it dwarfs the tiny capsule that contains the DNA, the genetic information. The DNA content must be a small proportion of the total, so why did I say that it was raining DNA rather than cellulose? The answer is that it is the DNA that matters. The cellulose fluff, although more bulky, is just a parachute, to be discarded. The whole performance, cotton wool, catkins, tree and all, is in aid of one thing and one thing only, the spreading of DNA around the countryside. Not just any DNA, but DNA whose coded characters spell out specific instructions for building willow trees that will shed a new generation of downy seeds. Those fluffy specks are, literally, spreading instructions for making themselves. They are there because their ancestors succeeded in doing the same. It is raining instructions out there; it's raining programs; it's raining tree-growing, fluff-spreading, algorithms. That is not a metaphor; it is the plain truth. It couldn't be plainer if it were raining floppy discs. (Dawkins, 1986, p. 111)

Our character [an atom of carbon] lies for hundreds of millions of years, bound to three atoms of oxygen, and one of calcium, in the form of limestone... The limestone rock ledge of which the atom forms a part lies on the surface. It lies within reach of man and his pickax... A blow of the pickax detached it and sent it on its way to the lime kiln, plunging it into the world of things that change. It was roasted until it separated from the calcium, which remained so to speak, with its feet on the ground and went to meet a less brilliant destiny, which we shall not narrate. Still firmly clinging to two of its three former oxygen companions, it issued from the chimney and took the path of the air. Its story, which was once immobile, now turned tumultuous. It was caught by the wind, flung down on the earth, lifted up ten kilometres high. It was breathed in by a falcon, descending into its precipitous lungs, but did not penetrate its rich blood and was expelled. It dissolved three times in the water of the sea, once in the water of a cascading torrent, and again was expelled. It travelled on the wind for eight years; now high, now low, on the sea and among the clouds, over forests, deserts, and limitless expanses of ice; then it stumbled into capture and the organic adventure... It had the good fortune to brush against a leaf, penetrate it, and be nailed there by a ray of the sun... Our atom of carbon enters the leaf, colliding with other innumerable (but here useless) molecules of nitrogen and oxygen. It adheres to a large and complicated molecule that activates it, and simultaneously receives the decisive message from the sky, in the flashing form of a packet of solar light: in an instant, like an insect caught by a spider, it is separated from its oxygen, combined with hydrogen and (one thinks) phosphorus, and finally inserted in a chain, whether long or short does not matter, but it is the chain of life. All this happens swiftly, in silence, at the temperature and pressure of the atmosphere, and gratis: dear colleagues, when we learn to do likewise we will ... have solved the problem of hunger in the world. (Levi, 1984, p225)[107]

There are valuable opportunities for "re-seeing" in accounts of how chimpanzee Washoe and orang-utan Chantek learned to use American Sign Language to communicate sophisticated ideas, express their needs and wants, and convey their feelings

(Gardner et al., 1989; Miles, 1994). Savage-Rumbaugh et al. (1998) describe similar fluency in communicating ideas exhibited by bonobo Kanzi. Bell and Russell (2000) discuss how such studies have the potential to shift students' views regarding the common belief that humans are different from animals in kind (not just degree) with respect to experiencing emotions, possessing communication skills and having a sense of individuality and personal history. Weston (1991) talks about another kind of "re-seeing" when he describes how his views shift each Spring when his primary focus of attention moves from his life as an academic in an urban-based educational institution to his life as a gardener working in what people in the UK would call an allotment or a smallholding and people in New Zealand would call a "lifestyle block".

> My life takes on a different shape. The 'we', for instance, that in my office seems to include only humans, now changes. 'We' are now my co-gardeners and beneficiaries – the plants themselves, obviously; the neighbour who plows and advises, the friends and soup kitchen that get the extra cucumbers and tomatoes, the raccoons who rummage in the compost pile, the horses whose manure fertilizes, the insects who make their homes among the vegetables and consume their more destructive cousins. The 'them' are the various threats: other plants and insects, the groundhogs and deer that take more than they need or destroy more than they get, the kid down the hill (quite human) who lobs baseballs into the corn. Species lines do not determine my allegiances here; rather, my allegiance is to one multi-species community and against others who emerge as invaders and disrupters. One small step for a man, one fairly significant transformation of consciousness. (p. 110)

There is a strong case for building such opportunities for consciousness changing and "re-seeing" into every student's educational experiences.

Kellert (2005) classifies experiences with nature into three groups: *direct* contact with plants, animals and habitat; *indirect* contact through zoos, botanical gardens and aquaria; and *vicarious* (or symbolic) contact via literature, movies and computer-based experiences. Not surprisingly, Kellert states that indirect or vicarious contact rarely offers the same degree of opportunity as direct experience for "experiencing challenge, adaptation, immersion, creativity, discovery, problem-solving, or critical thinking" (p. 85). Schultz (2000) goes further, and argues that "a trip to a zoo to see animals in cages, watching animals perform skits or trained shows, hearing inform-ation about animals or nature taught abstractly in a classroom, or environmentally destructive recreational behaviours (like off-road motorcycles, jet skis, and snow-mobiles) will likely lead to less perceived interconnection and more egoistic attitudes about nature" (p. 403). Nevertheless, I would argue that literature, art, photographs and movies can be powerful *adjuncts* to (not substitutes for) outdoor experiences; they can provide vicarious experience of exotic locations and places that are distant in both space and time. But they need to be carefully, imaginatively and sensitively presented. Sadly, in recent years there has been a marked shift in the nature of wildlife movies and TV shows, presumably in pursuit of bigger audiences and the associated advertizing revenue. The purely descriptive and informative, exemplified by programmes such as *The Living Planet* and *Life on Earth*, is increasingly being supplanted by a sensationalist emphasis on sex, violence and death (Cottle, 2004).

As Barker (2007) comments, the consumer demand for programmes with names such as *Jaws and Claws, Ultimate Killers, Maneaters, Untamed and Uncut* and *Caught in the Moment,* which might well be described as wildlife porn, "should not guide us into an assumption that this quick thrill actually helps people situate themselves as ecological beings. Indeed the effect is probably quite contrary in that extremes of the natural world used as shock tactics to engage, actually alienates us even further from nature" (p. 32). These experiences are quite likely to precipitate irrational fears of large predators and may build feelings of revulsion for snakes, spiders and insects. On a more positive note, well-chosen movies, television documentaries, literature, art and photography can play a significant role in stimulating interest in SSI, contextualizing science content and NOS knowledge, reflecting the personal, sociohistorical and economic dimensions of scientific and technological developments, and shifting students' perceptions, attitudes and values (Bailey & Watson, 1998; Littledyke, 1998; Bentley, 2000; McSharry & Jones, 2000; Odegaard, 2003; Stinner & Teichmann, 2003; McNaughton, 2004). So, too, can drama and role-play. Particularly noteworthy are the role-play activities developed by Colucci-Gray et al. (2006) to address conflicts between the economic needs of impoverished communities and environmental protection of fragile ecosystems. Related material concerns the sometimes ill-advised interventions (reckless and unethical interventions, as some would describe them) of Western business interests in the agricultural practices of developing countries. For example, as part of the so-called "Green Revolution", many farmers in India were persuaded by Western banks and business interests to cultivate high yielding varieties of grain. Unfortunately the high yield was dependent on extensive irrigation, sophisticated and expensive machinery, and widespread use of chemicals as fertilisers and insecticides. To cover these costs many farmers took out huge loans. When crops failed to produce the anticipated returns, farmers were unable to repay the loans and the banks seized the land. Meanwhile the emphasis on cultivation of grain meant insufficient land was available for growing the oilseeds and pulses that constitute the prime source of protein in many parts of India. As a striking contrast, Joanna Macy's (1985) account of how the Sarvodaya Shramadana Movement in Sri Lanka changed the values of the local community and assisted them in acquiring the social and organizational skills to gain control of the environment through collective action might inspire students and raise their awareness of what is possible in their community (see later discussion).

BROADENING STUDENTS' CONCEPTIONS OF ENVIRONMENT

As noted several times in this book, the language an author chooses to deploy carries a substantial cargo of implicit meaning and strongly signals underlying value positions on the matters under discussion. It both reflects the author's thinking and guides the reader's thinking. Metaphor and analogy play a key role here, as Prain (2006) illustrates in his discussion of Bowler's (1992) account of how our views of the natural environment were formed by the writing of Haeckel and Tansley.

> [Bowler] noted that scientists 'may be inclined to favour a particular view of nature because they can see a parallel with their preferred image of how human

> society functions'. He pointed out that Haeckel coined the term 'oecologie' to 'denote the study of the interactions between organisms and the external world', where the term was derived from the Greek expression 'oikos', referring to tasks and duties performed by family members within a household. Such a metaphor implied a benevolent, monistic system where all species had pre-determined complementary roles. Bowler (1992, p. 525–6) further notes that Tansley, who coined the expression 'ecosystem', sought to emphasize a more materialistic view of management processes in food chains, rejecting any notion of a community metaphor for how the system's parts interacted. (p. 186)

As commonly used, the word 'environment' seems to imply something external and separate from humanity. We should seek to shift our thinking (and the thinking of our students) by broadening the concept of environment to encapsulate the *whole* environment: natural, cultivated, constructed, linguistic, social, cultural, economic and temporal (past, present and future), as discussed in chapter 8. If historians are correct when they tell us that one has to understand the past in order to make sense of the present, and plan effectively and appropriately for the future, then the history of thinking about the environment plays a crucial role in building environmental literacy (Jurin & Hutchinson, 2005). It gives us understanding of how past societies have viewed their place in the world and why they have impacted on it in particular ways. In other words, whatever we currently perceive as the relationship between environment, economy and society is a direct outgrowth of our historical conceptions and understandings of our place in the environment.

> The study of environmental history should develop pupils' understanding of changing social formations and their use of nature. Pupils should understand how the transformation of nature allows social development, how human environments are socially constructed and how social relations shape environmental relations. (Huckle, 1991, p. 56)

Literature can be a particularly powerful vehicle here. Students living in Ireland or the United Kingdom would find much food for thought in William Wordsworth's Lake District-inspired poetry, Thomas Hardy's vivid descriptions of life and work in the "Wessex" countryside and Emily Brontë's atmospheric writing about Yorkshire's West Riding. The transition from rural life to industrialized society finds eloquent and thought-provoking expression in the work of George Eliot, Elizabeth Gaskell and D.H. Lawrence. Wonderfully evocative descriptions of urban environments can be found in the work of Charles Dickens (London), James Joyce (Dublin) and a host of contemporary writers. Teachers in other countries could, no doubt, easily compile a list of literary works that reflect their local environments, both past and present. The "Story Walk" programme described by Ballantyne et al. (2001b) is an intriguing blend of narrative and outdoor experience. By following the story of a friendship between Matthew (a young white boy) and Kara (an Aboriginal girl), who lived in Queensland in the mid-19th Century, and spending time in the various locations described in the story, Grade 5 students can explore cultural differences in perceptions of the environment, learn about the complex issues of water conservation and usage, and gain some insight into the events surrounding the displacement of Aboriginal people from their land in colonial times. We might ask students to talk about the conceptions of environment and environmental behaviour in the books they have read, the TV programmes and movies they have seen, and even in the music they listen to, and to note the extent to which it resembles or differs from their own views – an activity that can be usefully extended by getting students to interview a diverse cross section of people in the local community. Conversations with elderly people about their memories of the neighbourhood during their childhood is a way of addressing the "environmental generational amnesia" referred to in chapter 8. Together with autobiographies, poetry, novels and movies, such experiences can play an important part in teaching students about how things used to be and, perhaps, how they *should* be.

Returning to a point made earlier, language not only reflects our thinking and the values and traditions that underpin it, but also *guides* our thinking. Our choice of particular language directs our questions, establishes our priorities, signals our values, fixes the parameters of the discourse in which we engage, and so on. Shifting to different language stimulates our thinking, provokes reflection, and can trigger a change in beliefs, views and values. For example, shifting to a more gender inclusive language, and encouraging students to do so, is not just an exercise in political correctness; it can play a key role in changing students' attitudes, values and political consciousness. In the same way, changing our language can play a key role in changing the image of science we hold, our views about a whole range of SSI and environmental matters, and our stance on moral-ethical issues. Indeed, Kelly et al. (2000) have shown that getting students to write *about* science, and discussing the texts they produce in class, can be an effective way of extending the scope of science education to embrace wider sociocultural, political and economic issues.

> Through discussion centered on writing in science, the course participants... considered the contextual nature of science (e.g., issues of funding, audience, economic and political ramifications), expertise (e.g., considering speakers' roles in framing arguments), evidence (e.g., supporting conclusions with an evidential base) and responsibility (e.g., citizens' role in the use and under-standing of scientific knowledge). (p. 712)

It follows that writing and reading can be invaluable tools in disrupting the 'social script' that underpins anthropocentrism and promoting alternative views of the environment, including Lázló's (2001) "planetary ethic" and Berry's (2006) notion of "sustainability citizenship" (see chapter 8). Of particular interest in this context is the new generation of writing about the natural environment, such as works by Roger Deakin (2000, 2007), Kathleen Jamie (2004), Richard Mabey (2005), Robert MacFarlane (2007) and Mark Cocker (2008). Schwartz (1999) identifies the following books as especially effective in linking the environmental consciousness of primary school students with social and political change: Nadia Wheatley and Donna Rawlins (1988), *My Place* (a child's eye view of the ecological, sociocultural and political history of an Australian town between 1788 and 1988); Deborah Lee Rose (1990), *The People Who Hug(ged) Trees* (an adaptation of an ancient Indian folktale about the interdependence of people and trees); Laurence Anholt (1992), *Forgotten Forest* (about a group of children discovering a long-forgotten forest hidden behind high walls in the middle of a large and noisy city); Diane DiSalvio-Ryan (1994), *City Green* (how a group of people - old, young, abled and disabled, and of diverse ethnic backgrounds - respond to the demolition of an old building by creating an urban garden); and Byrd Baylor (1994), *The Table Where Rich People Sit* (exploring how a family living in the mountains collectively respond to the concerns of one of the children about lack of money by sharing their views about the value of life in and around their home). Schwartz (1999) explains how Baylor's book explores how the things that the family really values, like sunsets, the sounds of birds, coyotes howling, the wide open views, the shadows and colours of the desert, cactus blossoms, and the simple pleasure of wandering through open countryside, help the young girl to realize that the old wooden table at which the family eats really is the table where rich people sit. Nicholas Tucker (1989) presents a helpful discussion of how children's literature (including nursery rhymes) can be used to address our relationships with, and treatment of animals, while Caduto and Bruchac (1988), Gough (1993) and Korteweg et al. (2008) make a case for using stories from Indigenous cultures to focus or in some cases re-focus students' attention on a deeper moral-ethical understanding of the relationships between people and the natural environment. Burke and Cutter-MacKenzie (2008) draw on their experiences with young children and preservice teachers to provide some vey helpful advice on classroom use of children's literature in science and environmental education, while Hug (2008) gives much useful advice on how to select appropriate materials. Wason-Ellam (2008) makes an eloquent case for the use of illustrated stories, picture books and descriptive texts layered with photographs, narratives and poems.

> When children read both illustrations and narratives on winter camping, fishing in trout streams or hiking on rocky cliffs, there are moments of stillness, moments of intersection, moments of enlightenment, and moments of shared inquiry. Stories beget other stories. As children walk on their own ground, by foot or in their minds, they can relate memories of similar experiences that transport them back to craggy coastlines, majestic forests, or rolling prairies with expansive horizon lines. Story initiates query, roots them in place and keep their connections alive. Stories help them see where they are, how others live here, and how they themselves should live. (p. 282)

Drawing on research by Palmer (1993) and Chawla (1998, 1999) on the formative experiences of some of the foremost environmental educators, Corcoran (1999) builds a case for the use of "environmental autobiography" as a tool for stimulating and developing student teachers' thinking about environmental education issues. One major component of the preservice programme involves students recalling and reflecting on childhood experiences of nature that were of significance to them – if possible, involving visits to places strongly remembered from childhood. Corcoran comments that most students find this a powerful emotional experience: "Whether the wild places have been developed into malls and housing or left undisturbed, the return to childhood places, whether rural, suburban, or urban, evokes thought and feeling" (p. 181). As noted earlier, experiences leading to an aesthetic and/or emotional connection with the environment can be a major determinant of positive attitudes towards the environment and the environmentally responsible behaviour that may result. Building up oral histories by talking with elderly people in the community about their earlier lives, their work, how they spent their leisure time, and the changes they have seen, can be enormously enlightening for students and can help them to build a sense of place.

A SENSE OF PLACE

It is now 70 years since Lewis Mumford (1938) wrote the following: "We must create in every region people who will be accustomed, from school onward, to humanist attitudes, co-operative methods, rational controls. These people will know in detail where they live and how they live: they will be united by a common feeling for their landscape, their literature and language, their local ways, and out of their own self-respect they will have a sympathetic understanding with other regions and different local peculiarities. They will be actively interested in the form and culture of their locality, which means their community and their own personalities" (p. 386). Mumford's ideas, together with the kinds of issues discussed in the previous section of this chapter, reinforced by the long-standing concern of Aboriginal and/or Indigenous education with reinforcing or re-establishing a sense of place, have been taken up and developed by scholars such as Orr (1992, 1994, 1996), Prakash (1994), Thomashow, M. (1995), Sobel (1996, 1997, 2004), Earle and Diffenderfer (1997), Kriesberg (1999), Smith (2002, 2007), Vaske and Kobrin (2001), Thomashow, C. (2002), Hutchinson (2004), Semken (2005), Knapp (2007), Semken and Freeman (2008) and Endreny (2010) into the notion of *place-based education*, sometimes called pedagogy of place, place-based learning or bio-regionalism (Li, 2000; Williams, 2000). Place-based education takes students' own "place" or "places" – the schoolyard, neighbourhood, town and local community – as the primary resource for learning and the primary focus for learning. In Graham's (2007) words, "place-based education aims to strengthen children's connections to others, to their region, to the land, and to overcome the alienation and isolation that is often associated with modern society" (p. 378). This is not to say that national, regional and global issues are regarded as less important, or can simply be left for much later consideration, but it is to say that students should have a thorough grounding in what is local: the history, flora, fauna, landscapes, culture, economy, literature and art of the particular place in which they live, and an awareness of how our lives are tied to the lives of other people and other non-humans, as well as to the welfare of rivers, mountains, forests and the sky. And it is to say that if students are to understand these matters, they must be immersed in the activities of the local community[108]. In elaboration, David Orr (1992) cites the views of Garrett Hardin (1985) that "most global problems are, in fact, aggregations of national or local problems, for which effective solutions can only occur at the same level... In other words, the constituency for global change must be created in local communities, neighborhoods, and households from people who have been taught to be faithful first in little things" (p. 31). Hence the maxim, "Think globally, act locally" (René Dubos, 1972)[109]

Developing a sense of place means focusing learning on the immediate community in which students live, seeking out local resources, focusing on local issues and helping students learn how to ask and answer questions about the phenomena and events that surround them. Knowledge of place (*where* one is) is, of course, intertwined with knowledge of self (*who* one is)[110]. In the words of Smith and Williams (1991), "we are place-based creatures as much as the animals Darwin encountered on the Galapagos Islands, but instead of producing distinctive plumage or beaks or extravagant flowers, we have created different forms of cultural interaction appropriate for varying biotic communities and natural conditions" (p. 4). It follows that place-based education must be firmly linked to the characteristics of the natural and sociocultural environment in which students are located. Key questions include: Where are we? Who are we? and Why are we the way we are? In what seems at first glance to be an oxymoron, Smith (2002) points out some generalized components to place-based education that can be used as a template for curriculum building, whatever the specific context: local cultural and historical studies; local nature studies and experiences; local environmental monitoring, fieldwork and advocacy; identifying community-based issues, seeking diverse views and working towards solutions; involvement in community decision-making. In similar vein, Semken (2005) identifies five "essential characteristics" of place-based education: the content focuses directly on the characteristics of the place; it acknowledges and tries to integrate the diverse meanings that the place holds for students, teachers and the wider community; it includes substantial fieldwork; it supports principles of sustainability; it seeks to enrich the sense of place for both students and teachers. Sobel (1996) argues that the priority in early childhood should be on building empathy between the child and the natural world and cultivating a sense of connectedness through outdoor experience, song, dance, stories, picture books, photography and, where appropriate, the Aboriginal/ Indigenous stories that Knudtson and Suzuki (1992) refer to as *Wisdom of the Elders*[111] (see Korteweg et al., 2008). Next comes the stage of exploration: finding out what lives here and thinking about what might once have lived here; following a stream; exploring a cave, abandoned building or vacant lot; learning to cultivate plants and care for animals; finding favourite places and treasuring secret places (places that students will remember with joy well into their adult years, and which Chawla (2002) describes as the "sweet and evasive nothings" of childhood); talking with local people, especially elderly residents; painting, sketching, taking photographs and making maps. When students know their neighbourhood well, they are well positioned to identify problems, gather opinions, raise issues for consideration by others, engage in community-based activities and take individual and collective action along the lines discussed in chapter 3 and revisited later in this chapter. Indeed, as Chawla (2008) argues, learning about one's place necessarily includes learning to recognize common problems, learning how to organize and collaborate with others to investigate and solve problems, and learning how to build a vision for a better future. The opportunity to participate in real world activities is a key part of building a sense of agency and collective capacity to effect change. Of course, there isn't necessarily a common sense of place held by everyone living in a particular area. Conflicting views of place constitute the predominant aspect of a project focused on a long-standing dispute between development interests and conservation needs in the Zalmon Creek National Park of Northern Israel, a situation exacerbated by intense sociopolitical differences and asymmetric power relationships among local people (Tal & Alkaher, 2010). There is a series of commentaries on this paper in *Cultural Studies of Science Education*, 2010, issue 2.

David Gruenewald (2003a,b; 2005; 2008) has sought to combine the principal concerns of place-based education, especially the distinctive place-based urban education rooted in multiculturalism, antiracism and decolonization pedagogy (Haymes, 1995; Calabrese Barton, 1998a,b,c; 2002; Bouillon & Gomez, 2001; Seiler, 2001; Zacharia & Calabrese Barton, 2004), with consideration of issues relating to power, privilege, race, gender and class that is central to the critical pedagogy of Paolo Freire, Henry Giroux and Peter McLaren. The outcome is what he calls *critical pedagogy of place*. In seeking to recognize and eliminate the multiplicity of oppressions within communities, and by linking environmental degradation, urbanization, corporate hegemony, cultural homogenization and globalization, a critical pedagogy of place aims to identify and promote sociocultural practices that enhance the well-being of people and the places in which they live. It aims to: "(a) identify, recover, and create material spaces and places that teach us how to live well in our total environments (reinhabitation), and (b) identify and change ways of thinking that injure and exploit other people and places (decolonization)" (Gruenewald, 2003a, p. 9). A critical pedagogy of place is not just a grounding in the local, but a critiquing of the local, that is, working with students to identify, challenge and change the perspectives, values and aspirations that harm their own lives, the lives of others, and the well-being of both the natural and social environment. In Gruenewald's (2003a) words, "decolonization involves learning to recognize disruption and injury and to address their causes. From an educational perspective, it means unlearning much of what dominant culture and schooling teaches, and learning more socially just and ecologically sustainable ways of being in the world" (p. 9). Further discussion, elaboration and justification of critical pedagogy of place can be found in Bailey and Stegelin (2003), Furman and Gruenewald (2004), Stone and Barlow (2005), Alsop et al. (2007), Smith and Gruenewald (2007), Zandvliet and Fisher (2007), Gruenewald (2008) and McKenzie (2008). It has much in common with the eco-justice approach advocated by Bowers (2001).

> The pedagogy that strengthens the local traditions of intergenerational knowledge, skills, and patterns of mutual support that enable members of the community to be less dependent upon consumerism, and thus to have a smaller ecological footprint, requires the teacher and professor to adopt the role of the mediator, and to engage students in thick descriptions of the differences between their experiences in various cultural commons activities and experiences in the industrial/consumer culture. (p. 9)

Despite the very similar sentiments of these two theoretical frameworks, Bowers himself describes critical pedagogy of place as an oxymoron. His concern is that while use of the terms *decolonization* and *reinhabitation* by critical theorists creates an illusion of a culturally and ecologically sound approach to place-based education, they are "unable to recognize the nature and ecological importance of the cultural commons that exist in every community – and that represent alternatives to a consumer-dependent existence. In effect, their commitment to universalizing the process of decolonization without deep knowledge of the diverse cultural practices that have a smaller ecological impact meets the definition of an oxymoron where two contradictory positions are assumed to be compatible" (Bowers, 2008, p. 325). Bowers goes on to state: "Culturally informed knowledge of place takes account of different approaches to dwelling on the land, as well as the ability to listen to the keepers of community memory of past environmentally destructive practices and of sustainable traditions of community self-sufficiency. It is not driven by a Western ideology that takes for granted the progressive nature of change, or assumes that Western theorists possess the answers that the other cultures should live by" (p. 325). Not surprisingly, but with much sadness, Greenwood (2008) [formerly Gruenewald] accuses Bowers of a partial reading, decontextualization, and subsequent distortion of a field he characterizes as "plural and diverse". His response spells out very clearly an approach that is eminently suitable for the kind of issues-based, action-oriented curriculum being advocated in this book.

> The best place-based education, in my view, emerges from the particularities of places, the people who know them best (including people with indigenous roots), and the people who wonder about all the opportunities that might arise from action-oriented place study. What happened here? What is happening now? What should happen here? These historical, experiential, and ethical questions suggest multiple responses given that communities are culturally diverse and different people will tell different stories about the same community. The concepts of decolonization and reinhabitation, and a related set of questions (what needs to be conserved, transformed, restored, or created – here?), I suggested, can provide pragmatic direction for inquiry and action while helping to bring together educators working for social justice and those working for ecological sustainability. The juxtaposition of decolonization and reinhabitation is productive because the simple pairing demands a blended cultural and ecological lens on place and curriculum. It invites educators who think primarily about culture to consider environment more deeply; it invites educators who think primarily about environment to consider culture more deeply. (Greenwood, 2008, p. 339)

My own view, like the views of McKenzie (2008), Smith (2008) and Stevenson (2008b), is that the ideas expressed in Bowers (2001) and Gruenewald (2003a,b) neatly complement each other, and can be used to establish a programme that comprises both education *about* the community and education *for* the community. It follows that such a thrust can only be properly located *in* the community. In other words, students learn *about* the community and *for* the community *through*, *in* and *from* the community.

PREPARATION FOR ACTIVISM

As discussed in chapter 3, the key to action on socioscientific and environmental issues comprises a complex amalgam of appropriate knowledge (scientific knowledge, NOS knowledge and knowledge of scientific argumentation), attitudes and values that lead to personal investment in an issue and a sense of commitment and responsibility, high self-esteem, and a cluster of attributes comprised of personal and community identity, agency and self-efficacy, allied to a substantial measure of media literacy and political literacy. Consideration of how to bring about political literacy in students is well outside the scope of this book, save to say that it can and should begin in school. As Jackson (1968) observed, more than 40 years ago, schools are institutions in which the division between the weak and the powerful is very clearly drawn. Within the traditional authoritarian and hierarchical school system, it is inevitable that students will quickly learn that power and status are the most significant features of human relationships. Curriculum decisions and matters of school organization are in the hands of the teachers and administrators; students, the primary clients of the enterprise, are rarely, if ever, consulted. If the truth be told, in the contemporary world of school education, as noted earlier, teachers themselves are increasingly excluded from curriculum decision making. Real control is vested in government guidelines for the curriculum, educational standards documents, examination syllabuses and the elaborate mechanisms of national testing. If the kind of curriculum advocated in this book is to become a reality, it is crucial that teachers re-establish their role as curriculum decision makers (see discussion in chapter 10). It is crucial, too, that students are afforded a substantial measure of control. We need to provide students with opportunities to exert their (collective) will, build power and influence, and gain a measure of control over decision-making – for example, in shaping classroom rules, expectations and procedures, and participating in the development of curriculum, design of learning activities and selection of assessment/evaluation strategies. If we are serious in our attempts to enhance political literacy and cultivate activist leanings in our students, we need to provide opportunities for democratic participation in schools and classrooms.

What I have in mind is well-captured in the principles underpinning Apple and Beane's (1995) notion of "democratic schools": an open flow of information is maintained to keep people fully informed; critical reflection and analysis are employed to assess problems and policies; both individual and collective capabilities are deployed in the resolution of problems; the 'common good' is the principal concern; the dignity and rights of all members are respected; democracy represents an idealized set of values and schools actively seek to promote and extend a democratic way of life. In similar vein, Trafford (2008) defines a "democratic school" as one that cultivates an open and inclusive ethos, with mutual respect among all involved, engages in school-wide critical dialogue in which everyone is empowered, encouraged and sufficiently self-confident to participate, establishes an active and effective school council with clear expectations, a substantive measure of power and decision-making capability[112], builds effective mechanisms of support, fosters student leadership of a wide range of school activities, including substantial input into curriculum decision-making, and builds a senior management team that is reflective, critical, willing to listen and ready to take risks. Further guidance can be found in Laguardia and Pearl's (2005) seven attributes of a "democratic classroom": persuasive and negotiable leadership; inclusiveness; knowledge made universally available and organized for addressing and solving important problems; inalienable student and teacher rights; universal participation in decisions that affect one's life;

the development of optimum learning conditions for each class member; and equal encouragement. The need for a measure of harmony between the message of the curriculum and the medium of its delivery extends to the values of compassion, harmony, equality and justice inherent in the curriculum I am advocating. This means recognizing and utilizing the insights, experiences, perspectives, skills and qualities that individual learners bring to the classroom for the benefit of all. It means fostering and supporting cooperative learning and critical dialogue among students and between teachers and students. And it means sustained commitment to esteem-building and group-bonding processes within learning programmes. Issues of equity, social justice and more democratic school organization are also addressed by Calabrese Barton and Tobin (2001), Tate (2001), Calabrese Barton (2002) and Moore (2008) in their discussion of what *urban* science education means in the 21st century. The ultimate goal of school democratization is to critique and transform those classroom conditions that marginalize or silence minority voices.

Political literacy can be further developed by involvement in local research activities (as discussed below) and participation in community-based organizations that bring citizens together to grapple with serious local issues, particularly those often overlooked by government agencies. In confronting real local issues directly, students gain valuable first-hand experience of the ways in which competing social, political and economic interests impact on decision-making. Through participation in community-based activities, they gain access to ideas, experiences, people, institutions and sociopolitical structures that build both individual and collective capacity to address SSI and environmental issues in a responsible, thoughtful, critical and politically effective way, and build the commitment to engage in the struggle for greater freedom, equality and social justice.

There is no doubt that political apathy is increasingly widespread and that many citizens have lost faith and trust in politicians. It is also the case that opportunities to participate in key decision-making have declined substantially with the rise of mega-corporations and the increasingly convoluted bureaucracies of local, regional and national governments. What I am advocating in this book is that we strive to halt this decline in civic participation and seek to fire up citizens to seize the opportunity to take control of local matters. If this is to happen on any substantial and meaningful scale, students currently in school need opportunities to work together, take responsibility and engage in activities designed to effect change. We need to cultivate a sense of community and develop an awareness of ties to others and the forms of obligation, responsibility and support that nurture and sustain communities. For effective sociopolitical action there needs to be a symbiotic relationship between school and surrounding community. Traditional barriers between school and community need to be dissolved or rendered permeable, with community members present and active in the school, and students and teachers active and involved in the community. We should be encouraging students to use their interest and skills in contemporary communications technology, especially social media such as Facebook, MySpace and Twitter, to establish networks, express concerns, share thoughts and spread messages about the need for action. As discussed in chapter 3, new forms of ICT enable forms of participation that were not previously possible and may engage significant numbers of people who would previously have been uninvolved. They have the potential to facilitate the building of a more inclusive, participatory, socially just and politically engaged community (McCaughey & Ayers, 2003; Kahn & Kellner, 2004, 2005, 2006; van de Donk et al., 2004). Indeed, Cho (2010) suggests that it is the power and ready availability of new ICT (at least, in some parts of the world) that has, in part, enabled individual and local struggles to become the main site for social change. Remtulla (2008) identifies three categories of online political activity: *awareness and advocacy* usage sees the Internet and other forms of ICT as a means of accessing independent and alternative sources of information that may be ignored or suppressed by mainstream media – for example, the Independent Media Center (www.indymedia.org) and Wikinews (en.wikinews.org); *community-oriented sites* seek to spread awareness, share experiences and ideas and build networks within communities; and *action groups* endeavour to raise public support for actions related to specific issues (local, regional, national and international). We need to be aware, however, that social inequities and differential access to technological resources can restrict opportunities for those who are already marginalized, unheard or disregarded. They can be further disadvantaged, silenced or excluded from participation in addressing the very problems that most affect them. Massive efforts will be needed to ensure that online spaces, and the communities that use them, are open to everyone. Garrett (2006) discusses these and related matters in an extensive review of some key literature in sociology, political science and communications studies. Space precludes any further comment here, save to note that Garrett frames the discussion in terms of three interrelated factors: *mobilizing structures* (the mechanisms that enable individuals to organize and engage in collective action), *opportunity structures* (the conditions that facilitate or constrain activist behaviour), and *framing processes* (the ways in which messages are framed, contested or promoted, and disseminated).

By focusing on the community and the issues and problems that residents confront in their everyday lives, students come to recognize their own experiences as shared, social and political. It is through direct experience of confronting social and environmental problems in the immediate community that public issues acquire personal meaning for young people. For example, working in shelters for the homeless, participating in breakfast programmes, doing volunteer work in hospitals, drug rehabilitation centres, HIV-AIDS support groups and homes for the elderly, involvement in environmental clean-up projects, renovating dilapidated homes, replanting degraded areas, building and maintaining community gardens, creating parks and conservation areas, organizing community festivals and information fairs, producing a local newsletter or community blog, and so on. As Paolo Freire (1973) observed, people learn democracy through the exercise of democracy, or as Banks (2004) says: "democracy is best learned in a democratic setting where participation is encouraged, where views can be expressed openly and discussed, where there is freedom of expression for pupils and teachers, and where there is fairness and justice" (p. 13). By engaging in public issues at the local level, students see democratic processes in action and learn how to engage in and negotiate them. By working alongside others, they learn about the demands and difficulties of taking action and learn to develop effective coping strategies. Research suggests that participation in these kinds of activities in childhood and adolescence is associated with levels of civic participation, community service and political activism in adulthood up to four times higher than the norm (Chawla & Flanders Cushing, 2007). Carlson (2005) reports an interesting venture in Hampton, Virginia, in which the City Council established part-time, paid positions for two high school students to conduct regular surveys of public opinion, facilitate focus group discussions with their peers about local issues of concern, keep other young people informed about opportunities for community engagement, and to facilitate that engagement. By the time of the next City Council election, some two years later, the voting participation rate among eligible young adults was 29% higher than the national average.

We should make strenuous efforts to involve students in public hearings and town hall meetings, consensus conferences, study circles, focus groups, citizen juries/panels, negotiated rule-making forums, public/citizen advisory committees, and the like. It is through community-based activities that young people gain autonomy, a sense of worth, a sense of personal and civic identity, respect for other people's views, negotiation skills, and so on. When engaged with real problems and issues, students encounter real barriers and obstacles; working with community members to overcome these barriers cultivates students' competency and sense of competency. When people work together, there are opportunities for doing things that individuals would not even contemplate doing alone. By working on a sub-task within a group effort, individuals acquire a level of expertise that wouldn't be achieved alone, at least not so quickly and so painlessly. They also come into contact with perspectives on issues and problems that differ from their own (which can be regarded as part of the "re-seeing" experience discussed earlier). Sharing experiences, action strategies and success stories, as well as building friendships, can be inspirational and highly motivating, and can lead to lifelong sociopolitical activism. These experiences are immensely valuable because they run counter to the trend of growing social isolation of individuals and individual families, and counter to the values that underpin the pervasive competition and conspicuous consumption of contemporary society.

It is important to note that young people are more likely to participate in community activities if a parent, some other family member or a close friend is already active and/or expresses approval and gives them lots of support (Pancer & Pratt, 1999; Fletcher et al., 2000). The prevalence of references by young people to the influence of parents and other role models in forming their views and attitudes is sufficient testimony to the influence of the old on the young. It is also the case that adults are more likely to join activist groups if their children are already involved or have expressed a desire to be involved. Political power rests with adults, but children can influence the ways in which that power is exercised. Consumer power rests (ultimately) with adults, though children can and frequently do exert considerable power on family consumption practices, as discussed in chapter 5. Codes of behaviour, language patterns and tastes in music, fashion and movies adopted by young people frequently act, over time, to shift older people's views and behaviours in a similar direction. On a closely related theme, Ballantyne et al. (1998, 2001a,b) have sought to exploit the ability of students to influence their parents or guardians, especially on environmental issues, by researching the elements in curricula that encourage students to talk with them (usually at mealtimes) about what they have been doing in school environmental education courses. Among the identified features that can easily be incorporated into recommendations for course design are: novel learning experiences, fieldwork, research-oriented homework assignments, discussion of easily-implemented pro-environmental behaviours (walking to school, taking shorter showers, turning off unneeded lights), student presentations at parents' evenings or public meetings, publicizing the programme in the local newspaper, conducting surveys and interviews in the community, and inviting local people to be guest speakers.

Our behaviour and/or our actions in any situation are influenced by a complex of psychological and sociological constructs like locus of control, self-image, self-efficacy, identity, self-esteem and agency: (i) how we construe ourselves and others; (ii) what we think we are capable of achieving; (iii) the confidence we have in our knowledge, skills and understanding and our capacity to use them appropriately and effectively; (iv) the stability of our beliefs and values; (v) how we think we are perceived by others, including our perception of our standing within the various groups we inhabit, together with our understanding and acceptance of the roles that attend membership of those groups; and (vi) our feelings of acceptance, belonging, comfort and association. These constructs are negotiated within relationships between self and others, with gender, ethnicity, social class, religion, sexual orientation, sociocultural traditions and language interacting in complex ways with feelings, values and attitudes to build, re-build and develop a sense of identity. Rather than regarding this sense of identity as static and coherent, we should acknowledge that each of us holds multiple identities in relation to membership of groups based on family, ethnicity, friendships, employment, sport and leisure interests, political affiliations, religious beliefs, and so on, some of which are complementary and mutually supportive, others of which may be in conflict or even direct contradiction. Some of these identities are consciously chosen, others may be thrust upon us by force of circumstances (a common experience for the poor, marginalized and powerless). All are under siege by the world of advertizing, the culture of the shopping mall, the trend towards "hyperindividualism", and what Anthony Giddens (1991) calls "the globalizing juggernaut of late modernity" (see discussion in chapters 3 and 5). A major thrust of the science and technology education proposed in this book concerns the commitment to assisting students in building a sense of identity as thoughtful, critical and active citizens. It is my contention that students should be encouraged and enabled to use aspects of youth culture, particularly music, chat rooms and other communications media, to spread an alternative youth-oriented message concerning civic and environmental responsibility. Music, television and music are important sites for identity construction and reinforcement, gaining a better understanding of one's own experiences and the experiences of others, raising political awareness, and building the solidarity and sense of community that can lead to activism. For many urban youth in the United States, the rap music of hip-hop culture can be a particularly powerful vehicle, enabling them to put their feelings, emotions, needs, aspirations, hopes, joys, fears, disappointments and anger into a form that is respectful of their immediate cultural experiences and will be readily understand by their peers[113]. Ginwright and Cammarota (2007), for example, describe how youth in Oakland (California) organized what they call "guerilla hip-hop" – impromptu mobile concerts with music, rapping, distribution of leaflets and other forms of political education in local parks, shopping malls, street corners and other places where young people hang out.

Throughout this book I have been arguing that part of our role as teachers of science and technology is to foster students' sense of identity as scientifically and technologically literate citizens who are able and willing to work with others in the local community to take action on SSI and environmental problems, that is, to behave as thoughtful, critical and responsible citizens. To revisit the discussion above in somewhat different form, citizenship identity can be seen to comprise four dimensions: *personal* (one's individual attitudes, feelings and values in relation to citizenship matters); *social* (willingness and ability to work with others to establish both common and minority needs, interests, attitudes, values and aspirations); *spatial* (recognition of belonging to multiple overlapping communities at the local, regional, national and global levels); and *temporal* (awareness of past, present and future dimensions of citizenship) (Parker et al., 1999). We can encourage the development of a socially responsible activist identity by engaging students in activist activities, providing feedback, support, encouragement and evidence of success. Clearly, a sense of identity as a community member and activist is key to successful engagement in collective action, but that sense of identity is developed and enhanced *through* engagement. And, of course, it may sometimes be threatened and disrupted by that engagement if the experience is unsatisfying, confusing or disturbing. In other words, identity is both a prerequisite for and a product of activity. And this applies just as much to the teacher and other involved community members as it does to students.

Group discussions and reflection, reading, writing, role-playing, watching and making movies, and so on, can also play an important role in identity building. Augusto Boal's *Theatre of the Oppressed* (www.theatreoftheooppressed.org) strives to enhance people's capacity for action by enabling them to experience some of the ways in which they are oppressed and simultaneously contribute to oppression of others through their social, linguistic, economic and political power. Each play presents a situation of oppression that one of the characters seems unable to combat. Audience members are invited to replace the actor and to act out, on stage, a range of solutions, ideas and strategies of their own. The other actors improvize the reactions of their characters as they face a range of new situations and interventions. The original actor stays on the stage, but to one side, and might make suggestions to the spect-actor (Boal's term) who has replaced her/him. If the audience believes the spect-actor's comments and actions are unrealistic, they may call out "magic", and the spect-actor is required to modify the actions to conform more closely with the views of the audience. If this spect-actor fails to overthrow the oppression, the original actor resumes her/his character and continues the production until another spect-actor calls out "stop" and attempts a different inter-vention strategy. While such personal experiences are unavailable to most people, they do underline the considerable potential of role- play acticities.

LEARNING FROM THE EXPERIENCES OF OTHERS

Chapter 3 included discussion of how students can learn *about* action, learn *through* action and learn *from* action via a 3-stage apprenticeship approach based on *modelling, guided practice* and *application*. While guidelines deriving from this kind of discussion can be enormously helpful for teachers looking to implement a community-based, action-oriented approach to consideration of SSI and environmental problems, there may be much more value (in terms of practical advice and ins-piration) in listening to and/or reading the stories of those who have been intimately involved in such projects. As John Forester (2006) comments, "in fields of practical activity... we are likely to learn less from recipes or general rules for all times and places, and more from vivid examples of real work, exemplars of sensitive and astute practical-contextual judgement in families of messy and complex cases. Here we need not abstract lists of 'what worked' but specific stories of reconstructive action – not so much experimental results but experimental stories, not so much (or only) abstract rules (or principles alone) about 'what to do' as emotionally rich, morally entangled, contextually specified stories about 'how they really did it'" (p. 573). What follows in this chapter does not constitute rich and detailed stories, but it does constitute a guide to recently published literature that provides such stories. It includes examples from three broad groups of community-based, action-oriented projects of varying degrees of complexity, sophistication and political involvement, some of which would be regarded by Jensen and Schnack (1997) as "activities" and some as "actions". In *citizen science projects*, scientists design investigations and recruit volunteers from the community to assist with data collection and dissemination of findings. In student-scientist *partnerships*, scientists work alongside students to support, advise and monitor the design, conduct, interpretation and reporting of students' own investigations. An interesting variant is the so-called "science shop", usually a small-scale organization that conducts scientific research in response to needs articulated by individuals and groups lacking the resources to conduct research themselves (Farkas, 1999). The third category, which I am calling *participatory action research* (PAR), engages citizens in defining, conducting and evaluating investigations and interventions with the goal of learning more about the immediate environment and findings ways to improve conditions and situations. PAR puts emphasis on knowledge "from below" (from the grassroots), values knowledge produced through collaboration and action, makes that knowledge freely available within the community, accepts accountability to the people most affected by the issues and problems, and seeks to effect change. At its best, it falls into the category that Callon (1999) labels "co-production of knowledge" (see chapter 4): "By participating in the collective action of production and dissemina-tion of knowledge and know-how concerning it, the group does not experience its relationship with specialists in a mode of trust or mistrust since it is on an equal footing with them" (p. 92). Within such initiatives, it seems that the very act of seeking input from local residents can make the community more aware of and responsive to the needs and interests of *all* its citizens. While this is the ideal towards which we should strive, it is more likely that projects will be collabo-rations conforming to the "public debate model" described in chapter 4. Both approaches entail a commitment to seeking input from a diverse cross section of people, and listening to what they have to say. In public meetings, ordinary people sometimes feel intimidated or excluded by scientists and engineers (and by politicians and lawyers, too) who use overly technical language and present opinions as fact and options as restricted. This is where Pouliot's (2008) advice to teach very explicitly about the three models of citizen involvement can be very helpful: "the purpose of using the deficit, public debate and co-production models is not to augment the consensual character of discussions concerning SSI... it is to encourage citizen participation in the sociotechnical issues confronting society... it is to encourage students to develop a point of view concerning citizens' attitudes, interests and capacities (discursive and interpretative) that moves away from the deficit model; it is to prompt students to articulate representations that accord legitimacy to the statements and experience-based knowledge of citizens and to the collaboration of citizens in the process of producing scientific knowledge" (p. 68).

Even so, strenuous efforts will need to be made if all constituencies are to be represented and all voices heard. In many societies, it is the urban or rural poor, women and members of minority racial, cultural, ethnic and religious groups who are most likely to be excluded from public representation, and to have their needs, interests, views, attitudes, values and aspirations marginalized or ignored. We would do well to heed Spivak's (1988) warning that the space for dialogue is invariably structured in exclusionary terms that prescribe who can speak, what they can speak about and how they will be heard. Within any group of participants, however carefully and sensitively recruited, there is unlikely to be a level playing field within which fully autonomous speakers can express their views. There is the ever-present danger that systemic inequalities will be activated and create opportunities for what Taylor (2008) calls "selective silencing". Even the venue for a public meeting can impact the demographics of the gathering, with location in a church hall, school hall, local RSA[114], health centre, university lecture theatre or local council debating chamber playing a role in inclusion/exclusion and determining whose voices are heard. For example, on a Māori *marae* gender will be a key determinant of who speaks; in a community hall in Toronto ethnicity will be influential in positioning the debate; in a village hall in the English countryside it is likely to be social class that fixes the agenda. Participants need to be constantly vigilant lest activities undertaken in the name of participation result in patronizing tokenism rather than effective representation and participation of diverse groups; lest they reinforce social hierarchies, reflect the dominant hegemonic agenda, and distract attention from key issues of contention by insisting on early consensus. Despite good intentions and efforts to establish open and democratic processes, there is a danger that dominant individuals can (consciously or unconsciously) impose an agenda that supports particular versions of what is appropriate thought, behaviour and action (Rahneema, 1992; Boler, 2004; Barrett, 2008; Reid & Nikel, 2008). It is significant that following the large-scale national debate in the United Kingdom about the commercial growing of GM crops, involving a large number of local, regional and national events during the summer of 2003, the establishment of a Website that received 2.9 million hits and the return of 37,000 feedback forms (Irwin, 2008), the final report concluded: "It is profoundly regrettable that the open part of the process, far from being a 'public debate', instead became a dialogue mainly restricted to people of a particular social and academic background. The greatest failure of the debate is that it did not engage with a wider array of people" (House of Commons Committee, 2003, p. 15). It is also the case that community-based groups can fracture around differences in gender, race-ethnicity, sexuality, age and class-based identities. Much skilful and sensitive work is needed to keep diverse groups working well.

Evans and Plows (2007) argue that in much of the debate about collaboration the distinction between 'scientists' and 'the public' is misleading: 'scientist' is too narrow a category and 'the public', even when pluralized as 'publics', conflates groups that are in many respects quite distinct. Instead, they advocate use of the terms *experts*, who may be scientists, activists or others with relevant specialist knowledge and experience, and *lay citizens* or *non-experts*, who have no particular expertise relevant to the situation beyond that acquired through day-to-day living: "While it is true that experts will also be citizens somewhere and lay people in relation to other debates, the crucial argument is that in any specific case a citizen cannot be an expert and a non-expert at the same time. Moreover, it is only those who are non-experts with regard to the science in question who can authentically represent the lay perspective implied in calls for the democratization of science" (p. 829). Distinguishing between experts and non-experts, rather than between scientists and the public, should increase the range of individuals who can (and should) contribute their expertise to the debate, and ensure that a particular group does not usurp the position of representing the public at large. Evans and Plows (2007) also comment that the relative disinterest of non-expert citizens, where disinterest is interpreted as absence of specialized knowledge, vested interest and commitment to particular point of view rather than lack of interest, should be regarded as a virtue rather than a problem. By way of endorsement of their argument, I recall that many years ago I was approached by the New Zealand Physiotherapy Board to evaluate courses for physiotherapy education in two major educational institutions. When I said that I didn't know anything about physiotherapy, they replied that that was why I had been invited. Lack of specialized knowledge and absence of vested interest meant that I would have no preconceptions of what should and should not be included, and that I would ask all those infuriatingly naïve questions that 'experts' would not think of asking. None of the foregoing should be taken as an argument for excluding expertise. As Laessøe (2010) comments, it is not simply a case of "top-down is bad, bottom-up is good". Rather, it is a case of struggling for the most appropriate and effective balance of experts and non-experts in any particular situation.

Because citizen science projects bridge the gap between school and community, students quickly recognize the ways in which scientific literacy links with responsible citizenship, how personal and community values impregnate all considerations, and just how difficult it can be to resolve moral-ethical dilemmas and the competing needs of industry, community and environmental protection. Suitable partners include local scientific organizations, environmental and 'green groups', local universities, colleges and industries, ramblers, animal rights and antiracism groups, local residents' groups, organizations such as "friends of X, Y or Z", pond or stream reclamation groups, and other community-based initiatives. Particularly striking examples are the WWF-funded MIDAS project *Making Informed Decisions About Sustainability* described by Ratcliffe and Grace (2003), the collaboration of Grade 7 students with an environmental activist group as they worked to influence local government decision-making regarding local water supply to the Canadian West coast community of "Henderson Creek" (pseudonym), as described by Roth and Lee (2002, 2004), Roth and Désautels (2004), and Roth and Calabrese Barton (2004), and the collaboration between the Appalachian Regional Commission and local universities to provide a summer institute that enables science teachers and high school students to work with scientists to investigate local stream ecosystems, assess ecological risks and participate in decision-making and policy formation for the region (Mueller, 2009).

Dori and Tal (2000) describe an interesting arrangement in which each cohort of Grade 6 students in a high school in the Upper Galilee area of Israel works in groups alongside parents and 'experts' from the local high-tech industrial park on projects such as planning and implementing road improvement schemes, building a light industrial plant to produce marketable artifacts from recycled paper, and designing, manufacturing and marketing eco-friendly games and toys. At the conclusion of the 8-week project there is an 'open day' for the entire community, at which students present their reports, invited 'experts' make critical comments, and the community members vote for the project they consider to best reflect the needs, interests and aspirations of the community. Good use can be made of secondary data, too, as Jensen (2004) describes in his account of how a group of Grade 7 students worked with the Danish Board of Health on a study of alcohol consumption, alcohol-related disease, and road accidents involving inebriated drivers and pedestrians. Their investigation looked at existing data on the impact of levels of economic development, unemployment rate, social status and social conditions on alcohol consumption rates and incidence of alcoholism, and gathered first-hand data by means of interview on variations in sociocultural traditions (using recent immigrants as informants), and the impact of peer group pressure and advertizing. A detailed report of their findings, including guidelines for parents, was presented at a public meeting in the school.

Albone et al. (1995) list twenty-eight projects, half of which are field-based activities, involving cooperative research between practising scientists and school students, while Robinson (2004) provides information on sixteen field research opportunities open to students in a wide variety of fields, including marine biology, rain forest ecology, geology and archaeology. Similar opportunities may arise in aquaria, botanical gardens, zoos, outdoor pursuits centres, science centres and museums[115]. For example, Thomashow (2002) describes how a group of 15-year olds designed a 3-component exhibit for a local zoo to aid visitors in adopting the perspective of the animals on issues such as diminishing habitat, hardships and stresses of captivity, increasing levels of pollution and environmental degradation, and human impact on the lives and well-being of local flora and fauna. First, they designed a glass-bottomed model of the Illinois River - half sparkling clean and half choked with weeds and highly polluted. To experience the different river conditions, the participants were invited to cross the river as frogs, ducks or fish. The second component, a 3-storey rain forest teeming with wildlife, used a treasure hunt approach to guide people through the ecology of the canopy, the undergrowth and the soil. Each visitor was assigned a predator-prey identity that determined where and how the forest was negotiated. Finally, they designed and built a walk-through model of an oak tree, populated with the creatures that make their home in tree trunks. At the exit was a beehive where participants could search for nectar, do the "wiggle dance" to inform other bees of its location, or feed the Queen bee.

In discussing the potential of such sites for providing *doing* science experiences, Braund and Reiss (2006) draw useful distinctions among three learning contexts: the *actual* world (e.g., field trips and visits to industrial installations and research facilities), the *presented* world (e.g., science centres and zoos), and the *virtual* worlds available through information and communications technology - a categorization that reflects Kellert's (2005) classification of experiences with nature as direct, indirect and vicarious (see earlier discussion). With regard to the third category, Robinson (2004) provides valuable information on a number of online simulated research activities, while McEwan (2003) reports some interesting data on the effectiveness of a fieldwork investigation of a wetlands area compared with a combination of textbook study and simulated investigative work. While the latter resulted in much better cognitive understanding of swamp, marsh, bog and fen ecosystems, the fieldtrip was far superior in terms of learning gains in the affective domain. Many would assert that computer technology should not be used as a substitute for multisensory experiences in nature. As Knapp (1999) comments, "virtual field trips cannot possibly impact the human brain in the same way as unmediated experiences with heat, cold, physical elation or exhaustion, and dryness or wetness" (p. 26). Nevertheless, Moseley et al. (2010) show that computer-mediated experiences can help to build environmental sensitivity as well as environmental knowledge and awareness. Computer technology can also be an invaluable aid to citizen science projects concerned with environmental monitoring, as Karrow and Fazio (2010) describe in their account of *NatureWatch*, a suite of online programs devised by Environment Canada and Nature Canada. As the authors point out, the four programs (WormWatch, PlantWatch, IceWatch and FrogWatch) are sufficiently simple and user-friendly to enable people with very limited scientific background to collect and report data for uploading to Environment Canada's Ecological Monitoring and Assessment Network database, where it is made available to researchers and policy makers.

A citizen science project organized via The Birdhouse Network (TBN) of the Cornell University laboratory of ornithology involves the construction of nest boxes for bluebirds, tree swallows and American kestrels, subsequent monitoring of their use, and regular email communication with TBN staff. Brossard et al. (2005) report that involvement in the project has significant impact on participants' knowledge of bird biology, although they have not observed any significant change in NOS knowledge, attitudes to science and attitudes towards the environment. However, the authors note that most of those who have been involved already held biocentric views and so further change would not be expected. They also comment that a primary motivation for enrolling in TBN is an interest in birds rather than a desire to engage in scientific research, and since there is nothing in the construction and monitoring activities that makes *explicit* reference to the procedures of science, a positive impact on NOS understanding is unlikely. Writing a decade earlier, Bogner (1999) describes a similar project that was designed to bring students into close contact with a local endangered bird (a sub-species of swift). The programme, initiated by two Swiss conservation agencies, comprised a combination of classroom and outdoor work: studying the bird's natural history; constructing nesting boxes; writing letters to students in Senegal (to where the bird migrates in winter); and observing local bird behaviour. Most of the 75 students who participated in the programme expressed a stronger intention to act in an environmentally conscious manner in the future and reported an enhanced enjoyment of natural places.

Posch (1993) describes some fascinating work conducted under the auspices of the Environment and Schools Initiative Project, including a collaborative project involving five Italian secondary schools in which students collected data on the quality of ground and surface water in their immediate localities by means of chemical, bacteriological and micro-plankton analysis, data that was subsequently passed on to the water authority for appropriate action. Posch (1993) also reports on a project in which students from a Swedish high school studied two local lakes affected by acid rain and then worked with the local council to mobilize a community programme for improving lake water pH by adding lime, and on a project in Australia during which students found that coliform bacteria counts on the local beach were much higher than water safety regulations permitted and launched a public campaign to force the water authority to undertake upgrading of the local sewage treatment plant. Tompkins (2005) describes an initiative in which students worked in collaboration with local environmental agencies to monitor water quality in streams feeding Cayuga Lake (in New York's Finger Lakes area). The students reported good water quality but found evidence of substantial erosion. After studying various methods of stabilizing the riverbanks, the students repaired the damage. The action-oriented project described by Lloyd and Wallace (2004), involving students, teachers, community action groups, the local council and various environmental agencies, also focuses on better water management – in this case, the physical and biological well-being of some wetlands and rivers in South Australia. Of particular interest to teachers thinking about the kind of experiences they can/should provide for their students is Kathleen Hogan's (2000b) report of differences in experience and learning outcomes between a group of students who followed a school-based course on water quality and watershed management and a parallel group who worked in a citizen-run environmental management and advisory organization. Predictably, the school-based programme emphasized theoretical understanding and scientific thinking, while the agency-based experience emphasized what Hogan calls "practical savvy". In consequence, two very different images of environmental practitioners were promoted: those who are science-based and use careful scientific analysis to link the local or current situation to larger and historical trends, and those who are society-based and need to be able "to juggle and manage multiple projects simultaneously, on small budgets and short timelines" (p. 428). Hogan concludes that the day-to-day business of running the agency can sometimes interfere with the provision of worthwhile educational experiences for the students, and that a judicious blend of school-based study and hands-on, real world experience may be the ideal.

A very different kind of learning resulted from a water quality study conducted by students from a middle school in inner Detroit. As Wals (1996) reports, the students found that as they travelled down the Rouge River the water quality decreases and the presence of heavy industry increases, as does the population of African-Americans and working-class people. Awareness that environmental degradation and other hazards impact the poor and powerless more frequently and more severely than they impact the rich and powerful is exactly what stage 2 of the 4-stage curriculum model outlined in chapter 3 is trying to achieve. There was similar potential in the investigation of water quality conducted by Grade 10 students in a border community in the South West United States, although Rodriguez and Berryman (2002) don't discuss this aspect in their report, choosing to put more emphasis on the issues and difficulties encountered by novice teachers of Anglo-European background working in a predominantly Latino/a and impoverished school setting. Both these studies reveal why rivers and lakes are such valuable sites for investigation. First, they can provide quick and reliable information about pollution levels and general environmental health in the area. Second, because they link mountains and oceans (or lakes), farmland and cities, they provide students with an easily understood connection between the natural environment and the social environment. In addition, as sites for early human settlement, they often provide a rich historical perspective and may inform us about cultural diversity and changes in social and economic priorities. It is this potential for learning that led to the establishment of the Global Rivers Environmental Education Network (GREEN) in 1989 (see www.earthforce.org), the origins and early history of which are recounted by Stapp (2000). GREEN enables high school students, with the support of local environmental partners (located mainly in the Eastern United States), to study watershed usage, monitor the quality and quantity of river water, reflect on ways that land and water usage and cultural perceptions influence river systems, and present their findings and recommendations to appropriate governmental and non-governmental organizations. Some of the actions taken by students include establishing community-wide hazardous waste collection and disposal days, campaigning for laws to prohibit powerboats or significantly reduce speed limits in waters where manatees live, placing messages on the street to encourage people to stop dumping waste in storm drains, organizing radio announcements and newspaper postings on water quality monitoring, and launching a television campaign to draw public attention to the discharge of untreated sewage into the ocean. In similar vein, Landcare Australia involves schools and local community groups in projects to improve land and water management practices, rehabilitate degraded waterways, stabilize coastal environments, plant trees and restore wildlife habitats. The Web site (www.landcareheroes.com) provides details of a wide range of projects, among which subscribers can vote at 2-yearly intervals for the best project in each of 12 categories. The report on the overall winner (National People's Choice Award) for 2008, the 30-student Wyong Creek School, located near Gosford (NSW), describes the positive impact on the local environment achieved by the students: "They have brought their neighbouring creek back to life, and are now enjoying the return of platypus, echidna and kangaroo to the area. They are minimising waste in the school, have built vegetable gardens and are collecting their own water for the garden".

In seeking a reversal of the usual situation in which parents and members of the local community respond to the initiatives and agendas of the school by attending meetings and fund raising events, supporting student learning via family-oriented homework assignments, and so on, Alsop (2009) posed the question: How can schools better enhance the well-being of local communities and environments and serve the needs of citizens? His response was an initiative in which five science teachers, three researchers and 25 students in Grades 6 and 11 made video records of a series of community-based investigations, including work with a severely ill 5-year old child (sister to one of the participants) that involved gaining familiarity with ECGs and treatment of sleep disorders in order to provide both emotional support and science-based advice. Another project involved two students investigating the local fish market, seeking answers to questions such as: Where do the fish come from? How nutritious are they? Which species are in decline? Emphasis in all the projects that Alsop describes is on ownership, personalization and relevance to the community in which the students live. In describing and evaluating further work by members of the *Science and the City Team* (based at York University, Toronto), Alsop, Ibrahim & Team (2009) draw attention to the sense of ownership felt by the participants in their reference to "learning for *my* family, *my* community, *my* environment" (p. 90). They also note a "profound shift in roles and relationships: learners became teachers and teachers became learners" (p. 90). Video recording was also a prominent aspect of the work of Calabrese Barton and Tan (2009) with a group of 11-year olds investigating the phenomenon of urban heat islands in a Midwestern city in the United States. The multimedia documentary titled *Where da heat go?* (running time: 8 minutes, 40 seconds), which the authors describe as "liberally sprinkled with hip-hop music and bloopers", was made to educate the local community about urban heat islands. It incorporates an explanation of the phenomenon, locally generated data, and interviews with residents. Video production is an especially powerful learning experience because it requires students to frame the issue in a particular way, consider the needs and interests of the intended audience and how the message might be interpreted differently by different audiences, and think about and practice the techniques that filmmakers use to manipulate audience response. Adopting different roles, such as interviewer or interviewee, requires students to adopt different perspectives on the issue. As they gain experience with the tools and techniques used to frame messages, they build the capacity to deconstruct and challenge dominant themes in the video material to which they are exposed and the ability to construct alternatives, thus enhancing both their media literacy and their political literacy as well as leaning more about the particular SSI under consideration.

Takano et al. (2009) report on a community-based initiative in the Alaskan community of Russian Mission to address the increasing disconnection of young people from the land, which was seen by community Elders as a threat to young people's sense of identity and self-esteem, and a factor in the culture of drug and alcohol abuse that is now all-too-common in remote Northern communities. A critical place-based pedagogical approach was used to re-acquaint students with the language, customs, values, practical knowledge and subsistence skills of the Yup'ik way of life[116]. Although located in a startlingly different geographical context, a sense of place and a sense of community are also prominent in the detailed description provided by Lim and Calabrese Barton (2006) of two investigations carried out by students in Grades 6 to 8 in a poor district of New York City: first, a study of pigeons, including their number, colouring and patterning, diet, social groupings, mating behaviours, and so on; second, a survey and evaluation of local playgrounds. This second project culminated in the design and construction of a model playground – an exercise that entailed decisions about materials, safety considerations, construction budget and intended location. Unfortunately, shortage of time necessitated premature closure of the project. GET City (Green Energy Technologies in the City) is a year-long programme for 10-14 year-olds established in a youth centre in an economically impoverished area of a US city as a means of engaging local youth in local environmental issues. Calabrese Barton and Tan (2010) provide valuable insight into the ways in which a project to design and build a "green roof" arose and developed through the stories of three of the participants. Thomashow (2002) describes the involvement of high school students in the restoration of a piece of vacant land owned by the local council. After conducting soil and water analyses and a wildlife count, and overcoming some fairly stiff political opposition, the students were able to clean up the site, remove many of the invasive species, and replace them with indigenous plants and animals. Related motives of rehabilitation are evident in Smith's (2007) and Argyeman's (2008) detailed descriptions of action-oriented projects addressing issues of poor air quality and the incidence of asthma among students at a high school in inner city Boston (Massachusetts) that resulted in much stricter enforcement of vehicle emissions controls and a commitment from the local authority to institute anti-idling legislation. It is noteworthy that the students subsequently became involved in a successful campaign to prevent the siting of a bioterrorism laboratory in their neighbourhood. Jensen (2004) describes an ambitious project in which students from three nearby schools, together with teachers, parents and members of the local community, investigated traffic conditions in the neighbourhood. Their report to the local council, presented in a public meeting, incorporated evidence gathered from their use of transportable pedestrian crossings and speed limit signs to show how traffic speed could be reduced. The author reports that this work resulted in a number of significant changes, including the construction of a roundabout, the installation of a new flashing-light pedestrian crossing, reduction of the speed limit in the immediate vicinity of one of the schools and in the town's main shopping street, and (intriguingly) in the planting of trees alongside local cycle paths.

Even very young students can be involved in action-oriented projects, as Erminia Pedretti (1997) shows in her description of how an elementary school teacher and her Grades 3 and 4 students responded to the "septic tank crisis" in their school. The local council had determined that the septic tank system in the school was now at full capacity, no additional students would be enrolled, and even some existing students would be bussed to a neighbouring school. The council had drawn up five possible strategies for longer-term solution to the crisis, including school closure. Deeply concerned about this prospect, students asked the teacher (Julie) if they could evaluate the five plans and make a recommendation to the council. After studying septic tank systems and other waste management methods, school building codes and local government policy on land use, the students drew up an alternative

(6th) plan for presentation at a public meeting. Sadly, the students didn't get the opportunity to present their report and argue their case; a decision had already been made prior to the public meeting and the anticipated debate was no more than an information-giving session. By inviting the Superintendent of Schools to visit the school, listen to the children's views, and make a commitment to present them to both the Director of Education and the Environmental Action Committee for consideration in longer-term decision-making, Julie was able to avoid this disappointing experience turning into disillusion and subsequent apathy. Indeed, the students continued to express enthusiasm for addressing SSI and "getting involved" with local issues long after this project had finished. It should be relatively easy to involve young children in working around the school to remove litter, maintain recycling programmes for cans, bottles and paper, plant trees and flowers, renovate and refurbish dilapidated rooms and furniture, and so on - see, for example, the Eco-Sherriff programme described by Eder (1999). Involvement of students in this kind of work is not new; more than 40 years ago, as a rookie teacher at Sevenoaks School (Kent, UK), I worked alongside students on a similar scheme that rejoiced in the name of *Digweed Project*[117]. Sevenoaks School was also an early pioneer of engaging students in working in the surrounding community - for example, painting the houses of elderly people in the town, shopping for the less mobile, working as porters in the local hospital or as road crossing wardens, assisting in the local school for the visually impaired, and playing 5-a-side football and teaching guitar at a young offenders residential centre (White et al., 1965). A subsequent teaching position at Rannoch School (Perthshire) gave me experience of school-initiated community service of a different kind: operating the local fire service, ambulance service, mountain rescue team and loch patrol.

Hammond (2001) describes a project in which elementary school children, most of whom were recent immigrants from South East Asia with poorly developed English language skills, developed a community garden where 80 families were able to grow their own food and use the surplus in the school cafeteria. In densely populated urban areas, a community garden is sometimes the only green space where residents can enjoy nature and socialize with neighbours, and may be one of the few spaces where young and old regularly meet. In a multiethnic community, especially with recent immigrants, community gardens provide a valuable opportunity for sharing different experiences, attitudes and values, and for discussing gardening practices drawn from a range of cultural traditions. To take advantage of the educational potential of this situation, the Cornell University *Garden Mosaic* project involves students in gathering information about the neighbourhood, its gardens and its gardeners. As Krasny and Bonney (2003) report, the project title reflects the ethnic mix of the gardeners, often from non-industrialized parts of the world where agro-technology is unavailable. It reflects the range of gardening practices they use, including composting rather than using chemical fertilizers, intercropping, collecting rainwater and using raised beds and mounds to conserve water, using marigolds to repel nematodes and soap solution as an alternative to commercial insecticides. From conversations with the gardeners, students compile a Community Garden Inventory database, including stories, photographs, maps, gardening techniques (and where they originated) and advice for novice gardeners. The project may be extended to involve different ways of preparing, storing and cooking the produce of the garden, the establishment of a meals service for people in the neighbourhood, and the organization of social events focused on the garden. Creating and maintaining urban gardens for supplying local families with food was also an activity of the "Hunger Education" science programme resulting from what students in Grades K-6 learned about local hunger and malnutrition from visits and interviews with clients and workers associated with the Vermont Food Bank (Kiefer & Kiefer, 1999). In a development of the Garden Mosaic project, faculty members from Cornell University combined with a number of public schools in New York City and several local community organizations to provide a summer programme that engages young people in planning and implementing ways to improve their local community. Using the same approach as the gardens project, students formulate a course of action arranged into three components: what they can do themselves, without outside help; what they can do with adult assistance and additional resources; what needs to be done by others. Adults with experience in community action act as role models and mentors, while local politicians assist students in negotiating the political hurdles. Ideas, strategies and outcomes are shared with other school groups participating in the scheme.

In describing the underlying rationale of the *Growing up in Cities* project, Louise Chawla (2002b) writes: "The realities of most urban areas are that traffic dominates the streets; waste places and public open spaces are often barren or dangerous; children's hunger for trees does not appear to be shared by most developers and city officials; communities still have to fight to maintain their heritage and identity in the face of development pressures; most children have narrowly limited ranges of movement; and research with children and attention to their needs are emphatically not part of most urban policy planning and design and management practices" (p. 25). With funding from UNESCO, the project uses research methods very similar to the Garden Mosaic project to build participatory social networks and political coalitions to address the needs of children in 14 countries around the world: Argentina, Australia, England, India, Jordan, Lebanon. Norway, Papua New Guinea, Poland, South Africa, Sweden, United States, Venezuela and Vietnam (see Driskell, 2002). One key finding is that beyond the provision of an acceptable level of health and welfare, increased material prosperity doesn't seem to enhance children's sense of satisfaction. Indeed, satisfaction levels were highest in Sathyanagar, a self-built settlement on the outskirts of Bangalore, and in Boca-Barracas, a working class district of Buenos Aries. In both places children were accepted as valued participants within a stable and rich cultural framework and were relatively free to move around within the district. In contrast, reports Chawla (2002), a sense of alienation was prevalent among children in the research sites in Australia, England and the United States, where young people complained of boredom, lack of safe and unstructured play space, and general marginalization within the community and public affairs. She concludes that in order to meet young people's real needs, priorities need to shift away from increasing industrialization, production and consumption, and towards fostering sociocultural identity, establishing and maintaining valued roles for individuals within the community, and supporting community self-help action groups.

On a related theme, Zahur et al. (2002) describe the prodigious efforts of Haleema, a Lahore-based teacher and teacher educator, to help preservice primary school teachers gain greater understanding of their students and the lives they lead, and to use the science curriculum to bring about individual and community empowerment and action around health and environmental issues (particularly water pollution, irrigation systems, sewage disposal, recycling and air quality issues relating to the use of wood and coal for cooking). This case study shows the importance of this kind of action-oriented curriculum for impacting the lives of disadvantaged, marginalized and powerless groups – in this case, poor urban children in Lahore, Pakistan. Dos Santos (2009) targeted his intervention project on urban garbage disposal sites in socially disadvantaged areas of Brazilian cities, posing a range of questions to workers at the site, local residents, and officials in the city council departments responsible for public health and waste management: What is recycled and what is simply dumped? Is sorting done by hand? How are different materials recycled? Are the methods safe from an environmental and public health perspective? Why are safer and cleaner methods not already in use? Could new/alternative technologies be developed to replace existing methods? Is the flow of garbage increasing, decreasing or steady, and why? Who works in landfill sites? Are masks and protective clothing provided? Who lives in the vicinity of landfill sites? Who scavanges in landfill sites, and for what? Do people scavange for food? Why does our society throw away so much food? And so on. It could be argued that this kind of curriculum is even more important for the children of the more economically privileged and politically powerful because it is they who will, in later life, be best placed to make the kinds of changes we need to make if life on Earth is to be sustained in ways that are desirable and appropriate. On a related theme, it would be interesting for students to discuss the phenomenon of "dumpster diving", that is, the practice of gleaning food from supermarket dumpster bins. Through these activities, participants seek to draw attention to issues of food waste, overproduction and over-consumption, and to highlight the politics of malnutrition and starvation in the Third World (see www.dumpsterdiving.net). At a more organized level, Food Not Bombs (FNB), founded in Cambridge (Massachusetts) by eight antinuclear activists after the brief occupation of the nearby Seabrook nuclear power station on May 24th 1980, redistributes food donated by markets, shops and restaurants to the urban poor, generates income by sorting and trading more durable items gleaned from dumpsters and landfill sites, and participates in other anti-consumerist and antiwar activities. The Web site (www.foodnotbombs.net) states that FNB, which now has over 400 chapters worldwide, operates under the philosophy of *freeganism*: "an anti-consumerist lifestyle that embraces community, generosity, social concern, freedom, cooperation and sharing in opposition to society based on materialism, moral apathy, competition, conformity and greed". Other counter-cultural initiatives include the Slow Food Movement (Petrini, 2007) and Vandana Shiva's (2005) ambitious proposals for Earth Democracy through locally-based community efforts aimed at a more simple and sustainable lifestyle.

Earth Democracy allows us to break free of the global supermarket of commodification and consumerism, which is destroying our food, our farms, our homes, our towns, and our planet. It allows us to re-imbed our eating and drinking, our moving and working, into our local ecosystems and local cultures, enriching our lives while lowering our consumption without impoverishing others. (Shiva, 2008, p. 46)

IN SUMMARY

What is clear is that we need to compile detailed accounts of the experiences, successes and failures of these and similar efforts to engage students in action-oriented and/or community-based projects. Other teachers and community activists can learn a great deal from what Forester (2006) calls the "friction of actual practice", that is, learning through "the eyes and ears and hopes and dreads and difficulties and surprises of actual people, activists and ordinary – and often extraordinary – people who get up each morning and confront in messy detail the fears and distrust and scheming and self-interest and aggression of others that our abstractions otherwise so thinly render" (p. 569). Schusler et al. (2009) provide much helpful advice on how researchers can go about gathering this kind of oral history[118] by asking questions such as: How did this project come about? At whose initiative? Who has been involved? What barriers and problems were encountered? How were they addressed? What successes have there been? What failures? What have you learned? What surprised, delighted or disappointed you? What would you do differently if you were starting again? Would you do it again? At a more general level, we might ask: What motivates and inspires you to engage in this kind of work? What are your goals, hopes and expectations? Stories and personal accounts could be very useful components of teacher education projects aimed at fostering interest in issues-based, action-oriented approaches to school science and technology education. One such project, aimed at preservice primary and secondary teachers, is STEPWISE (Science and Technology Education for Promoting Wellbeing for Individuals, Societies and Environment). A major element of the programme, as described by Bencze and Alsop (2009 and Bencze et al. (2009), is encouragement and support of student teachers in their efforts to infuse their teaching with possibilities for WISE activism, including transforming personal behaviour, using contemporary ICT to educate others for change (within the school and beyond), "lobbying power brokers" in government and business to make changes, developing services that can improve WISE (e.g., more effective recycling programmes, safer recreational facilities), and disruptive activities such as "clogging up roads with cyclists" to prevent the passage of noisy and polluting trucks through the neighbourhood. Interviews with student teachers on completion of the course revealed that those most likely to implement this kind of curriculum in their classrooms were those with prior experience of WISE issues and/or prior exposure to activism. Those least likely to do so included those whose overall experience and stance towards science education was content-oriented and those holding very traditional NOS views. These and other teacher education issues are discussed at greater length in chapter 10.

Common sense tells us that not all community-based activities will be successful in promoting, developing and sustaining an activist stance. There is an ever-present danger that actions reflect the teacher's agenda rather than the interests and concerns of the students and a danger that students merely 'go through the motions' of engaging in action, without any real commitment or sense of empowerment, in order to satisfy the course requirements or meet the expectations of the teacher. At the extreme, teachers may be led to compile a list of approved, scripted and 'politically safe' actions in which to engage successive groups of students without ever engaging them in the critical debate that should precede and determine action. Lousley's (1999) research on the activities of four urban secondary school environment clubs, established to focus attention on such endeavours as naturalizing the school grounds, planting trees, recycling, and organizing an Earth Week Festival, shows that students are frequently directed towards uncontroversial issues, guided away from conflict, dissuaded from political debate and censored when their proposals seem likely to challenge school practices, local government policies or the interests of local businesses. In short, she says, "the hidden 'curriculum' of surveillance, regulation, and interrogation which structured the club experience taught the students not to rock the boat and it hints that the liberal-humanist offer of tangible, 'empowering' results – results which do not alter the relations of power and authority within the school and do not take up controversial and challenging issues – amounts to a false perception of 'making a difference' and an education in naïve conformism" (p. 297). In making a similar point, Simovska (2008) distinguishes between *token* participation and *genuine* participation in terms of "focus" (specified content versus knowledge building through critique and reflection), "outcomes" (acceptance of a particular set of beliefs, values and behaviours versus student autonomy, critical consciousness and ability to address novel and complex issues) and "target of change" (individuals and their specific lifestyle versus individuals in context, taking account of inter-personal relations, sociocultural factors, moral-ethical dimensions and existing organizational structures). The same concerns run through Roth's (2009b) urging of teachers not to subordinate experience of activism to the more general aims of schooling. Again, these are points that will be addressed, although only very briefly, in chapter 10.

MAKING IT HAPPEN

The ideas, principles and values advocated in this book with respect to critical consideration of SSI and environmental issues are drawn from a wide range of scientific, social, political, cultural, historical, aesthetic, emotional, moral-ethical and economic concerns. If students are to address complex, multi-faceted SSI in ways that are meaningful and productive, they will need relevant scientific knowledge, though whether this is best provided through prior instruction or on a "need-to-know" basis undoubtedly varies substantially from situation to situation (see chapter 2). What is beyond dispute is that students need well-developed skills for accessing and evaluating additional scientific knowledge and technological information as the need arises, and they need experience of adapting that knowledge to real life situations, that is, putting it into a form that Layton et al. (1993) call "practical knowledge for action" (see chapter 2). It almost goes without saying that students will need to balance the competing needs, interests and aspirations of all parties impacted by a particular SSI and take account of a wide range of sociocultural, economic and historical factors. As discussed in chapter 2, and at considerable length in Hodson (2009a), students will also need a robust understanding of the nature of science and scientific inquiry, including the ability to understand reports of scientific investigations and evaluate the quality of evidence and arguments used to substantiate knowledge claims. Since much of the science that is needed to address SSI, and much of the science that students are likely to encounter as adults, will be accessed from media reports and Internet sites, there is also an urgent need for high levels of media literacy, including the capacity to read between the lines, ascertain the underlying agenda, and recognize distortion and manipulation of information in pursuit of vested interests. In summary, students' ability to confront SSI requires (at least) the following: relevant conceptual and theoretical knowledge and ability to identify and access whatever additional scientific knowledge is deemed necessary for the specific issue and context under consideration; NOS knowledge, including awareness of the theory dependence of observation and experiment, the relationship of evidence to theory, the characteristics of good investigative design, the role and status of scientific knowledge and the sociocultural location of scientific practice; understanding of scientific argumentation, and the ability to evaluate scientific arguments and deploy them effectively; ability to identify and access other knowledge resources as needed (e.g., knowledge relating to economic, moral-ethical, legal, sociocultural, religious and historical dimensions of SSI); ability to evaluate evidence from many different perspectives, establish priorities, resolve conflicts and dilemmas, reach conclusions and decisions, and justify all decisions or proposed actions. Furthermore, many SSI are highly controversial and raise complex and difficult issues relating to both the *constitutive values* of science, medicine and engineering and the *contextual values* that impregnate the personal, social, cultural, economic and political context in which scientific and technological practice are embedded. Students need to be able to recognize that personal and social values and perspectives, personal experiences, emotions and feelings can play a major role in considering SSI, and will impact on decision-making. Chapters 2 and 6 looked at these matters at some length, while chapter 7 outlined some of the ways in which students might learn how to confront moral-ethical dilemmas and make key decisions about what they *ought* to do (or not do) and how they *ought* to proceed in particular circumstances.

A key part of the issues-based curriculum outlined in chapter 3 involves teachers preparing students for taking both direct and indirect action on SSI. As discussed previously, Jensen (2002) categorizes the knowledge that leads to action in terms of four key dimensions: (i) scientific and technological knowledge that informs the issue or problem; (ii) knowledge about the underlying social, political and economic issues, conditions and structures, and how they contribute to creating social and environmental problems; (iii) knowledge about how to bring about changes in society through direct or indirect action; and (iv) knowledge about the likely outcomes and directions of possible actions, and the desirability of those outcomes. Central to Jensen's framework is a strong measure of political literacy, constituting yet another additional demand on science teachers. Other factors impacting the likelihood of students taking action on SSI, either now or in the future, include personal investment or emotional involvement in the issue (what some would call "ownership"), overall attitude and stance on underlying values (and the capacity to reconsider one's values in the light of alternatives), commitment to resolving an issue, sense of responsibility, levels of self-esteem, and notions of identity, agency and personal empowerment. In chapter 6, I described some of the teaching and learning strategies for addressing SSI, including discussion and debates, role-play and multimedia case studies, and briefly outlined some of the research findings on the efficacy of particular approaches. Other chapters 'put a little more flesh on the bones' with regard to the personalization of issues, engaging students' emotions, developing a sense of place, building a sense of community, and helping students cultivate a sense of identity and feelings of self-efficacy as a social activist. Several of these elements are included in what Smith and Williams (1999, p. 6) refer to as "ecological education": (i) development of personal affinity with the Earth through practical experiences out-of-doors and through the practice of an ethic of care; (ii) grounding learning in a sense of place; (iii) induction of students into an experience of community; (iv) acquisition of practical skills needed to regenerate human and natural environments; (v) preparation for work as activists able to negotiate local, regional and national governmental structures in an effort to forge policies that support social justice and ecological sustainability; and (vi) critique of cultural assumptions upon which modern industrialized civilization has been built, exploring in particular how they have contributed to the exploitation of the natural world and human populations. If a broad definition of "ecology" is adopted, this approach lends itself to critical consideration of *all* SSI, not just environmental issues.

Converting this rhetoric into practical action in real classrooms is an extraordinarily tall order for teachers to undertake. It is a tall order for three reasons. First, because it radically changes the nature of the school curriculum and puts a whole raft of new demands on teachers. Second, because it challenges many of the assumptions on which schooling is traditionally based. Third, because it is predicated on a commitment to bringing about extensive and wide-ranging social change at local, regional, national and international levels. As David Orr (1992) observes, efforts to change society for the better have a rather dismal history: "Societies change continually, but seldom in directions hoped for... and with consequences that are anticipated" (p. 19). Can we do better this time? The brutal reality is that we have no choice. We have to learn how to live in an environmentally sustainable and ethically sound way – that is, meeting our own needs and interests without jeopardizing the prospects of future generations or those of people living elsewhere on the planet. And we have to develop the strength of purpose to implement the solutions and strategies we devise. Of course, the kind of radical curriculum change I envisage will only occur when sufficient teachers, teacher educators, curriculum developers and curriculum policy makers are convinced of the importance, desirability and feasibility of addressing SSI in the science classroom and encouraging socio-political action, and when there is commitment to teach and confidence in doing so through awareness of appropriate pedagogical strategies, capacity to organize the required classroom environment, and access to suitable resources. Kaya et al. (2009) provide some encouraging evidence that a purpose-built SSI-oriented or STSE-oriented programme for student teachers, especially when it models the content, context and teaching/learning methods advocated for use in schools, can have substantial positive impact on their views about the desirability and feasibility of planning and implementing an SSI/STSE approach. However, much more research into the problems that teachers face and strategies to overcome them, together with much more extensive development of case studies of good practice, will be necessary if SSI-based, action-oriented teaching is to become established. Cross and Price (1996) talk about the need build a *critical mass* of committed and capable teachers.

> Until a critical mass of science teachers' ideology of teaching changes, committed science teachers and teacher educators will face an uphill battle against dominant traditional practices, which we describe as a schooling of science that presents science to learners as unproblematic, and is characterized by content and certainty. (p. 320)

Although they do not claim that a critical mass yet exists, Sadler et al. (2006) report very encouraging evidence that teachers (at least in the sample of 22 middle school and high school teachers they interviewed) "may be reconceptualizing the nature of their teaching" (p. 371). Seven of the teachers stated that they are already using SSI, five supported the use of SSI but cited major constraints in their school preventing them from converting rhetoric into practice, and only five rejected the notion out of hand[119]. Pedretti (2003) found that twenty-five newly qualified teachers who had expressed positive attitudes towards an STSE or SSI orientation, and had fairly sophisticated views concerning the sociocultural embeddedness of scientific practice, put very little of their professed enthusiasm and commitment into practice during their first year of teaching. The list of barriers identified by the teachers in her study constitutes a succinct summary of the discussion in chapter 6 of problems, difficulties and barriers associated with an SSI-based curriculum: apprehension about dealing with values-laden issues and addressing moral-ethical dilemmas; concern that students may not be cognitively and emotionally ready to engage in discussion of SSI in any meaningful way; insufficient time to develop appropriate teaching and learning experiences; a general perception that the complexity and uncertainty of the decision-making phase associated with SSI-oriented teaching is difficult to translate into effective curriculum experiences; and little or no confidence in their ability to assess learning in this area. Although not mentioned by any of Pedretti's teachers, several of the science teachers with whom I have worked in Toronto and Hong Kong expressed a concern that some SSI are so highly charged emotionally and so potentially divisive that they are unsuitable for productive classroom discussion. My own view is that the emotions generated by SSI can be the most motivating aspect of this kind of curriculum and one of the major reasons why we should be using SSI in class. A major and consistently voiced concern of teachers is the requirement to engage with issues that are often controversial, ill-defined, messy, fluid and unlikely to have a clear and easily agreed solution. In an interview-based study conducted by Tan and Pedretti (2010) with teachers who were generally supportive of an environmental education thrust in the curriculum, major anxieties were expressed about having to deal with values issues, and even more concern was voiced about the possibility of engaging students in sociopolitical action.

When teachers are presented with significantly different ways of thinking about science education, as in the proposals advanced in this book, they need time to address the mismatches, resolve conflicts, establish new priorities and build what Mellado (1998) calls a "practical scheme of action". This is no easy task. As Bell and Gilbert (1996) point out, it has three key dimensions: the *personal* dimension (resolving conflicts, clarifying uncertainties, dealing with anxieties and coping with the increased stress and pressure); the *professional* dimension (acquiring new knowledge and skills that can be readily applied in the classroom); and the *social* dimension (reconsidering what it means to be a science teacher and forging an identity within the community of practitioners). Often when teachers are faced with teaching unfamiliar content or are put in situations where they feel uncertain or vulnerable, they revert to a formal, knowledge-dispensing mode of teaching. It is here that emotional literacy and emotional intelligence are important. Chapter 6 included a brief reference to these conceptions in relation to students dealing with emotionally charged SSI; Hargreaves (1998), Day and Leitch (2001), Zembylas (2001, 2002a,b, 2003a,b, 2004a,b), Isenbarger and Zembylas (2006) and Schutz and Zembylas (2009) discuss ways of dealing with the emotional issues arising when teachers are faced with new and complex demands. Also of vital importance is robust pedagogical content knowledge (PCK), a term coined by Shulman (1986, 1987) to designate the repertoire of related examples, explanations, demonstrations and historical episodes that enable experienced teachers to translate important items of curriculum content (in this case, NOS and SSI issues) into a form that makes them accessible, interesting and comprehensible to students. Since Shulman's early work establishing the notion of PCK, a large number of educators have extended, modified and refined it – notably, Lederman and Gess-Newsome (1992), Cochran et al. (1993), Tobin et al. (1994), van Driel et al. (1998, 2002), Gess-Newsome and Lederman (1999), Magnusson et al. (1999), Bullough (2001), Loughran et al. (2001, 2004, 2006, 2008), Halim and Meerah (2002), Borko (2004), de Jong and van Driel (2004), de Jong et al. (2005), Sperandeo-Mineo et al. (2005), Hashweh (2005), Abell (2008) and Berry et al. (2008, 2009). Although there is still no universally accepted definition of PCK, its overall meaning is clear: whatever knowledge, skills, attitudes and attributes are needed in order to provide coherent, purposeful, stimulating and effective curriculum experiences for all learners. It is knowledge that establishes connections between what students do in class and what scientists do in labs, and between key NOS ideas and the conceptual and methodological structure of science. It is knowledge that locates important items of scientific knowledge in the sociocultural circumstances surrounding both their creation and their contemporary deployment. It is knowledge that enables teachers to make ready connections between scientific ideas and the social, cultural, economic, political and moral-ethical issues they raise. While PCK has been an extensively researched area in science education, in general, there is still much to be done with respect to PCK for NOS-oriented and SSI-oriented teaching, although Bartholomew et al. (2004), as noted in chapter 6, have identified five overlapping and interacting "critical dimensions" that characterize and determine a teacher's ability to be effective in teaching *about* science: (i) teachers' knowledge and understanding of NOS and their confidence in, or anxiety about, teaching NOS; (ii) teachers' conceptions of their role (ranging from dispenser of information and knowledge to facilitator of learning); (iii) teachers' use of discourse (closed and authoritative versus open and dialogic); (iv) teachers' conception of learning goals (and the extent to which they are limited to knowledge gains or include the development of reasoning skills); and (v) the nature of classroom activities (particularly the shift from activities that are teacher selected, contrived and inauthentic to activities that are both owned by the students and scientifically authentic). It is clear that teachers' views of learning are crucial factors in their choice of pedagogical strategies. Those who subscribe to a transmission of knowledge view of learning are inclined to regard problem solving as a matter of applying rules and algorithms. In consequence, they prefer to lower the level of cognitive demand, 'spoon feed' students with correct answers, utilize 'standard problems' that are amenable to routine-focused approaches, and avoid problems that require students to adopt an independent approach because they believe students will find them frustrating and confusing. In contrast, those teachers who view learning as knowledge construction make greater cognitive demands on students and encourage more independent thinking (Zohar, 2008).

It is unlikely that a one-off teacher workshop or set of guidelines from the Ministry of Education will bring about the level of professional knowledge, expertise, confidence and emotional comfort needed. These attributes are acquired through experience and the interest, cooperation and support of other teachers with whom ideas, feelings, successes and failures can be shared. My inclination is to address this problem via a combination of action research (Pedretti & Hodson, 1995; Hodson et al., 2002; Forbes & Davis, 2008) and use of multimedia case studies of exemplary practice (Bencze et al., 2001, 2003, 2009; Hewitt et al., 2003; Wong et al., 2006; Yoon et al., 2006; Yung et al., 2007). Barnett and Hodson (2001) use the term *pedagogical context knowledge* for the knowledge that teachers use to inform decision-making in a particular educational situation: a cluster of (i) academic and research-based knowledge (science content knowledge, NOS knowledge, knowledge of how and why students learn, etc.), (ii) pedagogical content knowledge (as above), (iii) professional knowledge (knowledge acquired, much of it unconsciously, through active participation in the community of science teachers), and (iv) classroom knowledge (knowledge of their particular class and students). Action research enables teachers to explore their pedagogical context knowledge, resolve some of the tensions inherent in all classroom situations, and develop new approaches to addressing SSI.

Speculating further on appropriate forms of preservice and inservice education, and discussing ways to recruit teachers and to organize and implement such programmes, is well outside the scope of this book. However, it is important to raise one or two key issues – the most significant of which is to make the point that if we are to politicize students we need to politicize teachers, too. Because teachers hold a pivotal position between the state, parental influence, media power and the dictates of institutional norms, they have enormous opportunities to foster the development of democratic values and influence the attitudes of students. Using those opportunities wisely, effectively and responsibly requires a substantial measure of political awareness. Teachers need to turn the critical spotlight on schooling, curriculum, teaching and learning, assessment and evaluation strategies, on the knowledge, beliefs, values and aspirations that underpin them (see discussion in chapter 5), and on the ways in which key curriculum decisions are made – in particular, by whom they are made and in whose interests they are made. If critical thinking, creativity and skilful problem solving are to be developed by students, it is essential that those who are responsible for that education also possess these attributes. If we want students to address SSI in a critical and independent way, their teachers must be afforded the opportunity to do so, too. If we want students to acquire the capacity to work productively in a collaborative mode, their teachers must have this capacity, too. If we want students to experience sociopolitical action in pursuit of ideas and practices they consider important, and against those that they consider undesirable, then teachers need to have had these experiences. It is absurd to expect teachers to create the necessary experiences for students to develop these abilities if they, themselves, have not had similar experiences. It is unrealistic to expect students to have confidence in their own knowledge, skills and judgement (i.e., to be intellectually independent) if their teachers have been socialized into blind acceptance of the views and decisions of others. It is unrealistic to expect students to recognize the value of collaborative learning and collaborative action when their teachers are denied the opportunity to work collaboratively with their teaching colleagues. Action research provides such opportunities for teachers. It also creates opportunities to build the professional learning communities that can sustain and support teacher development and curriculum development over time, as in the studies reported by Akerson et al. (2009) and Berry et al. (2009). It is in this kind of forum that teachers can share 'war stories' and reflect on their triumphs and failures. Just as I argued for the value of sharing stories about engaging in sociopolitical action in chapter 9, so I am arguing for the value of sharing teacher stories about classroom and curriculum building issues as important sources of learning for other teachers (Connelly & Clandinin, 1990, 2000). As Fenstermacher (1997) observes, "Through narrative we begin to understand the actor's reasons for the action, and are thereby encouraged to make sense of these actions through the eyes of the actor. This understanding constitutes an enormous contribution to learning about and getting better at teaching" (p. 123) – exactly the point made in chapter 9 concerning the value of stories about sociopolitical action.

Adopting a top-down approach to STSE or SSI-oriented education would be particularly ironic. The use of centrally-generated curriculum materials or even the use of an approved textbook (a common practice in North America) would reinforce the notion that SSI can be clarified and decisions reached simply by applying a set of guidelines located in the text. Not only would this approach invite students to be passive consumers of someone else's knowledge, it would tell teachers that the solution to the educational problems of teaching about SSI is located in those materials and in the expertise of others. Thus, it would foster passivity in teachers. As Pedretti and Hodson (1995) remark, "It is perversely contradictory for advocates of a form of education that should be concerned with enhancing critical thinking and decision-making, and with encouraging personal action among science students, to deny science teachers the opportunity to utilize these same critical thinking and decision-making skills to develop their own teaching practices" (p. 468). It is not unreasonable to assert that a curriculum that aims to achieve a critical scientific and technological literacy should be based on a model of curriculum development that seeks to encourage and support teachers in becoming critically literate about their own educational practice. For me, a crucial principle underpinning curriculum building is that *all* curriculum knowledge should be regarded as problematic and subject to scrutiny, critical appraisal and revision. Nothing should be taken for granted, whether it is goals, content, teaching/ learning activities or assessment/ evaluation strategies. Nothing should be accepted just because it is 'handed down' from the Ministry of Education, School Board or Local Education Authority. Nothing should be retained in the curriculum simply because "it's the way we've always done it in this school". Significant teacher education and teacher professional development, especially in the directions required by the curriculum advocated in this book, cannot be achieved by legislation. Nor can the precise nature and extent of change be pre-determined. Ultimately, control of the direction and pace of development must rest with teachers. By ceding a substantial measure of control of the curriculum to teachers, action research creates the sense of ownership essential to effective, long-lasting and radical change. In short, the approach is predicated on the notion that teachers can (and must) become significant curriculum makers rather than mere implementers of curricula designed by others. It is also important to note that although the prospect of implementing an SSI-based, action-oriented curriculum may be daunting for some teachers, there is ample evidence that we all get better at it by doing it – as illustrated by the case studies in Hodson et al. (2002).

A broadly similar argument is used by Barrett and Pedretti (2006) in elaboration of their distinction between "STSE for social reproduction" and "STSE for social reconstruction"[120]. In the first approach, teachers are not expected to challenge the stated goals, dispute the content or deviate too much from the curriculum plan; in the second approach, it is essential that they do so.

> Teachers can only facilitate development of agency in their students effectively if they are free to alter the content and intent of the courses they teach. Further, as role models, teachers show the students what it means to be autonomous, able to make decisions and think critically about what constitutes equity and justice within society, and able to act on those decisions. If students perceive teachers as being uncritical, the teachers' ability to teach the students how to become agents of change is undermined. (p. 239)

The goal is that teachers will adopt the role that Henry Giroux (1988) refers to as *transformative intellectuals*.

> Central to the category of transformative intellectual is the necessity of making the pedagogical more political and the political more pedagogical. Making the pedagogical more political means inserting schooling directly into the political sphere by arguing that schooling represents both a struggle to define meaning and a struggle over power relationships... Making the political more pedagogical means utilizing forms of pedagogy that embody political interests that are emancipatory in nature; that is, using forms of pedagogy that treat students as critical agents; make knowledge problematic; utilize critical and affirming dialogue; and make the case for struggling for a qualitatively better world for all people... Transformative intellectuals... must speak out against economic, political and social injustices both within and outside of schools. At some time, they must work to create the conditions that give students the opportunity to become citizens who have the knowledge and courage to struggle in order to make despair unconvincing and hope practical. (pp. 127 & 128)

The kinds of changes I have in mind are not just a matter of learning a few new pedagogical skills. They are better described as becoming a different kind of teacher, that is, subscribing to a different image of what it means to be a science teacher. The notion of *identity* was briefly discussed in chapter 3, with regard to helping students build an identity as a social activist. Here the focus is on teacher identity. Constraints on space preclude a discussion of the extensive literature on science teacher identity and other closely related ideas (e.g., Helms, 1998; Beijard et al., 2000, 2004; Becher & Trowler, 2001; Danielewicz, 2001; Sachs, 2001; Alsup, 2006; Larochelle, 2007; Forbes & Davis, 2008; Moore, 2008; Lee & Witz, 2009), save to note that the kind of curriculum being advocated in this book is predicated on a sense of identity that is very different from the traditional subject-oriented image of a science teacher. Barrett and Nieswandt (2010) have used the notion of teacher identity to probe the views, intentions and classroom practices of preservice teachers concerning the inclusion of SSI (especially moral-ethical issues) in the curriculum. At one extreme, "model scientists" saw their role as preparing students for further study and/or a career in science. They did not see SSI as an important or even relevant aspect of the curriculum. At the other extreme, "model citizens" saw ethics as an integral part of scientific practice. The authors warn against seeing the four "archetypes" they identified (the others were "model individual" and "model teacher") as a hierarchy, pointing out that although model citizens may have sophisticated views about ethics in science, they might have naïve views about other aspects of science. Interestingly, there seemed to be little change in the student teachers' positions over the duration of the preservice programme, although there was a noticeable improvement in their ability to express their views.

Recognizing that it is often very difficult to change teachers' sense of identity, Pedretti et al. (2008) recommend an explicit focus in preservice teacher education programmes on the ideologies and images associated with teaching science and the ways in which they are manifested in the classroom and impact on student learning. Being aware of these influences and having access to alternatives through in-depth case studies is the first step in bringing about change. It is here that the metaphors used by teachers and teacher educators to describe or model their actual or ideal practice can be useful[121]. Tobin (1990, 1993) and Tobin and Tippens (1996) show how a change in metaphor can sometimes be a stimulus to initiating a shift in classroom practice. Connelly and Clandinin (1990, 2000), Clandinin and Connelly (1996), Wilson (2002) and Hart (2008a,b) point out the effectiveness of narrative and autobiography in sensitizing teachers to issues relating to images of teaching, sense of identity as a teacher, and classroom practice, especially when there are opportunities to share experiences, beliefs, values and attitudes with others in a critical but emotionally supportive environment.. Interestingly, Thomas and McRobbie (1999, 2001) have adapted these ideas and strategies for understanding, challenging and changing *students'* views of learning and developing their metacognitive awareness. Pedretti et al. (2008) also stress the importance of providing opportunities for student teachers to explore, clarify and rationalize their own views on controversial SSI and to work with others on the development of SSI-oriented curriculum materials. The STEPWISE project (Science and Technology Education for Promoting Wellbeing for Individuals, Societies and Environment), a more radical, educationally ambitious and politically exciting form of this programme, was discussed in chapter 9 (see Bencze & Alsop, 2009; Bencze et al., 2009). In essence, these programmes enable prospective teachers to experience the kind of activities advocated for the curriculum. This is clearly of great importance for serving teachers, too, as is the opportunity to develop, trial and evaluate curriculum materials in a supportive and critical relationship with other teachers. Again, I would argue that this is best provided via an action research approach, as exemplified in the case studies in Hodson et al. (2002).

Another major target for change is the nature of the assessment regime currently being promoted in many countries around the world. In chapter 5, I described these standardized and highly prescriptive schemes as philosophically unsound (because they are rarely, if ever, based on a valid model of science or scientific literacy), educationally worthless (because they trivialize teaching and learning), pedagogically dangerous (because they foster bad teaching), professionally debasing (because they de-skill teachers), socially undesirable (because they project a number of powerful messages about control and compliance) and morally repugnant (because they objectify people, regard knowledge as a commodity to be traded for marks and grades, disallow freedom of expression, and allow no scope for creativity). It is the concern with control and compliance that bothers me here. A curriculum organized and monitored along such lines is an ideal vehicle for those who seek to shape people towards some predetermined goals. It is disempowering because it rules out critical thinking. Goals are taken on trust; emphasis is on obedience and efficiency in effecting someone else's plans; there is no concern with valuing, criticizing, challenging and changing the goals or intended outcomes. By inculcating a willingness to accept someone else's prescriptions for approved behaviours and an acceptance of external control and management, such a curriculum creates a culture of compliance that has considerable adverse impact on both students and teachers. Education becomes a means of social reproduction, with all its existing inequalities, rather than a means of social reconstruction and a route to social justice. When the award of marks is restricted to the uncritical execution of carefully specified tasks, critique becomes devalued in the eyes of students, critical faculties atrophy through lack of use, and eventually, students lose all trust and confidence in their capacity to make judgements. Thereafter, decisions on all matters of importance are left to 'experts'. There are a number of contributing elements in this unedifying culture of certainty, control and compliance. First, emphasis on what Edwards and Mercer (1987) call "ritualized knowledge": the ability to use algorithms and standard procedures to solve standard problems, but not the capacity to generate new insights and under-standing or to confront novel problems in novel ways. Second, what Apple (1982) calls a "rules orientation": an awareness of rules and procedures, and the habit of following them. Third, increased dependability, in the sense of eagerness to comply with the rules as speedily and efficiently as possible in order to 'get the job done'. Fourth, internalization of someone else's goals and values. Fifth, dependence on 'experts' and holders of high positions in the institutional and social hierarchy for all decisions on matters of importance. Sixth, the promotion of science as the patient, systematic gathering of 'factual data' that will inevitably reveal secure and truthful knowledge about the world. In Cawthron and Rowell's (1978) memorable words, the scientist comes to be seen as "a depersonalized and idealized seeker after truth, painstakingly pushing back the curtains which obscure objective reality, and abstracting order from the flux, an order which is directly revealable to him through a distinctive scientific method" (p. 32). While these outcomes are not always the express intent of the curriculum and its assessment and evaluation procedures, or of the science teachers who implement it, they are often the outcome. They form a powerful unintended curriculum. Bencze and Alsop (2007) also direct criticism at many contemporary science curricula and assessment regimes for promoting elitism (rather than inclusion), conformity (rather than diversity), passivity (rather than self-motivation), confusion (rather than comprehension), naivety (rather than awareness), regulation (rather than self-determination) and individualism (rather than collectivism). Discussion of alternative, more appropriate forms of assessment and evaluation is outside the scope of this book, though I do wish to note the potential of Lorna Earl's (2003) categorization into assessment *of* learning, assessment *for* learning and assessment *as* learning.

It is important to acknowledge that much of what I am advocating for the science curriculum may be disturbing to some science teachers and Ministry of Education officials, and so is likely to meet some stern resistance from those who favour a more traditional approach. This more radical and critical stance towards science, scientists and scientific and technological practice is in direct conflict not only with the traditional school model of science but also with the image that universities and the science professions have tended to promote. Thus, there may also be opposition from scientists and from universities, as Fensham (1998) shows in three case studies from Australia. Blades (1997) and Gaskell (2002) also describe how university-based scientists were successful in mobilizing opposition to Ministry of Education attempts to implement new STS-oriented curricula in Alberta and British Columbia, respectively. There may be opposition from parents. Some may regard it as a 'soft option' to 'proper science' (i.e., abstract, theoretical science assessed by conventional means); others may be more concerned about politicization of students, and particularly about their engagement in social action. They may even be concerned that students express views and values at variance with those prevailing in the local community. Being critical of forestry clear-cutting, production and promotion of gas-guzzling SUVs and environmentally destructive mining practices in communities where many of the residents are employed in the forestry, mining and automobile-building industries is likely to stir up considerable opposition. Change may even be resisted by students, especially by the more academically successful ones. They, too, have expectations of science lessons and a vested interest in maintaining classroom practices that have served them well in the past. Navigating these multiple resistances to change will require considerable courage and determination, and high levels of support and encouragement. Teachers may find encouragement in accounts of teachers engaged in similar efforts to overthrow the stultifying shackles of convention, as in the stories told by bell hooks (1994) and Michael Newman (2006). The real breakthrough comes when individual teachers are able to find and work with like-minded colleagues to form pressure groups that can begin to influence key decision-making bodies. As Vincent and Désautels (2008) comment, "The success of any project to deconstruct the hierarchy of subject-disciplines will depend on the extent to which the related issues become broadly shared by the populace, and can, at that point, become the subject of society-wide debates" (p. 294). Perhaps educationists need to develop the educational equivalent of the public forums (consensus panels, citizen juries, focus groups, and the like) that have been used by scientists, governments and NGOs to directly engage the public. However, discussion of strategies for doing so is well beyond the scope of this book.

While my inclination would be to give over the entire science curriculum to the kind of issues-based and action-oriented approach described in chapter 3, I am not so naïve as to think that is likely to happen any time soon. Indeed, Nashon et al. (2008) note that although "high church" STS (to use Steve Fuller's (1993) term for science studies courses emphasizing academic and research issues in the history, philosophy and sociology of science) is rapidly gaining popularity at the university level, "low church" or activist and socially and environmentally responsible STS is losing ground in schools, at least in British Columbia (from where the authors write). As a compromise, it is possible to implement this kind of issues-based approach alongside a more conventional subject-oriented curriculum, provided that neither students nor teachers see it as a mere 'add-on' or motivational adornment.

Confrontation of issues and taking action need to be fully integrated into the curriculum. I am confident that students exposed to such issues, and the treatment of them advocated here, will be much more likely to give serious consideration to the moral-ethical, political and environmental aspects of SSI in their daily lives outside and beyond school. I am confident that such experiences will assist them in moving firmly and positively in the direction of Oxfam's (1997) conception of a *global citizen* as someone who is: "aware of the wider world and has a sense of his or her own role as a world citizen; respects and values diversity; has an under-standing of how the world works economically, politically, socially, culturally, technologically and environmentally; is outraged by social injustice; participates in and contributes to the community at a range of levels from the local to the global; is willing to act to make the world a more equitable and sustainable place; takes responsibility for his or her actions" (p. 2).

Of course, returning to an earlier point, there are teachers who will argue that politicization is not a legitimate goal of science and technology education (or of any school-based education, for that matter) and that sociopolitical action has no place in school. There are many teachers, educational administrators and members of the wider community who will perceive the capacity for effecting social change located in a body of students who are scientifically literate, environmentally aware, socially critical, and perhaps most controversially of all, politically literate, as a threat rather than a boon. "It is ironical", says McElroy (1986), "that the very success of political literacy education is what draws the most opposition. Politically literate students are seen as a threat to the established order of power and control. Hence potentially successful political action may be vigorously resisted while ineffective participation is lauded" (p. 106). Avoiding controversial issues, especially those with very significant political dimensions, is regarded by many teachers as taking a neutral view. In reality, it is not neutral. Because it fails to confront and challenge the underlying sociopolitical causes of environmental problems, for example, it implicitly supports current social practices, current institutions and current values. Thus, it has to be regarded as education for social reproduction[122]. There is no such thing as political non-involvement. Non-involvement is, in itself, a form of involvement by default and constitutes implicit support for the dominant ideology. Avoiding political matters is, in effect, leaving it for others to decide.

> The very nature of educational practice – its necessary directive nature, the objectives, the dreams that follow the practice – do not allow education to be neutral as it is always political... The question before us is to know what type of politics it is, in favour of whom and what, and against what and for whom it is realized. (Freire, 1993, p. 22)

> This is a great discovery, education is politics! After that, when a teacher discovers that he or she is a politician, too, the teacher has to ask, What kind of politics am I doing in the classroom? That is, in favour of whom am I being a teacher? By asking in favour of whom am I educating, the teacher must also ask against whom am I educating? (Freire & Shor, 1987, p. 46)

There may also be teachers who support an issues-based and action-oriented curri-culum in principle, but are uncertain about what constitutes appropriate, acceptable and worthwhile action. Many questions spring to mind. Who decides what is acceptable and responsible action? What are the relevant criteria? What is the balance to be drawn between socially acceptable actions that may be politically ineffective and effective actions that may be socially unacceptable – at least to some?[123] Will teachers be prepared to support student actions that provoke the disapproval of parents, school administrators, local politicians or local businesses? Are we prepared for a situation in which students who are well-coached in action skills choose to direct those skills against aspects of the institution in which they study and/or the community in which they live?[124] Those teachers who promote involvement and develop action skills are riding a tiger, but it is a tiger that may well have to be ridden if we really mean what we say about education for civic participation. I do not seek to minimize the difficulties that teachers face in deciding a course of action. All I can do is urge teachers and students to be critical, reflective, robust in argument and sensitive to diverse values and beliefs, but above all to have the courage and strength of will to do what they believe is right and good and just. In the words of Alberto Rodriguez (2001), we need the courage to "expand our gaze... and rise to the challenge of becoming cultural warriors for social change" (p. 290).

NOTES

[1] Roberts (2007) quotes the somewhat puzzling views of the former Director of *Project 2061*, James Rutherford, on the usefulness of a distinction between *science literacy* and *scientific literacy*: science literacy "refers to literacy with regard to science", that is, the goals of science education, and scientific literacy refers to "the properties of literacy, namely literacy that is scientifically sound no matter what content domain it focuses on" (p. 731). Liu (2009) argues that current notions of scientific literacy suffer from three major flaws: they are based on: (i) a deficit model (scientific literacy as the level of understanding needed if individuals are to understand the achievements of, and constraints upon, science and technology); (ii) a commodity model (scientific literacy as a state to be achieved or commodity to be acquired rather than a lifelong process of developing understanding); and (iii) a static model (scientific literacy as unproblematic, value-free and universally applicable).

[2] It is nearly twenty years since F. Sherwood Rowland (1993), then President of the American Association for the Advancement of Science, argued that "faulty communication" is the major obstacle to scientific progress and urged scientists to "sell the importance of science" through better communication.

[3] Drori (1998) argues that the oft-repeated assertion of a causal link between science education and economic development is a myth. It is, in Drori's words, both "empirically problematic and conceptually misleading" (p. 70).

[4] Duschl et al. (2007) try to capture some of the flavour of multidisciplinary/multidimensional scientific literacy in the notion of *scientific proficiency*: knowing, using and interpreting scientific explanations of the natural world; generating and evaluating scientific evidence and explanations; understanding the nature and development of scientific knowledge; participating productively in scientific practices and discourse.

[5] Berkowitz et al. (2003) define civics literacy as "the ability to use an understanding of social (political, economic, etc.) systems, skills and habits of mind for participating in and/or studying society" (p. 228).

[6] In this view of the environment as *text*, perceiving and reacting to the environment can be regarded as "reading", while acting in and on the environment can be regarded as "writing".

[7] Among "currents" with a long tradition in environmental education, Sauvé identifies naturalist, conservationist, problem-solving, systemic, scientific, humanist and value-centered traditions (her terms). More recent "currents" include holistic, bioregionalist, praxic, socially critical, feminist, ethnographic, eco-education and sustainable development/sustainability (again, her terms).

[8] In contrast, Fuller (2000) states that no matter how expert scientists may be in their own sphere of interest, they are rarely expert in evaluating that field in relation to others, and in many instances their ignorance of other fields is just as extensive as that of the non-scientific lay public.

[9] The most tangible outcome of this discussion document is *Twenty First Century Science* (www. 21stcenturyscience.org), developed for 14–16 year olds and comprising a core curriculum that explores the major explanatory theories of science, a set of "ideas-about-science" (dealing with topics such as keeping healthy, air quality and radiation hazards), and an additional academic programme for those who wish to study science at a more advanced level or an additional applied science course embracing topics such as forensic science, communications technology and agricultural science. The scheme defines a scientifically literate person as someone able to appreciate and understand the impact of science and technology on everyday life, take informed decisions about things that involve science (such as health, diet and energy resources), read and understand essential points of media reports about matters that involve science, reflect critically on the information included or omitted from such reports, and take part confidently in discussion with others about issues involving science.

[10] Berkowitz and Simmons (2003) also argue that confronting SSI requires both teachers and students to move substantially beyond the scope of STS curricula.

[11] In the Keselman et al. (2004) study, conducted in the United States, erroneous ideas held by students included the belief that HIV-AIDS can be expelled from the body through sweat and urine, and that contracting other sexually transmitted diseases reduces the risk of contracting HIV-AIDS by activating T-cells and thereby "arming the body" against the newcomer infection. In a study in Uganda, reported by Mutonyi et al. (2007), there was widespread belief that HIV-AIDS could be contracted through shaking hands or sharing toilet facilities with infected persons, that women engaging in sexual intercourse during menstruation will not contract HIV-AIDS because "the virus will come out with the menstrual flow", and that washing one's genitalia in Coca Cola immediately after sexual contact will substantially reduce the risk of infection. In a later study, Mutonyi et al. (2010) report that a number of students (aged 15–17) believe that government messages about HIV-AIDS are exaggerated in order to deter young people from sexual activity.

[12] Chiapetta and Fillman (2007) comment that the situation regarding biology textbooks in the United States, while not ideal, is considerably better than it was fifteen years ago. Following an analysis of eight books about science written for general readers, including Chalmers (1999), Cromer (1993), Dunbar (1995) and Wolpert (1992), McComas (2008) has generated a series of historical vignettes that provide a more authentic view of NOS than is common in textbooks. On a related point, it is important to note that an individual teacher's efforts to foster more sophisticated NOS views may be thwarted by a science department culture that promotes traditional views. This is especially the case for novice and student teachers confronted by an unsympathetic supervisory teacher (Akerson et al., 2010).

[13] Duggan and Gott (2002), Law (2002), Chin et al. (2004) and Aikenhead (2005) reach broadly similar conclusions from studies of the day-to-day work of people in science-related and technology-related professions. Aikenhead (2005) notes, for example, that nurses combine academic knowledge with experiential knowledge and emotions-related intuitive knowledge to make judgements about patients, such as knowing when they are uncomfortable, in distress or in need of close attention.

[14] The model is based on Immanuel Kant's tripartite classification of mental activities into cognition, affection and conation (Hilgard, 1980).

[15] Hogan and Maglienti (2001) have developed a 5-level scheme for rating students' overall judgement of a conclusion: Level 0 does not mention any relevant strengths and weaknesses of the conclusion; level 1 mentions some relevant strengths and weaknesses of the conclusion, but not the major ones, and uses agreement with personal inferences or views as a basis for judging the conclusion; level 2 mentions some strengths and weaknesses of the conclusion (although not the major ones) but does not base judgements on agreement with personal inferences or views; level 3 mentions the major strengths and weaknesses of the conclusion, but also uses agreement with personal inferences or views as a basis for judging the conclusion; level 4 mentions the major strengths and weaknesses of the conclusion, but does not base judgments on agreement with personal inferences or views.

[16] Newspapers consulted were: *The Globe and Mail*, *The Edmonton Journal* and *The Edmonton Sun*. Magazines consulted were: *Time*, *Newsweek*, *Maclean's*, *National Enquirer*, *Star*, *Reader's Digest*, *National Geographic*, *People*, *Better Homes & Gardens*, *Canadian Living*, *Chatelaine*, *Cosmopolitan* and *Sports Illustrated*.

[17] Interestingly, members of the lay public organized by the researchers into six focus groups that might be expected to have specialist interests in the issue (birdwatchers, charity workers, arable farmers, undergraduates, parents of young children and temporary UK residents originating in Developing countries) had little difficulty in identifying, and usually rejecting, the persuasive rhetoric of the pro-GM newspaper reports.

[18] The Internet was the most-used source of information on science and technology, followed by television (67% in 2009, 74% in 2000), books/magazines (63%, 76%) and family and friends (45%, 55%). Interestingly, those citing museums, zoos and aquaria had declined from 65% to 41% and those citing school science had declined from 68% to 34%.

[19] The beliefs that students hold prior to instruction have been variously termed: alternative frameworks, alternative or prior conceptions, mini-theories, naïve theories, children's science, and so on. Each term has its adherents and its particular justification, but there is no consensus beyond a general concern to avoid the term *misconceptions*. My own view on this convention is made clear in Hodson (1998a).

[20] In a particularly insightful study, Larson (1995) describes a student (Fatima) who consistently and successfully "plays the game of school" according to a set of invented rules and conventions (e.g., "Don't read the textbook, just memorize the bold-faced words and phrases"). Although they may not understand the material they reproduce in tests, students like Fatima often achieve acceptable grades and can make instrumental use of science education in pursuit of other goals.

[21] Aikenhead (2001a) has added a fifth category, "I want to know" students, who are just as interested in, and keen to learn science as "potential scientists" but have difficulty with science and/or its accompanying mathematics or find some aspects of science disquieting.

[22] In the words of Paolo Freire (1972), "Education thus becomes an act of depositing, in which the students are depositories and the teacher is the depositor. Instead of communicating, the teacher issues communiqués and makes deposits which the students patiently receive, memorize, and repeat. This is the 'banking' concept of education, in which the scope of action allowed to the students extends only as far as receiving, filing, and storing the deposits" (p. 58).

[23] The article on which the television documentary is based is titled "Skyful of Lies and Black Swans" (Gowing, 2009). "Skyful of lies" was the expression used by the military junta in Myanmar (Burma) to describe the messages being sent out of the country by pro-democracy activists during a surge in the protest movement in September 2007. The second part of Gowing's title is taken from the title of Nassim Taleb's influential book, The Black Swan: The Impact of the Highly Improbable (published in 2007). A black swan is a highly improbable event with three principal characteristics: it is unpredictable; it has a massive impact; and, after the fact, we concoct an explanation that makes it appear less random and more predictable than it was. The astonishing success of Google was a black swan; so was 9/11 and the global economic crisis of 2008–09. In typically provocative fashion, Taleb also notes that we are most convinced of our grasp of what we actually know the least about, and we are almost completely ignorant of the scope and meaning of what we do know.

[24] Barlex (2006) notes that one of the "winners and losers" examples in the Nuffield Design and Technology Project Study Guide describes "how the introduction of the Nile perch into Lake Victoria led to a large export-crop of Nile perch but a decline to almost extinction of the indigenous Enkejje fish, which kept the algae growing in the lake under control and was used by local people as a vital food-source for young children" (p. 185).

[25] Levels of xylene were recorded at 6300 times the US drinking water standards.

[26] Kyle's language here reflects a common tendency to see the environment in terms of a "green space", where wild nature survives, and a "brown space", where society's industrialization, pollution and contamination occur.

[27] Global carbon emissions average about 1 tonne per year per person. US per capita emissions exceed 5 tonnes per year, while Japan and the countries of Western Europe emit 2 to 5 tonnes per year per capita. Per capita emissions in the Developing world are about 0.6 tonnes per year, with more than fifty Developing countries having per capita emissions under 0.2 tonnes per year (Baer et al., 2000).

[28] Plans are already in place to move the entire population of 2500 from the Cartaret Islands in Papua New Guinea, where the highest point is a mere 1.5m above current sea level, to nearby Bougainville.

[29] As noted in chapter 7 (endnote 83), medical ethics is based on the four principals of autonomy, beneficence, non-maleficence and justice. The 2000 version of the Tenets of the Code of Ethics developed by the Institution of Engineers Australia is based on three guiding principles: to respect the inherent dignity of the individual; to act on the basis of a well informed conscience; to act in the interests of the community. Students might consider what a code of ethics for scientists might comprise.

[30] Disappointingly, the availability of cheap sources of energy (especially petrol and electricity in North America) seems to discourage conservation measures simply because the costs are low.

[31] There has been much concern surrounding a prediction by IPCC that the Himalayan glaciers would disappear entirely by 2035. In August 2010, an independent review team appointed by the UN praised the high quality of the IPCC work but recommended rigorous scrutiny of all scientific data before making far-reaching predictions. It also recommended that the term for IPCC Chair should be restricted to one period of IPCC assessment – a move that puts increasing pressure on the current

Chair, Rajendra Pachauri, who has been consistently criticized by Greenpeace for his environmentally-unfriendly lifestyle, to step down before the preparation of the 2014 report.

[32] Wenger's (1998) notion of "learning trajectory" is a useful thinking tool for teachers because it relates present and future senses of identity – in effect, who one wishes to be compared with who one is (or thinks one is) at present. A person with a *peripheral* learning trajectory doesn't feel part of the community of practice in question, but is interested in learning more about it. Those with an *inbound* learning trajectory see themselves as belonging to the community in the future. Individuals with an *insider* trajectory see themselves as already a part of the community, while those with a *boundary* trajectory see themselves as members of this community and capable of liaising with one or more other communities.

[33] Bandura (1977) identifies two critical components of self-efficacy: (i) belief in one's ability to perform the behaviour successfully (*efficacy expectation*), and (ii) belief that performance of the behaviour will have a desirable outcome (*outcome expectancy*). Both are impacted by experience and associated tangible evidence of success, positive emotional responses that result from verbal acknowledgement and reinforcement of one's success by others, and observation of the success of others adopting similar approaches.

[34] In a later publication dealing with the problem-solving nature of actions, Jensen (2004) differentiates between *scientific investigative actions* (for example, student-initiated testing of pollution levels in waterways) and *social investigative actions* (for example, interviewing people in the local community about a socioscientific issue). Mogensen and Schnack (2010) provide further elaboration of these distinctions.

[35] Schusler et al. (2009) identify five forms of (environmental) action: physical environmental improvements (e.g., restoring natural habitats); community education (e.g., organizing festivals and information fairs, producing newsletters and multimedia materials); inquiry (e.g., surveys and mapping, environmental monitoring, etc.); public issue analysis and advocacy for policy change (researching an issue and making recommendations); and products or services (e.g., growing food in community gardens, working in a food bank).

[36] Hodson (2008, 2009a) provides a detailed discussion of these research findings and the ways in which we should respond to them.

[37] Discussion of the role of aesthetic criteria in science can be found in Yang (1982), McAllister (1996) and Girod (2007).

[38] Merton first outlined this theoretical framework in a 1942 essay titled "Science and technology in a democratic order", published in the *Journal of Legal and Political Sociology*, 1, 115–126. The citations in this chapter refer to a subsequent work published in 1973 (see references).

[39] In later work, Merton (1973) refers to the norms of *originality* (which puts great value on priority of discovery and citation by others) and *humility* (an outward expression of disinterestedness).

[40] Gaskell (1992) argues that science teachers may also feel some vested interest in sustaining this image of science as a means of enhancing their own status in school.

[41] According to Pepper (1942), "a world hypothesis is determined by its root metaphor" (p. 96), of which there are six: *animism, mysticism, formism, mechanism, contextualism* and *organicism*. Cobern (1991) provides a helpful introduction to worldview theory in relation to science education; see also the special issue of *Science & Education*, 2009, 18(6 & 7).

[42] Carolyn Merchant (1980) argues that modern science has fundamentally misconceived the world by fragmenting reality, separating observer from observed, portraying the world as a mechanism and dismissing all non-objective aspects of science. It has done so in the drive to dominate nature, with the outcomes that are now all too evident.

[43] The term *mankind* is used here in preference to *humankind* because it lends increased force to Smolicz and Nunan's proposition. They used the term *man*, but at a time when authors were less sensitive to gendered language.

[44] While Ziman (2000) refers to contemporary scientific practice as *post-academic science*, Funtowicz and Ravetz (1993) call it *post-normal science* and Gibbons et al. (1994) and Nowotny et al. (2003) use the term *mode 2 science*. In his wonderfully detailed and insightful book, *The Scientific Life*,

Steven Shapin (2008) reminds us that for a number of scientists this current situation was foreshadowed by experiences during World War 2 and throughout the so-called Cold War: "The mobilization of American science during the Second World War – especially in the Manhattan Project and in the construction of radar, but spreading across much of the scientific landscape – propelled a generation of academic scientists into a world that was largely unfamiliar to them: the experience of large-scale organization; of teamwork; of interdisciplinary project-oriented research; of unlimited resources and severely limited time; of close contact with the sorts of people – especially the military and the commercial worlds – they had not known much about" (p. 64).

[45] Etzkowitz and Leydesdorff (1997, 2000) and Etzkowitz (2003) refer to a "triple helix" of university-industry-government relations.

[46] Levels of secrecy are highest of all, of course, in research conducted by and for the military (Relyea, 1994).

[47] See, for example, Broad and Wade (1982), Kohn (1986), Sarasohn (1993) and Judson (2004).

[48] Kim (2009) provides a wealth of detail concerning the work of the investigative journalists working for *PD-Notebook*, the hostility initially directed towards them in the Korean media, and their efforts to enlist the support of Hwang's co-workers, who did eventually 'blow the whistle' on the fraud.

[49] Although generally supportive of Harding's notion of strong objectivity, Donna Haraway (1997) notes that by equating *strong* with *good* (or desirable), Harding seems to imply some possibility of "ultimate strength" and, therefore, ultimate objectivity.

[50] Oakley (2009) documents the history of student protests against dissection in school, from California High School student Jennifer Graham's refusal to dissect a frog (in 1987), the school's insistence on a fail grade for the course and the subsequent court proceedings brought by her family, to the establishment of dissection choice policies in a number of US states and Canadian cities (see also Duncan, 2008).

[51] The term *ecological footprint* was first used by William Rees (1992). In his PhD thesis, for which Rees was supervisor, Mathis Wackernagel (1994) devised a method for measuring it. The concept was developed further, in relation to environmental sustainability, equity and justice, by Wackernagel and Rees (1996). As these authors state, the notion of *ecological footprint* "accounts for the flows of energy and matter to and from any defined economy and converts these into the corresponding land/water area required from nature to support these flows" (p. 3). It represents the "appropriated carrying capacity of terrestrial ecosystems necessary to support a given person, society, country, or product" (p. 11). In elaboration, Rees (1992) says: "For human beings, carrying capacity can be interpreted as the maximum rate of resource consumption and waste discharge that can be sustained indefinitely in a given region without progressively impairing the functional integrity and productivity of relevant ecosystems" (p. 125). The appropriated area necessary to support the habits of affluent countries has gradually increased throughout the 20th and 21st centuries, such that the current ecological footprint of a typical North American is "three times his/her fair share of the Earth's bounty. Indeed, if everyone on Earth lived like the average Canadian or American, we would need at least three such planets to live sustainably" (p. 13).

[52] There have been some counter moves by patient groups and health movements seeking to reject this increasing trend towards medicalization and to de-medicalize particular conditions. For example, Epstein (2008) refers to "fat acceptance activists who challenge the discourse of an obesity 'epidemic' and question epidemiological claims about the unhealthy effects of being overweight" (p. 510). Blume (1997, 1999) describes how some deaf activists have resisted the discriminatory designation "disabled", preferring a community identity based on a variance from other sections of the population, and have opposed the use of cochlear implants to amplify sound on the grounds that it represents an assault on deaf culture. In another variation on this theme, Zavetoski et al. (2004a) document the efforts of US army veterans to gain recognition of "Gulf War Syndrome" and other physical and psychological symptoms arising from combat stress and exposure to toxic materials.

[53] Some quarter century ago, Schumacher (1973) listed eight criteria for the "appropriateness" of a technology: it best suits the needs and lifestyle of the people who use it; it should not damage the environment and ecosystem, and should be sustainable; it should keep costs within the economic

means of the community; it should strive to use local resources; it should provide employment opportunities for local people; it should increase self-reliance; it should use renewable sources of energy and should be economical in use of non-renewable resources; it should fit the social and cultural environment. A detailed discussion of what counts as "appropriate technology" for sustainability in the 21st Century can be found in Wicklein (2001).

[54] In similar vein, Perlas (1995) identified seven key characteristics of sustainable agricultural practice: (i) based on integrative and holistic science; (ii) supports the development of human potential; (iii) culturally sensitive; (iv) utilizes appropriate technologies; (v) ecologically sound; (vi) socially just and equitable; and (vii) economically viable.

[55] Drawing on the work of Thayar (1990), Justin Dillon (1993) develops a framework for constructing a school technology curriculum around consideration of technologies variously classified as *consumptive, sustainable, management, nostalgic, revived* and *information technologies*.

[56] Webster and Johnson (2009) have outlined some suggestions for extending these principles to the design and management of schools, as well as to the curriculum, citing the supposedly carbon neutral city of Masdar (Abu Dhabi) and the proposals for the Dongtan eco-city on Chong Ming Island (Shanghai) as exemplars. At the time of writing, phase 1 of the Dongtan development is expected to be completed in time for the Shanghai Expo (May 1 – October 31, 2010).

[57] Chapter 7 includes a brief discussion of a futures-oriented, interactive "thinking tool" for students confronting SSI.

[58] See Juan Antonio Oposa et al. versus the Honorable Fulgencio Factoran, Jr., Secretary of the Department of the Environment and Natural Resources et al., Supreme Court of the Philippines, G.R. No.101083 (Phil); Reports Annotated Vol 224, p. 802. See also, the website for the International Conference on Environmental Compliance and Enforcement (www.inece.org/ 4thvol/oposa2).

[59] De Bono (1992) uses differently coloured hats to represent six different modes of thinking: red hat – consider emotions; yellow hat – itemize good points; black hat – itemize bad points; green hat – engage in creative thinking; white hat – assemble information; blue hat – organize one's thinking. The purpose of the six hats method is to encourage students to use all six modes of thinking to confront an issue or problem, and to switch easily among them.

[60] Farmelo (1997) states that consensus conferences had their origin in the United States in the mid 1970s as a way of assessing the benefits of new and expensive developments in medical technology, although Nelkin (1977) states that they owe their genesis to the "study circles" established by the Government of Sweden (also in the 1970s) to involve the public in forming policy on nuclear power and nuclear weapons. Abelson et al. (2003) provide a critique of the strengths and weaknesses of consensus conferences in comparison with other forms of public consultation such as citizen juries, citizen panels, deliberative polling and recruitment of focus groups. These other forms of public participation are discussed by Rowe and Frewer (2000, 2004, 2005), Jackson et al. (2005), Flynn (2008) and Levinson (2010). Further elaboration of the merits and shortcomings of consensus conferences can be found in Joss and Durant (1995), Joss (1998), Sclove (2000) and Blok (2007).

[61] Walton (1998) describes verbal exchanges in terms of five types of dialogue, each with a different purpose: *persuasion* dialogue (e.g., critical discussion), *information-seeking* dialogue (e.g., interview and expert consultation), *negotiation* dialogue (e.g., deal making), *inquiry* dialogue (e.g., a scientific inquiry or public inquiry) and *eristic* dialogue (e.g., a quarrel). Roth and Lucas (1997) describe student exchanges in terms of *acceptance* (one student proposes an argument or expresses a point of view, and the others simply agree), *contradictory confrontations* (simple statements of opposing views, with little or no attempt to resolve disagreements or seek consensus) and *collaborative argumentation* (the students critique each other's views and seek to reach an acceptable consensus).

[62] Although, as noted in chapter 2, a number of authors, including Watts and Alsop (1997), Hodson (1998a), Alsop and Watts (2002) and Alsop (2005), have argued strongly for a much greater emphasis on the affective dimensions of learning. See also, Olds (1990), Meredith et al. (1997) and Barton and Scott (2003).

[63] Students with *performance-oriented* goals are concerned with task completion, accumulating academic credit and gaining teacher approval; those with *learning-oriented* goals are primarily

concerned with acquiring and developing knowledge and understanding. Performance goals promote defensive learning strategies and avoidance of challenge. By contrast, students with learning goals are encouraged by challenge and are willing to risk displaying their ignorance in order to acquire skills and knowledge through experience. Learning-oriented students are likely to seek understanding through what Entwistle (1981) calls "deep processing"; performance-oriented students, with their tendency to seek affirmation through marks and grades, may be content to seek superficial recall through "surface processing" on the grounds that simple recall is what tests and examinations usually reward. Traditional teaching practices often serve to reinforce the bad habits of performance-oriented students and penalize the more productive strategies of those who are learning-oriented.

[64] Some years ago, Clive Carré (1981) compiled a similar collection. It may be of interest to note the kinds of changes that have occurred in students' feelings, emotions, attitudes and values in the intervening 20 years.

[65] Sadler (2009) provides a comprehensive review of research findings relating to SSI-oriented teaching and learning.

[66] The researchers note that the articles contained the same types of data in terms of quality, quantity and presentation, and were written in a similar style and with comparable rhetoric. More encouragingly, students in an earlier study by Walker and Zeidler (2003) regarded articles as being "more convincing" when they cite a wide range of background information, include input from a range of people, and utilize statistical data.

[67] Perhaps the most widely quoted comment on the precautionary principle, at least in the context of environmental concerns, can be found in the 1992 Rio Declaration on Environment and Development: "Where there are threats of serious irreversible damage, the lack of full scientific certainty should not be used as a reason for postponing cost effective measures to prevent environmental degradation" (Principle 15). Sandin (1999), Graham (2000), Rogers (2001) and Sandin et al. (2002) provide further discussion. Duggan and Gott (2002) report that while the "precautionary argument" is often very prominent in public discussion of risks, companies directly involved with installations and practices that might create that risk (in the authors' case studies, the siting of a cement kiln and a mobile phone transmission mast near residential areas) argue the converse: because there is no clear and incontrovertible evidence indicating that a particular action is unsafe, it can/should be assumed that it is safe.

[68] Students were asked to consider the use of gene therapy for eliminating Huntington's disease, correcting near-sightedness and enhancing intelligence, and to discuss the use of reproductive cloning as an infertility treatment, for "replacing" a deceased child, and as a source of organs for situations in which transplants are needed for siblings born earlier.

[69] Ivan Snook (1975) reassures us that we are guilty of indoctrination when, and only when, we intend students to believe a proposition (or set of propositions) in the absence of, or despite/regardless of, the evidence. Or when we deliberately suppress or distort evidence to the contrary.

[70] Elsewhere, Donnelly (2005) asks some very tough questions about the extent to which the goal of critical engagement with SSI is a realistic one for school science education. In essence, are the issues just too complex, wide-ranging and elusive for school age students? I wholeheartedly share his view that serious and meaningful consideration of SSI is rooted in disciplinary knowledge (science, philosophy, history, sociology, politics, economics, ethics and media studies) and is not susceptible to the kind of 'generic skills' approach fashionable in some quarters: "The capacity for any 'critical engagement' worth the name cannot be achieved so cheaply, or simply transferred from the conceptually pared-down scientific environments of the classroom to the complex and problematic domain of boundary science and its interactions with the real world. If such complex and demanding intellectual matters are divorced from their disciplinary foundation, they might easily be reduced to trivialities" (p. 300). I take these comments as reinforcement of my advocacy of a much higher curriculum profile for SSI and the politicization of school science education.

[71] Huckle (2001) describes a cooperative venture between geography and English teachers in which students conducted a web-based investigation of issues relating to genetically modified food. It is interesting and disappointing that science teachers were not involved.

72 Of course, opinions on these questions vary enormously (Milner et al., 1998), and it is clear that personal experiences play a key role in determining responses. For example, prenatal genetic testing for deafness is generally opposed by those who are deaf, largely on the grounds that it devalues deaf people (Middleton et al., 1998).

73 The Great Ape Project, established in 1993 by Peter Singer and Paolo Cavalieri, proposes that all governments grant rights to life, liberty and protection from physical and psychological torture to our closest non-human relatives: chimpanzees, bonobos, gorillas and orang-utans (Cavalieri & Singer, 1993). Countries such as New Zealand and the United Kingdom have taken steps to *protect* great apes, but no national parliament had declared that these animals should be invested with *rights* until June 2008, when the Spanish parliament's Commission for the Environment, Agriculture and Fisheries declared unqualified support for the Great Ape project. Keeping these animals in captivity will be allowed only for purposes of conservation and only under optimal conditions for the apes. Moreover, the resolution recommends that the government of Spain take steps in international forums "to ensure that great apes are protected from maltreatment, slavery, torture and extinction" (Singer, 2008, p. 35). Interestingly, and disappointingly, the Catholic Church in Spain has declared itself opposed to the legislation on the grounds that it "erodes the Biblical injunction that gives humans dominion over the earth, and it diminishes the unique and primary place of human beings in the order of things; a uniqueness coming from the possession of an immortal soul that gives intelligibility to the central Christian (and Islamic) doctrines of Redemption, Salvation and Judgement" (Matthews, 2009, p. 642). The significance of this position for the kind of curriculum I am advocating will become apparent in chapter 8.

74 It is estimated that the vaccine could prevent 280,000 premature deaths per year, worldwide. Because the vaccine is ineffective once infection has occurred it is essential that it be administered before an individual has sexual contact. Exasperatingly, some parents seem to be concerned that vaccination will encourage early sexual activity, and so there is considerable disagreement on when the vaccine should be administered and whether parents and guardians should have the right to withdraw their daughters from the programme, and/or claim the right to be informed if their daughters make a request to receive the vaccine against parental wishes. My view is that students should be invited to debate these questions and to speculate on whether parents would be likely to deny their children access to a vaccine able to provide 100% protection against other life-threatening conditions not associated with sexual activity. At the time of writing, there is still considerable debate about the optimum age for inoculation. The New Zealand government has chosen to make the vaccine available at age 13 – three years later than the manufacturers (Merck) and many health professionals recommend. The government of Ontario will also make the vaccine available at age 13 (in Grade 8); Nova Scotia has opted for inoculation at Grade 7 (age 12) and the more enlightened government of Newfoundland has opted for a Grade 6 (age 11) vaccination programme. In a deplorable cost-cutting exercise, the United Kingdom government has chosen *Cervarix* (active against only two strains of HPV) in preference to *Gardasil* (active against the four major strains and also providing protection against genital warts) for its mass vaccination programme for 12–13 year olds (Boseley, 2008).

75 Each translation of *eudaimonia* has its disadvantages. 'Flourishing' would seem to apply to all animals and plants, yet Aristotle was only concerned with rational beings. 'Happiness' has a major subjective dimension (if I think I am happy, then I am happy), yet Aristotle wishes to allow for incorrect judgements about whether one's life is *eudaimon* or not. He notes that one can have a mistaken conception of eudaimonia or what it is to live well as a human being, such as believing that it consists solely in a life of self-indulgence.

76 This does not mean that the right amount is a modest amount. Sometimes it might be appropriate to display a considerable amount of emotion, as in the case of righteous indignation. The "mean amount" is neither too much nor too little, and is sensitive to the needs and interests of the person(s) and situation.

77 Singer also provides a detailed treatment of ethical issues surrounding abortion, IVF technology and stem cell research.

[78] Richard Guy (1989) points out that the cannibalism to which intensively farmed turkeys are often prone – a problem that is 'solved' by de-beaking – can be avoided entirely by provision of more space and a more stimulating environment.

[79] From a utilitarian perspective, animal experiments conducted in pursuit of treatments for serious human diseases, and the means of preventing them, can be regarded somewhat differently, although Singer (1977) comments as follows: "either the animal is not like us, in which case there is no reason for performing the experiment; or else the animal is like us, in which case we ought not to perform on the animal an experiment that would be considered outrageous if performed on one of us" (p. 52).

[80] She notes that staunch defenders of the current regime of animal experiments continually warn us of "the scourges of infectious disease" and would have us believe that "every rat and mouse that dies in the laboratory does so in the service of keeping children out of wheelchairs". She concludes: "Let us not delude ourselves" (p. 106).

[81] Genetic engineering creates new "transgenic" species by inserting a gene from one species into another; cloning produces genetically identical duplicates of an organism by replacing the nucleus of an unfertilized ovum with the nucleus of a cell extracted from the organism to be cloned.

[82] Thomas Jefferson's declaration, in 1776, that certain truths are "self-evident" is a fine and important example of Haidt's notion of moral intuition.

[83] Dawson (2010) advocates an approach based on adaptation of the four ethical principles commonly used in medical education: *autonomy* (decisions by patients regarding their medical care should be informed and voluntary), *beneficence* (actions should benefit or enhance the welfare of the patient), *non-maleficence* (do not intentionally cause harm or injury), and *justice* (fair and equitable allocation of resources).

[84] What Stephen Jay Gould (1996) calls "the error of reification".

[85] See Jones and Tuskegee Institute (1993), Reverby (2000) and Gray (2001) for background details.

[86] Those responsible for British tests in Australia and French tests in the South Pacific were similarly guilty of unethical, if not criminal, conduct.

[87] The policy of increasing the nicotine content of cigarettes in order to enhance their addictive characteristics, described by Glantz et al. (1996) and Hilts (1996), is the focus of the 1999 movie *The Insider*. Miller (1992) and Proctor (1995) describe the ways in which the tobacco industry manipulated newspaper reports and advertizing material to "manufacture doubt" about the link between smoking and lung cancer, while Barnes et al. (2006) describe how studies of secondhand smoking were distorted by focusing on workplaces that provided designated smoking areas.

[88] The term *biophilia* was coined by E.O. Wilson (1984) to describe what he regards as an "innate human urge to affiliate with other forms of life" (p. 85).

[89] Gough et al. (2000) identify four stances towards the environment, each associated with a particular "myth of nature": for the *fatalist*, nature is capricious; *individualists* see it as benign; *hierarchists* see nature as benign within certain limits, but perverse if those limits are exceeded; *egalitarians* view nature as ephemeral, that is, "a delicate equilibrium that may be easily and irretrievably disrupted" (p. 41).

[90] Important studies include Boyes and Stanisstreet (1993, 1994, 1997, 1998), Boyes et al. (1993, 1999, 2008, 2009a,b), Francis et al. (1993), Bostrom et al. (1994), Read et al. (1994), Strommen (1995), Christidou and Koulaidis (1996), Dove (1996), Gambro and Switzhy (1996), Potts et al. (1996), Gowda et al. (1997), Rye et al. (1997), Christidou et al. (1997), Fisher (1998a,b), Koulaidis and Christidou (1998), Mason and Santi (1998), Wylie et al. (1998), Groves and Pough (1999), Meadows and Wiesenmayer (1999), Myers et al. (1999, 2000, 2004), Andersson and Wallin (2000), Gayford, (2000, 2002a), Summers et al. (2000, 2001), Jeffries et al. (2001), Khalid (2001, 2003), Pruneau et al. (2001, 2003), Daniel et al. (2004), Papadimitriou (2004), Österlind (2005), Pekel and Ozay (2005), Schreiner et al. (2005), Gautier et al. (2006), Kerr and Walz (2007), Michail et al. (2007), Pe'er et al. (2007), Desjean-Perrota et al. (2008), Kilinc et al. (2008), Zak and Munson (2008), Whitmarsh (2009), Menzel and Bögeholz (2009), Oztas and Kalipci (2009), Shepardson et al. (2009), Skamp et al. (2009); Taber and Taylor (2009), Campbell et al. (2010), Driver et al. (2010) and Kirkeby Hansen (2010).

91 Whitmarsh (2008) notes that people with personal experience of flooding differ very little from other people in their understanding of climate change and likely responses to it, although personal experience of air pollution does result in greater awareness of factors contributing to climate change and often precipitates responsible action such as using public transport. Similarly, people living in so-called "biodiversity hotspots" (where biodiversity is high, but acutely at risk) seem to be no more sensitive to biodiversity issues than those living elsewhere (Menzel & Bögeholz, 2010). However, Guisasola et al. (2007) report that science teachers living in Nevada, designated by the US government as a site for storage of nuclear waste, expressed more concern about nuclear issues than teachers elsewhere.

92 Blocker and Eckberg (1989) report some interesting findings among adults, particularly those with young children: men focus on the economic dimensions of environmental problems, women focus on the health issues. Having children, they argue, increases parents' attentiveness to consequences bearing on their sex-typed roles within the family: for mothers, concern for their children's health; for fathers, concern for the material well-being of the family.

93 Because of the abstract and seemingly agent-free nature of terms like "habitat loss", the underlying issues are easily ignored. Similarly, use of general terms like "pollution" may prevent students from distinguishing among pollutants and their individual consequences. Moreover, complex diagrams using boxes and arrows to represent notions like "greenhouse effect" can be very confusing for students.

94 Whereas many of the primary school children in Holden's (2007) study considered themselves to be "making a difference" already, citing environmental action, fundraising and contributing to campaigns of various kinds, the vast majority of the secondary school students admitted that they were not involved in any action for change and were unlikely to take action in the future.

95 The Oxford English Dictionary gives the first recorded use of this phrase as *The New York Times*, June 20th 1959: "Financing schools has become a problem about equal to having an elephant in the room. It's so big you just can't ignore it".

96 Some put the estimated figure as high as 11 billion.

97 See http://portal.unesco.org/education/en/

98 However, this doesn't mean that aerosols are now "environmentally friendly". The alternative propellants, including compressed hydrocarbons and nitrous oxide, are considered to be "greenhouse gases" and contribute to global warming. There are, however, many alternatives to aerosol cans.

99 Animal dissection not only betrays the teacher's anthropocentric views, and those of the scientific community being represented, but it can shift the views of students strongly in that direction – as, of course, it is intended to do. Solot and Arluke (1997) observed some disturbing shifts in the behaviour of a group of Grade 6 students during six hours of class activity focused on the dissection of foetal pigs: from initial apprehension, squeamishness and reluctance, through emotional distancing and loss of empathy for the pig, increasing indifference and objectification of the pig as "the specimen", to a total absence of respect for the pig and acts of pointless and savage mutilation.

100 In startling contrast, Al-Khalili (2008) states that scientists in the Islamic world, particularly in Iran and Malaysia, are untroubled by many of the ethical issues that surround stem cell research in the United Kingdom and the United States.

101 Knowledge of the natural world accumulated outside of conventional Western science is variously described as traditional knowledge, Aboriginal knowledge, Indigenous knowledge, traditional environmental or ecological knowledge (often using the acronym TEK), ethnoscience and folklore. I prefer to use the term *traditional knowledge* (TK) to denote knowledge accumulated by a group of people, not necessarily Indigenous, who by virtue of many generations of unbroken residence develop a detailed understanding of their particular place in their particular world. This definition includes, for example, the beliefs and practices of distinct social groups such as the fishing community in rural Trinidad described by June George (1999a) and the groups in South and East Asia designated "neo-indigenous" by Aikenhead and Ogawa (2007).

102 Gaia (or Gaea), the most important deity of the early Greeks, represented the Earth and was worshipped as the universal mother. With her son Uranus (the sky), she produced the Titans, the first race of Gods, of whom six were male (Oceanus, Cocus, Hyperion, Crius, Iapetus and Cronus) and

six were female (Theia, Rhea, Mnemosyne, Phoebe, Tethys and Themis). Cronus and Rhea had three daughters (Hestia, Demeter and Hera) and three sons (Hades, Poseidon and Zeus).

[103] It should be noted that fieldwork and the kind of outdoor experiences discussed in chapter 9 are key to developing this kind of understanding.

[104] Elizabeth Dowdeswell held the position from 1992 to 1997. The current Executive Director is Achim Steiner.

[105] Despite substantial research evidence reporting the positive impact of outdoor education on both cognitive and affective learning outcomes, the provision of such experiences in school science education is in sharp decline in many parts of the world (Rickinson et al., 2004).

[106] Wendell Berry (1987) refers to hedges and walls as "margins", juxtapositions between the domestic and the wild that are particularly rich in wildlife and present wonderful opportunities for encounters with animals.

[107] Levi then tells us that the plant in question is a vine, and that the molecule of which it is now a part "travels, at the slow pace of vegetal juices, from the leaf through the pedicel and by the shoot to the trunk, and from here descends to the almost ripe bunch of grapes". The wine made from the grapes is drunk and the glucose oxidized, but it was not oxidized immediately, says Levi, "its drinker kept it in his liver for more than a week, well curled up and tranquil, as a reserve aliment for a sudden effort; an effort that he was forced to make the following Sunday, pursuing a bolting horse. Farewell to the hexagonal structure: in the space of a few instants the skein was unwound and became glucose again, and this was dragged by the bloodstream all the way to a minute muscle fiber in the thigh, and here brutally split into two molecules of lactic acid, the grim harbinger of fatigue: only later, some minutes after, the panting of the lungs was able to supply the oxygen necessary to quietly oxidise the latter. So a new molecule of carbon dioxide returned to the atmosphere". After a long and complex journey, the carbon dioxide is photosynthesized again, and becomes part of the trunk of a Lebanon cedar. Five hundred years later, that particular bit of the tree trunk is consumed by a woodworm, which subsequently pupates and becomes a moth. Levi continues: "Our atom is in one of the insect's thousand eyes, contributing to the summary and crude vision with which it orients itself in space. The insect is fecundated, lays its eggs, and dies; the small cadaver lies in the undergrowth of the woods, it is emptied of its fluids, but the chitin carapace resists for a long time, almost indestructible. The snow and sun return above it without injuring it: it is buried by the dead leaves and the loam, it has become a slough, a 'thing', but the death of atoms, unlike ours, is never irrevocable. Here are at work the omnipresent, untiring, and invisible gravediggers of the undergrowth, the microorganisms of the humus. The carapace, with its eyes by now blind, has slowly disintegrated, and the ex-drinker, ex-cedar, ex-woodworm has once again taken wing" (pp. 225–231).

[108] My use of the term *community* is not meant to imply that there is a common set of beliefs, values, attitudes and aspirations among the residents of a particular area. Nor am I so naïve that I fail to recognize that communities are in constant change and that daily life is frequently characterized by dispute and contestation over resources and power. Although *communities* might be a more descriptively accurate term, I have chosen to let common usage prevail. When particularly important, I have used the expression sub-cultural groups to indicate particular communities within the overall community of residents.

[109] Dubos used this expression at the UN conference on the human environment in 1972, although some attribute an earlier use to David Brower, founder of Friends of the Earth, in 1969. Essentially the same expression – think global, act local – was used by Patrick Geddes (1915) in *Cities in Evolution* (p. 397). Even earlier, John Stuart Mill declared: "If individuals in a large state are to be able to participate effectively in the government of the 'great society' then the necessary qualities underlying this participation have to be fostered and developed at the local level" (see Pateman, 1970, p. 30).

[110] This complex of place and identity is encapsulated in the Māori concept of *turangawaewae*. Of course, any attempt to explain a culturally embedded notion by a person who is not a member of that particular ethnic group is fraught with dangers. Consequently, what follows here includes both a paraphrase and a number of direct quotations from the first person words of Māori educator Liz McKinley (in Kincheloe et al., 2006, p. 145). Each person, McKinley says, has a *turangawaewae*

(literally, a place to stand). It is not necessarily the place where I currently live; rather, it is about my ancestry – biological and social (*whakapapa*) – and is a place where I belong. "It is a place of identity – usually represented through a *marae* (ancestral meeting place), an *urupa* (burial site), and through features of the land that surrounds these places, such as mountains, rivers, lakes, and so on. When I introduce myself in my culture – anywhere in *Aotearoa* (New Zealand) - it is with these signifiers". Thus, people know "who I am – where I come from, where I belong, what my history is in relation to them, and how I relate to others from other tribal areas."

[111] Cajete (2000) has written extensively on the significance of place in the cultural life of First Nations peoples and Native Americans. Two quotations should suffice to convey the flavour of his writing: "All human development is predicated on our interaction with the soil, the air, the climate, the plants, and the animals of the places in which we live. The inner archetypes in a place formed the spiritually based ecological mind-set required to establish and maintain a correct and sustainable relationship with place... But people make a place as much as a place makes them. Native people interacted with the places in which they lived for such a long time that their landscapes became reflections of their very souls" (p. 187). "Native peoples' places are sacred and bounded, and their science is used to understand, explain, and honor the life they are tied to in the greater circle of physical life. Sacred sites are mapped in the space of tribal memory to acknowledge forces that keep things in order and moving. The people learn to respect the life in the places they live, and thereby to preserve and perpetuate the ecology" (p. 77).

[112] Helpful discussion of the potential and pitfalls of student councils can be found in Taylor and Johnson (2002), Fielding (2004), Shallcross et al. (2006), Carlsson and Sanders (2008), and Shallcross and Robinson (2008)

[113] Christopher Emdin (2010) provides an extended discussion of the ways in which a hip-hop based and hip-hop inspired science curriculum can play a key role in creating opportunities for marginalized and under-served youth to participate successfully in science education. I am proposing an extension to social activism.

[114] In New Zealand, the Returned Serviceman's Association (RSA) is the equivalent of the RSL (Returned Serviceman's League) in Australia and the British Legion in the UK.

[115] Important literature references include: Rennie and McClafferty (1996), Griffin (1998), Krapfel (1999), Ash and Klein (2000), Falk and Dierking (2000), Bencze and Lemelin (2001), Heering and Muller (2002), Pedretti (2002, 2004), Anderson et al. (2003), Braund and Reiss (2004), Black (2005), Kisiel (2006), Rahm (2006, 2008) Tal and Steiner (2006), Rennie (2007), Tal and Morag (2007), Tran (2007) and Nielsen et al. (2009).

[116] While Takano et al. (2009) use the spelling *Yup'ik*, Kawagley et al. (1995) and Kawagley and Barnhardt (1999) prefer *Yupiaq*. I have simply adopted the spelling of the particular article under discussion.

[117] Digweed was not a reference to pulling weeds, although there was a lot of that going on, but a commemoration of the student who first suggested the scheme as a component of the voluntary service programme.

[118] Much helpful advice on oral history methods can be found in McMahan and Rogers (1994), Yow (2005) and Janesick (2010), while reading George Ewart Evans' classic book, *Ask the Folk who Cut the Hay* (published by Faber and Faber in 1956), will quickly demonstrate the compelling nature of oral history.

[119] Sadler et al. (2006) found that teachers could be divided into five groups: those committed to including SSI in the curriculum and able to give examples of how they have addressed SSI in their classrooms; those committed to including SSI but unable to realize goals because of contextual constraints; those not committed to including SSI; those who do not consider SSI to be appropriate for the curriculum because they believe that science is "value free"; and those who believe that moral-ethical issues should be a cross-curricular concern.

[120] Barrett and Pedrett (2006) note that in the former approach controversial issues may be introduced but controversy is likely to be restricted to scientific aspects rather than social, cultural or moral-ethical aspects. In the latter approach controversial issues are introduced not just because they are interesting, but because they impact on students' lives, require an examination of underlying values, seek to politicize students and engage them in sociopolitical action.

[121] Commonly used metaphors include teacher as broadcaster, teacher as gardener, teacher as tour guide, teacher as police officer, entertainer, director, *agent provocateur*, negotiator, circus ring master, ship's captain, chair person, scaffolder, manager or role mode. In Hodson (2009a), I made extensive use of the metaphor *teacher as anthropologist* or "teacher as culture broker", as Aikenhead (2000, 2001a,b) calls it.

[122] There are, of course, many with a vested interest in social reproduction; there are many more who do not recognize that social reproduction is the outcome of most current educational practice.

[123] Newman (2006) identifies three categories of action, with increasing levels of social disapproval and illegality: (i) conventional actions such as voting, campaigning through emails, phone calls and letters, organizing meetings, pamphleteering, setting up Web sites, blogging, organizing petitions, lobbying officials, engaging in consumer boycotts, demonstrations and strike action; (ii) confrontational actions, including disrupting meetings, blockading a road, holding unsanctioned demonstrations, occupying buildings, hacking into Web sites, and so; and (iii) violent action such as damaging property, destroying GM crops, releasing animals from research establishments, engaging in actions likely to provoke violence in others, and injuring people.

[124] Clough (1998) reports a small-scale survey in which 23 out of 33 preservice teachers expressed the view that citizens are justified in breaking the law if their action will protect the environment, though the author doesn't indicate whether the respondents would be willing to undertake such an illegal action themselves, or had done so. I suspect this is not a view held by most preservice or serving teachers.

REFERENCES

Abd-El-Khalick, F. (2001). Embedding nature of science instruction in preservice elementary science courses: Abandoning scientism, but... *Journal of Science Teacher Education, 12*(3), 215–233.

Abd-El-Khalick, F. (2003). Socioscientific issues in pre-college classrooms. The primacy of learners' epistemological orientations and views of nature of science. In D. L. Zeidler (Ed.), *The role of moral reasoning on socioscientific issues and discourse in science education* (pp. 41–61). Dordrecht: Kluwer.

Abd-El-Khalick, F. (2005). Developing deeper understandings of nature of science: The impact of a philosophy of science course on preservice science teachers' views and instructional planning. *International Journal of Science Education, 27*(1), 15–42.

Abd-El-Khalick, F., & Akerson, V. L. (2004). Learning as conceptual change. Factors mediating the development of preservice elementary teachers' views of the nature of science. *Science Education, 88*(5), 785–810.

Abd-El-Khalick, F., & Akerson, V. (2009). The influence of metacognitive training on preservice elementary teachers' conceptions of the nature of science. *International Jornal of Science Education, 31*(16), 2161–2184.

Abd-El-Khalick, F., & Lederman, N. G. (2000a). Improving science teachers' conceptions of the nature of science: A critical review of the literature. *International Journal of Science Education, 22*(7), 665–701.

Abd-El-Khalick, F., & Lederman, N. G. (2000b). The influence of history of science courses on students' views of the nature of science. *Journal of Research in Science Teaching, 37*(10), 1057–1095.

Abd-El-Khalick, F., Waters, M., & Le, A-P. (2008). Representations of nature of science in high school chemistry textbooks over the past four decades. *Journal of Research in Science Teaching, 45*(7), 835–855.

Abell, S. K. (2008). Twenty years later: Does pedagogical content knowledge remain a useful idea? *International Journal of Science Education, 30*(10), 1405–1416.

Abelson, J., Forest, P.-G., Eyles, J., Smith, P., Martin, E., & Gauvibin, F.-P. (2003). Deliberation about deliberation: Issues in the design and evaluation of public consultation processes. *Social Science and Medicine, 57*, 239–251.

Abelson, R. P. (1986). Beliefs are like possessions. *Journal for the Theory of Social Behavior, 16*, 223–250.

Abram, D. (1996). *The spell of the sensuous: Perception and language in a more-than-human world.* New York: Pantheon Books.

Adúriz-Bravo, A., & Izquierdo-Aymeric, M. (2009). A research-informed instructional unit to teach the nature of science to pre-service science teachers. *Science & Education, 18*(9), 1177–1192.

Agyeman, J. (2008). Action, experience, behaviour and technology: Why it's just not the same? In A. Reid & W. Scott (Eds.), *Researching education and the environment: Retrospect and prospect* (pp. 267–276). London: Routledge.

Aikenhead, G. S. (1996). Science education: Border crossing into the subculture of science. *Studies in Science Education, 27*, 1–52.

Aikenhead, G. S. (1997). Towards a First Nations cross-cultural science and technology curriculum. *Science Education, 81*, 217–238.

Aikenhead, G. S. (2000). Renegotiating the culture of school science. In R. Millar, J. Leach, & J. Osborne (Eds), *Improving science education: The contribution of research* (pp. 245–264). Buckingham: Open University Press.

Aikenhead, G. S. (2001a). Students' ease in crossing cultural borders into school science. *Science Education, 85*, 180–188.

Aikenhead, G. S. (2001b). Integrating Western and Aboriginal science: Cross-cultural science teaching. *Research in Science Education, 31*(3), 337–355.

Aikenhead, G. S. (2002). Cross-cultural science teaching: *Rekindling traditions* for Aboriginal students. *Canadian Journal of Science, Mathematics and Technology Education, 2*(3), 287–304.

REFERENCES

Aikenhead, G. S. (2005). Research into STS science education. *Educación Quimica, 16*(3), 384–397.
Aikenhead, G. S. (2006). Towards decolonizing the Pan-Canadian science framework. *Canadian Journal of Science, Mathematics & Technology Education, 6*(4), 387–399.
Aikenhead, G. S., & Jegede, O. (1999). Cross-cultural science education: A cognitive explanation of a cultural phenomenon. *Journal of Research in Science Teaching, 36,* 269–287.
Aikenhead, G. S., & Ogawa, M. (2007). Indigenous knowledge and science revisited. *Cultural Studies of Science Education, 2*(3), 539–591.
Ainsworth, S. (2006). A conceptual framework for considering learning with multiple representations. *Learning and Instruction, 16,* 183–198.
Akerson, V. L., Abd-El-Khalick, F., & Lederman, N. G. (2000). Influence of a reflective activity-based approach on elementary teachers' conceptions of nature of science. *Journal of Research in Science Teaching, 37*(4), 295–317.
Akerson, V. L., Buzzelli, C. A., & Donnelly, L. A. (2010). On the nature of teaching nature of science: Preservice early childhood teachers' instruction in preschool and elementary settings. *Journal of Research in Science Teaching, 47*(2), 213–233.
Akerson, V., & Donnelly, L. A. (2010). Teaching nature of science to K-2 students: What under-standings can they attain? *International Journal of Science Education, 32*(1), 97–124.
Akerson, V. L., & Hanuscin, D. L. (2007). Teaching nature of science through inquiry: Results of a 3-year professional development program. *Journal of Research in Science Teaching, 44*(5), 653–680.
Akerson, V. L., Cullen, T. A., & Hanson, D.L. (2009). Fostering a community of practice through a professional development proram to improve elemtary teachers' views of nature of science and teaching practice. *Journal ofResearch in Science Teaching, 46*(10), 1090–1113.
Akerson, V. L., & Volrich, M. L. (2006). Teaching nature of science explicitly in a first-grade intern-ship setting. *Journal of Research in Science Teaching, 43*(4), 377–394.
Albala-Bertrand, L. (1992). *Reshaping education towards sustainable development.* Paris: UNESCO.
Albe, V. (2008a). When scientific knowledge, daily life experience, epistemological and social considerations interest: Students' argumentation in group discussion on a socio-scientific issue. *Research in Science Education, 38,* 67–90.
Albe, V. (2008b). Students' positions and considerations of scientific evidemnce about a controversial socioscientific issue. *Science & Education, 17,* 805–827.
Albone, A., Collins, N., & Hill, T. (1995). *Scientific research in schools: A compendium of practical experience.* Bristol: Clifton Scientific Trust.
Alerby, E. (2000). A way of visualizing children's and young people's thoughts about the environment: A study of drawings. *Environmental Education Research, 6,* 205–222.
Al-Khalili, J. (2008, July 31). While our scientists struggle with ethics, the Islamic world forges ahead. *The Guardian,* p. 29.
Allchin, D. (1999). Values in science: An educational perspective. *Science & Education, 8,* 1–12.
Allchin, D. (2004). Should the sociology of science be rated X? *Science Education, 88*(6), 934–946.
Alsop, S. (1999). Understanding understanding: A model for the public learning of radioactivity. *Public Understanding of Science, 8,* 267–284.
Alsop, S. (2001). Living with and learning about radioactivity: A comparative study. *International Journal of Science Education, 23*(3), 263–281.
Alsop, S. (2005). Bridging the Cartesian divide: Scinec education and affect. In S. Alsop (Ed.), *Beyond cartesian dualism: Encountering affect in the teaching and learning of science* (pp. 3–16). Dordrecht: Springer.
Alsop, S. (2009). Not quite the revolution: Science and technology education in a world that changed. In A. T. Jones, & M. J.deVries (Eds.), *International handbook of research and development in technology education* (pp. 319–328). Rotterdam/Taipei: Sense.
Alsop, S., & Watts, M. (2000). Facts and feelings: Exploring the affective domain in the learning of physics. *Physics Education, 35*(2), 132–138.
Alsop, S., & Watts, M. (2002). Unweaving time and food chains: Two classroom exercises in scientific and emotional literacy. *Canadian Journal of Science, Mathematics and Technology Education, 2*(4), 435–439.

Alsop, S., & Watts, M. (2003). Science education and affect. *International Journal of Science Education, 25*(9), 1043–1047.

Alsop, S., Dippo, D., & Zandvliet, D. B. (2007). Teacher education as or for social and ecological transformation: Place-based reflections on local and global participatory methods and collaborative practices. *Journal of Education for Teaching, 33*(2), 207–223.

Alsop, S., Ibrahim, S., & Members of the Science and the City Team. (2009). Feeling the weight of the world: Visual journeys in science and technology education. *Journal of Activist Science & Technology Education, 1*(1), 85–104.

Alsup, J. (2006). *Teacher identity discourses: Negotiating personal and professional spaces.* Mahwah, NJ: Lawrence Erlbaum Associates.

American Association for the Advancement of Science (AAAS). (1989). *Science for all Americans. A Project 2061 report on literacy goals in science, mathematics, and technology.* Washington, DC: Author.

American Association for the Advancement of Science (AAAS). (1993). *Benchmarks for scientific literacy.* Oxford: Oxford University Press.

Anderson, D., Lucas, K. B., & Ginns, I. S. (2003). Theoretical perspectives on learning in an informal setting. *Journal of Research in Science Teaching, 40*, 177–199.

Anderson, R. D. (2007). Teaching the theory of evolution in social, intellectual, and pedagogical context. *Science Education, 91*(4), 664–677.

Andersson, B., & Wallin, A. (2000). Students' understanding of the greenhouse effect, the societal consequences of reducing CO2 emissions and the problem of ozone layer depletion. *Journal of Resarch in Science Teaching, 37*(10), 1096–1111.

Andrew, J., & Robottom, I. (2001). Science and ethics: Some issues for education. *Science Education, 85*, 769–780.

Andriessen, J. (2007). Arguing to learn. In K. Sawyer (Ed.), *The Cambridge handbook of the learning sciences* (pp. 443–460). Cambridge: Cambridge University Press.

Andriessen, J., Baker, M., & Suthers, D. (Eds.). (2003). *Arguing to learn: Confronting cognitions in computer-supported collaborative learning environments.* Dordrecht: Kluwer.

Angell, M. (2004). *The truth about the drug companies: How they deceive us and what to do about it.* New York: Random House.

Apostolou, A., & Koulidis, V. (2010). Epistemology and science education: A study of epistemological views of teachers. *Research in Science & Technological Education, 28*(2), 149–166.

Apple, M. W. (1982). Curricular form and the logic of technical control: Building the possessive individual. In M. W. Apple (Ed.), *Cultural and economic reproduction in education: Essays on class, ideology and the state* (pp. 247–274). London: Routledge.

Apple, M. W. (1993). *Official knowledge: Democratic education in a conservative age.* New York: Routledge.

Apple, M. W. (1999). *Power, meaning and identity: Essays in critical educational studies.* New York: Peter Lang.

Apple, M. W. (2000). The hidden costs of reform. *Educational Policy, 14*, 429–435.

Apple, M. W. (2001a). *Educating the 'right' way: Markets, standards, God, and inequality.* New York: RoutledgeFalmer.

Apple, M. W. (2001b). Creating profits by creating failures: Standards, markets, and inequality in education. *International Journal of Inclusive Education, 5*(2&3), 103–118.

Apple, M. W., & Beane, J. A. (Eds.). (1995). *Democratic schools.* Alexandria, VA: Association for Supervision and Curriculum Development.

Applebaum, S., Barker, B., & Pinzino, D. (2006, April). *Socioscientific issues as context for conceptual understanding of content.* Paper presented at the annual meeting of the National Association for Science Teaching, San Francisco.

Appleyard, B. B. (1999). *Brave new worlds.* London: HarperCollins.

Arnstein, S. R. (1979). Eight rungs on the ladder of citizen participation. *Journal of the American Institute of Planners, 35*(4), 216–224.

REFERENCES

Arvai, J., Campbell, V. E. A., Baird, A., & Rivers, L. (2004). Teaching students to make better decisions about the environment: Lessons from the decision sciences. *Journal of Environmental Education, 36*(1), 33–42.

Ash, D., & Klein, C. (2000). Inquiry in the informal learning environment. In J. Minstrell, & E. H. van Zee (Eds.), *Inquiring into inquiry learning and teaching in science* (pp. 216–240). Washington, DC: American Association for the Advancement of Science.

Ashe, S., Caulkins, M., Judson, G., Ten Kate, Q. M., & Zandvliet, D. (2007). Sustainability: An open question. In D. Zandvliet & D. Fisher (Eds.), *Sustainable communities, sustainable environments: The contribution of science and technology education* (pp. 1–11). Rotterdam: Sense Publishers.

Astleitner, H. (2000). Designing emotionally sound instruction: The FEASP-approach. *Instructional Science, 28*, 169–198.

Au, T. K.-F., & Romo, L. F. (1999). Mechanical causality in children's 'folkbiology'. In D. L. Medin & S. Atran (Eds.), *Folkbiology* (pp. 355–401). Cambridge, MA: MIT Press.

Augoustinos, M., Russin, A., & LeCouteur, A. (2009). Representations of the stem-cell cloning fraud: From scientific breakthrough to managing the stake and interest in science. *Public Understanding of Science, 18*(6), 687–703.

Augoustinos, M., Crabb, S., & Shepherd, R. (2010). Genetically modified food in the news: Media representations of the GM debate in the UK. *Public Understanding of Science, 19*(1), 98–114.

Ausubel, D. P. (1968). *Educational psychology: A cognitive view.* New York: Holt, Rinehart & Winston.

Ayala, F. J. (2000). Arguing for evolution: Holding strong religious beliefs does not preclude intelligent scientific thinking. *The Science Teacher, 67*(2), 30–32.

Bäckstrand, K. (2003). Civic science for sustainability: Reframing the role of experts, policy-makers and citizens in environmental governance. *Global Environmental Politics, 3*(4), 24–41.

Bader, B. (2003). Interprétation d'une controverse scientifique; Stratégies argumentatives d'adolescentes et d'adolescents québécois. *Canadian Journal of Science, Mathematics and Technology Education, 3*(2), 231–250.

Baer, P., Harte, J., Haya, B., Herzog, A. V., Holdren, J., Hultman, N. E., Kammen, D. M., Norgaard, B., & Raymond, L. (2000). Climate change: Equity and greenhouse gas responsibility. *Science, 289*(5488), 2287.

Baier, A. (1985). *Postures of the mind.* Minneapolis. MN: University of Minnesota Press.

Bailey, B., & Stegelin, D. A. (2003). Creating a sense of place: Anchoring at-risk students within K-12 classrooms. *Journal of At-Risk Issues, 9*(2), 17–26.

Bailey, S., & Watson, R. (1998). Establishing basic ecological understanding in younger pupils: A pilot evaluation of a strategy based on drama/role lay. *International Journal of Science Education, 20*(2), 139–152.

Bakan, J. (2004). *The corporation: The pathological pursuit of profit and power.* New York: Free Press.

Bakhtin, M. M. (1981). *The dialogic imagination: Four essays.* Austin, TX: University of Texas Press.

Balcombe, J. (1997). Student/teacher conflict regarding animal dissection. *American Biology Teacher, 59*(1), 22–25.

Balcombe, J. (2000). *The use of animals in higher education: Problems, alternatives, and recommendations.* Washington, DC: The Humane Society Press.

Ballantyne, R., Connell, S., & Fien, J. (1998). Students as catalysts of environmental change: A framework for researching intergenerational influence through environmental education. *Environmental Education Research, 4*(3), 285–298.

Ballantyne, R., Fien, J., & Packer, J. (2001a). Programme effectiveness in facilitating intergenerational influence in environmental education: Lessons from the field. *Journal of Environmental Education, 32*(4), 8–15.

Ballantyne, R., Fien, J., & Packer, J. (2001b). School environmental education program impacts upon family learning: A case study analysis. *Environmental Education Research, 7*(1), 23–37.

Ballantyne, R., Packer, J., Hughes, K., & Dierking, L. (2007). Conservation learning in wildlife tourism settings: Lessons from research in zoos and aquariums. *Environmental Education Research, 13*(3), 367–383.

Ballantyne, R., & Packer, J. (2005). Promoting environmentally sustainable attitudes and behavior through free choice learning experiences: What is the state of the game? *Environmental Education Research, 11,* 281–295.

Balls, M., & Southee, J. (1989). Reducing animal experiments by questioning their necessity. In D. Paterson, & M. Palmer (Eds.), *The status of animals: Ethics, education and welfare* (pp. 111–122). London: Humane Education Foundation/CAB International..

Bandeira, F. P., Toledo, V. M., & López-Blanco, J. (2002). Tzotzil Maya ethnoecology: Landscape perception and management as a basis for coffee agroforest design. *Journal of Ethnobiology, 22,* 247–272.

Bandura, A. (1977). Self-efficacy: Toward a unifying theory of behavior change. *Psychological Review, 84*(2), 191–215.

Bandura, A. (1986). *Social foundations of thought and action: A social cognitive theory.* Englewood Cliffs, NJ: Prentice Hall.

Bandura, A. (1993). Perceived self-efficacy in cognitive development and functioning. *Educational Psychologist, 28*(2), 117–148.

Banks, J. (2004). *Diversity and citizenship education: Global perspectives.* San Francisco: Jossey-Bass.

Barab, S. A., Sadler, T. D., Heiselt, C., Hickey, D. T., & Zuiker, S. (2007). Relating narrative, inquiry, and inscriptions: Supporting consequential play. *Journal of Science Education and Technology, 16*(1), 59–82.

Barad, K. (2000). Reconceiving scientific literacy as agential literacy. In R. Reid, & S. Traweek (Eds.), *Doing science + culture* (pp. 221–258). New York: Routledge.

Barber, B. (1962). *Science and the social order.* New York: Collier.

Barker, S. (2007). Ecological education: Reconnecting with nature to promote sustainable behavious. In D. Zandvliet, & D. Fisher (Eds.), *Sustainable communities, sustainable environments: The contribution of science and technology education* (pp. 23–35). Rotterdam: Sense Publishers.

Barlex, D. (2006). Pedadgogy to promote reflection and understanding in school technology courses. In J. R. Dakers (Ed.), *Defining technological literacy: Towards an epistemological framework.* (pp. 179–195). New York: PalgraveMacmillan.

Barnes, D. (1988). Oral language and learning. In S. Hynds, & D. Rubin (Eds.), *Perspectives on talk and learning* (pp. 41–54). Urbana, IL: National Council of Teachers of English.

Barnes, D., & Todd, F. (1995). *Communication and learning revisited.* Portsmouth, NH: Heinemann.

Barnes, R. L., Hammond, S. K., & Glantz, S. A. (2006). The tobacco industry's role in the 16 cities study of secondhand tobacco smoke: Do the data support the stated conclusions? *Environmental Health Perspectives, 114*(12), 1890–1897.

Barnett, J., & Hodson, D. (2001). Pedagogical context knowledge: Toward a fuller understanding of what good science teachers know. *Science Education, 85*(4), 426–453.

Barnett, M. (1995). Literacy, technology and 'tecgnological literacy'. *International Journal of Technology and Design Education, 5*(2), 119–137.

Barr, G., & Herzog, H. (2000). Fetal pig: The high school dissection experience. *Society & Animals, 8*(1), 53–69.

Barraza, L. (1999). Children's drawings about the environment. *Environmental Education Research, 5*(1), 49–66.

Barrett, M. J. (2008). Participatory pedagogy in environmental education: Reproduction or disruption? In A. Reid, B. B. Jensen, J. Nikel, & V. Simovsla (Eds.), *Participation and learning: Perspectives on education and the environment, health and sustainability* (pp. 212–224). New York: Springer.

Barrett, S. E., & Nieswandt, M. (2010). Teaching about ethics through socioscientific issues in physics and chemistry: Teacher candidates' beliefs. *Journal of Research in Science Teaching, 47*(4), 380–401.

Barrett, S. E., & Pedretti, E. (2006). Contrasting orientations: STSE for social reconstruction or social reproduction? *School Science & Mathematics, 106*(5), 237–245.

Barry, J. (2006). Resistance is fertile: From environmental to sustainability citizenship. In A. Dobson, & B. Derek (Eds.), *Environmental citizenship* (pp. 21–48). Cambridge, MA: MIT Press.

REFERENCES

Bartholomew, H., Osborne, J., & Ratcliffe, M. (2004). Teaching students "ideas-about-science": Five dimensions of effective practice. *Science Education, 88*(5), 655–682.

Baskaran, A., & Boden, R. (2006). Globalization and the commodification of science. In M. Muchie, & X. Li (Eds.), *Globalisation, inequality and the commodification of life and well-being* (pp. 42–72). London: Adonis & Abbey.

Bateson, G. (2000). *Steps to an ecology of mind.* Chicago, IL: University of Chicago Press.

Bator, R. J., & Cialdini, R. B. (2000). The application of persuasion theory to the development of effective proenvironmental public service announcements. *Journal of Social Issues, 56*(3), 527–541.

Batson, C. D. (1994). Why act for the public good? Four answers. *Personality and Social Psychology Bulletin, 20,* 603–610.

Battiste, M. (Ed.). (2000). *Reclaiming indigenous voice and vision.* Vancouver: University of British Columbia Press.

Battiste, M., & Henderson, J. Y. (2000). *Protecting Indigenous knowledge and heritage.* Saskatoon: Purich Publishing.

Battiste, M., & Henderson, J. Y. (2005). Protecting Indigenous knowledge and heritage: A global challenge. In W. Caslin (Ed.), *Justice as healing: Indigenous ways* (pp. 240–244). St. Paul, MN: Living Justice Press.

Battistoni, R. M. (2002). *Civic engagement across the curriculum: A resource book for service-learning faculty in all disciplines.* Providence, RI: Campu Compact.

Bauer, M., & Gaskell, G. (Eds.). (2002). *Biotechnology: The making of a global controversy.* Cambridge: Cambridge University Press.

Bauman, Z. (2007). Collateral casualties of consumerism. *Journal of Consumer Culture, 7*(1), 25–56.

Becher, T., & Trowler, P. (2001). *Academic tribes and territories: Intellectual enquiry and the culture of disciplines* (2nd ed.). Philadelphia, PA: Open University Press.

Bechtel, R. B., Verdugo, V. C., & de Queiroz Pinheiro, J. (1999). Environmental belief systems: United States, Brazil, and Mexico. *Journal of Cross-cultural Psychology, 30*(1), 122–128.

Beck, U. (1992). *Risk society: Towards a new modernity.* London: Newbury Park.

Beck, U. (1997). *The reinvention of politics: Rethinking modernity in the global social order.* Cambridge: Polity Press.

Beck, U. (2000). Risk society revisited: Theory, politics and research programs. In B. Adam, U. Beck, & J. van Loon (Eds.), *The risk society and beyond: critical issues for social theory* (pp. 211–229). London: Sage.

Beck, U. (2000). *What is globalization?* Cambridge: Polity Press.

Beckford, C. L., Jacobs, C., Williams, N., & Nahdee, R. (2010). Aboriginal environmental wisdom, stewardship, and sustainability: Lessons from Walpole Island First Nations, Ontario, Canada. *Journal of Environmental Education, 41*(4), 239–248.

Beijard, D., Meijer, P. C., & Verloop, N. (2004). Reconsidering research on teachers' professional identity. *Teaching and Teacher Education, 20,* 107–128.

Beijard, D., Verloop, N., & Vermunt, J. D. (2000). Teachers' perceptions of professional identity: An exploratory study froma personal knowledge perspective. *Teaching and Teacher Education, 16*(7), 749–764.

Bell, A. C., & Russell, C. A. (1999). Life ties: Disrupting anthropocentrism in language arts education. In J. Robertson (Ed.), *Teaching about tolerance* (pp. 68–89). San Diego, CA: National Council of Teachers of English.

Bell, A. C., & Russell, C. L. (2000). Beyond human, beyond words: Anthropocentrism, critical pedagogy, and the poststructuralist turn. *Canadian Journal of Education, 25*(3), 188–203.

Bell, A. C., Russell, C. L., & Plotkin, R. (1998). Environmental learning and the study of extinction. *Journal of Environmental Education, 29*(2), 4–10.

Bell, B., & Gilbert, J. (1996). *Teacher development: A model from science education.* London: Falmer Press.

Bell, P. (2002). Using argument map representations to make thinking visible for individuals and groups. In T. Koschmann, R. Hall, & N. Miyake (Eds.), *CSCL-2: Carrying forward to conversation* (pp. 449–485). Mahwah, NJ: Erlbaum.

Bell, P. (2004). Promoting students' argument construction and collaborative debate in the science classroom. In M. C. Linn, E.A. Davis, & P. Bell (Eds.), *Internet environments for science education* (pp. 115–143). Mahwah, NJ: Lawrence Erlbaum.

Bell, P., & Linn, M. C. (2000). Scientific arguments as learning artefacts: Designing for learning from the web with KIE. *International Journal of Science Education, 22*(8), 797–818.

Bell, R. L. (2004). Perusing Pandora's box. In L. B. Flick & N. G. Lederman (Eds.), *Scientific inquiry and nature of science: Implications for teaching, learning, and teacher education* (pp. 427–446). Dordrecht: Kluwer.

Bell, R. L., & Lederman, N. G. (2003). Understandings of the nature of science and decision making on science and technology based issues. *Science Education 87*(3), 352–377.

Bell, R. L., Blair, L. M., Crawford, B. A., & Lederman, N. G. (2003). Just do it? Impact of a science apprenticeship program on high school students' understandings of the nature of science and scientific inquiry. *Journal of Research in Science Teaching, 40*(5), 487–509.

Bell, W. (1997). *Foundations of futures studies.* New Brunswick, NJ: Transaction Publishers.

Bencze, J. L. (2001). Subverting corporatism in school science. *Canadian Journal of Science, Mathematics and Technology Education, 1*(3), 349–355.

Bencze, L. (2004). School science for/against social justice. In S. Alsop, L. Bencze, & E. Pedretti (Eds.), *Analysing exemplary science teaching: Theoretical lenses and a spectrum of possibilities for practice* (pp. 193–202). London: Routledge-Falmer.

Bencze, J. L. (2008). Private profit, science, and science education: Critical problems and possibilities for action. *Canadian Journal of Science, Mathematics and Technology Education, 8*(4), 297–312.

Bencze, J. L. (2010). Exposing and deposing hyper-economized school science. *Cultural Studies of Science Education, 5,* 293–303.

Bencze, L., & Alsop, S. (2007, February). *School science for the people and the planet: Enabling education in a milieu of global economization.* Paper presented at the 3rd biennial 'Provoking Curriculu' conference, Banff, Alberta.

Bencze, J. L., & Alsop, S. (2009). Anti-capitalist/pro-communitarian science & technology education. *Journal of Activist Science & Technology Education, 1*(1), 65–84.

Bencze, J. L., Alsop,S., & Bowen, G. M. (2009). Student-teachers' inquiry-based actions to address socioscientific issues. *Journal of Activist Science & Technology Education, 1*(2), 78–112.

Bencze, L., Hewitt, J., & Pedretti, E. (2001). Multi-media case methods in pre-service science education: Enabling an apprenticeship for praxis. *Research in Science Education, 31*(2), 191–209.

Bencze, L., Hewitt, J., Pedretti, E., Yoon, S., Perris, K., & van Oostveen, R. (2003). Science-specialist student-teachers consider promoting technological design projects: Contributions of multi-media case methods. *Research in Science Education, 33*(2), 163–187.

Bencze, L., Hewitt, J., & Pedretti, E. (2009). Personalizing and contextualizing multimedia case methods in university-based teacher education: An important modification for promoting technological design in school science. *Research in Science Education, 39*(1), 93–109.

Bencze, L., & Lemelin, N. (2001). Doing science at a science centre: Enabling independent knowledge construction in the context of schools' museum visits. *Museum Management and Curatorship, 19*(2), 139–155.

Bennett, J., Grasel, C., Parchmann, I., & Waddington, D. (2005). Context-based and conventional approaches to teaching chemistry: Comparing teachers' views. *International Journal of Science Education, 27,* 1521–1547.

Bentley, M. L. (2000). Improvisational drama and the nature of science. *Journal of Science Teacher Education, 11*(1), 63–75.

Bentley, M., Fien, J., & Neil, C. (2004). *Sustainable consumption: Young Australians as agents of change.* Canberra: National Youth Affairs Research Scheme.

Berkowitz, A. R., Ford, M. E., & Brewer, C. A. (2005). A framework for integrating ecological literacy, civics literacy, and environmental citizenship in environmental education. In E. A. Johnson, & M. J. Mappin (Eds.), *Environmental education and advocacy: Changing perspectives of ecology and education* (pp. 227–266). Cambridge: Cambridge University Press.

REFERENCES

Berkowitz, M. W., & Simmons, P. (2003). Integrating science education and character education. In D. L. Zeidler (Ed.), *The role of moral reasoning on sociscientific issues and discourse in science education* (pp. 117–138). Dordrecht: Kluwer.

Berlak, A., & Berlak, H. (1981). *Dilemmas of schooling: Teaching and social change*. London: Methuen.

Berland, L. K., & McNeill, K. J. (2010). A learning progression for scientific argumentation: Understanding student work and designing supportive instructional contexts. *Science Education, 94*(5), 765–793.

Berland, L., & Reiser, B. (2009). Making sense of argumentation and explanation. *Science Education, 93*(1), 26–55.

Berry, A., Loughran, J., & van Driel, J. H. (2008). Revisiting the roots of pedgagogical content knowledge. *International Journal of Science Education, 30*(10), 1271–1279.

Berry, A., Loughran, J., Smith, K., & Lindsay, S. (2009). Capturing and enhancing science teachers' professional knowledge. *Research in Science Education, 39*(4), 575–594.

Berry, W. (1987). *Home economics*. San Franciso,: North Point Press.

Berry, W. (1989). *What are people for?* San Francisco: North Point Press.

Best, S., & Kellner, D. (2002). Biotechnology, ethics and the politics of cloning. *Democracy & Nature, 8*(3), 439–465.

Bevier, M. L., Evenchick, C. A., Thompson, J. C., & Wyss, J. A. (1997). Making geoscience relevant to First Nations students from the north coast of British Columbia. *Journal of Geoscience Education, 45*(2), 105–108.

Beyer, L. E. (1998). Schooling for democracy: What kind? In L. E. Beyer, & M. W. Apple (Eds.), *The curriculum: Problems, politics, and possibilities* (pp. 245–263). Albany, NY: State University of New York Press.

Bianchini, J. A. (1997). Where knowledge construction, equity, and context intersect: Student learning of science in small groups. *Journal of Research in Science Teaching, 34*, 1039–1065.

Bianchini, J. A. (1999). From here to equity: The influence of status on student access to and understanding of science. *Science Education, 83*, 577–601.

Bilimoria, P. (1991). Indian ethics. In P. Singer (Ed.), *A companion to ethics* (pp. 43–57). Oxford: Blackwell.

Bingle, W. H., & Gaskell, P. J. (1994). Scientific literacy for decision making and the social construction of scientific knowledge. *Science Education, 78*(2), 185–201.

Birdsall, S. (2011). Empowering students to act: Learning about, through and from the nature of action. *Australian Journal of Environmental Education*, in press.

Birke, L. (1986). *Women, feminism and biology*. New York: Methuen.

Birke, L. (1994). *Feminism, animals and science: The naming of the shrew*. Philadelphia: Open University Press.

Birkeland, J. (1993). Ecofeminism: Linking theory and practice. In G. Gaard (Ed.), *Ecofeminism: Women, animals, nature*. Philadelphia: Temple University Press.

Bixler, R. D., & Floyd, M. F. (1997). Nature is scary, disgusting, and uncomfortable. *Environment and Behavior, 29*(4), 443–467.

Black, E. (2003). *War against the weak: Eugenics and America's campaign to create a master race*. New York: Thunder's Mouth Press.

Black, G. (2005). *The engaging museum: Developing museums for visitor involvement*. London: RoutledgeFalmer.

Blades, D. (1997). *Procedures of power and curriculum change: Foucault and the quest for possibilities in science education*. New York: Peter Lang.

Bleier, R. (1984). *Gender and science: A critique of biology and its theories on women*. Oxford: Pergamon Press.

Blocker, T. J., & Eckberg, D. L. (1989). Environmental issues as women's issues: General concerns and local hazards. *Social Science Quarterly, 70*(3), 586–593.

Blok, A. (2007). Experts on public trial: On democratizing expertise through a Danish consensus conference. *Public Understanding of Science, 16*, 163–182.

Bloom, J. W. (1992a). The development of scientific knowledge in elementary school children: A context of meaning perspective. *Science Education, 76*(4), 339–413.

Bloom, J. W. (1992b). Contexts of meaning and conceptual integration: How children understand and learn. In R. A. Duschl & R. J. Hamilton (Eds.), *Philosophy of science, cognitive psychology, and educational theory and practice* (pp. 177–194). Albany, NY: State University of New York Press.

Bloor, D. (1974). Popper's mystification of objective knowledge. *Science Studies, 4*, 65–76.

Bloor, M. (2000). The South Wales Miners Federation: Miners' lung and the instrumental use of expertise, 1900–1950. *Social Studies of Science 30*(1), 125–40.

Blume, S. S. (1997). The rhetoric and counter-rhetoric of a 'bionic' technology. *Science, Technology & Human Values, 22*(1), 31–56.

Blume, S. S. (1999). Histories of cochlear implantation. *Social Science & Medicine, 49*, 1257–1268.

Bögeholz, S. (2006). Nature experience and its importance for environmental knowledge, values and action: Recent German empirical contributions. *Environmental Education Research, 12*(1), 65–84.

Bogner, F. X. (2002). The influence of a residential outdoor education programme to pupil's environmental perception. *European Journal of Psychology of Education, 18*, 19–34.

Bohm, D. (1980). *Wholeness and the implicate order.* London: Routledge & Kegan Paul.

Boler, M. (Ed.). (2004). *Democratic dialogue in education: Troubling speech, disturbing silence.* New York: Peter Lang.

Bong, M., & Skaalvik, E. M. (2003). Academic self-concept and self-efficacy: How different are they really? *Educational Psychology Review, 15*, 1–40.

Bonnett, M. (1999). Education for sustainable development: A coherent philosophy for environmental education? *Cambridge Journal of Education, 29*(3), 313–324.

Bonnett, M. (2002). Education for sustainablility as a frame of mind. *Environmental Eduucation Research, 8*(1), 9–20.

Bonnett, M. (2007). Environmental education and the issue of nature. *Journal of Curriculum Studies, 39*(6), 707–721.

Bonnett, M., & Williams, J. (1998). Environmental education and primary children's attitudes towards nature and the enviroment. *Cambridge Journal of Education, 28*(2), 159–174.

Borko, H. (2004). Professional development and teacher learning: Mapping the terrain. *Educational Researcher, 33*, 3–15.

Boseley, S. (2008, November 19). Where lives are cheap. *The Guardian.* Available at: www.guardian.co.uk.

Bostrom, A., Morgan, M.G., Fischoff, B., & Read, D. (1994). What do people know about global climate change? I. Mental models. *Risk Analysis, 14*(6), 959–970.

Bouillion, L., & Gomez, L. (2001). Connecting school and community with science learning: Real world problems and school-community partnerships as contextual scaffolds. *Journal of Research in Science Teaching, 38*(8), 899–917.

Boulter, C. J., & Gilbert, J. K. (1995). Argument and science education. In P. S. M. Costello, & S. Mitchell (Eds.), *Competing and consensual voices: The theory and practice of argumentation* (pp. 84–98). Clevedon, UK: Multilingual Matters.

Bowd, A. (1989). The educational dilemma. In D. Paterson & M. Palmer (Eds.), *The status of animals: Ethics, education and welfare* (pp. 111–122). East Haddam, CT: Humane Education Foundation/CAB International.

Bowers, C. A. (1997). *The culture of denial: Why the environmental movement needs a strategy for reforming universities and public schools.* Albany, NY: State University of New York Press.

Bowers, C. A. (2001). *Educating for eco-justice and community.* Athens, GA: University of Georgia Press.

Bowers, C. A. (2008). Why critical pedagogy of place is an oxymoron. *Environmental Education Research, 14*(3), 325–335.

Bowler, P. (1992). *The Fontana history of the environmental sciences.* London: HarperCollins.

Boyes, E., & Stanisstreet, M. (1993). The 'greenhouse effect': Children's perceptions of causes, consequences and cures. *International Journal of Science Education, 15*(5), 531–552.

Boyes, E., & Stanisstreet, M. (1994). The ideas of secondary school children concerning ozone layer damage. *Global Environmental Change, 4*, 311–324.

Boyes, E., & Stanisstreet, M. (1997). Children's models of understanding of two major global environmental issues (ozone hole and greenhouse effect). *Research in Science & Technological Education, 15*(1), 19–28.

REFERENCES

Boyes, E., & Stanisstreet, M. (1998). High school students' perceptions of how major global environmental effects might cause skin cancer. *Journal of Environmental Education, 29*(2), 31–36.

Boyes, E., Chuckran, D., & Stanisstreet, M. (1993). How do high school students perceive global climate change; what are its manifestations? What are its origins? What corrective actions can be taken? *Journal of Science Education and Technology, 2*(4), 541–557.

Boyes, E., Skamp, K., & Stanisstreet, M. (2009a). Australian secondary students' views about global warming: Beliefs about actions, and willingness to act. *Research in Science Education, 39*, 661–680.

Boyes, E., Skamp, K., & Stanisstreet, M. (2009b). Global warming responses at the primary-secondary interface: 2. Potential effectiveness of education. *Australian Journal of Environmental Education, 25*, 31–44.

Boyes, E., Stanisstreet, M., & Papantoniou, V.S. (1999). The ideas of Greek high school students about the 'ozone layer'. *Science Education, 83*(6), 724–737.

Boyes, E., Stanisstreet, M., & Zhang, Y. (2008). Combating global warming: The ideas of high school students in the growing economy of South East China. *International Journal of Environmental Studies, 65*(2), 233–245.

Brandt, C. B. (2008). Scientific discourse in the academy: A case study of an American Indian undergraduate. *Science Education, 92*(5), 825–847.

Braun, M., Buyer, R., & Randler, C. (2010). Cognitive and motional evaluation of two educational outdoor programs dealing with non-native bird species. *International Journal of Environmental & Science Education, 5*(2), 151–168.

Braund, M., & Reiss, M. (Eds.). (2004). *Learning science outside the classroom.* London: RoutledgeFalmer.

Braund, M., & Reiss, M. (2006). Towards a more authentic science curriculum: The contribution of out-of-school learning. *International Journal of Science Education, 28*(12), 1373–1388.

Brem, S. K., Russell, J., & Weems, L. (2001). Sciencqe on the web: Student evaluations of scientific arguments. *Discourse Processes, 32*(2&3), 191–213.

Brennan, A. (1994). Environmental literacy and educational ideal. *Environmental Values, 3*(1), 3–16.

Bricker, L., & Bell, P. (2008). Conceptualizations of argumentation from science studies and the learning sciences, and their implications for the practices of science education. *Science Education, 9*(293), 473–498.

Brickhouse, N. W. (2001). Embodying science: A feminist perspective on learning. *Journal of Research in Science Teaching, 38*(3), 282–295.

Britzman, D. P. (1992). The terrible problem of knowing thyself: Toward a poststructural account of teacher identity. *Journal of Curriculum Theorizing, 9*(3), 23–46.

Broad, W., & Wade, N. (1982). *Betrayers of the truth.* New York: Simon & Schuster.

Brock-Utne, B. (1987). *Educating for peace: A feminist perspective.* Oxford: Pergamon.

Brody, M. W., Tomkiewicz, W., & Graves, C. (2002). Park visitors' understanding, values and beliefs related to their experience at Midway Geyser Basin, Yellowstone National Park, USA. *International Journal of Science Education, 24*(11), 1119–1141.

Brossard, D., Lewenstein, B., & Bonney, R. (2005). Scientific knowledge and attitude change: The impact of a citizen science project. *International Journal of Science Education, 27*(9), 1099–1121.

Brown, B. E. (2004). Environmental ethics and cosmology: A Buddhist perspective. *Zygon, 39*, 885–900.

Brown, M. S., & Lyons, K. A. (1992). Holes in the ozone layer: A global environmental controversy. In D. Nelkin (Ed.), *Controversy: Politics of technical decisions* (pp. 59–79). Newbury Park, CA: Sage.

Bruchac, J. (1993). The circle is the way to see. In P. Piacenti (Ed.), *Story Earth: Native voices on the environment* (pp. 3–13). San Francisco: Mercury House.

Brundtland, G. H. (1987). *Our common future.* Report of the World Commission on Environment and Development. Oxford: Oxford University Press.

Brush, S. G. (1989). History of science and science education. *Interchange, 20*(2), 60–70.

Brusic, S. A. (1992). Achieving STS goals through experiential learning. *Theory into Practice, 31*(1), 44–51.

Bryant, B. (1995). *Environmental justice: Issues, policies and solutions.* Covelo, CA: Island Press.

Bryant, J., & Zillmann, D. (Eds.). (1986). *Perspectives on media effects.* Mahwah, NJ: Lawrence Erlbaum Associates.

Bryce, T. G. K. (2010). Sardonic science? The resistance to more humanistic forms of science education. *Cultural Studies of Science Education, 5*, 591–612.

Bryce, T., & Gray, D. (2004). Tough acts to follow: The challenges to science teachers presented by iotechnologgical progress. *International Journal of Science Education, 26*(6), 717–733.

Bucchi, M., & Neresini, F. (2008). Science and public participation. In E. J. Hackett, O. Amsterdamska, M. Lynch, & J. Wajcman (Eds.), *The handbook of science and technology studies* (pp. 449–472). Cambridge, MA: MIT Press.

Budgett-Meakin, C. (1992). *Making the future work: Appropriate technology – A teacher's guide.* London: Longman.

Buell, L. (1995). *The environmental imagination: Thoreau, nature writing, and the formation of American culture.* Cambridge, MA: The Belknap Press of Harvard University Press.

Bugliarello, G. (2000). Reflections on technological literacy. *Bulletin of Science, Technology & Society, 2*, 83–89.

Bullard, R. (1993). *Confronting environmental racism: Voices from the grassroots.* Boston: South End Press.

Bullard, R. D., & Johnson, G. S. (2000). Environmental justice: Grassroots activism and its impact on public policy decision making. *Journal of Social Issues, 56*(3), 555–578.

Bullough, R. V. J. (2001). Pedagogical content knowledge circa 1907 and 1987: A study in the history of an idea. *Journal of Teaching and Teacher Education, 17*, 655–666.

Bulte, A. M. W., Westbroek, H. B., De Jong, O., & Pilot, A. (2006). A research approach to designing chemistry education using authentic practices as contexts. *International Journal of Science Education, 28*(9), 1063–1086.

Buntting, C., & Jones, A. (2009). Unpacking the interface between science, technology and the environment: Biotechnology as an example. In A. T. Jones & M. J.deVries (Eds.), *International handbook of research and development in technology education* (pp. 275–285). Rotterdam: Sense Publishers.

Buntting, C., & Ryan, B. (2010). In the classroom: Exploring ethical issues with young pupils. In A. Jones, A. McKim, & M. Reiss (Eds.), *Ethics in the science and technology classroom: A new approach to teaching and learning* (pp. 37–53). Rotterdam: Sense Publishers.

Burbules, N., & Callister, T. (2000). *Watch IT: The risks and promises of information technology.* Boulder, CO: Westview Press.

Burbules, N., & Rice, S. (1991). Dialogue across differences: Continuing the conversation. *Harvard Educational Review, 61*(4), 393–416.

Burgess, A. (2004). *Cellular phones, public fears, and a culture of precaution.* Cambridge: Cambridge University Press.

Burke, G., & Cutter-MacKenzie, A. (2010). What's ther, what if, what then, and what can we do? An immersive and embedded experience of environment and place through children's literature. *Environmental Education Research, 16*(3–4), 311–330.

Burns, J. (1992). Students perceptions of technology and implications for an empowering curriculum. *Research in Science Education, 22*, 72–80.

Burri, R. V., & Dumit, J. (2008). Social studies of scientific imaging and visualization. In E. J. Hackett, O. Amsterdamska, M. Lynch, & J. Wajcman (Eds.), *The handbook of science and technology studies* (pp. 297–317). Cambridge, MA: MIT Press.

Bybee, R. W. (1993). *Reforming science education: Social perspectives and personal reflections.* New York: Teachers College Press.

Bybee, R. W. (1997). Towards an understanding of scientific literacy. In W. Graber & C. Bolte (Eds), *Scientific literacy: An international symposium* (pp. 37–68). Kiel: IPN, University of Kiel.

Bybee, R. (2001). Teaching about evolution: Old controversy, new challenges. *Bioscience, 51*, 309–313.

Bybee, R., & DeBoer, G. (1994). Research on goals for the science curriculum. In D. Gabel (Ed.), *Handbook of research on science teaching and learning* (pp. 357–386). New York: Macmillan.

Cachelin, A., Paisley, K., & Blanchard, A. (2009). Using the significant life experience framework to inform program evaluation: The Nature Conservancy's Wings & Water Wetlands Education program. *Journal of Environmental Education, 40*(2), 2–14.

REFERENCES

Caduto, M. J., & Bruchac, J. (1988). *Keepers of the earth: native American stories and environmental activities for children*. Golden, CO: Fulcrum.

Caine, R. N., & Caine, G. (1991). *Making connections: Teaching and the human brain*. Alexandria, VA: Association for Supervision and Curriculum Devlopment.

Cajas, F. (2001). The science/technology interaction: implications for science literacy. *Journal of Research in Science Teaching, 38*(7), 715–729.

Cajas, F. (2002). Role of research in imporoving technological concepts and skills: The context of technological literacy. *International Journal of Technology and Design Education, 12*(3), 175–188.

Cajete, G. (1994). *Look to the mountain: An eclogy of indigenous education*. Skyand, NC: Kivaki Press.

Cajete, G. (1999). *A people's ecology: Explorations in sustainable living*. Santa Fe, NM: Clear Light Publishers.

Cajete, G. (2000). *Native science: Natural laws of interdependence*. Santa Fe, NM: Clear Light Publishers.

Calabrese Barton, A. (1998a). Margin and center: Intersections of urban, homeless children and a pedagogy of liberation. *Theory into Practice, 37*(4), 296–305.

Calabrese Barton, A. (1998b). Teaching science with homeless children: Pedagogy, representation, and identity. *Journal of Research in Science Teaching, 35*, 379–394.

Calabrese Barton, A. (1998). Reframing 'science for all' through the politics of poverty. *Educational Policy, 12*, 525–541.

Calabrese Barton, A. (2002). Urban science education studies: A commitment to equity, social justice, and a sense of place. *Studies in Science Education, 38*, 1–38.

Calabrese Barton, A., & Tan, E. (2009). The evolution of da heat: Making a case for scientific and technology literacy as robust participation. In A.T. Jones & M. J. deVries (Eds.), *International handbook of research and development in technology education* (pp. 329–346). Rotterdam: Sense Publishers.

Calabrese Barton, A., & Tan, E. (2010). 'It changed our lives': Activism, science, and greening the community. *Canadian Journal of Science, Mathematics and Technology Education, 10*(3), 207–222.

Calabrese Barton, A. Tan, E., & Rivet, A. (2008). Creating hybrid spaces for engaging school science among urban middle school girls. *American Educational Research Journal, 45*(1), 68–103.

Calabrese Bartion, A., & Tobin, K. (2001). Urban science education. *Journal of Research in Science Teaching, 38*(8), 843–846.

Callicott, J. (1994). *Earth's insights*. Berkeley, CA: University of California Press.

Callon, M. (1999). The role of lay people in the production and dissemination of scientific knowledge. *Science, Technology and Society, 4*(1), 81–94.

Callon, M., Lascoumes, P., & Barthe, Y. (2009). *Acting in an uncertain world: An essay on technical democracy* (G. Burchall, Trans.). Boston: MIT Press.

Campbell, T., Medina-Jerez, W., Erdogan, I., & Zhang, D. (2010). Exploring science teachers' attitudes and knowledge about environmental education in three international teaching communities. *International Journal of Environmental & Science Education, 5*(1), 3–29.

Caplan, A. (Ed.). (1992). *When medicine went mad*. Totowa, NY: Humana Press.

Capra, F. (1977, December 10). The tao of physics: Reflections on the cosmic dance. *Saturday Review*, pp. 21–28.

Capra, F. (1983). *The turning point: Science, society and the rising culture*. New York: Bantam.

Capra, F. (1996). *The web of life: A new synthesis of mind and matter*. London: Harper Collins.

Carlson, C. (2005). Youth with influence: The youth planner initiative in Hampton, Virginia. *Children, Youth and Environments, 15*(2), 211–216.

Carlsson, M., & Sanders, D. (2008). School councils as an arena for pupils' participation in collaborative environmental education projects. In A. Reid, B. B. Jensen, J. Nikel, & V. Simovsla (Eds.), *Participation and learning: Perspectives on education and the environment, health and sustainability* (pp. 321–337). New York: Springer.

Carré, C. (1981). *Language, teaching and learning: Science*. London: Ward Lock.

Carson, R. (1965). *The sense of wonder*. New York: Harper & Row.

Carter, L. (2005). Globalisation and science education: Rethinking science education reforms. *Journal of Research in Science Teaching, 42*(5), 561–580.

Carter, L. (2008a). Globalization and science education: The implications of science in the new economy. *Journal of Research in Science Teaching, 45*(5), 617–633.

Carter, L. (2009). Globalisation and learner-centred pedagogies: Some thoughts. *Journal of Activist Science & Technology Education, 1*(1), 57–60.

Carter, L., & Dediwalage, R. (2010). Globalisation and science education: The case of 'Sustainability by the Bay'. *Cultural Studies of Science Education, 5*, 275–291.

Castano, C. (2008). Socio-scientific discussions as a way to improve the comprehension of science and the understanding of the interaction between species and the environment. *Research in Science Education, 38*(5), 565–587.

Cavalieri, P., & Singer, P. (Eds.). (1993). *The great ape project: Equality beyond humanity.* London: Fourth Estate.

Cawthron, E. R., & Rowell, J. A. (1978). Epistemology and science education. *Studies in Science Education, 5*, 31–59.

Celik, S., & Bayrakçeken, S. (2006). The effect of a 'science, technology and society' course on prospective teachers' conceptions of the nature of science. *Research in Science & Technological Education, 24*(2), 255–273.

Cell, E. (1984). *Learning to learn from experience.* Albany, NY: State University of New York Press.

Chalmers, A. F. (1999). *What is this thing called science?* (3rd ed.). Buckingham: Open University Press.

Chalmers, D., & Nicol, D. (2004). Commercialization of biotechnology: Public trust and research. *International Journal of Biotechnology, 6*, 116–133.

Chambers, D. W. (1983). Stereotypic images of the scientist: The draw-a-scientist test. *Science Education, 67*(2), 255–265.

Chapple, C. K. (Ed.). (2002). *Jainism and ecology: Nonviolence in the web of life.* Cambridge, MA: Harvard University Press.

Chapple, C. C., & Tucker, M. E. (2000). *Hinduism and ecology: The intersection of earth, sky and water.* Cambridge, MA: Harvard Divinity School.

Chawla, L. (1998). Significant life experiences revisited: A review of research on sources of environmental sensitivity. *Journal of Environmental Education, 29*(3), 11–21.

Chawla, L. (1999). Life paths into effective environmental action. *Journal of Environmental Education, 31*(1), 15–26.

Chawla, L. (2002). Spots of time: Manifold ways of being in nature in childhood. In P. H. Kahn, & S. R. Kellert (Eds.), *Children and nature: Psychological, sociocultural, and evolutionary investigations* (pp. 119–225). Cambridge, MA: MIT Press.

Chawla, L. (Ed.). (2002b). *Growing up in an urbanising world.* Paris/London: UNESCO.

Chawla, L. (2008). Participation and the ecology of environmental awareness and action. In A. Reid, B. B. Jensen, J. Nikel, & V. Simovsla (Eds.), *Participation and learning: Perspectives on education and the environment, health and sustainability* (pp. 98–110). New York: Springer.

Chawla, L., & Flanders Cushing, D. (2007). Education for strategic environmental behavior. *Environmental Education Research, 13*(4), 437–452.

Cheek, D. W. (1992). *Thinking constructively about science, technology, and society education.* Albany, NY: State University of New York Press.

Cheek, D. W. (2009). Social aspects of technology. In A. Jones & M. de Vries (Eds.), *International handbook of research and development in technology education* (pp. 167–174). Rotterdam: Sense Publishers.

Chen, D., & Novick, R. (1984). Scientific and technological education in an information society. *Science Education, 68*(4), 421–426.

Chenhansa, S., & Schleppegrell, M. (1998). Linguistic features of middle school environmental education texts. *Environmental Education Research, 4*(1), 53–66.

Chiapetta & Fillman. (2007). Analysis of five high school biology textbooks used in the United States for inclusion of the nature of science. *International Journal of Science Education, 29*(15), 1847–1868.

REFERENCES

Chin, P., Munby, H., Hutchinson, N. L., Taylor, J., & Clark, F. (2004). Where's the science? Understanding the form and function of workplace science. In E. Scanlon, P. Murphy, J. Thomas, & E. Whitelegg (Eds), *Reconsideraing Science Learning* (pp. 118–134). London: RoutledgeFalmer.

Chinn, C. A., & Samarapungavan, A. (2008). Learning to use scientific models: Multiple dimensions of conceptual change. In R. A. Duschl & R. E. Grandy (Eds.), *Teaching scientific inquiry: Recommendations for research and implementation* (pp. 191–225). Rotterdam: Sense Publishers.

Chinn, P. W. U. (2006). Preparing science teachers for culturally diverse students; Developing cultural literacy through cultural immersion, cultural translators and communities of practice. *Cultural Studies of Science Education, 1*(2), 367–402.

Chinn, P. W. U. (2007). Decolonizing methodologies and indigenous knowledge: The role of culture, place and personal experience in professional development. *Journal of Research in Science Teaching, 44*(9), 1247–1268.

Cho, K.-L., & Jonassen, D. H. (2002). The effects of argumentation scaffolds on argmentation and problem solving. *Educational Technology, Research & Development, 50*(3), 5–22.

Cho, S. (2010). Politics of critical pedagogy and new social movements. *Educational Philosophy and Theory, 42*(3), 310–325.

Chomsky, N. (1969). *American power and the new mandarins*. Harmondsworth: Penguin.

Chomsky, N. (1991). *Manufacturing consent: Thought control in democratic societies*. Boston: Beacon Press.

Chopra, S. (2009). Globalisation, food security, public health & prosperity focus on India. *Journal of Activist Science & Technology Education, 1*(1), 61–64.

Christidou, V., & Kouladis, V. (1996). Children's models of the ozone layer and ozone depletion. *Research in Science Education, 26*(4), 421–436.

Christie, M. (1991). Aboriginal science for the ecologically sustainable future. *Australian Science Teachers Journal, 37*, 26–31.

Clandinin, J., & Connelly, M. (1996). Teachers' professional knowledge landscapes: Teacher stories – stories of teachers – school stories – stories of schools. *Educational Researcher, 25*(3), 24–30.

Clark, D. B., & Sampson, V. D. (2007). Personally-seeded discussions to scaffold online argumentation. *International Journal of Science Education, 29*(3), 253–277.

Clark, D. B., & Sampson, V. D. (2008). Assessing dialogic argumentation in online environments to relate structure, grounds, and conceptual quality. *Journal of Research in Science Teaching, 45*(3), 293–321.

Clark, D. B., Sampson, V. D., Weinberger, A., & Erkens, G. (2007). Analytic frameworks for assessing dialogic argumentation in online environments. *Educational Psychology Review, 19*(3), 343–374.

Clark, D. B., Stegmann, K., Weinberger, A., Menekse, M., & Erkens, G. (2008). Technology-enhanced learning environments to support students' argumentation. In S. Erduran, & M. P. Jiménez-Aleixandre (Eds.), *Argumentation in science education: Perspectives from classroom-based research* (pp. 217–243). Dordrecht: Kluwer.

Clarkeburn, H. (2002). A test of ethical sensitivity in science. *Journal of Moral Education, 31*(4), 439–453.

Claxton, G. (1991). *Educating the inquiring mind*. London: Harvester Wheatsheaf.

Claxton, G. (1997). Science of the times: A 2020 vision of education. In R. Levinson & J. Thomas (Eds.), *Science today: Problem or crisis?* (pp. 71–86). London: Routledge.

Clough, N. (1998). Emerging from the tunnel: Some dilemmas in environmental education. In C. Holden & N. Clough (Eds.), *Children as citizens: Education for participation* (pp. 63–77). London: Jessica Kingsley Publishers.

Clover, D. E., Follen, S., & Hall, B. (2000). *The nature of transformation: Environmental adult education*. Toronto: Ontario Institute for Studies in Education of the University of Toronto.

Cobern, W. W. (1991). *World view theory and science education research*. NARST Monograph No.3. Manhattan, KS: National Association for Research in Science Teaching.

Cobern, W. (1995). Science education as an exercise in foreign affairs. *Science & Education, 4*(3), 287–302.

Cobern, W. W., & Aikenhead, G. S. (1998). Cultural aspects of learning science. In B. J. Fraser & K.G. Tobin (Eds.), *International handbook of science education* (pp. 39–52). Dordrecht: Kluwer.

Cobern, W. W., Gibson, A. T., & Underwood, S. A. (1999). Conceptualizations of nature: An interpretive study of 16 ninth graders' everyday thinking. *Journal of Research in Science Teaching, 36*(5), 541–564.

Cochran, K. R., Deruiter, J. A., & King, R. A. (1993). Pedagogical content knowing: An integrative model for teacher preparation. *Journal of Teacher Education, 44,* 263–270.

Cocker, M. (2008). *Crow country: A meditation on birds, landscapes and nature.* London: Cape.

Code, L. (1987). *Epistemic responsibility.* Hanover, MA: University of New England Press.

Code, L. (1991). *What can she know?* Ithaca, NY: Cornell University Press.

Code, L. (2000). How to think globally: Stretching the limits of imagination. In U. Narayan & S. Harding (Eds.), *Decentering the centre: Philosophy for a multicultural, postcolonial, and feminist world* (pp. 67–79). Bloomington, IN: Indiana University Press.

Cohen, M.J. (1990). *The world peace university field guide to connecting with nature: Creating moments that let earth teach.* Eugene, OR: World Peace University.

Cohen, S. (2001). *States of denial: Knowing about atrocities and suffering.* Cambridge: Polity Press.

Collins, A., Brown, J. S., & Newman, S. E. (1989). Cognitive apprenticeship: Teaching the craft of reading, writing, and mathematics. In L. B. Resnick (Ed.), *Knowing, learning, and instruction: Essays in honor of Robert Glaser* (pp. 453–494). Hillsdale, NJ: Lawrence Erlbaum.

Collins, H. M., & Evans, R. (2002). The third wave of science studies: Studies of expertise and experience. *Social Studies of Science, 32,* 235–296.

Colucci-Gray, L., Camino, E., Barbiero, G., & Gray, D. (2006). From scientific literacy to sustainability literacy: An ecological framework for education. *Science Education, 90*(2), 227–252.

Connell, S., Fien, J., Sykes, H., & Yenken, D. (1998). Young people and the environment in Australia: beliefs, knowledge, commitment and educational implications. *Australian Journal of Environmental Education, 14,* 39–48.

Connell, S., Fien, J., Lee, J., Sykes, H., & Yenken, D. (1999). If it doesn't directly affect you, you don't think about it: A qualitative study of young people's environmental attitudes in two Australian cities. *Environmental Education Research, 5*(1), 95–113.

Connelly, F. M., & Clandinin, D. J. (1990). Stories of experience and narrative enquiry. *Educational Researcher, 23*(7), 5–12.

Connelly, F. M., & Clandinin, D. J. (2000). Narrative understandings of teacher knowledge. *Journal of Curriculum and Supervision, 15*(4), 315–331.

Conner, L. (2004). Assessing learning about social and ethical issues in a biology class. *School Science Review, 86*(315), 45–51.

Conrad, P. (1999). Uses of expertise: Sources, quotes and voice in the reporting of genetics in the news. *Public Understanding of Science, 8,* 285–302.

Constantinou, C., Hadjilouca, R., & Papadouris, N. (2010). Students' epistemological awareness concerning the distinction between science and technology. *International Journal of Science Education, 32*(2), 143–172.

Conway, R. (2000). Ethical judgements in genetic engineering: The implications for technology education. *International Journal of Technology and Design Education, 10,* 239–254.

Cook, G., Robbins, P. T., & Pieri, E. (2006). 'Words of mass destruction': British newspaper coverage of the gentically modified food debate, expert and non-expert reactions. *Public Understanding of Science, 15,* 5–29.

Cook, V. (2008). The field as a 'pedagogical resource'? A critical analysis of students' affective engagement with the field environment. *Environmental Education Research, 14*(5), 507–517.

Cope, B., & Kalantzis (2000). Introduction – Multiliteracies: The beginnings of an idea. In B. Cope & M. Kalantzis (Eds.), *Multiliteracies: Literacy learning and the design of social futures* (pp. 3–37). London: Routledge.

Corbett, J. B., & Durfee, J. L. (2004). Testing public (un)certainty of science: media representation of global warming. *Science Communication, 26*(2), 129–151.

Corcoran, P. B. (1999). Environmental autobiography in undergraduate educational studies. In G. A. Smith & D. R. Williams (Eds.), *Ecological education in action: On weaving education, culture, and the environment* (pp. 179–188). Albany, NY: State University of New York Press.

Corcoran, P. B. (2004). What if? The educational possibilities of the Earth Charter. *Educational Studies, 36*(1), 108–117.

REFERENCES

Corcoran, P. B., & Sievers, E. (1994). Reconceptualizing environmental education: Five possibilities. *Journal of Environmental Education, 25*(4), 4–8.

Cornelius, I. L., & Herrenkohl, L. R. (2004). Power in the classroom: How the classroom environment shapes students' relationships with each other and with concepts. *Cognition and Instruction, 22*(4), 467–498.

Cornish, E. (1977). *The study of the future: An introduction to the art and science of understanding and shaping tomorrow's world.* Bethesda, MD: World Futures Society.

Corral-Verdugo, V., & Armendariz, L. I. (2000). The 'new environmental paradigm' in a Mexican community. *Journal of Environmental Education, 31*(3), 25–31.

Costa, V. B. (1995). When science is 'another world': Relationships between worlds of family, friends, school, and science. *Science Education, 79*, 313–333.

Cottle, S. (2004). Producing nature(s): On the changing production ecology of natural history TV. *Media, Culture and Society, 26*(1), 81–101.

Cotton, D. R. E. (2006). Teaching controversial environmental issues: neutrality and balanbce in the reality of the classroom. *Educational Research, 48*(2), 223–241.

Council of Ministers of Education, Canada. (1997). *Common framework of science learning outcomes.* Toronto: CMEC Secretariat.

Courtenay-Hall, P. (1997). Environmental education in a democratic society. In A. Wellington, A. Greenbaum, & W. Cragg (Eds.), *Canadian issues in environmental ethics* (pp. 363–385). Toronto: Broadview Press.

Courtenay-Hall, P., & Rogers, L. (2002). Gaps in mind: Problems in environmental knowledge-behaviour modelling research. *Environmental Education Research, 8*(3), 283–297.

Crasnow, S. (2008). Feminist philosophy of science: 'Standpoint' and knowledge. *Science & Education, 17*(10), 1089–1110.

Critchley, C. R. (2008). Public opinion and trust in scientists: The role of the research context, and the perceived motivation of stem cell researchers. *Public Understanding of Science, 17*, 309–327.

Cromer, A. (1993). *Uncommon sense: The heretical nature of science.* Oxford: Oxford University Press.

Cross, R. T., & Price, R. F. (1996). Science teachers' social conscience and the role of controversial issues in the teaching of science. *Journal of Research in Science Teaching, 33*, 319–333.

Cross, R. T., & Price, R. F. (2002). Teaching controversial science for social responsibility: The case of food production. In W.-M. Roth & J. Désautels (Eds.), *Science education as/for socioploitical action* (pp. 99–123). New York: Peter Lang.

Crossley, M., & Watson, K. (2003). *Comparative and international research in education: Globalisation, context and difference.* London: RoutledgeFalmer.

Cupitt, D. (1991). *What is a story?* London: SCM Press.

Curran, S. R., & de Sherbinin, A. (2004). Completing the picture: The challenges of bringing 'consumption' into the population-environment equation. *Population and Environment, 26*(2), 107–131.

Curtin, D. (1991). Toward an ecological ethic of care. *Hypatia, 6*, 60–74.

Curtin, D. (2007). Toward an ecological ethic of care. In J. Donovan & C. J. Adams (Eds.), *The feminist care tradition in animal ethics* (pp. 87–104). New York: Columbia University Press.

Dagher, Z. R., & BouJaoude, S. (1997). Scientific views and religious beliefs of college students: The case of biological evolution. *Journal of Research in Science Teaching, 34*, 429–445.

Dagher, Z. R., & BouJaoude, S. (2005). Students' perceptions of the nature of evolutionary theory. *Science Education, 89*(3), 378–391.

Dahlberg, L. (2005). The corporate colonization of online attention and the margimalization of critical communication. *Journal of Communication Inquiry, 29*(2), 160–180.

Dakers, J. R. (Ed.). (2006). *Defining technological literacy: towards an epistemological framework.* New York: PalgraveMacmillan.

Daly, H. E. (1991). *Steady-state economics.* Washington, DC: Island Press.

Daniel, B., Stanisstreet, M., & Boyes, E. (2004). How can we best reduce global warming? School students' ideas and misconceptions. *International Journal of Environmental Studies, 61*(2), 211–222.

Danielewicz, J. (2001). *Teaching selves: Identity, pedagogy and teacher education.* Albany, NY: State University of New York Press.

Danserau, D. F. (1985). Learning strategy research. In J. Segal, S. Chipman, & R. Glaser (Eds.), *Thinking and learning skills: Relating instruction to research* (Vol. 1, pp. 209–239). Hillsdale, NJ: Erlbaum.

Dass, P. M. (2005). Understanding the nature of scientific enterprise (NOSE) through a discourse with its history: The influence of an undergraduate 'history of science' course. *International Journal of Science and Mathematics Education,* (391), 87–115.

Dator, J. (Ed.). (2002). *Advancing futures: Futures studies in higher education.* Westport, CT: Praeger.

Davies, I. (2004). Science and citizenship education. *International Journal of Science Education, 26*(14), 1751–1763.

Davidson, S. K., Passmore, C., & Anderson, D. (2010). Learning on zoo field trips: The interaction of the agendas and practices of students, teachers, and zoo educators. *Science Education, 94*(1), 122–141.

Davis, M. (1999). *Ethics and the University.* London: Routledge.

Dawkins, R. (1986). *The blind watchmaker: Why the evidence of evolution reveals a universe without design.* New York: W.W. Norton.

Dawkins, R. (1998). *Unweaving the rainbow: Science, delusion, and the appetite for wonder.* New York: Houghton Mifflin.

Dawson, V. (2007). An exploration of high school (12-17 year old) students' understandings of, and attitudes towards biotechnology processes. *Research in Science Education, 37*(1), 59–73.

Dawson, V. (2010). Outcomes of bioethics education in secondary school science: two Australian case studies. In A. Jones, A. McKim, & M. Reiss (Eds.), *Ethics in the science and technology classroom: A new approach to teaching and learning* (pp. 69–86). Rotterdam: Sense Publishers.

Dawson, V., & Schibeci, R. (2003). Western Australian school students' understanding of biotechnology. *International Journal of Science Education, 25,* 57–69.

Dawson, V., & Taylor, P. (2004). Do adolescents' bioethical decisions differ from those of experts? *Journal of Biological Education, 34*(4), 184–188.

Dawson, V. M., & Venville, G. J. (2009). High school students' informal reasoning and argumentation about biotechnology: An indicator of scientific literacy? *International Journal of Science Education, 31*(11), 1421–1445.

Dawson, V. M., & Venville, G. (2010). Teaching strategies for developing students' argumentation skills about socioscientific issues in high school genetics. *Research in Science Education, 40,* 133–148.

Day, C., & Leitch, R. (2001). Teachers' and teacher educators' lives: The role of emotion. *Teaching and Teacher Education, 17,* 403–415.

Deakin, R. (2000). *Waterlog: A swimmer's journey through Britain.* London: Vintage.

Deakin, R. (2007). *Wildwood: A journey through trees.* London: Hamish Hamilton.

Dearden, R. F. (1981). Controversial issues in the curriculum. *Journal of Curriculum Studies, 13,* 37–44.

DeBoer, G. (2001). Scientific literacy: Another look at its historical and contemporary meanings and its relationship to science education reform. *Journal of Research in Science Teaching, 37*(6), 582–601.

DeBono, E. (1992). *Six thinking hats for schools. Book 3 (lower secondary).* Cheltenham (Victoria): Hawker Bornwlow Education.

Dei, G. J. S. (2010). The environment, climate change, ecological sustainability, and anti-racist education. In F. Kagawa & D. Selby (Eds.), *Education and climate change: Living and learning in interesting times* (pp. 89–105). London: Routledge.

De Jong, O., & Van Driel, J. (2004). Exploring the development of student teachers' PCK of the multiple meanings of chemistry. *International Journal of Science and Mathematics Education, 2,* 477–491.

De Jong, O., Van Driel, J., & Verloop, N. (2005). Preservice teachers' pedagogical content knowledge of using particle models when teaching chemistry. *Journal of Research in Science Teaching, 42,* 947–964.

De Jong, T. (2006). Scaffolds for scientific discovery learning. In J. Elen & D. Clark (Eds.), *Handling complexity in learning environments: Research and theory* (pp. 107–128). London: Elsevier.

De Klerk Wolters, F., Raat, J. H., & De Vries, M. J. (1990). Assessing students' attitudes towqards technology. In D. Layton (Ed.), *Innovations in science and technology education* (Vol. III, pp. 111–121). Paris: UNESCO.

REFERENCES

Delanty, G. (1999). Biopolitics in the risk society: The possibility of a global ethic of societal responsibility. In P. O'Mahony (Ed.), *Nature, risk and responsibility: Discourses of biotechnology* (pp. 37–51). Houndmills, UK: Macmillan.

De Luca, R. (2010). Using narrative for ethical thinking. In A. Jones, A. McKim, & M. Reiss (Eds.), *Ethics in the science and technology classroom: A new approach to teaching and learning* (pp. 87–101). Rotterdam: Sense Publishers.

Demastes, S. S., Good, R. G., & Peebles, P. (1995). Students' conceptual ecologies and the process of conceptual change in evolution. *Science Education, 79*(6), 637–666.

Department of Education (Republic of South Africa). (2002). *Revised national curriculum statement for grades R-9 (schools) – Natural sciences*. Pretoria: Department of Education [*Government Gazette*, Vol. 443, No. 23406].

De Silva, (1991). Buddhist ethics. In P. Singer (Ed.), *A companion to ethics* (pp. 58–68). Oxford: Blackwell.

Desjean-Perrota, B., Moseley, C., & Cantu, L. E. (2008). Pre-service teachers' perceptions of the environment: Does ethnicity or dominant residence experience matter? *Journal of Environmental Education, 39*(2), 21–31.

Dettmann-Easler, D., & Pease, J. L. (1999). Evaluating the effectiveness of residential environmental education programs in fostering positive attitudes towards wildlife. *Journal of Environmental Education, 31*(1), 33–39.

Devall, B., & Sessions, G. (1985). *Deep ecology*. Layton, UT: Peregrine Smith.

Devine-Wright, P., Devine-Wright, H., & Fleming, P. (2004). Situational influences upon children's beliefs about global warming and energy. *Environmental Education Research, 10*(4), 493–506.

De Vries, M. J. (2005). *Teaching about technology: An introduction to the philosophy of technology for non-philosophers* (Vol. 27). Dordrecht: Springer.

Diamond, I. (1994). *Fertile ground: Women, earth and the limits of control*. Boston: Beacon.

Diamond, I., & Orenstein, G. F. (1990). *Reweaving the world: the emergence of ecofeminism*. San Francisco: Sirerra Club Books.

Diamond, J. M. (1982). Man the exterminator. *Nature, 298*(5877), 787–789.

Dillon, P. J. (1993). Technological education and the environment. *International Journal of Science Education, 15*, 575–589.

Dillon, J. (2003). On learners and learning in environmental education: Missing theories, ignored communities. *Environmental Education Research, 9*(2), 215–226.

Dillon, J. (2009). On scientific literacy and curriculum reform. *International Journal of Environmental & Science Education, 4*(3), 201–213.

Dillon, J., & Tearney, K. (2002). Reconceptualising environmental education: Taking account of reality. *Canadian Journal of Science, Mathematics and Technology Education, 2*(4), 467–483.

Dimopoulos, K., & Koulaidis, V. (2003). Science and technology education for citizenship: The potential role of the press. *Science Education, 87*(2), 241–256.

Disinger, J. (1990). Environmental education for sustainable development. *Journal of Environmental Education, 21*(4), 3–6.

Dispensa, J. M., & Brulle, R. J. (2003). Media's social construction of environmental issues: Focus on global warming – a comparative study. *International Journal of Sociology and Social Policy, 23*(10), 74–105.

Djerking, L. D. (2005). Museums, affexct, and cognition: The view from another window. In S. Alsop (Ed.), *The affective dimensions of cognition: Studies from education in the sciences* (pp. 111–12). Dordrecht: Kluwer.

Dobson, A. (1996). Environment sustainabilies: An anlysis and a typology. *Environmental Politics, 5*(3), 401–428.

Dodds, R. E., Tseëlon, E., & Weitkamp, E. L. C. (2008). Making sense (of) scientific claims in advertising: A study of scientifically aware consumers. *Public Understanding of Science, 17*, 211–230.

Dogan, N., & Abd-El-Khalick, F. (2008). Turkish grade 10 students' and science teachers' conceptions of nature of science: A national study. *Journal of Research in Science Teaching, 45*(10), 1083–1112.

Dole, J. A., & Sinatra, G. M. (1998). Reconceptualizing change in the cognitive construction of knowledge. *Educational Psychologist, 33*(2/3), 109–128.

Donnelly, J. (1999). Interpreting differences: The educational aims of teachers of science and history, and their implications. *Journal of Curriculum Studies, 31*(1), 17–41.

Donnelly, J. (2004). Ethics and the science curriculum. *School Science Review, 87*(315), 29–32.

Donnelly, J. (2005). Reforming science in the school curriculum: A critical analysis. *Oxford Review of Education, 31*(2), 293–309.

Donnelly, L. A., Kazempour, M., & Amirshokoohi, A. (2009). High school students' perceptions of evolutuion instruction: Acceptance and evolution learning experiences. *Research in Science Education, 39*(5), 643–660.

Donovan, J., & Adams, C. J. (Eds.). (2007), *The feminist care tradition in animal ethics.* New York: Columbia University Press.

Dori, Y. J., & Herscovitz, O. (1999). Question posing capability as an alternative evaluation method: Analysis of an envionmental case study. *Journal of Research in Science Teaching, 36*, 411–430.

Dori, Y. J., & Tal, R. T. (2000). Formal and informal collaborative projects: Engaging industry with environmental awareness. *Science Education, 84*(1), 95–113.

Dori, Y. J., Tal, R., & Tsaushu, M. (2003). Teaching biotechnology through case studies: Can we improve higher order thinking skills of nonscience majors? *Science Education, 87*(6), 767–793.

Dos Santos, W. L. P. (2009). Scientific literacy: A Freirean perspective as a radical view of humanistic science education. *Science Education, 93*(2), 361–382.

Doster, E. C., Jackson, D. F., Oliver, J. S., Crockett, D. K., & Emory, A. L. (1997). *Values, dissection, and school science: An inquiry into students' construction of meaning.* Proceedings of the 1997 annual international conference of the Association for the Education of Science Teachers. Columbus, OH: ERIC Document service, ED405220.

Dove, J. (1996). Student teacher understanding of the greenhouse effect, ozone layer depletion and acid rain. *Environmental Education Research, 2*(1), 89–100.

Dowdeswell, E. (1996, February). *Sharing responsibilities in a competitive world.* A speech to the conference on sustainable industrial development. Amsterdam.

Drake, F. (2006). Mobile phone masts: Protesting the scientific evidence. *Public Understanding of Science, 15*(4), 387–410.

Driskell, D. (2002). *Creating better cities with children and youth: A manual for participation.* Paris: UNESCO.

Driver, L., Stanisstreet, M., & Boyes, E. (2010). Young people's views about nuclear power to reduce global warming. *International Journal of Environmental Studies, 67*(1), 1–3.

Driver, R., Leach, J., Millar, R., & Scott, P. (1996). *Young people's images of science.* Buckingham: Open University Press.

Driver, R., Newton, P., & Osborne, J. (2000). Establishing the norms of scientific argumentation in classrooms. *Science Education, 84*(3), 287–312.

Drori, G. S. (1998). A critical appraisal of science education for economic development. In W. W. Cobern (Ed.), *Socio-cultural perspectives on science education* (pp. 49–74). Dordrecht: Kluwer.

Dubiel, R. F., Hasiotis, S. T., & Semken, S. C. (1997). Hands-on geology for Navajo Nation teachers. *Journal of Geoscience Education, 45*(2), 113–116.

Duggan, S., & Gott, R. (2002) What sort of science education do we really need? *International Journal of Science Education, 24*, 661–679.

Dunbar, K. (1995). How scientists really reason: Scientific reasoning in real-world laboratories. In R. J. Sternberg & J. E. Davidson (Eds.), *The nature of insight* (pp. 365–395). Cambridge, MA: MIT Press.

Duncan, A. (2008). To dissect or not: Student choice-in-dissection laws ensure the freedom to choose. *Journal of Law & Education, 37*(2), 283–289.

Dunlap, R. E., Gallup, G. H., & Gallup, A. M. (1993). 'Of global concern': Results of the health of the planet survey. *Environment, 35*, 7–15 & 33–40.

Dunlap, R. E., & van Liere, K. D. (1978). The new environmental paradigm: A proposed measuring instrument and preliminary results. *Journal of Environmental Education, 9*(4), 10–19.

REFERENCES

Dunwoody, S. (1993). *Reconstructing science for public consumption: Journalism as science education*. Geelong: Deakin University Press.

Dunwoody, S. (1999). Scientists, journalists, and the meaning of uncertainty. In S. M. Friedman, S. Dunwoody, & C. L. Rogers (Eds.), *Communicating Uncertainty* (pp. 59–79). Mahwah, NJ: Lawrence Erlbaum Associates.

Duschl, R. A. (2008). Quality argumentation and epistemic criteria. In S. Erduran & M. P. Jiménez-Aleixandre (Eds.), *Argumentation in science education: Perspectives from classroom-based research* (pp. 159–178). Dordrecht: Kluwer.

Duschl, R. A., & Osborne, J. (2002). Supporting and promoting argumentation discourse in science education. *Studies in Science Education, 38*, 39–72.

Duschl, R. A., Schweingruber, H. A., & Shouse, A. W. (Eds.) (2007). *Taking science to school: Learning and teaching science in grades K-8*. Washington, DC: The National Academies Press.

Duster, T. (1990). *Backdoor to eugenics*. New York: Routledge. [2nd ed.: 2003].

Dyrenfurth, M., & Kozak, M. (Eds.). (1991). *Technolgoical literacy*. Peoria, IL: Glencoe, McGraw-Hill.

Dyson, S. (2005). *Ethnicity and screening for sickle cell/thalassaemia: Lessons for practices from the voices of experience*. New York: Elsevier Churchill Livingstone.

Eagles, P. F. J., & Demare, R. (1999). Factors influencing children's environmental attitudes. *Journal of Environmental Education, 30*(4), 33–37.

Earl, L. (2003). *Assessment as learning: Using classroom assessment to maximize student learning*. Thousand Oaks, CA: Corwin Press.

Earle, J., & Diffenderfer, M. (1997). Fostering a sense of place: Bioregional education in theory and practice. *International Journal of Environmental Education and Information, 16*(3), 225–236.

Eckberg, D. L., & Blocker, T. J. (1989). Varieities of religious involvement and environmental concetrns: Testing the Lynn White thesis. *Journal for the Scientific Study of Religion, 28*(4), 509–517.

Eckberg, D. L., & Blocker, T. J. (1996). Christianity, environmentalism, and the theoretical problem of fundamentalism. *Journal for the Scientific Study of Religion, 35*(4), 343–355.

Eckersley, R. (1999). Dreams and expectations: Young people's expected and preferred futures and their significance for education. *Futures, 31*(1), 73–90.

Eckersley, R. (2002). Future visions, social realities and private lives: Young people and their personal well-being. In J. Gidley & S. Inayatullah (Eds.), *Youth futures: Comparative research and transformatory visions* (pp. 31–42). London: Praeger.

Eder, E. (1999). From sceptiicism to the urge to take action, or from daily frustration to a solo initiative. *Cambridge Journal of Education, 29*(3), 355–365.

Edis, T. (2007). *An illusion of harmony: Science and religion in Islam*. Amherst, NY: Prometheus Books.

Edwards, D. (2006). *Ecology at the hearty of faith*. MaryKnoll, NY: Orbis Books.

Edwards, D., & Mercer, N. (1987). *Common knowledge: The development of understanding in the classroom*. London: Methuen.

Eggert, S., & Bögeholz, S. (2010). Students' use of decision-making strategies with regard to socioscientific issue: an application of the Rasch partial credit model. *Science Education, 94*(2), 230–258.

Eisenberg, N., & Miller, P. (1987). The relation of empathy to prosocial and related behaviors. *Psychological Bulletin, 101*, 91–119.

Elam, M., & Bertillson, M. (2003) Consuming, engaging and confronting science: The emerging dimensions of scientific citizenship. *European Journal of Social Theory, 6*(2), 233–251.

El-Hani, C. N., & Bandeira, F. P. S. (2008). Valuing indigenous knowledge: To call it 'science' will not help. *Cultural Studies of Science Education, 3*, 751–779.

Elliot, R. (1991). Environmental ethics. In P. Singer (Ed.), *A companion to ethics* (pp. 284–293). Oxford: Blackwell.

Elliott, J. (1999). Sustainable society and environmental education: Future perspectives and demands for the educational system. *Cambridge Journal of Education, 29*(3), 325–340.

Elliott, P. (2006). Reviewing newspaper articles as a technique for enhancing the scientific literacy of student-teachers. *International Journal of Science Education, 28*(11), 1245–1265.

Elshof, L. (2001). *Worldview research with technology teachers.* Toronto: Unpublished PhD thesis, University of Toronto.

Elshof, L. (2005). Teachers's interpretation of sustainable development. *International Journal of Technology and Design Education, 15*(2), 173–186.

Elshof, L. (2006). Productivism and the product paradigm in technological education. *Journal of Technology Education, 17*(2), 18–32.

Elshof, L. (2009a). Toward sustainable practices in technology education. *International Journal of Technology and Design Education, 19*(2), 133–147.

Elshof, L. (2009b). Transcending the age of stupid: Learning to imagine ourselves differently. *Journal of Activist Science & Technology Education, 1*(1), 44–56.

Emdin, C. (2010). *Urban science education for the hip-hop generation: Essential tools for the urban science educator and researcher.* Rotterdam: Sense Publsihers.

Emmons, K. M. (1997). Perceptions of the enviroment while exploring the outdoors: A case study in Belize. *Environmental Education Research, 3*(3), 327–344.

Endreny, A. H. (2010). Urban 5th graders' conceptions during a [lace-based inquiry unit on watersheds. *Journal of Research in Science Teaching, 47*(5), 501–517.

Engle, R. A., & Conant, F. R. (2002). Guiding principles for fostering productive disciplinary engagement: Explaining an emergent argument in a community of learners classroom. *Cognition and Instruction, 20*(4), 399–483.

English, L. D. (2002). Priority themes and issues in international research on mathematics education. In L. D. English (Ed.), *Handbook of international research in mathematics education* (pp. 3–15). Mahwah, NJ: Lawrence Erlbaum/National Council of Teachers of Mathematics.

Entwistle, N. (1981). *Styles of learning and teaching.* Chichester: John Wiley.

Epstein, S. (1995). The construction of lay expertise: AIDS activism and the forging of credibility in the reform of clinical trials. *Science, Technology & Human Values, 20*, 408–437.

Epstein, S. (1996). *Impure science: AIDS, activism, and the politics of knowledge.* Berkeley, CA: University of California Press.

Epstein, S. (1997). Activism, drug regulation, and the politics of therapeutic evaluation in the AIDS era: A case study of ddC and the 'surrogate markers' debate. *Social Studies of Science, 27*, 691–726.

Epstein, S. (2008). Patient groups and health movements. In E. J. Hackett, O. Amsterdamska, M. Lynch, & J. Wajcman (Eds.), *The handbook of science and technology studies* (pp. 499–539). Cambridge, MA: MIT Press.

Erduran, S. (2006). Promoting ideas, evidence and argument in initial teacher training. *School Science Review, 87*(321), 45–50.

Erduran, S., Simon, S., & Osborne, J. (2004). TAPping into argumentation: developments in the application of Toulmin's argument pattern for studying science discourse. *Science Education, 88*(6), 915–933.

Etzkowitz, H. (2003). Innovation in innovation: The triple helix in university-industry-government relations. *Social Science Information, 42*(3), 293–337.

Etzkowitz, H., & Leydesdorff, L. (Eds.). (1997). *Universities and the global knowledge economy: A triple helix of university-industry-government relations.* London: Cassell.

Etzkowitz, H., & Leydesdorff, L. (2000). The dynamics of innovation: From national systems and 'mode 2' to a triple helix of university-industry-government relations. *Research Policy, 29*(2), 109–123.

Etzkowitz, H., Fuchs, S., Gupta, M., Kemelgor, C., & Ranga, M. (2008). The coming gender revolution in science. In E. J. Hackett, O. Amsterdamska, M. Lynch, & J. Wajcman (Eds.), *The handbook of science and technology studies* (pp. 403–428). Cambridge, MA: MIT Press.

Etzkowitz, H., Kemelgor, C., & Uzzi, B. (Eds.). (2000). *Athena unbound: The advancement of women in science and technology.* Cambridge: Cambridge University Press.

Evans, R., & Plows, A. (2007). Listening without prejudice? Re-discovering the value of the disinterested citizen. *Social Studies of Science, 37*(6), 827–853.

Evernden, N. (1985). *The natural alien: Humankind and environment.* Toronto: University of Toronto Press.

Evernden, N, (1992). *The social construction of nature.* Baltimore: Johns Hopkins University Press.

REFERENCES

Falk, H., & Yarden, A. (2009). 'Here the scientists explain what I said': Coordination practices elicited during the enabctment of the results and discussion sections of adapted primary literature. *Research in Science Education, 39*, 349–383.

Falk, J. H. (2001). *Free-choice science education: How we learn science outside school.* New York: Teachers College Press.

Falk, J. H. (2009, April). *Public understanding of science: Where and why people learn science.* Paper presented at the annual conference of the National Association for Research in Science Teaching, Garden Grove, CA.

Falk, J. H., & Dierking, L. D. (2000). *Learning from museums: Visitor experiences and the making of meaning.* Walnut Creek, CA: Altamira Press.

Fang, Z. (2005). Scientific literacy: A systematic functional linguistics perspective. *Science Education, 89*(2), 335–347.

Farkas, N. (1999). Dutch science shops: Matching community needs with university R&D. *Science Studies, 12*, 33–47.

Farmelo, G. (1997) From big bang to damp squib? In R. Levinson & J. Thomas (Eds.), *Science today: Problem or crisis?* (pp. 175–191). London: Routledge.

Fedigan, L. (1986). The changing role of women in models of human evolution. *Annual Review of Anthropology, 15*, 25–66.

Fee, E. (1979). Nineteenth century craniology: The study of the female skull. *Bulletin of the History of Medicine, 53*, 415–433.

Felton, M. (2004). The development of discourse strategies in adolescent argumentation. *Cognitive Development, 19*, 35–52.

Fensham, P. J. (1988). Approaches to the teaching of STS in science education. *International Journal of Science Education, 10*(4), 346–356.

Fensham, P. J. (1998). The politics of legitimating and marginalizing companion meanings: Three Australian case stories. In D. A. Roberts & L. Östman (Eds.), *Problems of meaning in science curriculum* (pp. 178–192). New York: Teachers College Press.

Fenstermacher, G. D. (1997). On narrative. *Teaching and Teacher Education, 13*(1), 119–124.

Feyerabend, P. K. (1975). *Against method: Outline of an anarchistic theory of knowledge.* London: New Left Books.

Feynman, R. (1965). *The character of physical law.* Cambridge, MA: MIT Press.

Feynman, R. P. (1969). What is science? *The Physics Teacher, 7*(6), 313–320.

Fielding, M. (2004). Transformative approaches to student voice: Theoretical underpinnings, recalcitrant realities. *British Educational Research Journal, 30*(4), 295–311.

Fien, J. (Ed.). (1989). *Living in a global environment: Classroom activities in development education.* Brisbane: Australian Geography Teachers Association.

Fien, J. (1993a). *Environmental education: A pathway to sustainability?* Geelong: Deakin university Press.

Fien, J. (1993b). *Education for the environment: Critical curriculum theorizing and environmental education.* Geelong: Deakin University Press.

Fien, J. (1998). Environmental education for a new century. In D. Hicks & R. Slaughter (Eds.), *Futures education. World yearbook of education 1998* (pp. 245–258). London: Kogan Page.

Finch, P. (1989). Learning from the past. In D. Paterson & M. Palmer (Eds.), *The status of animals: Ethics, education and welfare* (pp. 64–72). East Haddam, CT: Humane Education Foundation/CAB International.

Finkler, K. (2000). *Experiencing the new genetics: Family and kinship on the medical frontier.* Philadelphia: University of Pennsylvania Press.

Finkler, K., Skrzynia, C., & Evans, J. P. (2003). The new genetics and its consequences for family, kinship, medicine and medical genetics. *Social Science and Medicine, 57*(3), 403–12.

Finson, K. D. (2002). Drawing a scientist: What we do and do not know after fifty years of drawing. *School Science & Mathematics, 102*(7), 335–345.

Finson, K. D. (2003). Applicability of the DAST-C to the images of scientists drawn by students of different racial groups. *Journal of Elementary Science Education, 15*(1), 15–27.

Fisher, B. (1998a). There's a hole in my greenhouse effect. *School Science Review, 79*(288), 93–99.

Fisher, B. W. (1998b). Australian students' appreciation of the greenhouse effect and the ozone hole. *Australian Science Teachers' Journal*, (4493), 46–55.

Fitzpatrick, F. L. (Ed.). (1960). *Policies for science education*. New York: Teachers College Press.

Fleming, R. (1986a). Adolescent reasoning in socio-scientific issues. Part I – Social cognition. *Journal of Research in Science Teaching, 23*, 677–687.

Fleming, R. (1986b). Adolescent reasoning in socio-scientific issues. Part II – Non-social cognition. *Journal of Research in Science Teaching, 23*, 689–698.

Fletcher, A. C., Elder, G., & Mekos, D. (2000). Parental influences on adolescent involvement in community activities. *Journal of Research on Adolescence, 10*(1), 29–48.

Flogaitis, E., & Agelidou, E. (2003). Kindergarten teachers' conceptions about nature and the environment. *Environmental Education Research, 9*(4), 461–478.

Flores, V. S., & Tobin, A. J. (2003). Genetically modified (GM) foods & teaching critical thinking. *American Biology Teacher, 65*(3), 180–184,

Flynn, B. (2008). Planning cells and citizen juries in environmental policy: Deliberation and its limits. In F. H. J. M. Coenen (Ed.), *Public participation and better environmental decisions: The promise and limits of participatory processes for the quality of environmentally related decision-making* (pp. 57–72). Dordrecht: Springer.

Foot, P. (1978). *Virtues and vices*. Oxford: Blackwell.

Foot, P. (2001). *Natural goodness*. Oxford: Clarendon Press.

Forbes, C. T., & Davis, E. A. (2008). Exploring preservice elementary teachers' critique and adaptation of science curriculum materials in respect to socioscientific issues. *Science & Education, 17*, 829–854.

Ford, M. (2008). Disciplinary authority and accountability in scientific practice and learning. *Science Education, 92*(3), 404–423.

Forester, J. (2006). Exploring urban practice in a democratising society: Opportunities, techniques and challenges. *Development Southern Africa, 23*(5), 569–586.

Fortner, R., Lee, J., Corney, J., Romanello, S., Luthy, B., et al. (2000). Public understanding of climate change: Certainty and willingness to act. *Environmental Education Research, 6*(2), 127–141.

Foster, C., Stanisstreet, M., & Boyes, E. (1994). Children's attitudes to the use of animals in education and research: What are their justifications and reservations? *School Science Review, 76*(275), 39–44.

Fourez, G. (1982). *Liberation ethics*. Philadelphia: Temple University Press.

Fourez, G. (1997). Scientific and technological literacy as a social practice. *Social Studies of Science, 27*(6), 903–936.

Fowler, S. R., Zeidler, D. L., & Sadler, T. D. (2009). Moral sensitivity in the context of socioscientific issues in high school science students. *International Journal of Science Education, 31*(2), 279–296.

Fox, M. F. (2001). Women, science, and academia: Graduate education and careers. *Gender & Society, 15*, 654–66.

France, B. (2007). Location, location, location: Positioning biotechnolgy education for the 21st century. *Studies in Sience Education, 43*, 88–122.

Francis, C., Boyes, E., Qualter, A., & Stanisstreet, M. (1993). Ideas of elemntary students about reducing the 'greenhouse effect'. *Science Education, 77*(4), 375–392.

Freire, P. (1972). *Pedagogy of the oppressed*. London: Penguin.

Freire, P. (1973). *Education for critical consciousness*. New York: Continuum.

Freire, P. (1993). *Pedagogy of the city*. New York: Continuum.

Freire, P. (2004). *Pedagogy of indignation*. Boulder, CO: Paradigm Publishers.

Freire, P., & Schor, I. (1987). *A pedagogy for liberation*. London: Macmillan.

Frewer, L. J., Howard, C., & Shepherd, R. (1997). Public concerns in the United Kingdom about general and specific applications of genetic engineering: Risk, benefit and ethics. *Science, Technology & Human Values, 22*(1), 98–124.

Frewer, L., Hunt, S., Brennan, M., Kuznesof, S., Ness, M., & Ritson, C. (2003). The views of scientiific experts on how the public conceptualise uncertainty. *Journal of Risk Research, 6*(1), 75–85.

REFERENCES

Friedman, S. M., Dunwoody, S., & Rogers, C. L. (Eds.). *Communicating uncertainty*. Mahwah, NJ: Lawrence Erlbaum Associates.

Fryer, P. (1984). *Staying power: The history of black people in Britain*. London: Pluto Press.

Fuller, S. (1993). *Philosophy, rhetoric, and the end of knowledge: The coming of science and technology studies*. Madison, WI: University of Wisconsin Press. [2nd ed., with Collier, J. H. (2004). *Philosophy, rhetoric, and the end of knowledge: A new beginning for science and technology studies*. Mahwah, NJ: Lawrence Erlbaum Associates].

Fuller, S. (2000). *The goverance of science: Ideology and the future of the open society*. Buckingham: Open University Press.

Fullick, P., & Ratcliffe, M. (Eds.). (1996). *Teaching ethical aspects of science*. Totton: Bassett Press.

Fung, Y. Y. H. (2002). A comparative study of primary and secondary school students' images of scientists. *Research in Science & Technological Education, 20*(2), 199–213.

Funtowicz, S. O., & Ravetz, J. (1993). Science for the post-normal age. *Futures, 25*, 739–755.

Furberg, A., & Ludvigsen, S. (2008). Students' meaning-making of socioscientific issues in computer mediated settings: Exploring learning through interaction trajectories. *International Journal of Science Education, 30*(13), 1775–1799.

Furman, G., & Gruenewald, D. (2004). Expanding the landscape of social justice: A critical ecological perspective. *Educational Administration Quarterly, 40*(1), 47–76.

Gaard, G. (Ed.). (1993). *Ecofeminism: Women, animals, nature*. Philadelphia: Temple University Press.

Gagel, C. W. (1997). Literacy and technology: Reflections and insights for technological literacy. *Journal of Industrial Teacher Education, 34*(3), 6–34.

Galbraith, D. (1999). Writing as a knowledge-constituting process. In D. G. M. Torrance (Ed.), *Knowing what to write: Conceptual processes in text production* (pp. 139–159). Amsterdam: Amsterdam University Press.

Gamarnikow, E., & Green, A. (2000). Citizenship, education and social capital. In D. Lawton, J. Cairns, & R. Gardner (Eds.), *Education for citizenship* (pp. 93–113). London: Continuum.

Gambro, J. S., & Switzky, H. N. (1996). A national survey of high school students' environmental knowledge. *Journal of Environmental Education, 27*, 28–33.

Gaon, S., & Norris, S. P. (2001). The undecidable grounds of scientific expertise: Science education and the limits of intellectual independence. *Journal of Philosophy of Education, 35*(2), 187–201.

Garcia-Mila, M., & Andersen, C. (2008). Cognitive foundations of learning argumentation. In S. Erduran, & M. P. Jiménez-Aleixandre (Eds.), *Argumentation in science education: Perspectives from classroom-based research* (pp. 29–46). Dordrecht: Kluwer.

Gardner, G. T., & Stern, P. C. (2002). *Environmental problems and human behavior*. Boston: Pearson Custom Publishing.

Gardner, R. A., Gardner, B. T., & Canfort, T. E. (Eds.). (1989). *Teaching sign language to chimpanzees*. Albany, NY: State University of New York Press.

Garrett, R. K. (2006). Protest in an information society: A review of literature on social movements and new ICTs. *Information, Communication and Society, 9*(2), 202–204.

Gaskell, J. (1992). Authentic science and school science. *International Journal of Science Education, 14*, 265–272.

Gaskell, J. (2002). Of cabbages and kings: Opening the hard shell of science curriculum policy. *Canadian Journal of Science, Mathematics and Technology Education, 2*(1), 59–66.

Gauch, H. G. (2009). Science, worldviews, and education. *Science & Education, 18*(6&7), 667–695.

Gaudelli, W. (2003). *World class: Teaching and learning in global times*. Mahwah, NJ: Lawrence Erlbaum Associates.

Gauld, C. F. (1982). The scientific attitude and science education: A critical reappraisal. *Science Education, 66*, 109–121.

Gautier, C., Deutsch, K., & Rebich, S. (2006). Misconceptions about the greenhouse effect. *Journal of Geoscience Education, 54*(3), 386–395.

Gayford, C. (2002a). Controversial environmental issues: A case study for the professional development of science teachers. *International Journal of Science Education, 24*(11), 1191–1200.

Gayford, C. G. (2002b). Environmental literacy: Towards a shared understanding. *Research in Science & Technological Education, 20*(1), 99–110.

Geddes, P. (1915). *Cities in evolution: An introduction to the town planning movement and to the study of civics.* London: Willimas & Norgate.

Geddis, A. (1991). Improving the quality of science classroom discourse on controversial issues. *Science Education, 75*, 169–183.

Gee, J. P. (2002). Identity as an analytic lens for research in education. *Review of Research in Education, 25*, 99–125.

Gee, J. P., Hull, G., & Lankshear, C. (1996). *The new work order: Behind the language of the new capitalism.* Boulder, CO: Allen & Unwin/Westview Press.

Gelbspan, R. (2005). Global warming and political power: The end of nature and beyond. *Organization & Environment, 18*(2), 186–192.

George, J. (1999a). Worldview analysis of knowledge in a rural village: Implications for science education. *Science Education, 83*(1), 77–95.

George, J. M. (1999b). Indigenous knowledge as a component of the school curriculum. In L. M. Semali, & J. L. Kincheloe (Eds.), *What is indigenous knowledge? Voices from the academy* (pp. 79–94). New York: Falmer Press.

George, J., & Glasgow, J. (1988). Street science and conventional science in the West Indies. *Studies in Science Education, 15*, 109–118.

Gess-Newsome, J., & Lederman, N. G. (1999). *Examining pedagogical content knowledge.* Dordrecht: Kluwer.

Gibbons, M., Limoges, C., Nowotny, H., Schwarzman, S., Scott, P., & Trow, M. (1994). *The new production of knowledge: The dynamics of science and research in contemporary societies.* London: Sage.

Gibson, D. G., Glass, J. I., Latigue, C., Noskov, V. N., Chuang, R.-Y., Venter, J. C., et al. (2010, May 20). Creation of a bacterial cell controlled by a chemically synthesized genome. *ScienceExpress,* 1–12 (10.1126). Available at: www.scienceexpress.org

Gibson-Graham, J. K. (1996). *The end of capitalism (as we knew it): A feminist critique of political economy.* Cambridge: Blackwell.

Giddens, A. (1991). *Modernity and self-identity: Self and society in the late modern age.* Cambridge: Polity Press.

Gidley, J., Bateman, D., & Smith, C. (2004). *Futures in education: Principles, practice and potential.* The strategic foresight monograph series, Monograph 5. Melbourne: Swinbourne University of Technology. Available from: www.swinburne.edu.au

Gidley, J. M. (1998). Prospective youth visions through imaginative education. *Futures, 30*(5), 395–408.

Gidley, J., & Inayatullah, S. (Eds.). (2002). *Youth futures: Comparative research and transformative visions.* London: Praeger.

Gillborn, D. (1997) Racism and reform. *British Educational Research Journal, 23*, 345–360.

Gilligan, C. (1982). *In a different voice: Psychological theory and women's development.* Cambridge, MA: Harvard University Press.

Ginwright, S., & Cammarota, J. (2007). Youth activism in the urban community: Learning critical civic praxis within community organizations. *International Journal of Qualitative Studies in Education, 20*(6), 693–710.

Girardot, N. J., Miller, J., & Xiaogan, L. (Eds.). (2001). *Daosim and ecology: Ways within a cosmic landscape.* Cambridge, MA: Harvard University Center for the Study of World Religions.

Girod, M. (2007). A conceptual overview of the role of beauty and aesthetics in science and science education. *Studies in Science Education, 43*, 38–61.

Girod, M., Rau, C., & Schepige, A. (2003). Appreciating the beauty of science ideas: Teaching for aesthetic understanding. *Science Education, 87*(4), 574–587.

Giroux, H. A. (1988). *Teachers as intellectuals: Toward a critical pedagogy of learning.* New York: Bergin & Garvey.

REFERENCES

Gitari, W. (2003). An inquiry into the integration of indigenous knowledges and skills in the Kenyan secondary science curriculum: A case study of human health knowledge. *Canadian Journal of Science, Mathematics and Technology Education, 3*(2), 195–212.

Gitari, W. (2006). Everyday objects of learning about health and healing and implications for science education. *Journal of Research in Science Teaching, 43*(2), 172–193.

Glantz, S. A., Slade, J., Hanauer, P., & Barnes, D. E. (1996). *The cigarette papers.* Berkeley, CA: University of California Press.

Glasson, G. E., Frykholm, J. A., & Mhango, N. A. (2006). Understanding the earth systems of Malawi: Ecological sustainability, culture, and place-based education. *Science Education, 90*(11), 660–680.

Glasson, G. E., Mhango, N., Phiri, A., & Lanier, M. (2010). Sustainability science education in Africa: Negotiating indigenous ways of living with nature in the third space. *International Journal of Science Education, 32*(1), 125–141.

Goldman, S. R., & Bisanz, G. L. (2002). Towqard a functional understanding of scientific genres: Implications for understanding and learning processes. In J. Otero, J. A. Leon, & A.C. Graesser (Eds.), *The psychology of science text comprehension* (pp. 19–50). Mahwah, NJ: Erlbaum.

Goldston, M. J. D., & Kyzer, P. (2009). Teaching evolution: Narratives from three Southern biology teachers in the USA. *Journal of Research in Science Teaching, 46*(7), 762–790.

Goleman, D. (1985). *Emotional intelligence: Why it can matter more than IQ.* New York: Bantam Books.

Goleman, D. (1996). *Emotional intelligence.* London: Bloomsbury Publishing.

Goleman, D. (1998). *Working with emotional intelligence.* New York: Bantam Books.

González-Gaudiano, E., & Meira-Cartea, P. (2010). Climate change education and communication: A critical perspective on obstacles and resistances. In F. Kagawa & D. Selby (Eds.), *Education and climate change: Living and learning in interesting times* (pp. 13–34). London: Routledge.

Gooch, G. F. (1995). Environmental beliefs and attitudes in Sweden and the Baltic states. *Environment & Behavior, 27*(4), 513–539.

Goodman, R. T., & Saltman, K. J. (2002). *Strange love, or how we learn to stop worrying and love the market.* Lanham, MD: Rowman & Littlefield.

Gott, R., & Duggan, S. (1996). Practical work: Its role in the understanding of evidence in science. *International Journal of Science Education, 18*(7), 791–806.

Gott, R., Duggan, S., & Roberts, R. (2003). *Concepts of evidence.* Available online at: www.dur.ac.uk/rosalyn.roberts'Evidence/cofev.htm

Gough, N. (1987). Learning with environments: Towards an ecological paradigm of education. In I. M. Robottom (Ed.), *Environmental education: Practice and possibility* (pp. 49–67). Geelong: Deakin University Press.

Gough, N. (1989). From epistemology to ecopolitics: Renewing a paradigm for curriculum. *Journal of Curriculum Studies, 21*, 225–241.

Gough, N. (1990). Healing the earth within us: Environmental education as cultural criticism. *Journal of Experiential Education, 13*(3), 12–17.

Gough, N. (1991, September). *Coyote, crocodile, chaos and curriculum: Premodern lessons for postmodern learning.* Paper presented at the annual conference of the North American Association for environmental Education, St Paul, MN.

Gough, N. (1993). Environmental education, narrative complexity and postmodern science/fiction. *International Journal of Science Education, 15*, 607–625.

Gough, S. (2002a). Increasing the value of the environment: A 'real options' metaphor for learning. *Environmental Education Research, 8*(1), 61–72.

Gough, S. (2002b). Whose gap? Whose mind? Plural rationalities and disappearing academics. *Environmental Education Research, 8*(3), 273–282.

Gough, S., Scott, W., & Stables, A.(2000). Beyond O'Riordan: Balancing anthropocentrism and ecocentrism. *International Research in Geographical and Environmental Education, 9*(1), 36–47.

Gould, S. J. (1981a). *The mismeasure of man.* Harmondsworth: Penguin.

Gould, S. J. (1981b). Evolution as fact and theory. *Discover, 2*, 33–37.

Gould, S. J. (1994). *Eight little piggies: Reflections in natural history.* New York: W.W. Norton.

Gould, S. J. (1995). *Dinosaur in a haystack: Reflections in natural history*. New York: Crown Trade Paperbacks.

Gould, S. J. (1996). *The mismeasure of man*. New York: Norton.

Government of Canada. (1991). *Prosperity through competitiveness*. Ottawa: Ministry of Supply and Services Canada.

Government of Canada. (2002). *A framework for environmental learning and sustainability in Canada*. Ottawa: Government of Canada. Available online at: www.ec.gc.ca

Gowda, M. V. R., Fox, J. C., & Magelky, R. D. (1997). Students' understanding of climate change: Insights for scientists and educators. *Bulletin of the American Meteorological Society, 78*(1), 2232–2240.

Gowing, N. (2009). *'Skyful of lies' and black swans: the new tyranny of shifting information power in crises*. Oxford: Reuters Institute for the Study of Journalism, University of Oxford.

Graber, D., McQuail, D., & Norris, P. (1998). *The politics of news, the news of politics*. Washington, DC: CQ Press.

Gräber, W., & Bolte, C. (Eds.). (1997). *Scientific literacy: An international symposium*. Kiel: Institut fur die Padagogik der Naturwiseenschaften (IPN) an der Universitat Kiel.

Gräber, W., Nentwig, P., Becker, H.-J., Sumfleth, E., Pitton, A., Wollweber, K., & Jorde, D. (2002). Scientific literacy: From theory to practice. In H. Behrendt, H. Dahncke, R. Duit, W. Gräber, M. Komorek, A. Kross, et al. (Eds.), *Research in science education – Past, present and future* (pp. 61–70). Dordrecht: Kluwer.

Graham, J. D. (2000). Perspectives on the precautionary principle. *Human and Ecological Risk Assessment, 6*(3), 383–385.

Graham, M. A. (2007). Art, ecology and art educationm: Locating art education in a critical place-based pedagogy. *Studies in Art Education, 48*(4), 375–392.

Gramsci, A. (1971). *Selection from the prison notebooks*. New York: International Publishers.

Gray, F. D. (2001). *The Tusgekee syphilis study: The real story and beyond*. Montgomery, AL: New South Books.

Greenberg, D. (2003). Conference deplores corporate influence on academic science. *The Lancet, 362*, 302–303.

Greenall Gough, A. (1990). Red and green: two case studies in learnin g through ecopolitical action. *Curriculum Perspectives, 10*(2), 60–65.

Greenwood, D. A. (formerly Gruenewald) (2008). A critical pedagogy of place: From gridlock to parallax. *Environmental Education Research, 14*(3), 336–348.

Gregory, J., & Miller, S. (1998). *Science in public*. Cambridge, MA: Perseus.

Griffin, J. (1998). Learning science through practical experiences in museums. *International Journal of Science Education, 20*(6), 643–653.

Griffith, J. A., & Brem, S. K. (2004). Teaching evolutionary biology: Pressures stress, and coping. *Journal of Research in Science Teaching, 41*(8), 791–809.

Griffiths, A. K., & Barman, C. R. (1995). High school students' views about the nature of science: Results from three countries. *School Science & Mathematics, 95*(2), 248–255.

Grim, J. (Ed.). (2001). *Indigenous traditions and ecology: The interbeing of cosmology and community*. Cambridge, MA: Harvard University Press.

Groves, F., & Pugh, A. (1999). Elementary pre-service teacher perceptions of the greenhouse effect. *Journul of Science Education and Technology, 8*(1), 75–81.

Gruenewald, D. (2003a). The best of both worlds: A critical pedagogy of place. *Educational Researcher, 32*(4), 3–12.

Gruenewald, D. (2003b). Foundations of place: A multidisciplinary framework for place-conscious education. *American Educational Research Journal, 40*(3), 619–654.

Gruenewald, D. (2005). More than one profound truth: Making sense of divergent criticalities. *Educational Studies, 37*, 206–215.

Gruenewald, D. (2008). Place-based education: Grounding culturally responsive teaching in geographical diversity. In D. Gruenewald & G. Smith (Eds.), *Place-based education in the global age* (pp. 137–154). New York: Lawrence Erlbaum Associates.

REFERENCES

Gruenewald, D., & Smith, G. (Eds.). (2008), *Place-based education in the global age*. New York: Lawrence Erlbaum Associates.

Guisasola, J., Robinson, M., & Zuza, K. (2007). A comparison of the attitudes of Spansih and American secondary school teachers toward global science and technology based problems/threats. *Journal of Environmental & Science Education, 2*(1), 20–31.

Guy, R. (1989). Ethical problems in farming practice. In D. Paterson & M. Palmer (Eds.), *The status of animals: Ethics, education and welfare* (pp. 87–94). East Haddam, CT: Humane Education Foundation/CAB International.

Haavelsrud, M. (2010). Peace learning: Universalism in interesting times. In F. Kagawa & D. Selby (Eds.), *Education and climate change: Living and learning in interesting times* (pp. 55–70). London: Routledge.

Habermas, J. (1971). *Knowledge and human interests*. Boston: Beacon Press.

Habermas, J. (1972). *Towards a rational society*. London: Heinemann.

Habermas, J. (1990). *Moral consciousness and communicative action*. Cambridge, MA: MIT Press.

Habermas, J. (1996). *Between facts and norms*. Cambridge, MA: MIT Press.

Haidt, J. (2001). The emotional dog and its rational tail: A social intuitionist approach to moral judgment. *Psychological Review, 108*(4), 814–834.

Halim, L., & Meerah, S. M. (2002). Science trainee teachers' pedagogical content knowledge and its influence on physics teaching. *Research in Science Education, 20*, 215–225.

Hall, E. (2004) Science and ethics: Give them a break. *School Science Review, 86*(315), 25–28.

Halstead, J. H. (1996). Values and values education in schools. In J. M. Halstead & M. J. Taylor (Eds.), *Values in education and education in values* (pp. 3–14). Lewes: Falmer Press.

Halverson, K. L., Siegel, M. A., & Freyermuth, S. K. (2009). Lenses for framing decisions: Undergraduates' decision making about stem cell research. *International Journal of Science Education, 31*(9), 1249–1268.

Ham, S. H., & Weiler, B. (2002). Interpretation as the centrepiece of sustainable wildlife tourism. In R. Harris, T. Griffin, & P. Williams (Eds.), *Sustainable tourism: A global perspective* (pp. 35–44). Oxford: Butterworth Heinemann.

Hamilton, C., & Denniss, R. (2006). *Affluenza: When too much is never enough*. Crows Nest (NSW): Allen & Unwin.

Hammond, L. (2001). Notes from California: An anthropological approach to urban science education for language minority families. *Journal of Research in Science Teaching, 38*, 983–999.

Hampson, J. (1989). Practical dilemmas and solutions. In D. Paterson & M. Palmer (Eds.), *The status of animals: Ethics, education and welfare* (pp. 100–110). East Haddam, CT: Humane Education Foundation/CAB International.

Hand, C. M., & van Liere, K. B. (1984). Religion, mastery-over-nature, and environmental concerns. *Social Forces, 63*(2), 555–570.

Hanegan, N. L., Price, L., & Peterson, J. (2008). Disconnections between teacher expectations and student confidence in bioethics. *Science & Education, 17*, 921–940.

Hansen, C. (1991) Classical Chinese ethics. In P. Singer (Ed.), *A companion to ethics* (pp. 69–81). Oxford: Blackwell.

Hansson, l., & Lindahl, B. (2010). 'I have chosen another way of thinking': Students' relations to science with a focus on worldview. *Science & Education, 19*(9), 895–918.

Haran, J., & Kitzinger, J. (2009). Modest witnessing and managing the boundaries between science and the media: A case study of breakthrough and scandal. *Public Understanding of Science, 18*(6), 634–652.

Haraway, D. J. (1989). *Primate visions: Gender, race, and nature in the world of modern science*. New York: Routledge.

Haraway, D. J. (1997). *Modest-witness@second-millennium.femaleman-meets-oncomouse: Feminism and technoscience*. New York: Routledge.

Hardin, G. (1985). *Filters against folly: How to survive despite economists, ecologists, and the merely eloquent*. New York: Penguin.

Harding, P., & Hare, W. (2000). Portraying science accurately in classrooms: Emphasizing open-mindedness rather than relativism. *Journal of Research in Science Teaching, 37*(3), 225–236.

Harding, S. (1986). *The science question in feminism*. Ithaca, NY: Cornell University Press.

Harding, S. (1991). *Whose science? Whose knowledge? Thinking from women's lives*. Ithaca, NY: Cornell University Press.

Harding, S. (1998). *Is science multicultural?* Bloomington, IN: Indiana University Press.

Harding, S. G. (Ed.). (2004). *The feminist standpoint theory reader*. New York: Routledge.

Harding, S. G., & Hintikka, M. (Eds.). (1983). *Discovering reality: Feminist perspectives on epistemology, metaphysics, methodology, and philosophy of science*. Dordrecht: Reidel.

Hargreaves, A. (1998). The emotional practice of teaching. *Teaching and Teacher Education, 14*, 835–854.

Hargreaves, I., Lewis, J., & Spears, T. (2002). *Towards a better mark: Science, the public and the media*. Swindon: Economic and Social Research Council.

Hargreaves Heap, S. P. (2002). Making British universities accountable: In the public interest? In P. Mirowski & E.-M. Sent (Eds.), *Science bought and sold: Essays in the conomics of science* (pp. 287–411). Chicago, IL: University of Chicago Press.

Hardwig, J. (1991). The role of trust in knowledge. *Journal of Philosophy, 88*, 693–708.

Harré, R. (1986). *Varieties of reason*. Oxford: Blackwell.

Harris, R., & Ratcliffe, M. (2005). Socio-scientific issues and the wuality of exploratory talk – What can be learned from schools involved in a 'collapsed day' project? *Curriculum Journal, 16*, 439–453.

Hart, L. A., Wood, M. W., & Hart, B. L. (2008). *Why dissection? Animal use in education*. Westport, CT: Greenwood Press.

Hart, P. (2007). Environmental education. In S. K. Abell & N. G. Lederman (Eds.), *Handbook on research in science education* (pp. 689–726). Mahwah, NJ: Lawrence Erlbaum.

Hart, P. (2008a). What comes before participation? Searching for meaning in teachers' constructions of participatory learning in environmental education. In A. Reid, B. B. Jensen, J. Nikel, & V. Simovsla (Eds.), *Participation and learning: Perspectives on education and the environment, health and sustainability* (pp. 197–211). New York: Springer.

Hart, P. (2008b). Elusive participation: Methodological challenges in researching teaching and participatory learning in environmental education. In A. Reid, B. B. Jensen, J. Nikel, & V. Simovsla (Eds.), *Participation and learning: Perspectives on education and the environment, health and sustainability* (pp. 225–240). New York: Springer.

Hart, P., & Nolan, K. (1999). A critical analysis of research in enviromental education. *Studies in Science Education, 34*, 1–69.

Hart, R. (1992). *Children's participation: From tokenism to citizenship*. UNICEF Innocenti Essays, No.4. Florence: International Child Development Centre, UNICEF.

Hart, R. A. (2008). Stepping back from 'the ladder': Reflections on a model of participatory work with children. In A. Reid, B. B. Jensen, J. Nikel, & V. Simovsla (Eds.), *Participation and learning: Perspectives on education and the environment, health and sustainability* (pp. 19–31). New York: Springer.

Harvey, D. (2000). *Spaces of hope*. Edinburgh: Edinburgh University Press.

Harwood, W. S., MaKinster, J. G., Cruz, L., & Gabel, D. (2002). Acting out science. *Journal of College Science Teaching, 31*(7), 442–447.

Hashweh, M. Z. (2005). Teacher pedagogical constructions: A reconfiguration of pedagogical content knowledge. *Teachers and Teaching: Theory and Practice, 11*, 273–292.

Hatano, G., & Inagaki, K. (1991). Sharing cognition through a collective comprehension activity. In R. L. Resnick, J. Levine, & S. Teasley (Eds.), *Perspectives on socially shared cognition* (pp. 331–348). Washington, DC: American Psychological Association.

Hatano, G., & Inagaki, K. (1992). Desituating cognition through the construction of conceptual knowledge. In P. Light, & G. Butterworth (Eds.), *Context and cognition: Ways of learning and knowing* (pp. 115–133). New York: Harvester Wheatsheaf.

Hatcher, A., Bartlett, C., Marshall, A., & Marshall, M. (2009). Tw-eyed seeing in the classroom environment: Concepts, approaches, and challenges. *Canadian Journal of Science, Mathematics and Technology Education, 9*(3), 141–153.

Haymes, S. (1995). *Race, culture and the city: A pedagogy for Black urban struggle*. Albany, NY: State University of New York Press.

REFERENCES

Heap, R. (2006). *Myth busting and tenet building: Primary and early childhood teachers' understanding of the nature of science*. Auckland: Unpublished MEd thesis, University of Auckland.

Heering, P., & Muller, F. (2002). Cultures of experimental practice – An approach in a museum. *Science & Education, 11*, 203–214.

Heilbroner, R. (1995). *Visions of the future: The distant past, yesterday, today, tomorrow*. New York: Oxford University Press.

Helmke, A., & van Aken, M. A. G. (1995). The causal ordering of academic achievement and self-concept of ability during elementary school: A longitudinal study. *Journal of Educational Psychology, 87*, 624–637.

Helms, J. V. (1998). Science and me: Subject matter and identity in secondary school science teachers. *Journal of Research in Science Teching, 35*(7), 811–834.

Hennessey, M. G. (2003). Metacognitive aspects of students' reflective discourse: Implications for intentional conceptual change teaching and learning. In G. M. Sinatra & P. R. Pintrich (Eds.), *Intentional conceptual change* (pp. 103–132). Mahwah, NJ: Lawrence Erlbaum.

Henry, M. (2000). Drama's ways of learning. *Research in Drama Education, 5*, 45–62.

Hermann, R. S. (2008). Evolution as a controversial issue: A review of instructional approaches. *Science & Education, 17*(8&9), 1011–1032.

Hess, D., Breyman, S., Campbell, N., & Martin, B. (2008). Science, technology, and social movements. In E. J. Hackett, O. Amsterdamska, M. Lynch, & J. Wajcman (Eds.), *The handbook of science and technology studies* (pp. 473–498). Cambridge, MA: MIT Press.

Hewitt, J., Pedretti, E., Bencze, L., Vaillancourt, B. D., & Yoon, S. (2003). New applications for multimedia cases: Promoting reflective practice in preservice teacher education. *Journal of Technology and Teacher Education, 11*(4), 483–500.

Hewson, P. W., & Thorley, N. R. (1989). The conditions of conceptual change in the classroom. *International Journal of Science Education, 11*, 541–543.

Hicks, D. (1988). *Education for peace: Issues, principles and practice*. London: Routledge.

Hicks, D. (1996). A lesson for the future: Young people's hopes and fears for tomorrow. *Futures, 28*(1), 1–13.

Hicks, D. (1998). Stories of hope: A response to the psychology of despair. *Environmental Education Research, 4*(2), 165–176.

Hicks, D. (2002*). Lessons for the future: The missing dimension in education*. London: Routledge-Falmer.

Hicks, D., & Bord, A. (2001). Learning about global issues: Why most educators only make things worse. *Environmental Education Research, 7*(4), 413–425.

Hicks, D., & Holden, C. (1995). Exploring the future: A missing dimension in environmental education. *Environmental Education Research, 1*(2), 185–193.

Hicks, D., & Holden, C. (1995). *Vision of the future: Why we need to teach for tomorrow*. Stoke-on-Trent: Trentham Books.

Hicks, D., & Holden, C. (2007). Remembering the future: What do children think? *Environmental Education Research, 13*(4), 501–512.

Hicks, D., & Holden, C. (Eds.). (2007b). *Teaching the global dimension: Key principles and effective practice*. London: Routledge.

Hicks, D., & Slaughter, R. (Eds.). (1998). *Futures education*. World yearbook of education 1998. London: Kogan Page.

Hicks, D., & Steiner, M. (Eds.). (1989). *Making global connnections: A world studies workbook*. Edinburgh: Oliver & Boyd.

High Level Group on Science Education. (2007). *Science education NOW: A renewal pedagogy for the future of Europe*. Brussels: European Commission.

Hildebrand, D., Bilica, K., & Capps, J. (2008). Addressing controversies in science education: A pragmatic approach to evolution education. *Science & Education, 17*(8&9), 1033–1052.

Hildebrand, G. (2007). Diversity, values and the science curriculum. In D. Corrigan, J. Dillon, & R. Gunstone (Eds.), *The re-emergence of values in science education* (pp. 45–60). Rotterdam: Sense Publishers.

Hilgard, E. R. (1980). The trilogy of mind: Cognition, affection, and conation. *Journal of the History of the Behavioral Sciences, 16*(2), 107–117.

Hill, J. R., & Hannafin, M. J. (2001). Teaching and learning in digital environments: The resurgence of resource-based learning. *Educational Technology Research and Development, 49*(3), 37–52.

Hill, R., Stanisstreet, M., O'Sullivan, H., & Boyes, E. (1999). Genetic engineering of animals for medical research: Students' views. *School Science Review, 80*(293), 23–30.

Hill, S. B., Wilson, S., & Watson, K. (2003). Learning ecology – A new approach to learning and transforming ecological conciousness: Experiences from social ecology in Australia. In E. O'Sullivan, & M. Taylor (Eds.), *Leaning toward ecological consciousness; Selected transformative practices* (pp. 47–64). New York: PalgraveMacmillan.

Hillcoat, J., Forge, K., Fien, J., & Baker, E. (1995). 'I think it's really great that someone is listening to you…': Young people and the environment. *Environmental Education Research, 1*, 159–171.

Hilts, P. J. (1996). *Smokescreen: The truth behind the tobacco industry cover-up.* Reading, MA: Addison Wesley.

Hines, J. M., Hungerford, H. R., & Tomera, A. N. (1986). Analysis and synthesis of research on responsible pro-environmental bahavior: A meta-analysis. *Journal of Environmental Education, 18*(2), 1–8.

Hines, S. D. (Ed.). (2003). *Multicultural science education: Theory, practice, and promise.* New York: Peter Lang.

Hipkins, R. (2004). Developing an ethic of caring through narrative pedagogy. *School Science Review, 86*(315), 53–58.

Hitzhusen, G. E. (2007). Judeo-Christain theology and the environment: Moving beyond scepticism to new sources for environment education in the United States. *Environmental Education Research, 13*(1), 55–74.

Hivon, M., Lehoux, P., Denis, J.-L., & Rock, M. (2010). Marginal voices in the media coverage of controversial health interventions: How do they contribute to the public understanding of science? *Public Understanding of Science, 19*(1), 34–51.

Ho, M.-W. (1997). The unholy alliance. *The Ecologist, 27*(4), 152–158.

Hochschild, A. R. (1983). *The managed heart: Commercialization of human feeling.* Berkeley, CA: University of California Press.

Hochschild, A. R. (1990). Ideology and emotion management: A Perspective and path for future research. In T. D. Kemper (Ed.), *Commercialization Research agendas in the sociology of emotions.* (pp. 117–142). Albany, NY: State University of New York Press.

Hochschild, A. R. (1993). Preface. In S. Fineman (Ed.), *Emotions in organizations* (pp. ix–xiii). Thousand Oaks, CA: Sage.

Hodson, D. (1992a). In search of a meaningful relationship: An exploration of some issues relating to integration in science and science education. *International Journal of Science Education, 14*, 541–562.

Hodson, D. (1992b). Assessment of practical work: Some considerations in philosophy of science. *Science & Education, 1*, 115–144.

Hodson, D. (1993a). In search of a rationale for multicultural science education, *Science Education, 77*, 685–711.

Hodson, D. (1993b). Against skills-based testing in science. *Curriculum Studies, 1*(1), 127–148.

Hodson, D. (1994). Seeking directions for change: The personalisation and politicisation of science education. *Curriculum Studies, 2*, 71–98.

Hodson, D. (1998a). *Teaching and learning science: Towards a personalized approach.* Buckingham: Open University Press.

Hodson, D. (1998b). Science fiction: The continuing misrepresentation of science in the school curriculum. *Curriculum Studies, 6*(2), 191–216.

Hodson, D. (1999). Going beyond cultural pluralism: Science education for sociopolitical action, *Science Education, 83*(6), 775–796.

Hodson, D. (2001). Inclusion without assimilation: Science education from an anthropological and metacognitive perspective. *Canadian Journal of Science, Mathematics and Technology Education, 1*(2), 161–182.

Hodson, D. (2003). Time for action: Science education for an alternative future. *International Journal of Science Education, 25*(6), 645–670.

Hodson, D. (2006). Why we should prioritize learning *about* science. *Canadian Journal of Science, Mathematics and Technology Education, 6*(3), 293–311.

Hodson, D. (2008). *Towards scientific literacy: A teachers' guide to the history, philosophy and sociology of science*. Rotterdam: Sense Publishers.

Hodson, D. (2009a). *Teaching and learning about science: Language, theories, methods, history, traditions and values*. Rotterdam: Sense Publishers.

Hodson, D. (2009b). Putting your money where your mouth is: Towards an action-oriented science curriculum. *Journal of Activist Science & Technology Education, 1*(1), 1–15. Available at http://www.wepaste.org/journal.html

Hodson, D. (2010). Science education as a call to action. *Canadian Journal of Science, Mathematics and Technology Education, 10*(3), 197–206.

Hodson, D. with Bencze, L., Nyhof-Young, J., Pedretti, E., & Elshof, L. (2002). *Changing science education through action research: Some experiences from the field*. Toronto: Imperial Oil Centre for Studies in Science, Mathematics & Technology Education in association with University of Toronto Press.

Hodson, D., & Hodson, J. (1998a). From constructivisn to social constructivism: A Vygotskian perspective on teaching and learning science. *School Science Review, 78*(289), 33–41.

Hodson, D., & Hodson, J. (1998b). Science education as enculturation: Some implications for practice. *School Science Review, 80*(290), 17–24.

Hodson, D., & Prophet, R. B. (1986). A bumpy start to science education. *New Scientist, 1521*, 25–28.

Hogan, K. (1998). *Sociocognitive roles in science group discourse*. Paper presented at the annual meeting of the National Association for Research in Science Teaching, San Diego, CA.

Hogan, K. (1999). Thinking aloud together: A test of an intervention to foster students' collaborative scientific reasoning. *Journal of Research in Science Teaching, 36*(10), 1085–1109.

Hogan, K. (2002a). Small groups' ecological reasoning while making an environmental management decision. *Journal of Research in Science Teaching, 39*(4), 341–368.

Hogan, K. (2002b). A sociocultural analysis of school and community settings as sites for developing environmental practitioners. *Environmental Education Research, 8*(4), 413–437.

Hogan, K., & Maglienti, M. (2001). Comparing the epistemological underpinnings of students' and scientists' reasoning about conclusions. *Journal of Research in Science Teaching, 38*(6), 663–687.

Hogan, K., & Pressley, M. (1997). *Scaffolding student learning: Instructional approaches and issues*. Cambridge, MA: Brookline Books.

Hogle, L. F. (2008). Emerging medical technologies. In E. J. Hackett, O. Amsterdamska, M. Lynch, & J. Wajcman (Eds.), *The handbook of science and technology studies* (pp. 841–873). Cambridge, MA: MIT Press.

Holden, C. (1998). Keen at 11, cynical at 18? Encouraging pupil participation in school and community. In C. Holden & N. Clough (Eds.), *Children as citizens: Education for participation* (pp. 46–62). London: Jessica Kingsley.

Holden, C. (2007). Young people's concerns. In D. Hicks & C. Holden (Eds.), *Teaching the global dimension: Key principles and effective practice* (pp. 31–42). London: RoutledgeFalmer.

Holdsworth, I., & Conway, B. (1999). Investigating values in secondary design and technology education. *International Journal of Technology and Design Education, 4*(3), 205–214.

Holland, D., Lachiotte, W., Skinner, D., & Cain, C. (1998). *Identity and agency in cultural worlds*. Cambridge, MA: Harvard University Press.

Holstermann, N., Grube, D., & Bögeholz, S. (2009). The influence of emotion on students' performance in dissection exercises. *Journal of Biological Education, 43*(4), 164–168.

Holton, G. (1975). On the role of themata in scientific thought. *Science, 188*(4186), 328–334.

Holton, G. (1978). *The scientific imagination: Case studies*. Cambridge: Cambridge University Press.

Holton, G. (1981). Thematic presuppositions and the direction of science advance. In A. F. Heath (Ed.), *Scientific explanation: Papers based on the Herbert Spencer lectures given in the University of Oxford* (pp. 1–27). Oxford: Oxford University Press.

Holton, G. (1988). *Thematic origins of scientific thought: Kepler to Einstein*. Cambridge, MA: Harvard University Press.

Hong, J. L., & Chang, N. K. (2004). Analysis of Korean high school students' decision-making process in solving a problem involving biological knowledge. *Research in Science Education, 34*, 97–111.

hooks, b. (1994). *Teaching to transgress: Education as the practice of freedom.* New York: Routledge.

Hornig Priest, S. (2006). The public opinion climate for gene technologies in Canada and the United States: Competing voices, contrasting frames. *Public Understanding of Science, 15*, 55–71.

House of Commons, Environment, Food and Rural Affairs Committee. (2003). *Conduct of the GM public debate.* Eighteenth report of session 2002–2003. London: HMSO.

Howe, E. M. (2007). Untangling sickle-cell anemia and the teaching of heterozygote protection. *Science & Education, 16*(1), 1–19.

Howe, E. M., & Rudge, D. W. (2005). Recapitulating the history of sickle-cell anemia research. *Science & Education, 14*, 423–441.

Howes, E. (2002). *Connecting girls and science: Constructivism, feminism and science education reform.* New York: Teachers College Press.

Hsu, S.-J. (2009). Significant life experiences affect environmental action: A confirmation study in Eastern Taiwan. *Environmental Education Research, 15*(4), 497–517.

Huckle, J. (1990). Environmental education: Teaching for a sustainable future. In B. Dufour (Ed.), *The new social curriculum* (pp. 150–166). Cambridge: Cambridge University Press.

Huckle, J. (1991). Education for sustainability: Assessing pathways to the future. *Australian Journal of Environmental Education, 7*, 43–62.

Huckle, J. (2001). Towards ecological citizenship. In D. Lambert & P. Machon (Eds.), *Citizenship through secondary geography* (pp. 144–160). London: RoutledgeFalmer.

Hug, B. (2008). Re-examining the practice of dissection: What does it teach? *Journal of Curriculum Studies, 40*(1), 91–105.

Hug, J. W. (2010). Exploring instructional strategies to develop prospective elementary teachers' children's literature book evaluation skills for science, ecology and environmental education. *Environmental Education Research, 16*(3–4), 367–382.

Hughes, G. (2000). Marginalization of socioscientific material in science-technology-society science curricula: Some implications for gender inclusivity and curriculum reform. *Journal of Research in Science Teaching, 37*(5), 426–440.

Hull, D. L. (1988). *Science as a process: An evolutionary account of the social and conceptual development of science.* Chicago: University of Chicago Press.

Hungerford, H., & Volk, T. (1990). Changing learner behaviour through environmental education. *Journal of Environmental Education, 21*(3), 8–21.

Hurd, P. D. (1958). Science literacy: Its meaning for American schools. *Educational Leadership, 16*(1), 13–16.

Hurd, P. D. (1998). Scientific literacy: New minds for a changing world. *Science Education, 82*(3), 407–416.

Hursthouse, R. (1991). Virtue theory and abortion. *Philosophy and Public Affairs, 20*(3), 223–246.

Hursthouse, R. (1999). *On virtue ethics.* Oxford: Oxford University Press.

Hutchinson, D. (1998). *Growing up green: Education for ecological renewal.* New York: Teachers College Press.

Hutchinson, D. (2004). *A natural history of place in education.* New York: Teachers College Press.

Hutchinson, F. (1996). *Educating beyond violent futures.* London: Routledge.

Hutchinson, F. (1997). Our children's futures: Are there lessons for environmental educators? *Environmental Education Research, 3*(2), 189–201.

Inden, R. B. (2000). *Imagining India.* Bloomington, IN: Indiana University Press.

Intemann, K. (2008). Increasing the number of feminist scientists: Why feminist aims are not srved by the underdetermination thesis. *Science & Education, 17*(10), 1065–1079.

IPCC. (2007). *Summary for policymakers of the synthesis report of the IPCC fourth assessment report.* Geneva: IPCC Secretariat.

Irez, S. (2006). Are we prepared?: An assessment of preservice science teacher educators' beliefs about nature of science. *Science Education, 90*(6), 1113–1143.

REFERENCES

Irwin, A. (1995). *Citizen science: A study of people, expertise and sustainable development*. London: Routledge.

Irwin, A. (2008). STS perspectives on scientific governance. In E. J. Hackett, O. Amsterdamska, M. Lynch, & J. Wajcman (Eds.), *The handbook of science and technology studies* (pp. 583–607). Cambridge, MA: MIT Press.

Irwin, A., Dale, A., & Smith, D. (1996). Science and hell's kitchen: The local understanding of hazard issues. In A. Irwin & B. Wynne, B. (Eds.), *Misunderstanding science? The public reconstruction of science and technology* (pp. 47–64). Cambridge: Cambridge University Press.

Isenbarger, L., & Zembylas, M. (2006). The emotional labour of caring in teaching. *Teaching and Teacher Education, 22*(1), 120–134.

Jablonka, E. (2003). Mathematical literacy. In A. J. Bishop, M. A. Clements, C. Keitel, & F. K. S Leung (Eds.), *Second international handbook of mathematics education* (pp. 75–102). Dordrecht: Kluwer.

Jackson, P. W. (1968). *Life in classrooms*. New York: Holt, Rinehart & Winston.

Jackson, R., Barbagallo, F., & Haste, H. (2005). Strngths of public dialogue on science-related issues. *Critical Review of International Social and Political Philosophy, 8*, 349–358.

Jallinoja, P., & Aro, A. R. (2000). Does knowledge make a difference? The association between knowledge about genes and attitudes toward gene tests. *Journal of Health Communication, 5*, 29–39.

Jameson, F. (1998). Notes on globilization as a philosophical issue. In. F. Jameson & M. Miyoshi (Eds.), *The cultures of globization* (pp. 33–54). Durham, NC: Duke University Press.

Jamie, K. (2004). *Findings*. London: Sort of Books.

Janesick, V. J. (2010). *Oral history for the qualitative researcher: Choreographing the story*. New York: Guilford Press.

Jarvis, T., & Rennie, L. J. (1996). Understanding technology: The development of a concept. *International Journal of Science Education, 18*(8), 977–992.

Jasanoff, S. (1997). Civilzation and madness: The great BSE scare of 1996. *Public Understanding of Science, 6*(4), 221–232.

Jasanoff, S. (Ed.). (2004). *States of knowledge: The co-production of science and social order*. London: Routledge.

Jasanoff, S. (2005). *Designs on nature: Science and democracy in Europe and United States*. Princeton, NJ: Princeton University Press.

Jeffrey-Clay, K. R. (1999). Constructivism in museums: How museums create meaningful environments. *Journal of Museum Education, 23*, 3–7.

Jeffries, H., Stanisstreet, M., & Boyes, E. (2001). Knowledge about the 'greenhouse effect': Have college students improved? *Research in Science & Technological Education, 19*(2), 205–221.

Jegede, O. (1998). Worldview presuppositions and science and technology education. In D. Hodson (Ed.), *Science and technology education and ethnicity: An Aotearoa/New Zealand perspective* (pp. 76–88). Wellington: The Royal Society of New Zealand.

Jenkins, E. (1990). Scientific literacy and school science education. *School Science Review, 71*(256), 43–51.

Jenkins, E. W. (1994a). Scientific literacy. In T. Husen & T. N. Postlethwaite (Eds.), *The international encyclopaedia of education*, (Vol. 9, 2nd ed., pp. 5345–5350). Oxford: Pergamon Press.

Jenkins, E. W. (1994b). HPS and school science education: Remediation or reconstruction? *International Journal of Science Education, 16*(6), 613–623.

Jenkins, E. (1997a). Technological literacy: Concepts and constructs. *Journal of Technology Studies, 23*(1), 2–5.

Jenkins, E. (1997b). Scientific and technological literacy: Meanings and rationales. In E. Jenkins (Ed.), *Innovations in science and technology education* (Vol. VI, pp. 11–39). Paris: UNESCO.

Jenkins, E. W., & Nelson, N. W. (2005). Important but not for me: Students' attitudes towards secondary school science in England. *Research in Science & Technological Education, 23*, 41–57.

Jenkins, E. W., & Pell, R. G. (2006). 'Me and the environmental challenges': A survey of English secondary school students' attitudes towards the environment. *International Journal of Science Education, 28*(7), 765–780.

Jensen, B. B. (2000b). Health knowledge and health education in the democratic health-promoting school. *Health Education, 100*(4), 146–153.

Jensen, B. B. (2002). Knowledge, action and pro-environmental behaviour. *Environmental Education Research, 8*(3), 325–334.

Jensen, B. B. (2004). Environmental and health education viewed from an action-oriented perspective: A case from Denmark. *Journal of Curriculum Studies, 36*(4), 405–425.

Jensen, B. B., & Schnack, K. (1997). The action competence approach in environmental education. *Environmental Education Research, 3*(2), 163–178.

Jensen, E. (2008). The dao of human cloning: Utopian/dystopian hype in the British press and popular films. *Public Understanding of Science, 17,* 123–143.

Jeong, H., Songer, N. B., & Lee, S.-Y. (2007). Evidentiary competence: Sixth graders' understanding for gathering and interpreting evidence in scientific investigations. *Research in Science Education, 37,* 75–97.

Jickling, B. (2003). Education and advocacy: A troubling relationship. In E. A. Johnson & M. J. Mappin (Eds.), *Environmental education and advocacy: Changing perspectives of ecology and education* (pp. 91–113). Cambridge: Cambridge University Press.

Jickling, B. (2005). Sustainable development in a globalizing world: A few cautions. *Policy Futures in Education, 3*(3), 251–259.

Jickling, B., & Spork, H. (1998). Education for the environment: A Critique. *Environmental Education Research, 4*(3), 309–329.

Jickling, B., & Wals, A. E. J. (2008). Globalization and environmental education: Looking beyond sustainable development. *Journal of Curriculum Studies, 40*(1), 1–21.

Jiménez-Aleixandre, M. P., & Pereiro Muñoz, C. (2002). Knowledge producers or knowledge consumers? Agumentation and decision making about environmental management. *International Jorunal of Science education, 24*(11), 1171–1190.

Jiménez-Aleixandre, M. P., & Pereiro Muñoz, C. (2005). Argument construction and change while working on a real environmental problem. In K. Boersma, M. Goedhart, O. de Jong, & H. Eijkelhof (Eds.), *Research and the quality of science education* (pp. 419–431). Dordrecht: Kluwer.

Jiménez-Aleixandre, M. P. (2008). Designing argumentation learning environments. In S. Erduran & M. P. Jiménez-Aleixandre (Eds.), *Argumentation in science education: Perspectives from classroom-based research* (pp. 91–116). Dordrecht: Kluwer.

Jiménez-Aleixandre, M. P., & Erduran, S. (2008). Argumentation in science education; An overview. In S. Erduran & M. P. Jiménez-Aleixandre (Eds.), *Argumentation in science education: Perspectives from classroom-based research* (pp. 3–27). Dordrecht: Kluwer.

Jiménez-Aleixandre, M. P., & Federico-Agraso, M. (2009). Justification and persuasion about cloning: Arguments in Hwang's paper and journalistic reported versions. *Research in Science Education, 39,* 331–347.

Jiménez-Aleixandre, M. P., Rodriguez, A. B., & Duschl, R. A. (2000). 'Doing the lesson' or 'doing science': Argument in high school genetics. *Science Education, 84*(6), 757–792.

Johnson, B. (2007). Education and research for sustainable living. In D. Zandvliet & D. Fisher (Eds.), *Sustainable communities, sustainable environments: The contribution of science abnd technology education* (pp. 85–95). Rotterdam: Sense Publishers.

Johnson, J. R. (1989). *Technology: Report of the Project 2061 phase I technology panel.* Washington, DC: American Association for the Advancement of Science.

Johnson, O. A. (Ed.). (1989). *Ethics: Selections from classical and contemporary writers.* New York: Holt, Rinehart & Winston.

Johnston, A., Southerland, S. A., & Sowell, S. (2006). Dissatisfied with the fruitfulness of 'learning ecologies'. *Science Education, 90*(5), 907–911.

Jonassen, D. H., & Land, S. M. (2000). *Theoretical foundations of learning environments.* Mahwah, NJ: Lawrence Erlbaum Associates.

Jones, A. (1997). Recent research in learning technological concepts and processes. *International Journal of Technology and Design Education, 7*(1–2), 83–96.

REFERENCES

Jones, A. (2006). The role and place of technological literacy in elementary science teacher education: International perspectives on contemporary issues and practice. In K. Appleton (Ed.), *Elementary science teacher education* (pp. 197–217). Mahwah, NJ: Lawrence Erlbaum Associates.

Jones, A. T., & de Vries, M. J. (Eds.). (2009). *International handbook of research and development in technology education*. Rotterdam: Sense Publishers.

Jones, A., McKim, A., Reiss, M., Ryan, B., Buntting, C., Saunders, K., et al. (2007). *Research and development of classroom-based resources for bioethics education in New Zealand*. Hamilton: Wilf Malcolm Institute of Educational Research, University of Waikato.

Jones, A., McKim, A., & Reiss, M. (Eds.). (2010), *Ethics in the science and technology classroom: A new approach to teaching and learning*. Rotterdam: Sense Publishers.

Jones, C. (1998a). The need to envision sustainable futures. In D. Hicks & R. Slaughter (Eds.), *Futures education*. World yearbook of education 1998 (pp. 231–243). London: Kogan Page.

Jones, C. (1998b). Planet eaters or star makers? One view of futures studies in higher education. *American behavioral Scientist, 42*(3), 470–483.

Jones, J. H., & Tuskegee Institute. (1993). *Bad blood: The Tuskegee syphilis experiment*. New York: Free Press.

Jones, L., & Reiss, M. J. (Eds.). (2007). *Teaching about scientific origins: Taking account of creationism*. New York: Peter Lang.

Joravsky, D. (1970). *The Lysenko affair*. Chicago: University of Chicago Press.

Joss, S. (1998). Danish consensus conferences as a model in participatory technology assessment: An impact tudy of consensus conferences on Danish Parliament and Danich public debate. *Science & Public Policy, 25*, 2–22.

Joss, S., & Durant, J. (Eds.). (1995), *Public participation in science: The role of consensus conferences in Europe*. London: Science Museum.

Judson, H. F. (2004). *The great betrayal: Fraud in science*. Orlando, FL: Harcourt.

Jukes, N., & Chiuia, M. (2003). *From guinea pig to computer mouse: Alternative methods for a progressive, humane education*. Leicester: InterNICHE.

Jurin, R. R., & Hutchinson, S. (2005). Worldviews in transition: Using ecological autobiographies to explore students' worldviews. *Environmental Education Research, 11*(5), 485–501.

Kahn, P. H. (1999). *The human relationship with nature: Development and culture*. Cambridge, MA: MIT Press.

Kahn, P. H. (2001). *Structural-developmental theory and children's experience of nature*. Paper presented at the biennial meeting of the Society for Research in Child Development. Minneapolis, MN: ERIC Document Reproduction Service, ED 453908.

Kahn, P. H. (2002). Children's affiliations with nature: Structure, development, and the problem of environmental generational amnesia. In P. H. Kahn & S. R. Kellert (Eds.), *Children and nature: Psychological, sociocultural, and evolutionary investigations* (pp. 93–116). Cambridge, MA: MIT Press.

Kahn, P. H., & Friedman, B. (2005). Enviromental views and values of children in an inner-city Black community. *Child Development, 66*(5), 1403–1417.

Kahn, P., & Kellert, S. (2002). *Children and nature: Psychological, sociocultural and evolutionary investigations*. Cambridge, MA: MIT Press.

Kahn, R. (2008). From education for sustainable development to ecopedagogy: Sustaining capitalism or sustaining life? *Green Theory and Praxis: The Journal of Ecopedagogy, 4*, 1–14.

Kahn, R., & Kellner, D. (2004). New media and internet activism: From the 'battle of Seattle' to blogging. *New Media and Society, 6*(1), 87–95.

Kahn, R., & Kellner, D. (2005). Oppositional politics and the internet: A critical/reconstructive approach. *Cultural Politics, 1*(1), 75–100.

Kahn, R., & Kellner, D. (2006). Reconstructing technoliteracy: A multiple literacies approach. In J. R. Dakers (Ed.), *Defining technological literacy: Towards an epistemological framework*. (pp. 253–273). New York: PalgraveMacmillan.

Kalland, S. (2000). Indigenous knowledge: Prospects and limitations. In R. Ellen, P. Parkes, & A. Bicker (Eds.), *Indigenous environmental knowledge and its transformations: Critical anthropological perspectives* (pp. 319–331). Amsterdam: Harwood Academic.

Kang, S., Scharmann, L. C., & Noh, T. (2005). Examining students' views on the nature of science: Results from Korean 6th, 8th, and 10th graders. *Science Education, 89*(2), 314–334.

Kaplan, S. (2000). Human nature and environmentally responsible behavior. *Journal of Social Issues, 56*(3), 491–508.

Kasser, T. (2002). *The high price of materialism.* Cambridge, MA: MIT Press.

Karrow, D. D., & Fazio, X. (2010). *NatureWatch,* schools and environmental education practice. *Canadian Journal of Science, Mathematics and Technology Education, 10*(2), 160–172.

Kawagley, A. O., & Barnhardt, R. (1999). Education indigenous to place: Western science meets Native reality. In G. A. Smith & D. R. Williams (Eds.), *Ecological education in action: On weaving education, culture, and the environment* (pp. 117–140). Albany, NY: SUNY Press.

Kawagley, A. O., Norris-Tull, D., & Norris-Tull, R. A. (1995). Incorporation of the world views of indigenous cultures: A dilemma in the practice and teaching of western science. In F. Finley, D. Allchin, D. Rhees, & S. Fifield (Eds.), *Proceedings of the third international history, philosophy and science teaching conference* (Vol. 1, pp. 583–588). Minneapolis, MN: University of Minnesota Press.

Kawagley, A. O., Norris-Tull, D., & Norris-Tull, R. A. (1998). The indigenous worldview of Yupiaq culture: Its scientific nature and relevance to the practice and teaching of science. *Journal of Research in Science Teaching, 35,* 133–144.

Kawasaki, K. (1996). The concepts of science in Japanese and western education. *Science & Education, 5,* 1–20.

Kaya, O. N., Yager, R., & Dogan, A. (2009). Changes in attitudes towards science-technology-society of pre-service science teachers. *Research in Science Education, 39*(2), 257–279.

Kaza, S., & Kraft, K. (Eds.). (2000). *Dharma rain: Sources of Buddhist environmentalism.* Boston: Shambala.

Keane, M. (2008). Science education and worldview. *Cultural Studies of Science Education, 3*(3), 587–613.

Kearney, M. (1984). *World view.* Novato, CA: Chandler & Sharp.

Kefford, R. F. (2006). Medical heat for climate change. *The Medical Journal of Australia, 184*(11), 582.

Keirl, S. (2006). Ethical technological liuteracy as democratic curriculum keystone. In J. R. Dakers (Ed.), *Defining technological literacy: Towards an epistemological framework.* (pp. 81–102). New York: PalgraveMacmillan.

Keliher, V. (1997). Children's perceptions of nature. *International Research in Geographical and Enviromental Education, 6*(3), 240–243.

Keller, E. F. (1985). *Reflections on gender and science.* New Haven, CT: Yale University Press.

Keller, E. F., & Longino, H. E. (Eds.). (1996). *Feminism and science.* Oxford: Oxford University Press.

Kellert, S. R. (1997). *Kinship to mastery: Biophilia in human evolution and development.* Washington, DC: Island Press.

Kellert, S. R. (2002). Experiencing nature: Affective, cognitive, and evaluative development in childhood. In S. R. Kellert (Ed.), *Children and nature: Psychological, sociological, and evolutionary investigations* (pp. 117–151). Cambridge, MA: MIT Press.

Kellert, S. (2005). *Building for life: Designing and understanding the human-nature connection.* Washington, DC: Island Press.

Kellner, M. (1991). Jewish ethics. In P. Singer (Ed.), *A companion to ethics* (pp. 82–90). Oxford: Blackwell.

Kelly, B. (2004). Applying emotional intelligence: Exploring the promoting alternative thinking strategies curriculum. *Educational Psychology in Practice, 20,* 221–240.

Kelly, G. J., Chen, C., & Prothero, W. (2000). The epistemological framing of a discipline: Writing science in university oceanography. *Journal of Research in Science Teaching, 17,* 691–718.

Kelly, T. (1986). Discussing controversial issues: Four perspectives on the teacher's role. *Theory and Research in Social Education, 14,* 113–138.

Kempton, T. (2004). Using paintings and cartoons to teach ethics in science. *School Science Review, 86*(315), 75–82.

Kempton, W., Boster, J. S., & Hartley, J. A. (1995). *Environmental values in American culture.* Cambridge, MA: MIT Press.

Kenyon, L., Kuhn, L., & Reiser, B. J. (2006). Using students' epistemologies of science to guide the practice of argumentation. In S. A. Barab, K. E. Hay, & T. D. Hickey (Eds.), *Proceedings of the 7th international conference of the learning sciences* (pp. 321–327). Mahwah, NJ: Lawrence Erlbaum.

Kerr, S. C., & Walz, K. A. (2007). 'Holes' in student understanding: Addressing prevalent misconceptions regarding atmospheric environmental chemistry. *Journal of Chemical Education, 84*(10), 1693–1696.

Keselman, A., Kaufman, D. R., & Patel, V. L. (2004). 'You can exercise your way out of HIV' and other stories: The role of biological knowledge in adolescents' evaluation of myths. *Science Education, 88*(4), 548–573.

Keselman, A., Kaufman, D. R., Kramer, S., & Patel, V. L. (2007). Fostering conceptual change and critical reasoning about HIV and AIDS. *Journal of Research in Science Teaching, 44*(6), 844–863.

Khalid, T. (2001). Pre-service misconceptions regarding three environmental issues. *Canadian Journal of Environmental Education, 6*(1), 102–120.

Khalid, T. (2003). Pre-service high school teachers' perceptions of three environmental phenomena. *Environmental Education Research, 9*(1), 35–50.

Khishfe, R. (2008). The development of seventh graders' views of nature of science. *Journal of Research in Science Teaching, 45*(4), 470–496.

Khishfe, R., & Abd-El-Khalick, F. (2002). Influences of explict and reflective versus implicit inquiry-oriented instruction on sixth graders' views of nature of science. *Journal of Research in Science Teaching, 39*(7), 551–578.

Khishfe, R., & Lederman, N. (2006). Teaching nature of science within a controversial topic: Integrated versus non-integrated. *Journal of Research in Science Teaching, 43*(4), 395–418.

Kiefer, J., & Kemple, M. (1999). Stories from our common roots: Strategies for building an ecologically sustainable way of learning. In G. A. Smith & D. R. Williams (Eds.), *Ecological education in action: On weaving education, culture, and the environment* (pp. 21–45). Albany, NY: State University of New York Press.

Kilinç, A., Stanisstreet, M., & Boyes, E. (2008). Turkish students' ideas about global warming. *International Journal of Environmental & Science Education, 3*(2), 89–98.

Kim, D. (1999). Environmentalism in developing countries and the case of a large Korean city. *Social Science Quarterly, 80*(4), 810–829.

Kim, H., & Song, J. (2006). The features of peer argumentation in middle school students' scientific inquiry. *Research in Science Education, 36*(3), 211–233.

Kim, J. (2009). Public feeling for science: The Hwang affair and Hwang supporters. *Public Understanding of Science, 18*(6), 670–686.

Kincheloe, J. L., McKinley, E., Lim, M., & Calabrese Barton, A. (2006). Forum: A conversation on 'sense of place' in science learning. *Cultural Studies of Science Education, 1*(1), 143–160.

King, P. M., & Kitchener, K. S. (1994). *Developing reflective judgment: Understanding and promoting intellectual growth and critical thinking in adolescents and adults.* San Franciso: Jossey-Bass.

King, P. M., & Kitchener, K. S. (2002). The reflective judgment model: Twenty years of research on epistemic cognition. In B. K. Hofer & P. R. Pintrich (Eds.), *Personal epistemology: The psychology of beliefs about knowledge and knowing* (pp. 37–61). Mahwah, NJ: Lawrence Erlbaum Associates.

King, P. M., & Kitchener, K. S. (2004). Reflective judgment: Theory and research on the development of epistemic assumptions through adulthood. *Educational Psychologist, 39*(1), 5–18.

Kirkeby Hansen, P. J. (2010). Knowledge about the greenhouse effect and the effects of the pozone layer among Norwegian pupils finishing compulsory education in 1989, 1993, and 2005 – What now? *International Journal of Science Education, 32*(3), 397–419.

Kisiel, J. (2006). An examination of fieldtrip strategies and their implementation within a natural history museum. *Science Education, 90*(3), 434–452.

Kisiel, J. F. (2010). Exploring a school-aquarium collaboration: An intersection of communities of practice. *Science Education, 94*(1), 95–121.

Kitcher, P. (1993). *The advancement of science: Science without legend, objectivity without illusions.* Oxford: Oxford University Press.

Kithinji, W. (2000). *An inquiry into the integration of Indigenous knowledges and skills in the Kenyan secondary science curriculum.* Toronto: Unpublished PhD thesis, University of Toronto.

Kleinman, S. S. (1998). Overview of feminist perspectives on the ideology of science. *Journal of Research in Science Teaching, 35*(8), 837–844.

Klosterman, M. L., & Sadler, T. D. (2010). Multi-level assessment of scientific content knowledge gains associated with socioscientific issues-based instruction. *International Journal of Science Education, 32*(8), 1017–1043.

Knain, E. (2001). Ideologies in school science textbooks. *International Journal of Science Education, 23*(3), 319–329.

Knapp, C. (1999). *In accord with nature: Helping students form an environmental ethic using outdoor experience and reflection.* Charleston, WV: ERIC Clearinghouse on Rural and Small Schools.

Knapp, C. E. (2007). Place-based curricular and pedagogical models: My adventures in teaching through community contexts. In D. Gruenewald & G. Smith (Eds.), *Place-based education in an era of globalization: Local diversity* (pp. 5–27). Mahwah, NJ: Lawrence Erlbaum Associates.

Knapp, D., & Benton, G. (2006). Episodic and semantic memories of a residential environmental education program. *Environmental Education Research, 12*, 165–177.

Knight, A. J. (2009). Perceptions, knowledge and ethical concerns with GM foods and the GM process. *Public Understanding of Science, 18*, 177–188.

Knorr-Cetina, K. D. (1981). *The manufacture of knowledge: An essay on the constructivist and contextual nature of science.* Oxford: Pergamon Press.

Knorr-Cetina, K. (1995). Laboratory studies: The cultural approach to the study of science. In S. Jasanoff, G. Markle, J. Peterson, & T. Pinch (Eds.), *Handbook of science and technology studies* (pp. 140–166). Thousand Oaks, CA: Sage.

Knorr-Cetina, K. D., & Mulkay, M. (1983). Introduction: Emerging principles in social studies of science. In K. D. Knorr-Cetina, & M. Mulkay (Eds.), *Science observed: Perspectives on the social study of science* (pp. 1–17). London: Sage.

Knudtson, P., & Suzuki, D. (1992). *Wisdom of the elders.* Toronto: Stoddart.

Kohlberg, L. (1971). From 'is' to 'ought': How to commit the naturalistic fallacy and get away with it. In T. Mischel (Ed.), *The study of moral development* (pp. 151–184). New York: Academic Press.

Kohlberg, L. (1973). The claim to moral adequacy of a highest stage of moral judgment. *Journal of Philosophy, 70*(18), 630–646.

Kohlberg, L. (1984). *The psychology of moral development.* San Francisco: Harper & Row.

Kola-Olusanya, A. (2005). Free-choice environmental education: Understanding where children learn outside of school. *Environmental Education Research, 11*(3), 297–307.

Kolbert, E. (2007). *Field notes from a catastrophe: A frontline report on climate change.* London: Bloomsbury.

Kollmuss, A., & Agyeman, J. (2002). Mind the gap: Why do people act environmentally and what are the barriers to pro-environmental behavior? *Environmental Education Research, 8*(3), 239–260.

Kolstø, S. D. (2000). Consensus projects: Teaching science for citizenship. *International Journal of Science Education, 22*(6), 645–664.

Kolstø, S. D. (2001a). Scientific literacy for citizenship: Tools for dealing with the science dimension of controversial socioscientific issues. *Science Education, 85*(3), 291–310.

Kolstø, S. D. (2001b). To trust or not to trust… Pupils' ways of judging information encountered in a socio-scientific issue. *International Journal of Science Education, 23*, 877–901.

Kolstø, S. D. (2004). Socio-scientific issues and the trustworthiness of science-based claims. *School Science Review, 86*(315), 59–65.

Kolstø, S. D. (2006). Patterns in students' argumentation confronted with a risk-focused socio-scientific issue. *International Journal of Science Education, 28*(14), 1689–1716.

REFERENCES

Kolstø, S. D., Bungum, B., Arnesen, E., Isnes, A., Kristensen, T., Mathiassen, K., et al. (2006). Sciences students' criticsl examination of scientific information related to socioscientific issues. *Science Education, 90*(4), 632–655.

Koren, P., & Bar, V. (2009). Pupils' image of 'the scientist' among two communities in Israel: A comparative study. *International Journal of Science Education, 31*(18), 2485–2509.

Korpan, C. A., Bisanz, G. L., Bisanz, J., & Henderson, J. M. (1997). Assessing literacy in science: Evaluation of scientific news briefs. *Science Education, 81*, 515–532.

Korteweg, L., Gonzalez, I., & Guillet, J. (2010). The stories are the people and the land: Three educators respond to environmental teachings in Indigenous children's literature. *Environmental Education Research, 16*(3–4), 331–350.

Kortland, K. (1996). An STS case study about students' decision making on a waste issue. *Science Education, 80*, 673–689.

Kosso, P. (2009). The large-scale structure of scientific method. *Science & Education, 18*(1), 33–42.

Koulaidis, V., & Christidou, V. (1998). Models of students' thinking concerning the greenhouse effect and teaching implications. *Science Education, 83*(5), 559–576.

Kourany, J. (2003). A philosophy of science for the twenty-first century. *Philosophy of Science, 70*(1), 1–14.

Kovac, J. (1999). Professional ethics in the college and university science curriculum. *Science & Education, 8*, 309–319.

Krapfel, P. (1999). Deepening children's participation through local ecological investigations. In G. A.Smith & D. R.Williams (Eds.), *Ecological education in action: On weaving education, culture, and the environment* (pp. 47–64). Albany, NY: State University of New York Press.

Krasny, M. E., & Bonney, R. (2003). Environmental education through citizen science and participatory action research. In E. A. Johnson & M. J. Mappin (Eds.), *Environmental education and advocacy: Changing perspectives of ecology and education* (pp. 292–319). Cambridge: Cambridge University Press.

Kress, G. (2003). *Literacy in the new media age.* New York: Routledge.

Kriesberg, D. A. (1999). *A sense of place: Teaching children about the environment with picture books.* Englewood, CO: Libraries Unlimited.

Krimsky, S. (2003). *Science in the private interest: Has the lure of profits corrupted biomedical research?* Lanham, MD: Rowman & Littlefield.

Kuhlemeier, H., van den Bergh, H., & Lagerweij, N. (1999). Environmental knowledge, attitudes, and behavior in Dutch secondary education. *Journal of Environmental Education, 30*(2), 4–14.

Kuhn, D. (1991). *The skills of argument.* Cambridge: Cambridge University Press.

Kuhn, D. (2010). Teaching and learning science as argument. *Science Education, 94*(5), 810–824.

Kuhn, D., Black, J., Keselman, A., & Kaplan, D. (2000). The development of cognitive skills to support inquiry. *Cognition and Instruction, 18*(4), 495–523.

Kuhn, D., Goh, W., iordanou, K., & Shaenfield, D. (2008). Arguing on the computer: A microgenetic study of developing argument skills in a computer-supported environment. *Child Development, 79*, 1311–1329.

Kumar, D. (2000). *Science, technology, and society education: Citizenship for the new millennium.* Dordrecht: Kluwer.

Kumar, D., & Berlin, D. (1998). A study of STS themes in state science curriculum frameworks in the United States. *Journal of Science Education & Technology, 7*(2), 191–197.

Kumar, D. D., & Chubin, D. E. (Eds.). (2000). *Science, technology, and society: A sourcebook on research and practice.* New York: Kluwer/Plenum.

Kutnick, P., & Rogers, C. (Eds.). (1994). *Groups in schools.* London: Cassell.

Kyle, W. C. (1996). Editorial: The importance of investing in human resources. *Journal of Research in Science Teaching, 33*, 1–4.

Kyle, W. (1997). Urban environmental quality: An emerging educational challenge. *Journal of Research in Science Teaching, 34*(1), 1–2.

Kyle, W. C. (1999). Science education in developing countries: Access, equity, and ethical responsibility. *Journal of the Southern African Association for Research in Mathematics and Science Education, 3*, 1–13.

Kyle, W. C. (2006). The road from Rio to Johannesburg: Where are the footpaths to/from science education? *International Journal of Science and Mathematics Education, 4*(1), 1–18.

Laessøe, J. (2010). Education for sustainable development, participation and socio-cultural change. *Environmental Education Research, 16*(1), 39–57.

Laguardia, A., & Pearl, A. (2005). Democratic education: Goals, principles and requirements. In A. Pearl & C. R. Pryor (Eds.), *Democratic practices in education: Implications for teacher education* (pp. 9–30). Lanham, MD: Rowan & Littlefield.

Lalley, J. P., Piotrowski, P. S., Battaglia, B., Brophy, K., & Chugh, K. (2010). A comparison of V-Frog © to physical frog dissection. *International Journal of Environmental & Science Education, 5*(2), 189–200.

Lambert, H., & Rose, H. (1996). Disembodied knowledge? Making sense of medical science. In A. Irwin & B. Wynne (Eds.), *Misunderstanding science? The public reconstruction of science and technology* (pp. 65–83). Cambridge: Cambridge University Press.

Lankshear, C. (2000). Literacy. In D. A. Gabbard (Ed.), *Knowledge and power in the global economy: Politics and the rhetoric of school reform* (pp. 87–94). Mahwah, NJ: Lawrence Erlbaum Associates.

Lankshear, C., Gee, J. P., & Hull, G. (1996). *The new work order: Behind the language of the new capitalism.* Boulder, CO: Westview Press.

Larner, W. (2000). Neo-liberalism: Policy, ideology, governmentality. *Studies in Political Economy, 63,* 5–26.

Larochelle, M. (2007). Disciplinary power and the school form. *Cultural Studies of Science Education, 2*(4), 711–720.

Larochelle, M., & Désautels, J. (2001). Les enjeux des désaccords entre scientifiques: Un aperçu de la construction discursive d'étudiants et étudiantes, *Canadian Journal of Science, Mathematics and Technology Education, 1,* 39–60.

Larson, J. O. (1995, April). *Fatima's rules and other elements of an unintended chemistry curriculum.* Paper presented at the American Educational Research Association annual meeting, San Francisco.

László, E. (2001). *Macroshift: Navigating the transformation to a sustainable world.* San Francisco: Berrett-Koehler.

Latour, B. (1987). *Science in action: How to follow scientists and engineers through society.* Cambridge, MA: Harvard University Press.

Latour, B. (1990). Drawing things together. In M. Lynch & S. Woolgar (Eds.), *Representation in scientific practice* (pp. 19–68). Cambridge, MA: MIT Press.

Latour, B., & Woolgar, S. (1979). *Laboratory life: The social construction of scientific facts.* Beverley Hills, CA: Sage.

Laudan, L. (1977). *Progress and its problems: Toward a theory of scientific growth.* Berkeley, CA: University of California Press.

Laugksch, R. C. (2000). Scientific literacy: A conceptual overview. *Science Education, 84*(1), 71–94.

Lave, J., & Wenger, E. (1991). *Situated learning: Legitimate peripheral participation.* Cambridge: Cambridge University Press.

Law, N. (2002). Scientific literacy: Charting the terrains of a multifaceted enterprise. *Canadian Journal of Science, Mathematics and Technology Education, 2*(2), 151–176.

Lawrence, D. (1988). *Enhancing self-esteem in the classroom.* London: Paul Chapman.

Lawton, T. C., Roseneau, J. N., & Verdun, A. (2000). *Strange power: Shaping the parameters of international relations and international political economy.* Burlington, VT: Ashgate.

Layton, D. (1986). Revaluing science education. In P. Tomlinson & M. Quinton (Eds.), *Values across the curriculum* (pp. 158–178). London: Falmer Press.

Layton, D. (1991). Science education and praxis: The relationship of school science to practical action. *Studies in Science Education, 19,* 43–79.

Layton, D. (1993). *Technology's challenge to science education: Cathedral, quarry or company store?* Buckingham: Open University Press.

Layton, D., Jenkins, E., MacGill, S., & Davey, A. (1993). *Inarticulate science?* Driffield: Studies in Education.

Lecourt, D. (1977). *Proletarian science? The case of Lysenko.* Manchester: Manchester University Press.

Lederman, M., & Bartsch, I. (Eds.). (2001). *The gender and science reader.* New York: Routledge.

REFERENCES

Lederman, N. G. (1992). Students' and teachers' conceptions of the nature of science: A review of the research. *Journal of Research in Science Teaching, 29*(4), 331–359.

Lederman, N. G., & Gess-Newsome, J. (1992). Do subject matter knowledge and pedagogical content knowledge constitute the ideal gas law of science teaching? *Journal of Research in Science Teaching, 3*, 16–20.

Lee, H., Abd-El-Khalick, F., & Choi, K. (2006). Korean science teachers' perceptions of the introduction of socioscientific issues into the science curriculum. *Canadian Journal of Scienmce, Mathematics and Technology Education, 6*(2), 97–117.

Lee, H., & Witz, K. G. (2009). Science teachers' inspiration for teaching socio-scientific issues: Disconnection with reform efforts. *International Journal of Science Education, 31*(7), 931–960.

Lee, S., & Roth, W.-M. (2002). Learning science in the community. In W.-M. Roth & J. Desautels (Eds.), *Science education as/for sociopolitical action* (pp. 37–66). New York: Peter Lang.

Lee, Y. C. (2010). Science-technology-society or technology-society-science? Insights from an ancient technology. *International Journal of Science Education, 32*(14), 1927–1950.

Lélé, S. (1991). Sustainable development: A critical review. *World Development, 19*(6), 607–621.

Lemke, J. L. (1998). *Teaching all the languages of science: Words symbols, images, and actions.* Available at http://academic.brooklyn.cuny.edu/education/jlemke/papers/barcelon.htm

Lemke, J. L. (2001). Articulating communities: Sociocultural perspectives on science education. *Journal of Research in Science Teaching, 38*(3), 296–316.

Lemons, J. (1991). Structure and function of environmental programmes. *The Environmentalist, 11*(4), 297–311.

Lemons, J. (1995, July 14–16). The role of the university, scientists, and educators in promotion of environmental literacy. In B. Jickling (Ed.), *A colloquium on environment, ethics, and education* (pp. 90–109). Whitehorse, Yukon: Yukon College.

Lester, B. T., Ma, L., Lee, O., & Lambert, J. (2006). Social activism in elementary science education: A science, technology, and society approach to teach global warming. *International Journal of Science Education, 28*(4), 315–339.

Levi, P. (1984). *The periodic table* (R. Rosenthal, Trans.). New York: Schoken Books.

Levinson, R. (1999). Let's sup a while. *New Scientist, 2173*(Feb 13th), 52.

Levinson, R. (2001).Should controversial issues in science be taught through the humanities? *School Science Review, 82*(300), 97–102.

Levinson, R. (2003, April). *Teaching biotehics in science: Crossing a bridge too far?* A Paper presented at the annual meeting of the National Association for Research in Science Teaching, Philadelphia.

Levinson, R. (2004). Teaching biotehics in science: Crossing a bridge too far? *Canadian Journal of Science, Mathematics and Technology Education, 4*(3), 353–369.

Levinson, R. (2006). Towards a theoretical framework for teaching controversial socio-scientific issues. *International Journal of Science Education, 28*(10), 1201–1224.

Levinson, R. (2008). Promoting the role of the personal narrative in teaching controversial socio-scientific issues. *Science & Education, 17*, 855–871.

Levinson, R. (2010). Scence education and democratic participation: An uneasy congruence? *Studies in Science Education, 46*(1), 69–119.

Levinson, R., Douglas, A., Evans, J., Kirton, A., Koulouris, P., Turner, S., et al. (2000). Constraints on teaching the social and ethical issues arising from developments in biomedical research: A view across the curriculum in England and Wales. *Critical Studies in Education, 41*(2), 107–120.

Levinson, R., & Turner, S. (2001). *Valuable lessons: The teaching of social and ethical issues in the school curriculum arising from developments in biomedical research – A research study of teachers.* London: The Wellcome Trust.

Levy-Leboyer, C., & Duron, Y. (1991). Global change: New challenges for psychology. *International Journal of Psychology, 26*, 575–583.

Lewis, A., Amiri, L., & Sadler, T. D. (2006, April). *Nature of science in the context of socioscientific issues.* Paper presented at the annual meetings of the National Association for Research in Science Teaching, San Francisco.

Lewis, J., & Leach, J. (2006). Discussion of socio-scientific issues: The role of science knowledge. *International Journal of Science Education, 28*(11), 1267–1287.

Lewis, T., & Gagel, C. (1992). Technological literacy: A critical analysis. *Journal of Curriculum Studies, 24*(2), 117–138.

Lewontin, R., & Levins, R. (1976). The problem of Lysenkoism. In H. Rose & S. Rose (Eds.), *The radicalisation of science* (pp. 2–64). London: Macmillan.

Lewthwaite, B., & Renaud, R. (2009). *Pilimmaksarniq*: Working together for the common good in science curriculum development and delivery in Nunavut. *Canadian Journal of Scvience, Mathematics and Technology Education, 9*(3), 154–172.

Li, H.-L. (2000). Bioregionalism and global education: A re-examination. In L. Stone (Ed.), *Philosophy of education: Proceedings of the 21st annual meeting of the Philslophy of Education Society* (pp. 394–403). Toronto: Philosophy of Education Society.

Liakopoulos, M. (2002). Pandora's box or pabacea? Using mnetaphors to create the public representations of biotechnology. *Public Understanding of Science, 11*, 5–32.

Lijmbach, S., Margadant-van Arcken, M., van Koppen, C. S. A., & Wals, A. E. J. (2002). 'Your view of nature is not mine!': Learning about pluralism in the classroom. *Environmental Education Research, 8*(2), 121–135.

Lim, M., & Calabrese Barton, A. (2006). Science learning and a sense place in a urban middle school. *Cultural Studies of Science Education, 1*(1), 107–142.

Lin, C.-C., & Tsai, C.-C. (2008). Exploring the structiural relationships between high school students' scientific epistemological views and their utilization of informaation commitments toward online science information. *International Journal of Science Education, 30*(15), 2001–2022.

Lin, E. (2002). Trend of environmental education in Canadian preservice teacher education programs from 1979–1996. *Canadian Journal of Environmental Education, 7*(1), 199–215.

Lind, G. (2008). The meaning and measurement of moral judgment competence revisited. In D. Fasko & W. Willis (Eds.), *Contemporary philosophical and psychological perspectives on moral development and education* (pp. 185–220). Cresskill, NJ: Hampton Press.

Lindahl, M. G. (2009). Ethics or morals: Understanding students' values related to genetic tests on humans. *Science & Education, 18*(10), 1285–1311.

Lindemann-Matthies, P. (2005). 'Loveable' mammals and 'lifeless' plants: How children's interest in common local organisms can be enhanced through observation of nature. *International Journal of Science Education, 27*(6), 655–677.

Lindemann-Matthies, P., & Kamer, T. (2006). The influence of an interactive educational approach on visitors' learning in a Swiss zoo. *Science Education, 90*(2), 296–315.

Linzey, A. (1989). Reverence, responsibility and rights. In D. Paterson & M. Palmer (Eds.), *The status of animals: Ethics, education and welfare* (pp. 20–50). East Haddam, CT: Humane Education Foundation/CAB International.

Lippman, A. (1998). The politics of health: Geneticization versus health promotion. In S. Sherwin (Ed.), *The politics of women's health: Exploring agency and autonomy* (pp. 64–82). Philadelphia: Temple University Press.

Listerman, T. (2010). Framing of science issues in opinion-leading news: International comparison of biotechnology issue coverage. *Public Understanding of Science, 19*(1), 5–15.

Liston, D. (2004). The allure of beauty and the pain of injustice in learning and teaching. In D. Liston & J. Garrison (Eds.), *Teaching, learning and loving: Reclaiming passion in educational practice* (pp. 101–116). New York: RoutledgeFalmer.

Little, A. W. (1996). Globalization and educational research: Whose context counts? *International Journal of Educational Development, 16*(4), 427–438.

Littledyke, M. (1998). *Live issues: Drama strategies for personal, social and moral education.* Birmingham: Questions Publishing.

Littledyke, M. (2004). Primaty children's views on science and environmental issues: Examples of environmental cognitive and moral development. *Environmental Education Research, 10*, 217–235.

Littledyke, M. (2008). Science education for environmental awareness: Approaches to integrating cognitive and affective domains. *Environmental Education Research*, (1491), 1–17.

Liu, S.-Y., & Lederman, N. G. (2002). Taiwanese gifted students' views of nature of science. *School Science & Mathematics, 102*(3), 114–123.

Liu, S.-Y., & Lederman, N. G. (2007). Exploring prospective teachers' worldviews and conceptions of nature of science. *International Journal of Science Education, 19*(10), 1281–1307.

Liu, X. (2009). Beyond science literacy: Science and the public. *International Journal of Environmental & Science Education, 4*(3), 301–311.

Lloyd, D., & Wallace, J. (2004). Imaging the future of science education: The case for making futures studies explicit in student learning. *Studies in Science Education, 39*, 139–177.

Locust, C. (1988). Wounding the spirit: Discrimination and traditional American Indian belief systems. *Harvard Educational Review, 58*(3), 315–330.

Longino, H. E. (1990). *Science as social knowledge: Values and objectivity in scientific inquiry.* Princeton, NJ: Princeton University Press.

Longino, H. (1994). The fate of knowledge in social theories of science. In F. T. Schmitt (Ed.), *Socializing epistemology: The social dimensions of knowledge* (pp. 135–157). Lanham, MD: Rowman and Littlefield.

Longino, H. (1997). Feminist epistemology as a local epistemology. *Proceedings of the Aristotelian Society* supplementary volume *71*(1), 19–36.

Longino, H. E. (2002). *The fate of knowledge.* Princeton, NJ: Princeton University Press.

Loughland, T., Reid, A., & Petocz, P. (2002). Young people's conceptions of environment: A phenomenographic analysis. *Environmental Education Research, 8*, 187–197.

Loughland, T., Reid, A., Walker, K., & Petocz, P. (2003). Factors influencing young people's conceptions of environment. *Environmental Education Research, 9*(1), 3–20.

Loughran, J., Berry, A., & Mulhall, P. (2006). *Understanding and developing science teachers' pedagogical content knowledge.* Rotterdam: Sense Publishers.

Loughran, J., Milroy, P., Berry, A. Gunstone, R., & Mulhall, P. (2001). Documenting science teachers' pedagogical content knowledge through Pap-eRs. *Research in Science Education, 31*, 289–307.

Loughran, J., Mulhall, P., & Berry, A. (2004). In search of pedagogical content knowledge for science: Developing ways of articulating and documenting professional practice. *Journal of Research in Science Teaching, 41*, 370–391.

Loughran, J., Mulhall, P., & Berry, A. (2008). Exploring pedagogical content knowledge in science: Teacher education. *International Journal of Science Education, 30*(10), 1301–1320.

Lousley, C. (1999). (De)Politicizing the environment club: Environmental discourses and the culture of schooling. *Environmental Education Research, 5*(3), 293–304.

Louv, R. (2005). *Last child in the woods: Saving our children from nature deficit disorder.* Chapel Hill, NC: Algonquin Books.

Lovelock, J. (1986, December 18). Gaia: The world as a living organism. *New Scientist,* (1939), 25–28.

Lovelock, J. (1991). *The ages of Gaia: A biography of our living Earth.* Oxford: Oxford University Press.

Lovelock, J. (2000). *Gaia: A new look at life on earth.* Oxford: Oxford University Press.

Lovelock, J. (2006). *The revenge of Gaia: Why the Earth is fighting back – and how we can still save humanity.* London: Allen Lane.

Lovelock, J. (2009). *The vanishing face of Gaia: A final warning – Enjoy it while you can.* London: Allen Lane.

Lucas, A. (1979). *Environment and environmental education: Conceptual issues and curriculum interpretations.* Kew (Victoria): Australian International Press.

Lucas, B., & Roth, W.-M. (1996). The nature of scientific knowledge and student learning: Two longitudinal case studies. *Research in Science Education, 26*(1), 103–127.

Luke, C. (2000). Cyber-schooling and technological change. In B. Cope & M. Kalantzis (Eds.), *Multiliteracies: Literacy learning and the design of social futures* (pp. 69–91). London: Routledge.

Luke, T. W. (1995). Sustainable development as a power/knowledge system: The problem of 'governmentality'. In F. Fischer & M. Black (Eds.), *Greening environmental policy: The politics of a sustainable future* (pp. 21–32). London: Paul Chapman.

Luke, T. W. (2001). Education, environment and sustainability: What are the issues, where to intervene, what must be done? *Educational Philosophy & Theory, 33*(2), 187–202.

Lukes, S. (1974). *Power: A radical view*. London: Macmillan.

Lunn, S. (2002). 'What we think we can safely say…': primary teachers' views of the nature of science. *British Educational Research Journal, 28*(5), 649–672.

Lynch, M. (1985). *Art and artefact in laboratory science: The social construction of scientific facts*. Beverley Hills, CA: Sage.

Lynch, M. (1997). *Scientific practice and ordinary actions: Ethnomethodology and social studies of science*. Cambridge: Cambridge University Press.

Ma, H. (2009).Chinese secondary school science teachers' understanding of the nature of science – Emerging from their views of nature. *Research in Science Education, 39*(5), 701–724.

Maby, R. (2005). *Nature cure*. London: Catto & Windus.

MacFarlane, R. (2007). *The wild places*. London: Granta Books.

MacIntyre, A. (1981). *After virtue: A study in moral theory*. London: Duckworth.

Macy, J. R. (1983). *Despair and personal power in the nuclear age*. Philadelphia: New Society Publishers.

Macy, J. (1985). *Dharma and development: religion as resource in the Sarvodaya self-help movement*. West Hartford, CT: Kumarian Press.

Macy, J., & Brown, M. Y. (1998). *Coming back to life: Practices to reconnect our lives, our world*. Gabriola Island, BC: New Society Publishers.

Madrazo, G. M. (2002). The debate over dissection: Dissecting a classroom dilemma. *Science Educator, 11*(1), 41–45.

Magntorn, O., & Helldén, G. (2005). Student-teachers' ability to read nature: Reflections on their own learning of ecology. *International Journal of Science Education, 27*(10), 1229–1254.

Magnusson, S., Krajcik, J., & Borko, H. (1999). Nature, sources, and development of pedagogical content knowledge for science teaching. In J. Gess-Newsome & N. Lederman (Eds.), *Examining pedagogical content knowledge: The construct and its implications for science Education* (pp. 95–132). Dordrecht: Kulwer.

Mahoney. M. J. (1979). Psychology of the scientist: An evaluative review. *Social Studies of Science, 9*(3), 349–375.

Maiteny, P. T. (2002). Mind the gap: Summary of research exploring 'inner' influences on pro-sustainability learning and behaviour. *Environmental Education Research, 8*(3), 299–306.

Malcolm, C., & Keough, M. (2004). The science teacher as curriculum developer: Do you think it will rain today? In B. Gray, P. Naidoo, & M. Savage (Eds.), *School science in Africa: Teaching to learn, learning to teach* (pp. 105–128). Cape Town: African Forum for Children's Literacy in Science & Technology/ Juta Academic.

Mansour, N. (2008). The experiences and personal religious beliefs of Egyptian science teachers as a framework for understanding the shaping and reshaping of their beliefs and practices about science-technology-society (STS). *International Journal of Science Education, 30*(12), 1605–1634.

Marcinkowski, T. (1991). The relationship between environmental literacy and responsible environmental behaviour in environmental education. In M. Maldague (Ed.), *Methods and techniques for evaluating environmental education* (pp.). Paris: UNESCO.

Marcinkowski, T., Volk, T., & Hungerford, H. (1990). *An environmental educational approach to the training of middle level teachers: A prototype programme*. Paris: UNESCO-UNEP International Environmental Education Programme, Education Series 30.

Marks, R., & Eilks, I. (2009). Promoting scientific literacyt using a sociocritical and problem-oriented approach to chemistry teaching: Concept, examples, experiences. *International Journal of Environmental & Science Education, 4*(3), 231–145.

Marsden, B. (2001). Citizenship education: Permeation or pervasion? Some historical pointers. In D. Lambert & P. Machon (Eds.), *Citizenship through secondary geography* (pp. 1–30). London: RoutledgeFalmer.

REFERENCES

Marsh, H. W., & Yeung, A. S. (1997). Causal effects of academic self-concept on academic achievement: Structural models of longitudinal data. *Journal of Educational Psychology, 89*, 41–54.

Marshall, J. D. (1995). Foucault and neo-liberalism: Biopower and busno-power. In *Philosophy of education. Proceedings of the Philosophy of Education Society*. Available on-line at: http://www.ed.uiuc.edu/EPS/PES-Yearbook/95_docs/marshall.html

Mason, L., & Boscolo, P. (2002, September 12–15). *Interpreting a controversy: Epistemological thionking and critical reading and writing on a 'hot' science topic*. Paper presented at the conference on Philosophical, Linguistic Foundations for Language and Science Literacy. Victoria, BC: University of Victoria.

Martin, B. (1999). Suppressing research data: Methods, context, accountability, and responses. *Acoountability in Research, 6*(4), 333–372.

Martin, L. M. W. (2004). An emerging research framework for studying informal learning and schools. *Science Education, 88*(Suppl. 1), S71–S82.

Martin, P., & Klein, R. G. (Eds.). (1984). *Quaternary extinctions: A prehistoric revolution*. Tucson, AZ: University of Arizona Press.

Martin-Hanson, L. M. (2008). First-year college students' conflict with religion and science. *Science & Education, 17*(4), 317–357.

Mason, L., & Santi, M. (1998). Discussing the greenhouse effect: Children's collaborative discourse reasoning and conceptual change. *Environmental Education Research, 4*(1), 67–86.

Matthews, B. (2005). Emotional development, science and co-education. In S. Alsop (Ed.), *Beyond cartesian dualism: Encountering affect in the teaching and learning of science* (pp. 173–186). Dordrecht: Springer.

Matthews, B., Kilbey, T., Doneghan, C., & Harrison, S. (2002). Improving attitudes to science and citizenship through developing emotional literacy. *School Science Review, 84*(307), 103–114.

Matthews, G., Zeidner, M., & Roberts, R. D. (2004a). *Emotional intelligence: Science and myth*. Cambridge, MA: MIT Press.

Matthews, G., Roberts, R. D., & Zeidner, M. (2004b). Seven myths about emotional intelligence. *Psychological Inquiry, 15*(3), 179–196.

Matthews, M. R. (2009). Science, worldviews and education: An introduction. *Science & Education, 18*(6&7), 641–666.

Maurial, M. (1999). Indigenous knowledge and schololing: A continuum between conflict and challenge. In L. M. Semali & J. L. Kincheloe (Eds.), *What is indigenous knowledge? Voices from the academy* (pp. 59–77). New York: Falmer Press.

Maxwell, N. (1984). *From knowledge to wisdom*. Oxford: Basil Blackwell.

Maxwell, N. (1992). What kind of inquiry can best help us create a good world? *Science, Technology & Human Values, 17*(2), 205–227.

Maybury-Lewis, D. (1991). *Millennium: Tribal wisdom of the modern world*. London: Viking.

Mbajiorgu, N. M., & Iloputaife, E. C. (2001). Combating stereotypes of the scientist among pre-service science teachers in Nigeria. *Research in Science & Technological Education, 19*(1), 55–67.

McAllister, J. W. (1996). *Beauty and revolution in science*. Ithaca, NY: Cornell University Press.

McCaughey, M., & Ayers, M. D. (Eds.). (2003). *Cyberactivism: Online activism in theory and politics*. New York: Routledge.

McClaren, M., & Hammond, B. (2005). Integrating education and action in enviromental education. In E. A. Johnson & M. J. Mappin (Eds.), *Environmental education and advocacy: Changing perspectives of ecology and education* (pp. 267–291). Cambridge: Cambridge University Press.

McClune, B., & Jarman, R. (2010). Critical reading of science-based news reports: Establishing a knowledge, skills and attitudes framework. *International Journal of Science Education, 32*(6), 727–752.

McComas, W. F. (1998). The principal elements of the nature of science: Dispelling the myths. In W. F. McComas (Ed.), *The nature of science in science education: Rationales and strategies* (pp. 41–52). Dordrecht: Kluwer.

McComas, W. F. (2008). Seeking historical examples to illustrate key aspects of the nature of science. *Science & Education, 17*(2&3), 249–263.

McCormick, R. (1997). Conceptual and procedural knowledge. *International Journal of Technology and Design Education, 7*(1–2), 141–159.

McCright, A. M., & Dunlap, R. E. (2000). Challenging global warming as a social problem: An anlysis of the conservative movement's counter claims. *Social Problems, 47*(4), 499–522.

McCright, A. M., & Dunlap, R. E. (2003). Defeating Kyoto: The conservative movement's impact on U.S. climate change policy. *Social Problems, 50*(3), 348–373.

McCurdy, R. C. (1958). Towards a population literate in science. *The Science Teacher, 25*(7), 366–369 + 408.

McElroy, B. (1986). Geography's contribution to political literacy. In J. Fien & R. Gerber (Eds.), *Teaching geography for a better world* (pp. 90–108). Brisbane: Australian Geography Teachers Association, with Jacaranda Press.

McEneaney, E. H. (2003). The worldwide cachet of scientific literacy. *Comparative Education Review, 47*(2), 217–237.

McEwan, S. J. (2003). A comparison of computer simulation versus textbook study and field experience for teaching about wetlands. In D. Hodson (Ed.), *OISE papers in STSE education*, (Vol. 4, pp. 183–214). Toronto: Imperial Oil Centre for Studies in Science, Mathematics & Technology Education.

McGinnis, J. R., & Simmons, P. (1999). Teachers' perspectives on teaching science-technology-society in local cultures: A sociocultural analysis. *Science Education, 83*, 179–211.

McGregor, S. (2003). Consumerism as a source of structural violence. Available at: www.kon.org/hswp/archive/consumerism.pdf

McIntosh, A. (2008). *Hell and high water: Climate change, hope and the human condition*. Edinburgh: Birlinn.

McKenzie, M. (2008). The places of pedagogy: Or, what can we do with culture through intersubjective experiences. *Environmental Education Research, 14*(3), 361–373.

McKenzie-Mohr, D. (2000). Promoting sustainable behavior: An introduction to community-based social marketing. *Journal of Social Issues, 56*(3), 543–554.

McKenzie-Mohr, D., & Smith, W. (1999). *Fostering sustainable behaviour: An introduction to community-based social marketing*. Gabriola Island, BC: New Society.

McKeown, R., & Hopkins, C. (2003). EE ≠ ESD: Defusing the worry. *Environmental Education Research, 9*(1).

McKibben, B. (1989). *The end of nature* (10th anniversary edit, 1999). New York: Anchor.

McKibben, B. (2007). *Deep economy*. New York: Henry Holt.

McKinley, E. (2005). Locating the global: Culture, language and science education for indigenous students. *International Journal of Science Education, 27*(2), 227–241.

McLaren, P., & Lankshear, C. (1993). Critical literacy and the postmodern turn. In C. Lankshear & P. McLaren (Eds.), *Critical literacy: Politics, praxis, and the postmodern* (pp. 379–419). Albany, NY: State University of New York Press.

McMahan, E. M., & Rogers, K. L. (Eds.). (1994). *Interactive oral history interviewing*. Hillsdale, NJ: Lawrence Erlbaum Associates.

McMurty, J. (1999). *The cancer stage of capitalism*. London: Pluto.

McNaughton, M. J. (2004). Educational drama in the teaching of education for sustainability. *Environmental Education Research, 10*(2), 139–155.

McNeill, K. L. (2009). Teachers' use of curriculum to support students in writing scientific arguments to explain phenomena. *Science Education, 93*(2), 233–268.

McNeill, K. L., & Krajcik, J. (2007). Middle school students' use of appropriate and inappropriate evidence in writing scientific explanations. In M. Lovett & P. Shah (Ed.), *Thinking with data* (pp. 233–265). New York: Taylor & Francis.

McNeill, K. L., & Krajcik, J. (2008). Scientific explanations: Characterizing and evaluating the effects of teachers' instructional practices on student learning. *Journal of Research in Science Teaching, 45*(1), 53–78.

REFERENCES

McNeill, K. L, Lizotte, D. J., Krajcik, J., & Marx, R. W. (2006). Supporting students' construction of scientific explanations by fading scaffolds in instructional materials. *Journal of the Learning Sciences, 15*(2), 153–191.

McPeck, J. E. (1981). *Critical thinking and education.* Oxford: Martin Robertson.

McSharry, G., & Jones, S. (2000). Role-play in science teaching and learning. *School Science Review, 82*(298), 73–82.

McVay, S. (1993). Prelude: A Siamese connection with a plurality of other mortals. In S. R. Kellert & E. O. Wilson (Eds.), *The biophilia hypothesis* (pp. 3–19). Washington, DC: Island Press.

Mellado, V. (1998). The classroom practice of preservice teachers and their conceptions of teaching and learning science. *Science Education, 82*(2), 197–212.

Mellor, M. (1997). *Feminism & ecology.* Oxford: Blackwell.

Mellor, M. (2003). Gender and environment. In H. Eaton & L. A. Lorentzen (Eds.), *Ecofeminism and globalization: Exploring culture, context, and religion* (pp. 11–22). New York: Rowman & Littlefield.

Menzel, S., & Bögeholz, S. (2009). The loss of diversity as a challenge for sustainable development: How do pupils in Chile and Germany perceive resource dilemmas? *Research in Science Education, 39*(4), 429–447.

Menzel, S., & Bögeholz, S. (2010). Values, beliefs and norms that foster Chilean and German pupils' commitment to protect biodiversity. *International Journal of Environmental & Science Education, 5*(1), 31–49.

Mercer, N. (1995). *The guided construction of knowledge: Talk amongst teachers and learners.* Clevedon, UK: Multilingual Matters.

Mercer, N. (1996). The quality of talk in children's collaborative activity in the classroom. *Learning and Instruction, 6*(4), 359–375.

Mercer, N. (2000). *Words and minds: How we use language to think together.* London: Routledge.

Mercer, N., & Wergerif, R. (1999). Is 'exploratort talk' productive talk? In K. Littleton & P. Light (Eds.), *Learning with computers: Analysing productive interaction* (pp. 137–168). London: Routledge.

Mercer, N., Wegerif, R., & Dawes, L. (1999) Children's talk and the development of reasoning in the classroom. *British Educational Research Journal, 25*(1), 95–110.

Merchant, C. (1980). *The death of nature: Women, ecology, and the scientific revolution.* San Francisco: Harper & Row.

Merchant, C. (1992). Ecofeminism. In R. D. de Oliveira & T. Corral (Eds.), *Terra femina* (pp. 2–22). Rio de Janeiro: Companhia Brasileira de Artes.

Merchant, C. (1996). *Earthcare: Women and the environment.* New York: Routledge.

Meredith, J. E., Fortner, R. W., & Mullins, G. W. (1997). Model of affective learning for nonformal science education facilities. *Journal of Research in Science Teaching, 34*(8), 805–818.

Merton, R. K. (1973). *The sociology of science: Theoretical and empirical investigations.* Chicago: University of Chicago Press.

Michael, M., & Brown, N. (2005). Scientific citizenships: Self-representations of xenotransplantation's publics. *Science as Culture, 14*(1), 39–57.

Michaels, S., & O'Connor, M. C. (1990). *Literacy as reasoning within multiple discourses: Implications for policy and educational reform.* Newton, MA: The Literacies Institute and Education Development Center.

Michaelson, M. G. (1987). Sickle cell anaemia: An 'interesting pathology'. In D. Gill & L. Levidow (Eds.), *Anti-racist science teaching* (pp. 59–75). London: Free Association Press.

Michail, S., Stamou, A. G., & Stamou, G. P. (2007). Greek primary school teachers' understanding of current environmental issues: An exploration of their environmental knowledge and images of nature. *Science Education, 91*(2), 244–259.

Middleton, A., Hewison, J., & Muller, R. F. (1998). Attitudes of deaf adults toward genetic testing for hereditary deafness. *American Journal of Human Genetics, 63*, 1175–1180.

Mies, M., & Shiva, V. (1993). *Ecofeminism.* London: Zed Books.

Milburn, C. (1989). Introducing animal welfare into the education system. In D. Paterson & M. Palmer (Eds.), *The status of animals: Ethics, education and welfare* (pp. 73–78). East Haddam, CT: Humane Education Foundation/CAB International..

Milburn, C. (1992). Editorial. *Humane Education, 3*(2), 2.

Miles, H. L. W. (1994). ME CHANTEK: The development of self-awareness in a signing orangutan. In S. T. Parker, R. W. Mitchell, & M. L. Boccia (Eds.), *Self-awareness in animals and humans: Developmental perspectives* (pp. 254–272). Cambridge: Cambridge University Press.

Millar, R., & Osborne, J. (Eds.). (1998). *Beyond 2000: Science education for the future.* London: King's College London School of Education.

Miller, J. D., & Kimmel, L. G. (2001). *Biomedical communications: Purposes, audiences, and strategies.* New York: Academic Press.

Miller, K. (1992, December). Smoking up a storm: Public relations and advertising in the construction of the cigarette problem 1953-4. *Journalism Monographs No. 136.*

Miller, P. H., Swalinski Blessing, J., & Schwartz, S. (2006). Gender differences in high-school students' views about science. *International Journal of Science Education, 28*(4), 363–381.

Milne, C. (1998). Philosophically correct science stories? Examining the implications of heroic science stories for school science. *Journal of Research in Science Teaching, 35*(2), 175–187.

Milner, K. K., Collins, E. E., Connors, G. R., & Petty, E. M. (1998). Attitudes of young adults to prenatal screening and genetic correction for human attributes and psychiatric conditions. *American Journal of Human Genetics, 76*, 111–119.

Minaya, Z., & Downing, J. (n.d.). *Matamoras: Toxic legacy.* Available at: http://journalism.berkeley.edu/projects/border/matamoras.html

Ministry of Education, New Zealand. (1993). *Science in the New Zealand curriculum.* Wellington: Learning Media.

Ministry of Education, New Zealand. (1996). *Pūtaiao: i roto i te marautanga o Aotearoa.* Te Whangauia Tar: Te Karauna.

Ministry of Education & Training (Ontario). (2000). *The Ontario curriculum grades 9 to 12: Program planning and assessment.* Toronto: Queen's Printer for Ontario.

Ministry of Education & Training (Ontario). (2007). *Shaping our schools, shaping the future: Environmental education in Ontario schools.* Report of the working group on environmental education. Toronto: Queen's Printer for Ontario.

Mintzes, B. (2002). For and against: Direct to consumer advertising is medicalising normal human experience. *British Medical Journal, 324*(7342), 908.

Mirowski, P., & Sent, E.-M. (2008). The commercialization of science and the response of STS. In E. J. Hackett, O. Amsterdamska, M. Lynch, & J. Wajcman (Eds.), *The handbook of science and technology studies* (pp. 635–689). Cambridge, MA: MIT Press.

Mitcham, C. (1994). *Thinking through technology: The path between engineering and philosophy.* Chicago: University of Chicago Press.

Mitchell, R. K., Agle, B. R., & Wood, D. J. (1997). Toward a theory of stakeholder identification and salience: Defini the principle of who and what really counts. *Academy of Management Review, 22*(4), 853–886.

Mitroff, I. I. (1974). *The subjective side of science: A philosophical inquiry into the psychology of the Apollo moon scientists.* Amsterdam: Elsevier.

Mitroff, I. I., & Mason, R.O. (1974). On evaluating the scientific contribution of the Apollo missions via information theory: A study of the scientist-scientist relationship. *Management Science: Applications, 20*, 1501–1513.

Mittelstaedt, R., Sanker, L., & Van der Veer, B. (1999). Impact of a week-long experiential education program on environmental attitude and awareness. *Journal of Experiential Education, 22*(3), 138–149.

Mohai, P., & Bryant, B. (1998). Is there a 'race effect' on concern for environmental quality? *Public Opinion Quarterly, 62*, 475–505.

Moje, E. B. (2008). Foregrounding the disciplines in secondary literacy teaching and learning: A call for change. *Journal of Adolescent and Adult Literacy, 52*(2), 96–107.

REFERENCES

Moje, E. B., Ciechanowski, K. M., Kramer, K., Ellis, L., Carrillo, R., & Collazo, T. (2004). Working toward third space in content area literacy: An examination of everyday funds of knowledge and discourse. *Reading Research Quarterly, 39*, 38–70.

Moje, E. B., Collazo, T., Carrillo, R., & Marx, W. R. (2001). 'Maestro, what is quality?': Language, literacy, and discourse in project-based science. *Journal of Research in Science Teaching, 38*(4), 469–498.

Moje, E. B., & Shepardson, D. P. (1998). Social interactions and children's changing understanding of electric circuits. In B. Guzzetti & C. Hynd (Eds.), *Perspectives on conceptual change* (pp. 17–26). Mahwah, NJ: Erlbaum.

Monhardt, R. M., Tillotson, J. W., & Veronesi, P. D. (1999). Same destination, different journeys: A comparison of male and female views on becoming and being a scientist. *International Journal of Science Education, 21*(5), 533–551.

Mooney, C. (2005). *The Republican war on science*. New York: Basic Books.

Moore, F. M. (2008). Agency, identity, and social justice education: Preservice teachers' thoughts on becoming agents of change in urban elementary science classrooms. *Research in Science Education, 38*(50), 589–610.

Morgensen, F., & Schnack, K. (2010). The action competence approach and the 'new' discourses of education for sustainable development, competence and quality criteria. *Environmental Education Research, 16*(1), 59–74.

Morrison, J., & Carmody, M. (1997, September-October). Working within the framework of Aboriginal culture: Indigenous initiatives for sustainable development through landcare. In P. Austin (Ed.), *Proceedings of the sicth international permaculture conference & convergence: designing for a sustainable future*. Perth. Available from: permaculturewest.org.au

Morrison, J. A., Raab, F., & Ingram, D. (2009). Factors influencing elementary and secondary teachers' views on the nature of science. *Journal of Research in Science Teaching, 46*(4), 384–403.

Moseley, C., & Norris, D. (1999). Preservice teachers' views of scientists. *Science and Children, 37*(1), 50–53.

Moseley, C., Herber, R., Brooks, J., & Schwarz, L. (2010). 'Where are the field investigations?' An investigation of the (implied) paradox of learning about environmental education in a virtual classroom. *Canadian Journal of Science, Mathematics and Technology Education, 10*(1), 27–39.

Moss, D. M., Abrams, E. D., & Robb, J. (2001). Examining student conceptions of the nature of science. *International Journal of Science Education, 23*(8), 771–790.

Moynihan, R. (2003). The making of a disease: Female sexual dysfunction. *British Medical Journal, 326*(7379), 45–47.

Moynihan, R., Heath, J., & Henry, D. (2002). Selling sickness: The pharmaceutical industry and disease mongering. *British Medical Journal, 324*(7342), 886–891.

Muchie, M., & Li, X. (2006). Conclusions: Alternative approaches to well-being attainment and measurement. In M. Muchie & X. Li (Eds.), *Globaliation, inequality and the comodification of life and well-being* (pp. 265–280). London: Adonis & Abbey.

Mueller, M. P. (2009). Educational reflections on the 'ecological crisis': Ecojustice, environmentalism, and sustainability. *Science & Education, 18*(8), 1031–1056.

Mulkay, M. (1979). *Science and the sociology of knowledge*. London: Allen & Unwin.

Mulkay, M. (1993). Rhetorics of hope and fear in the great embryo debate. *Social Studies of Science, 23*, 721–742.

Mumford, L. (1938). *The culture of cities*. New York: Harcourt, Brace.

Munby, H. (1980). Analyzing teaching for intellectual independence. In H. Munby, G. Orpwood, & T. Russell (Eds.), *Seeing curriculum in a new light: Essays from science education* (pp. 11–33). Toronto: OISE Press.

Mutonyi, H., Nielsen, W., & Nashon, S. (2007). Building scientific literacy in HIV/AIDS education: A case study of Uganda. *International Journal of Science Education, 29*(11), 1363–1385.

Mutonyi, H., Nashon, S., & Nielsen, W. (2010). Perceptual influence of Ugandan biology students' understanding of HIV/AIDS. *Research in Science Education, 40*, 573–588.

Myers, G., Boyes, E., & Stanisstreet, M. (1999). Something in the air: School students' ideas about air pollution. *International Research in Geographical and Environmental Education, 8*, 108–119.

Myers, G., Boyes, E., & Stanisstreet, M. (2000). Urban and rural air pollution: A cross-age study of school students' ideas. *International Journal of Environmental Education and Information, 19*(4), 263–274.

Myers, G., Boyes, E., & Stanisstreet, M. (2004). School students' ideas about air pollution: Knowledge and attitudes. *Research in Science & Technological Education, 22*(2), 133–152.

Myers, O. E., Saunders, C. D., & Birjulin, A. A. (2004). Emotional dimensions of watching zoo animals: An experience sampling study building on insights from psychology. *Curator, 47*(3), 299–321.

Nabhan, G. P., & Trimble, S. (1994). *The geography of childhood: Why children need wild places.* Boston: Beacon Press.

Nadeau, R., & Désautels, J. (1984). *Epistemology and the teaching of science.* Ottawa: Science Council of Canada.

Naess, A. (1989). *Ecology, community and lifestyle.* Cambridge: Cambridge University Press.

Nanji, A. (1991) Islamic ethics. In P. Singer (Ed.), *A companion to ethics* (pp. 106–118). Oxford: Blackwell.

Nashon, S., Nielsen, W., & Petrina, S. (2008). Whatever happened to STS? Pre-service physics teachers and the history of quantum mechanics. *Science & Education, 17*(4), 387–401.

National Research Council. (1996). *National science education standards.* Washington, DC: National Academy Press.

National Science Board. (1998). *Science and engineering indicators – 1998.* Arlington, VA: National Science Foundation.

Naylor, S., Keogh, B., & Downing, B. (2007). Argumentation and primary science. *Research in Science Education, 37*(1), 17–39.

Negra, C., & Manning, R. E. (1997). Incorporating environmental behaviour, ethics, and values into nonformal environmental education programs. *Journal of Environmental Education, 28*(2), 10–21.

Nelkin, D. (1977). *Technological decisions and democracy: European experiments in public participation.* Beverley Hills, CA: Sage.

Nelkin, D. (1987). *Selling science: How the press covers science and technology.* New York: Freeman.

Nelkin, D. (1995). *Selling science: How the press covers science and technology* (Rev. ed.). New York: Freeman.

Newman, M. (2006). *Teaching defiance.* San Francisco: Jossey Bass.

Newton, P., Driver, R., & Osborne, J. (1999). The place of argumentation in the pedagogy of school science. *International Journal of Science Education, 21*(5), 553–576.

Nicholson-Cole, S. A. (2005). Representing climate change futures: A critique on the use of images for visual communication. *Computers, Environment and Urban Systems, 29*(3), 255–273.

Nielsen, W. S., Nashon, S., & Anderson, D. (2009). Metacognitive engagement during field-trip experiences: A case study of students in an amusement park physics program. *Journal of Research in Science Teaching, 46*(3), 265–288.

Nieswandt, M. (2007). Student affect and conceptual understanding in learning chemistry. *Journal of Research in Science Teaching, 44*(7), 908–937.

Nisbet, M. C., & Lewenstein, B. V. (2002). Biotechnology and the American media. *Science Communication, 23*(4), 359–391.

Nisbett, R. E. (2003). *The geography of thought: How Asians think differently... and why.* New York: The Free Press.

Noble, D. D. (1998). The regime of technology in education. In L. E. Beyer & M. W. Apple (Eds), *The curriculum: Problems, politics and possibilities* (pp. 267–283). Albany, NY: State University of New York Press.

Noddings, N. (1984). *Caring: A feminine approach to ethics and moral education.* Berkeley, CA: University of California Press.

Noddings, N. (1995). *Philosophy of education.* Boulder, CO: Westview Press.

Norgaard, K. M. (2006). 'We don't really want to know': Environmental justice and socially organized denial of global warming in Norway. *Organization & Environment, 19*(3), 347–370.

REFERENCES

Norris, S. P. (1995). Learning to live with scientific expertise: Toward a theory of intellectual communalism for guiding science teaching. *Science Education, 79*(2), 201–217.

Norris, S. P., & Phillips, L. M. (1994). Interpreting pragmatic meaning when reading popular reports of science. *Journal of Research in Science Teaching, 31,* 947–967.

Norris, S. P., & Phillips, L. M. (2003). How literacy in its fundamental sense is central to scientific literacy. *Science Education. 87*(2), 224–240.

Norris, S. P., & Phillips, L. M. (2008). Reading as inquiry. In R. A. Duschl, & R. E. Grandy (Eds.), *Teaching scientific inquiry: Recommendations for research and implementation* (pp. 233–262). Rotterdam: Sense Publishers.

Norris, S. P., Phillips, L. M., & Korpan, C. A. (2003). University students' interpretation of media reports of science and its relationship to background knowledge, interest and reading difficulty. *Public Understanding of Science, 12,* 123–145.

Norris, S. P., Macnab, J. S., Wonham, M., & de Vries, G. (2009). West Nile Virus: Using adapated primary literature in mathematical biology to teach scientific and mathematical reasoning in high school. *Research in Science Education, 39,* 321–329.

Noss, R. (1998). New numeracies for a technological culture. *For the Learning of Mathematics, 18*(2), 2–12.

Nowotny, H., Scott, P., & Gibbons, M. (2001). *Re-thinking science: knowledge and the public in an age of uncertainty.* Cambridge: Polity Press.

Nowotny, H., Scott, P., & Gibbons, M. (2003). 'Mode 2' revisited: The new production of knowledge. *Minerva, 41*(3), 179–194.

Nuffield Biology. (1966). *Text 1: Introducing living things.* London/Harmondsworth: Longmans/Penguin.

Nussbaum, E. M., Hartley, K., Sinatra, G. M., Reynolds, R. E., & Bendixen, L. M. (2004). Personality interactions and scaffolding in on-line discussions. *Journal of Educational Computing* Research, *30,* 113–137.

Nussbaum, E. M., & Kardash, C. M. (2005). The effect of goal instructions and text on the generation of cunterarguments during writing. *Journal of Educational Psychology, 97,* 157–169.

Nussbaum, E. M., & Sinatra, G. M. (2003). Argument and conceptual engagement. *Contemporary Educational Psychology, 28,* 384–395.

Nussbaum, M. (1988). Non-relative virtues: An Aristotelian approach. In P. A. French, T. Uehling, & H. Wettstein (Eds.), *Ethical theory: Character and virtue.* Midwest Studies in Philosophy (Vol. XIII, pp. 32–53). Notre Dame, IN: University of Notre Dame Press.

Nussbaum, M. C. (1990). *Love's knowledge: essays on philosophy and literature.* Oxford: oxford University Press.

Nye, D. E. (1990). *Electrifying America: Social meanings of a new technology, 1880–1940.* Cambridge, MA: MIT Press.

Oakley, J. (2009). Under the knife: Animal dissection as a contested school science activity. *Journal of Activist Science & Technology Education, 1*(2), 59–67.

Odegaard, M. (2003). Dramatic science: A critical review of drama in science education. *Studies in Science Education, 39,* 75–102.

Odegaard, M. (2004). Gen-gangere: A science-in-drama project about knowledge, biotechnology and Ibsen's dramatic works. *School Science Review, 86*(315), 87–94.

Odora Hoppers, C. A. (2000). Globalization and the social construction of reality: Affirming or unmasking the inevitable? In N. P. Stromquist & K. Monkman (Eds.), *Globalization and education: Integration and contestation across cultures* (pp. 99–119). Lanham, MD: Rowman & Littlefield.

Odora Hoppers, C. A. (2002). *Indigenous knowledge and the integration of knowledge systems.* Claremont (South Africa): New Africa Books.

Office of Science and Technology and the Wellcome Trust. (2001). Science and the public: A review of science communication and public attitudes toward science in britain. *Public Understanding of Science, 10*(3), 315–330.

Ogawa, M. (1998). A cultural history of science education in Japan: An epic description. In W. W. Cobern (Ed.), *Socio-cultural perspectives on science education* (pp. 139–161). Dordrecht: Kluwer.

Ogunniyi, M. B. (2007a). Teachers' stances and practical arguments regarding a science-indigenous knowledge curriculum: Part 1. *International Journal of Science Education, 29*(8), 963–986.

Ogunniyi, M. B. (2007b). Teachers' stances and practical arguments regarding a science-indigenous knowledge curriculum: Part 2. *International Journal of Science Education, 29*(11), 1189–1207.

Olds, A. R. (1990). Sending them home alive. In E. Hooper-Greenhill (Ed.), *Museums and their visitors* (pp. 332–336). London: Routledge.

O'Neill, C., & Lambert, A. (1983). *Drama structures: A practical handbook for teachers.* Portsmouth, NH: Heinemann.

O'Neill, O. (1991) Kantian ethics. In P. Singer (Ed.), *A companion to ethics* (pp. 175–185). Oxford: Blackwell.

Opotow, S., & Weiss, L. (2000). Denial and the process of moral exclusion in environmental conflict. *Journal of Social Issues, 56*(3), 475–490.

Organization for Economic Cooperation and Development (OECD). (2003). *Assessment framnework – Mathematics, reading, science and problem solving knowledge and skills.* Paris: OECD.

Organization for Economic Cooperation and Development (OECD). (2006). *Assessing scientific, reading and mathematical literacy: A framework for PISA 2006.* Paris: OECD.

O'Riordan, T. (1983). The nature of the environmental idea. In T. O'Riordan & R. K. Turner (Eds.), *An annotated reader in environmental planning and management* (pp. 1–62). Oxford: Pergamon Press.

Orlans, F. B. (1988). Debating dissection. *The Science Teacher, 55*(8), 36–40.

Orr, D. W. (1992). *Ecological literacy: Education and the transition to a postmodern world.* Albany, NY: State University of New York Press.

Orr, D. W. (1994). *Earth in mind.* Washington, DC: Island Press.

Orr, D. W. (1996). Re-ruralizing education. In W. Vitek & W. Jackson (Eds.), *Rooted in the land: Essays on community and place* (pp. 226–234). New Haven, CT: Yale University Press.

Orr, D. W. (2002). Political economy and the ecology of childhood. In P. H. Kahn & S. R. Kellert (Eds.), *Children and nature: Psychological, sociocultural, and evolutionary investigations* (pp. 279–303). Cambridge, MA: MIT Press.

Osborne, J. (2001). Promoting argument in the science classroom: A rhetorical perspective. *Canadian Journal of Science, Mathematics and Technology Education, 1*(3), 271–290.

Osborne, J., Erduran, S., & Simon, S. (2004). Enhancing the quality of argumentation in school science. *Journal of Research in Science Teaching, 41*(10), 994–1010.

Osborne, K. (1991). *Teaching for democratic citizenship.* Toronto: Our Schools/Our selves.

Oscarsson, V. (1996). Pupils' views on the future in sweden. *Environmental Education Research, 2*(3), 261–177.

Österlind, K. (2005). Concept formationnin environmental education: 14-year olds' work on the intensified greenhouse effect and the depletion of the ozone layer. *International Journal of Science Education, 27*(8), 891–908.

Östman, L. (1998). How companion meanings are expressed by science education discourse. In D. Roberts & L. Östman (Eds.), *Problems of meaning in science curriculum* (pp. 54–70). New York: Teachers College Press.

Oulton, C., Dillon, J., & Grace, M. (2004). Reconceptualizing the teaching of controversial issues. *International Journal of Science Education, 26*(4), 411–423.

Oxfam (1997). *A curriculum for global citizenship.* London: Oxfam.

Oztas, F., & Kalipçi, E. (2009). Teacher candidates' perception level of environmental pollutant and their risk factors. *International Journal of Environmental & science Education, 4*(2), 185–195.

Pacey, A. (1983). *The culture of technology.* Oxford: Basil Blackwell.

Palefau, T. H. (2005). *Perspectives on scientific and technological literacy in Tonga: Moving forward in the 21st century.* Unpublished PhD thesis, University of Toronto, Toronto.

Palmberg, I. E., & Kuru, J. (2000). Outdoor activities as a basis for environmental responsibility. *Journal of Environmental Education, 31*(4), 32–36.

Palmer, J. A. (1993). Development of concern for the environment and the formative experiences of educators. *Journal of Environmental Education, 24*(3), 26–30.

REFERENCES

Palmer, J. A. (1998). *Environmental education in the 21st century: Theory, practice, progress and promise*. London: Routledge.

Palmer, J. A., & Suggate, J. (1996). Influences and experiences affecting the proenvironmental behaviour of educators. *Environmental Education Research, 2*(1), 109–121.

Palmer, J. A., Suggate, J., Bajd, B., & Tsaliki, E. (1998). Significant influences on the development of adults' environmental awareness in the UK, Slovenia and Greece. *Environmental Education Research, 4*(4), 429–444.

Pancer, S. M., & Pratt, M. W. (1999). Social and family determinants of community service involvement in Canadian youth. In M. Yates & J. Youniss (Eds.), *Roots of civic identity* (pp. 32–55). Cambridge: Cambridge University Press.

Papadimitriou, V. (2004). Prospective primary teachers' understanding of cliomate change, greenhouse gas effect, and ozone layer depletion. *Journal of Science Education and Technology, 13*(2), 299–307.

Parchmann, I., Grasel, C., Baer, A., Nentwig, P., Demuth, R., Ralle, B., et al. (2006). Chemie im Kontext: A symbiotic implementation of a context-based teaching and learning approach. *International Journal of Science Education, 28*(9), 1041–1062.

Park, J., Jeon, H., & Logan, R. A. (2009). The Korean press and Hwang's fraud. *Public Understanding of Science, 18*(6), 653–669.

Park, J.-H., & Chang, N.-K. (1998). The development and effects of a teaching strategy to foster environmental sensitivity. *International Journal of Science Education, 17*(2). 167–178.

Parker, W. C., Ninimiya, A., & Cogan, J. (1999). Educating world citizens: Toward multinational curriculum development. *American Educational Research Journal, 36*(2), 117–145.

Parsons, E. C. (1997). Black high school females' images of the scientist: Expression of culture. *Journal of Research in Science Teaching, 34*(7), 745–768.

Pascalev, A. (2003). You are what you eat: Genetically modified foods, integrity, and society. *Journal of Agricultural and Environmental Ethics, 16*, 583–594.

Patel, V. L., Kaufman, D. R., & Arocha, J. F. (1999). Conceptual change in the biomedical and health sciences domain. In R. Glaser (Ed.), *Advances in educational psychology* (pp. 329–392). Mahwah, NJ: Lawrence Erlbaum Associates.

Pateman, C. (1970). *Participation and democratic theory*. Cambridge: Cambridge University Press.

Patronis, T., Potari, D., & Spiliotopoulou, V. (1999). Students' argumentation in decision-making on a socio-scientific issue: Implications for teaching. *International Journal of Science Education, 21*, 745–754.

Pavlova, M. (2005). Social change: How should technology education respond? *International Journal of Technology and Design Education, 15*, 199–215.

Pavlova, M. (2006). Technology education for sustainable futures. *Design and Technology Education: An International Journal, 11*(2), 41–53.

Pavlova, M. (2009). Conceptualisation of technology education within the paradigm of sustainable development. *International Journal of Technology and Design Education, 19*(2), 109–132.

Payne, P. (1998a). Children's conceptions of nature. *Australian Journal of Enviromental Education, 14*, 19–26.

Payne, P. (1998b). The politics of nature: Children's conceptions, constructions and values. In W. L. Filho & M. Ahlberg (Eds.), *Environmental education for sustainability: Good environment, good life* (pp. 209–229). Frankfurt: Peter Lang.

Pedretti, E. (1997). Septic tank crisis: A case study of science, technology and society education in an elementary school. *International Journal of Science Education, 19*(10), 1211–1230.

Pedretti, E. (1999). Decision making and STS education: Explotring scientific knowledge and social responsibility in schools and science centres through an issues-based approach. *School Science & Mathematics, 99*, 174–181.

Pedretti, E. (2002). T. Kuhn meets T. Rex: Critical conversations and new directions in science centres and science museums. *Studies in Science Education, 37*, 1–42.

Pedretti, E. (2003). Teaching science, technology, society and environment (STSE) education: Preservice teachers' philsopohical and pedagogical landscapes. In D. L. Zeidler (Ed.), *The role of moral reasoning on socioscientific issues and discourse in science education* (pp. 219–239). Dordrecht: Kluwer.

Pedretti, E. (2004). Perspectives on learning through critical issues-based science center exhibits. *Science Education, 88*(Suppl. 1), S34–S47.

Pedretti, E., & Hodson, D. (1995) From rhetoric to action: Implementing STS education through action research. *Journal of Research in Science Teaching, 32*, 463–485.

Pedretti, E., & Soren, B. (2006). Reconnecting to the natural world through an immersive environment. *Canadian Journal of Science, Mathematics and Technology Education, 6*(1), 83–96.

Pedretti, E. G., Bencze, L., Hewitt, J., Romkey, I., & Jivraj, A. (2008). Promoting issues-based STSE perspectives in science teacher education: Problems of identity and ideology. *Science & Education, 17*, 941–960.

Pe'er, S., Goldman, D., & Yavetz, B. (2007). Environmental literacy in teacher training: Attitude, knowledge, and environmental behaviour of beginning teachers. *Journal of Environmental Education, 39*(1), 45–59.

Pekel, F. O., & Ozay, E. (2005). Turkish high school students' perceptions of ozone layer depletion. *Applied Environmental Education and Communication, 4*(2), 115–123.

Pella, M. O., O'Hearn, G. T., & Gale, C. W. (1966). Referents to scientific literacy. *Journal of Research in Science Teaching, 4*, 199–208.

Penney, K., Norris, S. P., Phillips, L. M., & Clark, G. (2003). The anatomy of junior high school science textbooks: An analysis of textual characteristics and a comparison to media reports of science. *Canadian Journal of Science, Mathematics and Technology Education, 3*, 415–436.

People for the Ethical Treatment of Animals (PETA). (2004). *How animals are collected and killed for dissection and the alternatives... You can choose.* The PETA gyuide to animals and the dissection industry. Norfolk, VA: PETA.

Pepper, D. (1996). *Modern environmentalism: An introduction.* London: Routledge.

Pepper, S. C. (1942). *World hypotheses: A study in evidence.* Berkeley, CA: University of California Press.

Perlas, N. (1995). The seven dimensions of sustainable agriculture. In V. Shiva & I. Moser (Eds.), *Biopolitics: A feminist and ecological reader on biotechnology* (pp. 234–266). London: Zed Books.

Perreault, G. (1979, October). *Futuristic world views: Modern physics and feminism – Implications for teaching/learning in higher education.* Paper presented at the annual conference of the World Future Society, Minneapolis, MN. Columbus, OH: ERIC Document Reproduction Service, No. 184 016.

Petrina, S. (1998). Multidisciplinary technology education. *International Journal of Technology & Design Education, 8*(2), 103–138.

Petrina, S. (2000a). The politics of technological literacy. *International Journal of Technology and Design Education, 10*(2), 181–206.

Petrina, S. (2000b). The political ecology of design and technology education: An inquiry into methods. *International Journal of Technology and Design Education, 10*(2), 207–237.

Petrini, C. (2007). *Slow food nation: Blueprint for changing the way we eat.* New York: Rizzoli.

Petryna, A. Lakoff, A., & Kleinman, A. (Eds.) (2006). *Global pharmaceuticals: Ethics, markets, practices.* Durham, NC: Duke University Press.

Pfeiffer, R. S. (1992). Teaching ethical decision making: The case study method and the RESOLVEDD strategy. *Teaching Philosophy, 15*(2), 175–184.

Phillips, L. M., & Norris, S. P. (1999). Interpreting popular reports of science: What happens when the reader's world meets the world on paper? *International Journal of Science Education, 21*(3), 317–327.

Phillips, L. M., & Norris, S. P. (2009). Bridging the gap between the language of science and the language of school science through the use of adapted primary literature. *Research in Science Education, 39*, 313–319.

Physicians Committee for Responsible Medicine (PCRM). (2007). *Conscientious objection in the classroom.* Washington, DC: PCRM.

Pickering, A. (Ed.). (1992). *Science as practice and culture.* Chicago: University of Chicago Press.

REFERENCES

Pike, G. (2000). A tapestry in the making: The strands of global education. In T. Goldstein & D. Selby (Eds.), *Weaving connections: Educating for peace, social and environmental justice* (pp. 218–241). Toronto: Sumach Press.

Pike, G., & Selby, D. (1987). *Global teacher, global learner*. London: Hodder & Stoughton.

Pilger, J. (2002). *The new rulers of the world*. London: Verso.

Pintrich, P. R. (1999). Motivational beliefs as resources for and constraints on conceptual change. In W. Schnotz, S. Vosniadou, & M. Carretero (Eds.), *New perspectives on conceptual change* (pp. 33–50). Amsterdam: Pergamon.

Pintrich, P. R., Marx, R. W., & Boyle, R. A. (1993). Beyond cold conceptual change: The role of Motivational beliefs and classroom contextual factors in the process of conceptual change. *Review of Educational Research, 63*, 167–199.

Plumwood, V. (1991). Nature, self, and gender: feminism, environmental philosophy, and the critique of rationalism. *Hypatia, 6*(1), 3–27.

Plumwood, V. (1993). *Feminism and the mastery of nature*. New York: Routledge.

Plumwood, V. (1999). Paths beyond human-centredness: Lessons from liberation struggles. In A. Weston (Ed.), *An invitation to environmental philosophy* (pp. 69–105). New York: Oxford University Press.

Pool, R. (1997). *Beyond engineering: How society shapes technology*. New York: Oxford University Press.

Poole, M. W. (1998). Science and science education: A Judeo-Christian perspective. In W. W. Cobern (Ed.), *Socio-cultural perspectives on science education* (pp. 181–201). Dordrecht: Kluwer.

Popper, K. R. (1966). The sociology of knowledge. In K. R. Popper (Ed.), *The open society and its enemies, volume II: the high tide of prophesy – Hegel, Marx and the aftermath* (pp. 212–223). Princeton, NJ: Princeton University Press. (Originally published in 1945)

Posch, P. (1993). Research issues in environmental education. *Studies in Science Education, 21*, 21–48.

Posner, G. J., Strike, K. A., Hewson, P. J., & Gertzog, W. A. (1982). Accommodation of a scientific conception: Toward a theory of conceptual change. *Science Education, 66*, 211–227.

Postel, S. (1992). Denial in the decisive decade. In L. R. Brown & L. Starke (Eds.), *State of the world 1992: A Worldwatch institute report on progress topwards a sustainable society* (pp. 3–8). New York: Norton.

Postman, N. (1992). *Technopoly: The surrender of culture to technology*. New York: Alfred A. Knopf.

Potts, A., Stanisstreet, M., & Boyes, E. (1996). Children's ideas about the ozone layer and opportunities for physics teaching. *School Science Review, 78*, 57–62.

Pouliot, C. (2008). Students' inventory of social actors concerned by the controversy surroiunding cellular telephones: A case study. *Science Education, 92*(3), 543–559.

Pouliot, C. (2009). Using the deficit model, public debate model and co-production of knowledge models to interpret points of view of students concerning citizens' participation in socioscientific issues. *International Journal of Environmental & Science Education, 4*(1), 49–73.

Prain, V. (2006). Learning from writing in secondary science: Some theoretical and practical implications. *International Journal of Science Education, 28*(2&3), 179–201.

Prakash, M. S. (1994). From global thinking to local thinking: Reasons to go beyond globalization toward localization. *Holistic Education Review, 7*(4), 50–56.

Prakash, M. S. (1999). Indigenous knowledge systems – ecological literacy through initiation into people's science. In L. M. Semali & J. L. Kincheloe (Eds.), *What is indigenous knowledge? Voices from the academy* (pp. 157–178). New York: Falmer Press.

Preston, R. (1991). Christian ethics. In P. Singer (Ed.), *A companion to ethics* (pp. 91–105). Oxford: Blackwell.

Price, R. F., & Cross, R. T. (1995). Conceptions of science and technology clarified: Improving the teaching of science. *International Journal of Science Education, 17*(3), 285–293.

Prime, R. (2006). *Hinduism and ecology: Seeds of truth*. London: Cassell & World Wildlife Fund.

Princen, T. (2003). Principles for sustainability: from cooperation and efficiency to sufficiency. *Global Environmental Politics*, (391), 33–50.

Proctor, R. N. (1995). *Cancer wars: How politics shapes what we know and don't know about cancer*. New York: Basic Books.

Pruneau, D., Moncton, U., Liboirin, L., & Vrain, E. (2001). People's ideas about climate change: A source of inspiration for the creation of educational programs. *Canadian Journal of Environmental Education, 6*(1), 58–76.

Pruneau, D., Gravel, H., Courque, W., & Langis, J. (2003). Experimentation with a socio-constructivist process for climate change education. *Environmental Education Research, 9*(4), 429–446.

Pruneau, D., Doyon, A., Langis, J., Vasseur, L., Ouellet, E., McLaughlin, E., et al. (2007). When teachers adopt environmental behaviours in the aim of protecting the climate. *Journal of Environmental Education, 37*(3), 3–12.

Prutzman, P., Burger, M. L., Bodenhamer, G., & Stern, L. (1978). *The friendly classroom for a small planet: A handbook on creative approaches to living and problem solving for children.* Gabriola Island, BC: New Society Publishers.

Purdue, D. (2000). *Anti-genetix: The emergence of the anti-GM movement.* Aldershot: Ashgate.

Putnam, H. (2004). *The collapse of the fact/value dichotomy.* Cambridge, MA: Harvard University Press.

Qualifications and Curriculum Authority (QCA). (1998). *Education for citizenship and the teaching of democracy in schools.* London: Author.

Qualifications and Curriculum Authority (QCA). (2000). *Citizenship at key stages 3 and 4: Initial guidance for schools.* London: Author.

Quart, A. (2003). *Branded: The buying and selling of teenagers.* Cambridge, MA: Perseus.

Rahm, J. (2007). Youths' and scientists' authoring of and positioning within science and scientists' work. *Cultural Studies of Science Education, 1*(3), 517–544.

Rahm, J. (2008). Urban youths' hybrid positioning in science practices at the margin: A look inside a school-museum-scientist partnership project and an after-school science prohgram. *Cultural Studies of Science Education, 3*(1), 97–121.

Rahmeena, M. (1992). Participation. In W. Sachs (Ed.), *The development dictionary* (pp. 116–131). London: Zed Books.

Ramey-Gassert, L., & Walberg, H. J. (1994). Re-examining connections: Museums as science learning environments. *Science Education, 78*(4), 345–363.

Rampal, A. (1992). Image of science and scientists: A study of school teachers' views. 1. Characteristics of scientists. *Science Education, 76*(4), 415–436.

Ratcliffe, M. (1997). Pupil decision-making about socio-scientific issues within the science curriculum. *International Journal of Science Education, 19*(2), 167–182.

Ratcliffe, M. (1999a). Evaluation of abilities in interpreting media reports of scientific research. *International Journal of Science Education, 21*(10), 1085–1099.

Ratcliffe, M. (1999b). Exploring aspects of scientific literacy in the classroom – Evidence based decision-making. In O. de Jong, J. Kortland, A. J. Waarlo, & J. Buddingh (Eds.), *Bridging the gap bwtween theory and practice: What research says to the science teacher* (pp. 51–67). Hatfield: International Council for Associations of Science Education.

Ratcliffe, M. (2007). Values in the science classroom – The 'enacted' curriculum. In D. Corrigan, J. Dillon, & R. Gunstone (Eds.), *The re-emergence of values in science education* (pp. 119–132). Rotterdam: Sense Publishers.

Ratcliffe, M., & Grace, M. (2003). *Science education for citizenship: Teaching socio-scientific issues.* Maidenhead: Open University Press.

Ratcliffe, M., Harris, R., & McWhirter, J. (2004). Teaching ethical aspects of science – Is cross-curricular collaboration the answer? *School Science Review, 86*(315), 39–44.

Ratcliffe, M., Harris, R., & McWhirter, J. (2005). Cross-curricular collaboration in teaching social aspects of genetics. In K. Boersma, M. Goedhart, O. de Jong, & H. Eijkelhof (Eds.), *Research and the quality of science education* (pp. 77–88). Dordrecht: Springer.

Räthzel, N., & Uzzell, D. (2009). Transformative environmental education: A collective rehearsal for reality. *Environmental Education Research, 15*(3), 263–277.

Rawls, J. (1957). Justice as fairness. *Journal of Philosophy, 54*, 653–662.

Rawls, J. (1971). *A theory of justice.* Cambridge, MA: Harvard University Press.

REFERENCES

Read, D., Bostrom, A., Morgan, M. G., Fischoff, B., & Smith, T. (1994). What do people know about global climate change? Survey studies of educated lay people. *Risk Analysis, 14*, 971–982.

Reah, D. (2002). *The language of newspapers*. London: Routledge.

Reardon, B. A. (1988). *Comprehensive peace education: Educating for global responsibility*. New York: Teachers College Press.

Rees, W. E. (1992). Ecological footprints and appropriated carrying capacity: What urban economics leaves out. *Environment and Urbanization, 4*(2), 121–130.

Regan, T. (1983). *The case for animal rights*. Berkeley, CA: University of California Press.

Regan, T. (1985). The case for animals' rights. In P. Singer (Ed.), *In defence of animals* (pp. 13–26). New York: Blackwell.

Reid, A., & Nikel, j. (2008). Differentiating and evaluating conceptions and examples of participation in environment-related learning. In A. Reid, B. B. Jensen, J. Nikel, & V. Simovsla (Eds.), *Participation and learning: Perspectives on education and the environment, health and sustainability* (pp. 32–60). New York: Springer.

Reid, A., Teamey, K., & Dillon, J. (2004). Valuing and utilizing traditional ecological knowledge: Tensions in the context of education and the environment. *Environmental Education Research, 10*(2).

Reid, N., & Yang, M.-J. (2002). Open-ended problem solving in school chemistry: A preliminary investigation. *International Journal of Science Education, 24*, 1313–1332.

Reigosa, C., & Jiménez-Aleixandre, M.-P. (2007). Scaffolded problem-solving in the physics and chemistry laboratory: Difficulties hindering students' assumption of responsibility. *International Journal of Science Education, 29*(3), 307–329.

Reis, P., & Galvão, C. (2004). The impact of socio-scientific controversies in Portuguese natural science teachers' conceptions and practices. *Research in Science Education, 34*(2), 153–171.

Reiser, B. (2002). Why scaffolding should sometimes make tasks more difficult for learners. In G. Stahl (Ed.), *Computer support for collaborative learning: Foundations for a computer supported collaborative learning community* (pp. 255–264). Hillsdale, NJ: Erlbaum.

Reiss, M. (1999). Teaching ethics in science. *Studies in Science Education, 34*, 115–140.

Reiss, M. J. (2007a). Teaching about origins in science: Where now? In L. Jones & M. J. Reiss (Eds.), *Teaching about scientific origins: Taking account of creationism* (pp. 197–208). New York: Peter Lang.

Reiss, M. J. (2007b). Imagining the world: The significance of religious worldviews for science education. *Science & Education, 18*, 783–796.

Reiss, M. (2008). The use of ethical frameworks by students following a new science course for 16–18 year-olds. *Science & Education, 17*, 889–902.

Reiss, M. J. (2009). Ethical reasoning and action in STSE education. In A. Jones & M. de Vries (Eds.), *International handbook of research and development in technology education* (pp. 307–318). Rotterdam: Sense Publishers.

Reiss, M. J. (2010a). Science and religion: Implications for science educators. *Cultural Studies of Science Education, 5*, 91–101.

Reiss, M. (2010b). Ethical thinking. In A. Jones, A. McKim, & M. Reiss (Eds.), *Ethics in the science and technology classroom: A new approach to teaching and learning* (pp. 7–17). Rotterdam: Sense Publishers.

Relyea, H. C. (1994). *Silencing science: National security controls and scientific communication*. Norwood, NJ: Ablex.

Remtulla, K. A. (2008). Democracy or digital divide? The pedagogical paradoxes of online activism. In D. E. Lind & P. R Carr (Eds.), *Doing democracy: Striving for political literacy and social justice* (pp. 267–280). New York: Peter Lang.

Rennie, L. J. (2007). Learning science outside of school. In S. K. Abell & N. G. Lederman (Eds.), *Handbook of research on science education* (pp. 125–167). Mahwah, NJ: Lawrence Erlbaum Associates.

Rennie, L. J., & Jarvis, T. (1995a). Children's choice of drawings to communicate their ideas about technology. *Journal of Research in Science Teaching, 37*, 784–806.

Rennie, L. J., & Jarvis, T. (1995b). English and Australian children's perceptions about technology. *Research in Science & Technological Education, 13*(1), 37–52.

Rennie, L. J., & Jarvis, T. (1995c). Three approaches to measuring children's perceptions about technology. *International Journal of Science Education, 17*(6), 755–774.

Rennie, L. J., & Johnston, D. J. (2004). The nature of learning and its implications for research on learning from museums. *Science Education, 88*(Suppl. 1), S4–S16.

Rennie, L. J., & McClafferty, T. P. (1996). Science centres and science learning. *Studies in Science Education, 27,* 53–98.

Rest, J. (1986). *Moral development: Advances in research and theory.* New York: Praeger.

Rest, J., Cooper, D., Coder, R., Masanz, J., & Anderson, D. (1974). Judging the important issues in moral dilemmas: An objective test of development. *Developmental Psychology, 10*(4), 491–501.

Rest, J. R., Bebeau, M. J., & Volker, J. (1986). An overview of the psychology of morality. In J. R. Rest (Ed.), *Moral development: Advances in research and theory* (pp. 1–39). New York: Praeger.

Reverby, S. M. (2000). *Tuskegee's truths: Rethinking the Tuskegee syphilis study.* Chapel Hill, NC: University of North Carolina Press.

Revised Nuffield Biology. (1974). *Teachers' guide 1.* London: Longman.

Rickinson, M. (2001). Learners and learning in environmental education: A critical review of the evidence. *Environmental Education Research, 7*(3), 207–317.

Rickinson, M., Dillon, J., Teamey, K., Morris, M. Y., Choi, M. Y., Sanders, D., et al. (2004). *A review of research on outdoor learning.* Field Studies Council Occasional Paper No. 87. NFER and King's College, London. Available from: www.field-studies-council.org

Rifkin, J. (1997). *The biotech century: Harnessing the gene and remaking the world.* New York: Tarcher/Putman.

Riggs, E. M. (2003). Indigenous knowledge and global science literacy: A perspective from North America. In V. J. Mayer (Ed.), *Implementing global science literacy* (pp. 33–52). Columbus,OH: The Ohio State University Press.

Riggs, E. M. (2005). Field-based education and indigenous knowledge: Essential components of geoscience education for Native American communities. *Science Education, 89*(2), 296–313.

Rippetoe, P., & Rogers, R. (1987). Effects of components of protection-motivation theory on adaptive and maladaptive coping with a health threat. *Journal of Personality and Social Psychology, 52,* 596–604.

Rist, G. (1997). *The history of development: From western origins to global faith.* London: Zed Books.

Roberts, D. A. (1983) *Scientific literacy: Towards balance in setting goals for school science programs.* Ottawa: Science Council of Canada.

Roberts, D. A. (2007). Scientific literacy/science literacy. In S. K. Abell & N. G. Lederman (Eds.), *Handbook of research on science education* (pp. 729–780). Mahwah, NJ: Lawrence Erlbaum Associates.

Roberts, R. M. (2005). Walking backwards into the future: Māori views on genetically modified organisms. *Indigenous Knowledge – WINHEC Journal.* Available at: www.win-hec.org

Robinson, G. (2004). Developing the talents of teacher/scientists. *Journal of Secondary Gifted Eduucation, 15*(4), 155–161.

Robinson, J. (2004). Squaring the circle? Some thoughts on the idea of sustainable development. *Ecological Economics, 48,* 369–384.

Robinson, J., & Tinker, J. (1997). Reconciling ecological, economic, and social imperatives: A new framework. In T. Schrecker (Ed.), *Surviving globalism: Social and environmental dimensions* (pp. 71–94). London: St. Martin's Press.

Robottom, I. M. (1987). Towards inquiry-based professional development in environmental education. In I. M. Robottom (Ed.), *Environmental education: Practice and possibility* (pp. 83–119). Geelong: Deakin University Press.

Rockefeller Brothers Fund. (1958). *The pursuit of excellence: Education and the future of America.* Garden City, NY: Doubleday.

Rodda, A. (1991). *Women and the environment.* London: Zed Books.

Rodriguez, A. J. (2001). Courage and the researcher's gaze: (Re)defining our roles as cultural warriors for social change. *Journal of Science Teacher Education, 12*(3), 277–294.

REFERENCES

Rodriguez, A. J., & Berryman, C. (2002). Using sociotransformative constructivism to teach for under-standing in diverse classrooms: A beginning teacher's journey. *American Educational Research Journal, 39*(4), 1017–1045.

Roe, A. (1961). The psychology of the scientist. *Science, 134*(3477), 456–459.

Rogers, L., Erickson, G., & Gaskell, J. (2007). Developing an ethically attentive practice: Authority, understanding, and values in science education. In D. Corrigan, J. Dillon, & R. Gunstone (Eds.), *The re-emergence of values in science education* (pp. 165–178). Rotterdam: Sense Publishers.

Rogers, M., & Tough, A. (1996). Facing the future is not for wimps. *Futures, 28*(5), 491–196.

Rogers, M. D. (2001). Scientific and technological uncertainty, the precautionary principle, scenarios and risk management. *Journal of Risk Management, 4*(1), 1–15.

Rokeach, M. (1960). *The open and closed mind.* New York: Basic Books.

Rolin, K. (2008). Gender and physics: Feminist philosophy and science education. *Science & Education, 17*(10), 1111–1125.

Romm, J. (2007). *Hell and high water: Global warming – the solution and the politics – and what we should do.* New York: William Morrow.

Rorty, R. (1991). *Objectivity, relativism and truth: Philosophical papers* (Vol. 1). Cambridge: Cambridge University Press.

Rose, H. (1997). Science wars: My enemy's enemy is – only perhaps – my friend. In R. Levinson & J. Thomas (Eds.), *Science today: Problem or crisis?* (pp. 51–64). London: Routledge.

Rose, M. A. (2007). Perceptions of *technological literacy* among science, technology, engineering, and mathematics leaders. *Journal of Technology Education, 19*(1), 35–52.

Roseik, J. (2003). Emotional scaffolding: An exploration of the teacher knowledge at he intersection of student emotion and the subject matter. *Journal of Teacher Education, 54*(5), 399–412.

Rosenau, J. (Ed.). (1992). *Governance without government: Order and change in world politics.* Cambridge: Cambridge University Press.

Rosenthal, R., & Jacobson, L. (1968). *Pygmalion in the classroom: Teacher expectation and pupils' intellectual development.* New York: Holt, Rinehart & Winston.

Ross, A. (2000). The metal labor problem. *Social Text, 18*(2), 1–31.

Rosser, S. (2004). *The science glass ceiling: Academic women scientists and the struggle to succeed.* New York: Routledge.

Roth, C. E. (1992). *Environmental literacy: Its roots, evolution, and direction in the 1990s.* Columbus, OH: ERIC Clearinghouse for Science, Mathematics, and Environmental Education. ED 348235/SE 053316.

Roth, W.-M. (2003). Scientific literacy as an emergent feature of collective human praxis. *Journal of Curriculum Studies, 35*(1), 9–23.

Roth, W.-M. (2009a). Activism or science/technology education as a by product of capacity building. *Journal of Activist Science & Technology Education, 1*(1), 16–31.

Roth, W.-M. (2009b). On activism and teaching. *Journal of Activist Science & Technology Education, 1*(2), 33–47.

Roth, W.-M. (2010). Activism: A category for theorizing learning. *Canadian Journal of Science, Mathematics and Technology Education, 10*(3), 278–291.

Roth, W.-M., & Alexander, T. (1997). The interaction of students' scientific and religious discourses: Two case studies. *International Journal of Science Education,19*, 125–146.

Roth, W.-M., & Calabrese Barton, A. (2004). *Rethinking scientific literacy.* New York: RoutledgeFalmer.

Roth, W.-M., & Lee, S. (2002). Scientific literacy as collective praxis. *Public Understanding of Science, 11*, 33–56.

Roth, W.-M., & Lee, S. (2004). Science education as/for participation in the community. *Science Education, 88*, 263–291.

Roth, W.-M., & Lucas, K. B. (1997). From 'truth' to 'invented reality': A discourse analysis of high school physics students' talk about scientific knowledge. *Journal of Research in Science Teaching, 34*, 145–179.

Roth, W.-M., McGinn, M., & Bowen, G. M. (1996). Applications of science and technology studies: Effecting change in science education. *Science, Technology & Human Values, 21*, 454–484.

Roth, W.-M., Riecken, J., Pozzer-Ardenghi, L., McMillan, R., Storr, B., Tait, D., et al. (2004). Those who get hurt aren't always being heard: Scientist-resident interactions over community water. *Science, Technology & Human Values, 29*(2), 153–183.

Rowe, G., & Frewer, L. J. (2000). Public participation methods: A framework for evaluation. *Science, Technology & Human Values, 25*(1), 3–29.

Rowe, G., & Frewer, L. J. (2004). Evaluating public participation exercises: A research agenda. *Science, Technology & Human Values, 29*(4), 512–56.

Rowe, G., & Frewer, L. J. (2005). A typology of public mechanisms. *Science, Technology & Human Values, 30*(2), 251–90.

Rowland, F. S. (1993). President's lecture: The need for scientific communication with the public. *Science, 260*, 1571–1576.

Rowlands, M. (1998). *Animal rights: A philosophical defence*. London: Macmillan.

Royal Society, The (1985). *The public understanding of science*. London: Royal Society.

Royal Society, The (2004). *Science in society report*. London: Royal Society.

Rubie-Davis, C. M. (2006). Teachers' expectations and student self-perceptions: Exploring relationships. *Psychology in the Schools, 43*(5), 537–552.

Rubin, A. (2002). Reflections upon the late-modern transition as seen in the images of the future held by young Finns. In G. Gidley & S. Inayatullah (Eds.), *Youth Futures: Comparative research and transformative visions* (pp. 99–109). Westport, CT: Praeger.

Rubin, E., Bar, V., & Cohen, A. (2003). The images of scientists and science among Hebrew- and Arabic-speaking pre-service teachers in Israel. *International Journal of Science Education, 25*(7), 821–846.

Ruddock, J. (1986). A strategy for handling controversial issues in the secondary school. In J. Wellington (Ed.), *Controversial issues in the curriculum* (pp. 6–18). Oxford: Basil Blackwell.

Rudge, D. W., & Howe, E. M. (2009). An explicit and reflective approach to the use of history to promote understanding of the nature of science. *Science & Education, 18*(5), 561–580.

Rudolph, J. L., & Stewart, J. (1998). Evolution and the nature of science: On the historical discord and its implications for education. *Journal of Research in Science Teaching, 35*(10), 1069–1089.

Ruether, R. R. (1975). *New woman, new earth: Sexist ideologies and human liberation*. New York: Seabury Press.

Rushton, J. P. (1997). Racial research and the final solution: Review essay. *Society, 34*(3), 78–82.

Rushton, J. P. (2000). *Race, evolution and behaviour: A life history perspective*. Port Huron, MI: Charles Darwin Research Institute.

Rushton, J. P., & Jensen, A. R. (2005). Thirty years of research on race differences in cognitive ability. *Psychology, Public Policy and Law, 11*, 235–294.

Russell, C. L. (1997). Approaches to environmental education: Towards a transformative perspective. *Holistic Education Review, 10*, 34–40.

Russell, C. L., & Bell, A. C. (1996). A pliticized ethic of care: Environmental learning from an ecofeminist perspective. In K. Warren (Ed.), *Women's voices in experiential education* (pp. 172–181). Dubuque, IA: Kendall Hunt.

Russell, C. L., & Hodson, D. (2002). Whalewatching as critical science education? *Canadian Journal of Science, Mathematics and Technology Education, 2*(4), 485–504.

Russell, C. L., Bell, A., & Fawcett, L. (2001). Negotiating the waters of Canadian environmental education. In T. Goldstein & D. Selby (Eds.), *Weaving connections: Educating for peace, social and environmental justice* (pp. 196–217). Toronto: Sumach Press.

Russell, C. L., & Russon, A. E. (2007). Ecotourism. In M. Beckoff (Ed.), *Encyclopedia of human-animal relationships: A global exploration or our connections with animals* (pp. 653–657). Westport, CT: Greenwood Publishing.

Russon, A. E., & Russell, C. L. (2004). Primate-focused ecotourism. *Folia Primatologica, 75*, 38–45.

Ryder, J. (2001). Identifying science understanding for functional scientific literacy. *Studies in Science Education, 36*, 1–44.

REFERENCES

Ryder, J., Leach, J., & Driver, R. (1999). Undergraduate science students' images of science. *Journal of Research in Science Teaching, 36*(2), 201–219.

Rye, J. A., Rubba, P. A., & Wiesenmayer, R. L. (1997). An investigation of middle school students' alternative conceptions of global warming. *International Journal of Science Education, 19*, 527–551.

Saarni, L. (1990). Emotional competence: How emotions and relationships become integrated. In R. A. Thompson (Ed.), *Socioemotional development: Nebraska symposium on motivation* (Vol. 36, pp. 115–182). Lincoln, NE: University of Nebraska Press.

Sachs, J. (2001). Teacher professional identity: Competing discourses, competing outcomes. *Journal of Educational Policy, 16*(2), 149–161.

Sadler, T. D. (2004). Informal reasoning regarding socioscientific issues: A critical review of research. *Journal of Research in Science Teaching, 41*(5), 513–536.

Sadler, T. D. (2009). Situated learning in science education: Socio-scientific issues as contexts for practice. *Studies in Science Education, 45*(1), 1–42.

Sadler, T. D., & Donnelly, L. A. (2006). Socioscientific argumentation: The effects of content knowledge and morality. *International Journal of Science Education, 28*(12), 1463–1488.

Sadler, T. D., & Fowler, S. R. (2006). A threshold model of content knowledge transfer for socioscientific argumentation. *Science Education, 90*(6), 986–1004.

Sadler, T. D., & Zeidler, D. L. (2003). Scientific errors, atrocities and blunders. In D. L. Zeidler (Ed.), *The role of moral reasoning on socioscientific issues and discourse in science education* (pp. 261–285). Dordrecht: Kluwer.

Sadler, T. D., & Zeidler, D. L. (2004). The morality of socioscientific issues: Construal and resolution of genetic engineering dilemmas. *Science Education, 88*(1), 4–27.

Sadler, T. D., & Zeidler, D. L. (2005). The significance of content knowledge for informal reasoning regarding socioscientific issues: Applying genetics knowledge to genetic engineering issues. *Science Education, 89*(1), 71–93.

Sadler, T. D., & Zeidler, D. L. (2005b). Patterns of informal reasoning in the context of socioscientific decision making. *Journal of Research in Science Teaching, 42*(1), 112–138.

Sadler, T. D., Amirshokoohi, A., Kazempour, M., & Allspaw, K. M. (2006). Socioscience and ethics in science classrooms: Teacher perspectives and strategies. *Journal of Research in Science Teaching, 43*(4), 353–376.

Sadler, T. D., Barab, S. A., & Scott, B. (2007). What do students gain by engaging in socioscientific inquiry? *Research in Science Education, 37*(4), 371–391.

Sadler, T. D., Zeidler, D. L., & Chambers, F. W. (2004). Students' conceptualizations of the nature of science in response to a socioscientific issue. *International Journal of Science Education, 26*(4), 387–409.

Sagan, C. (1995). *The demon-haunted world: Science as a candle in the dark.* New York: Random House.

Salmon, P. (1988). *Psychology for teachers: An alternative approach.* London: Hutchinson.

Salovey, P., & Meyer, M. V. (1990). Emotional intelligence. *Imagination, Cognition and Personality, 9,* 185–211.

Salovey, P., & Shaytor, D. (Eds.). (1997). *Emotional development and emotional intelligence: Educational implications.* New York: Basic Books.

Samarpungavan, A. (1997, March). *Children's beliefs about the boundaries of knowledge: Examples from biology learning.* Paper presented at the annual meeting of the American Educational Research Association, Chicago.

Sammel, A. (2003). Environmental education and the Ontario science curriculum: In where? About what? For whom? In D. Hodson (Ed.), *OISE papers in STSE education* (Vol. 4, pp. 31–47). Toronto: Imperial Oil Centre for Studies in Science, Mathematics and Technology Education.

Sammel, A., & Zandvliet, D. (2003). Science reform or science conform: Problematic epistemological assumptions with/in Canadian science reform efforts. *Canadian Journal of Science, Mathematics and Technology Education.*

Sampson, V., & Clark, D. (2006, June). Assessment of argument in science education: A critical review of the literature. In *Proceedings of the 7th international conference of the learning sciences* (pp. 655–661). Bloomington, IN. International Society of the Learning Sciences. Retrieved from www.isls.org

Sandell, K., & Öhman, J. (2010). Educational potentials of encounters with nature: Reflections from a Swedish outdoor perspective. *Environmental Education Research, 16*(1), 113–132.

Sandilands, C. (1993). On 'green'consumerism: Environmental privatization and 'family values'. *Canadian Women's Studies, 13*(3), 45–47.

Sandin, P. (1999). Dimensions of the precautionary principle. *Human and Ecological Risk Assessment, 5*(5), 889–907.

Sandin, P., Peterson, M., Hansson, S. O., Ruden, C., & Juthe, A. (2002). Five charges against the precautionary principle. *Journal of Risk Research, 5*(4), 287–299.

Sandoval, W. A., & Millwood, K. A. (2005). The qulaity of students' use of evidence in written scientific explanations. *Cognition and Instruction, 23*(1), 23–55.

Sapontzis, S. F. (1995). We should not allow dissection of animals. *Journal of Agricultural and Enviromental Ethics, 8*(2), 181–189.

Sarasohn, J. (1993). *Science on trial: The whistle blower, the accused, and the Nobel laureate.* New York: St. Martin's Press.

Sardar, S. (Ed.). (1999). *Rescuing all our futures.* Westport, CT: Greenwood Press.

Sardar, Z. (1989). *Explorations in Islamic science.* London: Mansell.

Saul, J. R. (1997). *The unconscious civilization.* New York: Free Press.

Saul, J. R. (2005). *The collapse of globalism and the reinvention of the world.* London: Atlantic Books.

Saunders, W. L. (1992). The constructivist perspective: Implications fand teaching strategies for science. *School Science & Mathematics, 92*, 136–141.

Sauvé, L. (1999). Environmental education between modernity and postmodernity: Searching for an integrating educational framework. *Canadian Journal of Environmental Education, 4*, 9–35.

Sauvé, L. (2005). Currents in environmental education: Mapping a complex and evolving pedagogical field. *Canadian Journal of Environmental Education, 10*, 11–37.

Savage-Rumbaugh, S., Shanker, S. G., & Taylor, T. J. (1998). *Apes, language, and the human mind.* New York: Oxford University Press.

Scharper, S. B. (2002). Green dreams: Religious cosmologies and environmental commitments. *Bulletin of Science, Technology & Society, 22*(1), 42–44.

Scherz, Z., & Oren, M. (2006). How to change students' images of science and technology. *Science Education, 90*(6), 965–985.

Schnack, K. (2008). Participation, education, and democracy: Implications for environmental education, health education, and education for sustainable development. In A. Reid, B. B. Jensen, J. Nikel, & V. Simovska (Eds.), *Participation and learning: perspectives on education and the environment, health and sustainability* (pp. 181–196). Dordrecht: Springer.

Schneider, J. J., Crumpler, T. P., & Rogers, T. (Eds.). (2006). *Process drama and mutiple literacies: Addressing social, cultural, and ethical issues.* Portsmouth, NH: Heinemann.

Schor, J. B. (2004). *Born to buy: The commercialized child and the new consumer culture.* New York: Scribner.

Schreiner, C., Henriksen, E. K., & Kirkeby Hansen, P. J. (2005). Climate education: Empowering today's youth to meet tomoorow's challenges. *Studies in Science Education, 41*, 3–50.

Schultz, P. W. (2000). Empathizing with nature: The effects of perspective taking on concern for environmental issues. *Journal of Social Issues, 56*(3), 391–406.

Schultz, P. W., Zelezny, L. C., & Dalrymple, N. (2000). A multinational perspective on the relation between Judeo-Christian religious beliefs and attitudes of environmental concern. *Environment and Behavior, 32*, 576–591.

Schumacher, E. F. (1973). *Small is beautiful: A study of economics as if people mattered.* London: Blond & Briggs.

Schumaker, J. F. (2001). Dead zone. *New Internationalist, 336*(July), 34–35.

REFERENCES

Schusler, T. M., Krasny, M. E., Peters, S. J., & Decker, D. J. (2009). Developing citizens and communities through youth environmental action. *Environmental Education Research, 15*(1), 111–127.

Schutz, P. A., & Zembylas, M. (Eds.). (2009). *Advances in teacher emotion research: The impact on teachers' lives.* Dordrecht: Springer.

Schwab, J. J. (1962). The teaching of science as enquiry. In J. J. Schwab & P. F. Brandwein (Eds.), *The teaching of science* (pp. 3–103). Cambridge, MA: Harvard University Press.

Schwartz, R. S., Lederman, N. G., & Crawford, B. A. (2004). Developing views of nature of science in an authentic context: An explicit approach to bridging the gap between nature of science and scientific inquiry. *Science Education, 88*, 610–645.

Shwarz, B. B., Neuman, Y., Gil, J., & Ilya, M. (2003). Construction of collective and individual knowledge in argumentative activity. *Journal of the Learning Sciences, 12*(2), 219–256.

Schweizer, D. M., & Kelly, G. J. (2001, April). *An investigation of student engagement in a global warming debate.* Paper presented at the NARST annual meetings, St Louis, MI.

Sclove, R. (1995). *Democracy and technology.* New York: Guilford Press.

Sclove, R. (2000). Town meetings on technology: Consensus conferences as democratic participation. In D. L. Kleinman (Ed.), *Science, technology and democracy* (pp. 33–48). Albany, NY: State University of New York Press.

Scruton, R. (1996). *Animal rights and wrongs.* London: Demos.

Secondary School Curriculum Review (SSCR). (1987). *Better science: Working for a multicultural society.* London: Heinemann/Association for Science Education.

Seethaler, S., & Linn, M. (2004). Genetically modified food in perspective: An inquiry-based curriculum to help middle school students make sense of tradeoffs. *International Journal of Science Education, 26*(14), 1765–1785.

Seiler, G. (2001). Reversing the 'standard' direction: Science emerging from the lives of African American students. *Journal of Research in Science Teaching, 38*(9), 1000–1014.

Seiter, E. (1993). *Sold separately: Children and parents in the consumer culture.* New Brunswick, NJ: Rutgers University Press.

Selby, D. (1994a). Humane education: The ultima thule of global education. *Green Teacher, 39*, 9–14.

Selby, D. (1994b). Humane education: The ultima thule of global education – Part two. *Green Teacher, 40*, 23–31.

Selby, D. (1995). *Earthkind: A teacher's handbook on humane education.* Trentham: Trentham Books.

Selby, D. (1995). Relational modes of knowledge: Learning process implications of a humane and environmental ethic. In B. Jicklng (Ed.), *Proceedings of a colloquium on environment, ethics, and education* (pp. 49–60). Whitehorse, Yukon: July.

Selby, D. (2000). Widening the circle of compassion and justice. In T. Goldstein & D. Selby (Eds.), *Weaving connections: Educating for peace, social and environmental justice* (pp. 268–296). Toronto: Sumach Press.

Selby, D. (2010). 'Go, go, go, said the bird': Sustainability-related education in interesting times. In F. Kagawa & D. Selby (Eds.), *Education and climate change: Living and learning in interesting times* (pp. 35–54). London: Routledge.

Seldon, S. (2000). Eugenics and the social construction of merit, race and disability. *Journal of Curriculum Studies, 32*(2), 235–252.

Select Committee on Science and Technology, House of Lords. (2000). *Science and society.* 3rd Report, Session 1999–2000. London: HMSO.

Semken, S. C. (1999). Aboriginal cultures and earth sciences. *GSA (Geological Society of America) Today, 9*(8), 18.

Semken, S. (2005). Sense of place and place-based introductory geoscience teaching for American Indian and Alaska Native undergraduates. *Journal of Geoscience Education, 53*(2), 149–157.

Semken, S., & Freeman, C. B. (2008). Sense of place in the practice and assessment of place-based science teaching. *Science Education, 92*(6), 1042–1057.

Semken, S. C., & Morgan, F. (1997). Navajo pedagogy and earth systems. *Journal of Geoscience Education, 45*, 109–112.

Settlage, J., & Meadows, I. (2003). Standards-based reform and its unintended consequences: Implications for science education within America's urban schools. *Journal of Research in Science Teaching*, *39*(2), 114–128.

Shafir, E., Simonson, I., & Tversky, A. (2004). Reason-based choice. In A. Tversky & E. Shafir (Eds.), *Preference, belief, and similarity: Selected writings* (pp. 937–962). Cambridge, MA: MIT Press.

Shaiko, R. G. (1987). Religion, politics, and environmental conbcern: A powerful mix of passions. *Social Science Quarterly*, *68*(1–2), 244–262.

Shallcross, T., & Robinson, J. (2008). Sustainability education, whole school approaches, and communities of action. In A. Reid, B. B. Jensen, J. Nikel, & V. Simovsla (Eds.), *Participation and learning: Perspectives on education and the environment, health and sustainability* (pp. 299–320). New York: Springer.

Shallcross, T., Pace, P., Robinson, J., & Wals, A. (Eds.). (2006). *Creating sustainable environments in our schools*. Stoke-on-Trent: Trentham Books.

Shamos, M. H. (1993). STS: A time for caution. In R. E. Yager (Ed.), *The science, technology, society movement* (pp. 65–72). Washington, DC: National Science Teachers Association.

Shamos, M. (1995). *The myth of scientific literacy*. New Brunswick, NJ: Rutgers University Press.

Shapin, S. (1979). Homo phrenologicus: Anthropological perspectives on an historical problem. In B. Barnes & S. Shapin (Eds.), *Natural order: Historical studies of scientific culture* (pp. 41–71). London: Sage.

Shapin, S. (2008). *The scientific life: A moral history of a late modern vocation*. Chicago: University of Chicago Press.

Sharp, P. (2001). *Nurturing emotional literacy*. London: David Fulton.

Shaull, R. (1970). Foreword. In P. Freire (Ed.), *The pedagogy of the oppressed*. New York: Seabury.

She, H.-C. (1995). Elementary and middle school students' image of science and scientists related to current science textbooks in Taiwan. *Journal of Science Education and Technology*, *4*(4), 283–294.

She, H.-C. (1998). Gender and grade level differences in Taiwan students' stereotypes of science and scientists. *Research in Science & Technological Education*, *16*(2), 125–135.

Shelley, P. B. (1927). A defence of peotry. In R. Ingpen & W. E. Peck (Eds.), *The complete works of Percy Bysshe Shelley* (Vol. 7, pp. 109–140). London: Ernest Bern.

Shen, B. S. P. (1975). Scientific literacy and the public understanding of science. In S. B. Day (Ed.), *The communication of scientific information* (pp. 44–52). Basel: Karger.

Shepard, P. (1982). *Nature and madness*. Athens, GA: University of Georgia Press.

Shepardson, D. P. (2005). Student ideas: What is an environment? *Journal of Environmental Education*, *36*(4), 49–58.

Shepardson, D. P., Niyogi, D., Choi, S., & Charusombat, U. (2009). Seventh grade students' conceptions of global warming and climate change. *Environmental Education Research*, *15*(5), 549–570.

Shepardson, D. P., Wee, B., Priddy, M., & Harbor, J. (2007). Students' mental models of the environment. *Journal of Research in Science Teaching*, *44*(2), 327–248.

Shepherd, L. (1993). *Lifting the veil: The feminine face of science*. Boston: Shambala Publications.

Sherborne, T. (2004). Immediate inspiration: Ready-made resources for teaching ethics. *School Science Review*, *86*(315), 67–72.

Sherin, B. L. (2001). How students understand physics equations. *Cognition and Instruction*, *19*(4), 479–541.

Shiva, V. (1989). *Staying alive: Women, ecology and development*. London: Zed Books.

Shiva, V. (1992). Recovering the real meaning of sustainability. In D. E. Cooper & J. A. Palmer (Eds.), *The environment in question: Ethics and global issues* (pp. 185–191). London: Routledge.

Shiva, V. (1993). *Monocultures of the mind: Perspectives on biodiversity and biotechnology*. Atlanta Highlands, NJ: Zed Books.

Shiva, V. (2005). *Earth democracy: Justice, sustainability and peace*. London: Zed Books.

Shiva, V. (2008). *Soil not oil: Climate change, peak oil and food insecurity*. London: Zed Books.

Short, P. C. (2010). Responsible environmental action: Its role and status in evvironmental education and environmental quality. *Journal of Environmental Education*, *41*(1), 7–21.

REFERENCES

Shortland, M. (1988). Advocating science: Literacy and public understanding. *Impact of Science on Society, 38*(4), 305–316.
Shulman, L. S. (1986). Those who understand: Knowledge growth in teaching. *Educational Researcher, 15*, 4–14.
Shulman, L. S. (1987). Knowledge and teaching: Foundations of the new reform. *Harvard Educational Review, 57*, 1–22.
Siegel, M. A. (2006). High school students' decision making about sustainability. *Environmental Education Research, 12*(2), 201–215.
Simmons, M. L., & Zeidler, D. (2003). Beliefs in the nature of science and responses to socioscientific issue. In D. L. Zeidler (Ed.), *The role of moral reasoning on socioscientific issues and discourse in science education* (pp. 81–94). Dordrecht: Kluwer.
Simon, S., Erduran, S., & Osborne, J. (2006). Learning to teach argumentation: Research and development in the science classroom. *International Journal of Science Education, 28*(2–3), 235–260.
Simonneaux, L. (2001). Role play or debate to promote students' argumentation and justification on an issue in animal tramsgenesis. *International Journal of Science Education, 23*(9), 903–927.
Simonneaux, L. (2008). Argumentation in socio-scientific contexts. In S. Erduran & M. P. Jiménez-Aleixandre (Eds.), *Argumentation in science education* (pp. 179–199). Dordrecht: Sprmnger.
Simonneaux, L., & Simonneaux, J. (2009). Students' socio-scientific reasoning on controversies from the viewpoint of education for sustainable development. *Cultural Studies of Science Education, 4*, 657–687.
Simovska, V. (2008). Learning *in* and *as* participation: A case stuidy from health-promoting schools. In A. Reid, B. B. Jensen, J. Nikel, & V. Simovsla (Eds.), *Participation and learning: Perspectives on education and the environment, health and sustainability* (pp. 61–80). New York: Springer.
Simpson, A., Hildyard, N., & Sexton, S. (1997). No patents on life! *Corner House Briefing 01*: Dorset: The Corner House. Available at: www.thecornerhouse.org.uk.
Simpson, J. S., & Parsons, E. C. (2009). African American perspectives and informal science educational experiences. *Science Education, 93*(2), 293–321.
Sinatra, G. (2005). The 'warming trend' in conceptual change research: The legacy of Paul R. Pintrich. *Educational Psychologist, 40*(2), 107–115.
Sinatra, G., & Pintrich, P. R. (2003). *Intentional conceptual change*. Mahwah, NJ: Lawrence Erlbaum.
Sinatra, G., Southerland, S. A., McConaughy, F., & Demastes, J. W. (2003). Intentions and beliefs in students' understanding and acceptance of biological evolution. *Journal of Research in Science Teaching, 40*, 510–528.
Singer, P. (1977). *Animal liberation: Towards an end to man's inhumanity to animals*. London: Granada Publishing.
Singer, P. (Ed.). (1991). *Companion to ethics*. Oxford: Blackwell.
Singer, P. (1993). *Practical ethics* (2nd ed.). Cambridge: Cambridge University Press.
Singer, P. (Ed.). (1993b). *In defence of animals*. Oxford: Basil Blackwell.
Singer, P. (2002). *Animal liberation*. New York: Harper Collins.
Singer, P. (2008, July 18). Of great apes and men. *The Guardian*, p. 35.
Sleeter, C. (1996). *Multicultural education as social activism*. Albany, NY: State University of New York Press.
Sivek, D. (2002). Environmental sensitivity among Wisconsin high school students. *Environmental Education Research, 8*(2), 155–170.
Skamp, K., Boyes, E., & Stanissteeet, M. (2009). Global warming responses at the primaryu-secondary interface: 2. Students' beliefs and willingness to act. *Australian Journal of Environmental Education, 25*, 15–30.
Slaughter, R. (1988). *Recovering the future*. Melbourne: Monash University, Graduate School of Environmental Science.
Slaughter, R. (Ed.). (2005). *Knowledge base of future studies* (Vols. 1–4). Millennium edition CD Rom. Brisbane: Foresight International.

Slaughter, S., & Leslie, L. (1997). *Academic capitalism: Politics, policies, and the entrepreneurial university*. Baltimore: Johns Hopkins University Press.

Slaughter, S., & Rhoades, G. (2004). *Academic capitalism and the new economy: Markets, state, and higher education*. Baltimore: Johns Hopkins University Press.

Smith, A. J., & Smith, K. (2004). Guidelines for humane education: Alternatives to the use of animals in teaching and training. *Alternatives to Laboratory Animals, 32*(1), 29–39.

Smith, C. L., Maclin, D., Houghton, C., & Hennessey, M. G. (2000). Sixth grade students' epistemologies of science: The impact of school science experiences on epistemological development. *Cognition and Instruction, 18*(3), 349–422.

Smith, D., & Carson, T. (1998). *Educating for a peaceful future*. Toronto: Kagan & Woo.

Smith, D. S. (2001). Place-based environmentalism and global warming: Conceptual contradictions of American environmentalism. *Ethics and International Affairs, 15*(2), 117–134.

Smith, D. V., & Gunstone, R. F. (2009). Science curriculum in the market liberal society of the twenty-first century: 'Re-visioning' the idea of science for all. *Research in Science Education, 39*(1), 1–16.

Smith, G. (2002). Place-based education: Learning to be where we are. *PhiDeltaKappan, 83*, 584–594.

Smith, G. A. (2007). Place-based education: Breaking through the constraining regularities of public school. *Environmental Education Research, 13*(2), 189–207.

Smith, G. (2008). Oxymoron or misplaced rectification. *Environmental Education Research, 14*(3), 349–352.

Smith, G., & Gruenewald, D. (2007). *Place-based education in the global age*. Mahwah, NJ: Lawrence Erlbaum Associates.

Smith, G. A., & Williams, D. R. (1999). Introduction: Re-engaging culture and ecology. In G. A. Smith & D. R. Williams (Eds.), *Ecological education in action: On weaving education, culture, and the environment* (pp. 1–18). Albany, NY: State University of New York Press.

Smith, M. R., & Marx, L. (Eds.). (1994). *Does technology drive history? The dilemma of technological determinism*. Cambridge, MA: MIT Press.

Smithson, I. (1997). Native Americans and the desire for environmental harmony: Challenging a stereotype. In P. J. Thompson (Ed.), *Environmental education for the 21st century* (pp. 163–177). New York: Peter Lang.

Smolicz, J. J., & Nunan, E. E. (1975). The philosophical and sociological foundations of science education: The demythologizing of school science. *Studies in Science Education, 2*, 101–143.

Snook, I. A. (1975). *Indoctrination and education*. London: Routledge & Kegan Paul.

Smyth, J. C. (1995). Environment and education: A view of a changing scene. *Environmental Education Research, 1*(3), 3–12.

Snively, G., & Corsiglia, J. (2001). Discovering indigenous science: Implications for science education. *Science Education, 85*, 6–34.

Snow, C. P. (1962). *The two cultures and the scientific revolution*. Cambridge: Cambridge University Press.

Sobel, D. (1996). *Beyond ecophobia: Reclaiming the heart in nature education*. Great Barrington, MA: Orion Society.

Sobel, D. (1997). Sense of place education for the elementary years. In *Coming home: Developing a sense of place in our communities and schools*. Proceedings of the 1997 forum. Columbus, OH: Eric Document Service, ED421312.

Sobel, D. (2004). *Place-based education: Connecting classrooms and communities*. Great Barrington, MA: The Orion Society Press.

Solomon, J. (1987). Social influences on the construction of pupils' understanding of science. *Studies in Science Education, 14*, 63–82.

Solomon, J. (1992). The classroom discussion of science-based social issues presented on television: Knowledge, attitudes and values. *International Journal of Science Education, 14*(4), 431–444.

Solomon, J. (1993). *Teaching science, technolgy and society*. Buckingham: Open University Press.

Solomon, J. (1998). About argument and discussion. *School Science Review, 80*(291), 57–62.

REFERENCES

Solomon, J. (2003). The UK and the movement for science, technology and society (STS) education. In R. Cross (Ed.), *A vision for science education: Responding to the work of Peter Fensham* (pp. 76–90). New York: RoutledgeFalmer.

Solomon, J., & Aikenhead, G. (Eds.). (1994). *STS education: International perspective on reform*. New York: Teachers College Press.

Solomon, M. (2001). *Social empiricism*. Cambridge, MA: MIT Press.

Solot, D., & Arluke, A. (1997). Learning the scientists' role: Animal dissection in middle schools. *Journal of Contemporary Ethnography, 26*(1), 28–54.

Song, J., & Kim, K.-S. (1999). How Korean students see scientists: The images of the scientist. *International Journal of Science Education, 21*(9), 957–977.

Sperandeo-Mineo, R. M., Fazio, C., & Tarantino, G. (2005). Pedagogical content knowledge development and pre-service physics teacher education: A case study. *Research in Scioence Education, 36*, 235–268.

Sperling, E. (2009). 'More than particle theory': Action-oriented citizenship through science education in a school setting. *Journal of Activist Science & Technology Education, 1*(2), 12–30.

Spinks, P. (2001). Science journalism: The inside story. In S. Stocklmayer, M. Gore, & C. Bryant (Eds.), *Science communication in theory and practice* (pp. 151–168). Dordrecht: Kluwer.

Spivak, G. C. (1988). Can the subaltern speak? In C. Nelson & L. Grossberg (Eds.), *Marxism and the interpretation of culture* (pp. 271–313). Chicago: University of Chicago Press.

Spretnak, C. (1994). Critical and constructive contributions to ecofeminism. In M. E. Tucker & J. A. Grim (Eds.), *Worldviews and ecology: Religion, philosophy, and the environment* (pp. 181–189). New York: Orbis Books.

Spring, D., & Spring, E. (1974). *Ecology and religion in history*. New York: Harper Row.

Stables, A. (1996). Paradox in compoubnd educational policy slogans: Evaluating equal opportunities in subject choice. *British Journal of Educational Studies, 44*(2), 159–167.

Stables, A. (1998). Environmental literacy: Functional, cultural, critical. The case of the SCAA guidelines. *Environmental Education Research, 4*(2), 155–164.

Stables, A., & Bishop, K. (2001). Weak and strong conceptions of environmental literacy: Implications for environmental education. *Environmental Education Research, 7*(1), 89–97.

Stables, A., & Scott, W. (1999). Environmental education and the discourses of humanist modernity: Redefining critical environmental literacy. *Educational Philosophy & Theory, 31*(2), 145–155.

Stanisstreet, M., & Williams, T.R. (1993). Children's views about animal experimentation. *School Science Review, 73*(265), 146.

Stanisstreet, M., Spofforth, N., & Williams, T. R. (1993). Attitudes of children to the uses of animals. *International Journal of Science Education, 15*, 411–425.

Stankiewicz, R. (1994). University firms: Spin-off companies from universities. *Science and Public Policy, 21*, 99–107.

Stapp, W. B. (2000). Watershed education for sustainable development. *Journal of Science Education and Technology, 9*(3), 183–197.

Steiner, C. (1997). *Achieving emotional literacy*. London: Bloomsbury.

Stelfox, H. T., Chua, G., O'Rourke, G. K., & Detsky, A. S. (1998). Conflict of interest in the debate over calcium channel antagonists. *New England Journal of Medicine, 338*(1), 101–106.

Stenhouse, L. (1970). Controversial value issues in the classroom. In W. G. Carr (Ed.), *Values in the curriculum* (pp. 103–115). Washington, DC: National Education Association.

Stenhouse, L. (1983). *Authority, education and emancipation*. London: Heinemann.

Sterba, J. (2001). *Three challenges to ethics: Environmentalism, feminism, and multiculturalism*. Oxford: Oxford University Press.

Stern, P. C. (2000). Toward a coherent theory of environmentally significant behavior. *Journal of Social Issues, 56*(3), 407–424.

Stern, P. C., & Dietz, T. (1994). The value basis of enviornmental concern. *Journal of Social Issues, 50*, 65–84.

Stern, P. C., Dietz, T., & Karlof, L. (1993). Values orientations, gender, and environmental concern. *Environment and Behavior, 25*, 322–348.

Stern, M., Powell, R. B., & Ardoin, N. M. (2008). What difference does it make? Assessing outcomes from participation in a residential environmental education program. *Journal of Environmental Education, 39*, 31–43.

Stevenson, R. B. (2008). A critical pedagogy of place and the critical place(s) of pedagogy. *Environmental Education Research, 14*(3), 353–360.

Stevenson, R. B. (2008). Tensions and transitions in policy discourse: Recontextualizing a decontextualized EE/ESD debate. In A. Reid & W. Scott (Eds.), *Researching education and the environment: Retrospect and prospect* (pp. 31–44). London: Routledge.

Stinner, A., & Teichmann, J. (2003). Lord Kelvin and the-age-of-the-earth debate: A dramatization. *Science & Education, 12*(2), 213–228.

Stocking, S. H. (1999). How journalists deal with scientific uncertainty. In S. M. Friedman, S. Dunwoody, & C. L. Rogers (Eds.), *Communicating uncertainty* (pp. 23–41). Mahwah, NJ: Lawrence Erlbaum Associates.

Stocking, S. H., & Holstein, L. W. (1993). Constructing and reconstructing scientific ignorance: Ignorance claims in science and journalism. *Science Communication, Utilization, 15*(2), 186–210.

Stocking, S. H., & Holstein, L. W. (2009). Manufacturing doubt: Journalists' roles and the construction of ignorance in a scientific controversy. *Public Understanding of Science, 18*, 23–42.

Stocklmayer, S. M., Rennie, L. J., & Gilbert, J. K. (2010). The roles of the formal and informal sectors in the provision of effective science education. *Studies in Science Education, 46*(1), 1–44.

Stolberg, T. L. (2010). Teaching Darwinian evolution: Learning from religious education. *Science & Education, 19*, 679–692.

Strommen, E. (1995). Lions and tigers and bears, oh my! Children's conceptions of forests and their inhabitants. *Journal of Research in Science Teaching, 32*(7), 683–698.

Stone, C. A. (1993). What is missing in the metaphor of scaffolding? In E. A. Forman, N. Minick, & C. A. Stone (Eds.), *Contexts for learning: Sociocultural dynamics in children's development* (pp. 169–183). New York: Oxford University Press.

Stone, C. A. (1998). The metaphor of scaffolding: Its utility for the field of learning disabilities. *Journal of Learning Disabilities, 31*, 344–364.

Stone, M., & Barlow, Z. (2005). *Ecological Literacy: Educating our children for a sustainable world.* San Francisco: Sierra Club Books.

Stromquist, N. P., & Monkman, K. (2000). Defining globalization and assessing its implications on knowledge and education. In N. P. Stromquist & K. Monkman (Eds.), *Globalization and education: Integration and contestation across cultures* (pp. 3–25). London: Rowman & Littlefield.

Sturgeon, N. (1997). *Ecofeminist natures: Race, gender, feminist theory, and political action.* New York: Routledge.

Suchting, W. A. (1995). The nature of scientific thought. *Science & Education, 4*, 1–22.

Summers, M., & Kruger, C. (2003). Teaching sustainable development in primary schools: Theory into practice. *The Curriculum Journal, 14*(2), 157–180.

Summers, M., Corney, G., & Childs, A. (2003). Teaching sustainable development in primary schools: An empirical study of issues for teachers. *Environmental Education Research, 9*(3), 327–346.

Summers, M., Kruger, C., Childs, A., & Mant, J. (2000). Primary school teachers' understanding of environmental issues: An interview study. *Environmental Education Research, 6*(4), 293–312.

Summers, M., Kruger, C., Childs, A., & Mant, J. (2001). Understanding the science of environmental issues: Development of a subject matter guide for primary teacher education. *International Journal of Science Education, 23*, 33–53.

Sumrall, W. J. (1995). Reasons for the perceived images of scientists by race and gender of students in grades 1-7. *School Science & Mathematics, 95*(2), 83–90.

Suzuki, D. (1998). *Earth time.* Toronto: Stoddart.

Sward, L. (1996, November). *Experiential variables affecting the environmental sensitivity of El Salvadoran environmental professionals.* Paper presented at the annual conference of the North American Association of Environmental Education. Burlington, CA.

REFERENCES

Sward, L. (1999). Significant life experiences affecting the environmental sensitivity of El Salvadoran environmental professionals. *Environmental Education Research, 5*(2), 201–206.

Symington, D., & Tytler, R. (2004). Community leaders' views of the purposes of science in the compulsory years of schooling. *International Journal of Science Education, 26*(11), 1403–1418.

Taber, F., & Taylor, N. (2009). Climate of concern – A search for effective strategies for teaching children about global warming. *International Journal of Environmental & Science Education, 4*(2), 97–116.

Tairab, H. H. (2001). How do pre-service and in-service science teachers view the nature of science and technology. *Research in Science & Technological Education, 19*(2), 235–250.

Takano, T., Higgins, P., & McLaughlin, P. (2009). Connecting with place: Implications of integrating cultural values into the school curriculum in Alaska. *Environmental Education Research,* (1593), 343–370.

Tal, T., & Alkaher, I. (2010). Collaborative environmental projects in a multicultural society: Working from within separate or mutual landscapes? *Cultural Studies of Science Education, 5,* 325–349.

Tal, T., & Kedmi, Y. (2006). Teaching socioscientific issues: Classroom culture and students' performance. *Cultural Studies of Science Education, 1*(4), 615–644.

Tal, T., & Morag, O. (2007). School visits to natural history museums: Teaching or enriching? *Journal of Research in Science Teaching, 44*(5), 747–769.

Tal, T., & Steiner, L. (2006). Patterns of teacher-museum staff relationships: School visits to the educational centre of a science museum. *Canadian Journal of Science, Mathematics and Technology Education, 6*(1), 25–46.

Taleb, N. N. (2007). *The black swan: The impact of the highly improbable.* New York: Random House.

Tan, M. (2009). Science teacher activism: The case of environmental education. *Journal of Activist Science & Technology Education, 1*(1), 32–43.

Tan, M., & Pedretti, E. (2010). Negotiating the complexities of environmental education: A study of Ontario teachers. *Canadian Journal of Science, Mathematics and Technology Education, 10*(1), 61–78.

Tang, K.-S., & Moje, E. B. (2010). Relating multimodal respresentations to the literacies of science. *Research in Science Education, 40*(1), 81–85.

Taskin, O. (2009). The environmental attitudes of Turkish senior high school students in the context of postmaterialism and the new environmental paradigm. *International Journal of Science Education, 31*(4), 481–502.

Tate, W. (2001). Science education as a civil right: Urban schools and opportunity-to-learn considerations. *Journal of Research in Science Teaching, 38*(9), 1015–1028.

Taylor, L. K. (2008). Beyond 'open-mindedness': Cultivating critical, reflexive approaches to democratic dialogue. In D. E. Lind & P. R Carr (Eds.), *Doing democracy: Striving for political literacy and social justice* (pp. 159–176). New York: Peter Lang.

Taylor, M. J., & Johnson, R. (2002). *School councils: Their role in citizenship and personal and social education.* Slough: NFER. Available at: www.nfer.ac.uk

Taylor, P. J. (2002). *We know more than we are, at first, prepared to acjknowledge: Journeying to develop critical thinking.* Available at: http://www.faculty.umb.edu/pjt/journey.html

Taylor, P., Lee, S. H., & Tal, T. (2006). Toward socio-scientific participation: Changing culture in the science classroom and much more. *Cultural Studies of Science Education, 1*(4), 645–656.

Ten Eyck, T. A. (2005). The media and public opinion on genetics and biotechnology: Mirrors, windows, or walls? *Public Understanding of Science, 14*(3), 305–316.

Thayar, R. L. (1990). Pragmatism in paradise: Technology and the American landscape. *Landscape, 30,* 1–11.

Thier, M., & Daviss, B. (2002). *The new science literacy: Using language skills to help students learn science.* Portsmouth, NH: Heinemann.

Thoma, S. J., & Rest, J. R. (1999). The relationship between moral decision making and patterns of consolidation and transition in moral judgment development. *Developmental Psychology, 35*(2), 323–334.

Thomas, G., & Durant, J. (1987). Why should we promote the public understanding of science? In M. Shortland (Ed.), *Scientific literacy papers* (pp. 1–14). Oxford: Oxford University Department for External Studies.

Thomas, G., & McRobbie, C. J. (1999). Using metaphors to probe students' conceptions of learning. *International Journal of Science Education, 21*(6), 667–685.

Thomas, G., & McRobbie, C. J. (2001). Using a metaphor for learning to improve students' metacognition in the chemistry classroom. *Journal of Research in Science Teaching, 35*(2), 222–259.

Thomas, J. (1997). Informed ambivalence: Changing attitudes to the public understanding of science. In R. Levinson & J. Thomas (Eds.), *Science today: Problem or crisis?* (pp. 137–150). London: Routledge.

Thomashow, C. (2002). Adolescents and ecological identity: Attending to wild nature. In P. H. Kahn & S. R. Kellert (Eds.), *Children and nature: Psychological, sociocultural, and evolutionary investigations* (pp. 259–278). Cambridge, MA: MIT Press.

Thomashow, M. (1995). *Ecological identity*. Cambridge, MA: MIT Press.

Thomashow, M. (2002). *Bringing the biosphere home: Learning to perceive global environmental change*. Cambridge, MA: MIT Press.

Thomson, N. (2003). Science education researchers as orthograp[hers: documenting Keiyo (Kenya) knowledge, learning and narratives about snakes. *International Journal of Science Education, 25*(1), 89–115.

Thoreau, H. (1949). *The journal of Henry David Thoreau* (Vol. 5, B. Torrey & F. H. Allen, Eds.). Cambridge, MA: Houghton Mifflin.

Tilbury, D. (1994). The critical learning years for environmental education. In R. Wilson (Ed.), *Environmental education at the early childhood level* (pp. 11–13). Washington, DC: North American Association for Environmental Education.

Timberlake, L. (1992). The dangers of environmental education. *Annual Review of Environmental Education, 5*, 3–6.

Tirri, K., & Pehkonen, L. (2002). The moral reasoning and scientific argumentation of gifted adolescents. *Journal of Secondary Gifted Education, 13*(3), 120–129.

Tobin, K. (1990). Changing metaphors and beliefs: A master switch for teaching. *Theory into Practice, 29*(2), 122–127.

Tobin, K. (1993). Referents for making sense of science teaching. *International Journal of Science Education, 15*(3), 241–254.

Tobin, K., & Tippens, D. (1996). Metaphors as seeds of conceptual change and the improvement of science teaching. *Science Education, 80*(6), 711–730.

Toh, S.-H., & Cawagas, V. F. (2010). Transforming the ecological crisis: Challenges for faith and interfaith education in interesting times. In F. Kagawa & D. Selby (Eds.), *Education and climate change: Living and learning in interesting times* (pp. 175–196). London: Routledge.

Tompkins, L. J. (2005). A case for community-based education: Students form partnerships to tackle local environmental issues. *The Science Teacher, 72*(4), 34–36.

Toulmin, S. E. (1958). *The uses of argument*. Cambridge: Cambridge University Press.

Trafford, B. (2008). Democratic schools: Topwards a definition. In J. Arthur, I. Davies, & C. Hahn (Eds.), *The Sage handbook of education for citizenship and democracy* (pp. 410–423). London: Sage.

Tran, L. U. (2007). Teaching science in museums: The pedagogy and goals of museum educators. *Science Education, 91*(2), 278–297.

Tronto, J. C. (1987). Beyond gender difference to a theory of care. *Signs: Journal of Women in Culture and Society, 12*(4), 644–663.

Tsai, C.-C. (2004a). Information commitments in Web-based learning environments. *Innovations in Education and Teaching International, 41*(1), 105–112.

Tsai, C.-C. (2004b). Beyond cognitive and metacognitive tools: The use of the Internet as an 'epistemological' tool for instruction. *British Journal of Educational Technology, 35*, 525–536.

Tucker, M. E., & Williams, D. R. (Eds.). (1997). *Buddhism and ecology: The interconnections of dharma and deeds*. Cambridge, MA: Harvard University Press.

REFERENCES

Tucker, N. (1989). Animals in children's literature. In D. Paterson & M. Palmer (Eds.), *The status of animals: Ethics, education and welfare* (pp. 167–172). East Haddam, CT: Humane Education Foundation/CAB International.

Turner, S. (2008). School science and its controversies; or, whatever happened to scientific literacy? *Public Understanding of Science, 17,* 55–72.

Tytler, R. (2007). *Re-imagining science education: Engaging students in science for Australia's future.* Camberwell (Victoria): Australian Council for Educational Research.

Tytler, R., Duggan, S., & Gott, R. (2001). Dimensions of evidence, the public understanding of science and science education. *International Journal of Science Education, 23*(8), 815–832.

UK Government. (1996). *Indicators of sustainable development for the United Kingdom.* London: HMSO.

Ulmer, G. L. (2003). *Internet invention: From literacy to electracy.* New York: Longman.

UNCED. (1992). *Promoting education and public awareness and training.* Agenda 21. Conches: Author. (chap. 36)

UNESCO-UNEP. (1976). The Belgrade Charter: A global framework for environmental education. *Connect: UNESCO-UNEP Environmental Education Newsletter, 1*(1), 1–2.

UNESCO. (2002). *Education for sustainability from Rio to Johannesburg: Lessons learnt from a decade of commitment.* World summit on sustainable development. Paris: Author.

UNESCO. (2005, January). *United Nations decade of education for sustainable development, 2005–2014.* International implementation scheme (draft). Paris: Author.

Ungar, S. (2000). Knowledge, ignorance and popular culture: Climate change versus the ozone hole. *Public Understanding of Science, 9*(3), 297–312.

United Nations. (1992, June). *Rio declaration on environment and development.* Report of the United Nations conference on environment and development. Rio de Janeiro.

US Environmental Protection Agency. (1998). *Guidance for incorporating environmental justice in EPA's NEPA compliance analysis.* Washington, DC: Author.

Uzzell, D. (1999). Education for environmental action in the community: New roles and relationships. *Cambridge Journal of Education, 29*(3), 397–413.

Uzzell, D. (2000). The psycho-spatial dimension of global environmental problems. *Journal of Environmental Psychology, 20*(4), 307–318.

van Damme, L. S. M., & Neluvhalani, E. F. (2004). Indigenous knowledge in environmental education processes: Perspectives on a growing research arena. *Environmental Education Research, 10*(3), 353–370.

van Dijck, J. (1998). *Imagenation: Popular images of genetics.* New York: New York University Press.

van Driel, J. H., de Jong, O., & Verloop, N. (2002). The development of pre-service chemistry teachers' pedagogical content knowledge. *Science Education, 86,* 572–590.

van Driel, J. H., Verloop, N., & De Vos, W. (1998). Developing science teachers' pedagogical content knowledge. *Journal of Research in Science Teaching, 35,* 673–695.

van Eijck, M., & Roth, W.-M. (2008). Representations of scientists in Canadian high school and college textbooks. *Journal of Research in Science Teaching, 45*(9), 1059–1082.

van Gorder, A. C. (2007). Pedagogy for the children of the oppressors: Liberative education for social justice among the world's privileged. *Journal of Transformmative Education,* (591), 8–32.

van Matre, S. (1979). *Sunship Earth: An acclimatization program for outdoor learning.* Martinsville, IN: American Camping Association.

van Matre, S. (1990). *Earth education: A new beginning.* Warrenville, IL: The Institute for Earth Education.

van Matre, S., & Johnson, R. (1988). *Earthkeepers: Four keys for helping youmg people live in harmony with the Earth.* Warrenville, IL: The Institute for Earth Education.

van Petegem, P., & Blieck, A. (2006). The environmental worldview of children: A cross-cultural perspective. *Environmental Education Research, 12*(5), 625–635.

van Zee, E. H., & Minstrell, J. (1997). Reflective discourse: Developing shared understandings in a physics classroom. *International Journal of Science Education, 19*(2), 209–228.

Vance, L. (1993). Ecofeminism and the politics of reality. In G. Gaard (Ed.), *Ecofeminism: Women, animals, nature* (pp. 118–145). Philadelphia: Temple University Press.

Varelas, M., Pappas, C. C., Kane, J. M., Arsenault, A., Hankes, J., & Cowan, B. M. (2008). Urban primary-grade children think and talk science: Curricular and instructional practices that nurture prticipation and argmentation. *Science Education, 92*(1), 65–95.

Varelas, M., Pappas, C. C., Tucker-Raymond, E., Kane, J., Hankes, J., Ortiz, I., et al. (2010). Drama activities as ideational resources for primary-garde children in urban science classrooms. *Journal of Research in Science Teaching, 47*(3), 302–325.

Varma, R. (2000). Changing research cultures in U.S. industry. *Science, Technology & Human Values, 25*(4), 395–416.

Vaske, J. J., & Kobrin, K. C. (2001). Place attachment and environmentally responsible behavior. *Journal of Environmental Education, 32*(4), 16–21.

Veerman, A. (2003). Constructive discussions through electronic dialogue. In J. Andriessen, M. Baker, & D. Suthers (Eds.), *Arguing to learn: Confronting cognitions in computer-supported collaborative learning environments* (pp. 117–143). Dordrecht: Kluwer.

Vincent, S., & Désautels, J. (2008). Teaching and learning democracy in education: Interweaving democratic citizenship into/through the curriculum. In D. E. Lund & P. R. Carr (Eds.), *Doing democracy: Striving for political lietarcy and social justice* (pp. 283–300). New York: Peter Lang.

Vlaardingerbroek, B. (1998). Challenges to reform: Botswana junior secondary school science teachers' perceptions of the development functions of science education. *International Journal of Educational Reform,* (793), 264–270.

Vygotsky, L. S. (1978). *Mind in society: The development of higher psychological processes.* Cambridge, MA: Harvard University Press.

Wackernagel, M. (1994). *Ecological footprint and appropriated carrying capacity: A tool for planning toward sustainability.* Unpublished PhD thesis, University of British Columbia, Vancouver.

Wackernagel, M., & Rees, W. (1996). *Our ecological footprint: Reducing human impact on the Earth.* Gabriola Island, BC: New Society Publishers.

Waetjen, W. (1993). Technological literacy reconsidered. *Journal of Technology Education, 4*(2), 5–11.

Wajcman, J. (2004). *Technofeminism.* Malden, MA: Polity Press.

Waks, L. J. (2006). Rethinking technological literacy for the global network era. In J. R. Dakers (Ed.), *Defining technological literacy: Towards an epistemological framework* (pp. 275–295). New York: PalgraveMacmillan.

Walker, K., Brady, I., & Young, G. (1999, April). *The social cultural influences on environmental understandings of NSW school students.* Paper presented at AERA annual conference, Montreal.

Walker, K. A., & Zeidler, D. L. (2003, March). *Students' understanding of the nature of science and their reasoning on socioscientific issues: A web-based learning inquiry.* Paper presented at the annual meeting of the National Association for Research in Science Teaching, Philadelphia.

Walker, K. A., & Zeidler, D. L. (2007). Promoting discourse about socio-scientific issues through saffgolded inquiry. *International Journal of Science Education, 29,* 1387–1410.

Wallace, R. M., Kupperman, J., Krajcik, J., & Soloway, E. (2000). Science on the web: Students on-line in a sixth-grade classroom. *Journal of the Learning Sciences, 9,* 75–104.

Wals, A. E. J. (1994). Nobody planted it, it just grew! Young adolescents' perceptions and experiences of nature in the context of urban environmental education. *Children's Enviroments, 11*(3), 177–193.

Wals, A. E. J. (1996). Back-alley sustainability and the role of environmental education. *Local Environment, 1*(3), 299–316.

Walsh, R. (1992). Psychology and human survivcal: Psychological approaches to contemporary global threats. In S. Staub & P. Green (Eds.), *Psychology and social responsbility: Facing global challenges* (pp. 59–87). New York: New York University Press.

Walshe, N. (2008). Understanding students' Conceptions of sustainability. *Environmental Education Research,* (1495), 537–558.

Walton, D. N. (1997). *Appeal to expert opinion: Arguments from authority.* University Park, PA: The Pennsylvania State University Press.

Walton, D. N. (1998). *The new dialectic: Conversational contexts of argument.* Toronto: University of Toronto Press.

REFERENCES

Warnock, M. (1996). Moral values. In J. H. Halstead & M. J. Taylor (Eds.), *Values in education and education in values* (pp. 45–53). London: Falmer.

Warnock, M. (1998). *An intelligent person's guide to ethics.* London: Duckworth.

Warren, K. J. (1990). The power and the promise of ecological feminism. *Environmental Ethics, 12,* 125–146.

Warren, K. (1996). Educating for environmental justice. *Journal of Experiential Education, 19*(3), 135–140.

Warren, K. (Ed.). (2000). *Ecofeminism: Women, culture, nature.* Bloomington, IN: Indiana University Press.

Warren, K. (2001). The power and the promise of ecological feminism. In M. Zimmerman, J. Callicott, G. Sessions, K. Warren, & J. Clark (Eds.), *Envirommental philosophy: From animal rights to radical ecology* (pp. 332–342). Englewood Cliffs, NJ: Prentice Hall.

Wason-Ellam, I. (2010). Children's literature as a springboard to place-based embodied learning. *Environmental Education Research, 16*(3–4), 279–294.

Watanabe, M. (1974). The conception of nature in Japanese culture. *Science, 183*(4122), 279–282.

Waterman, A. T. (1960). National science foundation: A ten year resume. *Science, 131*(3410), 1341–1354.

Watts, D. M. (1989). Case study 9: Science with rhyme and reason. In D. Bentley & M. Watts (Eds.), *Learning and teaching in school science* (pp. 102–105). Milton Keynes: Open University Press.

Watts, D. M. (Ed.). (2000). *Creative trespass: Fusing science and poetry in the classroom.* Hatfield, UK: Association for Science Education.

Watts, D. M. (2001). Science and poetry: Passion v. prescription in school science? *International Journal of Science Education, 23*(2), 197–208.

Watts, M. (2005). Orchestrating the confluence: A discussion of science, passion, and poetry. In S. Alsop (Ed.), *Beyond cartesian dualism: Encountering affect in the teaching and learning of science* (pp. 149–159). Dordrecht: Springer.

Watts, M., & Alsop, S. (1997). A feeling for learning: Modelling affective learning in school science. *The Curriculum Journal, 8*(3), 351–365.

Watts, M., Alsop, S., & Zylbersztajn, A. (1997). 'Events-centred-learning': An approach to teaching science, technology and societal issues in two countries. *International Journal of Science Education, 19*(3), 341–351.

Watts, D. M., & Barber, B. (1997). Poetry and science. *Primary Science Review, 50,* 7–9.

Weaver, W. (1966). Why is it so important that science be understood? *Impact of Science on Society, XVI*(1), 41–50.

Webster, K., & Johnson, C. (2009). *Sense and sustainability: Educating for a low carbon world.* Preston, UK: Terra Presta.

Wegner, G. P. (1991). Schooling for a new mythos: Race, anti-semitism and the curriculum materials of a Nazi race educator. *Paedogogica Historica, 27*(2), 189–213.

Weigold, M. F. (2001). Communicating science: A review of the literature. *Science Communication, 23*(2), 164–193.

Weil, Z. (2004). *The power and promise of humane education.* Gabriola Island, BC: New Society Publishers.

Weinstein, M. (2008). Captain America, Tuskegee, Belmont, and righteous guinea pigs: Considering scientific ethics through official and subaltern perspectives. *Science & Education, 17,* 961–975.

Wellington, J. (2001). What is science education for? *Canadian Journal of Science, Mathematics and Technology Education, 1*(1), 23–38.

Wellington, J. (2004). Ethics and citizenship in science education: Now is the time jump off the fence. *School Science Review, 86*(315), 33–38.

Wellington, J., & Osborne, J. (2001). *Language and literacy in science education.* Buckingham: Open University Press.

Wenger, E. (1998). *Communities of practice: Learning, meaning and identity.* Cambridge: Cambridge University Press.

West, D. (2004). *Democracy matters: Winning the fight against imperialism.* Harmondsworth: Penguin.

West, L. H. T., & Pines, A. L. (1983). How 'rational' is rationality? *Science Education, 67,* 37–39.

Westheimer, J., & Kahne, J. (2004). What kind of citizen? The politics of educating for democracy. *American Educational Research Journal, 41*(2), 237–269.

Weston, A. (1991). Non-anthropocentrism in a thoroughly anthropocentrized world. *Trumpeter, 8*(3), 108–112.

White, B., Paterson, N., Talbot, H., Sommerhof, G., Hoare, G., & Scragg, B. (1965). *Experiments in education at Sevenoaks.* London: Constable Young.

White, L. T. (1967). The historical roots of our ecologic crisis. *Science, 155*(3767), 1203–1207.

Whitmarsh, L. (2008). Are flood victims more concerned about climate change than other people? The role of direct experience in risk perception and behavioural response. *Journal of Risk Research, 11*(3), 351–374.

Whitmarsh, L. (2009). What's in a name? Commonalities and differences in public understanding of 'climate change' and 'global warming'. *Public Understanding of Science, 18*, 401–420.

Wicklein, R. C. (Ed.). (2001). *Appropriate technology for sustainable living.* New York: Council on Technology Teacher Education/McGraw Hill.

Williams, D. R. (2000). Re-coupling place and time: Bioregionalism's hope for situated education. In L. Stone (Ed.), *Philosophy of Education 2000* (pp. 404–407). Chapel Hill, NC: Philosophy of Education Archives.

Williams, J. D., & Snipper, G. C. (1990). *Literacy and bilingualism.* New York: Longman.

Williams, P. J. (2009). Technological literacy: A multiliteracicies approach for democracy. *International Journal of Technology & Design Education, 19*(1), 237–254.

Wilson, E. O. (1984). *Biophilia.* Cambridge, MA: Harvard University Press.

Wilson, T. (2002). Excavation and relocation: Landscapes of learning in a teacher's autobiography. *Journal of Curriculum Theorizing, 18*(3), 75–88.

Winner, L. (1977). *Autonomous technology: Technics-out-of-control as a theme in political thought.* Cambridge, MA: MIT Press.

Wolpert, L. (1992). *The unnatural nature of science.* London: Faber & Faber.

Wong, S. L., & Hodson, D. (2009). From the horse's mouth: What scientists say about scientific investigation and scientific knowledge. *Science Education 93*(1), 109–130.

Wong, S. L., & Hodson, D. (2010). More from the horse's mouth: What scientists say about science as a social practice. *International Journal of Science Education, 32*(11), 1431–1463.

Wong, S. L., Yung, B. H. W., Cheng, M. W., Lam, K. L., & Hodson, D. (2006). Setting the stage for developing pre-service science teachers' conceptions of good science teaching: The role of classroom videos. *International Journal of Science Education, 28*(1), 1–24.

Wood, D., Bruner, J. S., & Ross, G. (1976). The role of tutoring in problem solving. *Journal of Child Psychology and Psychiatry, 17*, 89–100.

Woodrum, E., & Hoban, T. (1994). Theology and religiosity effects on environmentalism. *Review of Religious Research, 35*(3), 193–206.

Woolnough, B., & Allsop, T. (1985). *Practical work in science.* Cambridge: Cambridge University Press.

Wu, Y.-T., & Tsai, C.-C. (2005). The information commitments: Evaluative standards and information searching strategies in web-based learning environments. *Journal of Computer Assisted Learning, 21*, 374–385.

Wu, Y.-T., & Tsai, C-C. (2007). High school students' informal reasoning on a socio-scientific issue: Qualitative and quantitative analyses. *International Journal of Science Education, 29*(9), 1163–1187.

Wyatt, S. (2008) Technological determinism is dead; long live technological determinism. In E. J. Hackett, O. Amsterdamska, M. Lynch, & J. Wajcman (Eds.), *The handbook of science and technology studies* (pp. 180–192). Cambridge, MA: MIT Press.

Wylie, J., Sheehy, N., McGuinness, C., & Orchard, G. (1998). Children's thinking about air pollution: A systems theory analysis. *Environmental Education Research, 4*(2), 117–137.

Wynne, B. (1989). Sheep farming after Chernobyl: A case study in communicating scientific information. *Environment Magazine, 31*(2), 10–15 & 33–40.

Wynne, B. (1991). Knowledges in context. *Science, Technology & Human Values, 16*(1), 111–121.

REFERENCES

Wynne, B. (1995). Public understanding of science. In S. Jasanoff, G. E. Markle, J. C. Petersen, & T. Pinch (Eds.), *Handbook of science and technology studies* (pp. 361–388). London: Sage.

Wynne, B. (1996). Misunderstood misunderstandings: Social identities and public uptake of science. In A. Irwin & B. Wynne (Eds.), *Misunderstanding science? The public reconstruction of science and technology* (pp. 19–46). Cambridge: Cambridge University Press.

Wynne, C. F., Stewart, J., & Passmore, C. (2001). High school students' use of meiosis when solving genetics problems. *International Journal of Science Education, 23*, 501–515.

Yager, R. E. (Ed.). (1996). *Science/technology/society as reform in science education.* Albany, NY: State University of New York Press.

Yager, R. E., & Lutz, M. V. (1995). STS to enhance total curriculum. *School Science & Mathematics, 95*, 28–35.

Yager, R. E., & Tamir, P. (1993). STS approach: Reasons, intentions, accomplishments, and outcomes. *Science Education, 77*, 637–658.

Yager, S. O., Lim, G., & Yager, R. (2006). The advantages of an STS approach over a typical textbook dominated approach in middle school science. *School Science & Mathematics, 106*, 248–260.

Yang, C. N. (1982). Beauty and theoretical physics. In D. W. Curtin (Ed.), *The aesthetic dimension of science.* 1980 Nobel conference (pp. 25–40). New York: Philosophical Library.

Yang, F.-Y. (2004). Exploring high school students' use of theory and evidence in an everyday context: The role of scientific thinking in environmental science decision-making. *International Journal of Science Education, 26*(11), 1345–1364.

Yang, F.-Y., & Anderson, O. R. (2003). Senior high school students' preference and reasoning modes about nuclear energy use. *International Journal of Science Education, 25*, 221–244.

Yearley, S. (2000). What does science mean in the 'public understanding of science'? In M. Dierkes & C. von Grote (Eds.), *Between understanding and trust: The public, science and technology* (pp. 217–236). Amsterdam: Harwood.

Yearley, S. (2008). Nature and the environment in science and technology studies. In E. J. Hackett, O. Amsterdamska, M. Lynch, & J. Wajcman (Eds.), *The handbook of science and technology studies* (pp. 921–947). Cambridge, MA: MIT Press.

Yeung, S. P.-M. (1998). Environmental consciousness among students in senior secondary schools: The case of Hong Kong. *Enviromental Education Research*, (493), 251–268.

Yoon, S., Pedretti, E., Bencze, L, Hewitt, J., Perris, K., & van Oostveen, R. (2006). Improving elementary preservice science teachers' self-efficacy beliefs through the use of cases and case-methods. *Journal of Science Teacher Education, 17*(1), 15–35.

Yore, L. D., Pimm, D., & Tuan, H-L. (2007). The literacy component of mathematical and scientific literacy. *International Journal of Science and Mathematics Education, 5*(4), 559–589.

Yore, L. D., & Treagust, D. F. (2006). Current realities and future possibilities: Language and science literacy – empowering research and informing instruction. *International Journal of Science Education, 28*(2–3), 291–314.

Young, R. M. (1987). Racist society, racist science. In D. Gill & L. Levidow (Eds.), *Anti-racist science teaching* (pp. 16–42). London: Free Association Books.

Yow, V. R. (2005). *Recording oral history: A guide for the humanities and social sciences.* Walnut Creek, CA: AltaMira Press.

Yung, B. H. W., Wong, A. S. L., Cheng, M. W., Hui, C. S., & Hodson, D. (2007). Benefits of progressive video reflection on pre-service teachers' conceptions of good science teaching. *Research in Science Education, 37*(3), 239–259.

Zacharia, Z., & Calabrese Barton, A. (2004). Urban middle schoolers' attitude toward a defined science. *Science Education, 88*(2), 197–222.

Zahur, R., Calabrese Barton, A., & Upadhyay, B. R. (2002). Science education for empowerment and social change: A case study of a teacher educator in urban Pakistan. *International Journal of Science Education, 24*(9), 899–917.

Zak, K., & Munson, H. (2008). An exploratory study of elementary preservice teachers' understanding of ecology using concept maps. *Journal of Environmental Education, 39*(3), 32–46.

Zandvliet, D., & Fisher, D. (Eds.). (2007). *Sustainable communities, sustainable environments: The contribution of science and technology education.* Rotterdam: Sense Publishers.

Zavestoski, S., Brown, P., McCormick, S., Mayer, B., D'Ottavi, M., & Lucove, J.C. (2004a). Patient activism and the struggle for diagnosis: Gulf War illnesses and other medically unexplained physical symptoms in the U.S. *Social Science & Medicine, 58*(1), 161–175.

Zavestoski, S., Morello-Frosch, R., Brown, P., Mayer, B., McCormick, S., & Altman, R. G. (2004b). Embodied health movements and challenges to the dominant epidemiological paradigm. *Research in Social Movements, Conflicts and Change, 25,* 253–278.

Zeidler, D. L., & Sadler, T. D. (2008a). The role of moral reasoning in argumentation: Conscience, character and care. In S. Erduran & M. P. Jiménez-Aleixandre (Eds.), *Argumentation in science education: Perspectives from classroom-based research* (pp. 201–216). Dordrecht: Springer.

Zeidler, D. L., & Sadler, T. D. (2008b). Social and ethical issues in science education: A prelude to action. *Science & Education, 17*(8&9), 799–803.

Zeidler, D. L., & Schafer, L. E. (1984). Identifying mediating factors of moral reasoning in science education. *Journal of Research in Science Teaching, 21,* 1–15.

Zeidler, D. L., Osborne, J., Erduran, S., Simon, S., & Monk, M. (2003). The role of argument during discourse about sociosvientific issues. In D. L. Zeidler (Ed.), *The role of moral reasoning on socio-scientific issues and discourse in science education* (pp. 97–116). Dordrecht: Kluwer.

Zeidler, D. L., Sadler, T. D., Applebaum, S., & Callahan, B. E. (2009). Advancing reflective judgment through socioscientific issues. *Journal of Research in Science Teaching, 46*(1), 74–101.

Zeidler, D. L., Sadler, T. D., Simmons, M. L., & Howes, E. V. (2005). Beyond STS: A research-based framework for socioscientific issues education. *Science Education, 89*(3), 357–377.

Zeidler, D. L., Walker, K. A., Ackett, W. A., & Simmons, M. L. (2002). Tangled up in views: Beliefs in the nature of science and responses to socioscientific dilemmas. *Science Education, 86*(3), 343–367.

Zeidner, H., Matthews, G., & Roberts, R. D. (2009). *What we know about emotional intelligence.* Cambridge, MA: MIT Press.

Zell, S. K. (1998). Ecofeminism and the science classroom: A practical approach. *Science & Education, 7*(2), 143–158.

Zembal-Saul, C., Munford, D., Crawford, B., Friedrichsen, P., & Land, S. (2002). Scaffolding preservice sciencev teachers' evidence-based arguments during an investigation of natural selection. *Research in Science Education, 32*(4), 437–463.

Zembylas, M. (2001). A paralogical affirmation of emotion's discourse in science teaching. In M. Osborne & A. Calabrese Barton (Eds.), *Teaching science in diverse settings: Marginalized discourses and classroom practice* (pp. 99–128). New York: Peter Lang.

Zembylas, M. (2002a). 'Structures of feeling' in curriculum and teaching: Theorizing the emotional rules. *Educational Theory, 52,* 187–208.

Zembylas, M. (2002b). Constructing genealofies of teachers' emotions in science teaching. *Journal of Research in Science Teaching, 39,* 79–103.

Zembylas, M. (2003a). Interrogating 'teacher identity': Emotion, resistance and self-formation. *Educational Theory, 53*(1), 107–127.

Zembylas, M. (2003b). Emotions and teacher identity: A post-structural perspective. *Teachers and Teaching, 9*(3), 213–238.

Zembylas, M. (2004a). Emotion metaphors and emotional labor in science teaching. *Science Education, 88*(3), 301–324.

Zembylas, M. (2004b). Emotional issues in teaching science: A case study of a teacher's views. *Research in Science Education, 34*(4), 343–364.

Zembylas, M., & Avraamidou, L. (2008). Postcolonial foldings of space and identity in science education: Limits, transformations, prospects. *Cultural Studies of Science Education, 3*(4), 977–998.

Zemplén, G. A. (2009). Putting sociology first: Reconsidering the role of the social in 'nature of science' education. *Science & Education, 18,* 525–559.

Zerubavel, E. (2006). *The elephant in the room: Silence and denial in everyday life.* Oxford: Oxford University Press.

REFERENCES

Ziman, J. (1998). Essays on science and society: Why must scientists become more ethically sensitive than they used to be? *Science, 282*(5395), 1813–1814.

Ziman, J. (2000). *Real science: What it is, and what it means.* Cambridge: Cambridge University Press.

Zimmerman, C., Bisanz, G. L., Bisanz, J., Klein, J. S., & Klein, P. (2001). Science at the supermarket: A comparison of what appears in the popular press, experts' advice to readers, and what students want to know. *Public Understanding of Science, 10*(1), 37–58.

Zohar, A. (2008). Science teacher education and professional development in argumentation. In S. Erduran & M. P. Jiménez-Aleixandre (Eds.), *Argumentation in science education: perspectives from classroom-based research* (pp. 245–268). Dordrecht: Springer.

Zohar, A., & Nemet, F. (2002). Fostering students' knowledge and argumentation skills through dilemmas in human genetics. *Journal of Research in Science Teaching, 39*(1), 35–62.

Zoller, U., Ben-Chaim, D., Pentimalli, R., & Borsese, A. (2000). The disposition towards critical thinking of high school and university science students: An inter-intra Israeli-Italian study. *International Journal of Science Education, 22*, 571–582.

INDEX

9 789460 914706